Global Risk and Contingency Management Research in Times of Crisis

Narasimha Rao Vajjhala
University of New York Tirana, Tirana, Albania

Kenneth David Strang
W3-Research, USA & RMIT University, Australia

IGI Global
PUBLISHER of TIMELY KNOWLEDGE

A volume in the Advances in Logistics, Operations, and Management Science (ALOMS) Book Series

Published in the United States of America by
IGI Global
Business Science Reference (an imprint of IGI Global)
701 E. Chocolate Avenue
Hershey PA, USA 17033
Tel: 717-533-8845
Fax: 717-533-8661
E-mail: cust@igi-global.com
Web site: http://www.igi-global.com

Library of Congress Cataloging-in-Publication Data

Names: Vajjhala, Narasimha Rao, 1978- editor. | Strang, Kenneth David, 1962- editor.
Title: Global risk and contingency management research in times of crisis / Narasimha Rao Vajjhala, and Ken Strang, editor.
Description: Hershey, PA : Business Science Reference, [2023] | Includes bibliographical references and index. | Summary: "This book provides an interdisciplinary approach to risk and contingency management, presenting work of researchers and practitioners that provides best practices and a look into the future of this field"-- Provided by publisher.
Identifiers: LCCN 2022013983 (print) | LCCN 2022013984 (ebook) | ISBN 9781668452790 (hardcover) | ISBN 9781668452806 (paperback) | ISBN 9781668452813 (ebook)
Subjects: LCSH: Risk management. | Crisis management.
Classification: LCC HD61 .G557 2023 (print) | LCC HD61 (ebook) | DDC 658.15/5--dc23/eng/20220603
LC record available at https://lccn.loc.gov/2022013983
LC ebook record available at https://lccn.loc.gov/2022013984

This book is published in the IGI Global book series Advances in Logistics, Operations, and Management Science (ALOMS) (ISSN: 2327-350X; eISSN: 2327-3518)

British Cataloguing in Publication Data
A Cataloguing in Publication record for this book is available from the British Library.

For electronic access to this publication, please contact: eresources@igi-global.com.

Advances in Logistics, Operations, and Management Science (ALOMS) Book Series

John Wang
Montclair State University, USA

ISSN:2327-350X
EISSN:2327-3518

Mission

Operations research and management science continue to influence business processes, administration, and management information systems, particularly in covering the application methods for decision-making processes. New case studies and applications on management science, operations management, social sciences, and other behavioral sciences have been incorporated into business and organizations real-world objectives.

The **Advances in Logistics, Operations, and Management Science** (ALOMS) Book Series provides a collection of reference publications on the current trends, applications, theories, and practices in the management science field. Providing relevant and current research, this series and its individual publications would be useful for academics, researchers, scholars, and practitioners interested in improving decision making models and business functions.

Coverage

- Information Management
- Services management
- Production Management
- Decision analysis and decision support
- Finance
- Risk Management
- Organizational Behavior
- Political Science
- Marketing engineering
- Computing and information technologies

IGI Global is currently accepting manuscripts for publication within this series. To submit a proposal for a volume in this series, please contact our Acquisition Editors at Acquisitions@igi-global.com or visit: http://www.igi-global.com/publish/.

The Advances in Logistics, Operations, and Management Science (ALOMS) Book Series (ISSN 2327-350X) is published by IGI Global, 701 E. Chocolate Avenue, Hershey, PA 17033-1240, USA, www.igi-global.com. This series is composed of titles available for purchase individually; each title is edited to be contextually exclusive from any other title within the series. For pricing and ordering information please visit http://www.igi-global.com/book-series/advances-logistics-operations-management-science/37170. Postmaster: Send all address changes to above address.

Titles in this Series

For a list of additional titles in this series, please visit: http://www.igi-global.com/book-series/advances-logistics-operations-management-science/37170

Handbook of Research on Global Networking Post-COVID-19
Ana Pego (Nova University of Lisbon, Portugal)
Business Science Reference • © 2022 • 400pp • H/C (ISBN: 9781799888567) • US $295.00

Increasing Supply Chain Performance in Digital Society
Ramona Diana Leon (Universitat Politecnica de Valencia, Spain) Raul Rodriguez (Universitat Politecnica de Valencia, Spain) and Juan Jose Alfaro Saiz (Universitat Politecnica de Valencia, Spain)
Business Science Reference • © 2022 • 315pp • H/C (ISBN: 9781799897156) • US $250.00

Sales Management for Improved Organizational Competitiveness and Performance
José Duarte Santos (Instituto Superior Politécnico Gaya, Portugal)
Business Science Reference • © 2022 • 325pp • H/C (ISBN: 9781668434307) • US $240.00

Handbook of Research on Post-Pandemic Talent Management Models in Knowledge Organizations
Mohammad Rafiqul Islam Talukdar (American International University-Bangladesh, Bangladesh) Carmen z. Lamagna (American International University-Bangladesh, Bangladesh) Charles Carillo Villanueva (American International University-Bangladesh, Bangladesh) Rezbin Nahar (American International University-Bangladesh, Bangladesh) and Farheen Hassan (American International University-Bangladesh, Bangladesh)
Business Science Reference • © 2022 • 415pp • H/C (ISBN: 9781668438947) • US $295.00

Global Air Transport Management and Reshaping Business Models for the New Era
Kannapat Kankaew (Suan Sunandha Rajabhat University, Thailand)
Business Science Reference • © 2022 • 300pp • H/C (ISBN: 9781668446157) • US $250.00

International Perspectives on Value Creation and Sustainability Through Social Entrepreneurship
Hesham Magd (Modern College of Business and Science, Oman) Dharmendra Singh (Modern College of Business and Science, Oman) Raihan Taqui Syed (Modern College of Business and Science, Oman) and David Spicer (Bradford University, UK)
Business Science Reference • © 2022 • 300pp • H/C (ISBN: 9781668446669) • US $250.00

Examining the Vital Financial Role of SMEs in Achieving the Sustainable Development Goals
Dalila Taleb (A. Belkaid University, Algeria) Mohammed El Amine Abdelli (University Of Brest, France) Afef Khalil (University Of Tunis Carthage, Tunisia) and Asma Sghaier (University Of Sousse, Tunisia)
Business Science Reference • © 2022 • 325pp • H/C (ISBN: 9781668448342) • US $250.00

IGI Global
PUBLISHER of TIMELY KNOWLEDGE

701 East Chocolate Avenue, Hershey, PA 17033, USA
Tel: 717-533-8845 x100 • Fax: 717-533-8661
E-Mail: cust@igi-global.com • www.igi-global.com

Editorial Advisory Board

Table of Contents

Detailed Table of Contents

COVID-19 has inflicted tremendous damage across countries and economies. Some of the world's most populous nations suffered high death rates as their political leaders publicly expressed skepticism of the advice of their public health leaders and sowed distrust in the public's mind. Many political leaders failed to understand its implications and attributed blame rather than identified public health solutions, which diluted public health messaging. In addition, central and state government leaders undermined attempts by local leaders to mount effective public health campaigns. Meanwhile, leaders most closely aligned themselves with the advice of public health experts fared better both in the measures of disease mitigation and economic displacement. The author compares results in various countries based on their response pattern, explores the literature on effective contingent and risk management that helps explain the divergence in success in battling COVID-19, and demonstrates that collective citizen trust in government is a significant predictor of effective crisis risk management.

This chapter demonstrates how to apply a novel Bayesian auditing statistical technique with a predictive probability distribution model to predict petroleum accidents. The goal was to first develop the petroleum oil spill patterns for a given population, develop a predictive distribution model, and validate that using Bayesian audit statistical techniques. Sample data were taken from a U.S.-based state and fixed interval random sampling was used to select the records for the audit. A beta distribution was generated illustrating the materiality parameters along with the misstatement results.

Risk management is an integral part of the project management process, and project failure is an area of concern in many organizations. This chapter explains and discusses a new maturity model for assessing and managing project risk in the automotive industry. The research design was two-fold. First, a case study analysis in a major German automotive company was undertaken to develop the maturity model. The approach was qualitative and inductive, using data provided by in-depth interviews. Second, this model was applied in two major projects currently underway in the company – one involving implementing a cloud-based ERP system and the other the program management function responsible for product development and launch. The model adds to existing risk management maturity models and is unique to the automotive industry. It can be used by risk and project managers and can be adapted to other industry sectors.

The author studies the explosive behaviors, causality relationships, and contagion effects between three financial markets using the daily closing prices of Bitcoin, gold, and West Texas Intermediate (WTI) oil prices for a sample period from July 19, 2010 to September 10, 2021. By employing the generalized supremum augmented Dickey-Fuller (GSADF) approach, the author finds significant evidence of bubble explosive behaviors in the Bitcoin and WTI prices—but not in the gold prices—and these periods mostly match with the periods of quantitative easing and financial stress. Besides, the test shows several short and long episodes of unilateral causal linkages from Bitcoin returns to oil price changes under homoscedasticity and heteroskedasticity assumptions. The results show no evidence for the contagion effect of bubbles between cryptocurrency and oil markets during the sample period.

The global pursuit of higher quality and corporate social responsibility are motivating corporations to set climate preservation goals and to employ quality theory processes, notably lean six sigma methods. One of the significant contemporary social responsibility initiatives is climate preservation. Climate conservation has been dramatically achieved through the increases efficient production of clean energy, such as hydroelectricity and nuclear power plants. However, advanced quality management processes are needed to effectively and safely operate electricity generation plants of any type due to their potential to cause significant man-made accidental disasters if certain critical processes become out of control. This chapter explores how lean six sigma quality theories were applied for risk management at a renewable energy hydroelectricity facility. Quality inspections were collected from a plant in New York, USA. A statistical process control model was developed based on the attribute and continuous inspection data.

The COVID-19 pandemic has altered the business landscape for several organizations throughout the world, emphasizing the significance of being able to respond, adapt, and set up crisis management processes in an attempt to withstand uncertain situations. The necessity of supply chain resilience and risk management is more evident than previously as organizations attempt to strengthen operations and business resilience. The authors conducted an empirical investigation within the Nigerian supply chain logistics setting to evaluate and compare the uncertainties, tactics, and strategies employed by two businesses in Nigeria's northeastern region, where insurgency and banditry are rampant, exacerbated by the novel COVID-19 pandemic. The chapter provides a theoretical approach to logistics and supply chain management, delving into the fundamental business processes of the Global Supply Chain Forum (GSCF) and the role of logistics in each of the emphasized businesses.

People fear uncertainty as it leads to risk in the pursuit of their journeys, where they seek success. The authors articulate that opportunity lies beyond risk, encouraging individuals and business organizations to take calculated risks. In this chapter, the authors will show how risk-based decisions become more feasible when the decisions are made in light of risk assessment tools available to business organizations. The chapter will orchestrate the impact of risk assessment tools (qualitative, quantitative, and hybrid risk assessment tools) on organizational effectiveness given their perceived benefits in the information technology industry in India.

In recent years, blockchain technologies are constantly transforming many business processes. A shared, distributed ledger has revolutionized transaction recording, handling trust, and robustness in business network participants. In the telecommunication sector, the primary concern of voice over internet protocol (VoIP) providers when exchanging calls is the transparent storage of call detail records (CDRs) to avoid billing discrepancies, disputes, and interruption of services. In this chapter, the authors aim to investigate the utilization of permissioned blockchain in carriers' business models in telecommunication. They propose a business model architecture based on hyperledger fabric for developing smart contracts, which are invoked to store information about each CDR generated and business cases. The necessary steps and configurations for integrating the different technologies and building a development network are presented. Finally, the performance testing results regarding the latency for a transaction submission are shown.

The core objective of this chapter is to explore the risks associated with organizational factors influencing the professional growth of women in the United Arab Emirates (UAE) during the pandemic. The collected data were summarized and coded using software R Studio, and the variables were encoded and reduced using the one-hot encoding method and principal component analysis (PCA). The researchers identified that organizational and situational factors have a high degree of impact on women's professional development, which creates a significant effect of discontent over the mindset of women employees even in uncertain conditions. The study covers women employees working only in two emirates, Dubai and Sharjah. It includes telecom, banking, education, and other governmental and non-governmental organizations. This chapter is valuable to all the policymakers of the entire corporate sector and government authorities to set the right things by observing diverse organizational factors that influence women employees.

Due to the COVID-19 outbreak, schools are closed in many countries worldwide. China is the first to develop a distance learning program of 'Schools Out, But Classes On' not to disrupt learning. Ethiopia closed schools on 16 March 2020 after it confirmed the first coronavirus on 13 March 2020. To avoid learning disruption, the Ethiopian Ministry of Education has tried to develop strategies to resume classes at home. Accordingly, radio and TV education programs are designed for primary education, secondary education programs, and online teaching for higher education. This chapter aimed to explore the educational inequality of rural students of Ethiopia using situational analysis. The findings unveil the multiple inequalities of rural students that make them disadvantaged compared to urban students. The available distance learning programs homogenize students, which can create educational inequality.

Many Canadians have built their wealth through the real estate business. There are two types of real estate: commercial real estate and residential real estate. In this chapter, risks relating to only residential real estate have been discussed due to two main reasons. Firstly, residential real estate occupies an important place in the income of the household sector. Secondly, in comparison to commercial real estate, it requires a smaller capital to do the business and build wealth. Residential real estate investors build wealth by investing in investment properties and generating current income through capital appreciation. However, there are multiple risks that an investor faces in managing investment properties. This chapter discusses how some risks can be averted before and after buying an investment property. The chapter points out that the essential part of the business is to buy the right property at the right place and at the right time.

Ulrich Beck, a German sociologist who does not need prior presentation, cast his diagnosis of risk society as a new emerging ethos where social class and hierarchies blurred before the figure of risk. Although he shed light on the post-industrial society of the 1990s, today, the society he studied seems pretty different. Hence, a new fresh insight should be placed. This chapter introduces readers to the conceptual foundations of Thana Capitalism, as it was critically debated in the author's book The Rise of Thana Capitalism and Tourism. The risk society sets the pace for a new facet of capitalism where the other´s pain remains the main commodity to exchange. Far from being a more egalitarian society, as Beck said, in the days of Thana capitalism, a ruling elite governs the destiny of a precaritized workforce. The novel The Hunger Games represents perfectly how this society works. Additionally, the author brings some reflection on the connection of Thana capitalism and the spectacle beyond the recent COVID-19 pandemic.

The reign of terror ignited by 9/11 and the resulting War on Terror has accelerated the effects on social imaginary. Beyond the economic aftermaths, 9/11 recreated the conditions towards a monopoly of radicalized discourse, which was mainly oriented toward demonizing the "Non-Western Other." Terrorism allowed the introduction of a conspiracy plot that marked some minority ethnicities as an enemy living within. At the bottom, these narratives punctuated that Muslim communities hate the society they inhabit. Such discourse changed forever the ways the "Other" is imagined. The chapter deals with HBO Saga Westworld, a futurist and dystopian world where robots (hosts) are subjected to torture, violence, and even sadist practices at the hands of wealthy tourists (guests). The formula in "Robots We Must Trust" is placed under the critical lens of scrutiny.

Foreword

It was an honor and a challenge to write a foreword for this global risk and contingency management in times of crisis book. The challenge stems from the fact that the 16 chapters were written by a score of prominent risk specialists who covered highly diverse risk and uncertainty topics. Additionally, the editors and I were under schedule pressure to make this book project successful. Being an experienced specialist in project risk management (PRM), I did not have much trouble with understanding the logic and value of most of the chapters. However, two chapters that touched on philosophical and futuristic aspects of risk in post-modern Western society were a stunning discovery to me: They harnessed the creative thinking of philosophers, sociologists, fiction writers, and Hollywood moviemakers to shape possible risk-related scenarios of our future.

After reading the abstracts and several chapters, I observed that the COVID-19 pandemic was often – but not always – the underlying crisis for explaining how technical risk management was, or could, be implemented. I applied a semi-structured methodology to categorize the peer-reviewed chapters into the theoretical PRM body of knowledge and then assign an approximate risk frontier coefficient. My methodology was heuristics and perception based, which is often all that a busy project manager may have available when forced to make quick complex decisions with highly variable and verbose business intelligence information. The PRM coefficient roughly classifies documentary evidence into five categories. It covers the entire spectrum of perceived uncertainties from complete risk ignorance to full determinism of uncertainty quantification. I must point out that the book chapters did not fit perfectly into one specific risk frontier coefficient. Therefore, to provide value to the readers, I adapted my methodology to categorize the scientific studies. I assigned a range rather than strictly categorize every chapter. The five PRM frontier coefficients are briefly enumerated below.

1. A clear-enough future characterized by slight variations (what we may describe as identifying general uncertainties in PRM);
2. A future with alternative outcomes characterized by probabilities (what we may consider to be uncertain events in PRM);
3. A few plausible futures requiring routine scenario analyses (these take a form of risk-based and economic-based project alternative decision making in PRM);
4. Many plausible futures requiring sophisticated scenario analyses (not used too often in PRM since the basis is often interdisciplinary or abstract factors like politics, policymaking, philosophy, sociology and conceptual studies);
5. Deeply unknown futures (in rudimental nomenclature these are often referred to and evaluated in PRM as black swans or unknown-unknowns).

These scales do not represent a good versus bad ranking, but rather, an approximate PRM risk frontier topical coverage. To elaborate further, to categorize information into a PRM frontier coefficient, one must also evaluate the system context as a whole, its scope and parts, its inside interactions, and its external influences. Thus, a PRM frontier coefficient ought to encompass the whole system as well as the level of uncertainty from deeply unknown (5) to clear-enough (1). Strictly speaking, only PRM frontiers 3 – 5 could be described as deep uncertainties in practice. To provide value to the reader, I briefly discuss how each of the 16 chapters correlated to the PRM frontier typology, in terms of two parameters: System as a whole (aka the subject of the study) and uncertainty articulation.

Chapter 1 analyses success of various anti-COVID-19 measures and health campaigns implemented in various countries and observed response patterns (uncertainty types 1 and 3). The undertaken risk analysis explains the divergence in success in battling COVID-19. It is demonstrated that the level of collective citizen trust in government is a significant predictor of effective crisis risk management. It shall be of high interest to UN, WHO and government officials as well as to healthcare workers.

Chapter 2 addresses an important environment protection risk related to oil spill incidents. A novel Bayesian auditing statistical technique has been developed resulting in a predictive probability beta-distribution model as opposed to traditional accident-per-period approach (uncertainty types 1 and 2). This highly efficient statistical technique utilizes random sampling of US oil spill incidents. Besides timely prediction of oil spill incidents, this inferential technique can be applied way beyond oil and gas industry where reliability, availability and maintainability risks are of major concern.

Chapter 3 shares experience of development and implementation of a new maturity model for risk management at a German automotive plant. The developed model has been used to deploy cloud-based enterprise risk system and to manage a product development program. This handles uncertainty types 1 and 2 in the automotive industry. Besides automotive risk and project managers this chapter should be of interest to risk specialists in other production industries.

Chapter 4 investigates effects of bubbles and causality among bitcoin, gold and oil markets based on price dynamics from July 2010 to September 2021 (uncertainty types 1 and 2). The working hypotheses have been tried using generalized supremum augmented Dickey-Fuller (GSADF) statistical test resulting in a conclusion that there is a significant evidence of bubble explosive behaviors in the bitcoin and oil prices, but not in the gold prices, mostly in periods of quantitative easing and financial stress. It should be of interest to investment, fintech, banking, etc. specialists.

Chapter 5 marries lean six sigma risk management with social and corporate responsibility initiatives aimed at climate conservation and clean energy production at a hydroelectricity generation plant in the State of New York, USA (uncertainty types 1 and 2). This methodology zeroes in on prevention of various man-made accidental disasters. A statistical six-sigma-process-control model was developed using inspection data to support this methodology. No doubts that this chapter would be highly appreciated by representatives of energy production facilities – both renewable and traditional – and any other corporations supporting clean energy initiatives.

Chapter 6 investigates one of the main risks encountered by businesses these days across the Globe – supply chain logistics vulnerability – which is one of core root causes of structural inflation (uncertainty types 1 – 3). This study delves into Global Supply Chain Forum (GSCF) fundamental processes. Although specifically it aims at Nigerian supply chain logistics impacted by COVID-19 pandemic. This chapter verifies ways to strengthen logistics operations and business resilience. It could be of interest to logistics specialists especially in the light of upcoming impacts of sanctions.

Chapter 7 is devoted to contribution of information technology industry of India in development of risk assessment tools (uncertainty types 1 – 3). It shall be of interest to risk management and organizational effectiveness specialists responsible for deployment of enterprise risk management systems in various industries – from banking and insurance to engineering, to education, to marketing.

Chapter 8 introduces risks associated with implementation of blockchain technology that may occur among telecommunication carriers (VOIP providers). Namely, transparent storage of Call Detail Records (CDRs) when exchanging calls might fail resulting in billing discrepancies, disputes, and interruption of services (uncertainty types 1 and 2). The authors come up with a permission blockchain business model architecture for VOIP providers based on hyper-ledger fabric to support smart contacts which allows reliable CDR storage. This chapter addressing the blockchain technology risk should be of high interest to blockchain, fintech, banking and IT specialists.

Chapter 9 sheds light on cyber security risk management in various industry sectors. It covers overall cyber security risk management system as well as specific risks such as increasing number of cyber-attacks during the COVID-19 pandemic (uncertainty types 1 and 2). This chapter should be of interest to risk management specialists who deal with cyber security risks in various industries.

Chapter 10 describes developments in healthcare informatics in times of COVID-19 pandemic as healthcare organizations have undergone real "stress tests" (uncertainty types 1 – 3). It shows how healthcare informatics allows mitigate healthcare challenges (e.g., treating of patients remotely, reducing exposure of personnel to COVID-19, etc.) through using telemedicine, drug delivery portals, drones, robots, big data, AI, etc. It shall be of lively interest to many healthcare professionals.

Chapter 11 reviews risks and challenges of big-data analytics implementation in fifty Indian enterprises (uncertainty types 1 and 2). This study has discovered five risks related to lack of human resources, data privacy and security, shortage of technological resources, deficiency of awareness and financial constraints. This chapter should be of keen interest to many corporate IT specialists.

Chapter 12 is devoted to organizational risks preventing professional growth of female employees in banking, education, government, etc. sectors of United Arab Emirates (UAE) during COVID-19 pandemic (uncertainty types 1 and 2). Collected survey data have been processed statistically. A resulting conclusion points to the fact that the discussed risks have a high impact on women's professional development and their mindsets. This chapter shall be of interest to corporate, government and non-government policymakers involved in handling of diversity factors.

Chapter 13 discusses COVID-19 impact on education in Ethiopia resulting in educational process disruption and inequality. It also points to ways to mitigate the impact (uncertainty types 1 - 3). It should be of interest to policymakers dealing with education programs – from UN to developing-country government officials – as well as to teachers, to students and to their parents.

Chapter 14 puts forward risks that may be encountered by Canadian residential real-estate investors (uncertainty types 1 – 3). Major mitigation measures are discussed to ensure wealth growth through real estate business by averting pertaining risks both prior to and after buying an investment property. It shall be of interest to North American, European, and Australian real-estate investors.

Chapter 15 presents a sociological study that investigates reasons why the Western society moves from traditional and more rational perception of risk (tabbed as "Risk Capitalism") to a way more emotional perception based on fear (tabbed as "Thana Capitalism"). A role of some epoch events like Chernobyl disaster and COVID-19 pandemic in this shift is thought through. Development of scenarios of "futures" utilizes review of dystopian novel and movie The Hunger Games: it is believed by the author that this novel and the movie represent perfectly how the "Thana-Capitalism" would work. Again, the same as chapter 16, chapter 15 utilizes intuitive scenario-building approach to shape "futures" (uncertainty types 3 – 5) and should be attractive to many people interested in futuristic risk studies.

Chapter 16, which could be considered a spin-off from chapter 15, was perceived as rather unconventional by typical representatives of enterprise, project, operations, etc. Honestly, it has been a double-taker to me as it prescribes deep shifts and associated risks occurring in the Western society after 9/11. Rather sensitive general topics related to "non-Western others" are discussed including specific implications for hospitality industry. Moreover, this chapter deals with futuristic post-modern Western society through analyzing a dystopian world introduced by the HBO Saga, Westworld as an object for philosophical thinking. This chapter points to an intrinsic value of artistic and philosophical intuitive approach for development of scenarios of "futures" (uncertainty types 3 – 5). It could be of curious interest to a broad auditorium.

This book being an impressive teamwork of the chapter authors and editors shall be well received by risk management professionals and decision makers working in various sectors from healthcare and cyber security to education, to operations, to finances.

Yuri Raydugin
Risk Services & Solutions Inc., Calgary, Canada

Yuri Raydugin *is Principal Consultant of Risk Services & Solution Inc, a Canadian consulting company. Previously, Yuri worked for Saudi Aramco, Royal Dutch Shell, TransCanada Pipelines, and SNC-Lavalin. He has been involved in risk management of capital mega and large projects with combined budget of more than $160B. Yuri has an engineering degree in nuclear physics from Urals Polytechnics Institute, Russia, a PhD in physics and mathematics from Russia's Academy of Sciences, and an MBA in business strategy from Henley Management College in England. He is a member of the Association of Professional Engineers and Geoscientists of Alberta (APEGA). Yuri is an author of several articles on project risk management as well as on various aspects of physics. He is the author of 'Modern Risk Quantification in Complex Projects: Non-linear Monte Carlo and System Dynamics Methodologies', Oxford University Press (2020) and 'Project Risk Management: Essential Methods for Project Teams and Decision Makers', John Wiley & Sons (2013) as well as the editor of 'The Handbook of Research on Leveraging Risk and Uncertainties for Effective Project Management', IGI Global (2017). Born and raised in Ekaterinburg, Russia, Yuri lives and works in Calgary, Alberta, Canada.*

Preface

INTRODUCTION

Figure 1. Thematic topic and keyword coverage

This book explores selected risk and contingency management topics in a crisis, including fear, artificial intelligence, healthcare pandemic, political instability, big data, internet terrorism, and others, as illustrated in figure 1. The editors created the thematic diagram using empirical evidence. The keywords and abstracts of the manuscripts from 21 subject matter expert authors across 10 countries were tabulated into frequencies and graphically modeled using font size to represent a percentage of reiteration (larger words indicate higher interpreted importance). Even more interesting is the post-hoc thematic model of the analysis for the entire book contents (discussed later). This initiative is an empirical extension of our previous project, which was focused on theoretical risk models (Strang, Korstanje, Vajjhala, 2018). This book focuses on how risk and contingency management were retrospectively applied by practitioners in a crisis, namely the COVID-19 pandemic, environmental conservation, climate control, economic volatility, healthcare supply chain constraints, internet cyber-security terrorism, inequality, and global political instability.

The intended audience for this book includes risk management practitioners and academics across numerous disciplines and industries. Most of the subject matter experts were academics and scholars with preexisting peer-reviewed publications. Still, selected contributors were specialists in economics, politics, social policy, terrorism, cryptocurrency, and statistical modeling. The industries included healthcare, financial 'fintech', oil and gas refining, automotive manufacturing, clean energy creation, hydroelectricity, education, engineering, internet cyber-security, artificial intelligence robots, big data analytics, tourism, real estate investment, and supply chain management. Clearly, the stakeholders for this book are decision-makers, practitioners, and researchers. Students, academic teachers, librarians, politicians, and content writers may also be interested in this. Therefore, this book ought to help instructors, undergraduate and post-graduate students by providing vital case studies in understanding how the organizations deal with a crisis.

This book could also be described as retrospective science since the authors often revisited recent studies and extended their findings or models based on actual pandemic experiences. Earlier projects may have been focused on disciplinary topics such as healthcare or education. In contrast, in this book, prior studies were expanded to collect data and or interpretations of how risk and contingency management was applied during a crisis. The Covid-19 coronavirus pandemic was typically the crisis scenario underpinning most of the book chapters. Yet, some researchers focused on other salient contexts, such as environmental conservation, economic sustainability, and global terrorism, including artificial intelligence, cyber-security, and big data risk management.

BOOK RATIONALE AND PROJECT MANAGEMENT METHODOLOGY

The rationale for creating this book was primarily to address the coronavirus pandemic, yet other issues also came to light. First, the definition of risk was grounded in the a priori literature. Risks can be identified, evaluated, mitigated, and evaluated, but the underlying uncertainty remains elusive yet always present across most industries (Strang, 2015; Strang, Korstanje & Vajjhala, 2018). This is why the topic needs to be iteratively researched. The editors extended the 2018 project to encompass new findings over the last 4-5 years after the coronavirus pandemic and global instability.

This book project finished approximately 6 months ahead of schedule, it was under budget, within agreed-upon scope and at acceptable quality levels. The project management was shared between Vajjhala and Strang. All chapters were double-blind peer-reviewed, with Vajjhala serving as the managing editor since Strang contributed two chapters. The initial design was created by Strang, while Vajjhala managed the book editing and peer reviews. The preface chapter summary was written by Vajjhala and completed by Strang, including the statistical analysis of the keywords. The foreword was initiated by Strang and written independently by a global risk management expert and scholar, Dr. Yuri Raydugin. Both editors received ethical approval to conduct this project, and no specific external funding was received. No conflicts of interest were reported. In other words, the primary motive for the editors underpinning this book was to advance the state-of-the-art in risk contingency management through collaboration as well as knowledge sharing. A secondary motive of the editors was to stimulate empirical and qualitative case study research on these topics.

CHAPTER OVERVIEW

In Chapter 1, "In Crisis Risk Management Across Nations: COVID-19 Wins When Trust Is Low," Colin Read contrasts the outcomes of the COVID-19 pandemic based on their response patterns, delving into the research on successful contingency and risk management to understand the disparity in pandemic success. According to the author, leaders who closely followed the advice of public health professionals performed better in terms of illness mitigation and economic displacement. The author successfully establishes that citizen trust in government is an essential predictor of good crisis risk management.

In Chapter 2, "Petroleum Industry Contingency Planning Using Auditing Theories and Inferential Statistics," Kenneth David Strang shows how to forecast petroleum accidents using a unique Bayesian auditing statistical technique combined with a predictive probability distribution model. The author develops petroleum oil leak patterns for a particular population, creates a predicted distribution model, and validates it using Bayesian audit statistical techniques in this chapter. The author used fixed interval random sampling to choose records for the audit using sample data from a state in the United States. The author demonstrated the materiality parameters and misstatement results using a beta distribution.

In Chapter 3, "Development and Application of a New Maturity Model for Risk Management in the Automotive Industry," Jose Irizar and Martin George Wynn explain and explore a new maturity model for project risk assessment and management in the automotive industry. The authors offer a case study analysis conducted in a major German automotive firm to develop a maturity model utilizing a qualitative and inductive approach based on data from in-depth interviews. The authors then apply this approach to two significant projects now underway at the company: one involving adopting a cloud-based ERP system and the other involving the product development and launch program management function. By establishing a new model particular to the automobile industry, the authors contribute to existing risk management maturity models. Risk and project managers can apply this model to other sectors as well.

In Chapter 4, "Does the Contagion Effect of Bubbles and Causality Exist Among Bitcoin, Gold, and Oil Markets?" Remzi Gök investigates the explosive behaviors, causation linkages, and contagion effects amongst three financial markets utilizing daily closing prices of Bitcoin, gold, and West Texas Intermediate (WTI) oil prices for a sample period of July 19, 2010, to September 10, 2021. The author used the Generalized Supremum Augmented Dickey-Fuller technique to discover considerable evidence of bubble explosive behaviors in Bitcoin and WTI prices—but not in gold prices—during periods of quantitative easing and financial stress. The author states that no evidence is available for the contagion effect of bubbles between cryptocurrency and oil markets during the sample period.

In Chapter 5, "How Lean Six Sigma Risk Management Was Used at a Clean Energy Plant?" Kenneth David Strang investigates how lean six sigma quality ideas were used to manage risk in a renewable energy hydroelectricity facility. Through quality inspections, the author gathered data from a plant in New York, USA. The author designs a statistical process control model based on attribute and continuous inspection data. Because of the potential for substantial man-made unintended disasters, if specific crucial processes fall out of control, the author contends that advanced quality management techniques are required to properly and safely operate any form of energy generation plant.

In Chapter 6, "Supply Chain Logistics Risk Mitigation: Impact of COVID-19 Pandemic," Edna Denga and Sandip Rakshit perform an empirical analysis in the Nigerian supply chain logistics setting to examine and compare the uncertainties, tactics, and strategies used by two enterprises in Nigeria's northeastern region. The authors concentrate on Nigeria's northeastern part, where insurgency and banditry are common, and the recent COVID-19 pandemic has aggravated the situation. The writers take a theoretical approach to logistics and supply chain management, diving into the global supply chain forum's key business processes and logistics functions in each highlighted industry. The findings of this study are relevant because supply chain resilience and risk management are becoming more visible in the post-pandemic environment as businesses try to increase their operations and company resilience.

In Chapter 7, "Risk Assessment in Information Technology Industry: An Imperative Phenomenon," Madhu Kishore Raghunath and Tulasi Devi investigate the effects of qualitative, quantitative, and hybrid risk assessment tools on organizational effectiveness, considering the perceived advantages in the Indian information technology industry. In this chapter, the authors show how risk-based decisions become more plausible when they are made using risk assessment tools available to corporate organizations. The authors argue that the opportunity is greater than the risk, encouraging individuals and businesses to take prudent risks.

In Chapter 8, "Minimizing Risk of Disputes Among Telecommunication Carriers With Blockchain Technologies," Evis Trandifili, Marenglen Biba, and Enes Cela study the use of permissioned blockchain in the business model of telecommunication carriers. The authors propose a business model architecture for the generation of smart contracts based on hyperledger fabric, which stores information about each call detail record generated and business cases. The authors outline the methods and configurations required to integrate the various technologies and create a development network. The authors provide the findings of performance tests related to transaction submission latency.

In Chapter 9, "Cybersecurity Risk: Assessment and Management," Natasha Cecilia Edeh and Ibiene Idu present a comprehensive overview of cybersecurity risk. The writers provide an overview of cybersecurity, vulnerabilities, frequent cyber threats/attacks, and why cybersecurity risk is crucial to businesses. The authors discuss cybersecurity threats in several industries and provide an overview of the multiple cyber-attacks during the covid-19 outbreak. The authors discuss the role of organizations in the handling and management of cybersecurity risks and the activities that governments, organizations, stakeholders, and individuals should take to minimize or manage cybersecurity risks.

In Chapter 10, "Healthcare Informatics During the COVID-19 Pandemic," Philip Eappen examines how healthcare companies used innovative healthcare informatics during the pandemic and how technology assisted in reducing healthcare delivery issues. The author discusses a variety of healthcare informatics applications that have been developed and utilized around the world, including telemedicine, drug delivery portals, drones, robots, big data, artificial intelligence, and a variety of other complex applications for remote patient care. The author also discusses different health informatics methods, such as telemedicine, that have helped healthcare staff avoid needless contact with contagious patients, averting numerous illnesses in hospitals.

In Chapter 11, "Consequences in Acceptance and Application of Big Data Analytics in Micro, Small, and Medium Enterprises in India," Rajasekhara Mouly Potluri explains the implications of accepting and using big data analytics in India's micro, small, and medium enterprises (MSMEs). The author presented conclusions based on experimental evidence on five critical problems that Indian MSMEs experience in accepting and implementing big data analytics: a lack of human resources, data privacy and security, a lack of technological resources, a lack of knowledge, and financial consequences. The author conducted research using various methods to collect responses from middle and top-level managers in fifty firms across five key commercial sectors. The outcomes of this study should aid MSMEs' organizational leadership in developing and planning short- and long-term information systems strategies.

In Chapter 12, "Risks Associated With Organizational Factor Influence on the UAE Women's Professional Growth During COVID-19," Rajasekhara Mouly Potluri and Sophia Johnson explore the risks associated with organizational factors influencing the professional growth of women in the United Arab Emirates (UAE) during the pandemic. The authors identified that organizational and situational factors have a high degree of impact on women's professional development, which creates a significant effect of discontent over the mindset of women employees even in uncertain conditions. This chapter covers women employees working only in two emirates, Dubai and Sharjah. This book chapter is valuable to all the policymakers of the entire corporate sector and government authorities to set the right things by observing diverse organizational factors that influence women employees.

In Chapter 13, "COVID-19 Pandemic, Distance Learning, and Educational Inequality in Rural Ethiopia," Degwale Gebeyehu Belay explores the educational inequality of rural students of Ethiopia using situational analysis. The findings of this chapter unveil the multiple inequalities of rural students that make them in a disadvantaged position compared to urban students. The author posits that the available distance learning programs homogenize students creating educational disparities. The author presents the strategies used by the Ethiopian Ministry of Education to avoid the disruption of learning during the pandemic. The plan included radio and TV education programs designed for primary education, TV programs for secondary education, and online teaching for higher education.

In Chapter 14, "Managing Risk in Wealth Building Through Residential Real Estate Business in Canada," Mahendra Singh Rawat and Mudit Rawat discuss the risks of investing in residential real estate in Canada. The authors claim that discussing just domestic real estate is crucial since residential real estate contributes significantly to household income and takes less capital to operate and develop wealth in comparison to commercial real estate. The authors discuss the hazards that an investor encounters when managing rental properties. This chapter explains how to avoid specific hazards before and after purchasing an investment property. The chapter emphasizes the importance of buying the right property at the right time and in the right location.

In Chapter 15, "From the Risk Society to COVID-19: Analysis of the Beck´s Risk Society – Towards a New Modernity," Maximiliano Emanuel Korstanje introduces readers to Thana Capitalism's intellectual foundations, as discussed in the book -"The Rise of Thana Capitalism and Tourism". Ulrich Beck, a German sociologist, defined risk society as a new developing ethos in which social class and hierarchies blurred in the face of risk. Beyond the recent COVID-19 outbreak, the author observes the relationship between Thana capitalism and spectacle.

In the book's final chapter, "Terrorism, Automated Hosts, and COVID-19: Critical Film Review on the HBO Saga *Westworld*," Maximiliano Emanuel Korstanje discusses the HBO series Westworld, which depicts a futuristic and dystopian society in which robots (hosts) are exposed to torture, violence, and even sadistic activities at the hands of wealthy tourists (guests). The author examines the argument in "Robots We Must Trust" through a critical lens. The author claims that the reign of terror sparked by 9/11 and the subsequent War on Terror have hastened the social imaginary's consequences. Beyond the economic fallout, the author claims that 9/11 re-created the circumstances for a monopoly of politicized rhetoric aimed primarily at demonizing the "Non-Western Other."

SYNOPSIS AND FUTURE RESEARCH

In this subsection, we, the editors, take the unusual approach of ending the book with no summary chapter, electing instead to ask the readers to conduct literature reviews to identify topics important to key stakeholders. Instead of a summary chapter, the editors present a visual synopsis of the themes emerging from the full manuscripts, a post-hoc empirical analysis of the thematic concepts in Figure 1. This ought to summarize which topics from Figure 1 were reiterated in the subject matter expert case studies. This summary is presented in Figure 2, an empirical risk contingency management synopsis. Therefore, Figure 2 extends Figure 1 with what was discussed and or modeled by the authors of this book. We argue these topics were the most important keywords in the risk contingency management discipline during a crisis, particularly (but not limited to) the global coronavirus pandemic of 2019-2022. Figure 2 was developed in a similar methodology as Figure 1 by tallying the frequencies of keywords and creating a graph where the size of the word reflects the importance (frequency) of the topic discussed by the book authors.

It is interesting to note from Figure 2, as contrasted with figure 1, that new topics arose in perceived importance, namely, real estate, cyber-security, healthcare assessment, artificial intelligence, robots, statistical models, capitalism, and social concerns. Without question, much of the emphasis was on technology, healthcare, COVID-19 pandemic, effective business decision-making processes, and data analytics.

Figure 2. Post-hoc keyword synopsis model

Based on the keyword synopsis model, the editors assert that state-of-the-art risk and contingency management coverage pertain to health and financial related crises. In the future, we argue more empirical and experimental research is needed to understand how decision makers and consumers will react to risks. We base this proposal on the fact that most nations globally have democratic political governance, so citizens have much more power compared to decades ago. Now with 'we the people' influencing national policies and organizational cultures, we anticipate a very different future world. We argue more consideration will be given to people rather than political pundits or leaders. We argue that risks such as man-made terrorism or wars could be reduced with better strategic management of politics and global relationships. We also argue that natural disasters and risks, including pandemics and climate warming, need to be addressed immediately at the highest level of authority; otherwise, the next book we will be writing may be focused on how decision-makers are handling the global apocalypse and evacuation to other planets.

Narasimha Rao Vajjhala
University of New York Tirana, Tirana, Albania

Kenneth David Strang
W3-Research, USA & RMIT University, Australia

REFERENCES

Strang, K. D. (2015). Risk Management Research. In Research Methods: Concepts, Methodologies, Tools, and Applications (pp. 362-389). Information Resource Management Association (IRMA). doi:10.4018/978-1-4666-7456-1.ch017

Strang, K. D., Vajjhala, N. R., & Korstanje, M. E. (2018). Global risk and contingency management overview. In K. D. Strang, M. E. Korstanje, & N. R. Vajjhala (Eds.), *Research, Practices, and Innovations in Global Risk and Contingency Management* (pp. xxii–xxix). IGI-Global. doi:10.4018/978-1-5225-4754-9

Chapter 1
In Crisis Risk Management Across Nations:
COVID-19 Wins When Trust Is Low

Colin Read
State University of New York, Plattsurgh, USA

ABSTRACT

COVID-19 has inflicted tremendous damage across countries and economies. Some of the world's most populous nations suffered high death rates as their political leaders publicly expressed skepticism of the advice of their public health leaders and sowed distrust in the public's mind. Many political leaders failed to understand its implications and attributed blame rather than identified public health solutions, which diluted public health messaging. In addition, central and state government leaders undermined attempts by local leaders to mount effective public health campaigns. Meanwhile, leaders most closely aligned themselves with the advice of public health experts fared better both in the measures of disease mitigation and economic displacement. The author compares results in various countries based on their response pattern, explores the literature on effective contingent and risk management that helps explain the divergence in success in battling COVID-19, and demonstrates that collective citizen trust in government is a significant predictor of effective crisis risk management.

INTRODUCTION

No socio-economic phenomenon since the Second World War has struck global economies and societies with more severity and displacement as has the Corona Virus Disease of 2019 (COVID-19). Failures of some political leaders to understand the implications of the disease, and their efforts to attribute blame rather than identify appropriate public health responses, had distracted the public and diluted public health messaging. Especially in Peru, Poland, Brazil, and the United States, countries that experienced the highest death rates among populous nations, political leaders had publicly expressed skepticism over the advice of their public health officials. In addition, central and state government leaders often undermined attempts by local leaders to mount effective public health campaigns. This chapter shows

DOI: 10.4018/978-1-6684-5279-0.ch001

that nations which cultivate the greatest level of public trust fared better in the measures of disease mitigation and in reduced economic displacement. The analysis compares the effectiveness of mitigation of disease deaths in various G20 countries based on the degree of trust of their citizens in public officials and explores the literature on effective contingent and risk management that helps explain the divergence in success in battling COVID-19.

BACKGROUND

Just two years ago, concerns over pandemic disease were rarely articulated. Yet, this lack of attention is not for want of academic study. For instance, in a seminal work, Crawford (2003) documented the potential for global pandemics over the past three centuries. Her analysis is a reminder that pandemics occur more frequently than many imagine and are often forgotten just as quickly as a cure arrives. Her message is one of vigilance and investment in public health. Since the World Health Organization (WHO) declared COVID-19 to be a pandemic on March 11, 2020, few have been untouched by the potential for infection. Worldometers, a leading reporter of statistics internationally, on the two-year anniversary of the WHO declaration reported that 6,056,843 people had died from COVID-19. On the same day, Lancet (2022) reported that, based on excess deaths over what would have normally been expected, fatalities may be three to four times the measured COVID-19 deaths. The direct deaths alone make COVID-19 comparable to the two most common causes of death in developed nations, heart conditions and cancer.

The larger COVID-19 indirect deaths measure considers not only direct deaths attributed to COVID-19, but also deaths that had not been attributed to any cause, deaths attributed to other causes related to COVID-19, or deaths arising by a lack of full access to the medical system that has been overloaded by COVID-19 patients. As the Lancet study shows, the actual rate of excess deaths is estimated to be 18.2 million people worldwide from January 1, 2020, to Dec. 31, 2022. These cumulative excess deaths were highest in India (4.07 million people) and the United States (1.13 million people). Readers worldwide surely recognize the profound nature of this once-in-a-century pandemic, and each likely has strongly held views of the success, failure, and appropriateness of disease mitigation measures, the initial source of the disease, or the effectiveness or necessity of local public health measures. This chapter seeks to explore the disconnect between the wide variety of our individual normative opinions regarding the pandemic, the representations of political leaders, and objective measures of our public health experts to the disease. As the analysis separates the positive from the normative aspects of the public discussion, the relationship between prevailing levels of trust in authority is correlated with success in disease mitigation as measured in mortality.

In the first section, the COVID-19 phenomenon is briefly described. The second section conducts a review of relevant literature. The significant and well-established epidemiological analysis is omitted, and instead the focus is on the socio-economic risk factors that contribute to the degree to which a community is sufficiently prepared to perform crisis risk management. In the third section, a simple hypothesis is postulated that relates one novel socio-economic measure, the degree of trust in government among citizens of G20 nations, and nations' incidence of COVID-19 deaths. Results and conclusion are discussed in the last two sections.

MAIN FOCUS OF THE CHAPTER

A Brief History of Covid-19

Readers are familiar with the history of SARS-COV-2019. The first official case reported to the World Health Organization occurred on December 31, 2019. The disease was identified and named by Chinese authorities a week later as 2019-nCoV. The WHO declared the disease a Public Health Emergency of International Concern on January 30, 2021 and named it COVID-19 on February 11, 2020.

While it remains unclear precisely when or where the first human case occurred, Chinese authorities responded quickly following the first identified case in Wuhan, China, by imposing the standard measure to combat communicable diseases suspected of respiratory transmission. Authorities locked down populations to prevent human-to-human mixing by requiring households to remain at home except for brief windows of time to secure provisions. The quick action of Chinese authorities resulted in a drop in cases in the infected region from thousands in January to dozens by March of that year. Meanwhile, the day following the WHO pandemic declaration, Italy recorded 250 deaths in just 24 hours, which led the WHO to declare Europe to be the pandemic's first epicenter. A little more than a week later, the first known death in the Americas occurred on February 20 of 2020 in Washington State. By early March, 100,000 cases had been identified, and, on March 11, 2020, the WHO declared COVID-19 a global pandemic. On March 13, the United States declared a state of emergency because of its rapid case escalation, especially in New York City and New York State. While its initial source remains unknown to date, most experts believe COVID-19 transitioned from another species to humans. Such species-to-species jumps are not uncommon for respiratory illnesses. A reasonable hypothesis for the COVID-19 jump comes from Mallapaty (2021), who documents studies of bats in Laos that carried a virus which most resembled human SARS-CoV-2.

The Cure

These unprecedented declarations resulted in an equally unprecedented search for cures to the disease and vaccinations to prevent further infections. Chinese scientists had very early identified and broadly shared the genetic code of the virus. By March 17, the Massachusetts-based pharmaceutical research and development firm Moderna used the sequence to create the first trial vaccine. Traditional therapies since the development of a vaccine for smallpox relied on live viruses in small doses, or in viruses that have been killed or neutralized. Exposure of such vaccines allows the human body to build various natural defensive measures. The Moderna approach, and a similar approach by Pfizer, instead relied on a novel technique called messenger RNA, or mRNA. The mRNA is a snippet of the virus that can reproduce within human cells themselves. These strands of ribonucleic acid (RNA) then replicate within our own cells that are, in turn, recognized as foreign bodies by the human immune system. In essence, the mRNA manufactures clones within our own body that are sufficiently similar to the actual COVID-19 virus to trigger an immune response as our body recognizes as foreign and creates responses to kill these RNA strings. Hence, our bodies create both a snippet of the virus and a stock of cells that can then fight the complete virus should the full COVID-19 virus present itself.

This approach would not result into an injectable vaccine that the United States Food and Drug Administration (FDA) could approve for routine human injection until December 11, 2020. Knowing that vaccines typically take years to develop, early public health interventions were designed to limit transmission. By early March of 2020, public health officials worldwide began to recommend measures to limit the spread of the disease. These early measures recommended frequent handwashing and social distancing, which was defined as six feet, or two meters of human-to-human separation based on previous studies involving transmission of viruses on airplanes.

Public Leadership

Many elected officials were unwilling to impose the strict measures some public health officials recommended. Other officials lacked sufficient guidance to make firm recommendations. Responses were typically correlated with the local rate of disease mortality. For instance, in Europe, especially Italy and Spain, residents were afflicted early and intensely, and governments responded with lockdowns. In another early intervener and one of the first national governments to respond, the United Kingdom imposed a stay-at-home lockdown rule on March 26 in the wake of successful lockdowns in Wuhan province in China. Their quick and dramatic response contained the disease by minimizing human contact while infected people overcame the virus, typically within two weeks.

Local Responses

By April 1, 2020, global cases had risen to one million people. On that same date, this author, who was serving as Mayor of the City of Plattsburgh in New York State, imposed a mask mandate for its residents. Having faced a significant exponential growth in cases in the city, this declaration, the first of its kind in the United States, produced a sharp decline in new infections, but not until the Upstate New York Community suffered a rash of hospitalizations and deaths. A few days after the local mask mandate, on April 6, the WHO released guidance that recommended wearing masks of some sort, based on an increasing consensus that COVID-19 was spread through aerosol projection from human exhalation. The Governor of New York subsequently denied a renewal of the Plattsburgh order and imposed a state-wide order later that month.

Such executive orders are often controversial. For instance, in Plattsburgh, some argued that a simple mask would not provide sufficient protection for the wearer unless it was an N95 mask, designed to remove 95% of airborne particulates. Others claimed that the demand for masks would deprive health care workers of that important element of personal protection equipment. Even today, many people fail to understand that masks in this setting are designed not to protect the wearer, but rather to protect the many people with whom an infected wearer may contact and inadvertently spread the disease. The mask was effective not in filtering air but rather in preventing the aerosol projection of the COVID-19 virus to others.

Countervailing Forces, Mutations, and Successful Therapies

By the summer of 2020, seasonal warming in the Northern Hemisphere allowed the outside air to absorb a greater amount of moisture from human exhalation. In addition, summer allows people to devote more time outside, with the attendant ability for the disease to disperse, rather than have it concentrate indoors. However, lack of sufficient confinement of the disease and a vastly increased infection base created the condition for mutations of the virus to develop and spread. By August of 2020, the Southern Hemisphere country of Peru, during their winter, identified a new Lambda variety. On the verge the

Fall of 2020, the Alpha variety appeared in the United Kingdom. Later that month, the world recorded its millionth documented death.

By November of that year, two pharmaceutical companies, Pfizer, in collaboration with BioNTech, and Moderna each documented results from clinical tests to show their developed mRNA vaccines were at least 90% effective in preventing serious disease, while a collaboration between the University of Oxford and AstraZeneca had demonstrated the effectiveness of a traditional vaccine. By the last day of 2020, the WHO recommended their use. At that time, a new and much more virulent mutation was discovered to be quickly spreading in India. By mid-spring of 2021, billions of doses of these various vaccines had been produced and, on April 27th, the billionth dose had been administered. If lockdowns, mask-wearing and social distancing were the first important public health tools for disease eradication, voluntary vaccinations became a second, and perhaps much more difficult hurdle.

The purpose of this paper is to describe the elements of public trust in its contribution to the effectiveness of these various measures recommended by local public health officials. It is the lag between the increasingly well-understood nature of disease transmission by public health scientists and the mandates or encouragement elected officials and public opinion leaders are willing to promulgate to protect their constituents that determines success in containing the spread of COVID-19.

LITERATURE REVIEW

The final story of COVID-19 has not yet been written. At the time of writing, the world is still reeling from yet another COVID-19 variant. Few experts are willing to state that another mutation could not create another new peak in infection. Epidemiologists and virologist will likely study this and related coronaviruses for many years to come. Few believe humankind will never encounter one again. But, while virologists may be preparing for the next mutation or version, the far greater challenge remains the interface between good public policy and politics. Indeed, since late in 2020, scientists and public health experts have agreed on viable ways to manage disease spread and mitigate its symptoms in those infected. If the story is not yet over, there are public policy lessons that leaders can glean on the path of the disease

Vaccines are effective from an objective public health perspective, but the challenge has been to ensure our leaders can through messaging, executive orders, and legislation encourage or mandate practices that can create a sufficiently large pool of protected citizens to prevent further spread of the disease. It is this herd immunity that ensures the virus has few victims to infect and within which it can multiply and then spread to other vulnerable victims. Such successful mitigation of infection risk is sufficient if virus carriers do not offer a ready environment for the virus to replicate inside susceptible humans. These phenomena are now understood from a scientific perspective, but the literature on the socio-political aspects of the problem is still nascent.

A Lethal Mixture of Politics and Policy

The experience in the United States is most enlightening for several reasons. First, the U.S. and Brazil are the only two large population (over 50 million people) nations in the world that experienced more than 300 documented deaths per 100,000 in population. Second, the U.S. suffered the worst outbreak early in the disease's progression, and hence was the first large democracy to confront the socio-political challenges associated with the disease. Third, the year of first infection in the United States was a presidential election year, with the incumbent president Donald Trump running for reelection partly on a platform of minimization of the seriousness of the disease. Fourth, the U.S. was suffering from economic displacements associated with the actions of some states that imposed strong measures to reduce human-to-human contact through forced lockdowns. Finally, turmoil over racial incidents resulting in large crowds of angry protestors that congregated in most major cities, while equally large assemblies of disease deniers erupted across the country. The nation had become divided in many ways, and hence trust in government was dropping.

The Politics of Lockdowns

These are the ingredients of a perfect storm for public health officials who must balance public health needs with economic interests. Fung (2020) well described this perfect storm and the ways in which public policy and political leadership must adapt to COVID-19 and future pandemics. Clark and Harley (2020) add that success in mitigating a pandemic requires sufficient capacity to manage these various contingencies necessary to maintain focus on the public health risk at hand. While a nation may have experience in dealing with each confounding factor that challenged public policy in 2020, it was difficult to simultaneously formulate economic policy to combat unemployment, social policy to deal with racial injustices, and public health policy to deal with a pandemic. Our political system is ill-suited for simultaneous, even if related crises. The authors outline the need for six risk management tools.

Capacity Building

Clark and Harley (2020) note that the first essential element to manage risk is the creation of sufficient public policy capital to manage our economy. The second is assurance that crisis management does not exacerbate social injustices and hence frustrate its uptake. Third, the risk management system must maintain sufficient reserves to deal effectively with unexpected shocks. Fourth, the authors identify the need to ensure that those who preserve the status quo can be swayed to participate in necessary mitigation efforts that often results in a redistribution of income or well-being. Fifth, society must manage the political agitation that will result in such a necessarily dynamic and typically uncertain environment. Finally, the authors note that various levels of our governance systems must work in concert over such a short period of time. In the case of the United States, these risk management challenges must also be conducted following several years of increasing political divisiveness and in a particularly divisive election year.

McConnell and Stark (2021) frame the problem in terms well-understood by politicians. They note that political leaders typically view issues as zero sum. This is in contrast with the positive sum approach public health experts and economists aim to attain. If some politicians are willing to use a pandemic for political gain, in the belief that their gain is their opponents' loss, the discussion is almost immediately diverted from the net societal gain over the obviously displacing costs necessary to combat a pandemic, and into conflicting political assertions. The use of a pandemic as a political tool is especially dangerous when fear, amplified by lockdowns and vaccination requirements, replaces rational discourse.

Such advocacy debates that result when fear replaces discourse are often designed to preserve or enhance political fortunes rather than solve challenges to society, as described by Cairney (2020). In addition, Brandstrom and Kuipers (2003) note that it is not uncommon for politics during periods of crisis management to degenerate into dysfunction. McConnell and Stark agree that risk management in times of crises is effective only to the degree that politicians can put their parochial interests and political fortunes aside. In addition, too often there is insufficient capacity for public sector risk management in times of crises. Boin et al (2006) note that capacity investment when there is no impinging risk is too often an uncertain investment that cannot compete readily for resources with more immediate and certain concerns.

The Clash of Culture and Pandemic Politics

Korstanje (2021) offers a case study of responses to COVID-19 within the broader context of accelerating social injustice and the interplay between economic rights and social responsibilities, especially considering a global pandemic. At the same time as nations were experiencing increased social unrest over a decade that were bookended by the Arab Spring and global George Floyd protests, governments were judged to lack sensitivity to social injustice while it asked so much of society, through lockdowns, social distancing, mask wearing, and then vaccinations. To manage a new and chronic public health risk while society was reeling over other societal risks became confusing and contradictory.

The universality of such perfect public policy storms was exacerbated by broader global communications through social media and through global migration and travel. Interestingly, such migration also meant that, like never before, viruses could easily spread globally. Certainly, the United States demonstrated the tragic results when, in the absence of federal leadership, various groups in a divided population dug in their respective heels. While the U.S. experience was not entirely unique, it was also emblematic of an alienated populist response in other nations such as Brazil. Altheide (2020) documented how the Twitter era and its exploitation by U.S. President Donald Trump frustrated social and public health policy and contributed to the spread of disinformation at a critical time. With respected public policy experts at his side, Trump offered solutions as if drawn from Internet conspiracy theorists, such as the use of strong household cleaning disinfectants to be ingested to ward off the respiratory virus. Altheide observed that the export of disinformation and political opportunism often dominated the political arena at a time when better information and a sense of common purpose were the best antidotes to a global pandemic.

Platteau et al (2020) continue with the dialog that culture and trust constitute a leg of the response stool, along with good public health, clinical innovation, and superior information. They note that various national identities, the demographics of nations, and the subcultures therein are diverse and require nuanced responses. For instance, young people will likely defy lockdowns in ways that older couples would easily embrace. These two groups also garner their information through different outlets, and their likelihood of becoming infected, infecting others, and of chronic illness also differ substantially. One size will not fit all, even when a charismatic and trusted leader can reach all citizens. Nuanced messaging and flexible public policies tailored to the needs and social norms of various demographics are necessary to combat the virus. There may also be cultural norms that entire cultures share, for instance an insistence on personal space versus an acceptance of crowding. However, no national identity is monolithic.

Successful Crisis Navigation

Despite these challenges, some leaders successfully navigated the management of public opinion and enhanced trust in public health prescriptions. Most notably, Mazey and Richardson (2020) describe the leadership of Jacinda Ardern, the Prime Minister of New Zealand, who exercised extraordinary public communication, leadership and compassion in her nation, which culminated in an incredibly low 1.8 COVID-19 deaths per 100,000, a rate that is but 0.6% that suffered in the United States. McConnell and Stark note that some nations manage to bring their citizens together in times of crisis. Winston Churchill in World War II and Volodymyr Zelensky in the wake of the 2022 Russian invasion of Ukraine were successful in public messaging that united their nations at critical junctures. They note that successful crisis management is often a deft combination of science and politics within an environment of fear and uncertainty.

Kleinfeld (2020) provides a commentary that postulates trust ought to impinge upon the effectiveness of crisis risk management. She argues that politicians' assertions that political ideology is more important than sound public health policy in the face of COVID-19 are unfounded. Kleinfeld asserts that trust is essential, and a high degree of trust can be obtained in a variety of economic systems. For instance, China has an authoritarian system, but also has a high degree of trust, as documented by the Edelman Trust Index described in the next section. On the other end of the authoritarian-democratic spectrum, New Zealand, with a high level of democracy, also posts an exceedingly high level of trust. As evidence of this trust, Goldfinch et al (2021) confirm that, in public opinion polls, 83% of New Zealanders either agree or strongly agree that they can trust their government, and this level of trust helps explain the superior COVID-19 results in that country.

Trust in Leadership

Recently, Wu (2021) argued that success in managing the COVID-19 pandemic is correlated with the level of social capital. In her review of the rapidly developing literature related to social capital in pandemic mitigation success, she observed a correlation between social capital and public health success but notes that more work must be done to formalize the relationship, especially in the development of measures of public trust and their effect in pandemic mitigation success. One can postulate that public trust in government is an essential factor in the implementation of successful public health policy. In the next section, the prevailing levels of trust among citizens are compared with the success of leaders of nations to manage a crisis more effectively and hence produce a better outcome in the face of a pandemic.

SOLUTIONS AND RECOMMENDATIONS: THE CORRELATION BETWEEN TRUST AND DISEASE MITIGATION

Myriad factors define the path of progress in managing the risk of a pandemic. Volumes are being written on how to convert a global pandemic to a more manageable endemic disease such as influenza. Titles in this edition treat various approaches and identify factors in our collective management of risk. The identification of one such factor is added to these analyses. In the spirit of Wu (2021), the intuitively appealing hypothesis is postulated: To what degree does public trust determine the success in which we manage pandemic risk?

A normalized measure of risk management success is used. While there are various databases that record the time series of COVID-19 deaths globally, the Worldometers website has consistently collected and reported COVID-19 deaths across various states in every nation since the onset of the disease. Their agents constantly collect, tabulate, and update data from over 5,000 COVID-19 reporting services worldwide. These sources include government agencies and media reports. Their methodology affords them the ability to produce the most complete and timely COVID-19 data worldwide, and subsets of their data is comparable to other trusted regional sources such as Coronavirus Resource Center at Johns Hopkins University in the United States. Their methodologies are more fully described at https://www.worldometers.info/coronavirus/about/, while their daily tabulations can be found at https://www.worldometers.info/coronavirus/. To normalize across countries of various sizes, total death rates per 100,000 people across nations on the date March 11, 2022 is employed. Countries are identified by the name recognized by the United Nations. To remove the effect of nations with vastly different risk management capacities, I confine the analysis to a subset of the G20 nations. These nations include Argentina, Australia, Brazil, Canada, China, the European Union, France, Germany, India, Indonesia, Italy, Japan, Mexico, Russia, Saudi Arabia, South Africa, South Korea, Turkey, the United Kingdom, and the United States. The European Union nations is further divided to include only their major constituent members.

Measures of public trust

If COVID-19 death rates are the dependent variable, a measure of public trust is used to capture the degree to which a nation has sufficient public leadership and messaging capacity to assemble in a crisis and trust that their leadership are not leading them astray. The index is the Edelman Trust Barometer 2022. Founded by Dan Edelman in 1952, Daniel J. Edelman, Inc. is a major public relations firm that subscribes to a strong Environment, Society, and Governance (ESG) ethic. Their annual index they construct "highlights ethical drivers such as integrity, dependability and purpose drive the trust capital of business." They add that, "in the wake of a global pandemic and an international reckoning with racial equality, we work to foster the trust of our clients, employees and partners through citizenship, our global corporate social responsibility mandate." The simplest of data is assembled as follows to determine the correlation between the level of public trust and the rate of COVID-19 deaths per 100,000 as shown in Table 1.

Table 1. A subset of G20 nations ranked by their COVID-19 death rate per 100,000

Edelman Trust Measure 2022	Country Ranked From Highest to Lowest Death Rate	COVID-19 Death Rate per 100,000
51	Brazil	3,041
43	USA	2,968
45	Argentina	2,767
53	Italy	2,597
32	Russia	2,462
59	Mexico	2,443
44	UK	2,376
45	Spain	2,162
50	France	2,137
48	South Africa	1,646
42	South Korea	1,646
46	Germany	1,494
54	Canada	972
75	Indonesia	545
74	India	368
72	Saudi Arabia	252
53	Australia	214
40	Japan	204
83	China	3

In this very simple model, the analysis seeks to determine the degree to which their index is a statistically significant determinant of risk management as measured by the rate of COVID-19 deaths. This analysis has also been repeated using their indices for different years with similar conclusions, but only the cross section in one year of the time series is reported. The null hypothesis is that the index of trust in a nation does not affect the risk management outcome of the COVID-19 normalized death rate.

Regression Results

When this simple regression is performed, the alternative hypothesis that higher degrees of national trust in government results in a lower COVID-19 death rate is accepted as shown in Table 2.

Table 2. Regression results of the dependence of COVID-19 deaths on national trust

Regression Statistics								
Multiple R	0.60332052							
R Square	0.36399565							
Adjusted R Square	0.32658363							
Standard Error	870.212558							
Observations	19							
ANOVA								
	df	***SS***	***MS***	***F***	***Significance F***			
Regression	1	7367764.394	7367764	9.729377	0.00624232			
Residual	17	12873588.24	757269.9					
Total	18	20241352.63						
	Coefficients	***Standard Error***	***t Stat***	***P-value***	***Lower 95%***	***Upper 95%***	***Lower 95.0%***	***Upper 95.0%***
Intercept	4085.13702	823.0416696	4.963463	0.000118	2348.670888	5821.60316	2348.67089	5821.60316
X Variable 1	-46.898517	15.0354555	-3.11919	0.006242	-78.620555	-15.176479	-78.620555	-15.1764786

This alternative hypothesis is accepted with a t-statistic of -3.12. In other words, the relation between COVID-19 deaths and public trust is statistically significant at the 99.4% confidence level. Since only one explanatory variable is employed, the overall regression is also significant, with an F-statistic of 9.73 and a level a significance of 99.4%, well above the threshold necessary to accept the interdependence of trust and crisis risk management effectiveness. There are myriad variables that affect the ability of a nation to manage crisis risk. Indeed, some of these variables could interact with the level of trust to which a nation's citizens subscribe. The level of trust can also shift over time, and the various constructors of the index provide an interesting narrative of shifting trust over time. However, the use of the index over different years did not produce significantly different results.

FUTURE RESEARCH DIRECTIONS

COVID-19 has acted as a most unfortunate laboratory for the study of effective public policy in risk mitigation at times of crises. World War II, racial strife in the United States in 1968, and Russia's invasion of Ukraine in 2022 are similar examples of national crises. A lesson learned is that, if one could predict the capricious nature of the human condition and the effectiveness of leadership to foster crisis risk management, public policy leaders could encourage various socio-political systems to invest sufficiently in the citizenry's capacity to trust its leadership to prevent the invariably painful and inferior responses at times of crisis.

However, the literature on capacity building notes that it is difficult to establish such capacity in advance. Few leaders run for office at the precise time of and mandate to manage a crisis. Instead, crises are thrust upon them. Society's measure is how it develops the capacity once it absorbs the inevitable. To do so depends on one essential element. The data show that various nations ultimately respond very differently. The key observation is that the ability of a nation's leaders to foster trust and put aside politics, at least temporarily, allows for successful crisis risk management.

Crisis managers often look to Prime Minister Jacinda Ardern's success in the experience of New Zealand to mitigate the COVID-19 pandemic. In a small country without numerous layers of competing bureaucracies, trust was maintained by articulating a unified message. Ardern recognized that sufficient degrees of communications and compassion are essential for risk mitigation. Indeed, it is likely that alternate measures of successful public communications would also perform well as an independent variable. This and other relevant variables are asserted to have been captured in the trust index and hence influence our success in crisis risk management.

Experts in crisis risk management understand at an intuitive level the ingredients necessary for success. For instance, Platteau et al (2020) describe the process by which some leaders can navigate culture to promote public health and economic resilience. The relationship between trust and risk management success is likely a fragile one. Leaders who practice misinformation and prevent accurate reporting may cultivate short-term message control and popularity, but will surely, sooner or later, violate the public's trust. Without being too metaphoric about the crisis arising from Russia's invasion, deception may allow a leader to win a battle, but, once the public realizes their trust has been violated, the leader may ultimately lose the war, especially in this age of social media.

An interesting extension of this model would be to explore the degree to which sound public policy can be frustrated through tensions between competing levels of government. Such a notion of political competition viewed through the lens of zero-sum games, has been suggested by McConnell and Stark (2021). Note, though, that if such political games hinder sound risk management, politics can convert what they consider to be a zero-sum game between leaders into a negative sum game for society and the economy overall.

Another interesting avenue for future research is the interplay between disease communicability and the style of modern social media communications. While intuition suggests that access to broader information channels should offer a potent public policy tool, evidence seems to suggest that social media instead amplified intransigence and frustrated the articulation of clear policy messages.

CONCLUSION

For better or worse, readers of this edition have all experienced the calamity of the first global pandemic in a century. Hopefully, readers fared better than many. Society will certainly be learning from this experience for decades to come, although the vagaries of politics suggest countries may not handle crisis risk management substantially better in the future. One can hope otherwise, though. Meanwhile as our epidemiologists and virologists work to prepare us better with hard science, and with tools to cope with the next pandemic, and our public health experts better absorb what happens when we tend to listen to politicians rather than objective public health practitioners, it is obvious at both an intuitive and empirical level that the confidence of a citizenry in their government and its perceived honesty and communicativeness set the landscape for crisis risk management success.

ACKNOWLEDGMENT

The author thanks the editor and two anonymous referees for insightful advice and guidance in the writing of this chapter. Their comments allowed me to significantly improve the exposition and the quality of the paper's conclusions.

This research received no specific grant from any funding agency in the public, commercial, or not-for-profit sectors.

REFERENCES

Altheide, D. L. (2020). Pandemic in the time of Trump: Digital Media Logic and Deadly Politics. *Symbolic Interaction, 43*(3), 514–540. doi:10.1002ymb.501

Boin, A., Hart, P., Stern, E., & Sundelius, B. (2006). *The Politics of Crisis Management: Public Leadership Under Pressure*. Cambridge University Press.

Brändström, A., & Kuipers, S. (2014). *From 'Normal Incidents' to Political Crises: Understanding the Selective Politicization of Policy Failure*. Cambridge University Press. doi:10.1111/1477-7053.t01-1-00016

Cairney, P. (2020). *Understanding Public Policy: Theories and Issues*. MacMillan International/Red Globe Press.

Clark, W., & Harley, A. (2020). *How COVID-19 has changed public policy*. Harvard Kennedy School. https://www.hks.harvard.edu/faculty-research/policy-topics/public-leadership-management/how-covid-19-has-changed-public-policy

Crawford, D. (2003). *The Invisible Enemy: A Natural History of Viruses*. Oxford University Press.

Fung, A. (2020). *How COVID-19 Has Changed Public Policy*. Harvard Kennedy School. https://www.hks.harvard.edu/faculty-research/policy-topics/public-leadership-management/how-covid-19-has-changed-public-policy

Goldfinch, S., Gauld, R., & Taplin, R. (2021). Trust in Government Soars in Australia and New Zealand During Pandemic. *The Conversation*. https://theconversation.com/trust-in-government-soars-in-australia-and-new-zealand-during-pandemic-154948

Kleinfeld, R. (2020). *Do Authoritarian or Democratic Countries Handle Pandemics Better?* Carnegie Endowment for International Peace. https://carnegieendowment.org/2020/03/31/do-authoritarian-or-democratic-countries-handle-pandemics-better-pub-81404

Korstanje, M. E., & George, B. (2021). *Mobility and Globalization in the Aftermath of COVID-19: Emerging New Geographies in a Locked World*. Palgrave MacMillan. doi:10.1007/978-3-030-78845-2

Lancet (2022). *Estimating excess mortality due to the COVID-19 pandemic: A systematic analysis of COVID-19-related mortality, 2020–21*. doi:10.1016/S0140-6736(21)02796-3

Mallapaty, S. (2021). Laos Bats Host Closest Known Relatives of Virus Behind Covid. *Nature, 24*(September). https://www.nature.com/articles/d41586-021-02596-2

Mazey, S., & Richardson, J. (2020). Lesson-Drawing from New Zealand and Covid-19: The Need for Anticipatory Policy Making. *The Political Quarterly*, *91*(3), 561–570. doi:10.1111/1467-923X.12893 PMID:32836413

McConnell, A., & Stark, A. (2021). Understanding Policy Responses to COVID-19: The Stars Haven't Fallen from the Sky for Scholars of Public Policy. *Journal of European Public Policy*, *28*(8), 1115–1130. Advance online publication. doi:10.1080/13501763.2021.1942518

Platteau, J. P., & Verardi, V. (2020). How to Exit COVID-19 Lockdowns: Culture Matters. CEPR.

Ries, T. (Ed.). (2020). *2020 Edelman Trust Barometer Global Report*. https://www.edelman.com/trust/2020-trust-barometer

Ries, T. (Ed.). (2022). *2022 Edelman Trust Barometer Global Report*. https://www.edelman.com/trust/2020-trust-barometer

Wu, C. (2021). Social Capital and COVID-19: A Multidimensional and Multilevel Approach. *Chinese Sociological Review*, *53*(1), 27–54. doi:10.1080/21620555.2020.1814139

ADDITIONAL READING

Barrios, J. M., Benmelech, E., Hochberg, Y. V., Sapienza, P., & Zingales, L. (2021). Civic capital and social distancing during the COVID-19 pandemic. *Journal of Public Economics*, *193*(1), 104–112. doi:10.1016/j.jpubeco.2020.104310 PMID:33199928

Bartscher, A. K., Seitz, S., Slotwinski, M., & Wehrhofer, N. (2021). Social capital and the spread of COVID-19: Insights from European countries. *Journal of Health Economics*, *80*(2), 56–64. doi:10.1016/j.jhealeco.2021.102531 PMID:34607120

Borgonovi, F., & Andrieu, E. (2020). Bowling Together by Bowling Alone: Social Capital and COVID-19. *Social Science & Medicine*, *265*(1), 45–67. doi:10.1016/j.socscimed.2020.113501 PMID:33203551

Ding, W., Levine, R., Lin, C., & Xie, W. (2020). *Social distancing and social capital: Why U.S. counties respond differently to COVID-19*. NBER Working Paper. https://www.nber.org/papers/w27393

Fraser, T., & Aldrich, D. P. (2021). The dual effect of social ties on COVID-19 spread in Japan. *Scientific Reports*, *11*(1), 1596. doi:10.103841598-021-81001-4 PMID:33452323

Fraser, T., Aldrich, D. P., & Page-Tan, C. (2020). *Bowling Alone or Masking Together? The Role of Social Capital in Excess Death Rates from COVID19*. https://papers.ssrn.com/sol3/papers.cfm?abstract_id=3744251

Taylor, M. W. (2014). *Viruses and Man: A History of Interactions*. Springer International Publishing. doi:10.1007/978-3-319-07758-1

Varshney, L. R., & Socher, R. (2020) *COVID-19 Growth Rate Decreases with Social Capital*. doi:10.1101/2020.04.23.20077321

Wu, C., Wilkes, R., Fairbrother, M. & Giordano, G. (2020). *Social Capital, Trust, and State COVID-19 Testing*. Contexts.

Chapter 2
Petroleum Industry Contingency Planning Using Auditing Theories and Inferential Statistics

Kenneth David Strang
https://orcid.org/0000-0002-4333-4399
W3-Research, USA & RMIT University, Australia

ABSTRACT

This chapter demonstrates how to apply a novel Bayesian auditing statistical technique with a predictive probability distribution model to predict petroleum accidents. The goal was to first develop the petroleum oil spill patterns for a given population, develop a predictive distribution model, and validate that using Bayesian audit statistical techniques. Sample data were taken from a U.S.-based state and fixed interval random sampling was used to select the records for the audit. A beta distribution was generated illustrating the materiality parameters along with the misstatement results.

INTRODUCTION

This chapter investigates if risk management techniques used in the auditing discipline could help identify and or prevent petroleum accidents. First the severity of the petroleum spill problem is briefly reviewed to establish the rationale for the current study. Next the relevant literature is reviewed to inform the methods. The methods are explained and a model is developed using sample data collected in the U.S.

Oil spill disasters happen more often around the world than environment conservationists would find acceptable (Liang, Ryvak, Sayeed, & Zhao, 2012; Mendelssohn et al., 2010; Strang & Nersesian, 2014). In the U.S. for example, there have been over 24,000 oil spills documented during the last two decades. In New York State there were at least 1,000 oil spills documented during the decade ending 2013 (Strang, 2015). Figure 1 depicts the frequency of oil spills in the USA during 2000-2020 based on the author's analysis of data obtained from the U.S. Bureau of Transportation Statistics (USBTS, 2022).

DOI: 10.4018/978-1-6684-5279-0.ch002

Figure 1 suggests the oil spill trend is decreasing since 2000, and as expected, the incidents were low during COVID-19 (2019-2020), which was as much data that were available at the time of the current study. Paradoxically and alarmingly, the analysis of the current study reveals that the volume of oil spilled actually increased dramatically to 714,416 gallons, just prior to the COVID-19 pandemic, which was the largest amount of annual oil spilled in almost two decades, since 2000. Overall, the data from figure 1 demonstrate that there were 24,245 known oil spills during the last two decades (2000-2020) resulting in a cumulative 3,781,384 gallons of oil contributing to pollution and critical resource wastage in the U.S.

Petroleum disaster prevention has been studied by several researchers, using inferential statistics and qualitative case studies. For example, Strang (2015) retrospectively analyzed 1005 oil spill accidents recorded by the New York State Department of Environment Conservation, in an attempt to develop an empirically-grounded environmental planning risk management model to prevent the frequency and severity of future human-caused petroleum-related accidents. Interestingly, Strang (2015) found gas service stations were likely have 4-8 times more petroleum accidents, and more so, repeat-offenders were common: If a gas station in New York had experienced a petroleum accident then it was 40% more likely to have a repeat occurrence. Nersesian and Strang (2013) described how a discrete probability distribution could be developed and tested with sample data to identify potential oil spills. Other researchers including Mendelssohn et al. as well as Matlow, Wray and Richardson (2012) used qualitative approaches to examine this oil disaster problem. The common finding across those studies was that novel techniques were proposed but there were no complete practice-based solutions for how to reduce petroleum accidents given the large geographic expanse of the earth.

Thompson (2012) made a salient point which was the impetus for the current study. In the U.S. he reviewed the problems arising from hydraulic fracturing of bedrock deep under the surface (fracking), with a finding that in addition to more accidents there were health implications including potable water table contamination and structural cracks in building foundations of nearby populations. His salient point was that more environmental audits were needed to prevent fracking problems. The current study takes his idea further, to examine if auditing theory, models and or procedures could be applied to detect petroleum accidents. The research question (RQ) in the current study became: Could risk-based statistical techniques used in the auditing discipline identify potential petroleum accidents?

This chapter makes a contribution to the petroleum contingency management body of knowledge by reviewing the literature and illustrating how to apply a novel Bayesian auditing statistical technique with a predictive probability distribution model to predict petroleum accidents. Prediction provides an important benefit in the contingency management practice because, if a decision maker can project a potential risk, then a contingency plan may be created to eliminate or mitigate any future occurrence. A statistical model can facilitate creating a contingency plan, but not all managers know how to do that. This chapter presents one possible approach.

Figure 1. Oil spill disasters across the U.S. during 2000-2020
(collected and analyzed by the author)

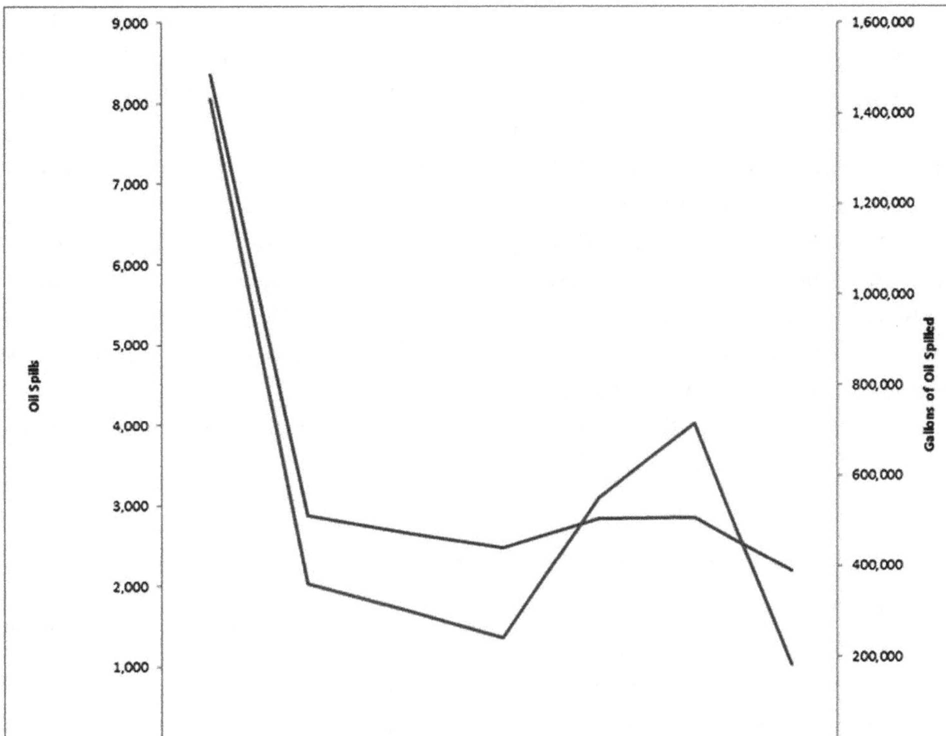

	2000	2015	2016	2017	2018	2019	2020
Incidents	8,354	2,873	2,663	2,472	2,834	2,855	2,194
Gallons spilled	1,431,370	361,482	301,723	241,204	549,914	714,416	181,275

PROBLEMS AND CONTROVERSIES IN PETROLEUM RISK MANAGEMENT

Uncertainty Quantification and Risk Analysis

Disasters are risk events or crises (Taleb, 2007). Disaster planning means to plan for mitigating against disasters (Simonovi, 2010). Since disasters are uncertain until they occur, risk management theories can be applied to estimate uncertainty and to develop strategic mitigation plans (Ginn, 1989). Man-made disasters are more uncertain due to the nature of human socio-cultural behavior (Adams & Berry, 2012; Goodwin & Strang, 2012; Wagner et al., 2009).

Uncertainty quantification is done in the assessment phase of risk management generally by applying probability theory and statistical techniques (Goodwin & Strang, 2012), to estimate the likelihood each event could occur (Taleb, 2007). The most difficult aspect of risk analysis is developing a probability distribution model, which can be easily applied to actual practice when needed (Nersesian & Strang, 2013). However, distributions are based on historical data to quantify uncertainty, so in order to apply this for contingency planning or petroleum accident prevention, the probabilities must be used to sample current data in order to detect an ensuing disaster early on before it occurs in full form (Goodwin & Strang, 2012).

Contingency Planning Distribution Models for Disasters

Probability distribution models can be based on actual data or theoretical models (Keppel & Wickens, 2004). Simulation generally relies on probability distributions to calculate risks within acceptable control intervals (Keppel & Wickens, 2004). Simulation does not have any such theoretical precepts built into its construct except a very critical assumption that past patterns, such as the probability distribution of price changes, or petroleum spills, hold for the future. It may be helpful to discuss how to build and interpret a distribution model applied to an actual earthquake disaster case study.

The case study data from Nersesian and Strang (2013) was applied to illustrate this point. In their case study situation, the idea was to have response teams for major earthquakes of magnitude 7 and above. The teams were actually helicopter carriers strategically placed in different areas of the world. In case of a major earthquake, the carrier proceeds at top speed to a location close to the earthquake. Even before the carrier arrives at its destination, helicopters full of men and equipment fly to the scene, administer first aid and come to the rescue of those trapped in the rubble. Then the helicopters return to the carrier for a second wave of food and temporary shelters.

Table 1. Example distribution frequencies of magnitude 7+ earthquakes (author)

Year	Earthquakes	Bin (class)	Frequency	Cumulative %
1994	12	10	0	0.00%
1995	18	11	2	10.53%
1996	17	12	3	26.32%
1997	16	13	1	31.58%
1998	12	14	0	31.58%
1999	20	15	2	42.11%
2000	16	16	3	57.89%
2001	15	17	2	68.42%
2002	13	18	3	84.21%
2003	15	19	0	84.21%
2004	16	20	2	94.74%
2005	11	21	0	94.74%
2006	11	22	1	100.00%
2007	18	23	0	100.00%
2008	12	24	0	100.00%
2009	17	25	0	100.00%
2010	22	>25	0	100.00%
2011	20	M=15.7 (SD= 3.246, N=19), Median=16		
2012	18	95% control interval (14.3, 17.2)		

In their case study, the helicopter carriers were the contingency plan to reach the earthquake victims because people trapped in rubble can only last a relatively short time. Many major earthquakes affect areas close to the ocean. For more inland locations, a military base often has to be used for helicopter refueling events. They estimated that a helicopter response team will require 20-40 days to complete a mission before it can be employed to respond to another earthquake. Their goal for the risk planning model was to determine how many helicopter carriers should be dedicated to responding to earthquakes of magnitude 7 and above for any given year. The first step in the analysis was to obtain a sample of the historical data on major earthquakes during 1989 through 2013 (N=19), which are listed in table 1, 'earthquakes' column. Next the developed class bins, and they counted the frequencies per bin class. They constructed a histogram using the summary data from table (not shown here). They calculated the mean number of earthquakes in the sample data was 15.7 (SD= 3.246, N=19), the median was 16, the range was 10-22 and the control intervals at the 95% confidence level were (14.3, 17.2).

As they explained in their study (Nersesian & Strang, 2013), the distribution can be used in risk planning to compare current data in order to estimate the risk of a disaster event occurring. Their logic was based on parametric statistics, specifically the *Central Limit Theorem (CLT)*. They used a *chi square goodness of fit* statistical test to determine if a current sample was similar to the distribution, and if so, the trend line could be used to forecast if and when a future earthquake disaster would likely occur, in any 95 out of 100 years (since the distribution was based on annual data). The applied the simulated earthquake distribution to determine how many helicopter emergency response teams would be needed in any given year. The result was that four helicopter response teams strategically placed could handle 73% of expected earthquakes and six teams could handle 98.4% of all expected earthquakes. Thus they asserted their inferential statistical modeling was effective for earthquake contingency planning.

The contingency planning distribution model developed by Nersesian and Strang (2013) has several limitations. One problem is that the normal distribution in CLT may not be appropriate for analyzing the number of petroleum disasters. Although they conceded that, they suggested a lognormal distribution was used by some scholars for estimating expected economic values when there was a high degree of uncertainty (Taleb, 2007), but a lognormal distribution is intended for continuous data types (Browne & Cudeck, 1993; Ozgur & Strasser, 2004) such as money or distance. Petroleum spills are events, which can be counted (although the volume or weight could be measured). A spill event is discrete in a binary sense: either it exists or it does not. Therefore, analysis of any type of disaster, natural or man-made, with respect to counting the events, requires a discrete probability distribution (Daniel, 1990). The common discrete distributions are binomial, chi square, Poisson, and hypergeometric (Levine et al., 2005; Strang, 2009).

Table 2. Petroleum spills by industry and year adapted from Nersesian & Strang (2013)

Industry	2004	2005	2006	2007	2008	2009	2010	2011	2012	Totals	Mean	SD	Median
Petroleum sales	14	24	27	21	18	21	4	9	9	147	16.3	7.8	18
Residential	25	15	18	21	10	17	17	14	17	154	17.1	4.2	17
Electricity generation	10	16	21	25	15	12	13	25	19	156	17.3	5.5	16
Business	20	15	23	13	15	13	13	12	18	142	15.8	3.8	15
Transportation system	14	14	8	14	9	9	9	12	16	105	11.7	3.0	12
Government	5	11	10	3	6	5	6	4	6	56	6.2	2.6	6
Interstate or road	4	8	2	4	4	7	5	7	8	49	5.4	2.1	5
Hospital	3	0	1	3	0	4	1	3	0	15	2.5	1.2	3
University	4	3	3	4	4	6	2	3	1	30	3.3	1.4	3
Water or port area	0	1	4	3	3	1	1	3	1	17	2.1	1.2	2
Park	2	1	1	2	0	1	1	2	1	11	1.4	0.5	1
Totals	101	108	118	113	84	96	72	94	96	882	98.0	14.3	96

Nersesian and Strang (2013) went further in their disaster risk planning model formulation by determining if a discrete probability distribution could be applied for risk analysis of empirical data from petroleum spills using actual data collected from New York State. Their procedures were interesting and worth replicating. After they collected 945 petroleum spill reports from the Department of Environmental Conservation inspectors, they calculated interrater reliabilities as a way to ensure the investigator causes were reliable (the reliability estimate was 98% which they considered good). Table 2 summarizes what they found, the petroleum spills by industry across years. They found there was a clear distinction between the industries with the highest average per year and the highest number of petroleum spills. The petroleum spills were most frequent in the following industries: Petroleum sales (e.g., gas stations), residential, electricity generation, businesses, and transportation systems. Secondly, those industries had the highest percentage of spills every year. They further analyzed the data into a distribution of oil spills by day of week (not shown). From that they determined 79% of the spills were caused in only a subset of the industries: Residential, business, electricity generation, petroleum sales and transportation systems. They also found most oil spills occurred on a weekday, the highest on Thursdays (49, for businesses). It is clear their discrete distribution statistical model could be used for oil disaster contingency planning, by simply creating public administration policies to increase audits on Thursdays, and targeting accident-prone industries such as gas stations.

There are parallels between contingency planning for petroleum disasters and risk management in auditing – both rely on CLT, normal distribution probabilities, data sampling and applying inferential statistical tests. Auditing of financial statements (and other documents) are typically required by law in most developed countries, including the U.S., namely for private, public and non-profit organizations. The audit processes are considered to be complex, the quality requirements are very high (to ensure no false accusations or missed law-breakers), and the associated costs may be substantial (Read, 2013). Auditors must use statistical techniques to determine the sample size and estimate if errors or monetary discrepancies significantly deviate from a prescribed percentage or monetary amount, which is called materiality (Callahan & Soileau, 2017). When the total errors in a statement exceed the materiality benchmark, the auditor would declare that the financial statements contain significant material misstatements, meaning the errors in the financial statements could impact decisions of stakeholders relying on those statements (e.g., investors, customers, partners).

Risk management in auditing takes the form of a four-phase framework, as briefly enumerated below:

1. Planning – using heuristics and regulations to determine what documents in the population needs to be sampled and using statistics to determine sample size;
2. Selecting – applying statistical sampling technique to identify which population records to collect;
3. Executing – collecting specific data and comparing to source documents, then calculating estimates including summary evidence of comparisons;
4. Evaluating – using inferential statistics to determine if there were material misstatements and concluding the audit processes based on the results (adapted from Johnstone, 2018).

Auditors are considered to be in the accounting discipline and they have transformed auditing practices from the classical statistical techniques of hypothesis testing to the Bayesian probability distribution approaches (Johnstone, 2018). The key difference with Bayesian auditing approaches as compared with hypothesis testing is that in the former subjective considerations (prior probabilities), namely the percentage of allowable error probabilities, are used to statistically test the data. In the Bayesian approach, the sample size planning uses materiality, expected tolerable errors, the likely underlying distribution (Binomial, Poisson, or Hypergeometric), the estimated population size, and optionally whether to use prior probabilities if available from similar audits (Derks, de Swart, van Batenburg, Wagenmakers & Wetzels, 2021). The selection can apply random interval, fixed interval, or sieve type sampling technique, whereby attribute or monetary items can be selected (e.g., all records with values over a certain amount).

According to Derks et al. (2021), in Bayesian auditing approaches statistical measurement parameters for the calculations are determined by the auditor with the common being a confidence level of 95%, and a significance level of .05 which becomes the materiality cutoff. Note that in most software being applied for Bayesian auditing, it appears that it is not mandatory to assign a prior probability namely the population misstatement. However, if available, this incorporates preexisting audit information. If prior probabilities are available, the statistical techniques may use gamma, beta or beta-binomial distribution parameters (Derks et al., 2021). It is clear that the Bayesian auditing approach would be a valuable statistical technique to apply for developing a petroleum disaster contingency planning model.

METHODOLOGY

This was a simulation study using retrospective archival data requested from a previous study of petroleum disasters by Strang (2015). A post-positivist ideology was applied, namely that quantitative data would be collected, and inferential statistical techniques would be used for analysis. Descriptive, inferential and nonparametric statistical techniques were applied using ubiquitous commercial software.

Procedures

First the database of prior oil spills was obtained, which was based on the New York State Department of Environmental Conservation (NYSDEC) investigations in the U.S. The goal of the audit was set to check if Strang (2015) made any errors in evaluating the NYSDEC investigator conclusions about whether the spill was serious enough to be considered a disaster, since some reports indicated no great amount was discharged, such when someone spilled a small amount of gas when refueling automobiles or when a tanker overturned without releasing anything. In other words, the purpose of the applied auditing technique would be to determine if the disaster prediction model developed from the NYSDEC reports was sufficiently accurate without any misstatements. If the model were considered accurate after the audit then it could be used for future petroleum disaster prediction by decision makers. Thus in this sense, the Bayesian audit would go hand—in-hand with the predictive disaster model development as a follow up statistical validation technique.

Then a subjective decision was made for the auditing parameters. Standard parameters were selected where possible. The rationale for this decision was that if using Bayesian auditing techniques to identify potential petroleum accidents, then the logic of similar oil disaster/auditing research should be followed (namely: Callahan & Soileau, 2017; Nersesian & Strang, 2013; Strang & Nersesian, 2014; Strang, 2015; Derks et al., 2021). Thus, auditing industry defaults were set as: 95% confidence level, .05 materiality, and a Poisson distribution which allows for discrete count data. The simulation was executed using the petroleum investigation reports as if an audit were being conducted.

RESULTS AND DISCUSSION

To reiterate, the Bayesian audit of the underlying data could be done prior to or after developing the probability distribution. The objective of the audit sampling procedure was to determine with a confidence of 95% whether the percentage of misstatements in the population (petroleum spill data collected/ interpreted from NYSDEC) was lower than the performance materiality of 5% .

In the planning phase, the most likely error in the sample was expected to be 0% . This was reasonable since Strang (2015) had reported the interrater reliabilities between the NYSDEC investigators was 98%. In this simulation case study, there were no prior probabilities, so the required sample size was calculated using a beta distribution with the parameters set to alpha = 1 and beta = 1. The sample size that was calculated as required for an accuracy materiality of 5%, assuming the sample contained 0 full errors, was calculated to be 58. This sample size was based on the beta distribution, the *a priori* assumption that every value of the misstatement is equally likely, and the expected errors. Statistically this means that if this sample is evaluated and the sum of (proportional) errors in the audited transactions is lower than (or equal to) 0, the maximum misstatement is determined to be below the performance materiality. In a practical sense, 58 of those 1005 records needed to be examined, after being randomly selected using the fixed interval sampling technique.

Figure 2. Bayesian audit beta distribution
(author)

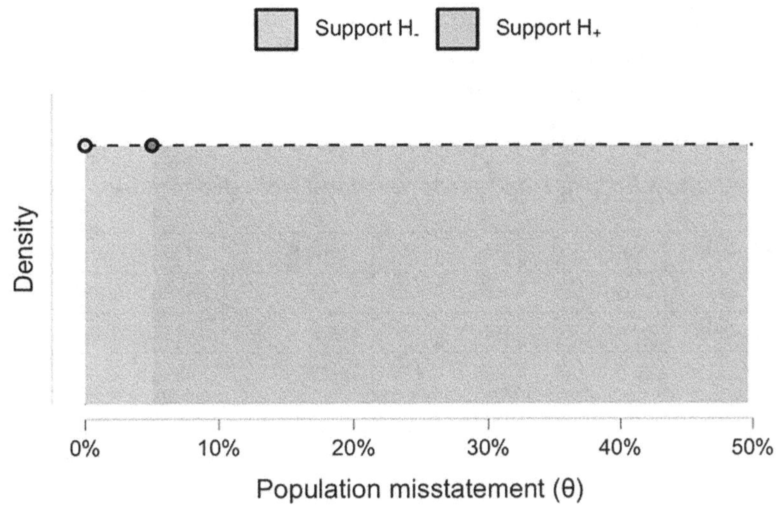

Figure 2 illustrates how the Bayesian auditing theory applied to the current study. The prior probability distribution (beta) on the misstatement in the population is shown in the shaded blue and orange regions. Again note the prior beta distribution parameters were $\alpha = 1$, $\beta = 1$. In Bayesian audit theory the prior beta distribution probabilities would be based on or derived from the assessments of the inherent and control risk, along with the expected errors. The expected errors (grey dot) receive the highest probability. The red dot represents the materiality, or expected / allowable errors. Figure 2 is the prior probability density beta distribution illustrating the expected misstatement in the population of oil spill records. Theoretically, the prior parameters $\alpha = 1, \beta = 1$ are derived from the assessments of the inherent and control risk, along with the expected errors. The expected errors (grey dot) receive the highest probability. The red dot represents the materiality (e.g., 5%).

The next step was to randomly select 58 records from the oil spill population dataset using the fixed interval sampling technique. After the records were selected, each one was evaluated. The record in the petroleum spill distribution database was checked against the NYSDEC investigator's report to determine if there were any errors. An error could be that the spill was so small or actually nothing escaped, but the researcher could have categorized the record as a spill since it was in the disaster distribution file, or alternatively, there could have been parameter errors. A new column or field was added to the audit sample of 58 in a spreadsheet to indicate if the record was an error, and if so it was flagged as 1=error otherwise that field was set to 0=no error. Interestingly, selection consisted of **58** sampling units, of which a total of 1 were misstated (there was an error). The information from this sample combined with the prior information results in a most likely error in the population of 1.667% and a 95% upper bound of 3.79%. The CLT deductive logic provides that there is a 95% probability that the misstatement in the population is lower than 3.79% with a precision of 1.667%.

The interpretation of this is that the error is acceptable because it was lower than 5% materiality level. Next the posterior Bayesian audit beta distribution probabilities may be calculated which could inform the development and audit of a future disaster prediction model. Table 4 summarizes the key estimates of the Bayesian audit beta distribution posterior probabilities. In Bayesian audit theory, consideration is given to classical theory where hypothesis testing is applied. The concept of a materiality being lower than the acceptable error is denoted as support for H- whereas being above the acceptable error would be states as support H+. Table 4 lists the audit beta distribution parameters, H-, H+, the ratio, mode if relevant, 95% upper interval and precision. A value of "NaN" means it was not available or relevant for that estimate's data. Table 4 parameters are visually portrayed in figure 3 as a beta distribution.

Table 4. Descriptive statistics for prior and posterior audit beta distribution

	Functional Form	Support H_-	Support H_+	Ratio $^{H}{}_{-}$ ¤ $_{H+}$	Mode	95% Upper Bound	Precision
Prior	beta(α = 1, β = 1)	0.050	0.050	1.000	NaN	0.050	0.051
Posterior	beta(α = 2, β = 58)	0.801	0.199	4.023	0.017	0.078	0.061
Shift		16.018	0.210	76.438	NaN	-0.872	

Note. H_-: The population misstatement is lower than materiality ($\theta < 0.05$). H_+: The population misstatement is equal to, or higher than, materiality (θ ³ 0.05).

Figure 3. Beta distribution of population misstatement
(author)

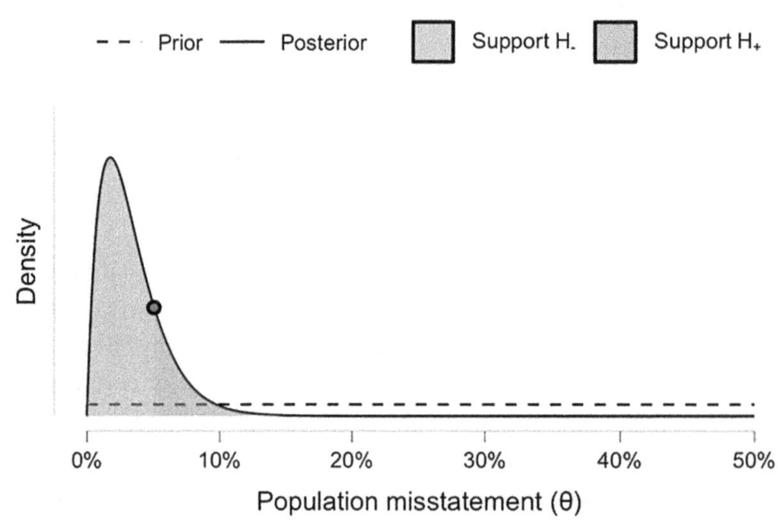

The objective of this audit sampling procedure was to determine with 95% confidence whether the misstatement in the population is lower than the specified performance materiality, in this case 5%. For the current data, the 5% upper bound on the misstatement is below the performance materiality. The conclusion on the basis of these results is that, with at least 95% confidence, the misstatement in the population is lower than the performance materiality.

However, if the misstatement were higher than the performance materiality, theoretically, an additional sample ought to be obtained, using the beta distribution parameters to calculate the additional sample size.

CONCLUSION

This paper demonstrated how to apply Bayesian auditing statistical techniques with a predictive probability distribution model to predict petroleum accidents. The goal was to first develop the petroleum oil spill patterns for a given population, develop a predictive distribution model, and validate that using a Bayesian audit statistical technique. Actually, the distribution model was developed in a different study, since that was a lengthy process, so as to afford discussion space towards explaining the Bayesian audit statistical techniques for validating that model.

This study was one of the few in the literature which demonstrated uncertainty estimation and applied risk analysis using discrete probability distributions for man-made petroleum spill disasters accompanied by Bayesian statistical audit techniques to validate the model. The literature review identified several similar studies of petroleum or similar type of chemical spill disaster accompanied by predictive model development, but none of the researchers applied auditing theory to validate their models. In most studies reviewed, Chi Square Goodness of Fit tests were performed to validate the model. However, those studies fell short of the evidence that would be required in a rigorous financial audit. Thus, this led to the idea that Bayesian auditing statistical techniques could be applied in conjunction with the development of a predictive petroleum accident prediction model, for use by stakeholders such as decision makers. In this way the concept for the current study was to apply auditing theory reasoning, by using statistical sampling techniques to evaluate if the probability model's underlying data contained more than a few errors, which in the financial industry would amount to material misstatements.

Some interesting ideas emerged from this study, of interest to environment conservation and auditing stakeholders. By itself, this Bayesian auditing approach is not useful in contingency planning since it relies on validating the data used to develop a probability distribution. Thus, this is a two-step process for practitioners and other stakeholders. However, the audit can be performed before the probability model is constructed, to validate the materiality of the data, before time is put into developing and testing the model. Bayesian auditing can also be applied in a post-hoc or retrospective fashion, to published scholarly studies, to determine if the model in an empirical were based on accurate data or misstatements of fact.

In terms of generalization, a municipality or an Emergency Management Systems (EMS) agency could use these methods - distribution probability analysis with Bayesian auditing techniques - for creating reliable models to predict petroleum spills (or disasters), on a day of the week or other time period, or by a certain type of industry/stakeholder. In fact, any nominal factor in the sample data could serve as the axis for the distribution (such as location, type of spill, time of day or season, just to name a few).

The main contribution this chapter made to the petroleum contingency management body of knowledge was by reviewing the literature and illustrating how to apply a novel Bayesian auditing statistical technique with a predictive probability distribution model to predict petroleum accidents. Prediction provides an important benefit in the contingency management practice because, if a decision maker can project a potential risk, then a contingency plan may be created to eliminate or mitigate any future occurrence. A statistical model can facilitate creating a contingency plan, but not all managers know how to do that. This chapter presented one possible approach using a case study.

The key argument the author made in the current study was that a statistically significant discrete distribution model was developed and validated from the sample data using Bayesian auditing techniques, which showed there was a difference in patterns as to when petroleum spills would likely occur within specific industries on certain weekdays. EMS agency planners would use this type of distribution to schedule first responder staff while municipalities could use the model to adjust tax rates by industry. There are many other possibilities for applying this.

The central benefit of this type of research to the community of practice is to show how it can be done, rather than to imply these specific results would generalize to another population. The data in this study was collected from New York State and validated using Bayesian auditing techniques. There is no claim made to generalize the findings to a specific population. Instead, the researchers suggest collecting data and testing it against the common probability distribution models, applying Bayesian auditing to validate the model, then probabilities could then be used to drive contingency planning for the future, so as to reduce uncertainty without having to calculate risk. That is a valuable benefit.

FUTURE RESEARCH DIRECTIONS

The author recommends additional distribution analysis should be attempted with other types of natural and man-made disasters, in combination with Bayesian auditing statistical techniques to validate the underlying data. This would require discrete probability distributions if event counts or the number of people affected or repeated spills by location were analyzed as the dependent variable.

The author also recommends researchers investigate additional dependent variables associated with natural and man-made disasters, such as the volume of spill content and distances between locations of spills. The authors plan a future study to examine the distances between disasters using a variation of logistics optimization analysis.

ACKNOWLEDGMENT

This research received no specific grant from any funding agency in the public, commercial, or not-for-profit sectors.

REFERENCES

Adams, L. M., & Berry, D. (2012). Who Will Show Up? Estimating Ability and Willingness of Essential Hospital Personnel to Report to Work in Response to a Disaster. *Online Journal of Issues in Nursing*, *17*(2), J1. doi:10.3912/OJIN.Vol17No02PPT02 PMID:22686116

Browne, M. W., & Cudeck, R. (1993). Alternative ways of assessing model fit. In J. S. Long (Ed.), *Testing Structural Equation Models*. Sage.

Callahan, C., & Soileau, J. (2017). Does Enterprise risk management enhance operating performance? *Advances in Accounting*, *37*(1), 122–139. doi:10.1016/j.adiac.2017.01.001

Daniel, W. W. (1990). Applied Nonparametric Statistics (2nd ed.). PWS Kent.

Derks, K., de Swart, J., van Batenburg, P., Wagenmakers, E.-J., & Wetzels, R. (2021). Priors in a Bayesian audit: How integration of existing information into the prior distribution can improve audit transparency and efficiency. *International Journal of Auditing*, *25*(3), 621–636. doi:10.1111/ijau.12240

Ginn, R. D. (1989). *Continuity Planning: Preventing, Surviving and Recovering from Disaster*. Elsevier Science Publishers Ltd.

Goodwin, Y., & Strang, K. D. (2012). Socio-cultural and multi-disciplinary perceptions of risk. *International Journal of Risk and Contingency Management*, *1*(1), 1–11. doi:10.4018/ijrcm.2012010101

Johnstone, D. (2018). Accounting Theory as a Bayesian Discipline. *Foundations and Trends in Accounting*, *13*(1-2), 1–266. doi:10.1561/1400000056

Keppel, G., & Wickens, T. D. (2004). *Design and Analysis: A Researcher's Handbook* (4th ed.). Pearson Prentice-Hall.

Levine, D. M., Stephan, D., Krehbiel, T. C., & Berenson, M. L. (2005). *Statistics for Managers using Microsoft Excel* (4th ed.). Pearson Prentice-Hall.

Liang, F.-Y., Ryvak, M., Sayeed, S., & Zhao, N. (2012). The role of natural gas as a primary fuel in the near future, including comparisons of acquisition, transmission and waste handling costs of as with competitive alternatives. *Chemistry Central Journal*, *6*(1), 1–24. doi:10.1186/1752-153X-6-S1-S4 PMID:22540989

Mendelssohn, I. A., Andersen, A. L., Baltz, D. M., Caffey, R. H., Carman, K. R., Fleeger, J. W., Joye, S. B., Lin, Q., Maltby, E., Overton, E. B., & Rozas, L. R. (2010). Oil impacts on coastal wetlands: Implications for the Mississippi River Delta Ecosystem after the Deepwater HorizonOil Spill. *Bioscience*, *62*(6), 562–574. doi:10.1525/bio.2012.62.6.7

Nersesian, R., & Strang, K. D. (2013). Risk planning with discrete distribution analysis applied to petroleum spills. *International Journal of Risk and Contingency Management*, *2*(4), 61–78. doi:10.4018/ijrcm.2013100105

Nersesian, R., & Strang, K. D. (2013). Risk planning with discrete distribution analysis applied to petroleum spills. *International Journal of Risk and Contingency Management*, *2*(4), 61–78. doi:10.4018/ijrcm.2013100105

Ozgur, C., & Strasser, S. E. (2004). A Study of the Statistical Inference Criteria: Can We Agree on When to use Z Versus t? *Decision Sciences Journal of Innovative Education*, *2*(2), 177–192. doi:10.1111/j.1540-4609.2004.00043.x

Read, C. (2013). Key risk and uncertainty theories impacting contemporary financial economics. *International Journal of Risk and Contingency Management*, *1*(4), 22–41.

Simonovi, S. P. (2010). *Systems approach to management of disasters: Methods and applications*. Wiley. doi:10.1002/9780470890363

Strang, K. D. (2009). Using recursive regression to explore nonlinear relationships and interactions: A tutorial applied to a multicultural education study. *Practical Assessment, Research & Evaluation*, *14*(3), 1–13.

Strang, K. D. (2015). Developing prescriptive environmental protection models from descriptive human accident behavior. *International Journal of Disaster Resilience in the Built Environment*, *6*(4), 81–96. doi:10.1108/IJDRBE-08-2013-0029

Strang, K. D., & Nersesian, R. (2014). Nonparametric estimation of petroleum accident risk to improve environmental protection. *Journal of Environment. Systems and Decisions*, *34*(1), 150–159. doi:10.100710669-013-9476-z

Taleb, N. N. (2007). *The black swan. The impact of the highly improbable*. Penguin.

Thompson, H. (2012). Fracking boom spurs environmental audit: As hydraulic fracturing unlocks new gas reserves, researchers struggle to understand its health implications. *Nature*, *485*(5), 557–560.

USBTS. (2022). *Oil Spills In and Around U.S. Waterways*. Bureau of Transportation Statistics, U.S. Department of Transportation.

Wagner, K. D., Brief, D. J., Vielhauer, M. J., Sussman, S., Keane, T. M., & Malow, R. (2009). The Potential for Ptsd, Substance Use, and HIV Risk Behavior Among Adolescents Exposed to Hurricane Katrina. *Journal of Substance Use & Misuse*, *44*(1), 1749–1767. doi:10.3109/10826080902963472 PMID:19895305

Chapter 3
Development and Application of a New Maturity Model for Risk Management in the Automotive Industry

Jose Irizar
University of Gloucestershire, UK

Martin George Wynn
https://orcid.org/0000-0001-7619-6079
University of Gloucestershire, UK

ABSTRACT

Risk management is an integral part of the project management process, and project failure is an area of concern in many organizations. This chapter explains and discusses a new maturity model for assessing and managing project risk in the automotive industry. The research design was two-fold. First, a case study analysis in a major German automotive company was undertaken to develop the maturity model. The approach was qualitative and inductive, using data provided by in-depth interviews. Second, this model was applied in two major projects currently underway in the company – one involving implementing a cloud-based ERP system and the other the program management function responsible for product development and launch. The model adds to existing risk management maturity models and is unique to the automotive industry. It can be used by risk and project managers and can be adapted to other industry sectors.

INTRODUCTION

The significance of managing risk has come to the fore in recent years in the context of cybersecurity and the rapid growth of the associated risks to organisations and society at large (Olakunle & Win, 2022). However, project risk management has been a fundamental discipline in most industry sectors for several

DOI: 10.4018/978-1-6684-5279-0.ch003

decades, and can be defined as the process that dynamically minimizes risk levels by identifying and ranking potential risk events, developing a response plan, and actively monitoring risk during project execution (Zwikael & Ahn, 2011). Although risk management has become a significant element of some of the most widely deployed industry standard methodologies, there is no universally agreed method for managing risk. Yet, as a recent industry report notes, "risk management has never been more important. Projects are under more pressure to deliver, and the costs of failure are higher than they have ever been" (Project Management.com, 2019, p.8). Application of integrated risk management methods can support early risk identification and assessment, thereby improving project outcomes and avoiding delays and cost overruns (Zayed, Amer, & Pan, 2008).

This research focuses on the development and application of a new maturity model for the assessment, monitoring and management of project risk capability in the automotive industry, specifically in a European context. Following this brief introduction, the next section explores relevant literature in this field, followed by a detailed explanation of the research methodology employed. Section 4 then presents the maturity model as built and verified, but also applies the model to two in-company projects. This provides an illustration of how the model can be used, in a manner that can be built upon by other researchers and practitioners. The final section draws together key themes covered in the chapter and assesses the contribution to research and practice.

LITERATURE REVIEW

Risk Dimensions

Holzmann (2012) views risk management as comprising five main activities, encompassing risk identification, risk assessment, risk allocation, and risk control. Other authors (Bannerman, 2008; Harwood, Ward, & Chapman., 2009) see risk appetite or treatment as an important dimension for overall risk management. This research combines elements drawn from these sources to focus on four main dimensions of risk management: risk identification, risk assessment, risk allocation and risk appetite; and it does not see risk in a purely negative context, but also recognises the potential of positive risks or opportunities.

Risk Identification

This is considered to have the highest impact on the effectiveness of project risk management and involves the detection and classification of all known and - as far as is possible - unknown, risks, thus producing the foundation upon which the overall risk management process can be established (Chapman, 2001). Risk identification is also perceived as the most influential risk management activity (de Bakker, Boonstra, & Wortmann, 2011; de Bakker et al., 2012), and particularly in complex projects is seen as an area in need of improvement (Harvett, 2013). Risk identification can be performed in a number of ways, such as filling in questionnaires, consulting experts or available documentation from previous projects, doing brainstorming sessions, or conducting interviews.

Risk Assessment

The stage in the risk management process at which each identified risk is assessed for its probability or likelihood of occurrence, and its impact - in terms of time, cost and quality - on either the project phase or the entire project, should it occur (Patterson, 2002). Risk assessment entails the study of the probability of occurrence and any associated consequences. Generally speaking, two broad categories of risk assessments have been used - qualitative risk assessment and quantitative risk assessments (Dawotola, Gelder, & Vrijling, 2012). Qualitative risk assessment makes use of descriptive scales for the assessment of probabilities, such as risk scores. These scores or rankings are subject to interpretation and therefore entail an inherent level of subjectivity (Dawotola et al., 2012). The application of qualitative risk assessment suffers some serious limitations, mainly the subjectivity of the values estimated. Qualitative risk analyses are flawed in the sense that they can produce wildly different results (Emblemsvåg & Kjølstad, 2006).

Risk Matrices

These are one of the most popular risk assessment methodologies employed across many industries, providing the graphical output that enables the communication of risk assessment. The development of risk matrices (RMs) has taken place in isolation from academic research in decision making and risk management – risk matrices produce arbitrary decisions and risk-management actions. These problems cannot be overcome because they are inherent in the structure of RMs (Thomas, 2013). Their theoretical basis is superficial and the validity of the qualitative information they employ is highly suspect. Assessments of the likelihood of occurrence and their impacts suffer all the shortcomings associated with subjective assessment (Wall, 2011).

Risk Allocation

This is a major task in the overall risk project management process (Harvett, 2013), and is based on the recognition that different parties have different objectives and perceptions of project risk, as well as varying capabilities for managing associated sources of uncertainty. Chapman and Ward (2007) consider risk allocation (or risk ownership as it is sometimes termed) a relevant phase within their formal process framework SHAMPU (Shape, Harness, And Manage Project Uncertainty). It involves allocating responsibility for managing project uncertainty to appropriate project parties. These allocations are fundamental because they can strongly influence the motivation of parties and the extent to which project uncertainty is assessed and managed by each party.

Risk allocation is related to the more general concept of business ownership which has seen a range of business functions take responsibility for various aspects of project delivery. In the past IT or engineering functions often owned exclusively the risk in their related projects. Now, it is often the case that the function in charge of the project helps business partners to take ownership of specific risks and assists them in making assessments and in following compliance mechanisms by themselves (Chobanova, 2014).

Project Risk Appetite

Sometimes called "risk treatment" or "risk propensity," reflects an organisation's attitude and strategy towards risk. It encompasses how risk is managed and whether exposure to risk should be reduced, or the impact of risk should be mitigated, transferred, externalized or accepted. These responses can be supported by a framework providing risk factor dependencies and priorities (Aloini et al., 2012). Harwood et al. (2009) see risk propensity as the organizational behavioural tendency towards taking reasonable risks, by recognising, assessing and managing risks. A risk-averse organisation is seen to have low risk appetite, and will take only those risks that are judged to be tolerable and justifiable.

A balanced treatment of risk would focus both on risk and reward. An overemphasized focus on risk versus reward may have considerable influence on strategic decisions such as entering new markets, developing new products or targeting new mergers and acquisitions (TowerGroup, 2014). Resultant executive inaction may lead to loss of potential revenue growth. Education and training in project risk management with subsequent additional experience in the organization can produce a better understanding of risk and reward. Risk management can then be understood as a protection shield, not an action stopper. Manager and employees learn through education and training to take and manage risks, not to avoid them. The organization will treat risk appropriately and not try to circumvent it.

Existing Maturity Models

The maturity concept has featured in a range of models used for assessing organizational capabilities encompassing the collective skills, abilities and expertise of an organization. Maturity can be understood as a measure of organizational performance, and such models have been developed to assess a range of organisational capabilities, including e-Government (Wynn et al., 2021), e-business (Wynn et al., 2013) and blockchain deployment (Bazaeea et al., 2020; Wang et al., 2016), and Artificial Intelligence utilisation (Vaish et al., 2021). There are two approaches to organizational maturity that can be applied in the development of such models. The Organisational Project Management Maturity Model (OPM3) measures organisational maturity based on the level of best practices deployment, while the Capacity Maturity Model Integration (CMMI) assesses maturity based on organisational process effectiveness (Man, 2007). Further, organisational capabilities may refer to both processes and projects (Maier et al., 2012). Assessing an organization's project risk management maturity level can help develop its project capability and performance. Risk management maturity reflects the organization's s211understanding of its risk portfolio and its attitude towards those risks. Organizations intending to implement or improve their project risk management need a framework against which they can benchmark their current practice (Zou et al., 2010), and maturity models can be used to identify the priority areas in need of improvement, and remedial actions can then be taken to increase performance (Hopkinson, 2012; Ciorciari & Blattner, 2008).

Hillson (1997) was an early proponent of risk maturity models. His approach consisted of four attributes (culture, process, experience and application) and four levels of maturity. His model (Table 1) is not industry specific and does not focus on risk in projects, but is a general organisational approach to risk. Yeo and Ren (2009) developed and tested a five-level maturity model (initial, repeatable, defined, managed, and optimizing) with three key capability areas: organization culture; risk management process; and risk management knowledge and technology, based on research of Asian offshore and marine projects. Similarly, Zou et al's. (2010) risk management maturity model was industry specific, in this case the construction industry in Asia and Australia. It had four maturity levels (initial, repeated, managed and optimized), and encompasses risk identification, risk assessment and risk appetite - but not risk allocation - in projects.

Table 1. Attributes of Hillson's Risk Maturity Model (Hillson, 1997)

	Level 1 - Naive	Level 2 - Novice	Level 3 - Normalised	Level 4 - Natural
Definition	Unaware of the need for management of risk. No structured approach to dealing with uncertainty. Repetitive & reactive management processes. Little or no attempt to learn from past or to prepare for future.	Experimenting with risk management, through a small number of individuals. No generic structured approach in place. Aware of potential benefits of managing risk, but ineffective implementation, not gaining full benefits.	Management of risk built into routine business processes. Risk management implemented on most or all projects. Formalised generic risk processes. Benefits understood at all levels of the organisation, although not always consistently achieved.	Risk-aware culture, with proactive approach to risk management in all aspects of the business. Active use of risk information to improve business processes and gain competitive advantage. Emphasis on opportunity management ("positive risk").
Culture	No risk awareness. Resistant/reluctant t to change. Tendency to continue with existing processes.	Risk process may be viewed as an additional overhead with variable benefits. Risk management only used on selected projects	Accepted policy for risk management. Benefits recognised & expected. Prepared to commit resources in order to reap gains.	Top-down commitment to risk management, with leadership by example. Proactive risk management encouraged & rewarded.
Process	No formal processes.	No generic format processes, although some specific formal methods may be in use. Process effectiveness depends heavily on the skills of the in-house risk team and availability of external support.	Generic processes applied to most projects. Formal processes, incorporated into quality system. Active allocation & management of risk budgets at all levels, Limited need for external support.	Risk-based business processes. "Total Risk Management" permeating entire business. Regular refreshing & updating of processes. Routine risk metrics with constant feedback for improvement
Experience	No understanding of risk principles or language.	Limited to individuals who may have had little or no formal training.	In-house core of expertise, formally trained in basic skills. Development of specific processes and tools.	All staff risk-aware & using basic skills. Learning from experience as part of the process. Regular external training to enhance skills.
Application	No structured application. No dedicated resources. No risk tools.	Inconsistent application. Variable availability of staff. Ad hoc collection of tools and methods.	Routine & consistent application to all projects. Committed resources. Integrated act of tools and methods.	Second-nature, applied to all activities. Risk-based reporting & decision-making. State-of-the-art tools and methods.

An extension of Hilson's maturity model is Hopkinson's (2012) Project Risk Maturity Model, which establishes a framework for assessing risk management capability against recognised standards. Hopkinson's model offers a working model to assess risk management capacity and applies it to an equipment procurement case study. Crawford (2006) identified some key issues for developing and applying project management related maturity models. One is the intrinsic subjectivity associated with the determination of an organisation's maturity. Crawford also concluded that, rather than necessarily striving to achieve the next level of maturity, organizations should instead determine their minimum level of maturity at which optimum value can be achieved (Crawford, 2006). Maier et al. (2012) established a roadmap to develop maturity grids for assessing organizational capabilities. They review existing maturity models and conclude that they offer a contemporary representation of different conceptualizations of organizational practices and capabilities that are viewed as important for success.

Provisional Conceptual Framework

Whilst some of these maturity models are of value in certain industry contexts, there is no maturity model specifically geared to project risk management in the automobile industry. This research addresses this gap by building and verifying a maturity model for the automotive industry in Europe. The initial conceptual framework for this model builds upon the four dimensions of risk discussed above – identification, assessment, allocation and appetite. These can be defined as:

Risk Identification

The process by which the project team detects prospective events which might affect the project and documents their characteristics (Holzmann, 2012).

Risk Assessment

The stage in risk management at which the identified risk is assessed for its probability (likelihood) of occurrence and its impact, in terms of time, cost and quality (Patterson & Neailey, 2002).

Risk Allocation

The assignment of the responsibility for managing specific project risks or uncertainty to appropriate project individuals or parties (Harvett, 2013).

Risk Appetite

The organizational (or individual) behavioural tendency regarding how to take reasonable risks (Aloini et al., 2012).

The research attempts to identify typical risk characteristics that can be associated with each of these four dimensions of risk at different stages of maturity in the risk management process. Like some of the models discussed above, the proposed model was assigned four stages with provisional stage labels of Rudimentary, Intermediate, Standardised and Corporate. Maturity models typically have either four or five stages, but in the five stage models, the difference between stages one and two is generally minimal, with stage one often describing a non-existent or minimal initial capability. Four stage models have the additional benefit of avoiding an assessor's tendency to select middle values (Zou et al., 2010). These stages can be defined as follows:

- **Rudimentary***:* the organisation has no sense of need for risk management; teams do not follow any common approach in managing risks. Project risk activities are reactive and no lessons learned or improvement process is established. Typically, no project risk plan exists.
- **Intermediate**: some project management practitioners undertake certain project risk management activities. Neither these activities, nor the systems and applications used to support risk manage-

ment, are standardised. The organisation does not gain the full benefit of implementing these risk management activities.

- **Standardised**: risk management is seen as part of core business processes, and risk responses and their effectiveness are reviewed in most projects. Systems and applications supporting risk management are accessible and lessons learned are established to improve the overall risk management process.
- **Corporate**: the entire organisation recognises and values risk management, which is integrated into other processes. Executives actively audit and support risk owners. Multi-user risk databases are widely available and used as part of continuous improvement programs.

RESEARCH METHODOLOGY

The research method was qualitative and inductive, based on in-depth interviews in a single company case study. The case study entails a "detailed investigation of one or more organisations, or groups within organisations, with a view to providing an analysis of the context and processes involved in the phenomenon under study" (Hartley, 2004, p. 323). This is exploratory research that adopts a qualitative approach. Project management success is complex, messy, and involves a range of stakeholders with different concerns and perceptions (Skinner, Tagg, & Holloway, 2000). A qualitative approach is particularly appropriate for research that seeks to explore real organizational goals, linkages and processes in organizations; to understand the failure of policies and practices (Marshall & Rossman, 2014).

The research builds explanations of risk management in practice from the ground up, based on interview evidence, observations, and analysis of available documentation. The interview is an important source for collecting data, and may take several forms (Yin, 2012). To achieve quality in data collection, interviews must be carefully planned. Data collection was undertaken through 12 semi-structured interviews, three follow-up in-depth interviews, an on-line survey, informal discussions, secondary material, and participant observation.

This research took place within the automotive industry, one of the leading manufacturing industries worldwide, where scientific method has an undeniable influence in manufacturing industry development. Operational research and systems engineering are two of the main academic disciplines that provide the basis for process improvements in this industry. The underlying theoretical perspective of these disciplines is positivism (Taylor, 1911), and the concept of separating planning from doing is reflected in the emphasis on planning and control in modern project management. Furthermore, rationality, universality, objectivity, value-free decision making, and the possibility of generating law-like predictions in knowledge are basic assumptions of modern project management (Gauthier & Ika, 2012). The traditional project management paradigm has been described as "rational, normative, positivist and reductionist" (Harvett, 2013, p.51).

The study aligns with recent academic research from authors such as Harvett (2013), Niebecker (2009) and Olsson (2006) all of which explicitly characterize their work on project risk management in practice as post-positivist. This study adopts a qualitative research approach that identifies descriptive labels specific to different risk management contexts. Some may suggest this is an interpretivist approach, but interpretivism, as an alternative to the positivist orthodoxy, assumes there is no absolute truth, but multiple realities and is based on subjectivity (Biedenbach & Müller, 2011). However, this research assumes there is an answer to the questions posed, even if the researchers must seek for the consensus views of the practitioners to validate what is known. For the interpretivist, all meaning is believed to be subjective, based on subjective perceptions and experiences with external environmental factors. This research adopts a post-positivist stance which looks for an objective, singular truth, thus differentiating it from the interpretivist paradigm (Phoenix et al., 2013).

The selected case study company was viewed as a reasonable example of a global automotive supplier organisation, because of its regional presence, customer mix, and product catalogue. The company has over 135,000 employees, around 200 production facilities in some 40 countries, sales of €35.2 billion in 2016, and a yearly investment on R&D of about €2 billion. It is highly dependent on the success of its new projects and the smooth launch of serial production for global customers. Project risk management is a fundamental aspect of its project management process, and is applied globally. Project risks are documented, evaluated and risk controls are applied, and the risk management process is reviewed regularly to adapt it to the market challenges. The unit of analysis is thus the entire organisation. Following Yin's (2012) distinctions of designs for case studies, the one chosen in this research is holistic as opposed to embedded, in which more than one unit of the organisation are the units of analysis (Saunders et al., 2009). In the application and testing of the model in 2022, two "live" business environments were used. The implementation of the cloud-based SAP Enterprise Resource Planning (ERP) product provided an ideal context for the application of the developed maturity model. The second project in which the maturity model was applied centred on the program management function responsible for product development (and launch). This represented a somewhat different application of the model – assessing a process or function rather than a defined project.

The initial research phase was conducted over an eighteen-month period and fourteen potential interviewees were initially invited, of which 12 accepted the invitation. These business leads were chosen because collectively they represented project managers of major projects with high impact to the organization. An initial semi-structured interview took place with these 12 personnel (Table 2), in which their previous experience with regards to project risk management and their understanding of the risk management dimensions were explored. The Participant Consent form and the project information sheet were sent in advance to the participants, together with an interview agenda and questionnaire.

Table 2. Roles and experience of the 12 interviewees

1. **Program Manager:** 8 years' experience as Project Manager – published chapters on project risk management, PMP
2. **European ERP Manager:** 12 years' experience in IT and project management as project manager and Steering Committee member, PhD in IT, PMP
3. **VP Program Management Global:** 25 years' experience in Project Management, responsible for the Project and Project Risk Management methodology, training, templates and business process methods defined/deployed through the global organization, PMP
4. **Global ERP Manager:** 20 years' experience, responsible for ERP competency center, responsible of several ERP rollouts worldwide, PMP
5. **Director, Global Program Management of business unit:** 20 years' experience, responsible of the global business unit programs, manager of 15 program managers, experience with Project Risk management quantitative methods such as Monte Carlo, PMP
6. **Chief Engineer, PMO lead:** 15 years' experience, responsible of the PMO, engineering programs methodologies and systems, PMP
7. **PMO / Program Systems Coordinator:** 10 years' experience, responsible for standard program management training and Program management systems development, PMP
8. **Senior Program Manager:** 15 years' experience – responsible for major programs, PMP
9. **Senior Program Manager:** 15 years' experience – responsible for major programs, PMP
10. **Director, Global Program Management business unit:** 10 years' experience, responsible of the global Engineered Fasteners & Components programs, manager of 10 program managers, PMP
11. **Applications Engineer and Project Manager:** 5 years' experience, Project Risk management expert, co-author of the internal project risk management procedures.
12. **Senior Vice President, business unit:** 15 years' experience - ultimate responsibility for 12 sites in 9 countries, acting as Sponsor and/or senior Steering Committee member on major customer programs.

The questions were grouped according to the four sequential project risk management dimensions. To support and balance these main questions, follow-up questions were developed to ensure breadth of discussion of each of the risk dimensions. The interview was introduced by a brief presentation using PowerPoint slides, to set the scene. Just four slides were discussed initially, and the remaining three slides were discussed in combination with questions. The interviews finished with a debriefing, requesting whether anything else could be relevant to the questions discussed, any other aspect that should be mentioned, or any question needing further elaboration. All 12 stakeholder interviews were transcribed verbatim, resulting in 135 pages of transcripts. These were then analysed and the initial version of the maturity model was constructed.

Having built the initial model from data collected through the 12 semi-structured interviews, this was then tested for validity and relevance (Maier et al., 2012). First, an online survey was undertaken involving six practitioners who were contacted by phone where the maturity model and the aim of the online survey was discussed. The responders were then requested to assign each of the 151 statements emanating from the interviews to one of the four maturity stages via an online form distributed via Google forms; a simple tool used to create and distribute questionnaires. The respondents answered the survey on their own with no influence from the researcher, and the responses were collected and stored in a repository. Secondly, three semi structured interviews were conducted.

Although the above procedures constituted a form of model validation, the model was subsequently used to assess risk maturity in the two live environments, as noted above, in 2022. The first of the interviewees was the program manager responsible for defining the standard process template configuration of the SAP implementation, and for the subsequent rollout of the system through several production facilities in different continents. The template is designed to meet funcional, legal and customer requirements, which will eventually be standardised with few exceptions, based on a defined governance model. The second interviewee was the head of the program management function. For both interviewees, the maturity model was explained in outline, and interviewees were provided with a brief description of the labels and the maturity stages applied to the four dimensions were briefly discussed, with one or two more detailed explanations. Intervieweees were then asked to relect upon the model and identify, in a series of logical steps, the labels that best represented their project or process environment. The interviewer provided guidance and support to help the interviewees in this procedure (Figure 1).

Figure 1. Guide for maturity model application

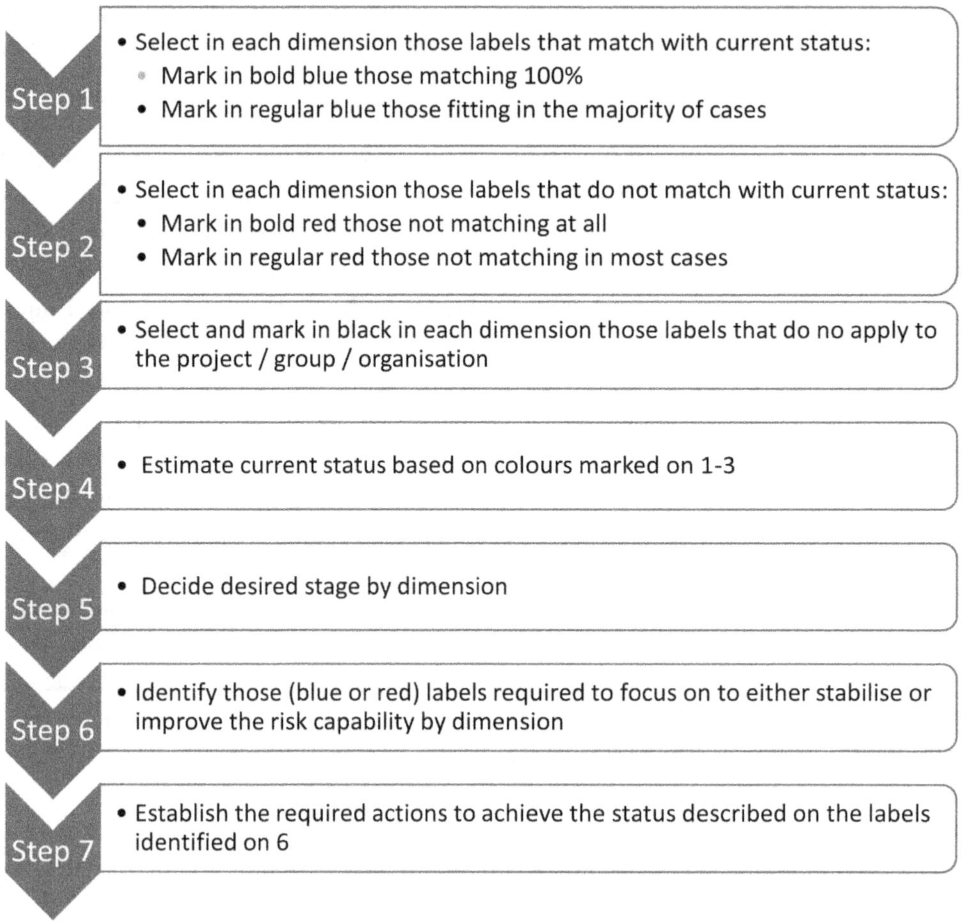

MATURITY MODEL PRESENTATION AND APPLICATION

The model, with its four stages of maturity, can be used to assess and understand the organisation's current project risk management capability and subsequently develop strategies to improve their risk management practice. The maturity model assesses four fundamental dimensions of project risk management, namely risk identification, assessment, allocation and appetite. There are 156 labels allocated to one of the four risk dimensions and one of the four stages in the model. The labels are grouped within the stages and dimensions into two types:

'people and organisation' and 'process and systems'. Following the verification process, the positioning of 51 of the labels was changed, 49 being changed by one stage in the model and two of the labels were relocated by two stages. The model is depicted in Figures 2-5, and summary descriptions of each stage of each of the four dimensions are included in appendices 1-4.

RThe application of the model in the two business environments noted in section 3 above is now discussed. In the web-based SAP ERP project, the maturity level for the Identification, Assessment and Allocation risk dimensions was assessed as Rudimentary, whilst Risk Appetite was seen as being at the

Figure 2. Maturity model: risk identification

IDENTIFICATION	RUDIMENTARY	Negative perception of risk	End users no involvement with risk identification process	Fear of raising risk concerns	Compliancy risks not identified even though may exist	Risk identification is ad-hoc, basic, hit and miss
	INTERMEDIATE	People make full use of their freedom to act	Lack of integration of all stakeholder views	Disagreement among stakeholders if an event is a risk, subjectivity	Some compliancy aspects addressed but may have omitted significant ones	Potentially significant risk items may be omitted in reporting
		Lack of knowledge regarding what risk or uncertainty mean	Risk identification process characterised by subjectivity	No visibility of risk identification tasks / activities in project plan	Isolated non coordinated risk identification	Risk description is ambiguous, misleading
			New risks identified as they occur	Some remaining subjectivity (cultural differences)	Only focused on individual risks, managed at lower levels within team	Lessons learned not standardised. Unstructured documentation
	STANDARDISED	End users have an active role in the identification process	Timely integration of previous phases	Clear risk classification (standard risks)	Set minimum frequency risk identification rules with senior members	Shared understanding of group approach to risk identification
		Recognises risk management but not ready to invest resources	Instructions with project categorization / risk sources identification	Routine planning reviews to aid risk identification	Bridge from the lessons learned into the risk identification process	Mechanism identifies gaps between planned tasks and resources available
		Use quantitative risk methods (Montecarlo) to avoid subjectivity	Established procedure for contradictory views (objectivise)	A risk identification process guide may be Visibility on new sourcing, 'make-or-buy' decisions	Visibility of implications of risks associated with all relevant suppliers	Structured accessible lessons learned & risk registers database (DB)
	CORPORATE	Earned Value (EV) monitoring highlights project performance shortfalls	Integrated process with involvement of all stakeholders	Formal communication regarding risk interrelations between projects	Top down approach related to project purpose and strategy	Real time reporting based on realistic data from all stakeholders

Figure 3. Maturity model: risk assessment

ASSESSMENT	RUDIMENTARY	No relationship between risk information and cost forecast	Responses based on weak understanding or delayed thus ineffective	Isolated non coordinated risk assessment No evidence of opportunities being pursued	No fall back plans for risk mitigation or management	Only considered if project in difficulty or imposed by management
	INTERMEDIATE	Higher focus on project issues than on risks is embedded in the culture	Description includes an indication about the source of risk	Lacks standard impact & probability estimate methodologies. This increases 'subjectivity'	Probability estimation accuracy is weak	Risk description is impact oriented, lacks context and of uncertain origin
		Management does not prioritise project issues over project risks	Quantitative schedule analysis is not used	Struggle with Probability Impact (P*I) threshold concept	Formal risk register maintenance Prescribed risk categorisatio	Use existing expertise and qualitative assessments
	STANDARDISED	FMEA, 6s, poka yoke used for quality management (in product design)	Clear procedure, minimum frequency to assess risk event - Evidence based	Realistic estimates, use existing expertise and qualitative assessments	Sound understanding of risk combined with use of Monte Carlo, decision tree	Description is useful for qualitative risk analysis Impact estimation includes secondary effects
		Planned costs consider risk management - Threshold based on $ or days	Visibility of high-impact risks, risks which became issues, risks clustering ability	Valid methods for risk prioritisation and risk quantification	Team members have good understanding of project's context and overall goal	Certain use of Quantitative Methods
		Considers secondary effects which extend beyond immediate impact	Measure project team members' performance regarding risk issues (commitment)	Steering Committee may challenge the risk process – escalate when required	Systems analyse and summarise risk categories by project, customer or industry	Project categorization is standard Attempts to prevent event from happening in first
	CORPORATE	Systemic risk assessment and continuous improvement	Ability to measure team members' performance	$ estimation of mitigated risk (Benefit of risk responses)	Risk management system integrated with other corporate systems	

Figure 4. Maturity model: risk allocation

ALLOCATION					
RUDIMENTARY	Some stakeholders reluctant to divulge new information on risk	Unwillingness to assign risk ownership - perceived as telling to the other person 'you are doing it wrong'	Reluctance to own risk	Isolated non coordinated risk allocation	Some departments do not feel responsible 'project manager will be hold responsible'
	No active recognition or support for good risk management practice		Risk perceived as intrusive, lot of work and not keen to talk about its ownership	Lack of risk disclosure with contracting parties	
INTERMEDIATE	Dependent on project managers' personality some of which are no open to others' input	Some program managers doing everything, but recognised as inefficient	Steering Committee meetings are pure status meetings	Only program management (and engineering) drive the risk allocation	In most cases assigned to project manager
		Only dotted line reporting to project manager 'my boss has not told me ...'	Suppliers provide risk information however not complete	Identify groups with potential but currently not involved	Constant communication with customer / vendors
STANDARDISED	There is expertise to assign risks across several groups	Team members' actions are aligned with achieving overall project objectives	Expertise within teams is recognised and harnessed	Formal agreements with risk sharing arrangements	Clear business guidelines regarding who is the risk-taker
	All people working in the project actually use the risk management plan	Autonomous functional risk allocation System accessible, customised and team trained	All risks have a risk owner with authority and who accepts responsibility	Clear procedure with minimum frequency rules to update risk ownership	Suppliers undertake complementary risk management
	Steering Committee audits, processes and supports the risk owners	Contracts with formal risk agreement bearing clear financial liabilities	Every team member provides input on items with commercial impact	Prescriptive risk classification and job descriptions enable allocation automation	All stakeholders are open in their disclosure of all risk information
CORPORATE	Good risk management practice, management audits the process and supports the risk owners		Escalation powers and procedures are in place	Consistently maintained multi-user concurrent access risk database is in place	

Figure 5. Maturity model: risk appetite

APPETITE					
RUDIMENTARY	Team members have little understanding of their responsibilities	Senior management makes little/no use of risk management	Lack of competency development plan for program managers	Executives fail to challenge the risk process, primary focus on issues	No project-specific risk management plan
	You raised the risk, you are in charge	No nominated risk manager		Fall back decision points are either not identified or ignored	Risk records cannot be retrieved reliably
INTERMEDIATE	Lack of standard quantitative methods, their use is a subjective decision	Review at fall back decision point but fails to result in decision	'Self-fulfilling prophecy', the less risk mitigation there is, the more issues are left open in the issue list	Mainly qualitative analysis	Steering committees are more akin to status boards
	Contribution to risk although not yet formally active in the program	Risk responses are rarely monitored		Trained teams	Diverse with limited access knowledge databases
STANDARDISED	Ability to commit resources without formal stakeholder confirmation	Highly integrated change management, readiness to take decisions	Clear, unambiguous and documented risk management process	Risk item details have adequate visibility in project phase gate exits	Top-down-approach to appropriate goals establishes the risk culture, strategic decisions first, aligned to project purpose
	The organisation's risk appetite statement is regularly updated	Promotes 'lessons learned' continuous improvement and standard practices	Responses to significant risks tackle risk at source	Resources and skills management address capacity risks	Risk responses consistently implemented Evidence available
	The value of risk management is recognized outside the project	Risk culture is encouraged – openness and respect of others' opinions	Risk awareness is reflected in certain level of compliance (SPICE, MAN5)	Audit trail is recorded	Risk management methodologies are more flexible and adaptable
	Stakeholders are aware of their role as risk takers with ability to cope with risk		Management requires risk response. Evidence available	Risk response effectiveness is reviewed	Systems can report original scope vs. outcomes (post mortem)
CORPORATE	Project risk management capability incorporated into process improvement	Risk management incorporated within other processes (planning, quality...)	Risk responses supported by 'Cost – Benefit' which also considers secondary risks	Lessons learned are effectively incorporated into a continuous improvement programme	

Intermediate stage. For the program management function, risk Identification was judged as being at the Intermediate stage, whereas Risk Assessment and Allocation were slightly more mature, being between the Intermediate and Standardised stages. Risk Appetite was assessed as being between Rudimentary and Intermediate stages.

Risk identification in the *web-based SAP ERP* project does not involve end-users, and the project manager registers potential risks in an ad-hoc manner, which are then formalised in status reports. Project sponsors and Steering Committee members do not encourage anticipation of risks, but rather significant risks (such as lack of resource availability) are identified as these occur. Project team members do not make full use of their freedom to act in this regard. These features and the selected labels suggest risk Identification, Assessment, and Allocation are clearly at the rudimentary stage. The project manager assessed the risk appetite as being at the Intermediate stage, having selected a combination of labels at Rudimentary and Intermediate stages as matching with current status of the project.

For Risk Identification in the *program management function,* a number of labels from the standardized stage relevant to industrialization projects were selected, such as "visibility on new sourcing, make of buy decisions" and "visibility of implications of risk associated with all relevant suppliers". However, there was no overall matching of labels at the Standardized stage for this dimension, which was assessed as Intermediate. Regarding Risk Assessment, several features suggested a Standardized stage rating, but certain crucial capabilities indicative of the Standardised stage were not available – for example, "Impact estimation includes secondary effects", "Certain use of Quantitative Methods" and "Considers secondary effects which extend beyond immediate impact". In terms of Risk Allocation, certain aspects remained weak – for example, not all people working on a project could actually use the risk management plan, making it difficult to provide input on items with commercial impact. The level of collaboration among stakeholders was sub-optimal as there are no "Contracts with formal risk agreement bearing clear financial liabilities", nor are "All stakeholders are open in their disclosure of all risk information." Both Risk Assessment and Allocation were judged to be between the Intermediate and Standardised stages. The assessment of the Appetite dimension was more varied, spanning the Rudimentary and Intermediate stages. There were some labels linked to the Rudimentary stage – for example "No nominated risk manager" - and not all project team members were trained in risk management, which is a requirement of the Intermediate stage. There was a clear failure to meet several of the specifications at Standardised stage, for example, there was no "Risk response effectiveness review", there was no recognition of the value of risk management, and there was a lack of systems functionality to provide variance reports regarding project original scope and project outcomes. Overall, Risk Appetite was deemed to be between Rudimentary and Intermediate stages.

Overall, the program management function attained a somewhat higher maturity rating than the web-based SAP ERP project. This possibly reflects the fact that for several years the program management function has adhered to the company's formal Global Development and Product Evolution Process (GDPEP), which includes elements of risk management. Although IT projects follow a similar process, working practices are not as well-developed as in the product development area, and this is clearly reflected in the maturity assessments.

A major benefit of using the model to assess risk maturity, is that it can provide the basis for an action plan to advance the organisation's capabilities in risk management. A review of the labels assigned to the current and following stages in the model can act as a trigger for new initiatives and follow-on actions (Tables 3 and 4). The SAP ERP project manager is now developing a formal method to train the program management staff on what risk is and how to manage it. He also proposes defining benchmarks for tracking and reporting risk in a standardized way. Although the risk register is currently kept up to date for the issuing of status reports, it has become a box ticking activity, and the project manager now plans to emphasise the significance of the register by making the communication and mitigation of risks a standard item on every Steering Committee meeting agenda. As regards risk appetite improvement, he is now stressing to colleagues the importance of evidence to support actions taken in response to risk alerts ("Management requires risk responses implemented with evidence available").

In the program management function, the functional head is now keen to underline the importance of formalising risk identification tasks and activities, in any project plan and associated work packages. He proposes the introduction of quantitative risk methods and advanced risk analysis training for all project managers in the function. He stresses the importance of usage of the project risk management plan by all project team members.

Table 3. Action plan to advance risk maturity in the SAP ERP project

Action plan by project / dimension	ERP system Implementation	
	Current / next stage	Suggested next steps
IDENTIFICATION	Rudimentary / Intermediate	• Integrate risk identification into the planning process. • Involve end users in the risk identification process • Improve and standardize lessons learned structure
ASSESSMENT	Rudimentary / Intermediate	• Integrate risk assessent into the project cost planning • Expand opportunity management to risk management • Train project team members on advanced risk analysis
ALLOCATION	Rudimentary / Intermediate	• Reinforce usage of project risk management • Train executives and senior management on project risk management for Steering Committee Members • Train project team members on advanced risk analysis
APPETITE	Intermediate / Intermediate	• Train executives and senior management on project risk management for Steering Committee Members • Train project team members on advanced risk analysis • Develop risk management reporting (to ensure risk responses monitoring)

Table 4. Action plan to advance risk maturity in the program management function

Action plan by project / dimension	New product developement project	
	Current / next stage	Suggested next steps
IDENTIFICATION	Intermediate / Standardised	• Increase knowledge and usage of quantitative risk methods • Improve usage and availability of lessons learned • Provide visibility of planned tasks against committed resources
ASSESSMENT	Intermediate / Standardised	• Expand the use of risk quantification and quantitative analysis • Train project team members on advanced risk analysis (e. g. consider secondary risk effects) • Develop risk management reporting
ALLOCATION	Intermediate / Standardised	• Train executives and senior management about the responsibilities of Steering Committee Members • Enforce usage of project risk management plan by all project team members
APPETITE	Intermediate / Standardised	• Ensure project risk management training for all project stakeholders including Steering Committee members

CONCLUSION

This chapter sets out a new maturity model for assessing risk management capability in the automotive industry in Germany. The model is based on 12 responsive interviews that provided the base material for model construction. The model was then validated and refined through an on-line survey and follow-up interviews with three of the original interviewees. It was then subsequently applied in two in-house environments, one concerning the implementation of the SAP ERP product, the other the program management function. The model can be used to gauge the capability level of an organization as a whole, or can be used to assess a particular project. Once an initial assessment of maturity stages has been made, the model can be used as a guide or for the development of action plans and initiatives to improve different aspects of risk management.

The model can be used in practice in a variety of ways and contexts and for different purposes. Company project practitioners may select the appropriate labels from each dimension to assess their risk management capability. Senior management and project practitioners can identify a desired maturity stage; identify gaps in their capabilities with the help of the label descriptors; and develop a list of actions required to reach the chosen stage. In a training or workshop session, the model can also be "deconstructed", removing the allocation of labels to specific maturity stages, with project participants selecting labels that appear most appropriate to the environment in which they work. Ensuing debate can then suggest the current maturity level for that particular project risk management environment.

Joustra (2010, p.3) refers to project risk management as a set of activities often perceived as a "bolt-on-extra" rather than being integrated with the project management process and organization. This maturity model can be seen as an integrating matrix that encompasses a range of elements relating to process and systems and to organizations and people. The matrix can also be viewed as a means of achieving improved communication within and across a project team, termed the "instrumental effect of risk management" by de Bakker et al. (2011, p.76). A communicative effect occurs when stakeholders deliberately use risk management to convey messages to others, with the aim of influencing their behaviour, synchronizing their perception, and making them aware of the context and their responsibilities. As PwC (2021) note, risk management systems and infrastructure "provide an integrated platform to communicate identified risks and escalate decisions to senior management, as well as sharing good practice across the organisation" (p. 2). The matrix stimulates action and increases the effectiveness of the action, synchronizing stakeholders' actions and perceptions, making a situation more predictable which can lead to less uncertainty (de Bakker, Boonstra, & Wortmann, 2014).

Overall, the model has limitations. It has been developed from a small sample of practitioners in the German automotive industry. However, the participants have over 200 years of relevant project management experience between them, providing a unique knowledge base that was explored in depth in the interviews. Previous knowledge and experience also informed judgements on the significance of specific factors, processes, or capabilities. The model is also aligned to the automotive industry and the particular type of projects that operate in this environment. The qualitative model provides a set of characteristics (labels) typifying different stages of risk management maturity, relating to both processes and systems, and to organisational and people aspects.

Future research directions will focus on using the model in different business environments, and developing its pedagogic and operational potential. The application of the model to date has provided valuable insights into the subjective phenomena of success and failure, and the link to the maturity concept has added to this area of knowledge. The model will be applied by the authors in other contexts in the host company, but would also benefit from application in other automotive organizations in other countries, and then in different industries. It has the potential to be developed into a more generic model with wider applicability, with more industry specific variations at a secondary level.

This chapter provides new knowledge on how to integrate multiple rationalities of risk management coexisting in a project with the objective of supporting rational and consistent decisions in projects. As a contribution to theory, the maturity model complements existing models, and is specifically oriented to the automotive industry, one of the major sectors in the global economy which is currently experiencing dramatic disruptions. Supplier dependencies and legal and normative changes are some of the issues constituting serious risk to this industry. As the OECD (2021) recently concluded "the maturity model will help an administration assess…. where they see themselves as to their current level of maturity and the kind of processes and broad outcomes they may wish to consider in order to improve their maturity." (p.7). The aim of this research was to support companies in the German automotive industry in achieving this endeavour.

REFERENCES

Aloini, D., Dulmin, R., & Mininno, V. (2012). Risk assessment in ERP projects. *Information Systems*, *37*(3), 183–199. doi:10.1016/j.is.2011.10.001

Bannerman, P. L. (2008). Risk and Risk management in software projects: A reassessment. *Journal of Systems and Software*, *81*(12), 2118–2133. doi:10.1016/j.jss.2008.03.059

Bazaeea, G., Hassanib, M., & Shahmansouri, A. (2020, September). Identifying Blockchain Technology Maturity's Levels in the Oil and Gas Industry. *Petroleum Business Review*, *4*(3), 43–61.

Berntzen, L. (2013). Citizen-centric eGovernment Services. In *CENTRIC 2013, The Sixth International Conference on Advances in Human oriented and Personalized Mechanisms, Technologies, and Services*. ThinkMind.

Biedenbach, T., & Müller, R. (2011). Paradigms in project management research: Examples from 15 years of IRNOP conferences. *International Journal of Managing Projects in Business*, *4*(1), 82–104. doi:10.1108/17538371111096908

Blakemore, M. (2006). *Think Paper 2: Customer-centric, citizen centric. Should Government learn directly from business?* Working paper, prepared for the e-Government unit, DG Information Society and Media, European Commision. Available at http://europa.eu.int/e-Government_research

Bollinger, R. (2010). *Lean Risk Management*. Project Management Institute.

Bryman, A., & Bell, E. (2011). *Business research methods*. Oxford University Press.

Chapman, C., & Ward, S. (2007). *Project risk management: processes, techniques and insights*. John Wiley & Sons.

Chapman, R. J. (2001). The controlling influences on effective risk identification and assessment for construction design management. *International Journal of Project Management*, *19*(3), 147–160. doi:10.1016/S0263-7863(99)00070-8

Chobanova, E. (2014). *Why You Should Share Your Risk With Business Partners*. Available at: http://www.executiveboard.com/it-blog/why-you-should-share-your-risk-with-business-partners/?utm_source=Tech&utm_medium=CIO-Banner&v2=banner

Ciorciari, M., & Blattner, P. (2008). *Enterprise risk management maturity-level assessment tool*. Paper presented at the 2008 Enterprise risk management symposium, Chicago, IL.

Crawford, J. K. (2006). The Project Management Maturity Model. *Information Systems Management*, *23*(2), 50–58. doi:10.1201/1078.10580530/46352.23.4.20060901/95113.7

Creswell, J. W. (2007). *Qualitative enquiry and research design: Choosing among five approaches*. Sage publications Ltd.

Dawotola, A. W., Gelder, P. H., & Vrijling, J. K. (2012). Design for acceptable risk in transportation pipelines. *International Journal of Risk Assessment and Management*, *16*(1-3), 112–127. doi:10.1504/IJRAM.2012.047570

de Bakker, K., Boonstra, A., & Wortmann, H. (2011). Risk management affecting IS/IT project success through communicative action. *Project Management Journal*, *42*(3), 75–90. doi:10.1002/pmj.20242

de Bakker, K., Boonstra, A., & Wortmann, H. (2012). Risk managements' communicative effects influencing IT project success. *International Journal of Project Management*, *30*(4), 444–457. doi:10.1016/j.ijproman.2011.09.003

de Bakker, K., Boonstra, A., & Wortmann, H. (2014). The communicative effect of risk identification on project success. *International Journal of Project Organisation and Management*, *6*(1-2), 138–156. doi:10.1504/IJPOM.2014.059749

Emblemsvåg, J., & Kjølstad, L. E. (2006). Qualitative risk analysis: Some problems and remedies. *Management Decision*, *44*(3), 395–408. doi:10.1108/00251740610656278

Gauthier, J.-B., & Ika, L. A. (2012). Foundations of Project Management Research: An Explicit and Six-Facet Ontological Framework. *Project Management Journal*, *43*(5), 5–23. doi:10.1002/pmj.21288

Hartley, J. (2004). *Case study research*. SAGE Publications.

Harvett, C. M. (2013). *A Study of Uncertainty and Risk Management Practice Related to Perceived Project Complexity* [PhD thesis]. Bond University.

Harwood, I. A., Ward, S. C., & Chapman, C. B. (2009). A grounded exploration of organisational risk propensity. *Journal of Risk Research*, *12*(5), 563–579. doi:10.1080/13669870802497751

Hillson, D. A. (1997). Towards a risk maturity model. *The International Journal of Project and Business Risk Management*, *1*(1), 35–45.

Holzmann, V. (2012). *Analyzing Lessons Learned to Identify Potential Risks in new Product Development Projects*. Paper presented at the 6th European Conference on Information Management and Evaluation, Cork, Ireland.

Hopkinson, M. (2012). *The project risk maturity model: measuring and improving risk management capability*. Gower Publishing, Ltd.

Jen, R. (2009). *Visual Ishikawa Risk Techique (VIRT) - An Approach to Risk Management.* PMI Virtual Library.

Joustra, S. B. (2010). *Towards the effective management of project risk in complex projects: A case study review.* Retrieved from www.sk.tbm.tudelft.nl

Khan, O., & Burnes, B. (2007). Risk and supply chain management: Creating a research agenda. *International Journal of Logistics Management, 18*(2), 197–216.

Krane, H. P., Olsson, N. O. E., & Rolstadås, A. (2012). How Project Manager-Project Owner Interaction Can Work Within and Influence Project Risk Management. *Project Management Journal, 43*(2), 54–67. doi:10.1002/pmj.20284

Lamberti, L. (2013). Customer centricity: The construct and the operational antecedents. *Journal of Strategic Marketing, 21*(7), 588–612.

Maier, A. M., Moultrie, J., & Clarkson, P. J. (2012). Assessing organizational capabilities: Reviewing and guiding the development of maturity grids. *Engineering Management. IEEE Transactions on, 59*(1), 138–159.

Man, T.-J. (2007). *A framework for the comparison of Maturity Models for Project-based Management* [Unpublished MBA thesis]. Utrecht University.

Marshall, C., & Rossman, G. B. (2014). *Designing qualitative research.* Sage publications.

Martínez Lamas, M., Quintas Ferrín, A., & Pardo Froján, J. (2012). *Project Risk Management in Automotive Industry. A Case Study.* Paper presented at the 6th International Conference on Industrial Engineering and Industrial Management.

McClure, D. (2007). *From the CIO trenches: Why some projects fail and others succeed.* Gartner Industry Research.

McDonald, N. (2006). *Think Paper 5: Is Citizen-centric the same as Customer-centric.* Ccegov Project. http://www. ccegov. eu/thinkpapers. asp

Namey, E., Guest, G., Thairu, L., & Johnson, L. (2008). Data reduction techniques for large qualitative data sets. *Handbook for Team-Based Qualitative Research, 2*, 137-161.

Niebecker, K. (2009). *Collaborative and cross-company project management within the automotive industry using the Balanced Scorecard* [PhD thesis]. University of Technology, Sydney.

OECD. (2021). *Enterprise Risk Management Maturity Model Maturity Model.* OECD Tax Administration Maturity Model Series, OECD. Retrieved March 6, 2022, from www.oecd.org/tax/forum-on-tax-administration/publications-and-products/enterprise-risk-managementmaturity-model.htm

Olakunle, O., & Win, T. (2022). Cybersecurity and Data Privacy in the Digital Age: Two Case Studies. In M. Wynn (Ed.), Handbook of Research on Digital Transformation, Industry Use Cases, and the Impact of Disruptive Technologies (pp. 117-131). IGI-Global.

Olsen, M. D., & Roper, A. (1998). Research in strategic management in the hospitality industry. *International Journal of Hospitality Management, 17*(2), 111–124.

Olsson, R. (2006). *Managing project uncertainty by using an enhanced risk management process* [Unpublished PhD thesis]. University of Västerås, Mälardalen.

Patterson, F. D. (2002). *Project risk management and its application into the automotive manufacturing industry* [PhD Thesis]. University of Warwick. Retrieved from http://search.ebscohost.com/login.aspx?direct=true&AuthType=ip,shib&db=edsble&AN=ethos.007151837&site=eds-live&scope=site&custid=s1123095

Patterson, F. D., & Neailey, K. (2002). A Risk Register Database System to aid the management of project risk. *International Journal of Project Management*, *20*(5), 365.

Phoenix, C., Osborne, N. J., Redshaw, C., Moran, R., Stahl-timmins, W., Depledge, M. H., . . . Wheeler, B. W. (2013). *Paradigmatic approaches to studying environment and human health: (Forgotten) implications for interdisciplinary research.* Retrieved from OAIster database.

Project Management.com. (2019). *Ineffective Risk Management – That's Risky!* White paper. PMI/Deltek. Retrieved January 19, 2022, from https://img.en25.com/Web/DeltekInc/%7Bb6abeb66-b499-4ee4-ae8d-022336a3b88e%7D_Ineffective_Risk_Management_%E2%80%93_That's_Risky_.pdf?elqTrackId=91ad96e2cb854183987f4c254d285ab0&elqaid=11820&elqat=2

PwC. (2021). *Enterprise Risk Management.* Pricewaterhouse Coopers LLP. Retrieved March 6, 2022, from https://www.pwc.co.uk/audit-assurance/assets/pdf/enterprise-risk-management.pdf

Rübesam, T. (2015). *Drug funding decision-making in hospital formulary committees in Germany* [Unpublished DBA thesis]. University of Gloucestershire.

Rubin, H. J., & Rubin, I. S. (2011). Qualitative interviewing: The art of hearing data. *Sage (Atlanta, Ga.).*

Saunders, M., Lewis, P., & Thornhill, A. (2009). *Research methods for business students.* FT/Prentice Hall.

Skinner, D., Tagg, C., & Holloway, J. (2000). Managers and Research: The Pros and Cons of Qualitative Approaches. *Management Learning*, *31*(2), 163–179.

Taylor, F. W. (1911). *The Principles of Scientific Management.* Harper and Brothers.

Thomas, P. (2013). *The Risk of Using Risk Matrices* (Masters Master's thesis). University of Stavanger. Retrieved from https://brage.bibsys.no/uis/bitstream/URN:NBN:no-bibsys_brage_45899/1/Thomas_Philip.pdf

TowerGroup. (2014). Reducing Risk Management's Organizational Drag. Executive Guidance. CIO Executive Board.

Vaish, R., Agrawal, A., & Kapoor, S. (2021). *AI maturity framework for enterprise applications.* IBM Corporation.

Wall, K. D. (2011). *The Trouble With Risk Matrices.* DRMI Working Papers Ongoing Research.

Wang, H., Chen, K., & Xu, D. (2016). *A maturity model for blockchain adoption. Financial Innovation, 2(12).* doi:10.118640854-016-0031-z

Wynn, M., Bakeer, A., & Forti, Y. (2021). E-government and digital transformation in Libyan local authorities. *International Journal of Teaching and Case Studies*, *12*(2), 119–139. doi:10.1504/IJTCS.2021.116139

Wynn, M., Turner, P., & Lau, E. (2013). E-business and process change: Two case studies (towards an assessment framework). *Journal of Small Business and Enterprise Development*, *20*(4), 913–933. doi:10.1108/JSBED-03-2012-0044

Yeo, K., & Ren, Y. (2009). Risk management capability maturity model for complex product systems (CoPS) projects. *Systems Engineering*, *12*(4), 275–294.

Yin, R. K. (2012). *Applications of case study research*. SAGE Publications Ltd.

Zayed, T., Amer, M., & Pan, J. (2008). Assessing risk and uncertainty inherent in Chinese highway projects using AHP. *International Journal of Project Management*, *26*(4), 408–419. doi:10.1016/j.ijproman.2007.05.012

Zou, P. X., Chen, Y., & Chan, T.-Y. (2010). Understanding and improving your risk management capability: Assessment model for construction organizations. *Journal of Construction Engineering and Management*, *136*(8). Retrieved March 6, 2022, from https://ascelibrary.org/doi/abs/10.1061/%28ASCE%29CO.1943-7862.0000175

Zwikael, O., & Ahn, M. (2011). The effectiveness of risk management: An analysis of project risk planning across industries and countries. *Risk Analysis*, *31*(1), 25–37.

KEY TERMS AND DEFINITIONS

Enterprise Resource Planning (ERP): An integrated software package that supports all main business functions. Examples include SAP, Oracle, Infor and Epicor.

Risk Allocation (or Risk Ownership): Involves allocating responsibility for managing project uncertainty to appropriate project parties. These allocations are fundamental because they can strongly influence the motivation of parties and the extent to which project uncertainty is assessed and managed by each party.

Risk Appetite (or Risk Treatment or Risk Propensity): Reflects an organisation's attitude and strategy towards risk. It encompasses how risk is managed and whether exposure to risk should be reduced, or the impact of risk should be mitigated, transferred, externalized or accepted.

Risk Assessment: Is the stage in the risk management process at which each identified risk is assessed for its probability or likelihood of occurrence, and its potential impact on either the project phase or the entire project.

Risk Identification: Involves the detection and classification of all known and - as far as is possible - unknown, risks, thus producing the foundation upon which the overall risk management process can be established.

APPENDIX 1: RISK IDENTIFICATION - MATURITY STAGE DESCRIPTIONS

Table 5.

Risk Identification
Rudimentary stage: Risks are identified in an *ad hoc* manner, and the process may be driven by one single group or individual, thus missing the opportunity to consider other groups' views and enhancements. Potentially high risks, such as those related to compliance, may remain unaddressed, as the process of identification is eventually subsumed within other project initiatives, and risk logs are not systematically updated during the project life cycle. The individuals involved in the project may well share a negative perception of risk and may be reluctant to bring these risks forward for discussion and review. End users who may have experience of the project environment have no involvement in the risk identification process.
Intermediate stage: The project plan does not show any specific work package or activities for project risk identification. Project records are maintained, but central documentation, such as lessons learned, is not standardised. The documentation is unstructured, and data searches on project history are cumbersome. Risk management tends to focus on individual risks managed at lower levels within the team. The activity may be a single action, without clarity on how to periodically review the validity of identified risks, conduct new identification sessions, monitor risk amelioration plans and communicate identified risks to all relevant stakeholders. Risks are often identified as they occur, leaving inadequate time to address them effectively. The documented risk item descriptions may be ambiguous, in many cases describing potential events instead of the root cause that originates the risk. Impact oriented risk descriptions with no insight into how to manage risks proactively are typical at this stage. Some compliance aspects are addressed, but the risk identification process may have failed to recognise some significant risks. Potentially significant risk items may be omitted in reporting. There is a lack of knowledge of the meaning and significance of risk and uncertainty which, together with the lack of involvement of specific stakeholders, increases the subjectivity of how potential events are documented as risks for the project. Several stakeholders and groups with significant involvement in the project do not contribute to risk identification.
Standardised stage: Some standard guide or developed documentation to support project risk identification may be used, but the process may not be known to all stakeholders nor implemented by the project management practitioners with due rigour. Practitioners follow specific project and risk management guidelines and instructions – these may provide a methodology to categorise the project's complexity based on several dimensions such as business impact, project team size or project schedule. Project planning and risk management are fully integrated. Routine planning reviews consistently use lessons learned logs, as well as risk register databases to aid risk identification. All stakeholders contribute to the process whereby their input and their views are considered. The risk register template provides clear risk classifications which can be mapped to established standard risks. Project categorisation establishes minimum frequency rules to perform risk identification. The project team adheres to these rules, and evidence regarding risk identification is documented, and senior members are involved in the process. A holistic view of the project is required in order to properly identify risks. Risk identification is performed at a group level, encouraging and integrating all stakeholders' views. Project team members are knowledgeable and use quantitative data and methods such as Monte Carlo simulation when required. Documentation, such as lessons learned logs and risk registers, is standardised to a certain level and regularly maintained. Records are accessible by all project team members. An active role for the end users is promoted. These are permanently informed about project progress, and they are actively involved in the testing and validation process.
Corporate stage: Use and monitoring of earned value (EV) management supports the identification of potential risk areas. A high maturity in risk identification allows a focus on the key risks. The risk identification process is driven by an initial iterative top-down approach based on the project's purpose and strategy. The risk prioritisation is based on the project's strategic goals. Risk analysis must focus on the right questions and the fundamental purpose of the project. The big picture needs to be understood from the beginning instead of adding risk effects from different areas. The project team ensures formal communication about the identified risk items within the organisation while keeping an overview of the interrelationship or impact of other projects' risks. There is good evidence that risk data emerging from all stakeholders is reported and documented in a timely manner. Systems supporting risk management are available to all stakeholders, and these enable real time reporting.

APPENDIX 2: RISK ASSESSMENT - MATURITY STAGE DESCRIPTIONS

Table 6.

Risk Assessment
Rudimentary stage: Risk assessment performed at the rudimentary stage is not regularly maintained. Changes in the project which could influence the impact or the likelihood of the event are not considered. As results are not reviewed regularly, risk information may become stale. The approach can be described as static as opposed to an active style. Risk assessment tends to be considered only when the project is in difficulty, or when it is imposed by senior management. Risk responses are often based on rapid decisions reflecting a poor understanding of the alternative courses of action. Sometimes there is a delay between risk identification and response implementation, which results in their ineffectiveness. The organisation focuses exclusively on threat management when addressing uncertainty and does not consider opportunity management. The assessment results are not reflected in the cost forecast. Typically, no fall-back plans are developed.
Intermediate stage: Risks are updated, and certain risk categorisation is assigned with the utilisation of risk register templates. Risk description tends to be impact-oriented and often lacks context and identification of relevant sources of uncertainty. Sometimes the risk descriptions provide some indication regarding the source of risks. However, probability estimation is weak. The project team deploys mainly qualitative assessments, e.g., a probability and impact matrix. Quantitative schedule analysis is not generally executed. In addition, existing expertise from previous projects is used as an input for these assessments. The lack of standards to estimate impacts and the difficulty in quantifying likelihood increases the subjectivity of the risk assessment results, and therefore any subsequent risk prioritisation. Individuals required to participate in risk assessment do not completely understand how to assign the likelihood and the impact of the potential risks. They struggle with how to rate the risk statements against prescribed risk tolerance thresholds. There is a lack of knowledge of the risk concept and its potential effect on the project outcomes. The organisation and management would rather deal with issues than with risks - it is embedded in the culture; resource constraints and a focus on problem-solving make it difficult to undertake an adequate risk assessment.
Standardised stage: Project categorisation is performed, based on several dimensions reflecting project complexity. The greater the complexity, the higher is the level of management attention and risk assessment detail. The project teams are capable and sufficiently knowledgeable to undertake risk assessment deploying quantitative quality methods. The team also uses certain risk analysis quantitative methods, such as Monte Carlo, decision trees or Bayesian belief networks, underpinned by a sound understanding of risk with significant thought put into identifying relevant sources of uncertainty. There are clear minimum frequency rules on when to perform risk assessments. Action response plans to the identified risks are regularly reviewed. The description of the risks documented in the risk register is useful for qualitative risk analysis. Some risk effects may extend beyond the immediate risk impact. These effects could also exacerbate other existing risks. Such secondary risks are considered in the assessment. There is a clear method to estimate the Overall Risk Priority Rating, which determines the threshold for taking a certain risk into the risk response plan or not. The threshold for taking events into the risk register's response plan is based on estimated costs or project delays in case of the event happening. Risk assessment is reviewed against the likelihood of any risk happening – a risk assessment at standardised level is one that aims at preventing the events from happening in the first place. Project reporting supports management with visibility of the high impact risks, with clustering and prioritisation functionalities. Systems provide risk aggregation by customers, groups of programs or project portfolios. Steering Committees challenge the assessment process and initiate appropriate escalation when required. A method is designed for the project manager to measure team members' commitment by means of their performance.
Corporate stage: The organisation assesses systemic risks based on past projects; this assessment can be part of a continuous improvement initiative. This initiative evaluates those risks in more detail and determines how to mitigate or change procedures or ways of working to minimise, if not eliminate, the potential impact on the project. Risk assessment includes the quantification of mitigated risks, benefit of risk responses and secondary effects. The project budget contains appropriate funding for overall risk costing. The project managers measure and monitor the project team members' performance against project deliverables. The risk register lists are the result of all stakeholders' and functions' inputs into an integrated system.

APPENDIX 3: RISK ALLOCATION - MATURITY STAGE DESCRIPTIONS

Table 7.

Risk Allocation
Rudimentary stage: Risk ownership is not reviewed and remains assigned to the same individual during the different project phases. Risk allocation is hampered by the lack of risk disclosure with the contracting parties, e.g., suppliers or external customers. Individuals from different functions involved in the project do not feel responsible for the program - it is the project manager that will be associated with the result - and therefore those functions do not feel responsible for the risk which remains with the project manager. Team members are mostly reluctant to own the risks. There is the general impression that assigning somebody a risk item equates to telling them they are doing something wrong. The reluctance of certain stakeholders, in particular suppliers, to divulge new information on risk prevents them being effectively allocated to individuals or groups. Individuals involved in the project perceive risks as intrusive. Being owners of a risk item represents for them an additional burden. In most cases, they do not feel motivated to talk about risk and the associated problems of risk ownership. The organisation does not actively recognise the support of good risk management practice.
Intermediate stage: Central risk allocation is carried out only by the project manager with most risks remaining with the project manager. These are characteristics of risk ownership centricity. Project managers maintain constant communication with third parties and customers to agree on risk accountability. However, there are groups with a critical role in the project who have little or no involvement in the risk allocation process. Suppliers provide risk information; nevertheless, this is sometimes not complete. Some project managers recognise the inefficiency of this centric approach, but sometimes they are reluctant to receive input from other team members or functions. This seems to be dependent on the personal attitude of the project manager. Some of them do everything, from assigning the risk, maintaining the risk registers, and even owning most of the actions documented in the risk response plan. Steering committees are more status boards; in their meetings, risk allocation is not reviewed. Individuals working on the project usually only report in a dotted line to the project manager, but direct line to their functions. This negatively influences risk ownership and therefore allocation. There is a lack of willingness to own risk by the project team members.
Standardised stage: There is a clear procedure to assign risks in the risk register. Clear instructions determine at what point in time these assignments are to be documented or reviewed, typically at the end of any given project phase. Organisations review and assess team members' expertise to assign risk items to the appropriate person. Functional groups involved in the project are able to assign the identified risks internally without much involvement from the project manager. By doing so, the project manager is released from risk allocation activity, allowing him/her to concentrate on other critical activities. The organisation has established guidelines to clearly identify and specify the risk taker, be it the project sponsor, the project manager, or the stream lead. The introduction of prescribed risk classification and job descriptions in the project provides the opportunity to introduce some automation in the risk allocation process. All identified risks have a risk owner with authority and skills to undertake the required actions from the response plan and who accept responsibility. The organisation has established guidelines to clearly identify and specify the risk taker. In some cases, risk ownership is documented in the contracts awarded to suppliers. The contracts contain formal risk agreements with clear financial liabilities for bearing risk. Collaboration and risk sharing are required between partners of different size. Risk sharing promotes risk disclosure; it is also a means of engaging the customer in the process. All stakeholders are open in their disclosure of all risk information. Suppliers operate risk management processes which are complementary to the ones used in the project. In terms of systems, risk registers are accessible and used by all members and functions. All team members are trained in the use of these systems. Steering committees audit the risk allocation process, and steering committee members actively support the risk owners and their mitigation actions. There is evidence that all people working on the project use the risk management plan. Risk project team members know enough about the ultimate project goal and align their actions accordingly.
Corporate stage: There is transparency of the escalation procedure of risk allocation for project team members. These procedures address the following: Who is the next person the risk is allocated to when I am not able to cope with the risk? Who needs to take a decision when the actions described in the risk response plan are well above my responsibility? In term of systems, the risk database is consistently maintained and enables multi-user concurrent access. Management actively rewards good risk management practice and supports the risk owners as contributors to project success. Good risk management practice continuously monitors and tries to improve the risk management processes, sets comprehensive and stretching targets, and promotes high-performing employees in regards to risk management.

APPENDIX 4: RISK APPETITE - MATURITY STAGE DESCRIPTIONS

Table 8.

Risk Appetite
Rudimentary stage: There is no project-specific risk management plan. Fall back decision points (such as a date, or the point in the project's schedule at which a decision on implementing the fall back should be taken) are either not identified or ignored. Risk records cannot be retrieved reliably. Senior management makes little or no use of risk management. Executives fail to challenge the documented project risks, as they feel uncertain as to how to deal with risks, and their comfort area remains on how to address issues. Team members have little understanding of their responsibilities. In some cases, there is no nominated risk manager. People avoid raising risk items. Team members are afraid that if they bring up their concerns, they may end up being made responsible for the potential risk. There is a general failure to offer competency development plans for program managers, resulting in a misalignment of employee competencies with the organisational strategy. This lack of potential development negatively affects the project management performance from the risk management perspective.
Intermediate stage: Risk is not at the top of the executive agenda. Risk responses are rarely monitored. Steering committees are typically status boards; risk is discussed only during phase exits or program reviews. However, management only adopts mainly qualitative risk analysis. There are no formalised standard quantitative methods - the use of these may vary from project to project, and the decision to use quantitative methods is left to the project manager or subject matter expert. Sometimes a fall-back decision point fails to result in a decision. Teams are typically trained in project risk management. Project team members start doing some risk identification and assessments. As the project moves forward, the project manager and team members typically come under time pressure and risk management falls increasingly behind. As the team is not able to cope with the execution of the planned risk mitigation actions, more issues are raised in the open issue list. As resources are assigned to address the issues, less time and resources are available for risk management. Functions still not active in the project at a certain point in time are requested to contribute with their risk assessment to consider potential future implications of current project developments or status. There are systems designed to document risks, but these are not common to all functions and may not be accessible to all project stakeholders.
Standardised stage: Project management is supported with guidelines and methods containing clear, unambiguous process descriptions. Companies train staff in project management specific to their industry, let their risk management process be assessed by auditors, and follow risk management process reference models. Risk items have adequate visibility at project phase exits and review. Executives request evidence for risk mitigation actions and dictate compliance with certain risk management activities. Responses to significant risks tackle risk at source. Importantly, risk response effectiveness is reviewed. Risk responses are consistently implemented. Executives and steering committees provide leadership in risk management. Executives request evidence of risk activities and challenge the risk management process. They support an iterative top-down approach to risk management which supports key strategy decisions first. The risk management methodology is used flexibly, and is adapted to project particularities. Project management practitioners within the organisation stress the importance of project governance, clarity of roles and responsibilities, authority, and competency. Management has the ability to quantify risks associated with capacity shortcomings. Project governance and project human resource management are integrated into the overall project plan. The risk management applications enable 'post-mortem' analysis which compares historical original project scope and outcomes. Project risk management applications enable audit trail functions.
Corporate stage: Risk management is integrated into project planning. The project plan considers routine activities that aid risk identification and assessment. Cost of risk responses is considered. Risk responses which are consistently implemented are supported by cost benefit analysis which also considers secondary risks. Lessons learned are effectively incorporated into a continuous improvement programme. Organisations have at their disposal all elements needed to perform continuous improvement initiatives in risk management. These include project history with risk registers; risk items detailing whether events occurred or not; results of mitigation actions; systems that support queries/aggregation. Project risk management capability is assessed and process improvements in risk management are implemented.

Chapter 4
Does Contagion Effect of Bubbles and Causality Exist Among Bitcoin, Gold, and Oil Markets?

Remzi Gök
https://orcid.org/0000-0002-9216-5210
Dicle University, Turkey

ABSTRACT

The author studies the explosive behaviors, causality relationships, and contagion effects between three financial markets using the daily closing prices of Bitcoin, gold, and West Texas Intermediate (WTI) oil prices for a sample period from July 19, 2010 to September 10, 2021. By employing the generalized supremum augmented Dickey-Fuller (GSADF) approach, the author finds significant evidence of bubble explosive behaviors in the Bitcoin and WTI prices—but not in the gold prices—and these periods mostly match with the periods of quantitative easing and financial stress. Besides, the test shows several short and long episodes of unilateral causal linkages from Bitcoin returns to oil price changes under homoscedasticity and heteroskedasticity assumptions. The results show no evidence for the contagion effect of bubbles between cryptocurrency and oil markets during the sample period.

INTRODUCTION

Global markets and economies have experienced several economic and financial crises, triggered by political instability or conflicts, since early 2000. While the effects of some were limited to the country or region in which the crises took place, others caused global-scale destruction in both markets and economies due to the rapid development of economic globalization and financialization of commodities, such as oil. In early 2020, the world witnessed for the first time in a century a virus pandemic that spread rapidly around the globe. In the early stages of the COVID-19 pandemic, people continued their daily lives instead of acting cautiously, thinking that a cure would be found soon. However, the rapid increase

DOI: 10.4018/978-1-6684-5279-0.ch004

in the death toll due to the pharmaceutical industry's inability to produce an effective vaccine against the virus in a short time had a shock effect on the markets, causing unexpected levels of uncertainty and high volatility, and a sharp deterioration in investors' risk appetite. Investors, who thought that this one was different from previous crises, tried to switch to cash instead of investing in safe-haven assets. Panic sales with the idea of "cash is king" caused asset prices to plunge rapidly. During the early period of uncertainty, the spot and futures prices of U.S. crude oil crashed into negative territory for the first time in history while Bitcoin and gold prices failed to act as a safe haven under extreme stock market conditions. In the following days, the markets calmed down as the uncertainty subsided, and investors searching for a safe haven caused prices to spike. The fact that individuals who were confined to their homes and who had no previous financial investment experience turned to the market to compensate for their income losses caused an excessive increase in asset prices. The question to be asked here is whether these behaviors created a positive or negative bubble in asset prices as in the past.

In the literature, a financial bubble has been defined as a rational or irrational deviation of the current price from its fundamental value. A rational asset bubble can be defined as a self-confirming divergence of asset prices from market fundamentals, which is equal to the expected present value of a stream of cash flows of dividend or coupon payments discounted with an appropriate rate, in response to extraneous variables (Diba & Grossman, 1988). On the one hand, a possible explanation for the formation of a rational bubble is that investors decide to hold or buy an overvalued asset with the expectation that they can sell it to someone else profitably. On the other hand, an irrational bubble emerges when investors are driven solely by psychological factors, such as sentiments, optimistic expectations, fashions, and fads, which are unrelated to the asset's fundamental value and the relationship between its fundamental value and market price is disrupted (Dale et al., 2005). Accordingly, investors with self-fulfilling beliefs fail to correctly and in a timely fashion identify bubble formations and, therefore, indulge in herding (Tran, 2017).

Numerous empirical papers study the existence of asset bubbles in financial markets, such as stock (Gürkaynak, 2008; Homm & Breitung, 2012), currency (Bettendorf & Chen, 2013; Gök, 2021), bond (Chiu & Yeh, 2019), commodity (Emekter et al., 2012; Brooks et al., 2015), oil (Zhang & Yao, 2016; Su et al., 2017), and cryptocurrency markets (Gemici, 2020; Geuder et al., 2019), using various techniques. Among these studies, Brooks et al. (2015) applied the regime-switching regression model to a broad range of commodities, such as oil, and the estimation results found supportive evidence of periodically collapsing speculative bubbles in oil prices, aka black gold, and attributed these extreme price movements to fundamental factors, such as temporary supply shocks, rather than to speculative attacks. By employing two different methods, Zhang and Yao (2016) revealed that crude oil and diesel prices contained a substantial speculative bubble component whereas the main driver of the gasoline price boom was found to be fundamentals. Concentrating on the 2007–08 price spike and 2014–16 price decline, Figuerola-Ferretti et al. (2020) examined the price fluctuations in oil markets and claimed that global economic activity was significant enough to be the main driver of a mildly explosive episode in oil markets during mid-2008, whereas neither the excess speculation nor the excess supply relative to demand, due to U.S. shale oil production, were decisive in the mildly negative explosive period during the 2014–16 price decline. On the other hand, Baumeister and Kilian (2016) conjectured that the oil price fall of 2014–16 resulted from the consequences of a negative shift in demand expectations. Fantazzini (2016), on the other hand, employed two sets of bubble detection approaches for WTI oil prices and argued that this market experienced a negative mildly explosive process from the end of 2014 until the beginning of 2015, which could not be explained by economic fundamentals alone, such as oil supply glut and demand. Sharma and Escobari (2018) interpreted price explosiveness in eight energy price series as evidence of price bubbles, which coincided with the Gulf War of 1991, the Asian crisis of 1997, and the 2007–09 global recession, and contended that the observed price implosion between December 2014 and March 2015 might have been caused by a supply glut—mostly stemming from the production of U.S. and non-OPEC nations—and the economic slowdown in China. Gharib et al. (2021) stated that explosive bubbles found in oil and gold prices could be attributed to fundamental and non-fundamental factors and to a combination of demand and supply issues, such as the COVID-19 pandemic, the oil price war between Saudi Arabia and Russia, and the depreciation of the U.S. dollar.

There is voluminous literature studying episodes of price bubbles in the oil market. Those papers, overall, conclude that gold prices exhibited multiple episodes of explosive behavior; however, there was no consensus among researchers (Lucey & O'Connor, 2013; Zhao et al., 2015) on the driving factors of that explosiveness. By using the bubble detection tests, Zhao et al. (2015) discovered multiple explosive behaviors in the gold price during the period from 1973 to 2014 and claimed that they coincided with financial crisis periods, suggesting the role of gold as a hedge or safe-haven asset for investors and as a leading harbinger of a financial crisis for policymakers. Similar observations were made by Bialkowski et al. (2015), who interpreted the gold price spike from 1979 to 1982 as a response to skyrocketing inflation, caused by the second oil crisis and amplified by a very expansive monetary and fiscal policy. Lucey and O'Connor (2013) used the gold lease rates as a measure of gold's fundamental value and found evidence of explosiveness in gold markets when not allowing the variance to switch between the two different regimes. Baur and Glover (2012) found that gold prices exhibited explosive behaviors, explained by increased chartists (feedback traders) activities in the market, between 2002 and 2012, with a short break during the recent financial crisis in 2008. Perifanis (2019) examined the price explosiveness in the WTI oil market over a long period spanning from 1947 to 2018. The results provide evidence to suggest that WTI prices exhibited several bubble episodes, coinciding with structural changes, including oil crises in 1973 and 1974, price collapse in 1985, price surge before the global financial crisis in 2008, and oil price rebound in 2012. The author concluded that the surges and bursts of the bubble episodes were the consequences of fundamentals' swift.

As an investment instrument, Bitcoin and other cryptocurrencies continued to attract the attention of investors and policymakers owing to their important implications for building risk-management strategies and for constructing monetary policies. Categorized as the "new gold" or "digital gold" by many financial media channels (Huynh et al., 2021) and specified as a form of commodity, in the same way as crude oil and gold, Bitcoin posted a 61.1% annual increase in value—from \$29,374 to \$47,319—and reached an approximate market value of \$897.6 billion as of December 29, 2021. However, whether Bitcoin has any intrinsic value or its price is fair has been highly debated in the existing literature (Baur et al., 2018; Cheah & Fry, 2015; Corbet et al., 2018; Gkillas et al., 2020). In a noteworthy paper, Cheah & Fry (2015) empirically estimated the fundamental value of Bitcoin and investigated whether a bubble exists in the market. The author found evidence to suggest that Bitcoin prices were prone to speculative bubbles and the fundamental value was zero. Rather than a currency or a security, its behaviors, according to White et al. (2020), more closely resembled a bubble event, an emerging asset class, or a technology-based product. However, the findings produced an ambiguous result in regard to whether Bitcoin is a commodity. Likewise, Baur et al. (2018) concluded that Bitcoin exhibited particularly different risk-return, volatility, and correlation characteristics compared to gold and the U.S. dollar. Geuder et al. (2019) reported evidence for the existence of multiple bubble episodes over the sample period, from March 2016 to September 2018, pointing to the development of the global monetary environment in favor of fiat currencies. Corbet et al. (2018) examined the effects of several indicators—the BlockChain position, the hash rate, and liquidity—on the existence of bubble behaviors in Bitcoin and Ethereum between 2009 and 2017. The authors detected several bubble episodes and concluded that the effect of each fundamental indicator on the price dynamics of both cryptocurrencies dissipates quickly. Bouri et al. (2019) studied the price explosiveness in seven cryptocurrencies during the period August 7, 2015 to December 31, 2017. The authors documented several bubble episodes in all cryptocurrencies, and Bitcoin, Dash, and Ethereum were found to be more subject to long-lived explosive periods, with an average of 20, 18, and 17 days, respectively. Additionally, the likelihood of the occurrence of explosivity in one cryptocurrency considerably increases with (depends on) the presence of explosivity in other cryptocurrencies.

In addition to studying bubble behaviors, researchers have paid a great deal of attention to the contagion effect of bubbles between financial markets using several techniques, such as causality tests Gharib et al. (2021) and network theory (Guo et al., 2021). For example, Guo et al., (2021) examined the contagion phenomenon between Bitcoin and other assets before and during COVID-19 period. The results showed that Bitcoin was relatively independent of other financial markets before the COVID-19 shock. During the COVID-19 period, however, the average market contagion between asset markets was found to be higher, faster, and easier. The effects on the contemporaneous and no contemporaneous causality relationship indicated close connections between Bitcoin and other instruments during the COVID-19 crisis: that is, gold and bond absorbed the spillover risks from the Bitcoin market while Bitcoin was connected to the contagion network of the MSCI USA Index and reacted to the fear level of the VIX Index during the pandemic. Gharib et al. (2021) studied the contagion effect of bubbles between the gold and oil spot markets using rolling causality and GSADF tests. They found evidence for the existence of multiple bubble episodes and a bilateral contagion effect during the COVID-19 period. Similar results were obtained by Gök (2021), who documented evidence of price explosiveness in and time-varying causal episodes between bond, currency, and gold markets in Turkey during and non-crisis periods. The authors also found that there was a one-way and bilateral contagion effect of bubbles in currency markets to bond and gold markets over the sample period of 2005-2021.

Other than those studying contagion effects, there are few research papers that look at the causality relationship between gold, oil, and Bitcoin markets. The relevant literature includes Balcilar et al. (2018), Yıldırım et al. (2020), and Gharib et al. (2021), on the causality relationship between gold and WTI; Kang et al. (2019) and Gkillas et al. (2020), on that between gold and Bitcoin; and Okorie and Lin (2020) and Gkillas et al. (2020), on that between WTI and Bitcoin. To fill the gap, we investigate the presence of multiple episodes of explosive behaviors and the contagion effects between three global financial markets—Bitcoin, with the largest market capitalization and trading volume among cryptocurrencies, gold, and WTI oil markets—during the last decade using the well-known method involving the GSADF (Generalized Supremum Augmented Dickey-Fuller) test and two rolling causality tests. Our findings reveal evidence to suggest the existence of mildly explosive bubble behaviors in the Bitcoin and WTI oil prices but not in the gold prices. Using both rolling causality tests, we detected unidirectional causal episodes between markets, mostly coinciding with the quantitative easing programs—launched by the Fed in the U.S. and the European Central Bank (ECB)—and extreme market conditions. However, there is no evidence for a contagion effect of bubbles between Bitcoin and WTI oil markets given that their causal episodes do not overlap during the sample period.

The layout of the paper proceeds as follows. The selected econometrics methods, for bubble detection and causality tests, are outlined in the methodology section. We briefly describe our data and present and discuss the results in the data and empirical findings section. Finally, the conclusion section offers concluding remarks.

METHODOLOGY

GSADF Bubble Detection Test

In this section, we will briefly describe the real-time monitoring procedure, depending on the PSY approach proposed by Phillips et al. (2015, PSY hereafter) and Phillips and Shi (2020). In fact, the PSY procedure was introduced to identify and to date-stamp explosive behaviors in underlying asset prices as well as for use as an early warning device for crises. When comparing other bubble tests, including the PWY approach introduced by Phillips et al. (2011), the recursive evolving algorithm of PSY has good size and power properties and offers greater flexibility in the revealing of multiple episodes of exuberance and collapse within the sample period. It is argued that this test has the advantage of detecting bubbles despite a potential misspecification of the fundamental market process. While other approaches rely on subjective judgment in their deviations from the fundamentals or the moderate states, this method stands out as a formal statistical test for the presence of bubbles (Su et al., 2017). It can be formally used to test for both the positive (upward trending bubble) and negative (downward trending bubble) behaviors and applied to data at any frequency. Requiring the formation of a bubble as a prerequisite for a price collapse, however, gives a major shortcoming prominence (Fantazzini, 2016). Another two problems that can affect the performance of the recursive evolving procedure are the presence of heteroscedasticity and multiplicity, but the authors suggest using the wild bootstrap approach proposed by Harvey et al. (2016) to simultaneously overcome the two issues in testing.

This procedure, which can be easily implemented in practical work, starts with the following regression with intercept:

$$\Delta y_t = \alpha_{\tau_1,\tau_2} + \beta_{\tau_1,\tau_2} y_{t-1} + \sum_{i=1}^{m} \xi^i_{\tau_1,\tau_2} \Delta y_{t-i} + \varepsilon_t \tag{1}$$

In Equation (1), Δy_t denotes the first difference of underlying series, y_t, at time t; m, selected by information criteria, represents the number of lags to remedy serial correlation problems in the residuals, ε_t, from which should follow a normal distribution. The two subscripts, τ_1 and τ_2, are the standard fraction of the total sample, T, and signify the starting and ending points of a subsample period.

After defining the relevant Equation (1), we can test the null hypothesis of a unit root, $H_0 : \beta_{\tau_1,\tau_2} = 0$, against the alternative hypothesis of explosive behavior, $H_1 : \beta_{\tau_1,\tau_2} > 1$. The required ADF t-statistics calculated for each subsample are denoted by $ADF_{\tau_1}^{\tau_2}$. In this setting, PSY proposes a statistic based on the supremum t-statistics, which provides the largest ADF statistic and can be expressed as given:

$$PSY_{\tau^*}\left(\tau_0\right) = \sup_{\tau_1 \in \left[0, r^* - \tau_0\right], \tau_2 = r^*} \left\{ADF_{\tau_1}^{\tau_2}\right\} \tag{2}$$

where r^* is equal to τ_2 and τ_1 is the starting point and allowed to vary within a feasible range, namely $\left[0, r^* - \tau_0\right]$. Further, τ_0 denotes the minimum window required to initiate the repression and is recommended to be set as $\tau_0 = 0.01 + 1.8 / sqrt\left(T\right)$. If the estimated test statistic is greater than the right tail critical value obtained using the wild bootstrap approach of Harvey et al. (2016) with the R package "*exuber*" of Vasilopoulos et al. (2018), then the null can be rejected in favor of the explosive alternative.

In the case of null rejection, it is time to date-stamp the origination and termination dates of a bubble or crisis period. The origination (termination) point of a bubble episode is assumed to be where the PSY test statistic for the first (second) time exceeds (falls below) its critical value. For a subsample period that contains only one episode of explosive behaviors between τ_s and τ_e points, the estimated origination and termination dates for these points can be obtained by the stopping times

$$\hat{\tau}_s = \inf_{r^* \in \left[\tau_0, 1\right]} \left\{ r^* PSY_{\tau^*}\left(\tau_0\right) > cv_{\tau^*}\left(\beta_T\right) \right\} \tag{3}$$

$$\hat{\tau}_e = \inf_{r^* \in \left[\hat{\tau}_s, 1\right]} \left\{ r^* PSY_{\tau^*}\left(\tau_0\right) < cv_{\tau^*}\left(\beta_T\right) \right\} \tag{4}$$

where $cv_{\tau^*}\left(\beta_T\right)$ denotes the quantile of the distribution of the PSY test statistic in Equation (2) for a preferred significance level.

Recursive Evolving Causality Test

Here, we follow the recursive evolving causality procedure recently proposed by Shi et al. (2018). This approach starts with the unrestricted VAR(p) in a multivariate regression format as given:

$$y_t = \Pi x_t + \varepsilon_t \,\&\, t = 1, \ldots, T \tag{5}$$

In the equation, y_t is a k-vector time series, i.e., $y_t = \left(y_{1t}, y_{2t}\right)'$, while $x_t = \left(1, y'_{t-1}, y'_{t-2}, \ldots, y'_{t-p}\right)'$ and $\Pi_{2x(2p+1)} = \left[\varphi_0, \varphi_1, \ldots, \varphi_p\right]$. For the hypothesis testing, $H_0 : y_{2t} \nrightarrow y_{1t}$, the Wald test takes the following form:

$$\mathcal{W} = \left[Rvec\left(\hat{\Pi}\right)\right]' \left[R\left(\hat{\psi} \otimes \left(X'X\right)^{-1}\right)R'\right]^{-1} \left[Rvec\left(\hat{\Pi}\right)\right] \tag{6}$$

where $X' = [x_1,...,x_T]$ is the observation matrix of the regressors, $\hat{\varepsilon}_t = y_t - \hat{\Pi}x_t$, $\hat{\psi} = T^{-1}\sum_{t=1}^{T}\hat{\varepsilon}_t\varepsilon'_t$, and $vec(\hat{\Pi})$ signifies the (row vectorized) $2(2p+1)\times 1$ coefficient of the ordinary least squares estimator, $\hat{\Pi}$, while R denotes the $p\times 2(2p+1)$ selection matrix. Under H_0 and the assumption of conditional homoscedasticity, the Wald statistic is asymptotically χ_p^2.

Following the PSY procedure, Shi et al. (2018) introduced a real-time-varying causality test based on the supremum Wald statistic sequences, using three different algorithms: forward recursive, rolling window, and recursive evolving window. From this point on, we will only provide the information necessary for the last algorithm since it gives the best finite sample performance (as indicated by the authors) when compared with the other procedures. As such, the Wald statistic of the recursive evolving algorithm for each subsample regression over $[f_1, f_2]$ with a sample size fraction of $f_w = f_2 - f_1 \geq f_0$ can be defined as $\mathcal{W}_{f_2}(f_1)$ and the supremum Wald statistic is given by

$$\mathcal{SW}_f(f_0) = \sup_{(f_1, f_2)\in \wedge_0, f_2 = f} \left\{\mathcal{W}_{f_2(f_1)}\right\} \tag{7}$$

where f_0 is the necessary minimum (fractional) window size to estimate the model while

$$\wedge_0 = \{(f_1, f_2)0 < f_0 + f_1 \leq f_2 \leq 1,$$

and $0 \leq f_1 \leq 1 - f_0\}$ for some minimal sample size in the regressions.

Based on the recursive evolving algorithm, the dating rules are given by the following crossing time for a single simple switch case:

$$\hat{f}_s = \inf_{f\in[f_0,1]}\left\{f\mathcal{SW}_f(f_0) > crtv\right\} \& \hat{f}_e = \inf_{f\in[\hat{f}_s,1]}\left\{f\mathcal{SW}_f(f_0) < crtv\right\} \tag{8}$$

where $\hat{f}_s$ and $\hat{f}_e$ represent the estimated first chronological observations, whose test statistics are greater or lower than the critical value of the $\mathcal{SW}_f$ statistics at any reasonable significance level for the origination, and termination points in the causal linkage, respectively. Those points are investigated for each episode i with $i \geq 2$ conditions in the sample ranges of $[\hat{f}_{i-1s}, 1]$ and $[\hat{f}_{ie}, 1]$.

DATA AND EMPIRICAL FINDINGS

Data

Our dataset includes daily observations of Bitcoin, gold, and oil spot prices, spanning from July 19, 2010 to September 10, 2021, with 2,804 daily closing prices in U.S. dollars. They are obtained from www.coinmarketcap.com, https://www.gold.org (World Gold Council), and www.eia.gov (U.S. Energy Information Administration). We give the results of the descriptive and unit root tests for the continuously compounding return series, calculated as the first log differences, in Table 1. It reveals that the average daily returns are positive for all series. Bitcoin returns show the highest volatility (6.08%), with a minimum value (-46.5%) and a maximum value (52.1%), followed by oil and gold returns, with a standard deviation of 3.19% and 1.0%, respectively. All returns series are far from normally distributed, with significantly negative skewness and significantly positive excess kurtosis. Further, the unit root results of the Dickey and Fuller (ADF, 1979), the Phillips and Perron (PP, 1988), and the Shin and Schmidt (KPSS, 1992) tests indicate nonstationarity in levels but stationarity in first differences for all prices.

Table 1. Descriptive statistics

		R_BITCOIN	R_GOLD	R_WTI
Mean		0.0047	0.0001	0
Median		0.0022	0	0.0008
Maximum		0.5208	0.0513	0.4258
Minimum		-0.4647	-0.096	-0.7203
S. Deviation		0.0608	0.0101	0.0319
Skewness		-0.12**	-0.54***	-3.12***
Kurtosis		10.36***	6.48***	122.02***
JB		12547.13***	5033.6***	1743350.03***
N		2803	2803	2803
ADF	Level	-1.9657	-1.5985	-2.0672
	First Diff.	-22.4926***	-53.8902***	-10.9134***
PP	Level	-0.9430	-1.5004	-2.0938
	First Diff.	-52.3632***	-53.9271***	-60.0016***
KPSS	Level	0.7023***	1.1679***	0.5208***
	First Diff.	0.0793	0.1144	0.0492

Note: The asterisks ** and *** denote, respectively, the rejection of the null hypothesis at a 95% and 99% level of confidence. **Source:** Author's own calculation.

We present the rolling correlation estimations using a 123-day window in Figure 1. On the one hand, the findings reveal that gold returns positively and strongly correlate with Bitcoin returns, and positively but weakly correlate with WTI price changes during the whole sample period. The correlation coefficient between Bitcoin and WTI price changes is significantly negative for the whole period. The results of the overlapping rolling windows of the linear correlation estimations, on the other hand, show that all returns series exhibit significant variation in the direction and strength of the co-movement: that is, the correlation coefficients switch signs from positive (negative) to negative (positive) depending on the market conditions. Our findings are in line with Gharib et al. (2021), who argue that this linear estimation may be insufficient to fully reflect the dependence between financial market returns.

Figure 1. Rolling Correlation Estimation between Bitcoin, Gold, and Oil Prices (w=123)
Note: *The asterisk *** denotes the rejection of the null hypothesis at a 99% level of confidence.*

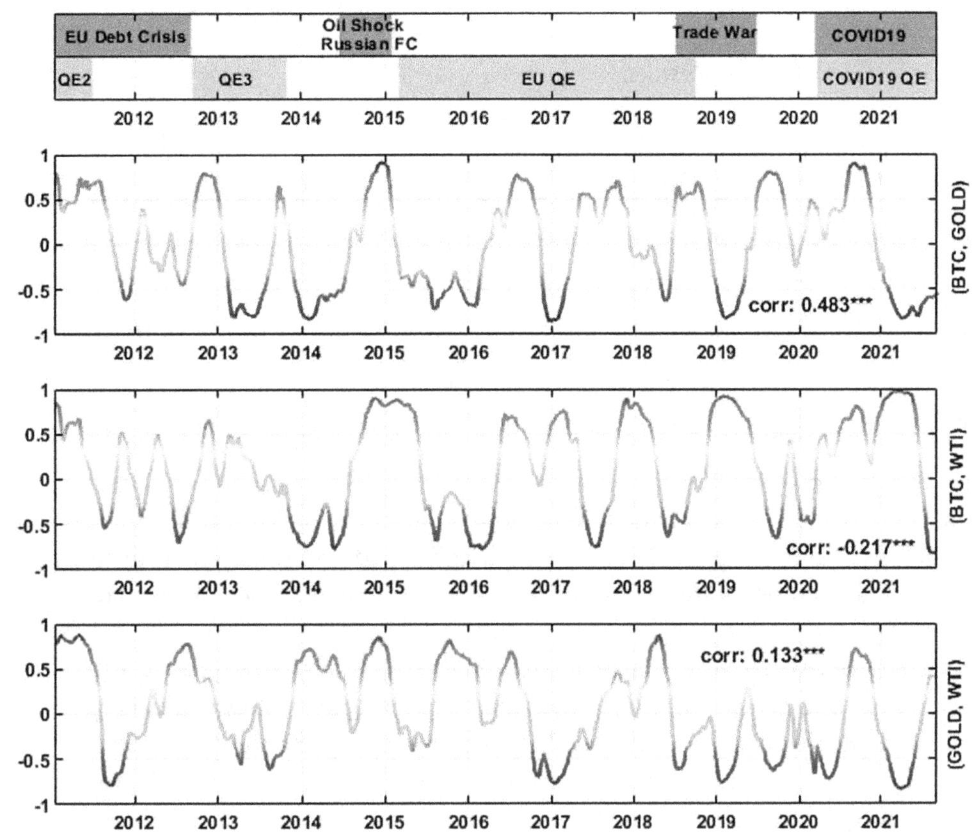

GSADF Test Results

We report the GSADF test statistics along with the critical values obtained by the wild bootstrap procedure introduced by Harvey et al. (2016) using 5,000T iterations, with a minimal estimation window,

$$r_0 = \text{round}(T \times \left(0.01 + 1.8 / \sqrt{T}\right),$$

which gives a positive integer of 123 observations in Table 2. The null hypothesis of no explosiveness, $H_0 : \beta = 1$, in asset prices is rejected against the alternative hypothesis, $H_1 : \beta > 1$, for Bitcoin and WTI at the 5% and 10% significance level, respectively, but not gold spot prices. In other words, the findings show strong evidence of multiple explosive behaviors in the cryptocurrency and oil markets, with 15 and three episodes, lasting 472 and 62 days, respectively. The results allow us to study the timing of explosive behavior periods and are in line with Geuder et al. (2019) and Gemici (2020) for Bitcoin; Fantazzini (2016), Su et al. (2017), and Sharma and Escobari (2018) for WTI crude oil. However, the result of no explosive behaviors in the gold prices contradicts with Ozgur et al. (2021), who revealed that each precious metal—gold, palladium, platinum, rhodium—had at least one episode of explosive behavior, with varying durations, during 1980–2019.

Table 2. The PSY (GSADF) Test Results.

Variables	Test Statistics	10%	5%	1%	Length	Duration
BITCOIN	25.3653**	17.656	20.618	28.009	15	472 [104]
GOLD	2.9991	3.749	4.323	5.558	-	-
WTI	3.611*	3.351	3.9	5.106	3	62 [42]

Source: Author's own calculation.

Notes: ** and * denote rejection of the null hypothesis at the 5% and 10% significance levels, respectively. The statistics and their critical values are obtained through using the R package of "psymonitor" (Caspi et al., 2018) and "exuber" (Vasilopoulos et al., 2018), respectively. To remedy the multiplicity issue in the recursive procedure, the empirical size is controlled over a 140-day period, by taking $\tau_b = 123 + 140 - 1 = 262$ observations for each bootstrapped sample.

The identified origination and termination dates of bubble episodes, lasting at least three days for two markets, are illustrated in Figure 2. The major financial and economic events during the last decade are shaded by different colors in the top panel. The BSADF sequence (blue line) and its critical values for the 90% level of confidence (red line) are depicted on the left-hand axis whereas the time path of relevant asset prices (black line) is given on the right-hand axis. The middle panel shows that the BSADF statistics exceed six times the critical value of 1.2428, suggesting six mildly explosive episodes with different durations in Bitcoin prices. We observe three positive mildly and short-lived explosive episodes in 2011: that is, they originate and terminate, respectively, between February 1 and February 13; March 25 and May 19; and May 23 and June 15, and they all coincide with the second quantitative easing program launched by the FED as part of its expansionary monetary policy. The empirical results indicate one short and one long positive mildly bubble episode, between July 31 and August 16, 2012 and January 25 and April 10, 2013. The origination of the second bubble may be attributed to the third quantitative easing program of the FED while the termination date may be related to the end of the controversial bond-buying program. In line with Corbet et al. (2018) and Enoksen et al. (2020), we notice a positive financial bubble between November 4, 2013 and December 13, 2013, lasting 29 days. There are three short-lived mildly bubble episodes between June 2016 and March 2017, and this finding concur with the results from Gemici (2020) and Enoksen et al. (2020). The second longest-lived bubble episode, however, starts on May 1 and ends on September 13, 2017. After two days, the third-largest episode of explosive behaviors emerges in Bitcoin prices and persists until January 12, 2018. Two short positive mildly bubble episodes are detected over the period May–June 2019 and may be caused by the trade war between the U.S. and China. We dated a short and—the longest—long positive mildly explosive episode during the ongoing COVID-19 pandemic crisis, i.e., from November to December 2020 and between December 12, 2020 and May 17, 2021.

Notice from the bottom panel that we detect only three bubble episodes in the WTI crude oil spot prices. The first and the longest-lived episode—a negative mildly explosive behavior—starts on December 2, 2014 and ends on February 2, 2015, and this finding agrees with the results from Figuerola-Ferretti et al. (2020), Sharma and Escobari (2018), and Su et al. (2017), who argued that this explosiveness might be driven by the surge in global oil supply, the economic slowdown in China, and non-fundamental factors such as speculation activities. After three weeks, a short and negative mild bubble episode originates and terminates in five days. In 2020, the test detects a short-lived negatively mildly bubble episode, lasting 15 days, from March 12 to April 1, coinciding with the day after the WHO declared COVID-19 a pandemic and with a substantial increase (from 53.90 to 75.47) in the VIX Index. Oil prices fell to their lowest levels, i.e., plunged from \$18.31 to -\$36.98 in one day, for the first time in history with COVID-19-related low demand. Besides, the price war between Saudi Arabia and Russia (from March 8 to June 3, 2020) facilitated a 35.7% fall in the price of oil during this negative bubble period. This result partially reinforces the findings of Gharib et al. (2021), who detect two short and mildly explosive episodes from March 6 to April 1 and from April 14 to April 29 in 2020.

Figure 2. Date-stamping periods of explosive behaviors in Bitcoin and Oil Markets
Note: *We plot the historical path of weekly observations for the VIX Index, where the red shaded bars in the top panel denote the crisis periods of the European sovereign debt crisis, the Russian financial crisis, oil price shocks, the trade war between the U.S. and China, and the ongoing COVID-19 pandemic crisis. Likewise, the quantitative easing periods launched by the FED and the ECB during and after the crisis periods, including financial and pandemic crises, are represented by the green shaded bars. The gray shadows in the two bottom panels show explosive episodes lasting at least four weeks (>$\log_{10}(T = 2804)$=3.45), following the suggestion of the PWY procedure.*

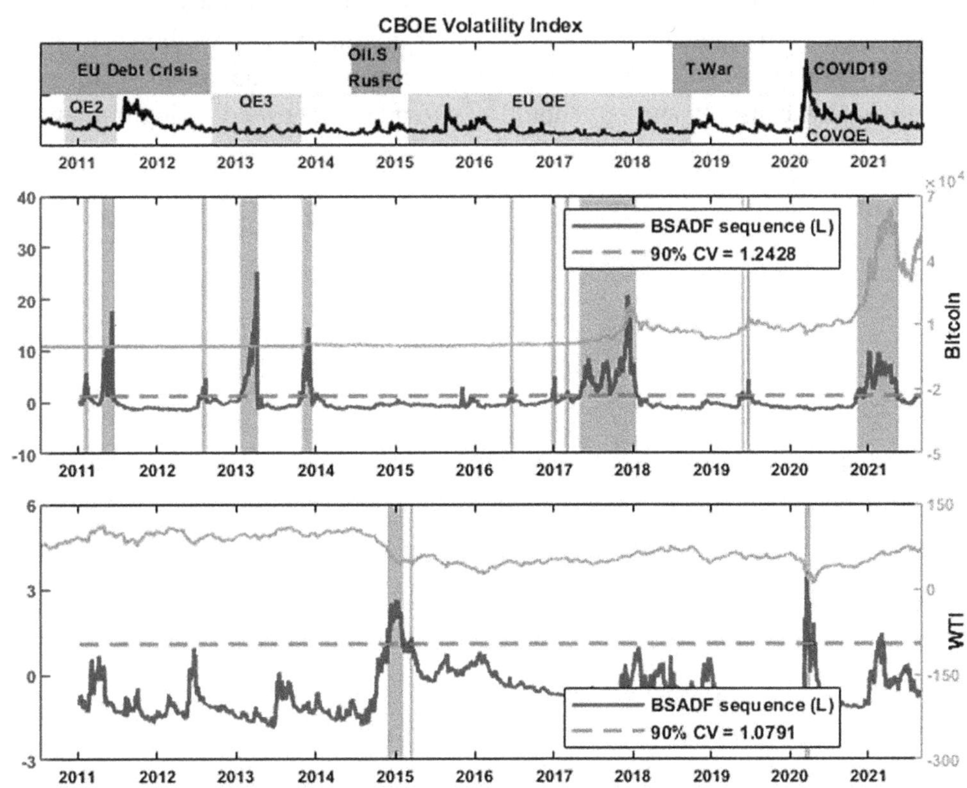

Time-Varying Linear and Nonlinear Causality Tests Results

Following the procedure in Gharib et al. (2021), we examine the contagion effect of bubbles in gold and oil markets by employing two causality tests: the symmetrical causality test of Hacker and Hatemi-J

(2012) and the recursive evolving causality test proposed by Shi et al. (2018). As a yardstick for analyzing causality, we must check the integration order of the underlying asset prices. The unit root results suggest that all variables are integrated into the first order, therefore we select $d = 1$ for two causality test applications.

After determining the integration order, we proceed to test the parameter stability, nonlinearity, and breakpoint of residuals. Testing causal linkages using the full sample VAR model and assuming parameter constancy and nonexistence of structural breaks may produce unreliable outcomes (Balcılar et al., 2019). To this end, we employ three tests and report the results in Table 3. The results regarding the parameter stability of VAR models—through the application of the Andrews (1993) test and using three different statistics—are given in the top panel. The null hypothesis of stability of parameters can be rejected at the 1% significance level for each test and all equations, except for the Exp LR F-statistic for the VAR model comprising WTI (as an independent) and Bitcoin 4 (as a dependent) with a constant. Next, we employ the Bai and Perron (2003) test of multiple structural breaks to detect 1 to M globally determined breaks, allowing error distributions to change across the breaks and a 15% trimming from each end of the sample. The results (UDMax) suggest the presence of breakpoints in all cases at the 1% significance level. Last, we conduct the Broock et al. (BDS, 1996) test on the regression residuals for nonlinearity and we report the results built on 5,000 bootstrap repetitions in Table 3. The findings related to the BDS z-statistic indicate strong evidence of nonlinearity at all dimensions ranging from 2 to 6, implying a nonlinear relationship between return series for all equations. All three results taken together indicate that the causality analysis should be extended to a time-varying framework.

Table 3. Parameter stability, breakpoint, and BDS nonlinearity test results

PANEL A - Quandt-Andrews unknown breakpoint test (H_0: No breakpoints within 15% trimmed data)						
Independent	**DL(BTC)**		**DL(GOLD)**		**DL(WTI)**	
Dependent	**DL(GOLD) [5]**	**DL(WTI) [8]**	**DL(BTC) [5]**	**DL(WTI) [8]**	**DL(BTC) [8]**	**DL(GOLD) [8]**
Sup LR	4.006***	7.249***	4.755***	5.123***	3.1***	4.709***
Exp LR	1.389***	2.068***	1.141**	1.367***	0.758	1.786***
Ave LR	2.573***	3.265***	2.089***	2.373***	1.435**	3.496***
PANEL B - Bai-Perron tests of 1 to M globally determined breaks (H_0: No structural break against an unknown number of breaks)						
UDMax	43.587***	115.577***	41.134***	70.43***	73.149***	75.099***
Breakpoints	2018-10-02	2020-01-13	2012-03-23	2019-12-24	2012-04-24	2013-09-12
	-	-	2013-11-19	-	2013-12-19	-
	-	-	2016-05-18	-	2015-10-01	-
	-	-	-	-	2017-12-19	-
	-	-	-	-	2019-12-18	-
PANEL C - The BDS test (H_0: underlying data (residual) is independently and identically distributed (iid)						
Res(INDV)	**DL(BTC)**	**DL(BTC)**	**DL(GOLD)**	**DL(GOLD)**	**DL(WTI)**	**DL(WTI)**
m = 2	14.62***	15.34***	2.57***	2.42**	15.8***	15.44***
m = 3	17.29***	17.99***	4.83***	4.6***	18.93***	18.77***
m = 4	19.48***	20.04***	6.16***	5.8***	20.67***	20.71***
m = 5	21.31***	21.79***	7.25***	6.83***	22.37***	22.47***
m = 6	23.39***	23.86***	8***	7.56***	23.98***	24.25***
Res(DEPV)	**DL(GOLD)**	**DL(WTI)**	**DL(BTC)**	**DL(WTI)**	**DL(BTC)**	**DL(GOLD)**
m = 2	2.57**	15.8***	14.62***	15.44***	15.34***	2.42**
m = 3	4.83***	18.93***	17.29***	18.77***	17.99***	4.6***
m = 4	6.16***	20.67***	19.48***	20.71***	20.04***	5.8***
m = 5	7.25***	22.37***	21.31***	22.47***	21.79***	6.83***
m = 6	8***	23.98***	23.39***	24.25***	23.86***	7.56***

Source: Author's own calculation.

Note: The asterisks ** and *** demonstrate significance at a 10%, 5%, and 1% level, i.e., show the rejection of the null hypothesis of parameter stability, no structural breaks, or linearity, respectively. Besides, "m" represents the embedding dimensions. Numbers in the brackets are optimal lag lengths determined by AIC for each VAR model.

We report the findings regarding time-varying rolling linear and nonlinear recursive causality tests evolving under the homoscedastic and heteroskedasticity assumptions in Figure 3. In the top panel, we show the explosive episodes in Bitcoin and WTI crude oil spot prices to identify the contagion effect of bubbles by matching causal episodes in those markets. In the next two panels, the recursive evolving causality test results between Bitcoin and oil prices, along with the relevant bootstrapped critical values at the 10% level of significance, under two assumptions are given. Notice that in Figure 3 the findings reveal that there is a one-way causal linkage, running from Bitcoin returns to oil price changes, under two assumptions. We plot six and 11 causality episodes, with different durations, under the homoscedastic and heteroscedastic assumptions, respectively. For example, Bitcoin returns Granger-cause oil price changes before 2020, with four causal episodes and 16-, 14-, 11-, and 72-day durations under the heteroscedastic assumption, coinciding with the FED's third quantitative easing period and the trade war between the U.S. and China. In 2020, the rolling window approach detects two short episodes of causality with a five-day break before the COVID-19 crisis. Starting from the second half of 2020, the test finds four causality episodes under the homoscedastic assumption, lasting 37, 50, 5, and 12 days. In 2021, however, the test detects two causality periods under the homoscedastic assumption, whereas the heteroscedastic-consistent recursive evolving algorithm discovers three episodes during the same period. During the sample period, we notice the longest causality episode, starting on April 4 and ending on September 10, in 2021 under the two assumptions with a slight difference, i.e., 106 vs. 102 days. The results suggest that cryptocurrency price movement may be helpful in predicting oil price changes.

Figure 3. The contagion effect of bubbles and rolling causality relationship between Bitcoin and WTI oil returns

Note: *The parameters for the causality are defined as d=1 (the integration order), x=0, f0 = 0.20, contrsize = 32, IC_flag=20, alpha = 0.95, and M = floor(f0*nob) + contrsize – 1 (in the main function) and nboot = 499 (in the boostrap_RGC_MW.m). The green bar in plots shows the periods where the null hypothesis is rejected at the 5% significance level under the homoscedastic (top) and heteroscedastic (bottom) assumptions. Likewise, the red shaded areas in plots shows the causality periods where the null hypothesis is rejected at the 5% significance level for the symmetric causality test.*

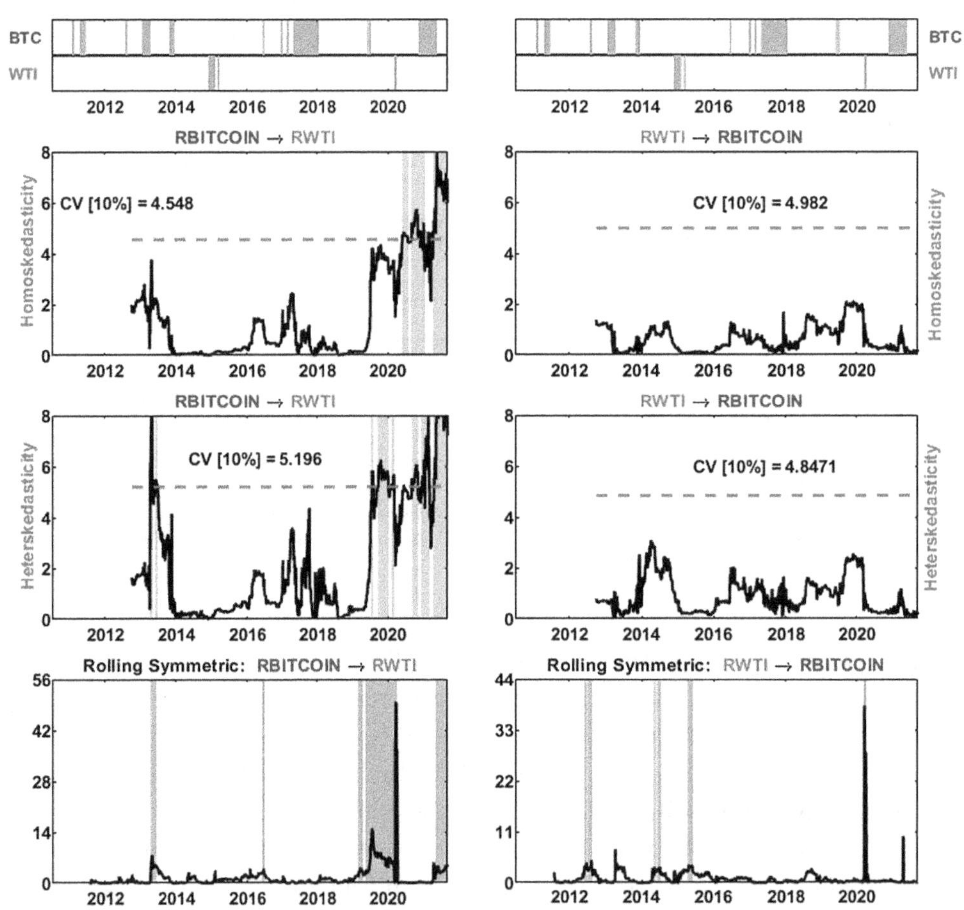

Our time-varying causality test results (see the bottom panel), using the symmetric causality procedure of Hacker and Hatemi-J (2012), show both unidirectional and bidirectional causal linkages, unlike the recursive test. In 2012, we find two short causality episodes running from oil to Bitcoin, from June 4 to July 3 and from July 17 to August 17, 2012. The direction of causality changes to reverse in 2013 and Bitcoin returns Granger-cause oil price changes for two short periods, lasting 12 and 17 days. In 2014, we detect three short episodes of causality running from oil to Bitcoin. The test provides evidence for Bitcoin Granger-causing oil returns for a short period in 2016 and three short episodes in 2019, the last one of which lasts 193 days, starting in May 2019 and ending in March 2020. In the first month of the pandemic crisis, a bilateral causality relationship emerges. We plot four episodes of causality running from Bitcoin to oil in 2021, lasting 4, 24, 15, and 37 days, from May to September. All these results of the two techniques taken together indicate that there is no evidence for the contagion effect of bubbles given that the causality periods and bubble episodes in Bitcoin and WTI oil prices do not match.

Figure 4. Rolling causality relationships between Bitcoin and gold returns

Note*: The parameters for the causality are defined as d=1 (the integration order), x=0, f0 = 0.20, contrsize = 32, IC_flag=20, alpha = 0.95, and M = floor(f0*nob) + contrsize – 1 (in the main function) and nboot = 499 (in the boostrap_RGC_MW.m). The green bar in plots shows the periods where the null hypothesis is rejected at the 5% significance level under the homoscedastic (top) and heteroscedastic (bottom) assumptions. Likewise, the red shaded areas in plots shows the causality periods where the null hypothesis is rejected at the 5% significance level for the symmetric causality test.*

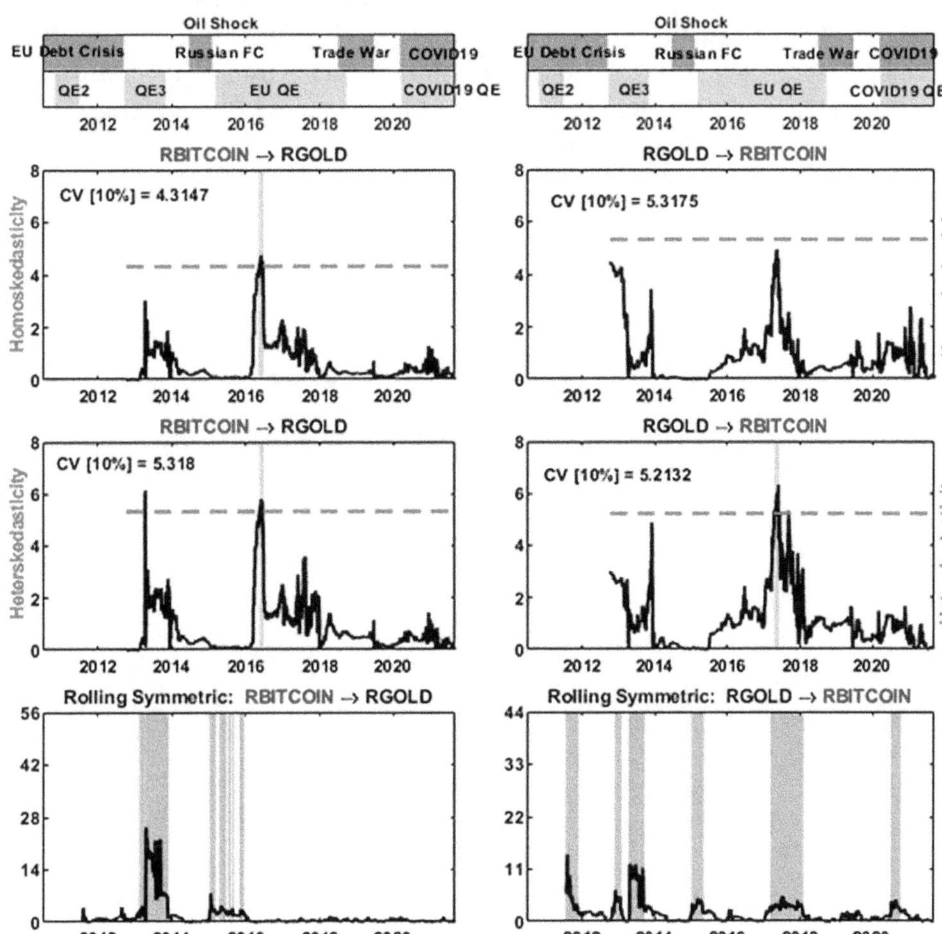

Figure 4 depicts the causality results for the pairing of Bitcoin and gold. This time, we add the time paths of financial/economic crisis and quantitative easing periods in the top panel. Visual inspection suggests a superior performance of the symmetric causality over the recursive evolving approach given the duration of the causal episodes. Under the homoscedasticity assumption, the recursive evolving approach shows a unilateral linear causal linkage, from Bitcoin returns to gold returns, between May 11 and June 13, 2016, with a one-day break. This result might be caused by the falling oil prices due to weak global growth. Under the heteroskedasticity assumption, however, we detect four short causal periods. The recursive evolving approach finds evidence of Granger causality running from Bitcoin to gold returns during the same period, i.e., from May 19 to June 13, 2016. In 2017, however, the test uncovers three short episodes of reverse causality, beginning on April 25 and ending on May 24, with some small breaks. Given the unprecedented interest from investors and policymakers, Bitcoin exhibited a similar path with gold prices in the first half of 2017 and had nearly doubled its price from $1,265 to $2,443, implying that gold returns are relevant drivers in causing and forecasting future movements in Bitcoin prices.

The bottom panel in Figure 4 shows that there exist strong linear causal linkages between gold and Bitcoin returns. The test, for example, detects several unilateral causal episodes before 2013. However, the causality seems to be bidirectional from April 17 to July 19 and August 7 to September 4, in 2013; and in 2015, from January 21 to January 28, February 10 to February 26, and April 15 to April 23. Those causality periods might be driven by the FED's announcement to slow the pace of quantitative easing in May 2013 and by the ECB's quantitative easing starting in 2015. After 2017, the causality is unidirectional—with eight episodes and lasting 241 days with some breaks—from gold returns to Bitcoin price changes. In the second half of 2020, gold price changes Granger-cause Bitcoin returns with no reverse direction from July 14 to August 3 and August 18 to October 6.

Figure 5. Rolling causality relationships between gold and oil returns

Note*: The parameters for the causality are defined as d=1 (the integration order), x=0, f0 = 0.20, contrsize = 32, IC_flag=20, alpha = 0.95, and M = floor(f0*nob) + contrsize – 1 (in the main function) and nboot = 499 (in the boostrap_RGC_MW.m). The green bar in plots shows the periods where the null hypothesis is rejected at the 5% significance level under the homoscedastic (top) and heteroscedastic (bottom) assumptions. Likewise, the red shaded areas in plots shows the causality periods where the null hypothesis is rejected at the 5% significance level for the symmetric causality test.*

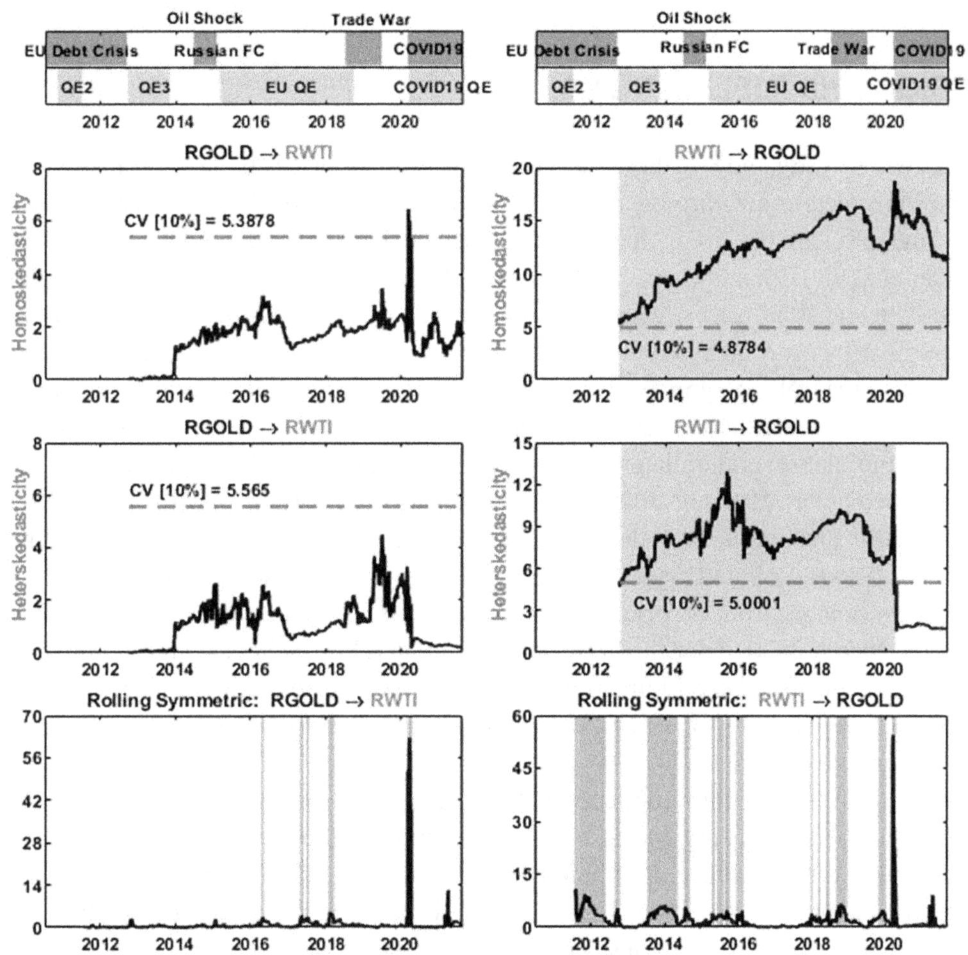

The time-varying causality between gold returns and oil price changes is highlighted in Figure 5 and the findings are intriguing. Under both assumptions, the causality is unilateral and runs from oil price changes to Bitcoin returns with no reverse direction during the whole sample period, except for the heteroskedasticity assumption where the time-varying Wald statistics remain below the critical value at the 10% significance level from March 31, 2020, until the end of the sample period, coinciding with the ongoing pandemic crisis and implying that oil prices seem to have lost their ability to forecast gold returns during COVID-19 under the heteroskedasticity assumption. However, the rolling symmetric causality results indicate that the causality is linear and unilateral from the oil market to the cryptocurrency market and vice versa over different periods. Before April 2016, the bootstrapped causality test shows strong episodes of unilateral causality from oil markets to gold markets, with 13 subperiods and lasting 525 days. Among these episodes, we notice two long-lived periods, from September 9, 2011 to May 10,

2012 (the longest episode, lasting 168 days) and from September 19, 2013 to April 24, 2014. However, we find strong evidence for gold Granger-causing oil from April 21 to April 29 in 2016, and May 2 to May 17, and June 29 to July 10, in 2017. The test identifies two episodes of bidirectional causality, confirming the existence of a linear feedback mechanism between markets, in March 2018 (six days) and from March 24 to April 13 in 2020, concurring with the onset of the pandemic crisis.

CONCLUSION AND IMPLICATIONS

In this chapter, we investigated whether gold, WTI, and Bitcoin prices exhibit explosive behaviors and contagion bubble effects or not, through the applications of PSY and rolling causality tests. The findings, supporting some previous papers, including Fantazzini (2016), Su et al. (2017), Sharma and Escobari (2018), Geuder et al. (2019), and Gemici (2020), revealed strong evidence of multiple explosive behaviors in the Bitcoin and WTI prices, which coincide mostly with the periods of quantitative easing and financial turmoil. However, no evidence was found for bubble episodes in gold prices. The causality test results showed that rolling symmetric causality offered a better finite sample performance than the recursive evolving approach under both assumptions. Regarding the results of the recursive evolving approach, we found that several unilateral causality episodes, running from Bitcoin returns to oil price changes, intensified before 2014 and 2020 and during the COVID-19 period with some breaks. Since the episodes of causality and bubble periods did not overlap, we take this result as evidence of no contagion effect of bubbles between oil and cryptocurrency markets. The results also documented unidirectional causation impacts running from oil price changes to gold returns during the entire period and between October 2012 to March 2020 under the homoscedasticity and heteroskedasticity assumptions. Further, there were both unidirectional and bidirectional causal episodes between Bitcoin and gold returns, with five and 20 episodes and lasting 73 and 672 days, indicating higher predictability of using Bitcoin returns for gold returns and vice versa.

Overall results have significant implications for investors for asset allocation and hedging purposes among three financial instruments during both normal and crisis periods. For policymakers, however, the findings highlight the existence of bubble periods in Bitcoin and oil prices and suggest taking precautionary actions to control them—such as lowering demand by increasing transaction costs or taxes or increasing supply—before they collapse and cause devastating consequences in the financial markets. Whether psychological and political risk factors and social media posts have led to significant causal and contagion effects on the financial markets is left for future research.

REFERENCES

Andrews, D. W. K. (1993). Tests for parameter instability and structural change with unknown change point. *Econometrica*, *61*(4), 821–856. doi:10.2307/2951764

Bai, J., & Perron, P. (2003). Computation and analysis of multiple structural change models. *Journal of Applied Econometrics*, *18*(1), 1–22. doi:10.1002/jae.659

Balcilar, M., Ozdemir, Z. A., & Shahbaz, M. (2018). On the time-varying links between oil and gold: New insights from the rolling and recursive rolling approaches. *International Journal of Finance & Economics*, *24*(3), 1047–1065. doi:10.1002/ijfe.1704

Baumeister, C., & Kilian, L. (2016). Forty years of oil price fluctuations: Why the price of oil may still surprise us. *The Journal of Economic Perspectives*, *30*(1), 139–160. doi:10.1257/jep.30.1.139

Baur, D. G., Dimpfl, T., & Kuck, K. (2018). Bitcoin, gold and the US dollar–A replication and extension. *Finance Research Letters*, *25*, 103–110. doi:10.1016/j.frl.2017.10.012

Baur, D. G., & Glover, K. (2012). A gold bubble? SSRN *Electronic Journal.* Retrieved from https://papers.ssrn.com/sol3/papers.cfm?abstract_id=2166636 doi:10.2139/ssrn.2166636

Bettendorf, T., & Chen, W. (2013). Are there bubbles in the Sterling-Dollar exchange rate? New evidence from sequential ADF tests. *Economics Letters*, *120*(2), 350–353. doi:10.1016/j.econlet.2013.04.039

Bialkowski, J., Bohl, M. T., Stephan, P. M., & Wisniewski, T. P. (2015). The gold price in times of crisis. *International Review of Financial Analysis*, *41*, 329–339. doi:10.1016/j.irfa.2014.07.001

Bouri, E., Shahzad, S. J. H., & Roubaud, D. (2019). Co-explosivity in the cryptocurrency market. *Finance Research Letters*, *29*, 178–183. doi:10.1016/j.frl.2018.07.005

Broock, W. A., Scheinkman, J. A., Dechert, W. D., & LeBaron, B. (1996). A test for independence based on the correlation dimension. *Econometric Reviews*, *15*(3), 197–235. doi:10.1080/07474939608800353

Brooks, C., Prokopczuk, M., & Wu, Y. (2015). Booms and busts in commodity markets: Bubbles or fundamentals? *Journal of Futures Markets*, *35*(10), 916–938. doi:10.1002/fut.21721

Caspi, I., Phillips, P. C. B., & Shi, S. (2018). *Real time monitoring of asset markets with psymonitor.* R package version 0.0.1. https://itamarcaspi.github.io/psymonitor

Cheah, E. T., & Fry, J. (2015). Speculative bubbles in Bitcoin markets? An empirical investigation into the fundamental value of Bitcoin. *Economics Letters*, *130*, 32–36. doi:10.1016/j.econlet.2015.02.029

Chiu, C. L., & Yeh, C. C. (2019). Whether the multiple bubbles exist in the bond markets of developed countries? *International Journal of Information and Management Sciences*, *30*, 271–282.

Corbet, S., Lucey, B., & Yarovaya, L. (2018). Datestamping the Bitcoin and Ethereum bubbles. *Finance Research Letters*, *26*, 81–88. doi:10.1016/j.frl.2017.12.006

Dale, R. S., Johnson, J. E., & Tang, L. (2005). Financial markets can go mad: Evidence of irrational behaviour during the South Sea Bubble. *The Economic History Review*, *58*(2), 233–271. doi:10.1111/j.1468-0289.2005.00304.x

Diba, B. T., & Grossman, H. I. (1988). Explosive rational bubbles in stock prices? *The American Economic Review*, *78*(3), 520–530.

Dickey, D. A., & Fuller, W. A. (1979). Distribution of the estimators for autoregressive time series with a unit root. *Journal of the American Statistical Association*, *74*(366a), 427–431.

Emekter, R., Jirasakuldech, B., & Went, P. (2012). Rational speculative bubbles and commodities markets: Application of duration dependence test. *Applied Financial Economics*, *22*(7), 581–596. doi:10.1080/09603107.2011.619496

Enoksen, F. A., Landsnes, C. J., Lučivjanská, K., & Molnár, P. (2020). Understanding risk of bubbles in cryptocurrencies. *Journal of Economic Behavior & Organization*, *176*, 129–144. doi:10.1016/j.jebo.2020.05.005

Fantazzini, D. (2016). The oil price crash in 2014/15: Was there a (negative) financial bubble? *Energy Policy*, *96*, 383–396. doi:10.1016/j.enpol.2016.06.020

Figuerola-Ferretti, I., McCrorie, J. R., & Paraskevopoulos, I. (2020). Mild explosivity in recent crude oil prices. *Energy Economics*, *87*, 104387. doi:10.1016/j.eneco.2019.05.002

Gemici, E. (2020). Testing for multiple bubbles in cryptocurrency market. In A. Akinci (Ed.), *Interdisciplinary Public Finance, Business and Economics Studies* (Vol. 3, pp. 107–118). Peter Lang Publishing.

Geuder, J., Kinateder, H., & Wagner, N. F. (2019). Cryptocurrencies as financial bubbles: The case of Bitcoin. *Finance Research Letters*, *31*, 179–184. doi:10.1016/j.frl.2018.11.011

Gharib, C., Mefteh-Wali, S., & Jabeur, S. B. (2021). The bubble contagion effect of COVID-19 outbreak: Evidence from crude oil and gold markets. *Finance Research Letters*, *38*, 101703. doi:10.1016/j.frl.2020.101703 PMID:32837382

Gkillas, K., Bouri, E., Gupta, R., & Roubaud, D. (2020). Spillovers in higher-order moments of crude oil, gold, and Bitcoin. *The Quarterly Review of Economics and Finance*, *x*, xxx–xxx. doi:10.1016/j.qref.2020.08.004

Gök, R. (2021). Identification of Multiple Bubbles in Turkish Financial Markets: Evidence From GSADF Approach. *Marmara Üniversitesi İktisadi ve İdari Bilimler Dergisi*, *43*(2), 231–252.

Guo, X., Lu, F., & Wei, Y. (2021). Capture the contagion network of Bitcoin–Evidence from pre and mid COVID-19. *Research in International Business and Finance*, *58*, 101484. doi:10.1016/j.ribaf.2021.101484 PMID:34518717

Gürkaynak, R. S. (2008). Econometric tests of asset price bubbles: Taking stock. *Journal of Economic Surveys*, *22*(1), 166–186. doi:10.1111/j.1467-6419.2007.00530.x

Hacker, S., & Hatemi-J, A. (2012). A bootstrap test for causality with endogenous lag length choice: Theory and application in finance. *Journal of Economic Studies (Glasgow, Scotland)*, *39*(2), 144–160. doi:10.1108/01443581211222635

Harvey, D. I., Leybourne, S. J., Sollis, R., & Taylor, A. R. (2016). Tests for explosive financial bubbles in the presence of non-stationary volatility. *Journal of Empirical Finance*, *38*, 548–574. doi:10.1016/j.jempfin.2015.09.002

Homm, U., & Breitung, J. (2012). Testing for speculative bubbles in stock markets: A comparison of alternative methods. *Journal of Financial Econometrics*, *10*(1), 198–231. doi:10.1093/jjfinec/nbr009

Huynh, T. L. D., Ahmed, R., Nasir, M. A., Shahbaz, M., & Huynh, N. Q. A. (2021). The nexus between black and digital gold: Evidence from US markets. *Annals of Operations Research*, 1–26. doi:10.100710479-021-04192-z PMID:34316086

Kang, S. H., McIver, R. P., & Hernandez, J. A. (2019). Co-movements between Bitcoin and Gold: A wavelet coherence analysis. *Physica A*, *536*, 120888. doi:10.1016/j.physa.2019.04.124

Lucey, B. M., & O'Connor, F. A. (2013). Do bubbles occur in the gold price? An investigation of gold lease rates and Markov Switching models. *Borsa Istanbul Review*, *13*(3), 53–63. doi:10.1016/j.bir.2013.10.008

Okorie, D. I., & Lin, B. (2020). Crude oil price and cryptocurrencies: Evidence of volatility connectedness and hedging strategy. *Energy Economics*, *87*, 104703. doi:10.1016/j.eneco.2020.104703

Ozgur, O., Yilanci, V., & Ozbugday, F. C. (2021). Detecting speculative bubbles in metal prices: Evidence from GSADF test and machine learning approaches. *Resources Policy*, *74*, 102306. doi:10.1016/j.resourpol.2021.102306

Perifanis, T. (2019). Detecting west Texas intermediate (WTI) prices' bubble periods. *Energies*, *12*(14), 2649. doi:10.3390/en12142649

Phillips, P. C., & Perron, P. (1988). Testing for a unit root in time series regression. *Biometrika*, *75*(2), 335–346. doi:10.1093/biomet/75.2.335

Phillips, P. C., & Shi, S. (2020). Real time monitoring of asset markets: Bubbles and crises. In Handbook of Statistics 42 (pp. 61–80). Elsevier Science.

Phillips, P. C., Shi, S., & Yu, J. (2015). Testing for multiple bubbles: Historical episodes of exuberance and collapse in the SP500. *International Economic Review*, *56*(4), 1043–1078. doi:10.1111/iere.12132

Phillips, P. C., Wu, Y., & Yu, J. (2011). Explosive behavior in the 1990s NASDAQ: When did exuberance escalate asset values? *International Economic Review*, *52*(1), 201–226. doi:10.1111/j.1468-2354.2010.00625.x

Sharma, S., & Escobari, D. (2018). Identifying price bubble periods in the energy sector. *Energy Economics*, *69*, 418–429. doi:10.1016/j.eneco.2017.12.007

Shi, S., Phillips, P. C., & Hurn, S. (2018). Change detection and the causal impact of the yield curve. *Journal of Time Series Analysis*, *39*(6), 966–987. doi:10.1111/jtsa.12427

Shin, Y., & Schmidt, P. (1992). The KPSS stationarity test as a unit root test. *Economics Letters*, *38*(4), 387–392. doi:10.1016/0165-1765(92)90023-R

Su, C. W., Li, Z. Z., Chang, H. L., & Lobonţ, O. R. (2017). When will occur the crude oil bubbles? *Energy Policy*, *102*, 1–6. doi:10.1016/j.enpol.2016.12.006

Tran, T. B. N. (2017). Speculative bubbles in emerging stock markets and macroeconomic factors: A new empirical evidence for Asia and Latin America. *Research in International Business and Finance*, *42*, 454–467. doi:10.1016/j.ribaf.2016.02.004

Vasilopoulos, K., Pavlidis, E., & Spavound, S. (2018). *Econometric analysis of explosive time series*. R foundation for statistical computing. https://github.com/kvasilopoulos/exuber

White, R., Marinakis, Y., Islam, N., & Walsh, S. (2020). Is Bitcoin a currency, a technology-based product, or something else? *Technological Forecasting and Social Change*, *151*, 119877. doi:10.1016/j.techfore.2019.119877

Yıldırım, D. Ç., Cevik, E. I., & Esen, Ö. (2020). Time-varying volatility spillovers between oil prices and precious metal prices. *Resources Policy*, *68*, 101783. doi:10.1016/j.resourpol.2020.101783

Zhang, Y. J., & Yao, T. (2016). Interpreting the movement of oil prices: Driven by fundamentals or bubbles? *Economic Modelling*, *55*, 226–240. doi:10.1016/j.econmod.2016.02.016

Zhao, Y., Chang, H. L., Su, C. W., & Nian, R. (2015). Gold bubbles: When are they most likely to occur? *Japan and the World Economy*, *34*, 17–23. doi:10.1016/j.japwor.2015.03.001

ADDITIONAL READING

Claessens, S., & Forbes, K. (Eds.). (2013). *International financial contagion*. Springer Science & Business Media.

Granger, C. W. (1969). Investigating causal relations by econometric models and cross-spectral methods. *Econometrica*, *37*(3), 424–438. doi:10.2307/1912791

Halaburda, H., & Sarvary, M. (2016). Beyond bitcoin. *The Economics of Digital Currencies.*

Junttila, J., Pesonen, J., & Raatikainen, J. (2018). Commodity market based hedging against stock market risk in times of financial crisis: The case of crude oil and gold. *Journal of International Financial Markets, Institutions and Money*, *56*, 255–280. doi:10.1016/j.intfin.2018.01.002

Lee, J. H., & Phillips, P. C. (2016). Asset pricing with financial bubble risk. *Journal of Empirical Finance*, *38*, 590–622. doi:10.1016/j.jempfin.2015.11.004

Phillips, P. C., & Shi, S. P. (2018). Financial bubble implosion and reverse regression. *Econometric Theory*, *34*(4), 705–753. doi:10.1017/S0266466617000202

Segendorf, B. (2014). What is bitcoin. *Sveriges Riksbank Economic Review*, *2014*, 2–71.

YarovayaL.BrzeszczynskiJ.GoodellJ. W.LuceyB. M.LauC. K. (2020). Rethinking Financial Contagion: Information Transmission Mechanism During the COVID-19 Pandemic. Available at SSRN 3602973. doi:10.2139/ssrn.3602973

Yousaf, I., Ali, S., Bouri, E., & Saeed, T. (2021). Information transmission and hedging effectiveness for the pairs crude oil-gold and crude oil-Bitcoin during the COVID-19 outbreak. *Economic Research-Ekonomska Istraživanja*, 1–22.

KEY TERMS AND DEFINITIONS

Asset Bubble: It represents extreme (rational or speculative) price acceleration and deceleration, which cannot be explained by the market fundamentals.

Bitcoin: It can be described as a decentralized digital or virtual currency, and it is the world's largest cryptocurrency in terms of market capitalization.

Contagion: It represents the transmission of negative shocks or crises from a particular market/ economy or region to another.

Financial Crisis: It is a situation when financial instruments and assets decrease suddenly and significantly in value. The 2007-2008 global financial crisis –originated in the US and spread out to other economies in a short time– is known as the worst economic disaster since the stock market crash of 1929

Gold: Gold is the most precious (a soft and yellow) metal that has been used as a common commercial medium of exchange, as a store of value, and as valuable jewelry. The price of gold can be affected by several factors including the production, demand, reserves, the value of the U.S. dollar, market volatility, inflation rates, geopolitical risks, financial/economic or pandemic crises, etc.

Granger Causality: Briefly, it shows the relationship of cause and effect between underlying variables. Broadly speaking, however, it is a statistical hypothesis test for determining whether using one variable's current information increases the prediction probability of the future value of another variable.

WTI: It stands for West Texas Intermediate, and it is among the most heavily traded crude oil grades in the world (with Brent crude oil) and its price is tremendously sensitive to production and demand factors.

Chapter 5
How Lean Six Sigma Risk Management Was Used at a Clean Energy Plant

Kenneth David Strang
https://orcid.org/0000-0002-4333-4399
W3-Research, USA & RMIT University, Australia

ABSTRACT

The global pursuit of higher quality and corporate social responsibility are motivating corporations to set climate preservation goals and to employ quality theory processes, notably lean six sigma methods. One of the significant contemporary social responsibility initiatives is climate preservation. Climate conservation has been dramatically achieved through the increases efficient production of clean energy, such as hydroelectricity and nuclear power plants. However, advanced quality management processes are needed to effectively and safely operate electricity generation plants of any type due to their potential to cause significant man-made accidental disasters if certain critical processes become out of control. This chapter explores how lean six sigma quality theories were applied for risk management at a renewable energy hydroelectricity facility. Quality inspections were collected from a plant in New York, USA. A statistical process control model was developed based on the attribute and continuous inspection data.

INTRODUCTION

It is important to study how quality theories such as lean six sigma may be used for risk management in the clean energy production sector. Continuous process checking or improvement in electricity generation are needed due to the global pursuit of higher quality and corporate social responsibility (Peinado, Graeml, & Vianna, 2018). Decision makers at energy creation companies are moving in the direction of setting climate preservation goals and to employ quality theory processes, notably lean six sigma methods (Strang, 2017a).

One of the significant contemporary social responsibility initiatives is climate preservation. Climate conservation has been dramatically achieved through the increases efficient production of clean energy,

DOI: 10.4018/978-1-6684-5279-0.ch005

such as hydroelectricity and nuclear power plants. However, advanced quality management processes are needed to effectively and safely operate electricity generation plants of any type due to their potential to cause significant man-made accidental disasters if certain critical processes become out of control (Nersesian & Strang, 2017).

This chapter explores how lean six sigma quality theories were applied for risk management at a renewable energy hydroelectricity facility. Quality inspections were collected from a plant in New York, USA. A statistical process control model was developed in an easy-to-use spreadsheet software package, based on collected attribute and continuous inspection data.

The main contribution of this chapter is to show how lean six sigma was applied in a clean energy manufacturing plant. This may generalize more broadly, globally, to other hydro-electric, wind, solar, nuclear and even fossil-fuel based energy utilities, because lean six sigma is a primarily risk prevention or mitigation methodology not a risk management estimation technique. The lean tools allow a company to detect problems that have occurred not ones that will occur. When a process is out of control the problem has already started. However, it can dramatically reduce subsequent problems at an energy generation plant if problems can be detected early on, so they may be brought back into control. For example, the near-fatal nuclear plant overheating at Three Mile Island in the U.S. was an example of a process out of control, but it was accidentally detected by a diligent employee. By comparison the nuclear explosion disaster in Chernobyl Ukraine was an example of a process out of control that was not detected in time, with catastrophic results. By illustrating how lean six sigma was applied in a simple easy to use spreadsheet application, this may be of interest to all levels of management working at energy production plants, including nuclear, solar, wind, fossil-fuel as well as hydro (like the current study). In other words the risk detection and mitigation approaches in this chapter, namely lean six sigma, should generalize widely to all types of energy creation around the world.

THEORETICAL BACKGROUND

Issues and Controversies in Electricity Generation

It is important to study clean electrical energy risk management because there is global uncertainty about the future existence of renewable resources (IEA, 2015), there is social discontent with fossil fuel climate pollution (Kallakuri, Vaidyanathan, Kelly, & Cluett, 2016), there is a risk of global terrorism at nuclear plants, and there is political instability around energy resource sites in some countries (Barbour, Radcliffe, Ding, Li, & Wilson, 2016; Breckenridge, Zimbardo, & Sweeton, 2010). It is surprising the potential for generating solar, hydro and wind electricity easily surpasses fossil fuels during in the peak demand daytime hours (lo Storto & Capano, 2014; Pedraza, 2012). However, the problem is that we do not have good risk management of natural energy resources like wind, solar and hydro nor do we have a battery capable of storing clean energy when natural resources are not available (Geth, Brijs, Driesen, Belmans, & Kathan, 2015; Kadiyala, Kommalapati, & Huque, 2016; Zafirakis, Chalvatzis, Daskalakis, & Baiocchi, 2016). This problem occurs because wind and solar are unreliable due to atmospheric limitations and weather variations (Geth et al., 2015; Koohi-Kamali, Rahim, Mokhlis, Tyagi, & Panwar, 2013). For example, a high capacity 300 kWh lead battery costs between $100,000-200,000 but can store only about the amount of electricity that a small-to-medium sized solar, wind or hydro system could generate in a day, and they have a much shorter lifespan (Bruninx et al., 2016; McConnell, Forcey, & Sandiford,

2015; Park, Kim, & Lee, 2016). Unfortunately may factors such as human resources, man-made disasters, and uncertainty impact the generation of clean renewable hydroelectricity so we need better models that incorporate risk and client energy demand (Nersesian & Strang, 2017). Thus, there is a need to study better clean natural energy generation and risk management to address the aforementioned uncertainty.

Pumped hydro storage is the technique used by 99% all electricity generation facilities over 150 Giga Watts (GW) around the world (Blakers, 2015). Pumped hydro storage systems are simple, they produce clean energy, and they are renewable (Barbour et al., 2016; Boicea, 2014). In a pumped hydro storage system water is moved into a reservoir or tank at a higher elevation using excess non-peak energy to be released later to generate electricity by spinning turbines to meet higher demand periods (Kusakana, 2016; Park et al., 2016). The problem with pumped hydro storage facilities is that they can be expensive to construct, they need regular quality inspections, and the environment may be damaged in doing so (Jimanez, Capilla, Carrian, & Alameda-Hernandez, 2016; Ma, Yang, & Lu, 2014). Furthermore, there may be aesthetic concerns and legal issues associated with land use (Foley, Leahy, McKeogh, Li, & Morrison, 2015; Zafirakis et al., 2016).

Several approaches have been proposed to reduce the cost and environmental damage associated with developing pumped hydro storage systems (Bruninx et al., 2016). Novel designs include using compressed gas containers (de Boer, Moll, Benders, & Grond, 2014; Wang, Wang, Wang, & Yao, 2013), weights (Vasel-Be-Hagh, Carriveau, & Ting, 2013), tall buildings (Fonseca & Schlueter, 2013), and underground caves (Olsen, Paasch, Lassen, & Veje, 2015). The idea of using underground caves is renewable, it is the least expensive and the most environmentally friendly (Elahee, 2013; Olsen et al., 2015; Segurado, Costa, Carvalho, & Duia, 2014). Nevertheless, the existing literature contains only theoretical proposals rather than pumped hydro storage case studies.

The increasing global demand for electricity and climate conservation are two forces which have pushed many countries towards evaluating novel concepts for electricity generation and storage (Boicea, 2014; lo Storto & Capano, 2014; Whittingham, 2012). An emergent risk in electricity generation is domestic or global terrorism (Korstanje, Strang & Tzanelli, 2019)). Electricity generation is not necessarily the problem because solar and wind are adequate except they are not available everywhere or anytime (Ashok, 2007; Margeta & Glasnovic, 2011). Very few locations have consistently strong enough wind (Blakers, 2015; Jamil, Ahmad, & Jeon, 2016) and only approximately 66% of the world population resides in feasible solar zones with direct angle sunlight (Jafar, 2000; Margeta & Glasnovic, 2010). However, risk management is lacking in many hydroelectricity plants.

Another global factor impacting the consumers is the lack of efficiency associated with the electricity production in some countries (Koleva & Mladenov, 2014). The USA trails the developed nations in terms of the efficiency that the country produces renewable climate-friendly electricity, particularly hydroelectricity. Germany, Japan, Italy, France, United Kingdom, China and Spain were the most energy efficient countries ahead of the USA (Kallakuri et al., 2016). This is interesting to see that China ranks higher than USA in efficient clean energy production since that is contrary to the public perception in America. One reason that China outranks USA is due to its lower demand and communist government that is capable of controlling the social as well as economic factors. Another reason that China ranks high despite its reliance on importing coal from Australia and using it for traditional fossil fuel electricity plants is that they have high numbers of renewable hydro plants (IEA, 2015). A limitation with the ACEEE statistics is that their measurement methodology to rank renewable energy generation does not address socio-cultural risks such as flooded land due to dams, the quality of living conditions building or appliance codes and the risk of terrorism (Strang, 2015a). Nonetheless the work of ACEEE illustrates what is possible for effective clean energy production in countries much smaller than USA, with less favorable land resources, and all nations in the top ranks had lower GDP levels as compared to USA.

Americans often forget that they are a small population on the planet and their ways of using fossil fuel to generate electricity are not universally practiced. Biomass has become a popular renewable source of materials used to generate electricity in fossil fuel type plants (Bansal, Kumar, & Gupta, 2013). Biomass is a natural product of solar energy consisting of wood shrub and grass. In tropical and sub-tropical regions, common biomass products are the chilauney tree, laber, katus, utis, mawa, panisas, malata, marich, bamboo and palmetto bushes (Mishra, 2010). Biomass products are burned to produce heat which is converted into electricity so these are not exactly clean energy methods because smoke pollution is created but the output is considered less hazardous for the ozone as compared with coal or oil (Mishra, 2010). The attraction of biomass products is their abundance and renewability (Mishra, 2010). The problem for northern climates of USA is that land is controlled, most productive vegetation is used for agriculture, farming, or forestry and what is left is insufficient to meet the customer demands of a technology-driven generation. Additionally, social groups in the USA are against any type of fuel burning method for electricity generation since the output is carbon dioxide (greenhouse gas).

Inspection Component Weaknesses of Electricity Generation and Storage

Hydroelectric plants work on the principle of kinetic moving energy. Water flows naturally or is redirected to turn blades using gravity in a turbine whereby the kinetic form is changed to mechanical energy. A turbine can produce electricity by a generator rotor which is turned by the flowing water. Thus, the mechanical energy is converted into another energy format as electricity. The phrases hydroelectric power, hydroelectricity or hydropower are used because water was the initial source of the energy creation. The terms green, clean and renewable are associated with hydroelectricity because it comes from a natural renewable clean source – water.

Aesthetics and environmental conservation are becoming increasingly important in society. A well-designed small hydropower system can be aesthetically pleasing and clean because it can blend with its surroundings and have minimal negative environmental impacts. Small hydropower has a huge, as yet untapped potential in most areas of the world. The biggest advantage of a small hydropower system is that it is the only clean and renewable small source of energy available round the clock because solar and wind are typically available only for shorter durations – if at all – every day. Hydropower is clean because it is free from many issues and controversies that continue to impede large hydro, like the submergence of forests, siltation of reservoirs, rehabilitation and relocation and seismological threats. Other benefits of small hydroelectricity systems are user-friendliness, low cost and short gestation periods.

Furthermore, small hydroelectricity systems are especially valuable in remote areas with limited or no electricity. This is a beneficial system for both developed, developing and emerging countries. For example, Austria is a developed country with more than 1,000 small hydro plants scattered throughout its mountainous terrain (Dell, Egger, & Grabl, 1996; Geth et al., 2015). At the microeconomic level, some developing countries, rural civilizations have made the switch from firewood for cooking to electricity, thus limiting deforestation and reducing carbon emissions. At the macroeconomic level, rural communities in developed countries such as South Africa, China and Nepal have been able to attract new industries, mostly related to agriculture, due to their ability to provide power from small hydroelectricity plants.

Chhetri, Islam and Pokharel (2009) raised an important consideration when thinking about risk management of green energy creation and storage. They suggested a major constraint was the dependency of most people on a scarce few utility companies or limited fuel sources. They suggested renewable energy creation should be community-based and decentralized so that it is more responsive to demand as well as fault tolerant to a single large natural or man-made disaster. Furthermore they pointed to the success of establishing effective micro hydro generation plants in both developed and emerging nations. Oseni (2012), Erdogdu (2011) and Basnyat (2004) independently found that rural communities preferred decentralized electricity plants and that hydro power was more economical to build as well as operate due to the lack of trained personnel in the region.

Micro hydro facilities typically produce from 1-5 mWatts of electricity per second, enough to power a small city or village. When combined with other methods a micro hydro facility could act as a storage system (Ehnberg & Bollen, 2005) or serve as the primary energy generation point (Pimenta & Assireu, 2015). Decentralization of energy creation and storage using micro hydro plants is becoming attractive to emerging countries that have less infrastructure to reliably and effectively handle their overall electricity demand (Purvins, Papaioannou, Tzimas, & Oleinikova, 2012). However, micro hydro plants still require land, water (initially at least and small quantities for topping up), plus they have an operational cost due to human resources (Armstrong & Bulkeley, 2014). The human resources are needed in any system for safety monitoring and administration so this alone is not a limiting factor as compared to other electricity generation methods. Also the stakeholders become dependent on the electricity so proactive risk management is needed to avoid power outages.

A special case of hydroelectric power is a pumped storage facility where excess power from the base demand load plants is used to drive pumps that fill an artificial or natural reservoir at a higher altitude that can be later used to generate hydroelectricity by flowing through turbines at a lower elevation. A turbine may be a pump and a turbine. When consumer power demand exceeds base load capacity, such as during mornings before work hours and at night when people return home from work, the hydro turbine pumps become generators, feeding the stored energy of the stored water back into the grid, much like a very large storage battery – this is why the term stored hydroelectricity or pumped hydroelectricity is used.

Interestingly, stored micro pumped hydropower is becoming a popular alternative to dirty energy creation methods such as fossil fuel. It is also being considered when integrated with solar or wind power systems because of the electricity storage potential generated in off peak demand cycles and available to fulfill consumer energy requirements in peak periods. Denmark has the highest proportion of wind electricity generation plants in the world, although unfortunately peak supply does not coincide with peak demand (Olsen et al., 2015). Nonetheless Denmark exports its excess wind electricity to Norway, where it is used to pump water up to its pumped storage reservoirs (Olsen et al., 2015).
There are two broad categories of hydroelectricity turbines:

1. Impulse turbines (such as the Pelton) where a jet of water is sprayed on the runner, which is designed to reverse the direction of the jet and thereby extract momentum from the water - this turbine is suitable for high heads and small discharges;
2. Reaction turbines (mainly the Francis or Kaplan systems), which run with the full flow of water and generate hydrodynamic lift forces to propel the runner blades – these turbines are suitable for medium to low heads and medium to large discharges.

The Pelton hydroelectricity turbine was patented in 1890 and it was first used in the 1930s for high head projects like the Hoover Dam in the USA. The Pelton turbine is used within many large hydro facilities today and it is capable of rotational speeds of up to 1,300 rpm from water jets aimed at cupped blades. Pelton turbines are used for high head height hydroelectricity sites (50 feet to 6,000 feet). Pelton turbines are capable of producing 200 megawatts of hydroelectricity.

The Francis reaction turbine was developed in 1914. It has a runner with fixed vanes, usually nine or more. In this system the water flow enters the turbine in a alight radial direction to the shaft and the water is discharged in an axial direction almost perpendicular, in order to generate the electricity through mechanical energy conversion. A Francis turbine can operate from 10 feet to 2,000 feet of head and can generate as much as 800 megawatts of hydroelectricity energy.

Ahmadian, Falconer and Bockelmann-Evans (2014) proposed a unique tidal system to generate power. Their design had two variations, the first using only the incoming tide, and the second using both incoming and outgoing ties. In this way it could act as a type of storage system when combined with alternative methods that could produce electricity at other times. A significant advantage of their idea was that tidal systems are renewable and more reliable than either wind which varies considerably (Goel, Singh, Murthy, & Kishore, 2011) or sun because clouds or vapor can block direct rays even near the equator. Segurado, Madeira, Costa, Carvalho and Duia (2016) extended that idea by combining a tidal generation facility with a pumped hydro storage system. Tides are not totally reliable though since they are subject to solar gravity pulls from the moon and planets. Also there are occasional surges which could damage such a facility (Ahmadian & Falconer, 2012). The biggest limitation is that the plant would have to be located near an ocean with a strong tide and with firm bedrock to house the facility (Ahmadian, Falconer, & Bockelmann-Evans, 2012). Additional concerns may be from negative impact to the fish habitat and the tourism industry where the large structures are visible (McConnell et al., 2015). Interestingly, Raluy, Serra and Uche (2005) came up with an idea to combine a tidal energy creation/storage plant with a water desalination system. This may be attractive to countries such as Australia where water is in short supply but the country continent is surrounded by several oceans with strong currents and tides.

Some hydro systems have been built on a river that is only a few feet or a meter deep such as in Bangladesh (Islam, Karim, Rahman, Gupta, & Masum, 2013). According to the American Society of Civil Engineers (ASCE), dams will usually be necessary to build a hydro electricity generation plant and this obviously impacts the environment in a negative manner due to the flooding of adjacent wildlife habitats (Tortajada, 2015). However, with a pumped hydro plant, dams may not be needed. Connolly, Leahy and MacLaughlin (2010) wrote a software program that could analyze geographical features and topographical relief data to identify potential sites for small pumped hydro plants. Their concept was useful with respect to identifying contrasting land elevations where nearby water sources existed. However, the program was only as good as the data input. Additionally, they did not encompass the socio-economic factors such as were their native people's rights on the land, what was the cost of the land, was the area prone to droughts, as well as other environmental constraints. Nonetheless their program would be valuable when used in combination with other methods to prioritize potential sites.

Wang, Wang, Wang and Yao (2013) proposed a novel idea that used sealed storage cylinders to store energy potential combined with a hydro facility. Their design starts with a pumped hydro facility where water is sent downhill through turbines to generate electricity. Park, Kim and Lee (2016) built on that idea by designing a hydro-based generation system that used compressed air and gas to store excess energy for later use. In these systems compressed air is used to store the excess energy storage and it is released to pump the water or to turn turbines. These solutions were unique but would require expensive components to compress the air and a large tight high-pressure tank. By comparison, a hydro container would not require a sealed cylinder or expensive pressure pumps, so it would be cheaper to construct and maintain them (Strang, 2019). Additionally compressed air has the potential risk of an explosion due to external heat, overfilling or metal fatigue.

Solar, wind and hydro facilities are the most economical clean and renewable energy generation source methods (Islam et al., 2013). Hydro remains the cheapest and most reliable since it uses kinetic energy to turn the turbines producing electricity without additional conversion or loss as would be the case in photo voltaic units that are able to utilize only 20% of the incoming solar potential (Chhetri et al., 2009; Strang, 2019). Wind is almost as effective as water but has less gravitational force. Also wind facilities must be shut down during high winds, hurricanes, or when there is a risk of any type of storm, which requires more monitoring and further reduces availability.. Thus, hydro is the more economical, effective and efficient green method for an electricity storage system.

Tam, Blomquist and Kartsounes (2007) wrote a paper presenting a theoretical design for an underground pumped hydro storage facility where two caverns at different levels were used. The impetus for such a design was to store electrical energy by harnessing off-peak traditional fossil fuel energy in order to reuse it during peak demand times by producing hydroelectricity. Their paper was focused on the state-of-the-art in hydro turbines and they discussed how various penstock head heights impacted the electricity generated versus the cost to pump the water back into a surface reservoir. An interesting point they made was that any type of hydro generation system could never operate at 100% efficiency due to mechanical resistance (including the pipes) as well as electrical impedance (voltage losses). In fact, typical hydro generation efficiencies ranged from 42% to 76% at the highest when all factors were included. Furthermore they pointed out that efficiency was lost both on the generation cycle through the turbines and more on the return trip where water was pumped back uphill to the higher level reservoir or storage container(s). Nonetheless, they researched the costs of comparative electrical generation alternatives and found that hydro was overall much cheaper, renewable (if continuous water were available) and cleaner. They recommended, as with any electricity generation proposal, that research should be done on penstock head sizing, turbine efficiency versus performance, cavern/storage chamber geology, and overall system efficiency versus stakeholder goals.

Olsen, Paasch, Lassen and Veje (2015) published an interesting theoretical paper about using underground reservoirs for a pumped hydroelectric storage facility. Their case was very similar to many aspects of this study. They suggested a large amount of storage container construction expense could be saved if an existing underground cavern or container already existed. All that would be needed is to have two approximately equal sized containers, as long as one was at lower gravitational elevation. Two pipes would be needed between them if there was no air escape on the lower level reservoir. A pipe located would be located at the bottom of the upper level container for feeding the hydro turbines to generate electricity, and either reverse pump-turbines could return the water or an additional pipe would be needed with pumps to return the water from the lower to the upper level (assuming there was an air escape route on the lower reservoir). As they discussed, these were simple structural mechanics. They did not advance beyond the initial work of Tam, Blomquist and Kartsounes (2007) except to mention that the use of underground reservoirs that already existed provide the benefits of lower construction (as the containers already existed and needed only sealing and piping), aesthetics since the entire facility would be hidden, and provision for continuous independent surface land use (e.g., agriculture or other appropriate activities may be conducted in parallel).

However, such a facility would function only as a storage system since the net production would be negative considering that slightly more energy would be needed overall return the water back up to the upper level as compared to what would be generated (de Boer et al., 2014). Nonetheless, such a facility would surpass all the previous designs from the literature with respect to being renewable, green, environmentally friendly and aesthetically suitable for placement within a community (since the facility would be hidden from view). As implied by Olsen, Paasch, Lassen and Veje (2015), the surface land may be used independently for appropriate activities such as agriculture, farming, storage and so on.

Uddin (2012) provided an informative discussion of the geotechnical factors and constraints for designing an underground hydroelectricity storage facility. He applied his design to an underground facility located in the northwestern region of Alabama, USA. His case study was focused on using caverns in hard rock formations as the reservoir. He discussed engineering challenges associated with sealing the cavern, reinforcing it, and how to address other geological, hydrological, geochemical, geothermal, and geotechnical factors. He also provided some guidelines about the anticipated cost for building such a plant including which types of reversible turbines to use based on reservoir size and total electricity demand. His study was limited to a small design that was an open loop system (did not return all water back to the reservoir). Also it was not clear if the design was successful or implemented.

These were the only theoretical studies found in the scholarly literature discussing a feasible underground hydro electrical storage facility. There was only one applied case study of an underground hydro storage facility found in the literature (e.g., Uddin, 2012).

Several researchers studied geothermal electricity generation systems which use wells 1-4KM deep. A closed loop geothermal system taps into hot underground water at 150-300C temperatures which rise as a gas through a production pipe to generate electricity on the surface in an evaporator heat exchanger system and after cooling it is returned back into an injection well using gravity (Atlason & Unnthorsson, 2014). The average temperatures below 1KM range from 60C to over 300C, the latter if the location has tectonic plate cracks or is close to a magma layer. According to Atlason and Unnthorsson (2014) the temperature must be close to 150C to be usable for generating electricity. On the other hand much lower temperatures between 30-60C are being used for geothermal heating systems (Chaudhry, Raza, & Hayat, 2009; Kazem, 2011; Pedraza, 2012). Although water is commonly used for geothermal systems, other gases are more efficient in heating quickly so they are used in closed loop systems (Atlason & Unnthorsson, 2014). Even with closed loop systems, some chemicals such as CO_2 and sulfur sometimes escape but any pollution from a geothermal systems tends to be minimal (if any) in comparison to fossil fuel plants. Hot dry rock systems are common almost everywhere at the 1KM depth (Atlason & Unnthorsson, 2014). With hot rock systems, water or gases are pumped down through an injection well, heated, and they evaporate to the surface into an evaporator heat exchange system. Geothermal systems are much cheaper to build as they require only two small diameter wells and a simple evaporator heat exchanger followed by a steam hydro generator, and appropriate cabling with substation to the nearest high voltage grid. However, geothermal systems do not provide storage as they only generate electricity although they could do so if a large underground dry rock reservoir were available.

Hydro Facility Risk Management Decision Making Models

Although there was only one case study of an underground hydro generation storage facility located in the literature, there were many examples of decision making models for managing risks or operating hydro plants. Gu, Bakke, Zhou, Osborn, Bo and Guo (2014) published an interesting paper describing a simulation model for storing electricity. Their idea was to use wind to generate energy which would be used to pump water into an elevated container system with hydro turbines at the bottom where another equivalent sized reservoir resided. The concept was that wind would be used to generate electricity to operate the pumps to keep the upper containment area loaded, and secondly excess electricity would be fed into a smart grid for nearby cities to utilize as needed. The limitations of their model were that it was simulated, the containers and reservoir were above ground, they needed to be constructed, a large amount of land needed to be purchased close to a city, and an expensive wind generation facility also needed to be built. Bobinaite and Juozapaviaiene (2011) pointed out that building an integrated hydro and a wind electricity generation facility would require a large investment many times more than an equivalent system of one fuel type. Also, wind is not reliable, and unless the hydro system has a continuous supply of water, both of these require a third facility such as a traditional fossil fuel or nuclear plant to enable continuous supply (Foley et al., 2015).

Zafirakis, Chalvatzis, Baiocchi and Daskalakis (2013) analyzed the cost and benefit of compressed air versus pumped hydro energy storage facilities. Their decision making model included relevant factors to represent customer demand, operational costs and production expenses. Their model was particularly useful for evaluating comparative projects using net present value as the basis for selecting the best design. A major limitation with their model was the lack of a risk management function except through the net present value rate which does not truly represent operational uncertainty. This type of decision making model is driven by economics more so than by clean renewable energy approaches unless the projects are prescreened for those criteria. Thus, in that sense their model was valuable, but it does not help a manager make decisions about building and operating a hydro storage facility. As McNabola, Coughlan and Williams (2014) assert, decision making for hydro based plants must include factors for energy demand, capacity, water availability, water sustainability and both internal (e.g., operating availability) as well as external risks like disasters, fires or drought. At minimum risk must be included into a decision making model (Ghadikolaei, Ahmadi, Aghaei, & Najafi, 2012).

Earlier the idea of using geographical information system data for decision making was introduced based on the work of Connolly, Leahy and MacLaughlin (2010). Jimanez, Capilla, Carrian and Alameda-Hernandez (2016) extended their idea by developing a multicriteria decision making model that used using geographical information systems along with other factors to assist in selecting the site for upper reservoirs in pumped hydro storage systems. The strength of their model was being able to add managerial factors. However, the model was basically a project selection mechanism since it helped to locate the site of a surface reservoir based on land relief features and water source availability. Therefore, operational and risk factors were missing from the model.

Gupta, Saini and Sharma (2011) developed an interesting decision making model for a hybrid energy generation system of hydro and traditional methods using integer programming. This was partly based on their earlier work on a hybrid smart city design that featured multiple methods of energy creation using biomass and solar cells for the main generation, with diesel generators as backup and a small hydro system for storage (Gupta, Saini, & Sharma, 2010). Their integer programming model was useful for its intended purpose of determining the optimal switching between the various energy creation sources using constraints such as material supply, environmental conditions (e.g., sunshine) and customer electricity demand. The major limitation of their model was that it was deterministic meaning that all of the constraints must be first entered into the model – no probability or risk factors could be used. Secondly, as with the earlier literature, the facility would be expensive to build since solar, hydro, and the other components would be needed in addition to purchasing the land. Another issue was that their model required technical programming to develop the model which would require expensive human resources be available for maintaining or changing it, as compared with using ubiquitous spreadsheet software. Nonetheless this was a step in the right direction by capturing the critical factors and producing a software-based decision making model.

Ma, Yang and Lu (2014) published an interesting paper discussing the feasibility of using pumped hydro versus traditional industrial batteries to store electrical energy generated in Hong Kong from other traditional methods. They asserted that with the cost of current precious metals needed for large scale industrial battery construction that it was cheaper to build a pumped powered hydro facility. However as they pointed out, technology is always evolving so we must keep an open mind about future storage innovations – if a municipality invested in only pumped hydro globally then they could miss a paradigm shift if economical battery storage devices are invented. A strategic design compromise between pumped hydro and traditional battery storage technology would be to build hydro facilities with appropriate conversion features to allow for a retrofit should cheaper solutions emerge, especially as the plant begins to age and requires extensive maintenance.

Risk management decision making models for hydro electricity generation and storage should be based on rigorous inspections of the supply components using lean six sigma quality theories. There are few studies of how quality can be applied for risk management at underground hydroelectric plants. However, Kusakana (2016) developed a programming solution for risk management which consisted mostly of scheduling the production of a distributed hybrid pumped hydro storage facility around inspections. The strength of his model was that it integrated pumped hydro process capability with another primary electricity generation source and it included a priority scheduling mechanism for known quality inspections. A weakness of the model was the lack of operational uncertainty due to unforeseen factors and there was no lean six sigma quality theory applied. A methodology to overcome the aforementioned limitations would be to develop a quality inspection model using statistical process control in order to manage the significant energy creation risks.

Lean Six Sigma Quality Theory in Risk Management

Lean six sigma (LSS) risk management is important to discuss because successful companies are using it. A look at the NYSE SNP500 listed company prospectus briefs illustrates that many of the top companies apply lean six sigma quality processes, including Motorola, GE, IBM, Allied Signal, Texas Instruments, ABB, Navistar, Citibank as well as others. We could attribute much of present day LSS open model development to Toyota and Motorola. Obviously LSS is an important method to consider for risk management and especially at high risk energy creation plants such as hydroelectricity production.

LSS is considered to be a set of theories and tools in the operations management body of knowledge (Peinado et al., 2018; Strang, 2015b). According to Peinado, Graeml, and Vianna (2018), LSS is described as a vision and philosophical commitment to consumers to offer the highest quality, lowest cost products, in the most efficient, effective safe manner. A present day enhancement of this would be to comply with environmental conservation goals. A benchmark for product and process capability comparison is to become the ‘best in class’ of any industry, e.g., energy production or hydroelectricity for the current study. LSS practitioners use statistical tools and methods to help measure, analyze, improve, and control the processes, as well as to help decision makers conduct risk management of the entire operation (Peinado et al., 2018). In fact, most of the techniques in LSS are based on statistical theories such as the Central Limit Theorem and distribution testing (Strang, 2019). The generally-accepted LSS techniques include visual process mapping, structure trees, rational subgrouping, components search, base-lining, Pareto analysis, Gauge R&R variance analysis, tolerance analysis, hypothesis testing, design of experiments

(DOE), regression, and statistical process control (SPC). In SPC, the focus of the current study, there are two categories of risk management quality control techniques, the first being attribute charts based on count data such as number of pump defects, and the second based on continuous value data such as water volume measurements. In other disciplines, such as manufacturing, LSS approaches include various diagramming matrices, project management, quality function deployment and voice-of-customer/voice-of-engineer/mind-of-designer analysis (Strang & Chan, 2010), which are also considered to be part of the LSS body of knowledge.

A key metric which demonstrates LSS quality levels is 99.9997% performance for products and processes. The 99.9997% refers to the six sigma range of deviation, on each side, from the mean, in a normal distribution model. Figure 1 is a visual representation of what six sigma is as compared to other common statistical distribution parameters. Most stakeholders may find this high level of quality difficult to understand in everyday terms outside of manufacturing or high risk energy production facilities. In figure 1, the sigma represents statistical deviation of the mean such as how much water in cubic feet a hydro plant penstock feeder pipe can hold without leaking, as measured several times to form an average – a mean. The formula for the standard deviation (SD) is shown at the top right of the model. In simple terms the SD is the sum of differences of each observation measurement from the overall mean, adjusted by how many samples were taken from the entire population (e.g., the entire day shift at a hydro plant). Parts per million (PPM) is often used to represent very small units such as in the pharmaceutical or environmental conservation industries. In the figure PPM is used to illustrate how many items would be represented by each sigma or SD quality level, shown in lines below the distribution. The increasing levels of LSS quality are shown below the distribution in figure 1, such that progressing from 1SD to 6SD would be equivalent to that penstock pipe leaking 317,300 gallons if the quality level were only 1SD as compared to leaning 0.002 gallons if a 6SD quality level were achieved. The percentages in the middle of the SD lines indicate the percent of the observations would be expected to fall within the SD ranges, in 95 out of 100 samples from the population. For with 1SD LSS quality level, 68.27% of the observations would be expected to have a mean within 1SD of the historical population mean (e.g., from company records or as compared to a best-in-class hydro plant). In the case of a 6SD or six sigma quality level, 99.9999998% of the observations from the penstock pipe would be expected to fall in the range of the historical mean plus or minus 6SD, in 95 out of 100 samples during the shift.

Figure 1. Visual model of a lean quality control distribution showing the meaning of six sigma

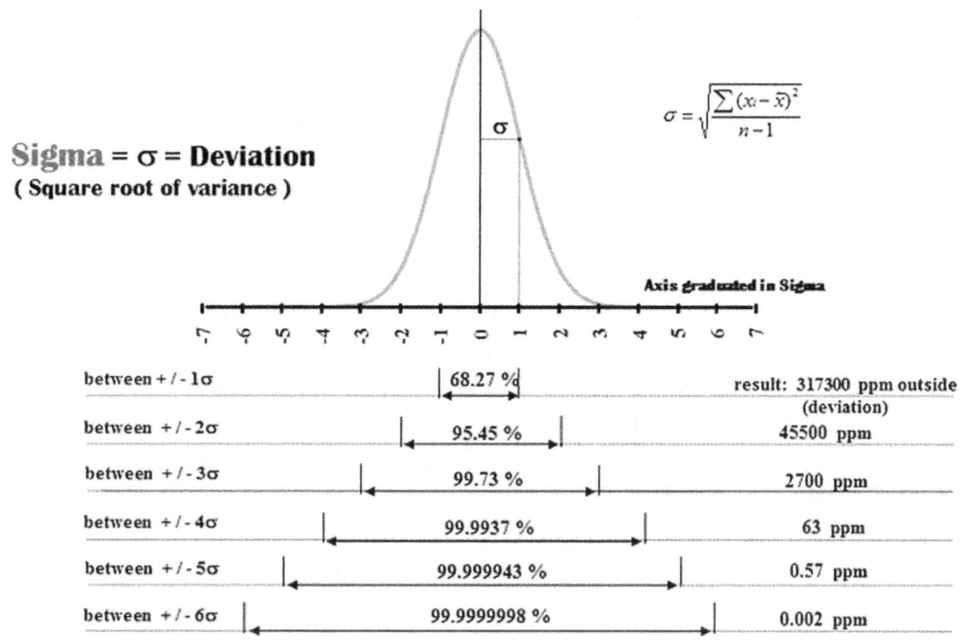

It may help practitioners from outside the energy creation industry to understand the risk management importance of LSS statistical significance if other common anecdotes are given, using a LSS 6SD of 0.002 PPM as compared to 1000 PPM which is roughly 3.5SD. In the U.S. healthcare industry, a LSS 1000 PPM failure would be equivalent to 4000 incorrect drug prescriptions issued to patients over a year. In the medical industry this quality failure would be akin to 3000 newborn babies falling out of doctor or nurse hands at hospitals over a year. Since the world has experienced the COVID-19 coronavirus pandemic, a snail mail example would illustrate how LSS could help risk management – deviation from a 3.5SD would be like USPS losing 400 letters over a year. By comparison, if those companies achieved a 6SD using LSS, we could anticipate only 13 wrong drug prescriptions across the U.S. in a year, only 10 new born babies being dropped at hospitals per year, and only 1 lost letter per year.

There were few studies in the literature where LSS was applied in energy creation facilities as a risk management technique, either for identification, assessment (measurement), or mitigation. Generally, LSS is applied for process control measurement, in other words, it detects a problem that is current occurring, that a process if out of control, so early detection is paramount in energy creation plants, otherwise catastrophic explosions and substantive environmental damage may occur.

Verma, Sharma, and Badar (2021) discussed a single case study of a LSS technique applied at an electronics manufacturing plant in India. Specifically, they explained how the value stream mapping (VSM) process was applied to allow quality control or assembly line managers to measure the worker process efficiencies in terms of materials used versus actual production. The VSM process uses a calculation based on takt time, which compares work team efficiency in terms of units produced divided into time needed. The takt time calculation helps to separate the necessary value-added processes from the non-value added processes, the latter is considered waste in LSS. The VSM is a visual method to capture all pertinent factors in the production process, similar in some ways to a predictive model, it shows inputs, processes, and outputs, along with the takt time measure of efficiency. Verma, Sharms and Bader (2021) modified the takt time calculation using an entropy-based mathematical model in VSM to include temperature and energy consumption as factors of production. They illustrated how VSM could identify the value-added and non-value-added steps in manufacturing, to calculate energy use and waste. They claimed this allowed plant managers to identify the maximum rejection or rework for workstations. The successfully illustrated how VSM in LSS could be modified and applied by practitioners for sustainable manufacturing. However, the VSM technique would not likely be applicable to a clean energy creation plant since the production factors are natural, with humans operating as controls not units of labor. There is no identifiable supply chain to the clean energy production industry, at least not after the facility is built (except of course for maintenance), since the resources are natural, including wind, solar, or water. Notwithstanding this, some clean energy production plants use bio degradable inputs, such as garbage, so VSM may be applicable in those scenarios or in fossil fuel plants such as coal or crude oil.

Yadav, Gahlot, Kaswan, Rathi, and Singh (2022), published an interesting literature review with a proposed framework illustrating how green LSS could be applied in many industries. They claimed the green version of LSS was actually LSS used for environmental conservation or carbon dioxide (CO^2) emission reduction. Their framework was an input, process, output flow similar to a SIPO chart or VSM from LSS. The main contribution of their paper was to identify the substantive literature of various stheories about how LSS techniques could be used for environment conservations or climate control, in others for environmental sustainability. They reviewed 35 applied LLS-related papers in a detailed form of meta-analysis. They identified several examples of successful LSS implementation in manufacturing, food processing, construction, mining, and public administration (e.g., government) industries. The implications from their paper were that companies across most industries are using LSS techniques for quality control which are perceived to support or improve environmental sustainability. However, none of the published papers specifically reviewed the quantitative statistical process control (SPC) family of LSS techniques applied to the energy creation industry, clean or otherwise.

METHODOLOGY

A pragmatic research ideology was applied for this case study because no formal method was suited to develop a quantitative risk management model using this unique case study of an underground hydro facility (Strang, 2015b). This was an action research project at the organizational level of analysis with an embedded case study to develop a lean six sigma risk management model based on SPC for operations of a clean energy production hydro storage plant.

Literature reviews, public record searches, field research of comparative cases and informant interviews were used to collect data. Quantitative analysis was performed using parametric and nonparametric statistical techniques to develop a model as well as to evaluate the results (Strang, 2015b). The study was conducted objectively by an independent research team with ethical approval but without direct involvement of the sponsors or stakeholders. All data were collected from publically accessible sources with the exception of informant interviews. Therefore competitively sensitive information was not revealed to genuinely protect stakeholder interests.

The 95% level of confidence was applied for all statistical tests unless otherwise specified. Distance, volume, and capacity measurements are converted to the metric system where needed and all numbers are rounded to whole units to facilitate global-minded executive decision making.

Case Study Site

The purpose of this chapter was to illustrate an application of LSS in an atypical setting, at a hydroelectricity generation plant located in a New York State remote park. The fact that it was remote, in located inside a state park, and operated on a large natural water body (near Lake George, NY) were the attributes that made this case study unique for sharing with stakeholders. As discussed, LSS is typically used to detect if a process is out of control, meaning that a problem or defect has already occurred, but LSS can also be used to detect such problems early enough to prevent disasters. This is the main reason that this case study site was selected, in order to illustrate an actual application of LSS in a hydro-electricity.

The analysis data were collected from site visits, surveys and applications recorded with the USA Federal Energy Regulatory Commission (FERC). Historical data were collected from news archives and through informant interviews held with local residents and engineers.

The case study site is located at the Lachute Hydroelectric in Ticonderoga, New York, USA. The site is located in Essex County, in the northern region of New York State, USA, within the general boundaries of the Adirondack Park Preserve. The Adirondack Park is a large protected natural preserve encompassing 6 million acres, thus making it the largest park in the contiguous USA, with mountains over 4000 feet high (1,220 meters), containing more than 2,800 lakes and 1,500 miles (938 KM) of rivers fed by over 30,000 miles (18,750 KM) of streams (Adirondack, 2016). The abundance of streams and rivers provide a renewable clean water source for the site. There is ample electricity produced through hydro and other methods but recently there has been a demand for storing electricity to accommodate peak demand and due to unforeseen events impacting existing generation plants.

The case study site plant is positioned on the Lachute Park. The reservoir is a fed by a short fast-moving river near the Vermont-New York State border, connecting Lake George with Lake Champlain. The source of water is the 32-mile (51 km) long Lake George which is known as the cleanest natural water lake in New York and is used as potable drinking water for residents surrounding the lake. Lake George is a popular vacation area for New Your City residents including the rich and famous along with corporate executives. The high priced residents along its shores generate significant tax revenues which go to pay for the protection and monitoring by the Lake George Park Commission. By comparison, sewage and water treatment systems flow into other lakes including Lake Champlain. The most interesting geographic aspect of the area is a 230 feet (70 m) drop in elevation in the 3½-mile (6 km) voyage. Interestingly, this is a drop-distance (at a lesser water volume) nearly twice the more-sudden altitude change of the well-known landmark Niagara Falls (167 ft (52 m). Lachute means water falls which came from the early French population who were killed when New York State was taken over by the British and later the land became part of the USA.

The Lachute Hydroelectric plant is owned by the Lachute Hydro Company. There are two hydroelectricity facilities on this outlet of Lake George. The first is the case study site focus which is located in the upper falls area beside a large reservoir with a capacity of 5.2 MW capable of generating 22,373 MWh per year using a 179 days average operating cycle. We have measured the efficiency of this plant to be 90.7% when operating. For reference purposes, the second Lachute hydroelectricity plant is located in the lower falls area adjacent to Bicentennial Park. This second site has a capacity of 3.8MW and has been generating 16,878 MHh per year during 185 days (7x24). The operational efficiency of this second site was at or near 98% when running. Both of these operational efficiency rates are outstanding in the hydroelectricity generation industry. Lean six sigma quality theories are essential to achieve that.

RESULTS AND DISCUSSION

LSS Risk Management Model

Data were collected from a typical inspection event, and a subset of the inspection observations were selected for the case study. A LSS SPC model was developed using Microsoft Excel spreadsheet but the author believes the formulas would also work in any other spreadsheet software package including Google Sheets or Apple Mac products. A laptop or desktop computer was required – the model would not function correctly for data entry on a smartphone, although a version completed on a laptop and shared could be viewed. LSS SPC was applied within the model using formulas acting on data entered into cells.

Figure 2 depicts the results of the study. It shows the risk management model with inspection data from the hydroelectricity plant. The data entry fields in figure 1 are located at the top left, namely the requirement, units, Gauge R&R variances and the type of distribution desired for SPC analysis. The list of requirements are the items selected for inspection, actually these were a small subset of the over 200 elements in production, so as to illustrate how this risk management model works. An inspection description/author block appears at the bottom left of the model as shown in figure 2.

In figure 2, the two data areas in the center are partitioned by either continuous (measured units) or attribute (defects count) data types. Either continuous or attribute fields are used for each data entry requirement. Depending on the nature of the inspected item, either continuous or attribute data would be collected, and then entered into the appropriate line of the model at the center portion of figure 2 (in the spreadsheet). The right most column in figure 2 represents the LSS SPC process capability calculations, or indexes of quality. The bottom portion of the SPC column in figure 2 aggregates and summarizes the key LSS metrics. The model source code is being shared by the author for research purposes (contact the corresponding author for a copy).

Figure 2. LSS SPC Model for Hydroelectricity Plant Risk Management

Data Entry Area					Continuous Data						Attribute Data		SPC Process Capability		
#	Requirement	Units	GRR	Distribution	Mean	σ	Shape	Scale	USL	LSL	Opp/Unit	dpu	dpmo	Z_{LT}	Z_{ST}
1	Forebay	1	12	Normal	12	0.05			12	11			500000.0	0.0	1.50
2	Intake infrastructure	1	21	Normal	20	0.025			22	18			0.0	>4.5	>6
3	Penstock	1	23	Weibull			1	2	25	19			999928.9	-3.8	-2.30
4	Surge chamber	1	31	Exponential	1				23	22			0.0	>4.5	>6
5	Hydraulic turbines	2	24	Attribute							4	1	250000.0	0.7	2.17
6	Power supply area	1	2	Normal	2	0.001							0.0	>4.5	>6
7	Draft tube	1	3	Normal	2	0.06							0.0	>4.5	>6
8	Tailrace	1	3	Normal	3	0.07							0.0	>4.5	>6
9	Batteries	3	1.5	Normal	2	0.8							0.0	>4.5	>6
10	Workareas	3	19	Attribute							9	1	111111.1	1.2	2.72
														Total Opps	21
														Service DPU	3.49993
														Service DPMO	166663.3
														Service RTY	3.02%
														Service Zst	2.47

Evaluation Description:	Non-tech visual inspection
Service Site:	Lachute upper plant, NY
Prepared by:	Dr. Kenneth D. Strang
Date:	9/1/2019

In figure 2, 10 hydroelectricity plan inspection requirements were selected from the case study to operationalize the LSS/SPC risk management model. These were the forebay area, the intake structure, the penstock pipe going to the top of the dam, the surge pressure chamber, the electricity generating hydraulic pelton turbines, the power supply assembly, the draft tube in the output channel, the tailrace, the temporary DC storage batteries, and the work-areas where employees travel which must be safe.

The SPC area of the model in figure 2 contains the LSS theory application. This represents the process capability measure of inherent statistical variability in a process or component at the hydroelectric plant. The goal of SPC is to use parametric and nonparametric statistics to ensure the inherent variability is in control or as desired and that no adverse conditions are present. The process capability study will compare the process specification (the goal or required benchmark) to the process output observed from the inspection to determine statistically if the process can meet the 6SD level of quality. All the measurements collected in the 'GRR' and continuous or attribute data columns are examined to determine if the total range of inherent variation is stable. The reason underlying the need to measure and reduce process capability in LSS is that the less the variation there is in a process, the more capable it will be of meeting the customer's specification, including for hydroelectricity plants clean energy, no accidents and no power brown outs. This is the key difference between statistics and LSS: the latter focuses on the customer, identifies defects or variances in the product/service, and then attempts to eliminate defects or process variations. In comparison, statistics attempts to find significant differences based on hypotheses and from that, deductions or inferences are made to generalize or predict future behavior. LSS practitioners try to identify and fix defective process behavior while researchers in statistics often try to forecast behavior of any type.

Process capability was determined by collecting and analyzing data through control charts. The control charts must indicate stability before capability calculations can be made. Histograms were used at first to examine the distribution pattern of individual values and verify a normal, Weibull, Exponential, or Beta distribution (they were in the model but not shown in figure 2). When analysis indicated a stable process using SPC and a distribution test, several indices were calculated at the lower right. If SPC indicated the process was non-stable, the index was still calculated, by considering the centering of the process. The process capability ratio describes what portion of the specification the process is taking up and it should be no greater than 75% in order for the process to be considered capable. The process performance index adjusts for the effect of non-centered distributions. The control limits in SPC and process capability are noted in figure 2 as USL and LSL, meaning upper service limit and lower service limit. USL and LSL are theoretically comparable to the confidence intervals of the sample average when using parametric statistical techniques such as t-tests or ANOVA. The generic theory for process capability is: Upper service limit – lower service limit / 6*SD.

The process capability from the hydroelectricity plan inspection was summarized at the bottom right of figure 1. The 'Total Opps' referred to count type inspections, it was the total number or operators multiplied by the number of items inspected, which was 21. The 'Service DPU' estimated the process capability of the data processing units, the defect counts, which was low at 3.49993%. The service DPU calculation adjusts the DPU with a six sigma variance based on a distribution analysis of USL and LSL. The 'Service DPMO' calculates the process capability rate of the service DPU per total operators, which was 166663.3 in figure 2. The 'Service RTY' creates a form of odds ratio of service DPU, based on an exponential distribution, which was 3.02%. The 'Service Zst' calculated the overall process performance index which was 2.47 in the model. Generally this should be close to 1.33 per benchmark. This signals a second more detailed inspection ought to be performed to double check the measures, and if any processes were found to be out of variation tolerances, a detailed plant maintenance would be ordered.

CONCLUSION AND FUTURE RESEARCH

Four attributes of this chapter make it unique and generalizable to the clean energy hydroelectricity production community of practice. The study applied a pragmatic research ideology using free spreadsheet software that could be utilized by practitioners or researchers, based on a literature review, comparative field case study data collection, and parametric statistical techniques. A unique actual hydroelectricity facility based in New York USA was used as the case study (data was collected from the site and from informants). A SPC model was developed to apply LSS theories for risk management. Finally, an easy to use and maintain spreadsheet-based decision making model was fully explained which could be used by managers, practitioners or other researchers.

The main contribution of this chapter was to show how lean six sigma was applied in a clean energy manufacturing plant. The LSS case study was in an atypical setting, at a hydroelectricity generation plant located in a New York State remote park. The fact that it was remote, located inside a state park, and operated on a large natural water body (near Lake George, NY) were the attributes which made this case study unique for sharing with stakeholders. As discussed, LSS is typically used to detect if a process is out of control, meaning that a problem or defect has already occurred, but LSS can also be used to detect such problems early enough to prevent disasters, as discussed in this chapter. This is the main reason that this case study site was selected, in order to illustrate an actual application of LSS in a hydro-electricity.

This may generalize more broadly, globally, to other hydro-electric, wind, solar, nuclear and even fossil-fuel based energy utilities, because lean six sigma is a primarily risk prevention or mitigation methodology not a risk management estimation technique. The lean tools allow a company to detect problems that have occurred not ones that will occur. When a process is out of control the problem has already started. However, it can dramatically reduce subsequent problems at an energy generation plant if problems can be detected early on, so they may be brought back into control. For example, the near-fatal nuclear plant overheating at Three Mile Island in the U.S. was an example of a process out of control, but it was accidentally detected by a diligent employee. ompareson the nuclear explosion disaster in Chernobyl Ukraine was an example of a process out of control that was not detected in time, with catastrophic results. By illustrating how lean six sigma was applied in a simple easy to use spreadsheet application, this may be of interest to all levels of management working at energy production plants, including nuclear, solar, wind, fossil-fuel as well as hydro (like the current study). In other words the risk detection and mitigation approaches in this chapter, namely lean six sigma, should generalize widely to all types of energy creation around the world.

Furthermore, the success of this case study hydroelectricity plant provides motivation to other American states and to other countries for exploring risk management using LSS techniques in the clean renewable energy field. There is significant corporate social responsibility on large corporations and utilities to produce energy without utilizing fossil fuel sources or further polluting the environment. Furthermore, the case study identified important best-practices from the literature, recommending for instance to use LSS theory as part of risk management.

The limitations of this study are that while the concepts and risk management decision making model may not generalize to any other pumped hydro facility, on or below ground since it was a single site case study based in New York. These limitations give rise to the need for conducting more studies of how to use LSS for risk management in other clean energy production facilities as well as in other industries around the world.

REFERENCES

Adirondack. (2016). *Discover the Adirondack Park*. Adirondack Council. Retrieved December 30, 2016, from the World Wide Web: https://www.adirondackcouncil.org/

Ahmadian, R., Falconer, R., & Bockelmann-Evans, B. (2012). Far-field modelling of the hydro-environmental impact of tidal stream turbines. *Renewable Energy*, *38*(1), 107–116. doi:10.1016/j.renene.2011.07.005

Ahmadian, R., & Falconer, R. A. (2012). Assessment of array shape of tidal stream turbines on hydro-environmental impacts and power output. *Renewable Energy*, *44*(1), 318–327. doi:10.1016/j.renene.2012.01.106

Ahmadian, R., Falconer, R. A., & Bockelmann-Evans, B. (2014). Comparison of hydro-environmental impacts for ebb-only and two-way generation for a Severn Barrage. *Computers & Geosciences*, *71*(C), 11–19. doi:10.1016/j.cageo.2014.05.006

Armstrong, A., & Bulkeley, H. (2014). Micro-hydro politics: Producing and contesting community energy in the North of England. *Geoforum*, *56*(1), 66–76. doi:10.1016/j.geoforum.2014.06.015

Ashok, S. (2007). Optimised model for community-based hybrid energy system. *Renewable Energy*, *32*(7), 1155–1164. doi:10.1016/j.renene.2006.04.008

Atlason, R., & Unnthorsson, R. (2014). Ideal EROI (energy return on investment) deepens the understanding of energy systems. *Energy*, *67*(1), 241–245. doi:10.1016/j.energy.2014.01.096

Bansal, A. K., Kumar, R., & Gupta, R. A. (2013). Economic analysis and power management of a Small Autonomous Hybrid Power System (SAHPS) using Biogeography Based Optimization (BBO) algorithm. *IEEE Transactions on Smart Grid*, *4*(1), 638–648. doi:10.1109/TSG.2012.2236112

Barbour, E., Radcliffe, J., Ding, Y., Li, Y., & Wilson, I. A. G. (2016). A review of pumped hydro energy storage development in significant international electricity markets. *Renewable & Sustainable Energy Reviews*, *61*(1), 421–432. doi:10.1016/j.rser.2016.04.019

Basnyat, M. B. (2004). Rural electrification through renewable energy in Nepal. *World Review of Science, Technology and Sustainable Development*, *1*(1), 74–80. doi:10.1504/WRSTSD.2004.004857

Blakers, A. (2015). Sustainable Energy Options. *Asian Perspective*, *39*(4), 559–590. doi:10.1353/apr.2015.0025

Bobinaite, V., & Juozapaviaiene, A. (2011). Assessment of performance efficiency of enterprises producing electricity in hydro and wind power plants. *Business: Theory and Practice*, *12*(2), 193–202.

Boicea, V. A. (2014). Energy storage technologies: The past and the present. *Proceedings of the IEEE*, *102*(11), 1777–1794. doi:10.1109/JPROC.2014.2359545

Breckenridge, J. N., Zimbardo, P. G., & Sweeton, J. L. (2010). After years of media coverage, can one more video report trigger heuristic judgments? A national study of American terrorism risk perceptions. *Behavioral Sciences Of Terrorism & Political Aggression*, *2*(3), 163–178. doi:10.1080/19434471003768826

Bruninx, K., Delarue, E., Dhaeseleer, W., Dvorkin, Y., Kirschen, D. S., & Pandzic, H. (2016). Coupling Pumped Hydro Energy Storage with Unit Commitment. *IEEE Transactions on Sustainable Energy*, *7*(2), 786–796. doi:10.1109/TSTE.2015.2498555

Chaudhry, A. M., Raza, R., & Hayat, S. A. (2009). Renewable energy technologies in Pakistan: Prospects and challenges. *Renewable & Sustainable Energy Reviews*, *13*(6-7), 1657–1662. doi:10.1016/j.rser.2008.09.025

Chhetri, A. B., Islam, M. R., & Pokharel, G. R. (2009). Sustainability of micro-hydrosystems - A case study. *Energy & Environment*, *20*(4), 567–585. doi:10.1260/095830509788707356

Connolly, D., Leahy, M., & MacLaughlin, S. (2010). Development of a computer program to locate potential sites for pumped hydroelectric energy storage. *Energy*, *35*(1), 375–381. doi:10.1016/j.energy.2009.10.004

de Boer, H. S., Moll, H., Benders, R., & Grond, L. (2014). The application of power-to-gas, pumped hydro storage and compressed air energy storage in an electricity system at different wind power penetration levels. *Energy*, *72*(1), 360–370. doi:10.1016/j.energy.2014.05.047

Dell, G., Egger, C., & Grabl, A. (1996). Renewable energy in Austria. *Renewable Energy*, *9*(1-4), 1116-1119.

Ehnberg, S. G. J., & Bollen, M. H. J. (2005). Reliability of a small power system using solar power and hydro. *Electric Power Systems Research*, *74*(1), 119–127. doi:10.1016/j.epsr.2004.09.009

Elahee, M. K. (2013). Potential of hydropower in mauritius: Myth or reality? *Energy Sources. Part A, Recovery, Utilization, and Environmental Effects*, *35*(10), 921–925. doi:10.1080/15567036.2010.514592

Erdogdu, E. (2011). An analysis of Turkish hydropower policy. *Renewable & Sustainable Energy Reviews*, *15*(1), 689–696. doi:10.1016/j.rser.2010.09.019

Foley, A. M., Leahy, P. G., McKeogh, E. J., Li, K., & Morrison, A. P. (2015). A long-term analysis of pumped hydro storage to firm wind power. *Applied Energy*, *137*(1), 638–648. doi:10.1016/j.apenergy.2014.07.020

Fonseca, J. A., & Schlueter, A. (2013). Novel approach for decentralized energy supply and energy storage of tall buildings in Latin America based on renewable energy sources: Case study of informal vertical community Torre David, Caracas - Venezuela. *Energy*, *45*(2), 131–143. doi:10.1016/j.energy.2013.02.019

Geth, F., Brijs, T., Driesen, J., Belmans, R., & Kathan, J. (2015). An overview of large-scale stationary electricity storage plants in Europe: Current status and new developments. *Renewable & Sustainable Energy Reviews*, *52*(1), 1212–1227. doi:10.1016/j.rser.2015.07.145

Ghadikolaei, H. M., Ahmadi, A., Aghaei, J., & Najafi, M. (2012). Risk constrained self-scheduling of hydro/wind units for short term electricity markets considering intermittency and uncertainty. *Renewable & Sustainable Energy Reviews*, *16*(7), 4734–4743. doi:10.1016/j.rser.2012.04.019

Goel, P. K., Singh, B., Murthy, S. S., & Kishore, N. (2011). Isolated wind-hydro hybrid system using cage generators and battery storage. *IEEE Transactions on Industrial Electronics*, *58*(4), 1141–1153. doi:10.1109/TIE.2009.2037646

Gu, Y., Bakke, J., Zhou, Z., Osborn, D., Bo, R., & Guo, T. (2014). A novel market simulation methodology on hydro storage. *IEEE Transactions on Smart Grid*, *5*(2), 1119–1128. doi:10.1109/TSG.2013.2289915

Gupta, A., Saini, R. P., & Sharma, M. P. (2010). Steady-state modelling of hybrid energy system for off grid electrification of cluster of villages. *Renewable Energy*, *35*(2), 520–535. doi:10.1016/j.renene.2009.06.014

Gupta, A., Saini, R. P., & Sharma, M. P. (2011). Modelling of hybrid energy system-Part I: Problem formulation and model development. *Renewable Energy*, *36*(2), 459–465. doi:10.1016/j.renene.2010.06.035

IEA. (2015). Key world energy statistics. International Energy Association (IEA).

Islam, M. S., Karim, S. A., Rahman, M. G., Gupta, S. D., & Masum, M. S. (2013). A case study of the notion and model of micro hydro power plant using the kinetic energy of flowing water of Burinadi and Meghna Rivers of Bangladesh. *Engineering Journal (New York)*, *17*(4), 47–60.

Jafar, M. (2000). Renewable energy in the South Pacific - Options and constraints. *Renewable Energy*, *19*(1-2), 305–309. doi:10.1016/S0960-1481(99)00045-2

Jamil, M., Ahmad, F., & Jeon, Y. J. (2016). Renewable energy technologies adopted by the UAE: Prospects and challenges - A comprehensive overview. *Renewable & Sustainable Energy Reviews*, *55*, 1181–1194. doi:10.1016/j.rser.2015.05.087

Jimanez, A., Capilla, J. A., Carrian, J. A., & Alameda-Hernandez, E. (2016). Optimal site selection for upper reservoirs in pump-back systems, using geographical information systems and multicriteria analysis. *Renewable Energy*, *86*(1), 429–440. doi:10.1016/j.renene.2015.08.035

Kadiyala, A., Kommalapati, R., & Huque, Z. (2016). Evaluation of the life cycle greenhouse gas emissions from hydroelectricity generation systems. *Sustainability (Switzerland)*, *8*(6), 12–25. doi:10.3390u8060539

Kallakuri, C., Vaidyanathan, S., Kelly, M., & Cluett, R. (2016). *The 2016 International Energy Efficiency Scorecard* (E1602). Washington, DC: American Council for an Energy-Efficient Economy (ACEEE).

Kazem, H. A. (2011). Renewable energy in Oman: Status and future prospects. *Renewable & Sustainable Energy Reviews*, *15*(8), 3465–3469. doi:10.1016/j.rser.2011.05.015

Koleva, E. G., & Mladenov, G. M. (2014). Renewable energy and energy efficiency in Bulgaria. *Progress in Industrial Ecology*, *8*(4), 257–278. doi:10.1504/PIE.2014.066798

Koohi-Kamali, S., Rahim, N. A., Mokhlis, H., Tyagi, V. V., & Panwar, N. L. (2013). Emergence of energy storage technologies as the solution for reliable operation of smart power systems: A review. *Renewable & Sustainable Energy Reviews*, *25*(1), 135–165. doi:10.1016/j.rser.2013.03.056

Korstanje, M. E., Strang, K. D., & Tzanelli, R. (2019). Tourism security after climate change. In M. E. Korstanje (Ed.), *The Anthropology of Tourism Security*. https://eprints.whiterose.ac.uk/147935/

Kusakana, K. (2016). Optimal scheduling for distributed hybrid system with pumped hydro storage. *Energy Conversion and Management*, *111*(1), 253–260.

lo Storto, C., & Capano, B. (2014). Productivity changes of the renewable energy installed capacity: An empirical study relating to 31 European countries between 2002 and 2011. *Energy Education Science and Technology, Part A. Energy Science and Research*, *32*(5), 3061–3072.

Ma, T., Yang, H., & Lu, L. (2014). Feasibility study and economic analysis of pumped hydro storage and battery storage for a renewable energy powered island. *Energy Conversion and Management*, *79*(1), 387–397. doi:10.1016/j.enconman.2013.12.047

Margeta, J., & Glasnovic, Z. (2010). Feasibility of the green energy production by hybrid solar + hydro power system in Europe and similar climate areas. *Renewable & Sustainable Energy Reviews*, *14*(6), 1580–1590. doi:10.1016/j.rser.2010.01.019

Margeta, J., & Glasnovic, Z. (2011). Exploitation of temporary water flow by hybrid PV-hydroelectric plant. *Renewable Energy*, *36*(8), 2268–2277. doi:10.1016/j.renene.2011.01.001

McConnell, D., Forcey, T., & Sandiford, M. (2015). Estimating the value of electricity storage in an energy-only wholesale market. *Applied Energy*, *159*(1), 422–432. doi:10.1016/j.apenergy.2015.09.006

McNabola, A., Coughlan, P., & Williams, A. P. (2014). Energy recovery in the water industry: An assessment of the potential of micro-hydropower. *Water and Environment Journal: the Journal / the Chartered Institution of Water and Environmental Management*, *28*(2), 294–304. doi:10.1111/wej.12046

Mishra, A. K. (2010). Alternate Sources of Energy Gadgets for the Sikkim State of NE Region. *Agricultural Engineering Today VO*, *34*(4), 29.

Nersesian, R., & Strang, K. D. (2017). Feasibility approaches to reduce the unreliability of gas, nuclear, coal, solar and wind electricity production. *International Journal of Risk and Contingency Management*, *6*(1), 54–69. doi:10.4018/IJRCM.2017010104

Olsen, J., Paasch, K., Lassen, B., & Veje, C. T. (2015). A new principle for underground pumped hydroelectric storage. *Journal of Energy Storage*, *2*(1), 54–63. doi:10.1016/j.est.2015.06.003

Oseni, M. O. (2012). Improving households' access to electricity and energy consumption pattern in Nigeria: Renewable energy alternative. *Renewable & Sustainable Energy Reviews*, *16*(6), 3967–3974. doi:10.1016/j.rser.2012.03.010

Park, J.-H., Kim, C.-G., & Lee, Y.-H. (2016). Efficient energy storage method by multistage pump of the energy storage system using CFD. *International Journal of Energy Research*, *40*(5), 685–691. doi:10.1002/er.3432

Pedraza, J. M. (2012). The Current and Future Role of Renewable Energy Sources for the Production of Electricity in Latin America and the Caribbean. *International Journal of Energy and Environmental Engineering*, *20*(5), 415–477.

Peinado, J., Graeml, A. R., & Vianna, F. (2018). Operations management body of knowledge and its relevance to manufacturing and service organizations. *Revista de Gestão*, *25*(4), 373–389. doi:10.1108/REGE-03-2018-0049

Pimenta, F. M., & Assireu, A. T. (2015). Simulating reservoir storage for a wind-hydro hydrid system. *Renewable Energy*, *76*(1), 757–767. doi:10.1016/j.renene.2014.11.047

Purvins, A., Papaioannou, I. T., Tzimas, E., & Oleinikova, I. (2012). Effects of variable renewable power on a country-scale electricity system: High penetration of hydro power plants and wind farms in electricity generation. *Energy*, *43*(1), 225–236. doi:10.1016/j.energy.2012.04.038

Raluy, R. G., Serra, L., & Uche, J. (2005). Life cycle assessment of desalination technologies integrated with renewable energies. *Desalination*, *183*(1-3), 81–93. doi:10.1016/j.desal.2005.04.023

Segurado, R., Costa, M., Carvalho, M. G., & Duia, N. (2014). Integrated analysis of energy and water supply in islands. Case study of S. Vicente, Cape Verde. *Energy*, *92*(Part 3), 639–648.

Segurado, R., Madeira, J. F. A., Costa, M., Carvalho, M. G., & Duia, N. (2016). Optimization of a wind powered desalination and pumped hydro storage system. *Applied Energy*, *177*, 487–499. doi:10.1016/j.apenergy.2016.05.125

Strang, K. D. (2015a). Exploring the relationship between global terrorist ideology and attack methodology. *Risk Management Journal, 17*(2), 65-90. https://link.springer.com/article/1010.1057/rm.2015.1058

Strang, K. D. (2015b). *Handbook of Research Design in Business and Management*. New York: Palgrave Macmillan. Retrieved from http://kennethstrang.com/ABIS/ResearchDesignHandbook[ISBN9781137484956]-Strang@Palgrave(2015).pdf doi:10.1057/9781137484956

Strang, K. D. (2017). Feasibility of a hidden renewable energy hydro power storage battery. *Journal of Energy Storage*, *13*(3), 164–175. doi:10.1016/j.est.2017.07.001

Strang, K. D., & Chan, C. E. L. (2010). Simulating e-business innovation process improvement with virtual teams across Europe and Asia. *International Journal of E-Entrepreneurship and Innovation*, *1*(1), 22–41. doi:10.4018/jeei.2010010102

Tam, S. W., Blomquist, C. A., & Kartsounes, G. T. (2007). Underground pumped hydro storage—An overview. *Energy Sources*, *4*(4), 329–351. doi:10.1080/00908317908908068

Tortajada, C. (2015). Dams: An essential component of development. *Journal of Hydrologic Engineering*, *20*(1), 1–10. doi:10.1061/(ASCE)HE.1943-5584.0000919

Uddin, N. (2012). *Geotechnical issues in the creation of underground reservoirs for massive energy storage.* Paper presented at the IEEE Geothermal Innovations, Birmingham, AL. 10.1109/JPROC.2011.2161969

Vasel-Be-Hagh, A., Carriveau, R., & Ting, D. S.-K. (2013). Energy storage using weights hydraulically lifted above ground. *The International Journal of Environmental Studies*, *70*(5), 792–799. doi:10.1080/00207233.2013.810043

Verma, N., Sharma, V., & Badar, M. A. (2021). Entropy-Based Lean, Energy and Six Sigma Approach to Achieve Sustainability in Manufacturing System. *Arabian Journal for Science and Engineering*, *46*(8), 8105–8117. doi:10.100713369-021-05826-x PMID:34189013

Wang, H., Wang, L., Wang, X., & Yao, E. (2013). A novel pumped hydro combined with compressed air energy storage system. *Energies*, *6*(3), 1554–1567. doi:10.3390/en6031554

Whittingham, M. S. (2012). History, evolution, and future status of energy storage. *Proceedings of the IEEE, 100*, 1518-1534. 10.1109/JPROC.2012.2190170

Yadav, V., Gahlot, P., Kaswan, M. S., Rathi, R., & Singh, M. (2022). Sustainable Green Lean Six Sigma Methodology and Application Status: A Perspective Review. In A. K. Dubey, A. Sachdeva, & M. Mehta (Eds.), *Recent Trends in Industrial and Production Engineering* (pp. 251–266). Springer Singapore. doi:10.1007/978-981-16-3135-1_26

Zafirakis, D., Chalvatzis, K. J., Baiocchi, G., & Daskalakis, G. (2013). Modeling of financial incentives for investments in energy storage systems that promote the large-scale integration of wind energy. *Applied Energy*, *105*(1), 138–154. doi:10.1016/j.apenergy.2012.11.073

Zafirakis, D., Chalvatzis, K. J., Daskalakis, G., & Baiocchi, G. (2016). The value of arbitrage for energy storage: Evidence from European electricity markets. *Applied Energy*, *149*(1), 150–161. doi:10.1016/j.apenergy.2016.05.047

Chapter 6
Supply Chain Logistics Risk Mitigation:
Impact of the COVID-19 Pandemic

Edna Mngusughun Denga
https://orcid.org/0000-0002-2121-242X
American University of Nigeria, Nigeria

Sandip Rakshit
American University of Nigeria, Nigeria

ABSTRACT

The COVID-19 pandemic has altered the business landscape for several organizations throughout the world, emphasizing the significance of being able to respond, adapt, and set up crisis management processes in an attempt to withstand uncertain situations. The necessity of supply chain resilience and risk management is more evident than previously as organizations attempt to strengthen operations and business resilience. The authors conducted an empirical investigation within the Nigerian supply chain logistics setting to evaluate and compare the uncertainties, tactics, and strategies employed by two businesses in Nigeria's northeastern region, where insurgency and banditry are rampant, exacerbated by the novel COVID-19 pandemic. The chapter provides a theoretical approach to logistics and supply chain management, delving into the fundamental business processes of the Global Supply Chain Forum (GSCF) and the role of logistics in each of the emphasized businesses.

INTRODUCTION

Supply chain risks are categorized into disruption risks and operational, the operational risks are related to common disruptions in SC operations, like lead-time and demand fluctuations, whereas the disruption risks are mostly related to incidents that occur seldom but have large consequences (Hosseini et al., 2019), in regards to duration, significant uncertainty, and ripple effects dispersion, epidemic outbreaks are a specific example of SC hazards (Ivanov, 2020). Volatility and unpredictability in supply chain are

DOI: 10.4018/978-1-6684-5279-0.ch006

fundamental characteristics of supply chain management(SCM) and can emerge in every firm. Natural catastrophes (tornados, flooding, hurricanes, quakes, tsunamis), man-made disasters (nuclear plant disruptions, inadvertent toxic spillages, Conflicts, acts of terrorism), and legal disputes or strikes are all examples of supply chain disruptions that cause uncertainty and volatility. The deterioration of the globe's ecological system, combined with socioeconomic instability, is escalating the frequency and intensity of natural catastrophes, subjecting supply chains to more disruptions to the point where specific incidents can have enormous financial as well as non-financial consequences for supply chains, businesses, and society. Disruptions are fundamental problems in logistics risk management, as they endanger logistics personnel' safety, damage products ((Hazen, Russo, Confente, & Pellathy, 2021)), and obstruct effective logistical operations. Hence, productive risk management preserves a broad variety of stakeholders (Miller, 2017) and assists organizations gain a competitive edge.

Uncertainty is defined by researchers working in strategic management and organizational theory as the volatility of environmental variables that influence organization's performance or the scarcity of relevant information about these variables (Wang, Wang, & Chan, 2021). The presence of uncertainty in internal and external environmental factors reduces the predictability of company effectiveness and increases the risk (Jha, Sharma, Kumar, & Verma, 2021; Moncef & Monnet Dupuy, 2021. The Coronavirus (COVID-19) pandemic has impacted several Supply chain logistics around the world (Araz et al., 2020). COVID-19's impacts wreaked havoc on the world economy, paralyzing major industries (Ivanov, 2020). According to Fortune (2020), the outbreak has a negative impact on more than 94 percent of top 1000 businesses. SCRM aims to increase a company's performance by ensuring SC robustness and increasing SC resilience. Organizations' capability to reorganize their competences is essential for their sustainability and success in conditions of extreme uncertainty, such as the COVID-19 outbreak. As a result, organizations that can restructure and redeploy their resources in a tumultuous environment are better able to create capacities to buffer the effects of SC disruptions.

Since supply chain logistics encompasses the entire process of conveying products from raw material processing to customer delivery, focusing on supply chain risk management is a step toward increasing the adoption and growth of sustainable practices. (Seuring & Müller, 2008; Shokouhyar, Pahlevani, & Mir Mohammad Sadeghi, 2019; Silva, Alves, Dias, & Nascimento, 2019). Logistics plays an essential role in an organization's quest for sustainability because it represents the integrated management of all the activities required to move products through the supply chain (Li, Yan, Zhang, & Yan, 2021). Whereas robustness describes a firm's ability to sustain its planned performance in the face of a disruption (or series of disruptions), resilience refers to the capacity to recover its performance despite absorbing the disruption impacts. With supply shortages, a lack of responsiveness, and production halts, the COVID-19 pandemic has put the robustness and resilience of supply chain logistics to the test in various industries (Ivanov and Dolgui, 2020). Examining how organizations have gained from previous disruptions to enhance mitigation measures is essential to reducing recovery time during possible risks or disruptions. In essence, understanding supply chain logistics risk management is important and a top priority for both academics and practitioners.

BACKGROUND

There is no other field of business operations that is as diverse or covers as much scope as logistics. Logistics is associated with delivering goods and services where they are required at the specific time desired (Subiyanto, 2021). It is impossible to imagine marketing, manufacturing, or foreign trade without logistics (Paula, Campos, Pagani, Guarnieri, & Kaviani, 2020). Previous research has shown that logistics plays a strategic role in a firm's performance. It is one of the vital elements of supply chain management (SCM) and a primary source of competitive advantage (Afum et al., 2021; Kawa & Świątowiec-Szczpańska, 2021). Logistics, particularly in SCM, extends beyond the functional level to include business processes. Logistics approach influences all business processes in the supply chain because it encapsulates the fundamental SCM business operations and has a significant effect on their effectiveness and efficiency. In other words, it affects firms' ability to meet their customers' needs at the lowest possible cost (Afum et al., 2021).

The COVID-19 pandemic is forcing a significant shift in how supply chains and logistics are maintained. Prior to the pandemic, most organizations focused their supply chains on cost reduction and just-in-time delivery, culminating in low inventory levels (Simchi-Levi 2020; Dohale et al. 2021). The COVID-19 epidemic showed the flaws in this method in a variety of sectors, prompting adjustments. COVID-19, according to Choi, Rogers, and Vakil (2020), this caused considerable difficulties and disruptions for organizations that were not well-prepared due to the complexities of their supply chains logistics. These disruptions in supply chain logistics possess rapid and negative consequences for production plants, vendors, warehousing facilities, and transportation linkages, some of which can become inaccessible for a duration of time. In some circumstances, organizations only become aware of their supply chain's vulnerability after a disruption has occurred (Bier, Lange, and Glock 2020). Furthermore, product shortages and delays in delivery rapidly spread, resulting in further negative consequences for supply chain performance and resilience.

Supply chain risk management is essential for establishing organizational resilience and long-term viability. The strengthening of supply-chain resilience is an organization's competence to monitor the environment, avert unexpected disruptions, and proactively deploy capabilities to mitigate risks and assist in alleviating vulnerability (Gligor et al., 2019). Supply chains' information-based, physical, and economic flows (Silva, Alves, Dias, & Nascimento, 2019) can be disrupted in a wide variety of ways, from natural catastrophes like fire, eruption, cyclones, or pandemics like the COVID-19, to activities management problems like vendor interruptions, low quality, or inadequate inventory (Rai et al., 2006). Pandemic outbreaks are a unique category of logistical supply chain disruption. They are particularly harmful due to their rapid spread throughout diverse geographical locations. COVID-19 is a new form of extremely infectious coronavirus that is wreaking havoc on supply chains around the world (Choi 2020; Ivanov 2020a), The development of organizations' capacities is an important part of rebounding from supply chain disruptions and establishing resilience. A reaction and recovery capability is required to mitigate the impact and to be able to recover after disruptions. Organizations' supply chains logistics will be much more exposed if they fail to create readiness, reaction, and recovery capabilities.

Organizations search through a disruption management strategy that incorporates discovery, recovery, and redesign. In several scenarios, the process is aided by an organization's peculiar risk management framework, which includes identification of risks, evaluation, mitigation, and monitoring (Moncef & Monnet Dupuy, 2021). Although supply chain logistic disruption and risk is a well-studied topic, research studies have so far focused primarily on the response to natural catastrophes as leading causes of supply chain disruptions or risks, rather than less intense but more prevalent daily operational disruptions. The chapter addresses a significant gap in the literature by addressing the scarcity of studies on operational disruptions, helping to extend the view of supply chain logistics disruptions and risks during crisis times. While all sorts of occurrences necessitate identical actions to cope with supply chain interruptions, the origins of the disruptions or risk, the relevant information in choosing a mitigating or recovery plan, and most importantly, the proactive measures are all distinct. Thus, it is imperative to investigate how firms potentially leverage SC risk management (SCRM) strategies to deal with the disruptions caused by terrorism, banditry and the COVID-19 outbreak. This chapter aims to identify and analyze the actions taken by organizations during and after operational constraints and risks in supply chain logistics.

Furthermore, most supply chain and logistics literature has been written from developed economies rather than developing countries. As a result, an attempt will be undertaken to investigate how organizations in a developing country like Nigeria manage supply chain logistics constraints (both man-made and natural), capitalize on opportunities in the country's most crisis-prone territory, and mitigate constraints, risks, and disruptions. This is conducted through empirical investigation within the Nigerian supply chain logistics setting to analyze and compare the challenges faced and strategies adopted by two organizations situated in the north-eastern region of Nigeria, where the religious and political insurgency is rampant. Owing to the clear specific disparities in current comprehension of the aforementioned issues, the chapter explores supply chain logistics constraints or risks faced by companies amid insurgency exacerbated by COVID- 19 Pandemic in the northeast, the opportunities available as well as the strategies adopted by companies to mitigate supply chain logistics challenges and finally, the effectiveness of these strategies.

REVIEW OF LITERATURE

Supply Chain

The term "supply chain" is typically described as the coordination of businesses that bring products or services to the market (Orr & Jadhav, 2018; Zimon, Madzik, & Sroufe, 2020). A supply chain includes manufacturers, suppliers, transporters, warehouses, wholesalers, retailers, other intermediaries, and even customers. Any product traded on the consumer goods market goes through a series of business-to-business transactions as it advances from raw material to finished product (Jha et al., 2021). This is a life cycle process comprised of physical, information, financial, and knowledge flows. The primary goal is to satisfy final consumer demand with products and services from a network of interconnected suppliers (Paciarotti, Piotrowicz, & Fenton, 2021).
An integrated supply chain model typically includes three interlinked flows:

- Material flows have three main phases (purchasing, transformation, and distribution).
- Informational flows (digital data interchange or blog linkages).
- Financial flows (which include payments to subcontractors and suppliers for goods and services as well as payments made by customers to retailers for the final product (Jha et al., 2021; Sharma, Raut, Govindarajan, & Narkhede, 2021).

SCM involves integrating activities and processes among supply chain members. SCM was developed to control the flow of information, products, and services through a network of customers, businesses, and supply chain partners (Zsidisin, Bresler, Hazen, Snider, & Wilkerson, 2020). Since its emergence as a concept in the 1980s, supply chain management has undergone significant changes and extensions. Since the supply chain is a network of businesses providing services and product lines to the final customers, supply chain management must concentrate on the relationships between both the firm and its connection of suppliers and customers (Hazen et al., 2021; Zimon et al., 2020). Therefore, supply chain management must include all activities in which a company interacts with its buyers and suppliers, which must be wide-ranging and impact most facets of business management.

Logistics

An element of a supply chain's larger framework and is the activity considered necessary to move and place inventory within a supply chain. It is a method of creating value by timing and placing inventory and integrating a company's order processing, inventory, shipping regulation, warehousing, materials handling, and packaging via a facility network. Integrated logistics is critical for efficient supply chain connectivity because it connects and synchronizes the entire supply chain as a single continuous operation. Whereas the purpose of logistical work has principally continued to remain consistent over the years, the context in which it is carried out has changed significantly concurrently with technological innovation and management advancement. According to the 5 Right Principles, logistics is the process of conveying the right product to the right location at the right time, under the right conditions, and at the right price for the right customer.

Logistics management is defined by the Council of Logistics Management (CLM) as the "process of planning, implementing, and managing the reliable, effective flow and storage of products, services, and relevant information from the point of origin to the point of consumption in an attempt to meet customer specifications and demands." Salam and Khan (2020) define logistics as the structure and execution of the physical, managerial, and information frameworks necessary to facilitate services and goods to travel across space and time. Logistics entails scheduling and managing all variables that will influence the delivery of the right product to the right place on time and within. Superior logistical effectiveness is a central task where organizations adopting integrated supply chain management initiatives benefit from a significant performance improvement. Due to the fierce competition in the market, logistics management is viewed as a crucial source of competitive advantage. As a result of integrated supply chain management, the value of logistics activities can only soar as it facilitates supply chain partners to enhance the utilization of their inter-organizational logistics. According to Sweeney (2018), a logistics tactic that encompasses the entire supply chain is considered necessary; this aggregate strategy will form the basic catalyst for logistic strategy in each supply chain but again distribution networks, modes of transportation, carrier monitoring, inventory control, warehousing, order processing, and other related activities must all be investigated (Nag et al., 2014).

The Council of Logistics Management characterizes Logistics activities in supply chain to include "key" and "support" activities, as well as some of the decision making affiliated with each of the activities (Tien et al., 2019). Key and support activities are segregated as the former generally occur throughout logistics channel (hub), whereas the latter takes place contingent on the industrial sector or particular scenario within a specific firm. Key activities add value to the total cost of logistics or are critical to the impactful synchronization and accomplishment of logistics tasks (Lambert et al., 2008). The key activities are represented below:

Figure 1. Key logistics activities in supply chain
Source: (Authors, 2022)

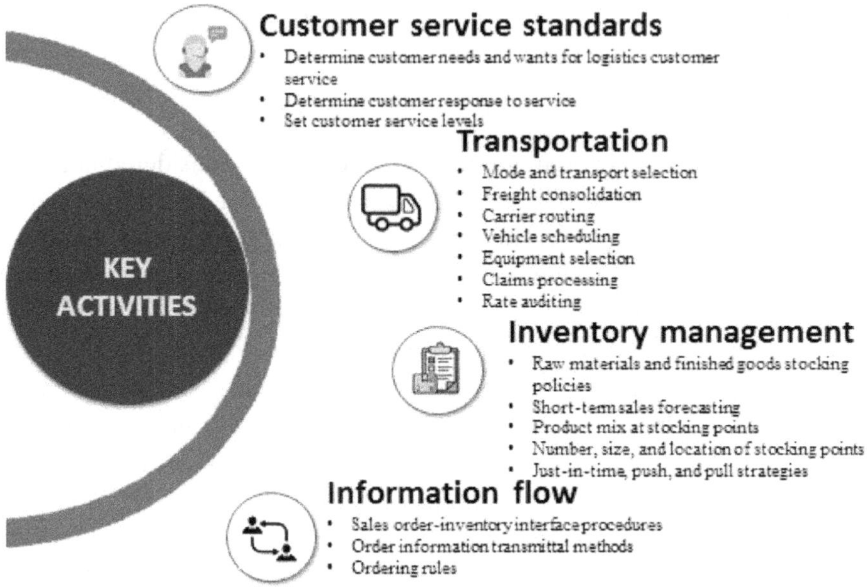

Support activities

In this context, Support Activities is viewed as contributing to the logistics task. However, one or more of the support activities may not be included in a company's logistics task mix. They include;

Figure 2. Support logistics activities in supply chain
Source: (Authors, 2022)

Logistics' Role in Supply Chain Management

To assist organizations in building, establishing, and consolidating supply chain structures, there are primarily two process-based supply chain management frameworks: Supply Chain Operations Reference model (SCOR) and the Global Supply Chain Forum (GSCF). Our focus will, however, be on the Global Supply Chain Forum (GSCF), as it explains a conceptual framework of pivotal relationships among internal functional areas and external parties such as customers and suppliers, as well as the development of performance metrics to recognize viable opportunities to strengthen operational efficiency and integrate strategic goals. The eight relevant processes in the GSCF model are depicted below, along with the role of logistics strategies in each:

Customer Relationship Management

Customer relationship management establishes the framework for developing and maintaining customer relationships. Decisions are made about which customers seem paramount to the firm's present and future growth and sustainability. As part of the company's business objective, major customers and customer segments are prioritized (Lambert & Schwieterman, 2012). Organization managers categorize customers based on their life span worth and channel products and services to significantly boost loyalty. Close cross-functional relationships are established with existing pivotal clients, whereas others are maintained in a conventional salesperson-to-client relation (Hazen, Russo, Confente, & Pellathy, 2021). Cross-functional client team members create product and service agreements (PSA) to satisfy the requirements of valued customers and segments of several other customer bases. The PSAs describe the relationship's concepts, key performance metrics, and how risk factors and incentives will be distributed. The logistics function contributes to the customer relationship management process by creating logistics capabilities of the organization that can personalize PSAs with existing clients and layout predefined PSAs for targeted customers. Logistics skills form a crucial source of differentiating factors for an organization.

Supplier Relationship Management

As the name implies, this business process reflects supplier relationship management. Supplier relationship management is the process that delineates how a business communicates with its vendors (Alora & Barua, 2021). In the same way that a firm ought to cultivate robust relationships with existing major customers, it must nurture strong relations with a specific segment of its suppliers while managing arms-length (transaction-based) relationships with others. It is the responsibility of supplier relationship management to design and manage PSAs. The intended outcome for all relationships is a win scenario where both parties profit. Logistics managers assist in calculating the cumulative cost of ownership of purchase requisitions so that suppliers can be assessed and segmented. While identifying prerequisites for suppliers, the inability to include logistics total costs such as transport costs, inventory carrying costs, order costs, receiving costs, quality-related costs, and the cost affiliated with service inadequacies may eventually lead to the relatively high overall cost of ownership firms. Therefore, such expenses need to be considered when choosing and assessing suppliers.

Customer Service Management

The Customer Service Management Process ought not to be conflicted with customer support in logistics. The activities deemed necessary to respond to customer demands are the primary focus of logistics customer service. The customer service management process, on the other hand, entails pre-emptively tracking the PSAs and direct intervention on the customer's behalf as considered necessary. The advancement of information systems and cooperation mechanisms between many functional departments is essential to implement customer service management (Palang & Tippayawong, 2019). Logistics managers assist in developing trigger points and indicators to enable customer service top management to monitor logistics-related commitments made to customers in PSAs proactively. This necessitates visibility of logistics activities, which entails using information technology to track the flow of products and identify and rectify scenarios that might lead to service disruptions. Logistics activities are widely dispersed geographically, and logistics managers should facilitate surveillance capabilities and vital contact points to the customer service management team.

Demands Management Process

Demand management determines how demand can be synchronized with supply chain capabilities. Forecasting, synchronization, lowering demand variations, boosting supply chain agility, and establishing business continuity management strategies for possible future supply disruption or unforeseen shifts in demand are all components of the method. Management can complement supply and demand action and implement the strategy with minimum interference if the right process is initiated (Butt, 2021). Logistics' major contribution to this process is input into the projections design process. Therefore, the forecast should be for the appropriate timescale and with a suitable degree of product specifics also based on geography dispersal. People in the logistics function might also facilitate in determining the viability and economic advantages of collaborative efforts. Another essential aspect of the demand management process is developing contingency management strategies to respond to internal or external occurrences that interrupt the supply-demand equilibrium.

Order Fulfillment Process

Order fulfillment is the process of creating, filling, and distributing customer requests. To accomplish such responsibilities, the cross-functional order fulfillment process team can create a network and procedures that allow the firm to encounter customers' demands while minimizing overall deliverable cost (Zimon et al., 2020). The goal is to create a smooth workflow from suppliers to the company and its multiple customer segments. Because many operating activities are implemented within the logistics function, order fulfillment is frequently regarded as a logistics domain. At the operational level, the order fulfillment process incorporates various logistics activities such as order filling and delivery, enabling the logistics function to contribute significantly to resources. Logistics top management is actively involved in the architecture of the network and the appraisal of the key competencies necessary by the order fulfillment process at the tactical level. It also aids in evaluating the value generated for customers by the order fulfillment process.

Manufacturing Flow Management Process

Manufacturing flow management is associated with ascertaining and incorporating manufacturing agility through the supply chain. In moving products efficiently across plants, firms and their vendors' operational activities need to be engaged by demand. Suitable cross-functional participation is required to interconnect end-customer demand to the firm's and its suppliers' manufacturing processes. The logistics abilities, along with those of customers and suppliers, can capitalize or restrict the extent of manufacturing flexibility in a supply chain. The relevant logistics skills must be implemented and monitored for a specific level of manufacturing flexibility. Logistics managers can recognize such capabilities and the cost implications affiliated with the desired level of manufacturing flexibility for the other team members. Logistics capabilities beyond mandated are ineffective, while those that fall short limit manufacturing flexibility (Lambert & Schwieterman, 2012).

Product Development and Commercialization Process

Product development and commercialization offer the structure for designing and introducing innovations into the market in the form of new products in partnership with key customers and suppliers. The procedure empowers management to efficiently organize the stream of new products across the supply chain and aids in the ramp-up of production, logistics, marketing, and other similar activities to boost the product's commercial viability. Logistics can assist or hinder the new product development and commercialization process. Furthermore, logistics managers estimate associated costs with the sourcing, manufacturing, and distribution of new products. As a result, logistics is a significant cost driver for product profit margins (Do et al., 2021). Product proliferation tends to increase the intricacy of operational activities and flattens up the market into progressively smaller, less financially viable pieces, necessitating logistics managers to help evaluate the effectiveness of stock-keeping units (SKU) proliferation.

Returns Management Process

Returns management is a supply chain management technique for managing operations such as returns, reverse logistics, gatekeeping, and avoidance in an organization and between involved parties. When correctly implemented, the process empowers managers to effectively manage the downstream flow of products and identify opportunities to eliminate redundant returns and regulate usable resources. The term "avoidance" pertains to the process of assessing rates of return, ascertaining underlying causes, and instituting initiatives that minimize the frequency of return requests. The screening of the return request coupled with the product being returned promptly in the reverse flow is known as gatekeeping. Logistics managers provide data and analytical expertise considered necessary to perform reverse flow network assessment (Huang, Yang, & Wong, 2016). Discovering avoidance opportunities that limit the series of return requests is critical to the returns management process. Logistics managers must be committed to instituting avoidance opportunities, alterations in product development, advertising campaigns, or the inclusion of better product manual are a few examples

SUPPLY SHOCKS

A supply shock occurs when the supply of goods and services abruptly surges or drops. This sudden and unexpected shift has an impact on the equilibrium cost of goods and services, as well as the overall price level of the economy. In the near run, a negative supply shock will shift the overall supply curve leftward, lowering output and raising prices, whereas a positive supply shock shifts the aggregate supply curve rightward, boosting output and lowering prices. Natural disasters, such as COVID -19, and geo-political upheavals, such as acts of war or terrorism, can trigger supply shocks by constraining output or disrupting the supply chain. The flow of commodities between countries was impeded when COVID-19 prompted lockdowns, quarantines, plant closures, and long-term social distance around the world, as movement restriction tactics were imposed, cutting off the supply of imports and generating material supply shock. Apart from supply shock, industries also experienced demand shock, which interrupted supply chains resulting in revenue losses. Supply and demand shocks are frequently intertwined, and they can even create a vicious cycle. Guerrieri et al. (2020) investigated the pandemic to determine how negative supply shocks induces a significant shift in demand in comparison to the shock itself. Modeling on numerous parts of the economy revealed that supply shocks from COVID-19 spurred panic buying in consumers, culminating in a quick surge in demand, accompanied by a decline as workers' paychecks and purchasing power were lost.

Risk Management

A future outcome and the likelihood of an outcome are the two basic components of risk. According to Ellegaard (2008), risk management(RM) provides opportunities to learn, which reduces the possibility of risks happening and their consequences on supply chain operations, because organizations are more prepared to effectively tackle risks if they are knowledgeable of them ahead of time. Identification, categorization, and evaluation are the three key processes in risk management (Hunter, & Roh, 2021). Identification entails assessing all potential dangers in a given situation. Risks are grouped into relatively homogenous categories for further exploration and risk mitigation strategies in classification. Gaudenzi and Borghesi (2006) emphasized the four important processes in risk evaluation in compliance with RM benchmarks: (1) risk assessment, (2) risk reporting/selection and decision making, (3) risk mitigation, and (4) risk tracking/monitoring. Researchers have worked to improve this generalized procedure by establishing risk management conceptual frameworks for use in SCM, with a specific emphasis on risk mitigation strategies. Different scholars have emphasized the significance of linking risk mitigation strategies to risk classifications and its origin (Oke and Gopalakrishnan, 2009).

According to Tang (2006), supply chain risk management (SCRM) is a partnership between supply chain players to minimize risk and generate profit. SCRM is a consistent activity requiring huge dedication from members since it can influence the firm's operational and financial dimensions. The underlying identification of risk variables or sources is a prevalent discussion point running through these various investigations. Unsurprisingly, substantial effort has gone into identifying important risk variables in SCM so that proactive or reactive techniques might be triggered. Risk mitigation tactics that are proactive focus on preventing risk.

On the other hand, reactive risk mitigation techniques plan for the emergence of a risk event to reduce its adverse economic effect. Tang (2006) further conceptualizes risk elements as operational and disruptions. Disruption risk factors are linked to substantial risks induced by natural or artificial catastrophes like COVID -19, earthquakes, hurricanes, floods, terrorist attacks, or economic recessions.

METHODOLOGY

The literature on methodologies indicates several different approaches contingent on the essence of the investigation and the research prepositions. Two key techniques appear to predominate in a broad sense, namely qualitative and quantitative methods. Nevertheless, combining the two methods has increased the vast scope of research topologies, including multiple versions of the mixed method (i.e., partly qualitative, and partly quantitative) method, such as sequential and embedded mixed method (Messina, Barros, Soares, & Matopoulos, 2020). This is exploratory research as it expands the scope of logistics activities in the supply chain and risk-mitigating strategies. Tsay, Gray, Noh, and Mahoney (2018) argue that qualitative research and case studies are the best approaches for SCM as it is still regarded as an emerging area — in other words, an extremely specialized field to the organizational setting, which is still in its exploratory stage. In addition to SCM, the current research paper addresses logistics and adopts qualitative research. According to Davis and Mentzer (2006), it is the most acknowledged and beneficial method in addressing this topic. These authors also advocated for the use of interviews when dealing with logistics. Furthermore, the use of case studies in exploratory logistics research has increased over the years, which is consistent with many prior calls in the literature for their use. Since this research sought to address the research question, formulated using "how" and "what," the case studies are descriptive and exploratory. Below is the summary of steps of this case study-based research:

- A conceptual overview as well as a highlight of the research questions
- The development of a research protocol and questionnaire
- Selecting and contacting companies for interviews
- Pilot test and questionnaire adjustments
- Performing the case studies
- The case study evaluation includes interview summaries, data collection, strict data interpretation, and pattern recognition.
- Including closing remarks and discussion of the findings

The two businesses were chosen using non-probability sampling. The following criteria were used to select the case studies, a common characteristic shared by all firms was recognition of the significant contribution of logistics in cumulative organizational effectiveness; second, companies operating in Nigeria's northeastern region where terrorism is prevalent; and third, companies that had adopted the concept of supply chain and logistics in their business processes. The analysis process was iterated upon and discussed among the authors. Various strategies were debated and tested, and the final version presented. There are two vital approaches to analyzing qualitative data that are large such as content analysis and grounded analysis. While the former encompasses interrogating data for previously evaluated ideas and constructs, the latter entails allowing the data to "speak for itself," directing the researcher to interpret the data. The authors' assessment entailed an appropriate blend of the two approaches, incorporating the strengths and minimizing the weaknesses of the two alternative options.

Data Source and Instrumentation

Primary data was obtained from telephone communications with the companies' logistics departments, outlining the study's objectives and authenticating their suitability to participate in it. The communication was formally established through e-mail, which also included the research protocol and questionnaire. Subsequent phone calls and e-mails were made to the companies to schedule the interviews at their convenient time; the interview sessions were recorded and compiled. This information was augmented with data obtained from companies' webpages, reports, and other internal documentary evidence. A qualitative approach involving semi-structured interviews with the logistics head of the selected companies was also explored to gain insight into the supply chain logistics of the companies. Before the distribution of the questionnaire, all confidential issues were mutually agreed upon. The following were addressed by the degree of confidentiality:

- The names and specific characteristics of the companies' product lines must not be disclosed.
- The names of the companies must not be disclosed, but an overall description about what they manufacture/ provide is authorized.
- Names of logistics personnel must not be mentioned.

Because of the agreed-upon privacy concerns issues, the companies were labeled company A and company B. The authors used the four qualitative criteria: credibility, transferability, dependability, and Confirmability, to guarantee the reliability of this research. The credibility criterion entails determining whether the qualitative research findings are credible from the participant's research perspective. Validity and reliability are given special consideration. To ensure that the research findings are credible from the perspective of key informants, the authors addressed the credibility criterion by allowing interviewees to give an opinion on data summaries. Dependability accentuates the importance of researchers properly accounting for the different circumstances in which research was undertaken. Thus, transferability is challenging in this context. The use of semi-structured interviews with specially selected respondents from a variety of firms, on the other hand, is designed to provide some possibly beneficial new insight into the aims to established experimentally. The authors meticulously documented the complete research procedure from the design phase to data collection and data analysis.

Data Collection and Analysis

Semi-structured interviews based on the description of disruptive in form of risks occurrences according to the interview protocol were also used to obtain data. A total of ten interviews were performed at organizations facilities, resulting in about 10 hours of recordings. All respondents were instructed to recollect five risks or obstacles they had encountered or facing, as well as how they were addressed, according to the interview protocol. The interviewee profiles chosen for this study comprised supply managers, logistics managers, and service delivery managers, as we are looking into the risks that organizations confront and the solutions, they use in supply chain logistics. We were able to gather diverse opinions on the obstacles faced operating in the region during unforeseen events by involving managers who executed various company functions related to supply chain and logistics. To conduct the data analysis, all the interviews were recorded, transcribed, and afterwards coded using MAXQDA® software. Additional materials presented during the interviews, such as a list of risks and disruptive events, a checklist of components with relevant logistical risk categories, and mitigating strategies were also used for data triangulation to ensure construct validity. The transcripts of the interviews were also submitted to the interviewees for review.

FINDINGS

Case-by-Case Assessment

Within-case evaluation offers a comprehensive view of the organizational framework of the organizations studied but also assists in characterizing each of these organizations' starting point in terms of supply chain logistics risks and disruptive occurrences, mitigation measures, and accessible opportunities.

Company A is a worldwide corporation based in Boston, Massachusetts, with operations in 24 countries. It is a large independent investor, owner, and provider of wireless and broadcasting telecommunications property investment and one of the world's largest real estate investment trusts. With worldwide operations of more than 214,000 transmission sites and over 43,000 in the United States, Canada, and 171,000 globally, the company has a strong presence in the communications industry. The company offers tailored services through in-building systems, outdoor multiple antenna systems, other right-of-way alternatives, controlled rooftops, and solutions that accelerate networking advancement, in addition to leasing space on wireless and broadcasting towers. All interviewees seemed to be aware of a proper risk management procedure and risk planning processes. Thus, the risk management strategy is notably well-established. Furthermore, the availability of many detectors on employees' devices and generators, batteries, and other assets enables proactive detection and response to disturbances. According to their clearance, the back office and managers have total visibility over their assets on sites enrolled into the system, which improves proactivity.

Remote monitoring systems (RMS) are typically utilized to identify events and auxiliary systems in various domains employed. The RMS detects potential disruptions automatically. Still, the operator must query the system to look for these occurrences. Direct internal lines, e-mail, and face-to-face meetings are other means to convey current or anticipated interruptions. Such incidents are caused by disruptions in the delivery of services, such as network outages, shortages of equipment spare parts, and supplier and shareholder insolvency in certain circumstances. The existence of formalized guidelines and a good standard of coordination among employees of various teams enable the organization to be aware of its surroundings and give flexibility. Visibility, transparency, lessons gained, and a proactive mindset is all characteristics of its resilient culture. Several vendors, intensive on-the-job training of site security guards, involvement of independent freelancers, fuel buffers in safe areas, and loads of spare parts supplies all support it swiftly recovering from disruptions or risks. The managers interviewed could not quantify the monetary losses associated with the occurrences of risks and interruptions affecting operations. Still, they qualitatively interpreted them in dimensions of network failures lasting hours and field personnel delays in reaching sites.

Company B is a leading pharmaceutical in Nigeria that market, distribute and sell 10 SKUs in the form of over-the-counter medications pills or suspension. Over the years of its operation, it has shaped the pharmaceutical architecture of the business, playing pivotal roles in the birth of a new generation of industry leaders, with Innovation, excellence, passion, integrity, and ownership as the five core values which have assisted it in establishing a world-class organization that has garnered the respect and admiration of the most ferocious competition. The company has developed and nurtured an appropriate structure that has enabled it continuously to rise the ranks. It has well-established risk management procedures in place, which is kept up to date through two daily online meetings where all region managers are invited to discuss potential risky scenarios for the day, as well as a system that focuses on providing information about identifying risks, with the assessment and subsequent management delegated to various managers' expertise.

When it comes to coping with disruptions, company B is primarily reactive, attempting to be more proactive. Phone calls, e-mail, and face-to-face meetings with internal and external stakeholders are other means to convey existing or anticipated disruptions or risks that lead to delivery delays and stock shortages. A combination of the two recovery procedures is used to recover from a disruption. To mitigate most of the disruptions associated with a single vendor, practices such as a flexible structure and task realignment allow the organization to adjust orders or put some independent logistics providers on reserve. Techniques like the use of numerous suppliers, different delivery options, and surplus stock are employed by the organization. Interviewees were able to estimate the financial losses associated with disruption and risks and interpret it qualitatively in terms of delays and shortage of stock, necessitating clients to switch to other competing brands. The comparison is shown in Table 1.

Table 1. Risks and mitigating strategies

	Company A	Company B
Constraints and risks	Boko haram insurgency Asset theft Communal and Ethnic clashes Kidnapping Poor Access Road Contractors' unwillingness to execute projects in the region Destruction of Telecommunication equipment Additional Operational cost Delay in delivery of materials and network equipment due to COVID-19 Suspension of site construction resulting from materials storage brought about by COVID-19	Destruction of Companies warehouse and Facilities Poor road network Armed Robbery and Banditry Kidnapping Ethnic crisis High operational cost Delay in delivery time which leads to inventory risk Long distance among major towns Shortage of products due to production halts from COVID-19
Mitigating Strategies	Tank capacity enlargement Deployment of Hybrid system Use of Armed Security Personnel Installation of remote monitoring system Asset tracking system Employment of locals as site guards Installation of mobile application for distress call. Shut down operations and withdrew from location where telecommunication facilities were bombed by insurgence. Dual vendor contracting such as Generators' maintenance among others Engaged in a mix of local and overseas sourcing to diversify risks brought about by COVID-19. Created Collaborations	Relocation of Warehouse Supplying directly to wholesalers' warehouses Use of alternative route Hiring of indigenous locals Outsourcing to third party logistics providers Use of Security Escorts Local sourcing of products owing to border restrictions Prioritized critical categories of products like hand sanitizers
Opportunities	High intensity of sun rays Vast Land mass thus, Land purchase inexpensive COVID-19 has culminated in a spike in data traffic and the usage of broadband services as a function of work from home.	High demand of company's products and services due to COVID-19 effects and poor conditions of displaced Persons Expand product line to include hand sanitizers and facemasks.

Source: (Authors, 2022)

DISCUSSION OF RESULTS

The Chapter's overarching goal is to investigate the challenges faced by companies operating in terrorist-prone areas and the opportunities available and strategies employed by such firms to mitigate them. The analysis is based on relevant empirical data, first presented in the tabular format, followed by selected direct quotes from the interviews that illustrate the critical issues presented by the target respondents. Tang (2006) categorizes potential risks as operational and disruptive. The term "operational risk elements" refers to factors that seem to be inherently unpredictable, such as customer requirements and expenses. Disruption risk variables are linked to significant risks caused by natural catastrophic events such as COVID-19, earthquakes, hurricanes, floods, terrorist attacks, or economic downturns. Logistics safety is strongly intertwined with logistics challenges, and any vulnerability in a logistics process can potentially disrupt the entire procedure. Respondents were asked to identify the various challenges their companies encounter doing business in the northeast.

Company A faced several challenges, including the theft of assets such as generators and batteries as a direct consequence of hardship in the region, exacerbated by the state of the economy, rendering business operational costs higher than in other regions. The Boko Haram insurgency has culminated in the bombing of company masts while making some sites inaccessible and thus abandoned. An instance offered by a participant supported this fact: *The federal government's recent demands for telecommunications to fully shut down services in several local governments in the region to combat banditry and insurgency have brought our business to a halt.*

The company is also facing rampant kidnapping of its employees, with huge sums of money requested and paid before their release. Poor access roads raise operating costs significantly, as confirmed by a respondent: *Shutting down facilities and kidnapping our field staff has resulted in revenue loss for the company and supply chain partners, penalties are also paid to customers for our company's failure to do so avoid outages on our sites.* Communal clashes among various ethnic groups aggravate the turbulent business environment; several of the company's projects are yet to be executed in the region since contractors are afraid of traveling to such areas, hindering the company from taking full advantage of the opportunities available in the region. Company B has experienced a communal crisis, which has resulted in many restrictions in transporting their products since they market, distribute, and sell over-the-counter drugs, causing an increase in delivery time delays and more money spent on other logistics activities such as warehousing. Due to the volatile environment, the company has suspended the distribution of its products in certain areas, leading to a significant loss of market share. A participant shared an incident that exemplifies this: *our delivery van was burnt recently, with the driver narrowly escaping death.*

According to participant responses, firms operating in that region face value streams and the external environment. Practitioners define value streams as having three main metrics: time, cost, and product quality. They encompass natural, political, social, and monetary policy interruptions, all of which can be negatively impacted by specific elements in the supply chain network. Delay is the divergence from the intended delivery time; contract agreement issues, fluctuating transport rates, and increased costs at a location can upsurge the targeted optimum logistics cost; massive product disparity, shipment loss, and disruption are linked to unforeseen product quality inadequacies. Such research results are consistent with Norrman and Henkow (2014), who observed that supply chains are adversely affected by time, cost, and quality; thus, logistics managers appropriately classify any loss or damage into these three types of failures constraints or risks. In addition, natural disasters, human-caused disruptions, and economic uncertainty have been recognized as external environment contingency elements. These aspects are challenging to manage, and while some can be predicted, they cannot be entirely mitigated at the firm or supply chain level.

Mitigating Strategies Adopted by Case Study Organizations

According to Company A respondents, the high intensity of the sun's rays in the region enables solar on their site, resulting in lower operating costs. The extensive landmark makes it relatively easy to acquire lands for site purposes at a cost lower when compared to other regions in Nigeria. To mitigate the challenges, the company has installed a hybrid system on their sites that uses solar, batteries, and generators to reduce the frequency of visits to sites by personnel who are routinely targeted for kidnapping. Remote visibility is another strategy employed to monitor events in real-time, and asset tracking systems use to keep tabs on their movements to reduce the ongoing theft that is highly prevalent in the region. The turbulent environment has necessitated the replacement of small diesel tanks with larger tank capacities to lessen the regular visits to sites for diesel supply which is frequently accomplished using armed escorts in notoriously risky areas. When visiting troubled areas, the company employs armed security. Additionally, the company has installed an app that allows personnel to alert the head office when in distress to ensure timely assistance. The epidemic prompted the company to collaborate with others, allowing them to benefit from each other's functions and competencies.

Company B has benefited from the Boko Haram insurgency, which has triggered a demographic change and population movement into some sections of the region. It has opened opportunities for the company to gain a sizeable market share as it is involved in the marketing and selling of basic information necessities. It has relocated its warehouse from crisis-prone areas to safer territories a distance away to mitigate the challenges. Given the products' relatively high weight and volume ratios, the products must be stocked in depots in the Northeast if they are to be delivered on time to accomplish the desired level of product accessibility and fill rate. Long hauls at full truckloads about 30 tons by road with a mix of different SKUs are deployed to reduce transportation costs per unit. To mitigate the various challenges encountered in the region, the company has further outsourced logistics activities in dangerous or high-risk zones to logistics service providers (LSP). In addition, the company follows alternative routes to towns or cities known to be relatively safe to distribute products to their wholesalers and retailers. Security escorts are frequently hired to accompany the company's delivery van to supply products. Indigenous locals who reside in those communities and are educated are hired to supply products since they are familiar with the terrain. COVID- 19 prompted the company to adopt local sourcing as it is a low-effort technique as it entails seeking smaller supplier pool in the immediate area and does not necessitate major infrastructural upgrades. This strategy has a long-term benefit since it improves the company's supply chain resilience. Prioritizing essential categories is a simple, short-term method that merely requires the company to shift its emphasis to an existing category during a risk event like the COVID-19 in order to deal with the disruption's consequences.

Company A and company B mitigation strategies generally involve a blend of acceptance, avoidance, postponement, speculation, hedging, control, share, and transfer. Company A utilized hedging strategies such as dual contracting with various vendors; generators maintenance, spare parts, diesel supply, and grid maintenance are sourced from multiple suppliers. Dual sourcing is an adopted hedge against reliability, quantity, disruption, cost, and opportunistic behavior hazards. The hedging strategy is implemented via a stratified segment of suppliers, clients, and infrastructure, ensuring that a singular occurrence does not significantly impact all entities at about the same time, and it is particularly beneficial for supply risk management. In contrast, multiple contracting can lessen efficiency variance. One notable advantage of this strategy to supply chain networks lies in the fact that it improves sustainability. The company's acceptance strategy, which includes an asset tracking system, the deployment of a hybrid system, and the expansion of tank capacity, assumes that the probability of occurrence will be close to zero or the negative effect will be insignificant. The company ignores risks that can be assimilated into the extant environment.

Acceptance of prospective damage is also required when the precise cost of other strategies seems to be considerably higher than the cumulative cost of likely destruction. Control mitigating strategies that encompass the effort to prevent threat by both a significant decrease in the likelihood of an incident happening and activities to lessen the implications of linked possibility were also incorporated by the company by enlisting the services of armed security personnel for their employees when an emergency arises for them to visit sites in locations where threats are high.

Company B adapted the shared or transferred strategy by recruiting logistics service providers in transporting goods and warehouse management and incentivizing distributors to load up shipments from the designated collection point. It also incorporated risk avoidance strategies by re-vamping the decentralized element of the supply chain through the diverging of supplies to the regional hubs established in cities less affected by the insurgency. Compared to straightforward shipment to resellers, this initiative will significantly raise the unit transportation costs due to the poor transport links, storage of goods, handling, and operational expenses. The company also implemented control strategies such as hiring locals to reduce attacks by indigenous peoples attempting to confiscate their goods and employing armed to the teeth security officers to safeguard, retaliate or strike when they encounter armed robbers or bandits. Alternative pathways are also embarked on when necessary to avoid attacks on company delivery vehicles. This strategy aims to reduce risk by lowering the likelihood of an incident happening and taking steps to counteract the adverse effects of induced damage.

In the nutshell, even though risk mitigation techniques deployed reactively revealed more promising signals of effectiveness, the impact of the COVID-19 pandemic throughout 2020 demonstrated that organizations' supply chain resilience was typically low. One possible explanation for the lack of resiliency is that sectors did not expect pandemic threats to cause such huge demand and supply shocks in the midst of statewide lockdowns. An analysis of the implemented solutions revealed that there is no such thing as a one-size-fits-all strategy that can be applied to any organization, as each tactic has its own range of strengths and weaknesses.

Effectiveness of the Mitigating Strategies

The effectiveness of the diverse strategies employed by the two companies could be measured by the desire to sustain presence and long-term customer satisfaction until further negotiated settlement of the insurgency instead of withdrawing entirely. This symbolizes a trade-off around sustaining a presence in the area and withdrawing completely, which might also render re-entry into the area after hostilities are tricky and expensive. The third research question focuses on the efficacy of the various companies' strategies for alleviating supply chain logistics obstacles in the region. According to Company A participants, the strategies have significantly positive effects since the frequency of generator servicing, and diesel supply on sites has been immensely curtailed, saving money and reducing the regularity of site visits by field personnel targeted for kidnapping. The solar system enabled by the high intensity of the

Table 2. SCM and logistics in two companies: a unified perspective

Variables	Company A	Company B
Sector	Telecommunication	Pharmaceutical
Types of products/ services	Provider of wireless towers, in-building and outdoor DAS, small cell and Wi-Fi networks, managed rooftops, and network deployment services for wireless and telecom infrastructure	Markets, distribute and sells ten SKUs of pharmaceutical products in tablets and suspension forms. They are primarily over- the-counter (OTC) products.
SCM model used	SCOR model	Adopted a hybrid of SCOR model and the company's model, focusing on customer service.
Existing key business processes	The supply chain is categorized into four processes: demand and supply planning (DSP), purchasing, external trade, customer support, and distribution, information technology, logistics, development, business planning	There are four business processes: supply chain, marketing, finance, and human resources. The supply chain process is divided into six sub processes: supply, strategic planning, production, sales and operational activities planning, distribution (warehousing and transportation), and logistics service management.
Logistics area in the company	Three sub processes: supply, Distribution (warehousing and transportation), and logistics service management	The scope of logistics includes five theoretical processes (CRM, Supplier relationship management, order fulfillment, returns management and demand management)
Relationship between logistics and supply chain	The scope of logistics includes four theoretical processes (customer service management, order fulfillment, customer relationship management, and supplier relationship management)	The scope of logistics includes five theoretical processes (CRM, Supplier relationship management, order fulfillment, returns management and demand management)

Source: (Authors, 2022)

sun in north-eastern Nigeria has lessened diesel consumption, culminating in lower operational costs. The unified perspective is shown in Table 2.

CONCLUSION

Organizations were impacted by the COVID-19 pandemic due to a combined effect of supply and demand shocks, which hampered economic growth while also wreaking havoc on businesses performance. Nevertheless, many organizations were able to survive disruptions by implementing proactive and reactive supply chain risk management measures. The chapter thoroughly investigated supply chain logistical constraints, risks and disruptions organizations in north-eastern Nigeria confront due to Boko haram insurgency, banditry, and communal clashes, further aggravated by the recent COVID -19 pandemic. A theoretical approach to logistics and supply chain management, the main business operations of the GSCF and the function of logistics in each of the highlighted businesses is explain in detailed. The chapter's theoretical contributions are primarily related to a deeper understanding of how organizations can address supply chain logistics disruptions and risks by implementing mitigation strategies to accelerate recovery. Additionally, it makes a unique contribution to supply chain risk management by exploring ways decision-makers at the operational level manage information to get improved visibility in a turbulent external environment dominated by the disruption caused by human beings and successfully implement recovery strategies during disruptive occurrences.

REFERENCES

Afum, E., Agyabeng-Mensah, Y., Acquah, I. S. K., Baah, C., Dacosta, E., Owusu, C. S., & Amponsah Owusu, J. (2021). Examining the links between logistics outsourcing, company competitiveness and selected performances: The evidence from an emerging country. *International Journal of Logistics Management, 32*(3), 1068–1090. doi:10.1108/IJLM-05-2020-0205

Alora, A., & Barua, M. K. (2021). The effect of supply chain disruptions on shareholder wealth in small and mid-cap companies. *Supply Chain Management, 26*(2), 212–223. doi:10.1108/SCM-05-2020-0200

Bier, T., Lange, A., & Glock, C. H. (2020). Methods for Mitigating Disruptions in Complex Supply Chain Structures: A Systematic Literature Review. *International Journal of Production Research, 58*(6), 1835–1856. doi:10.1080/00207543.2019.1687954

Butt, A.S. (2021). Strategies to mitigate the impact of COVID-19 on supply chain disruptions: a multiple case analysis of buyers and distributors. *The International Journal of Logistics Management*. . doi:10.1108/IJLM-11-2020-0455

Choi, T.-M. (2020). Innovative 'Bring-Service-Near-Your- Home' Operations under Corona-Virus (COVID-19/SARSCoV- 2) Outbreak: Can Logistics become the Messiah? *Transportation Research Part E: Logistics and Transportation, 140*, 101961. doi:10.1016/j.tre.2020.101961 PMID:32346356

Davis, B. R., & Mentzer, J. T. (2006). Logistics service driven loyalty: An exploratory study. *Journal of Business Logistics, 27*(2), 53–73. doi:10.1002/j.2158-1592.2006.tb00217.x

Do, Q. N., Mishra, N., Wulandhari, N. B. I., Ramudhin, A., Sivarajah, U., & Milligan, G. (2021). Supply chain agility responding to unprecedented changes: Empirical evidence from the UK food supply chain during COVID-19 crisis. *Supply Chain Management, 26*(6), 737–752. doi:10.1108/SCM-09-2020-0470

Dohale, V., Ambilkar, P., Gunasekaran, A., & Verma, P. (2021). Supply Chain Risk Mitigation Strategies during COVID- 19: Exploratory Cases of 'Make-to-Order' Handloom Saree Apparel Industries. *International Journal of Physical Distribution & Logistics Management*. Advance online publication. doi:10.1108/IJPDLM-12-2020-0450

Ellegaard, C. (2008). Supply risk management in a small company perspective. *Supply Chain Management, 13*(6), 425–434. doi:10.1108/13598540810905688

Gaudenzi, B., & Borghesi, A. (2006). Managing risks in the supply chain using the AHP method. *International Journal of Logistics Management, 17*(1), 114–136. doi:10.1108/09574090610663464

Hazen, B. T., Russo, I., Confente, I., & Pellathy, D. (2021). Supply chain management for circular economy: Conceptual framework and research agenda. *International Journal of Logistics Management, 32*(2), 510–537. doi:10.1108/IJLM-12-2019-0332

Hosseini, S., Ivanov, D., & Dolgui, A. (2019). ReviewofQuantitativeMethods for Supply Chain ResilienceAnalysis. *Transportation Research Part E, Logistics and Transportation Review, 125*, 285–307. doi:10.1016/j.tre.2019.03.001

Huang, Y.-C., Yang, M.-L., & Wong, Y.-J. (2016). Institutional pressures, resources commitment, and returns management. *Supply Chain Management, 21*(3), 398–416. doi:10.1108/SCM-04-2015-0144

Ivanov, D. (2020a). Predicting the Impacts of Epidemic Outbreaks on Global Supply Chains: A Simulation-Based Analysis on theCoronavirusOutbreak (COVID-19/SARS-CoV-2) Case. *Transportation Research Part E, Logistics and Transportation Review, 136*, 101922. doi:10.1016/j.tre.2020.101922 PMID:32288597

Ivanov, D. (2020b). Viable Supply Chain Model: Integrating Agility, Resilience and Sustainability Perspectives – Lessons from and Thinking Beyond the COVID-19 Pandemic. *Annals of Operations Research*. Advance online publication. doi:10.100710479-020-03640-6 PMID:32836614

Ivanov, D. (2021a). Supply Chain Viability and the COVID- 19 Pandemic: A Conceptual and Formal Generalisation of Four Major Adaptation Strategies. *International Journal of Production Research, 59*(12), 3535–3552. doi:10.1080/00207543.2021.1890852

Jha, A., Sharma, R. R. K., Kumar, V., & Verma, P. (2021). Designing supply chain performance system: a strategic study on Indian manufacturing sector. *Supply Chain Management: An International Journal*. . doi:10.1108/SCM-05-2020-0198

Kawa, A., & Światowiec-Szczpańska, J. (2021). Logistics as a value in e-commerce and its influence on satisfaction in industries: a multilevel analysis. *Journal of Business & Industrial Marketing*. . doi:10.1108/JBIM-09-2020-0429

Lambert, D. M., & Schwieterman, M. A. (2012). Supplier relationship management as a macro business process. *Supply Chain Management, 17*(3), 337–352. doi:10.1108/13598541211227153

Li, Q., Yan, R., Zhang, L., & Yan, B. (2021). Empirical study on improving international dry port competitiveness based on logistics supply chain integration: evidence from China. *The International Journal of Logistics Management*.

Messina, D., Barros, A. C., Soares, A. L., & Matopoulos, A. (2020). An information management approach for supply chain disruption recovery. *International Journal of Logistics Management, 31*(3), 489–519. doi:10.1108/IJLM-11-2018-0294

Moncef, B., & Monnet Dupuy, M. (2021). Last-mile logistics in the sharing economy: Sustainability paradoxes. *International Journal of Physical Distribution & Logistics Management, 51*(5), 508–527. doi:10.1108/IJPDLM-10-2019-0328

Nag, B., Han, C., & Yao, D. (2014). Mapping supply chain strategy: An industry analysis. *Journal of Manufacturing Technology Management, 25*(3), 351–370. doi:10.1108/JMTM-06-2012-0062

Oke, A., & Gopalakrishnan, M. (2009). Managing disruptions in supply chains: A case study of a retail supply chain. *International Journal of Production Economics, 118*(1), 168–174. doi:10.1016/j.ijpe.2008.08.045

Orr, S., & Jadhav, A. (2018). Creating a sustainable supply chain: The strategic foundation. *The Journal of Business Strategy, 39*(6), 29–35. doi:10.1108/JBS-11-2017-0157

Paciarotti, C., Piotrowicz, W. D., & Fenton, G. (2021). Humanitarian logistics and supply chain standards. Literature review and view from practice. *Journal of Humanitarian Logistics and Supply Chain Management*, *11*(3), 550–573. doi:10.1108/JHLSCM-11-2020-0101

Palang, D., & Tippayawong, K. Y. (2019). Performance evaluation of tourism supply chain management: The case of Thailand. *Business Process Management Journal*, *25*(6), 1193–1207. doi:10.1108/BPMJ-05-2017-0124

Paula, I. C., Campos, E. A. R., Pagani, R. N., Guarnieri, P., & Kaviani, M. A. (2020). Are collaboration and trust sources for innovation in the reverse logistics? Insights from a systematic literature review. *Supply Chain Management*, *25*(2), 176–222. doi:10.1108/SCM-03-2018-0129

Rafele, C. (2004). Logistic service measurement: A reference framework. *Journal of Manufacturing Technology Management*, *15*(3), 280–290. doi:10.1108/17410380410523506

Salam, M. A., & Khan, S. A. (2020). Lessons from the humanitarian disaster logistics management. *Benchmarking*, *27*(4), 1455–1473. doi:10.1108/BIJ-04-2019-0165

Seuring, S., & Müller, M. (2008). From a literature review to a conceptual framework for sustainable supply chain management. *Journal of Cleaner Production*, *16*(15), 1699–1710. doi:10.1016/j.jclepro.2008.04.020

Sharma, V., Raut, R. D., Govindarajan, U. H., & Narkhede, B. E. (2021). Advancements in urban logistics toward smart, sustainable reforms in developing enabling technologies and markets. *Kybernetes*. doi:10.1108/K-01-2021-0026

Shokouhyar, S., Pahlevani, N., & Mir Mohammad Sadeghi, F. (2019). Scenario analysis of smart, sustainable supply chain on the basis of a fuzzy cognitive map. *Management Research Review*, *43*(4), 463–496. doi:10.1108/MRR-01-2019-0002

Silva, M. E., Alves, A. P. F., Dias, P., & Nascimento, L. F. M. (2019). The role of orientation towards sustainability in supply chains. *Benchmarking: An International Journal*. doi:10.1108/BIJ-07-2017-0184

Stock, J. R., & Lambert, D. M. (1992). Becoming a "World Class" Company With Logistics Service Quality. *International Journal of Logistics Management*, *3*(1), 73–81. doi:10.1108/09574099210804822

Subiyanto, E. (2021). Investigating the logistics costs model: Recent update in Indonesia. *Journal of Science and Technology Policy Management*, *12*(2), 331–350. doi:10.1108/JSTPM-03-2020-0034

Sweeney, E., Grant, D. B., & Mangan, D. J. (2018). Strategic adoption of logistics and supply chain management. *International Journal of Operations & Production Management*, *38*(3), 852–873. doi:10.1108/IJOPM-05-2016-0258

Tang, C. S. (2006). Perspectives in supply chain risk management. *International Journal of Production Economics*, *103*(2), 451–488. doi:10.1016/j.ijpe.2005.12.006

Tsay, A. A., Gray, J. V., Noh, I. J., & Mahoney, J. T. (2018). A Review of Production and Operations Management Research on Outsourcing in Supply Chains: Implications for the Theory of the Firm. *Production and Operations Management*, *27*(7), 1177–1220. doi:10.1111/poms.12855

Wang, M., Wang, B., & Chan, R. (2021). Reverse logistics uncertainty in a courier industry: A triadic model. *Modern Supply Chain Research and Applications*, *3*(1), 56–73. doi:10.1108/MSCRA-10-2020-0026

Zimon, D., Madzik, P., & Sroufe, R. (2020). Management systems and improving supply chain processes. *International Journal of Retail & Distribution Management*, *48*(9), 939–961. doi:10.1108/IJRDM-04-2019-0107

Zsidisin, G. A., Bresler, A., Hazen, B., Snider, K. F., & Wilkerson, T. H. (2020). Research in defense logistics: Where are we and where are we going? *Journal of Defense Analytics and Logistics*, *4*(1), 3–17. doi:10.1108/JDAL-07-2019-0012

Zubairu, N., Dinwoodie, J., Govindan, K., Hunter, L., & Roh, S. (2021). Supply chain strategies as drivers of financial performance in liquefied natural gas networks. *Supply Chain Management*, *26*(5), 579–591. doi:10.1108/SCM-08-2020-0389

ADDITIONAL READING

Duong, A. T. B., Vo, V. X., Do Sameiro Carvalho, M., Sampaio, P., & Truong, H. Q. (2022). Risks and supply chain performance: Globalization and COVID-19 perspectives. *International Journal of Productivity and Performance Management*. Advance online publication. doi:10.1108/IJPPM-03-2021-0179

Herold, D. M., Nowicka, K., Pluta-Zaremba, A., & Kummer, S. (2021). COVID-19 and the pursuit of supply chain resilience: Reactions and "lessons learned" from logistics service providers (LSPs). *Supply Chain Management*, *26*(6), 702–714. doi:10.1108/SCM-09-2020-0439

Hohenstein, N.-O. (2022). Supply chain risk management in the COVID-19 pandemic: Strategies and empirical lessons for improving global logistics service providers' performance. *International Journal of Logistics Management*. Advance online publication. doi:10.1108/IJLM-02-2021-0109

Márcia, M. P. M. R. L. C. A. (2016). Logistics activities in supply chain business process A conceptual framework to guide their implementation. *International Journal of Logistics Management*, *27*(1), 6–30. doi:10.1108/IJLM-04-2014-0068

Um, J., & Han, N. (2021). Understanding the relationships between global supply chain risk and supply chain resilience: The role of mitigating strategies. *Supply Chain Management*, *26*(2), 240–255. doi:10.1108/SCM-06-2020-0248

Wang, M. (2018). Impacts of supply chain uncertainty and risk on the logistics performance. *Asia Pacific Journal of Marketing and Logistics*, *30*(3), 689–704. doi:10.1108/APJML-04-2017-0065

Wang, M., Asian, S., Wood, L. C., & Wang, B. (2020). Logistics innovation capability and its impacts on the supply chain risks in the Industry 4.0 era. *Modern Supply Chain Research and Applications*, *2*(2), 83–98. doi:10.1108/MSCRA-07-2019-0015

Wang, M., Jie, F., & Abareshi, A. (2015). Evaluating logistics capability for mitigation of supply chain uncertainty and risk in the Australian courier firms. *Asia Pacific Journal of Marketing and Logistics*, *27*(3), 486–498. doi:10.1108/APJML-11-2014-0157

KEY TERMS AND DEFINITIONS

COVID-19: COVID-19 is a contagious respiratory disease induced by a novel coronavirus variant that infects people.

Logistics: The process of acquiring, storing, and transporting materials to their ultimate destination.

Risk Management: The act of detecting, evaluating, and managing threats to a firm's capital and profitability.

Risk Mitigation: Entails the creation of plans that aim to control, eliminate, or potentially reduce risk to a manageable level.

Supply Chain: A web of people, organizations, resources, activities, and technologies associated with the production and distribution of a product.

Supply Chain Disruptions: Any occurrence that interrupts the manufacture, sale, or delivery of goods. Natural catastrophes, global wars, and pandemics are all examples of supply chain disruptions.

Supply Chain Management: Is the process of designing, planning, executing, controlling, and monitoring supply processes with the goal of generating net value, constructing a sustainable network, harnessing logistics, coordinating demand and supply, and tracking progress.

Supply Shock: An unforeseen incident that alters the supply of a product or service, culminating in an unanticipated price adjustment.

Chapter 7
Risk Assessment in the Information Technology Industry:
An Imperative Phenomenon

K. Madhu Kishore Raghunath
https://orcid.org/0000-0002-8134-5718
GITAM University, Visakhapatnam, India

S. L. Tulasi Devi
https://orcid.org/0000-0002-1285-4447
National Institute of Technology, Warangal, India

ABSTRACT

People fear uncertainty as it leads to risk in the pursuit of their journeys, where they seek success. The authors articulate that opportunity lies beyond risk, encouraging individuals and business organizations to take calculated risks. In this chapter, the authors will show how risk-based decisions become more feasible when the decisions are made in light of risk assessment tools available to business organizations. The chapter will orchestrate the impact of risk assessment tools (qualitative, quantitative, and hybrid risk assessment tools) on organizational effectiveness given their perceived benefits in the information technology industry in India.

INTRODUCTION

The information technology industry is one of the key drivers in placing India on the world map and at present India holds the top spot for off-shoring destinations for world IT companies. India's IT & ITeS industry grew to US$ 181 billion in 2018-19. Exports from the industry increased to US$ 137 billion in FY19 while domestic revenues (including hardware) advanced to US$ 44 billion. Information technology industry in India has been blooming at its brightest with its reliable on-shore and off-shore services

DOI: 10.4018/978-1-6684-5279-0.ch007

to global clients. The information technology industry is also in line to reach US$ 350 billion by 2025 where one can envisage the opportunities and exposure an organization will witness.

As India moves ahead into the future, existing emerging technologies present not only a gamut of opportunities for top IT firms in India but also exposure to a range of risk factors thriving from the internal and external environment. Nikolić & Ružić (2009) opined that Information technology, as a platform with an exponential rate of development and application in different spectrums of business, necessitates effective risk assessment to protect it from evolving risk factors within the industry.

The range of services provided by these information technology companies include: System integration- Software development, implementation and support- Network integration- Web-based development- Offshore development, delivery and support- Communication services- Desktop management- Data centre set-up, management and support- IT Consultancy (Operating system, Security, network design, etc.)- eBusiness solution development- Data mining, data storage, data warehousing and data processing- Cloud related services and finally big data and analytics.

Different types of risks involved in IT projects include technology risks, resource risks, scope risks, vendor risks, requirement risks, procurement risks, design risks, project complexity risks, planning and control risks, organizational and environmental risks and eventually information security risks.

Eventually, risk assessment within IT companies has become a necessity as numerous threats and vulnerabilities affect its operations in different ways. Risk identification, analysis and evaluation envisage operational efficiency by providing suitable measures and controls to manage risk factors to an acceptable level or mitigate it completely.

RISK ASSESSMENT AND ORGANISATIONAL EFFECTIVENESS

Risk assessment & management articulates the need for effective decision making with regard to identifying and mitigating risk scenarios for business entities to achieve their predetermined goals. Combination of risk management with sustainable decision making has garnered significant consideration and contributions from researchers in a variety of disciplines. It includes risk decision making under risk which is mostly attributed to risk assessment tools. Arias & Stern, (2011) reviewed that risk assessment tools are effective with different applications in mitigating risk elements in projects. Hull (2010) also emphasized the role of a deterministic risk management approach in illustrating and understanding a company's risk appetite. The following review of literature will further visualize the importance of risk assessment and management from different perspectives. Yue, et al (2021); Heyerdahl, A. (2022) also opined that risk assessment is a crucial component of effective and successfull policy compliance under crisis situation.

Callahan & Soileau (2017) ideated that enterprise risk assessment and management systems are designed to reinvigorate achievement of entity objectives, wherein firms with higher levels of enterprise risk assessment and management are characterized by higher operating performance compared to their competitors utilizing performance metrics related to earnings.

CGMA (2016) enunciated that risk assessment tools render decision making a superior exercise, such that it enhances organizational competitive position, it's brand's reputation, quality of its people and its intellectual capital. Further Raghunath & Devi (2018) articulated in their study that it is inevitable and imperative for organizations to try different combinations of risk assessment models to mitigate risk scenarios and enhance risk based decision making, which paves way for organizational success.

Junior & Carvalho (2013) in his research surveyed 415 projects at different levels of complexity in different industrial sectors and pointed out that risk management has a significant and positive impact on project success. They further mentioned that risk factors of different nature required specific mitigation strategies to be put in place to ensure better results. Lastly, they posited that periodically risk management ensures better safety.

Marhavilas et al (2011) have classified risk analysis and assessment tools into three major categories: (a) the qualitative, (b) the quantitative, and (c) the hybrid techniques. They also identified that most of risk assessment work was done in relation to quantitative risk assessment tools with a high frequency of (65.63%) followed by qualitative assessment tools with (27.68%) but hybrid tools remain to be explored further as it remains very low at (6.70%).

Dallat et al (2017) in a broad perspective ideated that with the present business environment swamped with a plethora of risk factors, there is a dire need for a paradigm shift and a new level of synergy that can be provided through the use of risk management and assessment tools.

Antonioni et al (2009) iterated that "domino effect" as a quantitative risk assessment tool for escalating hazard on-site and off-site, is of fundamental requisite to identify critical equipment and to address risk mitigation action. Aven (2010) illustrated that although the use of risk assessment and uncertainty analysis for decision-making may take different perspectives, there is a shared and common understanding that these tools provide useful decision support in a way that their outcomes facilitate the decision-makers in taking a prudent decision.

REVIEW OF LITERATURE

Banyahmad, H. (2011) articulated in his research that high failure rate of IT projects, cost & schedule overruns and failure to deliver expected requirements make IT project risk management an important topic. Implementation of risk management practices within these IT projects will eventually enhance project performance and facilitates organizational success.

Gholami, S. (2012) opined that effective management of critical risk factors (financial risks, managerial risks, technical risks, behavioral risks and political risks) within the information technology industry is the key to achieving efficiency within various financial, operational and strategic activities within organizational decision making.

Talet, et al (2014) suggested that as IT project management activities are affected by risk factors of the varied spectrum where a holistic knowledge and implementation of risk management techniques act as a significant requirement for successful implementation of IT projects.

Bakker, et al (2011) stated risk management and assessment as an instrumental phenomenon of rational decision making within various IT projects. It is also posited that the use of risk management and assessment techniques envisage a positive influence on project success by mitigating and managing various predominant risk factors in and around the business environment.

Raz and Michael (2001) in their study within software and high-tech industries analyzed 38 risk management tools under six groups to study their effectiveness towards Risk Management Contribution (RMC) and Project Management Performance (PMP). Finally, they concluded that tools like Risk probability assessment, Responsibility assignment and Simulation were highly significant towards risk management contribution (RMC) and other tools Checklists, Risk time frame assessment and Cost-benefit analysis were highly significant towards project management performance.

Majdara and Nematollahi (2008) articulated that risk assessment tools are powerful methods of evaluating safety with their features like graphical event/fault tree developing interface, performing importance analysis, different administrative levels, and handling time-dependent failure data. Eventually, risk assessment tools are found to be effective tools for solving risk scenarios in design & operation phases, scheduling tests, maintenance activities and for training purposes.

Leveson (2004) expressed in his work that existing traditional risk assessment methods are not assessing risk in a manner that is consistent with currently accepted models of accident causation. He further emphasizes that the majority of risk assessment methods are focused more on human error aspects of systems operations, which obviously fails to identify the emergent aspects of risk scenarios. Salmon et al (2017) concluded that the majority of current risk assessment methods are not fully explored for identifying risk in contemporary socio-technical systems. It is also argued that whilst existing methods are useful in identifying key risks, there are other aspects of risk assessment, which are to be explored further in the future.

NEED FOR THE STUDY

The specific need for this study arises for the reason that Alhakami & Slovic (1994) have posited long back that though analytical approaches to decision making treat risk and perceived benefits as distinct concepts, the cases of their dependence are very frequent. There are studies where researchers have observed an inverse relationship between risk and perceived benefit across diverse hazards. Renn (2017) & Slovic (2016) also illustrated in their study that the greater the perceived benefit, the lower the risk, and vice versa. It was further articulated that when the benefit dimensions are salient, it leads to inhibited risk. With such implications made in past studies, there was a dire need to test the psychological benefits present in the decisions of risk assessment experts to reinvigorate the claim leading to an inverse relationship and large disparity between risk and benefit judgments.

OBJECTIVES OF CHAPTER

1. To study and report the impact of risk assessment tools on organisational effectiveness of the IT industry, in view of their perceived benefits (Functionality, Innovativeness, Responsiveness, Credibility and Security)
2. To provide the best portfolio of risk assessment tools to Risk managers, Entrepreneurs and Business Leaders.

RISK ASSESSMENT TOOLS

Risk assessment tools used in diverse industries do vary in line with their organizational operations, prevailing risk scenarios and the environment in which they are operating. From the pilot study conducted in the information technology industry, it has been found out that though the risk assessment process conducted in different organizations is completely different for their needs and requirements, their toolkit for risk assessment consisted of similar tools. Figure 1, represents the risk assessment tools and techniques which are adopted and implemented predominantly in various operations of the information technology industry. Although there are various risk assessment tools available under each category of qualitative, quantitative and hybrid risk assessment tools, only the most preferred tools which were ranked the most during the pilot study were considered for the research. Henceforth the following risk assessment tools are considered to fulfil the objectives of this study. Chionis, et al (2022) also articulated that though effective risk management is highly based on risk perception and communication, very limited emphasis is given to these components.

Figure 1. Risk assessment tools

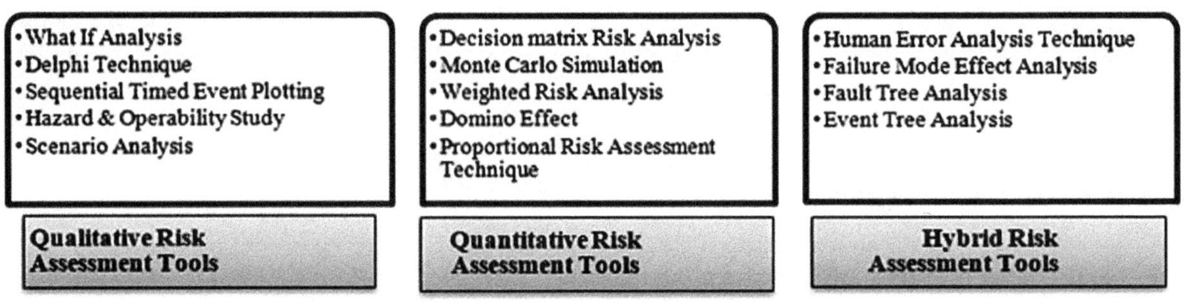

1. **Qualitative Risk Assessment:** Quantitative risk assessment is used in events where it is difficult to express a numerical measure of risk. Qualitative techniques are based on an analytical estimation process where probabilities and consequences are determined qualitatively. These qualitative tools require less effort and cost in evaluating risk events and conditions, yet they provide an appropriate level of information for handling risk scenarios.
2. **Quantitative Risk Assessment:** A Quantitative Risk Assessment (QRA) is a formal and systematic approach to quantifying the risks within operations of various engineering processes. It is an essential tool to support the knowledge of risk exposure to employees, environment, company assets and its reputation. QRA further assists to make effective decisions by managing the risks within the entire system by assigning numerical values to both impact and likelihood of various risk scenarios. Ultimately the quantitative measure of risk calculated by the statistical model is used to judge whether or not it is acceptable.
3. **Hybrid Risk Assessment:** Hybrid risk assessment tools are a detailed composition of qualitative, quantitative and semi-quantitative. Having the attributes of both qualitative and quantitative tools hybrid techniques provides a great efficacy in dealing with risks that are complex due to their ad hoc character, to prevent a wide spreading of risk scenarios.

CONCEPTUAL FRAMEWORK

The conceptual framework is representation of whole concept in nutshell. Figure 2, sums up the whole concept in single diagram, where authors study and test the impact of risk assessment tools on organizational effectiveness. The relationship between the risk assessment tools, perceived benefits and their impact on organizational effectiveness has been explored in detail and put on display through statistical inferences to give a clear picture to the readers of this book chapter.

Figure 2. Conceptual framework

RISK BASED DECISION MANAGEMENT STRATEGY

The question of decision making under risk and uncertainty is there for long now and one important thing that reader have to understand is that, for risk the outcome is unknown with known probability distribution of outcome and for uncertainty both outcome and probability are not known. Therefore decision making under risk have more objective orientation and decision making under uncertainty being subjective (with no information availability) is affected with biased outcomes (De Groot & Thurik, 2018).

Speaking about the risk management strategy of every organisation, the strategy always reciprocates the objectives of its organisational framework such as risk assumptions, risk tolerance, risk prioritization, risk management foundation and the boundaries of the risk based decisions as it is represented in figure 3. The risk strategy further translates into a systematic risk assessment methodology where the risk assessment models are evaluated based on the model specific assessment approach by analysing all the critical factors.

Figure 3. Organisational Risk Management Strategy

METHODOLOGY AND HYPOTHESES

Data required for the primary study was collected through an online survey, using a structured questionnaire (Closed-ended questions) via email communication to the employees at various levels of IT companies in India. A pilot study questionnaire was developed initially to find out information regarding risk management systems, strategies and policies in different information technology companies and then based on information gathered; the main questionnaire was developed with the help of academicians and risk management experts and employees. The main questionnaire was further tested for face validity and content validity by various experts and academicians. After rounds of revisions, the questionnaire was validated and data was collected on a five-point scale [Strongly disagree (1), Disagree (2), Neutral (3), Agree (4), Strongly agree (5)].The five-point scale was derived from the risk related literature from the Project Management Body of Knowledge [PMBOK] and through discussions with the project management practitioners. The target population aimed for this study were employees who had knowledge of risk management and the various tools used for risk assessment and management in their respective organizations. Therefore target population from whom the information was gathered mainly constituted of risk supervisors (9%), risk managers (28%), risk management teams & committees (31%), risk management directors (7%), chief financial officers (8%) and other employees (17%) working in IT companies. A descriptive statistical method was used to measure the significant impact of risk assessment models on organizational business decisions. An inferential Regression test has been used to test the hypotheses using the SPSS version 20.0 and to demonstrate the significance level of each risk assessment models. To study and establish the relationship between the dependent and independent variables, the following null hypotheses have been framed.

$H_{01:}$ Functionality under Quantitative risk assessment tools does not have an impact on Organizational Effectiveness of Information Technology industry.

H_{02}: Innovativeness under Quantitative risk assessment tools does not have an impact on Organizational Effectiveness of Information Technology industry.

$H_{03:}$ Responsiveness under Quantitative risk assessment tools does not have an impact on Organizational Effectiveness of Information Technology industry.

$H_{04:}$ Credibility under Quantitative risk assessment tools does not have an impact on Organizational Effectiveness of Information Technology industry.

$H_{05:}$ Security under Quantitative risk assessment tools does not have an impact on Organizational Effectiveness of Information Technology industry.

ANALYSIS AND INTERPRETATION

There are many decisions that a company has to take when it comes to improving the organizational performance in the short-run as well as the long-run succession of a business entity. Given the volatile business conditions with different dimensions of the organization as well society posing threat to business decisions, companies are in dire need of inculcating different risk assessment models within their organizations. The success or failure of an organization can be measured on how decisions are taken and how safe they are taken which acts as a prelude to overcast the impact of risk factors ready to decimate organizational growth (Patro& Raghunath, 2015; Raghunath& Devi, 2018). Thus, this section as an inherent part of the study will analyse the significance of tools in view of perceived benefits. As a part of achieving reliability within the model, average variance extracted, composite reliability and internal reliability (Cronbach's alpha) values are observed in table1. As articulated and presented all the constructs have a good composite reliability value and Cronbach alpha values (>.70) and average variance extracted is also fine as all the indicators have AVE above(.50) except security under qualitative risk assessment tools and functionality under hybrid risk assessment tools which is still valid as their composite reliability value is (> .70). Eventually, all the constructs are reliable and consistent enough to support a causal relationship among variables.

SIGNIFICANCE OF INDIVIDUAL RISK ASSESSMENT TOOLS IN AUTOMOBILE INDUSTRY

Adaptation of risk management process is very important for every organization in this contemporary business world and readers also have witnessed a take on the impact of risk assessment models on organizational effectiveness. As business entities move forward, an additional outlook on how significant individual risk assessment tools are on organizational effectiveness becomes a prerogative. Henceforth an in-depth analysis of individual risk assessment tools within the IT industry will provide the readers and stakeholders with a platform for decision making in the interest of organizational success.

Table 1. Results of Indicator Reliabilities in Final Iteration

	Qualitative Risk Assessment Tools				Quantitative Risk Assessment Tools				Hybrid Risk Assessment Tools			
	Code	**AVE**	**CR**	**Cronbach Alpha**	**Code**	**AVE**	**CR**	**Cronbach Alpha**	**Code**	**AVE**	**CR**	**Cronbach Alpha**
Functionality	Fun_Qlty1	0.5	0.78	0.92	Fun_Qty1	0.57	0.8	0.83	Fun_Hyd2	0.58	0.89	0.91
	Fun_Qlty3				Fun_Qty4				Fun_Hyd3			
	Fun_Qlty4				Fun_Qty5				Fun_Hyd4			
	Fun_Qlty5											
Innovativeness	Inno_Qlty1	0.6	0.87	0.92	Inno_Qty2	0.51	0.8	0.83	Inno_Hyd1	0.59	0.83	0.88
	Inno_Qlty2				Inno_Qty3				Inno_Hyd2			
	Inno_Qlty3				Inno_Qty4				Inno_Hyd3			
	Inno_Qlty4								Inno_Hyd5			
Responsiveness	Resp_Qlty1	0.6	0.9	0.84	Resp_Qty1	0.56	0.7	0.89	Resp_Hyd1	0.5	0.77	0.78
	Resp_Qlty2				Resp_Qty2				Resp_Hyd2			
	Resp_Qlty3				Resp_Qty3				Resp_Hyd3			
	Resp_Qlty4											
Credibility	Cred_Qlty1	0.6	0.86	0.87	Cred_Qty2	0.61	0.8	0.75	Cred_Hyd1	0.56	0.84	0.82
	Cred_Qlty2				Cred_Qty3				Cred_Hyd3			
	Cred_Qlty3				Cred_Qty5				Cred_Hyd4			
									Cred_Hyd5			
Security	Secu_Qlty2	0.5	0.79	0.83	Secu_Qty2	0.49	0.8	0.8	Sec_Hyd1	0.52	0.7	0.91
	Secu_Qlty3				Secu_Qty3				Sec_Hyd2			
	Secu_Qlty4				Secu_Qty4				Sec_Hyd3			
	Secu_Qlty5				Secu_Qty5				Sec_Hyd4			
									Sec_Hyd5			
Organizational Effectiveness	OE_Qlty1	0.7	0.91	0.89	OE_Qtty_1	0.62	0.9	0.87	OE_Hyd_1	0.57	0.87	0.84
	OE_Qlty2				OE_Qtty_3				OE_Hyd_2			
	OE_Qlty3				OE_Qtty_4				OE_Hyd_4			
	OE_Qlty5				OE_Qtty_6				OE_Hyd_6			
	OE_Qlty6								OE_Hyd_7			

Table 1, presents an comprehensive representation of risk assessment tools and theiry reliability indicators which are all according to the cut of value so that the study can be reliable and effective.

Significance of individual Risk Assessment Tools in IT Industry

Impact of risk assessment tools under the broader categories of qualitative, quantitative and hybrid have been analyzed with the help of inferential statistics and the results derived do constitute a lot of significance for risk based decision making by managers. But for an in-depth analysis of risk assessment tools (Qualitative-Quantitative-Hybrid), individual tools should be tested for their significance, which would ultimately reinvigorate the risk management process and provide significant insights for risk managers.

Significance of Individual Risk Assessment Tools Under Functionality

Table 2 articulates the significance of various individual risk assessment tools from functionality aspect within an organization. As illustrated the broad categories of Qualitative-Quantitative-Hybrid tools are further dissected into 14 individual tools.

Going through the functionality aspect of qualitative assessment tools, it is apparent that What if analysis (β= .192; P-value= 0.001) is positively significant towards organizational effectiveness i.e. with every one standard deviation increase in what if analysis, organizational effectiveness increases by .192 standard deviation. Scenario Analysis (β= -.132; P-value= 0.037) on the other side is negatively significant towards organizational effectiveness. Other qualitative tools like Delphi Technique (β= -.079; P-value=0 .264), STEP Technique (β= .097; P-value= 0.172) and HAZOP Study (β= -.148; P-value= 0.055) are all insignificant towards organizational effectiveness.

Table 2. Functionality inferential statistics

Functionality		Unstandardized Coefficients		Std. Coefficients	t	Sig.
		B	Std. Error	Beta		
	(Constant)	-.066	.032		-2.094	.038
Qualitative Models	What if analysis	.172	.053	.192	3.276	.001
	Delphi Technique	-.067	.060	-.079	-1.121	.264
	STEP Technique	.075	.048	.097	.960	.172
	HAZOP Study	-.128	.066	-.148	-1.933	.055
	Scenario Analysis	-.112	.053	-.132	-2.104	.037
Quantitative Models	DMRA	.194	.072	.198	3.660	.000
	Monte-Carlo	.233	.093	.235	2.54	.028
	Weight Risk Analysis	.098	.049	.113	2.008	.047
	Domino Effect	.184	.064	.215	2.860	.000
	PRAT	.003	.039	.004	.086	.932
Hybrid Models	HEAT	-.229	.053	-.250	-4.349	.000
	FMEA	.435	.062	.407	6.985	.000
	Fault Tree Analysis	.208	.078	.203	2.676	.008
	Event Tree Analysis	.221	.079	.224	2.797	.006
a. Dependent Variable: OE						

Quantitative individual risk assessment tools have performed better as most of the tools such as DMRA (β= .198; P-value= 0.000), Weight Risk Analysis (β= .113; P-value= 0.047, Domino Effect (β= .215; P-value= 0.000) and Monte-Carlo (β= .235; P-value= 0.028) are positively significant towards organizational effectiveness. On the flip side, Proportional Risk Assessment Tech. (β= .004; P-value= 0.932) though have a positive impact, it is highly insignificant.

The final categories are hybrid risk assessment tools and the best part about these tools was that all individual tools FMEA (β= .407; P-value= 0.000), Fault Tree Analysis (β= .203; P-value= 0.008), Event

Tree Analysis (β= .224; P-value= 0.006) and Human Error Analysis Tech. (β= -.250; P-value= 0.000 were highly significant with regard to organization effectiveness.

Significance of Individual Risk Assessment Tools Under Innovativeness

Innovativeness of risk assessment tools is one of the cornerstones for making effective risk based decisions on part of managers and table 3, visualizes the significant impact of risk assessment tools in view of their innovativeness in dealing with risk scenarios.

Qualitative risk assessment tools being the first category, it can be observed that all the risk assessment tools: What if analysis (β= -.036; P-value= 0.481), Delphi Technique (β= .026; P-value= 0.646), STEP Technique (β= -.054; P-value= 0.245), HAZOP Study (β= -.048; P-value= 0.163) and Scenario Analysis (β= .021; P-value= 0.676) are all insignificant towards organizational effectiveness. This postulates that innovativeness aspect within qualitative tools has no impact on organizational effectiveness. With quantitative tools also the same phenomena is observed as most of the tools: DMRA (β=0.039; P-value= 0.441), Weight Risk Analysis (β=-.068; P-value=0.235) and Domino Effect (β= -.040; P-value=0.471) are all insignificant towards organizational effectiveness. The only exception being Monte-Carlo (β=0.151; P-value=0.045) which is positively significant and Proportional Risk Assessment Technique (β=-.137; P-value=0.021) though positively related it has negative impact on organizational effectiveness.

Table 3. Innovativeness inferential statistics

Innovativeness		Unstandardized Coefficients		Std. Coefficients	t	Sig.
		B	Std. Error	Beta		
	(Constant)	.083	.018		4.492	.000
Qualitative Models	What if analysis	-.031	.044	-.036	-.707	.481
	Delphi Technique	.022	.049	.026	.460	.646
	STEP Technique	-.048	.041	-.054	-1.168	.245
	HAZOP Study	-.045	.032	-.048	-1.404	.163
	Scenario Analysis	.018	.043	.021	.419	.676
Quantitative Models	DMRA	.036	.047	.039	.773	.441
	Monte-Carlo	.139	.051	.151	2.031	.045
	Weight Risk Analysis	-.061	.051	-.068	-1.193	.235
	Domino Effect	-.036	.049	-.040	-.723	.471
	PRAT	-.123	.053	-.137	-2.329	.021
Hybrid Models	HEAT	.159	.044	.173	3.575	.000
	FMEA	.136	.042	.154	3.216	.002
	Fault Tree Analysis	.068	.057	.077	1.19	.237
	Event Tree Analysis	-.092	.056	-.105	-1.66	.100
a. Dependent Variable: OE						

Innovativeness with regard to qualitative and quantitative risk assessment tools have been on insignificant side but with hybrid risk assessment tools, it can be observed that tools such as Human Error Analysis Technique (β= 0.173; P-value=0.000) and FMEA (β=.154; P-value=0.002) are highly significant with a positive association with organizational effectiveness. At the same time, other tools like Fault Tree Analysis (β= .077; P-value=0.237) and Event Tree Analysis (β=-.105; P-value=0.100) have showcased an insignificant impact.

Significance of Individual Risk Assessment Tools Under Responsiveness

Responsiveness is the act of reacting quickly and when an organization is dealing with a plethora of risk scenarios, they expect their risk assessment tools to be as responsive as possible. Hereby with the help of table 4, readers will come across various individual risk assessment tools and their significance to respond. Responsiveness being a critical benefit that managers look forward, the following analysis will give them an idea of how responsive these tools are.

A birds-eye view of qualitative risk assessment tools and their responsiveness explains a lot of how significant the tools are towards organizational effectiveness. Most of the tools such as: What if analysis (β=0.501; P-value=0.000), Delphi Technique (β= 0.103; P-value=0.048), STEP Technique (β=0.537; P-value=0.000) under this category are significant cum positively correlated to organizational effectiveness. Whereas HAZOP Study (β=-0.127; P-value=0.026) though significant, is negatively associated with organizational effectiveness. The only tools that do not hold any ground is Scenario Analysis (β=0.061; P-value=0.309) which is statistically insignificant.

Responsiveness on the part of quantitative risk assessment tools seems to be totally on the downside as DMRA (β=0.091; P-value=0.372), Weight Risk Analysis (β=-0.075; P-value=0.113), Domino Effect (β=0.006; P-value=0.907) and Proportional Risk Assessment Technique (β=0.501; P-value=0.135) are completely insignificant towards organizational effectiveness. Monte-Carlo (β=0.089; P-value=0.009) is the only tool that is significant.

Hybrid risk assessment tools are analogous to quantitative risk assessment tools as most of the hybrid tools: Human Error Analysis Tech. (β=-0.022; P-value=0.675), Fault Tree Analysis (β=-0.077;

Table 4. Responsiveness inferential statistics

Responsiveness		Unstandardized Coefficients		Std. Coeff.	t	Sig.
		B	Std. Error	Beta		
	(Constant)	-0.066	0.026		-2.511	0.013
Qualitative Models	What if analysis	0.494	0.053	0.501	9.359	0.000
	Delphi Technique	0.087	0.044	0.103	1.996	0.048
	STEP Technique	0.499	0.055	0.537	9.025	0.000
	HAZOP Study	-0.113	0.05	-0.127	-2.253	0.026
	Scenario Analysis	0.051	0.05	0.061	1.022	0.309
Quantitative Models	DMRA	0.066	0.074	0.091	0.896	0.372
	Monte-Carlo	.085	.029	.089	2.778	.009
	Weight Risk Analysis	-0.069	0.043	-0.075	-1.597	0.113
	Domino Effect	0.005	0.045	0.006	0.117	0.907
	PRAT	0.523	0.037	0.501	1.202	0.135
Hybrid Models	HEAT	-0.018	0.043	-0.022	-0.42	0.675
	FMEA	-0.156	0.052	-0.173	-2.981	0.003
	Fault Tree Analysis	-0.066	0.045	-0.077	-1.457	0.147
	Event Tree Analysis	-0.011	0.033	-0.013	-0.32	0.749
a. Dependent Variable: OE						

P-value=0.147) and Event Tree Analysis (β=-0.013; P-value=0.749) are insignificant in terms of their responsiveness. Whereas FMEA (β=-0.173; P-value=0.003) though significant, it has a negative association with organizational effectiveness.

Significance of Individual Risk Assessment Tools Under Credibility

Credibility in terms of qualitative risk assessment tools depicted in table 5, looks promising as most of the tools: Delphi Technique (β=0.327; P-value=0.000), STEP Technique (β=0.149; P-value=0.013) and Scenario Analysis (β=0.376; P-value=0.000) displays positive beta value, with p-values being highly significant towards organizational effectiveness. What if analysis (β=-0.115; P-value=0.019) on the other hand is negatively significant towards organizational effectiveness. The only tool that stand insignificant is HAZOP Study (β=-0.072; P-value=0.195).

Quantitative risk assessment tools seems to be not that effective as most of the tools: DMRA (β=0.153; P-value=0.062), Weight Risk Analysis (β=0.142; P-value=0.162) and PRAT (β=-0.072; P-value=0.072) are highly insignificant towards organizational effectiveness except Monte-Carlo (β=0.421; P-value=0.000) and Domino Effect (β=0.274; P-value=0.00) which are positive and highly significant.

Hybrid tools with their credibility aspect look in balance as tools: Human Error Analysis Tech. (β=0.113; P-value=0.010) and FMEA (β=0.256; P-value=0.000) are positively associated with orga-

Table 5. Credibility inferential statistics

Credibility		Unstandardized Coefficients		Std. Coeff.	t	Sig.
		B	Std. Error	Beta		
	(Constant)	-.111	.022		-5.125	.000
Qualitative Models	What if analysis	-.103	.043	-.115	-2.369	.019
	Delphi Technique	.108	.029	.327	3.687	.000
	STEP Technique	.135	.054	.149	2.517	.013
	HAZOP Study	-.063	.038	-.072	-1.682	.195
	Scenario Analysis	.376	.038	.376	9.917	.000
Quantitative Models	DMRA	.148	.027	.153	2.550	.062
	Monte-Carlo	.392	.035	.421	11.157	.000
	Weight Risk Analysis	.253	.046	.142	5.518	.162
	Domino Effect	.300	.037	.074	8.195	.130
	PRAT	-.066	.037	-.072	-1.813	.072
Hybrid Models	HEAT	.094	.036	.113	2.629	.010
	FMEA	.225	.044	.256	5.072	.000
	Fault Tree Analysis	-.164	.058	-.187	-1.817	.116
	Event Tree Analysis	-.035	.033	-.043	-1.083	.281
a. Dependent Variable: OE						

nizational effectiveness with high significant value and tools such as Fault Tree Analysis (β=-0.187; P-value=0.116) and Event Tree Analysis (β=-0.043; P-value=0.281) are both statistically insignificant in terms of their credibility aspect.

Significance of Individual Risk Assessment Tools Under Security

The level of security envisaged by risk assessment tools is always high and as it is depicted in table 6, various risk assessment tools are tested for their level of significance in terms of security. Risk managers within every organization do expect their risk assessment tools to be as secure as possible.

It is evident from table 5.72, that qualitative risk assessment tools: What if analysis (β=-0.43; P-value=0.526), Delphi Technique (β=0.076; P-value=0.092) and HAZOP Study (β=0.017; P-value=0.742) are all insignificant towards organizational effectiveness and STEP Technique (β=-0.081; P-value=0.049) and Scenario Analysis (β=0.101; P-value=0.032) though are statistically significant, former is negatively associated and the later has with positive beta value, which denotes positive association with organizational effectiveness.

The performance of Quantitative tools seems to be better than qualitative tools as Domino Effect (β=0.171; P-value=0.002) and Proportional Risk Assessment Tech. (β=0.348; P-value=0.000) are highly

Table 6. Security inferential statistics

Security		Unstandardized Coefficients		Std. Coeff.	t	Sig.
		B	Std. Error	Beta		
	(Constant)	-.011	.020		-.567	.572
Qualitative Models	What if analysis	-.038	.060	-.043	-.636	.526
	Delphi Technique	.076	.045	.076	1.695	.092
	STEP Technique	-.067	.034	-.081	-1.982	.049
	HAZOP Study	.014	.042	.017	.330	.742
	Scenario Analysis	.094	.043	.101	2.168	.032
Quantitative Models	DMRA	-.043	.041	-.053	-1.037	.302
	Monte-Carlo	.071	.063	.075	1.122	.264
	Weight Risk Analysis	.091	.052	.102	1.750	.082
	Domino Effect	.152	.048	.171	3.150	.002
	PRAT	.320	.044	.348	7.233	.000
Hybrid Models	HEAT	-.328	.045	-.358	-7.342	.000
	FMEA	.533	.044	.499	9.096	.000
	Fault Tree Analysis	.092	.029	.109	3.175	.002
	Event Tree Analysis	.038	.059	.038	.638	.524
a. Dependent Variable: OE						

significant with positive association towards organizational effectiveness where other tools DMRA (β=-0.53; P-value=0.302), Monte-Carlo (β=0.075; P-value=0.264) and Weight Risk Analysis (β=0.102; P-value=0.082) are all statistically insignificant.

Eventually, hybrid tools are the ones with the most impact as individual tools under this category are witnessed to be highly significant with high positive beta values. Human Error Analysis Tech. (β=-0.358; P-value=0.000), FMEA (β=0.499; P-value=0.000) and Fault Tree Analysis (β=0.109; P-value=0.002) are all positively significant towards organizational effectiveness and Event Tree Analysis (β=0.038; P-value=0.524) is though have positive beta value the effect is completely insignificant.

FINDINGS OF THE STUDY

Findings Based on Descriptive Statistical Analysis

1. Under functionality, STEP technique under qualitative tools, Monte carlo under quantitative tools and Fault Tree Analysis were highly preferred.
2. Innovativeness was highly anticipated by HAZOP study under qualitative tools, Domino effect under quantitative tools and Fault Tree Analysis under hybrid tools.
3. Responsiveness concept was mostly credited to Delphi technique under qualitative tools, PRAT under quantitative tools and HEAT under hybrid tools.

4. For achieving credibility Scenario analysis under qualitative tools, Domino effect under quantitative tools and FMEA hybrid tools were preferred.
5. Security was highly envisaged by What if analysis under qualitative tools, WRA under quantitative tools and HEAT under hybrid tools.

Findings Based on Inferential Statistical Analysis (Individual Tools)

1. In terms of functionality, it has been found that What if analysis under qualitative tools. DMRA, Monte carlo, WRA & Domino effect under quantitative tools, FMEA, Fault Tree Analysis & Event Tree Analysis under hybrid tools are all positively significant towards organizational effectiveness whereas Scenario analysis and HEAT were negatively significant.
2. As of innovativeness, Monte carlo under quantitative tools, HEAT & FMEA under hybrid tools are positively significant towards organizational effectiveness, with PRAT being negatively significant.
3. Under the responsiveness aspect, What if analysis & STEP technique, Delphi technique as qualitative tools & Monte carlo under quantitative tools were all positively significant towards organizational effectiveness. On the other side, all the hybrid tools were insignificant.
4. From the credibility point of view, Delphi technique, STEP technique & Scenario analysis under qualitative tools, DMRA, Monte carlo, WRA & Domino effect under quantitative tools and finally HEAT & FMEA under hybrid tools are all significant towards organizational effectiveness. Whereas, What if analysis is the only tool with significant impact.
5. Scenario analysis under qualitative tools, Domino effect & PRAT under quantitative tools and finally FMEA & Fault Tree Analysis are all positively significant towards organizational effectiveness. Whereas STEP technique, DMRA and HEAT analysis are all negatively significant.

MANAGERIAL IMPLICATIONS

Based on findings from inferential statistics of individual tools, managers and entrepreneurs will come across the risk assessment tools that are significant towards achieving organisational effectiveness. Therefore all the finding in terms of inferential statistics individual risk assessment tools can be applied in Information Technology companies to achieve the best results in future. In the process of studying the impact of risk assessment tools on organizational effectiveness, risk managers have also provided some suggestions with regard to risk assessment tools to ensure better risk assessment within the IT industry.

1. Fault Tree Analysis and Event Tree Analysis should be used together to develop accident analysis technique which can thoroughly investigate the accidents.
2. Weighing factors for risk dimensions under WRA could be extended to make them comparable and relate them to measure the risk scenarios.
3. DMRA and HAZOP can be incorporated into computer automated toolkits to optimize their effectiveness.
4. Companies should envisage a unique graphical type of techniques for effective analysis.
5. HAZOP study can be further extended into development of Domino effects according to requirements to enhance better risk management.

FUTURE SCOPE FOR FURTHER RESEARCH

The landscape of risks globally has changed enormously, and with their occurrences becoming more unexpected and their effects becoming more profound, risks need to be taken seriously than ever before. In the present changing times, it is very much required for organizations to understand the importance of risk assessment and risk management in various aspects of the business as they reinvigorate risk based decision making.

As a part of continual improvement process the following points will reinvigorate the future studies in enterprise risk assessment and management.

1. The present study has been focussed only in metropolitan cities. In future, the scope can be expanded to other national and global areas to enhance radical thinking and explore new observations in the area of risk assessment and risk management.
2. Further, the present study can be extended to other industries within the nation to optimise the efficient use of risk assessment tools in view of their perceived benefits.

Lastly, as risk decisions are characterized by uncertainty and emergency, risk assessment framework should be developed in an efficient way to handle futuristic risk scenarios to capture knowledge dimensions and time dynamics of risk scenarios.

CONCLUSION

The landscape of risks globally has changed enormously and with their occurrences becoming more unexpected and their effects becoming more profound, risks need to be taken seriously more than ever before now. In these contemporary situations, it is very much prerequisite for organizations to understand the importance of risk assessment and risk management as they reinvigorate risk-based decision making.

Risk is imminent all over the world and for business organizations, it becomes more inevitable to manage risk in their every activity. One may not prevent every possible risk that may come up in the industry. But as it has been said "prevention is better than cure", risk assessment and risk management as an established field of science provide important insights in facilitating effective risk-based decision making within organizations. The hypotheses developed as a part of this study for analyzing the impact of risk assessment tools will further reinvigorate the confidence within managers and entrepreneurs in making informed decisions under uncertain environments.

Apart from providing great insights into an innovative way of exploring risk assessment tools, the present chapter has also taken a significant stride in the area of enterprise risk management for various good reasons. As the future is always uncertain it is expected that the existing risk assessment and management tools will build a strong platform for risk managers, future entrepreneurs and other interested stakeholders in managing the risk scenarios with a more innovative outlook and ultimately these tools will help them in overcoming future challenges posed by a gamut of risk factors underlying beneath every business opportunity.

REFERENCES

Alhakami, A. S., & Slovic, P. (1994). A psychological study of the inverse relationship between perceived risk and perceived benefit. *Risk Analysis*, *14*(6), 1085–1096. doi:10.1111/j.1539-6924.1994.tb00080.x PMID:7846317

Antonioni, G., Spadoni, G., & Cozzani, V. (2009). Application of domino effect quantitative risk assessment to an extended industrial area. *Journal of Loss Prevention in the Process Industries*, *22*(5), 614–624. doi:10.1016/j.jlp.2009.02.012

Arias, J. C., & Stern, R. (2011). Review of risk management methods. *Business Intelligence Journal*, *4*(1), 51–78.

Aven, T. (2010). On how to define, understand and describe risk. *Reliability Engineering & System Safety*, *95*(6), 623–631. doi:10.1016/j.ress.2010.01.011

Baker, S., Ponniah, D., & Smith, S. (1999). Risk response techniques employed currently for major projects. *Construction Management and Economics*, *17*(2), 205–213. doi:10.1080/014461999371709

Banyahmad, H. (2011). *Key challenges of information technology project risk management*. Academic Press.

Callahan, C., & Soileau, J. (2017). Does enterprise risk management enhance operating performance? *Advances in Accounting*, *37*, 122–139. doi:10.1016/j.adiac.2017.01.001

Chionis, D., Karanikas, N., Iordan, A. R., & Svensson-Dianellou, A. (2022). Risk perception and communication factors in aviation: Insights from safety investigators. *Journal of Risk Research*, 1–16. doi:10.1080/13669877.2022.2038246

Dallat, C., Salmon, P. M., & Goode, N. (2017). Risky systems versus risky people: To what extent do risk assessment methods consider the systems approach to accident causation? A review of the literature. *Safety Science*.

De Groot, K., & Thurik, R. (2018). Disentangling risk and uncertainty: When risk-taking measures are not about risk. *Frontiers in Psychology*, *9*, 2194. doi:10.3389/fpsyg.2018.02194 PMID:30498464

Gholami, S. (2012). Critical risk factors in outsourced support projects of IT. *Journal of Management Research*, *4*(1), 1.

Heyerdahl, A. (2022). Risk assessment without the risk? A controversy about security and risk in Norway. *Journal of Risk Research*, *25*(2), 252–267. doi:10.1080/13669877.2021.1936610

Hull, T. (2010, April). A deterministic scenario approach to risk management. In *2010 Enterprise Risk Management Symposium* (pp. 1-7). Academic Press.

Leveson, N. (2004). A new accident model for engineering safer systems. *Safety Science*, *42*(4), 237–270. doi:10.1016/S0925-7535(03)00047-X

Majdara, A., & Nematollahi, M. R. (2008). Development and application of a Risk Assessment Tool. *Reliability Engineering & System Safety*, *93*(8), 1130–1137. doi:10.1016/j.ress.2007.09.007

Marhavilas, P. K., Koulouriotis, D., & Gemeni, V. (2011). Risk analysis and assessment methodologies in the work sites: On a review, classification and comparative study of the scientific literature of the period 2000–2009. *Journal of Loss Prevention in the Process Industries*, *24*(5), 477–523. doi:10.1016/j.jlp.2011.03.004

Nikolić, B., & Ružić-Dimitrijević, L. (2009). Risk Assessment of Information Technology Systems. *Issues in Informing Science & Information Technology, 6*.

Patro, C. S., & Raghunath, K. M. K. (2015). Impetus to supply chain decisions with IT tools: An empirical study. *International Journal of Enterprise Information Systems*, *11*(3), 52–67. doi:10.4018/IJEIS.2015070104

Raghunath, K. M. K., & Devi, S. L. T. (2018). Supply Chain Risk Management: An Invigorating Outlook. *International Journal of Information Systems and Supply Chain Management*, *11*(3), 87–104. doi:10.4018/IJISSCM.2018070105

Raghunath, K. M. K., Devi, S. L. T., & Patro, C. S. (2017). An Empirical Take on Qualitative and Quantitative Risk Factors. *International Journal of Risk and Contingency Management*, *6*(4), 1–15. doi:10.4018/IJRCM.2017100101

Raghunath, K. M. K., & Devi, S. T. (2018). Effectiveness of Risk Assessment Models in Business Decisions: Reinforcing Knowledge. *International Journal of Sociotechnology and Knowledge Development*, *10*(2), 35–53. doi:10.4018/IJSKD.2018040103

Raz, T., & Michael, E. (2001). Use and benefits of tools for project risk management. *International Journal of Project Management*, *19*(1), 9–17. doi:10.1016/S0263-7863(99)00036-8

Renn, O. (2017). *Risk governance: coping with uncertainty in a complex world*. Routledge. doi:10.4324/9781849772440

Salmon, P. M., Walker, G. H. M., Read, G. J., Goode, N., & Stanton, N. A. (2017). Fitting methods to paradigms: Are ergonomics methods fit for systems thinking? *Ergonomics*, *60*(2), 194–205. doi:10.1080/00140139.2015.1103385 PMID:26799501

Slovic, P. (2016). *The perception of risk*. Routledge. doi:10.4324/9781315661773

Talet, A. N., Mat-Zin, R., & Houari, M. (2014). Risk management and information technology projects. *International Journal of Digital Information and Wireless Communications*, *4*(1), 1–10.

Yue, R. P. H., Lau, B. H., Chan, C. L., & Ng, S. M. (2021). Risk perception as a double-edged sword in policy compliance in COVID-19 pandemic? A two-phase evaluation from Hong Kong. *Journal of Risk Research*, 1–15. doi:10.1080/13669877.2021.1936612

ADDITIONAL READING

Patro, C. S., & Raghunath, K. M. K. (2015). Impetus to supply chain decisions with IT tools: An empirical study. *International Journal of Enterprise Information Systems*, *11*(3), 52–67. doi:10.4018/IJEIS.2015070104

Raghunath, K. M. K., & Devi, S. L. T. (2018). Supply chain risk management: An invigorating outlook. *International Journal of Information Systems and Supply Chain Management*, *11*(3), 87–104. doi:10.4018/IJISSCM.2018070105

Raghunath, K. M. K., Devi, S. L. T., & Patro, C. S. (2017). An empirical take on qualitative and quantitative risk factors. *International Journal of Risk and Contingency Management*, *6*(4), 1–15. doi:10.4018/IJRCM.2017100101

Raghunath, K. M. K., & Devi, S. T. (2021). Effectiveness of Risk Assessment Models in Business Decisions: Reinforcing Knowledge. In *Research Anthology on Small Business Strategies for Success and Survival* (pp. 1076–1096). IGI Global. doi:10.4018/978-1-7998-9155-0.ch053

Raghunath, K. M. K., Patro, C. S., & Sirisha, K. (2019). Paraphernalias of Entrepreneurship–A Contemplating Outlook. *International Journal of E-Entrepreneurship and Innovation*, *9*(1), 47–62. doi:10.4018/IJEEI.2019010105

Rao, V. P., Patro, C. S., & Raghunath, K. M. K. (2015). Employee welfare is the key: An insight. *International Journal of Business and Administration Research Review*, *3*(11), 40–47.

KEY TERMS AND DEFINITIONS

Organisational Effectiveness: Organisations ability to produce desired results as per the established parameter of performance.

Perceived Benefits: These are the perception of positive consequences that an organisation expects as the outcome of its actions.

Risk: The possibility of unexpected variation in the expected results is called risk.

Risk Assessment: The process of evaluating and appraising existing measures of security and controls by assessing their adequacy in response to the impending threats faced by the organization, so as to identify, evaluate, and report them periodically.

Risk Assessment Tools: Tools developed to assess risk for particular outcomes that helps in evaluating and appraising the efficiency of risk assessment.

Risk Factors: Variables/components that lead to unexpected variation in results.

Risk Management: The process of assessing and evaluating the various internal and external threats within organisation, so to mitigate them and bring stability within organisations.

Chapter 8
Minimizing Risk of Disputes Among Telecommunication Carriers With Blockchain Technologies

Evis Trandafili
Polytechnic University of Tirana, Albania

Marenglen Biba
University of New York, Tirana, Albania

Enes Cela
University of New York Tirana, Tirana, Albania

ABSTRACT

In recent years, blockchain technologies are constantly transforming many business processes. A shared, distributed ledger has revolutionized transaction recording, handling trust, and robustness in business network participants. In the telecommunication sector, the primary concern of voice over internet protocol (VoIP) providers when exchanging calls is the transparent storage of call detail records (CDRs) to avoid billing discrepancies, disputes, and interruption of services. In this chapter, the authors aim to investigate the utilization of permissioned blockchain in carriers' business models in telecommunication. They propose a business model architecture based on hyperledger fabric for developing smart contracts, which are invoked to store information about each CDR generated and business cases. The necessary steps and configurations for integrating the different technologies and building a development network are presented. Finally, the performance testing results regarding the latency for a transaction submission are shown.

DOI: 10.4018/978-1-6684-5279-0.ch008

INTRODUCTION

VoIP technologies have gained significant role in the telecommunication industry. VoIP stands for Voice over IP and as its name suggests, voice detected by a microphone is sampled and converted to binary data which serve as the data portion of a network packet. These packets are then transmitted over an IP network to the end user who is taking part in the conversation (Chakraborty. et al. 2019).

Rather than using the PSTN/ISDN infrastructure to make phone calls, it is possible to set up calls and transmit the voice over the IP network. Given that no dedicated infrastructure is necessary to transmit the voice, the cost of a call is lower than what PSTN/ISDN providers have to offer. In the telecommunication business it has been taken advantage of this fact, and a global network of providers offer their services to route phone calls to the desired destinations.

Figure 1. Simple call routing diagram

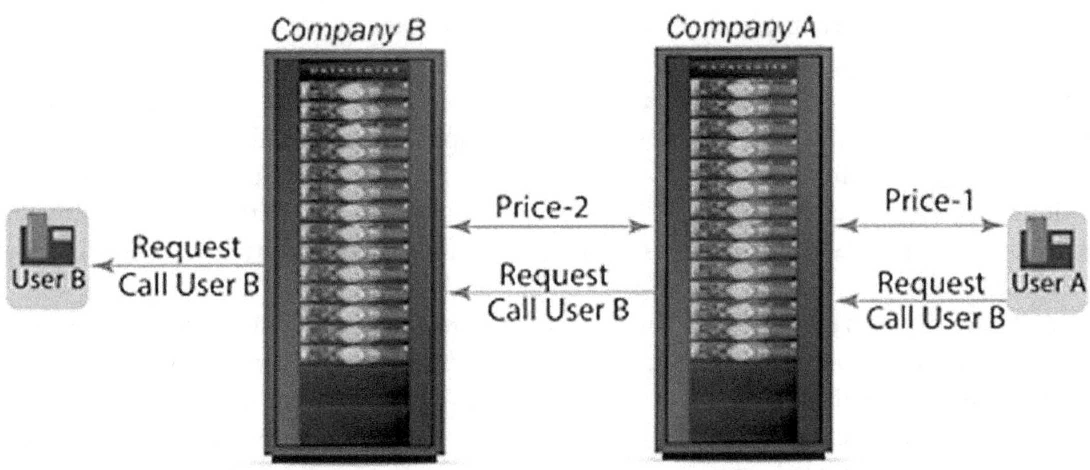

As shown in Figure 1, company A takes call requests from user A and routes them to company B, which "knows" how to terminate the call to user B.

In telecommunications, whoever starts the call is charged for it (not including roaming services). In such cases, company B charges company A, which in turn will charge user A. The billing takes effect only when the calls are answered and taking in consideration 1/1 billing increments, user A and company A will be charged for the number of seconds the call was in answered state. The price is obviously agreed beforehand between the communicating parties: Price-1 between user A and company A, and Price-2 between company B and company A (Swale and Collins 2013).

In real scenarios, company A can send millions of call requests to company B in the span of a month, and the billing needs to be precise. But this is not always the case. There are many occasions when companies raise disputes for unfair bills. Each call is attached a Call Detail Record (CDR). This piece of information contains all that is needed to calculate the cost of a call. It includes data such as the start, answer, end time of the call, its duration etc. Each company has its own set of CDRs for all the calls exchanged between them. This means that company A expects to be charged a certain amount of money for the traffic it has routed to company B on a given period. When the bill it receives from company B exceeds expectations, issues may arise and this process can lead to a formal dispute among both companies resulting in complex legal procedures with related significant costs for both companies.

When a dispute is raised there is a need to check in detail the traffic to figure out where the discrepancies reside. In many occasions, company B does not allow traffic towards it until the dispute is resolved and it closes the route. Also, company A would not want to send calls without knowing how they are being charged. They risk being charged more than they are charging user A, hence losing money on each call. For company B this means losing a customer for some time, which will lower its revenue and can lead to missing the business targets that have been set. Meanwhile, company A has one provider less for the traffic it receives from user A, and if it is a big amount of traffic, it can be difficult to find alternative routes.

To solve this problem in this paper the authors have considered the use of blockchain technologies. This technology would make sure that both parties have the same information on their CDRs, and that each call is charged with the same billing increment and at the same time. The price of the call differs based on its destination, so a price list is exchanged between companies containing the prices for each destination offered. So, the companies should store in a blockchain network the prices of each route and all CDRs. Through this approach, once the information is stored in the blockchain network, it becomes immutable and none of the parties can claim different values. This would avoid any kind of dispute among the Carriers as all billing information would be completely stored in the blockchain network and could be used by both billing teams to reconcile any discrepancy that they might find in their internal local billing systems. Effectively, once the data are stored in the network, there is no possibility that any Carrier finds different data locally leading therefore to a very safe and effective procedure for avoiding the risk of disputes.

The objective of this paper is to introduce a model for implementing a distributed storage of CDRs over the blockchain network. They implement the model in real world Carrier scenarios and perform thorough testing to show the effectiveness of the proposed approach. In addition, the authors have carried out some performance testing in order to check whether the proposed approach supports scalability in the case of millions of records involved.

BACKGROUND AND RELATED WORKS

Blockchain is a shared distributed ledger that facilitates the process of recording transactions and tracking assets in a business network (Narayanan. et al. 2016). This technology aids in building trust among business participants through these attributes:

- Distributed and sustainable: The ledger is shared and replicated among participants in real time
- Secure private and indelible: Access is allowed only to trusted parties that have the right cryptographic credentials.
- Transparent and auditable: Participants have access to the same records and can validate every transaction.
- Consensus-based and transactional: A transaction must be acknowledgment from all relevant participants before updating the ledger.
- Orchestrated and flexible: Blockchain networks can evolve to better suit the business process.

Depending on the need of the application, blockchain can be divided into three types: Public blockchain, Private blockchain and Consortium blockchain. Public blockchains are publicly accessible and there is no restriction on who can participate. It is fully distributed, and no single node has complete control over the network. Private blockchains, also known as permissioned blockchains, have restrictions on who can participate. Only pre-chosen entities can have access to the network. In Consortium blockchains, some nodes control the consensus process and others are allowed to participate in the transactions (Narayanan. et al. 2016).

Recently there is a growing body of work on the use of blockchain in many different and various areas such as: smart agriculture (Awan et al, 2020); governance (Zavolokina et al, 2020); consensus algorithms (Alsaqqa et al, 2020), robotics (Queralta and Westerlund, 2019), logistics (Issaoui et al, 2020), smart manufacturing (Jiahe et al, 2020), insurance (Nizamuddin and Abugabah, 2021) and many more.

Hyperledger is an open source collaborative effort created to advance cross-industry blockchain technologies (Elli et al 2018). It is a global collaboration, hosted by The Linux Foundation, including leaders in finance, banking, IoT, supply chain, manufacturing and technology. Hyperledger Fabric is one of the blockchain projects within Hyperledger. It has a ledger, uses smart contracts, and is used by participants to manage transactions. Hyperledger Fabric is a private and permissioned blockchain. Parties need to enroll through a trusted Membership Service Provider to participate in the network. There are different nodes, each with its own role on the network, defined by Hyperledger Fabric.

Orderer Nodes

In distributed public blockchains, Ethereum or Bitcoin, any node can participate in the consensus process where transactions are ordered and put into blocks. These systems use a probabilistic consensus algorithm which guarantees ledger consistency to a high degree. But there can still be cases where different participants have different views on the ledger. Hyperledger Fabric, instead, uses orderer nodes for transaction ordering. Orderer nodes, together, form an ordering service, and blocks are guaranteed to be final and correct, thus there is no possibility of ledgers forking as they do in public blockchains (Elli et al 2018). In addition to their ordering roles, orderer nodes also maintain the list of organizations that are allowed to create channels. This list is kept in the orderer system channel, which also works with blockchain principles. Orderers enforce basic access control for channels, restricting who can read and write data to them.

Peer Nodes

Peers are a fundamental part of the network as they host ledgers and smart contracts. Peers can have multiple ledgers and chaincodes, making design more flexible. A peer actually hosts instances of ledgers and smart contracts, thus avoiding single points of failure. Applications always connect to peers when they need to access the ledgers and chaincodes. Through a peer connection, they can execute chaincodes to query or update the ledger. The result of the query is returned immediately, since the ledger is stored locally, and it is sure to be correct. Meanwhile, updates involve a few more steps, including orderer nodes and validations from other peers to satisfy policies set by administrators. Peers interact with each-other and applications via channels. By joining a channel, these nodes agree to collaborate to collectively share and manage identical copies of the ledger associated with that channel (Elli et al 2018).

Certificate Authorities

A node is able to participate in the blockchain network, via the means of a digital identity issued by an authority trusted by the system. In most cases, an identity has the form of cryptographically validated digital certificates and are issued by a Certificate Authority. Certificate Authorities (CAs) can be Root Cas or Intermediate CAs. Any of them is allowed in a Fabric blockchain network and each participant can use its own CA.

Chaincodes and Smart Contracts

Businesses need to define a set of contracts which when taken together form the business model that determines how every transaction is made between the parties. In the blockchain network these contracts are expressed in the form of executable programs, which are automatically enforced on every transaction. The smart contract defines the transaction logic that controls the life cycle of a business object. It is then packaged into a chaincode and deployed into the Hyperledger network. An important aspect of the smart contract in Hyperledger Fabric is the endorsement policy. When instantiated on a peer node, an endorsement policy is defined. The endorsement policy indicates the organizations on a network that must sign the transaction for it to be valid. This is what makes Hyperledger Fabric different from other blockchains.

The Ledger

In the ledger it is stored the current state of a business object. In Hyperledger, the ledger is composed of the world state database and the blockchain. The world state is a cache that stores the current state of the business objects. Meanwhile, in the blockchain it is stored the history of changes made to the state of such objects. Using smart contracts, applications can update the state of an object, hence updating the world state database, but the history of the changes is immutable and cannot be changed.

The blockchain is structured as a sequential log of linked blocks, where each block contains a sequence of transactions representing a query or an update to the world state. The blocks are created from the ordering service where each block's header includes a hash of the block's transactions and a copy of the hash of the prior block's header. The first block of the ledger does not contain any transaction information and it is known as the genesis block. It is created when first starting the ordering service.

Figure 2. The blockchain structure
(Hyperledger, 2020)

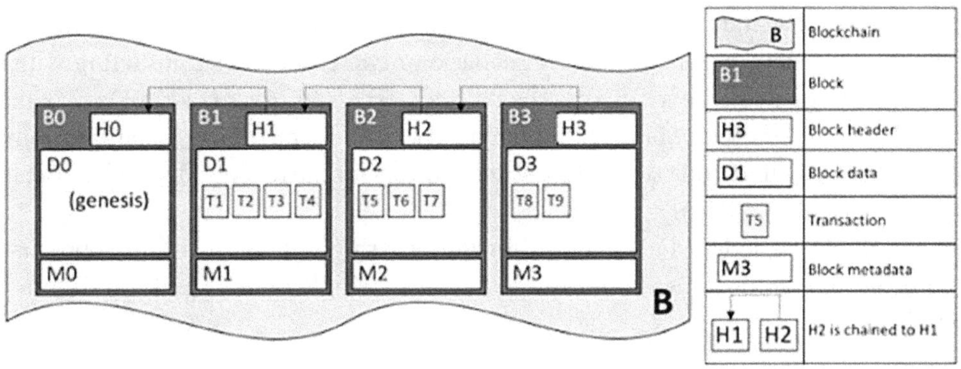

Transaction Flow

A transaction consists of six stages from the request initiation to updating the ledger, which is known as the transaction flow. The six stages are:

1. Transaction Initiation: a client initiates a request to update the ledger by sending it to the necessary peers in order to satisfy the chaincode endorsement policy. These peers then generate a transaction proposal, which is a request to invoke a function developed in the chaincode.
2. Signature verification and transaction execution: the endorsing peer that get the client request make sure that the proposal is well formed, not submitted in the past, it has a valid signature, and that the client is authorized to submit the transaction. It then uses the proposal inputs as arguments for the function to be invoked, and it executes the chaincode outputting a set of values. These values, along with the peer signature form a response that is sent back to the client.
3. Responses inspection: the client gets proposal responses from every endorsing peer it sent a request to. After checking the signatures, if the transaction was only a read operation it does not submit it to the ordering service. If the transaction must be submitted to the ordering service, it first checks that the endorsement policy is fulfilled and that all the peers sent back the same values.
4. Assemble endorsements into a transaction: the application sends the transaction containing the read/write sets, channel ID, and endorsing peers signatures to the ordering service. The ordering service gets transactions from all channels, sorts them chronologically for each channel, and creates the blocks for each channel.
5. Transaction validation: the blocks are sent to all peers on a channel which ensure that they are valid, having fulfilled endorsement policy, and that no changes were made to the ledger for the read set variables since they were created.
6. Update ledger: each peer adds the blocks to the channel's chain and generates an event to notify the client whether the transaction was validated or invalidated.

BUSINESS MODEL OF VOIP PROVIDERS

In this section we will illustrate through an example how the voice carriers implement their business scenarios. This example will focus on a simple scenario of two companies transacting with each other, where organization Org1 is the buyer, makes the call requests, and organization Org2 is the seller, receives the call requests. For each organization there is a peer node (peer0.org1.example.com and peer0.org2.exmple.com) a CouchDB node (the database technology for the ledger), and a Certificate Authority (the Fabric CA) (CouchDB, 2020).

According to the Hyperledger Fabric docs, for the ordering service a cluster mode using Raft or Kafka should be used in production, but for this example the single orderer node configuration is used: orderer.example.com.

Figure 3. Hyperledger Fabric Network Topology

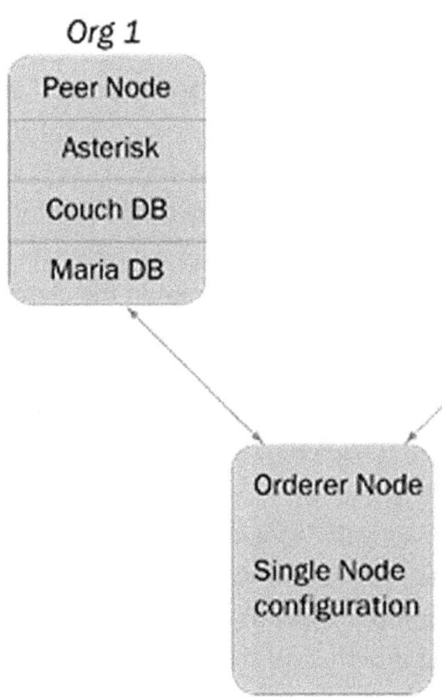

Asterisk, described in the next section, is installed on both peer nodes to make and receive calls. As suggested from the Hyperledger Fabric developing team (CouchDB, 2020), the CouchDB is replicated locally for each peer. This is done to be able to perform rich and frequent queries without affecting the blockchain network performance. Every CDR stored in the ledger is also stored in the MariaDB databases installed on the peers. Telecommunications providers need to make frequent queries to the CDR tables to monitor the performance of the routes and to generate many different reports. Issuing all these queries to the ledger database would take its toll on the performance that is why MariaDB is used locally.

DESIGN OF SOLUTION

Technologies Used

There are three main parts in this project, which correspond to the main tasks that are to be fulfilled. Firstly, there is the need to make and route calls using the Session Initiation Protocol (SIP, 2020). Asterisk, an open source technology from Digium is used as the software for this purpose. Secondly, CDRs generated from Asterisk need to be stored in a relational database, MariaDB is used in this case. And lastly, the CDRs generated need to be checked and put on the blockchain network. Hyperledger Fabric is the technology which will provide the blockchain network components and functionalities. These components, peer nodes, CAs, orderers etc., are all hosted on containers, so Docker is installed to support this requirement. CentOS 7 Servers are used for this project.

Asterisk

Asterisk is an open source framework for building communications applications (Asterisk 2020). It offers the possibility to configure SIP trunks and dialplans to receive and route voice calls. For this purpose, two files are important to configure. /etc/asterisk/sip.conf is where SIP trunks are configured for authentication, voice codecs supported etc. The information in this file is used when setting up calls. For each SIP trunk, there is the possibility to define a dialplan context where you can configure where the call is routed, at minimum. Asterisk offers a set of applications and functions that are used for this purpose. The file where contexts reside is /etc/asterisk/extensions.conf.

SIP is an application-layer control protocol that can establish, modify, and terminate multimedia sessions (conferences) such as Internet telephony calls (SIP, 2020). It is a request/response protocol based on HTTP. Each transaction consists of a request for a particular method and at least one response. For a basic answered voice call the messages exchanged include INVITE, 100 Trying, 180 RINGING, 200 OK, BYE. The initiating party sends an INVITE request which marks the start of the call. The first response is a 100 Trying, and when the B-party of the call indicates ringing, 180 Ringing is sent to the A-party. When the call is answered, 200 OK is sent, and the voice packets are permitted to go through to enable communication. For the transmission of the voice packets is used the Real Time Protocol (RTP).

MariaDB

Asterisk is configured to generate CDRs for the calls that go through, and each CDR is stored on MariaDB database, which is an open-source fork version of MySQL relational databases (MariaDB, 2020). The database used for storing the CDRs has at least one table, whose columns match the attributes of the CDR. An ODBC plugin is installed to enable Asterisk to connect to this database and perform the insert queries for each CDR after the call is hung up.

Docker

A container is a software package that contains everything the software needs to run. This includes the executable program as well as system tools, libraries, and settings. Containers are not installed like traditional software programs, which allows them to be isolated from the other software and the operating system itself. This makes them different from other virtualization techniques that utilize a hypervisor to act as an intermediate layer. Container virtualization is also called OS-level virtualization and it allows multiple isolated instances to be run on a single host.

Docker is an open-source engine that automates the deployment of applications into containers (Turnbull, 2014). During installation of Hyperledger Fabric, many docker images are downloaded, which include the base images for the nodes of the blockchain network. These containers are brought up and made to interact with each-other using YAML files and Docker Compose. Docker Compose consumes a YAML file where it is specified a set of containers to be started. The YAML files are custom made to fit the topology of the Hyperledger Fabric network, but the containers used are the ones provided by the developers of Hyperledger.

It is possible to manage the cluster of nodes using Docker Swarm, or Kubernetes, but for this project the network is set up manually. The file transfer between nodes is managed by the network administrator. The IPs of each node have been hard-coded on the YAML files used by Docker Compose.

Blockchain Network Setup

The blockchain network is composed of three servers. Two of them acting as peer nodes and one as the orderer. The installation should suit these functionalities. In peer nodes must be installed Asterisk, MariaDB, Docker and Docker Compose, and Hyperledger Fabric. For the orderer node only Hyperledger Fabric is enough. The development of the project consists of four stages:

1. Blockchain network setup
2. Smart contract development and instantiation
3. Setting up Asterisk and MariaDB
4. Solution for automatically updating the ledger

The Hyperledger Fabric configuration files shown in the next sections are based – with some modification to suit the network of this project – on the sample files that come together with the Fabric download.

Creating the blockchain network means determining the roles of the servers, creating the credentials that different nodes will use to securely communicate with each-other, and making sure that they can communicate together. There are two important files that must be created in order to fulfill the first two tasks. The first one is crypto-config.yaml. This file contains the network topology and it is consumed by cryptogen to generate a set of certificates and keys for each organization described there. Cryptogen is a tool that generates x509 certificates, and it is included in the Hyperledger Fabric binaries downloaded in the installation phase.
The contents of crypto-config.yaml are as below:

```
OrdererOrgs:
  - Name: Orderer
    Domain: example.com
    Specs:
    - Hostname: orderer
PeerOrgs:
  - Name: Org1
```

```
    Domain: org1.example.com
    Template:
      Count: 1
    Users:
      Count: 1
  - Name: Org2
    Domain: org2.example.com
    Template:
      Count: 1
    Users:
      Count: 1
```

In this file it is defined how the peers will address the orderer node, in this case orderer.example.com. So, the format is hostname.domain. Also there has been defined how many peer nodes and users are there for each organization and how to address them. There is defined only one peer and one user per organization. The peer count starts from zero, so the names of the peers are peer0.org1.example.com and peer0.org2.example.com. After writing this file, cryptogen is used to create the credentials. What matters is that the paths leading to the cryptogen binary and the crypto-config file are correct. After completion, a new directory will be created in the current working directory named crypto-config, containing the x509 certificates and keys generated for each node and user.

The second important file is configtx.yaml. This file defines the network members, the consortium consisting of the two organization and the channels that are to be created for chaincode instantiation. The contents of this file are as below:

```
---
Organizations:
    - &OrdererOrg
        Name: OrdererOrg
        ID: OrdererMSP
        MSPDir: crypto-config/ordererOrganizations/example.com/msp
    - &Org1
        Name: Org1MSP
        ID: Org1MSP
        MSPDir: crypto-config/peerOrganizations/org1.example.com/msp
        AnchorPeers:
            - Host: peer0.org1.example.com
              Port: 7051
    - &Org2
        Name: Org2MSP
        ID: Org2MSP
        MSPDir: crypto-config/peerOrganizations/org2.example.com/msp
        AnchorPeers:
            - Host: peer0.org2.example.com
              Port: 7051
```

```
Orderer: &OrdererDefaults
    OrdererType: solo
    Addresses:
        - orderer.example.com:7050
    BatchTimeout: 2s
    BatchSize:
        MaxMessageCount: 10
        AbsoluteMaxBytes: 99 MB
        PreferredMaxBytes: 512 KB
    Kafka:
        Brokers:
            - 127.0.0.1:9092
    Organizations:
Application: &ApplicationDefaults
    Organizations:
Profiles:
    TwoOrgsOrdererGenesis:
        Orderer:
            <<: *OrdererDefaults
            Organizations:
                - *OrdererOrg
        Consortiums:
            SampleConsortium:
                Organizations:
                    - *Org1
                    - *Org2
    OneOrgOrdererGenesis:
        Orderer:
            <<: *OrdererDefaults
            Organizations:
                - *OrdererOrg
        Consortiums:
            SampleConsortium:
                Organizations:
                    - *Org2
    ChannelTest:
        Consortium: SampleConsortium
        Application:
            <<: *ApplicationDefaults
            Organizations:
                - *Org2
    Channel12:
        Consortium: SampleConsortium
        Application:
```

```
            <<: *ApplicationDefaults
            Organizations:
                - *Org1
                - *Org2
```

Important settings of this file are the locations of Membership Service Provider (MSP) directories for each member, which makes it possible to include root certificates for each organization in the orderer genesis block. This means that any network node that wishes to communicate with the orderer will have its identity checked, so unauthorized nodes cannot make requests to submit transactions. Also, the orderer configuration has been specified, which in this case is solo - a single node. The channel which includes both organizations is Channel12.

This file is consumed by another Hyperledger Fabric tool installed along with Fabric called configtxgen in order to create the orderer genesis block, the channel configuration transaction, and the anchor peer transactions. The commands issued in the terminal for each configuration artifact are:

```
../bin/configtxgen -profile TwoOrgsOrdererGenesis -channelID voip2orgs-sys-
channel -outputBlock ./channel-artifacts/genesis.block
../bin/configtxgen -profile Channel12 -outputCreateChannelTx ./channel-arti-
facts/channel12.tx -channelID channel12
../bin/configtxgen -profile Channel12 -outputAnchorPeersUpdate ./channel-arti-
facts/Org1MSPanchors.tx -channelID channel12 -asOrg Org1MSP
../bin/configtxgen -profile Channel12 -outputAnchorPeersUpdate ./channel-arti-
facts/Org2MSPanchors.tx -channelID channel12 -asOrg Org2MSP
```

These artifacts are outputted in a previously created directory called channel-artifacts.
The last step for setting up the network is writing the Docker Compose files to start up Docker containers.

Running Services With Docker Compose

To run the network in Docker containers are needed four files. The first file is peer-base.yaml that contains basic, common configurations for all peer and orderer nodes. This file is extended by the other three, which define specific configurations for each container. The contents of the base file are as below:

```
version: '2'

services:
  peer-base:
    image: hyperledger/fabric-peer
    environment:
      - CORE_VM_ENDPOINT=unix:///host/var/run/docker.sock
      # the following setting starts chaincode containers on the same
      # bridge network as the peers
      # https://docs.docker.com/compose/networking/
      - CORE_VM_DOCKER_HOSTCONFIG_NETWORKMODE=voip2orgs_fabric
```

```
      - FABRIC_LOGGING_SPEC=ERROR
      #- FABRIC_LOGGING_SPEC=DEBUG
      - CORE_PEER_TLS_ENABLED=true
      - CORE_CHAINCODE_LOGGING_LEVEL=ERROR
      - CORE_PEER_GOSSIP_USELEADERELECTION=true
      - CORE_PEER_GOSSIP_ORGLEADER=false
      - CORE_PEER_PROFILE_ENABLED=true
      - CORE_PEER_TLS_CERT_FILE=/etc/hyperledger/fabric/tls/server.crt
      - CORE_PEER_TLS_KEY_FILE=/etc/hyperledger/fabric/tls/server.key
      - CORE_PEER_TLS_ROOTCERT_FILE=/etc/hyperledger/fabric/tls/ca.crt
    working_dir: /opt/gopath/src/github.com/hyperledger/fabric/peer
    command: peer node start

  orderer-base:
    image: hyperledger/fabric-orderer
    environment:
      - FABRIC_LOGGING_SPEC=ERROR
      - CORE_CHAINCODE_LOGGING_LEVEL=ERROR
      - ORDERER_GENERAL_LISTENADDRESS=0.0.0.0
      - ORDERER_GENERAL_GENESISMETHOD=file
      - ORDERER_GENERAL_GENESISFILE=/var/hyperledger/orderer/orderer.genesis.
block
      - ORDERER_GENERAL_LOCALMSPID=OrdererMSP
      - ORDERER_GENERAL_LOCALMSPDIR=/var/hyperledger/orderer/msp
      # enabled TLS
      - ORDERER_GENERAL_TLS_ENABLED=true
      - ORDERER_GENERAL_TLS_PRIVATEKEY=/var/hyperledger/orderer/tls/server.key
      - ORDERER_GENERAL_TLS_CERTIFICATE=/var/hyperledger/orderer/tls/server.
crt
      - ORDERER_GENERAL_TLS_ROOTCAS=[/var/hyperledger/orderer/tls/ca.crt]
      - ORDERER_KAFKA_TOPIC_REPLICATIONFACTOR=1
      - ORDERER_KAFKA_VERBOSE=true
      - ORDERER_GENERAL_CLUSTER_CLIENTCERTIFICATE=/var/hyperledger/orderer/
tls/server.crt
      - ORDERER_GENERAL_CLUSTER_CLIENTPRIVATEKEY=/var/hyperledger/orderer/tls/
server.key
      - ORDERER_GENERAL_CLUSTER_ROOTCAS=[/var/hyperledger/orderer/tls/ca.crt]
    working_dir: /opt/gopath/src/github.com/hyperledger/fabric
    command: orderer
```

There are two services described in this file. The first one is the peer service namely: peer-base. It is built on the fabric-peer docker image which was downloaded during Hyperledger installation. Some environment variables are included in the configuration that determine how this container will function. These specify that TLS is going to be used for communicating and the location of certificates is included also. The logging level is set to error to not produce a lot of output during ledger queries or updates. The working directory for the container is specified and lastly the command to run after the container is started, in this case peer node start starts the Hyperledger Fabric peer service.

The second service describes the orderer service. This time the fabric-orderer image is used to build the container. As with the peer service, TLS is enabled, and the location of certificates is specified. Logging is set to ERROR and the command issued to start the service is orderer.

The files that start the node containers are peer0-org1.yaml and peer0-org2.yaml. The contents for Org1's peer file are as below:

```
version: '2'
volumes:
  peer0.org1.example.com:
networks:
  fabric:
services:
  peer0.org1.example.com:
    container_name: peer0.org1.example.com
    extends:
      file: peer-base.yaml
      service: peer-base
    environment:
      - CORE_PEER_ID=peer0.org1.example.com
      - CORE_PEER_ADDRESS=peer0.org1.example.com:7051
      - CORE_PEER_LISTENADDRESS=0.0.0.0:7051
      - CORE_PEER_CHAINCODEADDRESS=peer0.org1.example.com:7052
      - CORE_PEER_CHAINCODELISTENADDRESS=0.0.0.0:7052
      - CORE_PEER_GOSSIP_BOOTSTRAP=peer0.org2.example.com:7051
      - CORE_PEER_GOSSIP_EXTERNALENDPOINT=peer0.org1.example.com:7051
      - CORE_PEER_LOCALMSPID=Org1MSP
      - CORE_LEDGER_STATE_STATEDATABASE=CouchDB
      - CORE_LEDGER_STATE_COUCHDBCONFIG_COUCHDBADDRESS=couchdb0:5984
      - CORE_LEDGER_STATE_COUCHDBCONFIG_USERNAME=
      - CORE_LEDGER_STATE_COUCHDBCONFIG_PASSWORD=
      - CORE_CHAINCODE_EXECUTETIMEOUT=300
    extra_hosts:
      - "peer0.org2.example.com:91.205.172.208"
      - "orderer.example.com:178.63.22.17"
    volumes:
        - /var/run/:/host/var/run/
        - ./crypto-config/peerOrganizations/org1.example.com/peers/peer0.org1.
example.com/msp:/etc/hyperledger/fabric/msp
        - ./crypto-config/peerOrganizations/org1.example.com/peers/peer0.org1.
example.com/tls:/etc/hyperledger/fabric/tls
        - ./crypto-config/peerOrganizations/org2.example.com/peers/peer0.org2.
```

```
example.com/msp:/etc/hyperledger/fabric/org2/msp
        - ./crypto-config/peerOrganizations/org2.example.com/peers/peer0.org2.
example.com/tls:/etc/hyperledger/fabric/org2/tls
        - peer0.org1.example.com:/var/hyperledger/production
    ports:
      - 7051:7051
    networks:
      - fabric
    depends_on:
      - couchdb0
  couchdb0:
    container_name: couchdb0
    image: hyperledger/fabric-couchdb
    environment:
      - COUCHDB_USER=
      - COUCHDB_PASSWORD=
    ports:
      - "5984:5984"
    networks:
      - fabric
  ca0:
    image: hyperledger/fabric-ca
    environment:
      - FABRIC_CA_HOME=/etc/hyperledger/fabric-ca-server
      - FABRIC_CA_SERVER_CA_NAME=ca-org1
      - FABRIC_CA_SERVER_TLS_ENABLED=true
      - FABRIC_CA_SERVER_TLS_CERTFILE=/etc/hyperledger/fabric-ca-server-con-
fig/ca.org1.example.com-cert.pem
      - FABRIC_CA_SERVER_TLS_KEYFILE=/etc/hyperledger/fabric-ca-server-
config/${CA0_PRIVATE_KEY}
      - FABRIC_CA_SERVER_PORT=7054
    ports:
      - "7054:7054"
    command: sh -c 'fabric-ca-server start --ca.certfile /etc/hyperledger/
fabric-ca-server-config/ca.org1.example.com-cert.pem --ca.keyfile /etc/hy-
perledger/fabric-ca-server-config/${CA0_PRIVATE_KEY} -b admin:adminpw -d'
    volumes:
      - ./crypto-config/peerOrganizations/org1.example.com/ca/:/etc/hy-
perledger/fabric-ca-server-config
    container_name: ca_peerOrg1
    networks:
      - fabric
  cli:
    container_name: cli
```

```
    image: hyperledger/fabric-tools
    tty: true
    stdin_open: true
    environment:
      - SYS_CHANNEL=voip2orgs-sys-channel
      - GOPATH=/opt/gopath
      - CORE_VM_ENDPOINT=unix:///host/var/run/docker.sock
      - CORE_PEER_ID=cli
      - CORE_PEER_ADDRESS=peer0.org1.example.com:7051
      - CORE_PEER_LOCALMSPID=Org1MSP
      - CORE_PEER_TLS_ENABLED=true
      - CORE_CHAINCODE_EXECUTETIMEOUT=300
      - CORE_PEER_TLS_CERT_FILE=/opt/gopath/src/github.com/hyperledger/fabric/
peer/crypto/peerOrganizations/org1.example.com/peers/peer0.org1.example.com/
tls/server.crt
      - CORE_PEER_TLS_KEY_FILE=/opt/gopath/src/github.com/hyperledger/fabric/
peer/crypto/peerOrganizations/org1.example.com/peers/peer0.org1.example.com/
tls/server.key
      - CORE_PEER_TLS_ROOTCERT_FILE=/opt/gopath/src/github.com/hyperledger/
fabric/peer/crypto/peerOrganizations/org1.example.com/peers/peer0.org1.exam-
ple.com/tls/ca.crt
      - CORE_PEER_MSPCONFIGPATH=/opt/gopath/src/github.com/hyperledger/fabric/
peer/crypto/peerOrganizations/org1.example.com/users/Admin@org1.example.com/
msp
    working_dir: /opt/gopath/src/github.com/hyperledger/fabric/peer
    command: /bin/bash
    extra_hosts:
        - "peer0.org2.example.com:91.205.172.208"
        - "orderer.example.com:178.63.22.17"
    volumes:
        - /var/run/:/host/var/run/
        - ./../chaincode/:/opt/gopath/src/github.com/chaincode
        - ./crypto-config:/opt/gopath/src/github.com/hyperledger/fabric/peer/
crypto/
        - ./channel-artifacts:/opt/gopath/src/github.com/hyperledger/fabric/
peer/channel-artifacts
    depends_on:
      - peer0.org1.example.com
    networks:
      - fabric
```

In one Docker Compose file one can describe more than one services that he wishes to start. In this file are configured: a peer service that runs the Hyperledger Fabric peer software; a couchdb service, a

NoSQL database used for the ledger; a certificate authority service (ca); a cli service which is used to access indirectly the peer container.

For the peer service the settings extend those of the peer-base service in peer-base.yaml file. The environment variables of this peer define that the ledger database to be used is couchdb and include the username and password to access the database, and the host and port number (couchdb1:5984). Since the installation does not take place in only one machine, extra_hosts are used to let the peer know where it can reach the orderer and peer0.org2.example.com. extra_hosts add entries to the /etc/hosts file in the same way as they are entered in the YAML file. It is important to mount the directories containing the digital certificates and keys created with cryptogen, otherwise the peer will not be able to prove its identity. A volume with the same name is defined and mounted in /var/hyperledger/production to provide data persistence when the containers are restarted. Port 7051 is exposed for this container so that it can be reached from outside in this same port.

For the couchdb service the image used is fabric-couchdb that was downloaded during installation of Hyperledger Fabric. In the environment variables section are defined the user and password that a client must use to access it. These credentials must exactly match the ones defined in the peer's environment variables. The port exposed for this container is 5984, which also matches the one configured for the peer.

The image used for the certificate authority service is fabric-ca. In the environment variables section is defined the location for the TLS certificate and key and the port where the service will listen for requests. This port is later exposed for access. The CA server certificates created with cryptogen are mounted in the same way as done with the peer service.

The cli service is used to run commands indirectly on the peer container. That is why the command issued upon startup is /bin/bash. The smart contracts will be installed and instantiated using this service, and it is important to mount the directory containing their source code.

All these services are on the same network declared at the beginning named fabric.

The configuration is just about the same in the peer0-org2 file with exception of the extra_hosts section. The contents of the file are as below:

```
version: '2'
volumes:
  peer0.org2.example.com:
networks:
  fabric:
services:
  peer0.org2.example.com:
    container_name: peer0.org2.example.com
    extends:
      file: peer-base.yaml
      service: peer-base
    environment:
      - CORE_PEER_ID=peer0.org2.example.com
      - CORE_PEER_ADDRESS=peer0.org2.example.com:7051
      - CORE_PEER_LISTENADDRESS=0.0.0.0:7051
      - CORE_PEER_CHAINCODEADDRESS=peer0.org2.example.com:7052
      - CORE_PEER_CHAINCODELISTENADDRESS=0.0.0.0:7052
```

```
        - CORE_PEER_GOSSIP_BOOTSTRAP=peer0.org1.example.com:7051
        - CORE_PEER_GOSSIP_EXTERNALENDPOINT=peer0.org2.example.com:7051
        - CORE_PEER_LOCALMSPID=Org2MSP
        - CORE_CHAINCODE_EXECUTETIMEOUT=300
        - CORE_LEDGER_STATE_STATEDATABASE=CouchDB
        - CORE_LEDGER_STATE_COUCHDBCONFIG_COUCHDBADDRESS=couchdb1:5984
        - CORE_LEDGER_STATE_COUCHDBCONFIG_USERNAME=
        - CORE_LEDGER_STATE_COUCHDBCONFIG_PASSWORD=
      extra_hosts:
        - "orderer.example.com:178.63.22.17"
        - "peer0.org1.example.com:195.201.242.35"
      volumes:
          - /var/run/:/host/var/run/
          - ./crypto-config/peerOrganizations/org2.example.com/peers/peer0.org2.
example.com/msp:/etc/hyperledger/fabric/msp
          - ./crypto-config/peerOrganizations/org2.example.com/peers/peer0.org2.
example.com/tls:/etc/hyperledger/fabric/tls
          - ./crypto-config/peerOrganizations/org1.example.com/peers/peer0.org1.
example.com/msp:/etc/hyperledger/fabric/org1/msp
          - ./crypto-config/peerOrganizations/org1.example.com/peers/peer0.org1.
example.com/tls:/etc/hyperledger/fabric/org1/tls
          - peer0.org2.example.com:/var/hyperledger/production
      ports:
        - 7051:7051
      networks:
        - fabric
      depends_on:
        - couchdb1
    couchdb1:
      container_name: couchdb1
      image: hyperledger/fabric-couchdb
      environment:
        - COUCHDB_USER=
        - COUCHDB_PASSWORD=
      ports:
        - "5984:5984"
      networks:
        - fabric
    ca1:
      image: hyperledger/fabric-ca
      environment:
        - FABRIC_CA_HOME=/etc/hyperledger/fabric-ca-server
        - FABRIC_CA_SERVER_CA_NAME=ca-org2
        - FABRIC_CA_SERVER_TLS_ENABLED=true
```

```
      - FABRIC_CA_SERVER_TLS_CERTFILE=/etc/hyperledger/fabric-ca-server-con-
fig/ca.org2.example.com-cert.pem
      - FABRIC_CA_SERVER_TLS_KEYFILE=/etc/hyperledger/fabric-ca-server-
config/${CA1_PRIVATE_KEY}
      - FABRIC_CA_SERVER_PORT=7054
    ports:
      - "7054:7054"
    command: sh -c 'fabric-ca-server start --ca.certfile /etc/hyperledger/
fabric-ca-server-config/ca.org2.example.com-cert.pem --ca.keyfile /etc/hy-
perledger/fabric-ca-server-config/${CA1_PRIVATE_KEY} -b admin:adminpw -d'
    volumes:
      - ./crypto-config/peerOrganizations/org2.example.com/ca/:/etc/hy-
perledger/fabric-ca-server-config
    container_name: ca_peerOrg2
    networks:
      - fabric
  cli:
    container_name: cli
    image: hyperledger/fabric-tools
    tty: true
    stdin_open: true
    environment:
      - SYS_CHANNEL=voip2orgs-sys-channel
      - GOPATH=/opt/gopath
      - CORE_VM_ENDPOINT=unix:///host/var/run/docker.sock
      - CORE_PEER_ID=cli
      - CORE_PEER_ADDRESS=peer0.org2.example.com:7051
      - CORE_PEER_LOCALMSPID=Org2MSP
      - CORE_PEER_TLS_ENABLED=true
      - CORE_CHAINCODE_EXECUTETIMEOUT=300
      - CORE_PEER_TLS_CERT_FILE=/opt/gopath/src/github.com/hyperledger/fabric/
peer/crypto/peerOrganizations/org2.example.com/peers/peer0.org2.example.com/
tls/server.crt
      - CORE_PEER_TLS_KEY_FILE=/opt/gopath/src/github.com/hyperledger/fabric/
peer/crypto/peerOrganizations/org2.example.com/peers/peer0.org2.example.com/
tls/server.key
      - CORE_PEER_TLS_ROOTCERT_FILE=/opt/gopath/src/github.com/hyperledger/
fabric/peer/crypto/peerOrganizations/org2.example.com/peers/peer0.org2.exam-
ple.com/tls/ca.crt
      - CORE_PEER_MSPCONFIGPATH=/opt/gopath/src/github.com/hyperledger/fabric/
peer/crypto/peerOrganizations/org2.example.com/users/Admin@org2.example.com/
msp
    working_dir: /opt/gopath/src/github.com/hyperledger/fabric/peer
    command: /bin/bash
```

```
    extra_hosts:
      - "orderer.example.com:178.63.22.17"
      - "peer0.org1.example.com:195.201.242.35"
    volumes:
        - /var/run/:/host/var/run/
        - ./../chaincode/:/opt/gopath/src/github.com/chaincode
        - ./crypto-config:/opt/gopath/src/github.com/hyperledger/fabric/peer/
crypto/
        - ./channel-artifacts:/opt/gopath/src/github.com/hyperledger/fabric/
peer/channel-artifacts
    depends_on:
      - peer0.org2.example.com
    networks:
      - fabric
```

In orderer.yaml is defined the orderer service. The orderer node will run only this service, so only the orderer service is defined in this file, as shown below:

```
version: '2'
volumes:
  orderer.example.com:
networks:
  fabric:
services:
  orderer.example.com:
    container_name: orderer.example.com
    extends:
      file: peer-base.yaml
      service: orderer-base
    extra_hosts:
        - "peer0.org1.example.com:195.201.242.35"
        - "peer0.org2.example.com:91.205.172.208"
    volumes:
        - ./channel-artifacts/genesis.block:/var/hyperledger/orderer/orderer.
genesis.block
        - ./crypto-config/ordererOrganizations/example.com/orderers/orderer.
example.com/msp:/var/hyperledger/orderer/msp
        - ./crypto-config/ordererOrganizations/example.com/orderers/orderer.
example.com/tls/:/var/hyperledger/orderer/tls
        - orderer.example.com:/var/hyperledger/production/orderer
    ports:
      - 7050:7050
    networks:
      - fabric
```

The configurations of this file extend the orderer-base service in the peer-base.yaml file. In a similar fashion to other services, extra_hosts are used to add the public IP addresses of the other two servers in this container. The orderer will listen to port 7050 for requests, so this port is exposed to be reachable from the peers. The genesis block generated with configtxgen is mounted on the container filesystem so the orderer can only follow requests from allowed peers.
The commands executed to start the containers are:

```
docker-compose -f peer0-org1.yaml up -d
docker-compose -f peer0-org2.yaml up -d
docker-compose -f orderer.yaml up -d
```

Smart Contract Development and Instantiation

Hyperledger Fabric allows for chaincode developing in different languages. Currently, languages such as Go, Java and Nodejs are supported. For this project the programming is done using JavaScript.

The Business Case Concept

A route to a destination has a few features more other than its price. All of them are discussed between companies before reaching an agreement on doing business. The traits of the route are stored digitally in the form of a business case. The business cases are thought of as private or public ones, the difference being in that only public ones are stored on the blockchain network.

Public business cases – in this paper referred to as HLF (stands for Hyperledger Fabric) business cases – describe information that both the buyer and the seller of the route know. This information includes the price per minute of an answered call, route type, prefixes toward which calls can be terminated etc. The managers of both the buyer and the seller have agreed on these terms, so a business case is created with this information and it can be stored on the blockchain network, as both parties know about it. Storing it in the ledger means that the terms are immutable, and no discrepancies will arise at a later time.

Different from the ones just explained, private business cases should not be stored on the ledger. The reason is because the information they store is sensitive and if revealed it could be damaging to the business. Privately, companies store in the form of a business case information about their buyer and their seller of the route, the terms they have reached an agreement with both the buyer and the seller, and the calculated Return on Investment for that route. If the buyer or the seller were to get this information, they could directly do business together, hence eliminating the middle man and increasing profit.

The Business Cases Chaincode

Having said that, there is the need to develop a smart contract for storing the public business cases in the ledger. This smart contract must give the possibility to create new business cases, update existing ones, and to query the ledger for a business case by some sort of ID.
The business case smart contract code developed in JavaScript is as below:

```
'use strict';
const shim = require('fabric-shim');
const util = require('util');

let Chaincode = class {

  async Init(stub) {
    console.info('=========== Instantiated businesscase chaincode
===========');
    return shim.success();
  }

  async Invoke(stub) {
    let ret = stub.getFunctionAndParameters();
    console.info(ret);

    let method = this[ret.fcn];
    if (!method) {
      console.error('no function of name:' + ret.fcn + ' found');
      throw new Error('Received unknown function ' + ret.fcn + ' invocation');
    }
    try {
      let payload = await method(stub, ret.params);
      return shim.success(payload);
    } catch (err) {
      console.log(err);
      return shim.error(err);
    }
  }

  async queryBC(stub, args) {
    if (args.length != 1) {
      throw new Error('Incorrect number of arguments. Expecting BCNumber.');
    }
    let BCNumber = args[0];

    let BCAsBytes = await stub.getState(BCNumber); //get the business case
from chaincode state
    if (!BCAsBytes || BCAsBytes.toString().length <= 0) {
      throw new Error(BCNumber + ' does not exist: ');
    }
    console.log(BCAsBytes.toString());
    return BCAsBytes;
  }
```

```
  async initLedger(stub, args) {
    console.info('============= START: Initialize Ledger ===========');
    console.info('============= END: Initialize Ledger ===========');
  }

  async createBC(stub, args) {
    console.info('============= START: Create BC ===========');
    if (args.length != 9) {
      throw new Error('Incorrect number of arguments. Expecting 9');
    }

    var BC = {
      docType: 'BusinessCase',
      destination: args[1],
      buyer: args[2],
      seller: args[3],
      price: args[4],
      prefixList: args[5],
      techPrefix: args[6],
      trafficType: args[7],
      status:args[8]
    };

    await stub.putState(args[0], Buffer.from(JSON.stringify(BC)));
    console.info('============= END: Create BC ===========');
  }

  async changeBCStatus(stub, args) {
    console.info('============= START: changeBCStatus ===========');
    if (args.length != 1) {
      throw new Error('Incorrect number of arguments. Expecting 1');
    }

    let BCAsBytes = await stub.getState(args[0]);
    let BC = JSON.parse(BCAsBytes);
    BC.status = "Non Active";

    await stub.putState(args[0], Buffer.from(JSON.stringify(BC)));
    console.info('============= END: changeBCStatus ===========');
  }
};
shim.start(new Chaincode());
```

The functions developed in this smart contract are initLedger, Invoke, queryBC, createBC and changeBCStatus.

initLedger is used only once after the chaincode has been instantiated in the channel for the purpose of initializing the ledger.

Invoke is a function used to invoke other functions. It reads the name of the function passed as an argument and calls that function in the smart contract passing the rest of arguments to the function called.

queryBC is the function that gives the possibility to read the ledger. It takes one argument which is the business case ID and returns the business case if it exists.

createBC is used to create new business cases in the blockchain network. It takes many arguments in order to complete the information of the business case. This information includes the route's destination name; the names of the buyer and seller companies; the price of the route; the list of prefixes toward which calls can be completed; a technical prefix that must be added before the number called by the buyer; the traffic type, if the caller ID goes through unchanged or not; the status of the business case.

changeBCStatus is a function used to change the status property of the business case to "Not Active". Business cases, when created, are active. This means that the route is opened for traffic on the terms described by the business case. In case one of the terms changes, the business case must be updated. Rather than updating it, a new one is created instead, and the old one is changed to not active, which means that no route exists with those terms between the two companies. This function does not take any arguments, because there is only one possibility, if the function is called the status is set to "Not Active".

The package.json file for this chaincode should be as shown below:

```
{
    "name": "businesscase",
    "version": "1.0.0",
    "description": "businesscase chaincode implemented in node.js",
    "engines": {
        "node": ">=8.4.0",
        "npm": ">=5.3.0"
    },
    "scripts": {
        "start": "node businesscase.js"
    },
    "engine-strict": true,
    "license": "Apache-2.0",
    "dependencies": {
        "fabric-shim": "~1.4.0"
    }
}
```

In the dependencies section is included the fabric-shim module which provides the chaincode interface along with implementation to support communication with Hyperledger Fabric peer nodes.

The business cases are usually created by account managers. An interface could be created to retrieve information needed for the parameters of the functions in a client application and perform the operations from there.

Setup and Configuration

With both Asterisk and MariaDB installed, there is the need to connect Asterisk to a MySQL back-end to store CDRs. For that purpose, ODBC is installed and used. The steps to do so can be found in Asterisk's documentation (Asterisk, 2020). Asterisk creates an ID for each call and stores it in the cdr_table. This variable is named uniqueid, but according to the documentation there is no guarantee that this ID will be unique across all channels. So, a new ID is created to distinguish a call in the Hyperledger network. This new ID is composed of the uniqueid, SIP call ID, and the EPOCH at the time the call is started. The first member of the blockchain network to receive a call generates this ID and it passes it along until the last member of the blockchain network receives it. This member is going to forward the call outside the network, so it must not forward the Hyperledger Fabric ID for the call.

It would be costly to create a separate mechanism to distribute the ID between Asterisk servers, because a communication would be set up and teared down for each call. The method used to let the Asterisk peer know of the ID is including it in the INVITE SIP message that starts the call. Asterisk provides an application called SIPAddHeader which gives the opportunity to add non-standard headers to the SIP INVITE. To read this header a function named SIP_HEADER is used, which stores the content of the header in a variable.

PERFORMANCE TESTING

Invoking the Chaincode From Command Line

To test the performance of the solution, the configuration script was modified to limit the number of transactions to submit to the peer software. First, some calls were generated using sipp, a tool to simulate SIP traffic with different scenarios. After accumulating several calls in the cdr_to_be_inserted table, insert_to_hlf.php was executed manually with different settings regarding the transactions per second limit. The command executed from this script was slightly modified to write the time of completion for each command on a text file. Eleven iterations were made with different TPS values starting from one to one hundred. After each test, the contents of the text file were gathered, and an average time of execution was calculated. Tests were made only for the chaincode that stores CDRs on the blockchain network, as this is the chaincode that would be mostly used in a real scenario. The results of the tests are shown in the table 1.

Table 1. Latency test results using command line

Transactions per Second	Latency(s)
1	0.26
10	6.530
20	11.485
30	16.019
40	20.831
50	28.315
60	34.642
70	39.955
80	47.781
90	53.058
100	56.670

Invoking the Chaincode From Client Application

Before starting with this test, the smart contract for the CDRs was re-programmed in order to make it possible for a client application to invoke it. The same testing method is used with eleven iterations starting from 1 CDR to 100. The results are presented in the table 2.

Table 2. Latency test results using Node SDK

Transactions per Second	Latency(s)
1	3.59
10	7.31
20	14.02
30	21.36
40	28.06
50	37.01
60	42.40
70	51.11
80	56.19
90	64.19
100	69.99

Submitting CDRs in Bulk

For this method, a new function is created in the CDR chaincode giving the possibility to insert multiple CDRs at the same time in one transaction. The chaincode is still invoked using the Node SDK. The new function is presented in Table 3.

Table 3. Latency test results in bulk insertion

Batch Size	Latency(s)
1	3.42
10	3.79
20	4.50
30	4.62
40	5.09
50	5.04
60	5.52
70	5.81
80	6.17
90	6.75
100	6.94

Results Assessment

Previous versions of Hyperledger Fabric (before version 1.0) were lacking in performance, but with newer version releases the developing team has addressed a lot of issues regarding performance (Elli, 2018). With the release used in this paper (version 1.4), the performance achieved during testing is about 3,500 transactions per second with a latency of less than one second. According to (Thakkar et al, 2018), changing different aspects of transaction processing, the performance of Hyperledger Fabric could go up to 20,000 transactions per second. From the test results the latency is not in these levels but taking into consideration that the testing is done in a development network, and the number of queries performed for each CDR, the results are promising, at least for the third method tested. For the first two methods the latency is very high compared to the third one.

Figure 4. Performance comparison of input methods

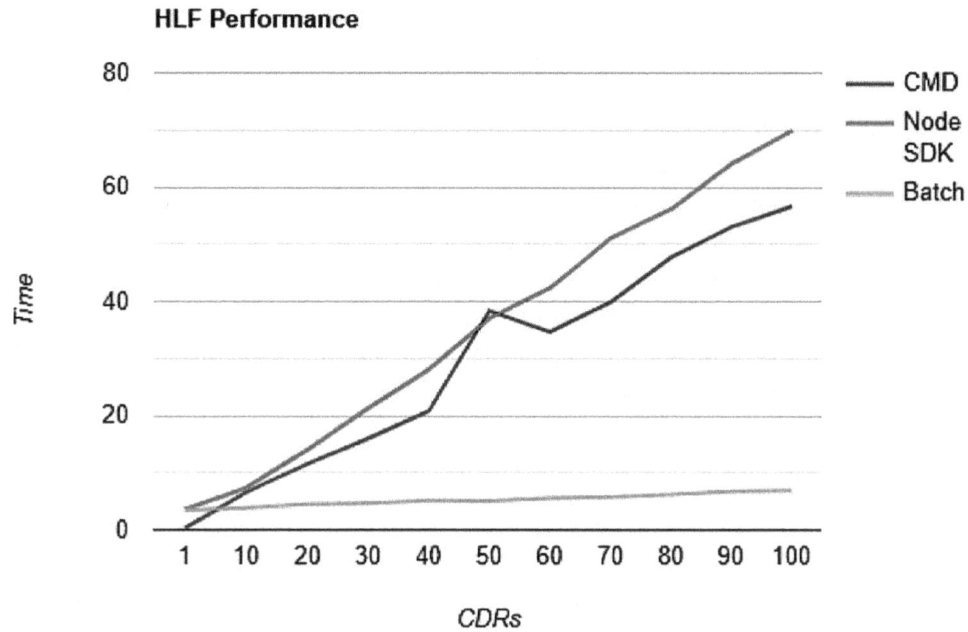

The reason is because when submitting CDR using the first two methods, a transaction was needed for each CDR. The peer that had to submit these was heavily loaded, as it needed to check the responses for every transaction and then submit these. While the network might be able to handle thousands of transactions, a single peer is not able to do so. In the third method all CDRs are included in a batch, which is then submitted in a single transaction. The number of CDRs is variable but the transaction still remains a single one, explaining the almost constant latency in the yellow line.

CONCLUSION

In this paper the authors have presented a blockchain-based approach for avoiding risk of disputes among Carriers in telecommunications. In particular, it has been proposed an approach for using Hyperledger Fabric as a framework for storing Call Detail Records (CDRs) and Business Cases in a blockchain network. The necessary steps and configurations for integrating the different technologies and building a development network were presented. Lastly performance tests regarding the latency for a transaction submission were made and the results show the effectiveness of the proposed approach.

From the point of view of avoiding dispute risks, through the proposed approach once the information is stored in the blockchain network, it becomes immutable and none of the parties can claim different values from those in the network. This would avoid any kind of dispute among Carriers as all billing information would be completely stored in the blockchain network and could be used by both billing teams to reconcile any discrepancy that they might find in their internal local billing systems due to internal system anomalies. Effectively, once the data are stored in the network, there is no possibility that each Carrier finds different data locally leading therefore to a very safe and effective procedure for avoiding the risk of disputes.

From the performance point of view, it is recommended to keep the number of transactions as low as possible in a peer, and if there is the possibility to accumulate data before being submitted to the blockchain network, this option should be preferred. Although this approach makes it harder to query the ledger for a single CDR, there is no real need to do so, because the information stored in the ledger is replicated in local MySQL databases. It is far more efficient and simpler to make these queries locally, instead of loading the blockchain network. Lastly, the latency may not be in milliseconds, but it is still suitable for this business scenario because the numbers approach the number of calls that could go through an Asterisk server in real scenarios.

As future work the authors plan to extend experiments to a larger number of transactions that involve also cluster installations. Very often, switching systems used by Carriers are installed in cluster architectures and it is interesting to investigate how the proposed approach would scale also for the scenario where softswitch nodes are organized under a cluster which as a single entity produces a very high number of CDRs.

REFERENCES

Alsaqqa, S., & Almajali, S. (2020). Blockchain Technology Consensus Algorithms and Applications: A Survey. *International Journal of Interactive Mobile Technologies*, *14*(15), 142. Advance online publication. doi:10.3991/ijim.v14i15.15893

Asterisk. (2020). https://www.asterisk.org/

Awan, S., Ahmed, S., Nawaz, A., Maghdid, S., Zaman, K., Ali, M. Y., Khan, Z., & Saeed, S. (2020). BlockChain with IoT, an Emergent Routing Scheme for Smart Agriculture. *International Journal of Advanced Computer Science and Applications*, *11*(4). Advance online publication. doi:10.14569/IJACSA.2020.0110457

Chakraborty, T., Misra, I. S., & Prasad, R. (2019). Overview of VoIP Technology. In *VoIP Technology: Applications and Challenges. Springer Series in Wireless Technology*. Springer. doi:10.1007/978-3-319-95594-0_1

CouchDB as the State Database. (2020). *CouchDB as the State Database — Hyperledger - Fabricdocs Master Documentation*. https://hyperledger-fabric.readthedocs.io/en/release-1.4/couchdb_as_state_database.html

Elli, A., Barger, A., Bortnikov, V., Cachin, C., Christidis, K., De Caro, A., & Enyeart. (2018). Hyperledger Fabric: A Distributed Operating System for Permissioned Blockchains. *Proceedings of the Thirteenth EuroSys Conference on - EuroSys '18*, 1–15. 10.1145/3190508.3190538

Hyperledger. (2020). *Hyperledger – Open Source Blockchain Technologies*. https://www.hyperledger.org/

Hyperledger - Fabricdocs Master Documentation. (2020). *Introduction — Hyperledger-Fabricdocs Master Documentation*. https://hyperledger-fabric.readthedocs.io/en/release-1.4/blockchain.html

Issaoui, Y., Khiat, A., Bahnasse, A., & Ouajji, H. (2020). Smart Logistics: Blockchain trends and applications. *Journal of Ubiquitous Systems and Pervasive Networks.*, *12*(2), 9–15. doi:10.5383/JUSPN.12.02.002

Maria, D. B. (2020). *Maria DB 2020*. https://mariadb.org/documentation/

Narayanan, A., Bonneau, J., Felten, E., Miller, A., & Goldfeder, S. (2016). *Bitcoin and cryptocurrency technologies: a comprehensive introduction*. Princeton University Press.

Nizamuddin, N., & Abugabah, A. (2021). Blockchain for automotive: An insight towards the IPFS blockchain-based auto insurance sector. *Iranian Journal of Electrical and Computer Engineering*, *11*(3), 2443–2456. doi:10.11591/ijece.v11i3.pp2443-2456

Queralta, J. P., & Westerlund, T. (2019). *Blockchain-Powered Collaboration in Heterogeneous Swarms of Robots*. Cryptography and Security.

SIP. (2019). *RFC 3261 - SIP: Session Initiation Protocol*. https://tools.ietf.org/html/rfc3261#page-8

Swale, R., & Collins, D. (2013). Carrier Grade Voice Over IP (3rd ed.). McGraw-Hill.

Thakkar, P., Nathan, S., & Viswanathan, B. (2018). Performance Benchmarking and Optimizing Hyperledger Fabric Blockchain Platform. In *2018 IEEE 26th International Symposium on Modeling, Analysis, and Simulation of Computer and Telecommunication Systems (MASCOTS)*. 10.1109/MASCOTS.2018.00034

Turnbull, J. (2014). *The Docker Book*. Lulu.com.

Xu, J., Tian, Y., Ma, T., & Al-Nabhan, N. (2020). Najla Al-Nabhan. Intelligent manufacturing security model based on improved blockchain. *Mathematical Biosciences and Engineering*, *17*(5), 5633–5650. doi:10.3934/mbe.2020303 PMID:33120570

Zavolokina, L., Ziolkowski, R., Bauer, I., & Schwabe, G. (2020). Management, Governance and Value Creation in a Blockchain Consortium. *MIS Quarterly Executive*, *19*(1), 1–17. Advance online publication. doi:10.17705/2msqe.00022

ADDITIONAL READING

Islam, A., & Shin, S. Y. (2019, October). BUAV: A blockchain based secure UAV-assisted data acquisition scheme in Internet of Things. *Journal of Communications and Networks (Seoul)*, *21*(5), 491–502. doi:10.1109/JCN.2019.000050

Manogaran, G., Alazab, M., Shakeel, P. M., & Hsu, C.-H. (2022, March). Blockchain Assisted Secure Data Sharing Model for Internet of Things Based Smart Industries. *IEEE Transactions on Reliability*, *71*(1), 348–358. doi:10.1109/TR.2020.3047833

Manogaran, G., Alazab, M., Shakeel, P. M., & Hsu, C.-H. (2022, March). Blockchain Assisted Secure Data Sharing Model for Internet of Things Based Smart Industries. *IEEE Transactions on Reliability*, *71*(1), 348–358. doi:10.1109/TR.2020.3047833

Singh, S., Hosen, A. S. M. S., & Yoon, B. (2021). Blockchain Security Attacks, Challenges, and Solutions for the Future Distributed IoT Network. *IEEE Access: Practical Innovations, Open Solutions*, *9*, 13938–13959. doi:10.1109/ACCESS.2021.3051602

KEY TERMS AND DEFINITIONS

Blockchain: Shared, immutable ledger that facilitates the process of recording transactions and tracking assets in a business network.

Call Details Record: A record in the database of the telecommunication platform containing the details of a voice call.

Carrier: A provider of trans receiver functionalities via mobile communication system to users of mobile devices that are sold, rented, leased, or otherwise provided to them with such providers' trademarks.

Hyperledger: A multi-project open source collaborative effort hosted by The Linux Foundation, created to advance cross-industry blockchain technologies.

Session Initiation Protocol (SIP): A signaling protocol used for initiating, maintaining, and terminating real-time sessions that include voice, video and messaging applications.

Smart Contract: Programs stored on a blockchain that run when predetermined conditions are met.

Softswitch: A call-switching node in a telecommunications network, based not on the specialized switching hardware of the traditional telephone exchange, but implemented in software running on a general-purpose computing platform.

Voice Over Internet Protocol (VoIP): A technology that allows you to make voice calls using a broadband Internet connection instead of a regular (or analog) phone line.

Chapter 9
Cybersecurity Risk:
Assessment and Management

Natasha Cecilia Edeh
American University of Nigeria, Nigeria

Ibiene Idu
American University of Nigeria, Nigeria

ABSTRACT

This chapter gives an all-inclusive view of cybersecurity risk. The main aim of this chapter is to explain what cybersecurity risk entails. This chapter starts by describing why cybersecurity risk is vital to organizations. The authors explain cybersecurity, vulnerabilities, and common cyber threats/attacks. This chapter also highlights some literature on cybersecurity risks in different sectors and gives an idea about the numerous cyber-attacks during the COVID-19 pandemic. The other sections of this chapter explain risk, risk assessment methods/approaches used in determining the level and type of risk, and risk management frameworks alongside examples from literature and how they were employed to manage risks. Finally, this chapter concludes with the role of organizations in handling and managing cybersecurity risks and the steps governments, organizations, stakeholders, and individuals should take when trying to mitigate or manage cybersecurity risks now and in the future.

INTRODUCTION

As businesses embrace digital change and use advanced technology solutions to boost corporate development and efficiency, cybersecurity risk has risen to the top of their priority list (Lee, 2021). Furthermore, many businesses are becoming increasingly reliant on third- and fourth-party merchants or plans. While these tools might help to unlock and grow businesses, they also offer new risks and increase the size of cyber-attacks (Rea-Guaman, San Feliu, Calvo-Manzano, & Sanchez-Garcia, 2018).Organisations/businesses must constantly prioritize the protection of their assets and information technology setup (Bada, Sasse, & Nurse, 2014). During the Covid-19 pandemic, securing and safeguarding organisations from cybersecurity attacks became extremely difficult because to ensure continuity, organisations abruptly

DOI: 10.4018/978-1-6684-5279-0.ch009

had to transition to remote work, and protecting against new cyber dangers became a major worry for most businesses (Pranggono & Arabo, 2021). One of the most typical blunders organisations make is failing to grasp the full scope of the risk they are taking on when dealing with these additional resources like third-party vendors (Fedele & Roner, 2022; Hasan, Ali, Kurnia, & Thurasamy, 2021). Organisations may better manage and mitigate risks-including cybersecurity risk-before they become major problems when everyone in the organisation knows what to look for and what to do if an issue rises (Bada et al., 2014). When it comes to cyber threats, organisations tend to place more emphasis on outside threats and the technical aspects than internal threats. Gundu (2019) argued that employees in organisations (which includes internal threats) routinely engage in risky behaviours as well as inexperienced mistakes that jeopardize the security, privacy, and credibility of the organisation's data. The effects of human factors in cybersecurity was further stressed by Jeong, Mihelcic, Oliver, and Rudolph (2019) Their research, which looked at the subjective and frequently intricate nature of human variables, found that there is still a strong technical focus on cybersecurity that ignores human factors. Many organisations invest heavily on cybersecurity protection but fail to properly educate their workers on cybersecurity threats resulting in a cybersecurity risk management gap (Aldawood & Skinner, 2019b). This suggests that procedures to mitigate cybersecurity risks in an organisation will not be effective if the workers are not knowledge about these how to use them. A study by Sadok, Alter, and Bednar (2020) also concluded that Corporate policies that emphasize information security are frequently separated from daily work practices and routines, and the great majority of employees are not included in risk assessment or the development of security standards. A literature review was conducted to meet the desired objectives of this study, and because it is repeatable, it also serves as a foundation for future research. The literature review was conducted based on previous research that employed a literature review approach (Humayun, Niazi, Jhanjhi, Alshayeb, & Mahmood, 2020). For these reasons, this chapter aims to provide insights on how to effectively assess and manage cybersecurity risk by asking the question; How effective are the approaches for assessing and managing cybersecurity risks considering human factors?

BACKGROUND

Cyber Security

This can be defined as the state of being safeguarded from unlawful or unauthorized use of electronic data, as well as the steps are taken to do so (Park, Shi, Zhang, Kontovas, & Chang, 2019). It is a field that aims to protect computer systems against attacks, which can include control systems, vital infrastructure, and technology transportation systems (Priyadarshini, 2018). Cybersecurity attacks can result in a variety of risks affecting vital infrastructure and continuation of business including production and performance deterioration, absence of vital services, and regulatory violations (Kure, Islam, & Razzaque, 2018).

Threat

A is an incident's ability to have a negative influence on your organisation's systems and assets. These could be activities performed to profit from security breaches while also having a negative influence on them (Humayun et al., 2020). All purposeful crimes against others utilizing a computer are referred to as "cyber security threats." Cyber security threats might target a single computer, a system, a network, or a collection of them. Scam, robbery, network disabling, data exploitation, and harassment are among the offenses. Studies have shown that there are several types of cyber security threats or attacks some of which are listed and explained below based on a report by sobers (2021).

1. The most common sort of cyberattack is a malware attack. Malware is a harmful software, such as spyware, ransomware, viruses, and worms, that is placed on a computer when a user clicks on a malicious link or email. Malware can block access to essential network components, harm the system, and collect confidential information, among other things, once it has gained access to the system. The average cost of a malware assault, according to Accenture, a professional services firm that specializes in information technology services and consulting, is USD 2.6 million.
2. Phishing: An email-based attack in which the email receiver is duped into giving private data or downloading malware by clicking on a link in the message. Cybercriminals send phishing emails that appear to come from reputable sources. Over 80% of reported cyber issues are due to phishing attacks.
3. Denial of Service Attack: A cyber attacker takes control of a large number of devices and uses them to call the operations of a target system, such as a website, making it crash due to a demand overload.
4. SQL injection: This attack uses any of the known SQL vulnerabilities to run malicious code on the SQL server. When fraudsters try to access a database by downloading malicious SQL scripts, it is referred to as a SQL injection attack. Once the malicious actor has gained access to the SQL database, he or she can view, modify, or remove data contained within. Nearly 65.1 percent of all web application assaults are caused by SQL injection.
5. When cyber thieves insert themselves in the middle of a two-way conversation, this is known as a Man in the Middle (MitM) assault. Once the attacker has deciphered the message, they may screen and take sensitive information, as well as provide the user with various incorrect responses. MitM is vulnerable to 95 percent of HTTPS servers, according to Netcraft.
6. Password attack: A cyber attacker can gain access to a vast amount of data with the appropriate password. Social engineering is a sort of password assault used by cybercriminals that are primarily reliant on human interaction and frequently involves duping people into violating common security procedures. Getting into a password database or guessing openly are two other methods of password assaults.
7. Ransomware: Ransomware is a sort of computer attack whereby the attacker encrypts or locks the data of the victim and threatens to circulate or prevent access to the data except a ransom is paid. By 2021, ransomware attacks are expected to cost global companies USD 20 billion.
8. The activity of exploiting human flaws through manipulation in order to achieve a harmful aim is known as social engineering. As a result of the pandemic, individuals and organisations are more vulnerable to social engineering challenges than ever before. The most popular targets of cyber attackers are huge telecommunication corporations and other comparable organisations with large client bases and a large collection of sensitive data.

Organisations may have known and undisclosed weaknesses in their organisational infrastructure, which can result in security invasions and other issues (Humayun et al., 2020).

Vulnerability

Is a security flaw, a fault, or a vulnerable part that allows cybercriminals to access an organisation's data, equipment, or other resources without authorization (Ulven & Wangen, 2021).The possibility of a threat exploiting a vulnerability causing a loss or damage to assets in an organisation is characterized as a risk (Sardi, Rizzi, Sorano, & Guerrieri, 2020).

Cybersecurity Risk/Cyber Risk

This refers to the likelihood of an organisation being exposed to or losing money as a result of a cyber-attack or data breach (Sardi et al., 2020). The potential loss or injury to an organisation's technological infrastructure, use of technology, or reputation is a better, more comprehensive description. People's activities, as well as system and technology failures, are key cyber risks (Wang & Alexander, 2021). Allodi and Massacci (2017) also in their research stated that people's behaviours are a source of operational risk; however, cybersecurity risks are usually caused by a "human" or "sentient actor" who initiates the attack. Based on these definitions cyber-attacks can be classified into:

- **Targeted attacks**: these incidents are defined as attacks that are directed primarily or virtually solely at certain facilities and often necessitate a high level of sophistication. According to recent surveys, only a small percentage of cyberattacks against companies and consumer systems are of this nature.
- **Untargeted attacks**: Attacks that are untargeted are those in which the targets are not distinguishable from one another by any unique trait or characteristic and are simply reached by the attack.

LITERATURE OF CYBERSECURITY RISKS IN DIFFERENT SECTORS

(Sardi et al., 2020) in their paper, studied literature on cyber risk in the healthcare sector using a methodical and rigorous technique to highlight the true expertise on this topic. To begin, they looked at the primary bibliometric data on cyber risk to determine the main publication trend on the subject. Additionally, they sorted the selected papers based on the principal risk they were dealing with. They completed the study by pointing out that there were insufficient studies on cyber risk in the healthcare sector and advising that the health sector, particularly in light of the Covid-19 pandemic, requires novel management methods to combat cyber-attacks.

Another study by Kure et al. (2018) focuses on a cybersecurity risk management approach for a cyber-physical system (CPS). This paper stresses the importance of managing cybersecurity risks of a cyber-physical system and evaluates risks from the investor model, cyber, and physical system components, as well as their linkages, based on existing risk management practices and standards. The method allows for the identification of key CPS assets as well as the assessment of the effect of vulnerabilities on those assets. It also depicts a cyber-attack situation with a cascade effect of threats and also vulnerabilities to the assets. The attack model aids in determining the proper risk levels and mitigation procedures. The findings reveal that the risk in a critical infrastructure CPS is mostly determined by cyber-physical attack situations and the organisation's setting.

Ulven and Wangen (2021) stressed the fact that since higher education's demand for information security will continue to rise, and without adequate risk management, serious data breaches have already happened and are likely to occur again in the near future. By examining current literature of known assets, threatening circumstances, actors that pose a threat, and vulnerabilities in higher education, they used a Comprehensive Literature Review (CLR) Model to synthesize research in cybersecurity risk. The study's goal was to improve on existing knowledge of cybersecurity's most serious risks. The research outlined nine strategic cyber risks, each with a frequency explanation and a description of the consequences based on the assembled dataset.

Pandey, Singh, Gunasekaran, and Kaushik (2020) did a study to look at cybersecurity risks in globalized supply chains (SCs) because it has been shown by research to have a bigger impact on SC performance. The researchers identified cyber security risks in global SCs and then classified these cyber security risks from a strategic stance. The goal was to detect various cyber security risks and cyber-attacks in worldwide SCs in order to improve performance. By providing a framework for understanding cyber security risks in terms of the causes of these risks and how to effectively handle them, the conclusion derived from this study provides valuable management awareness.

Alahmari and Duncan (2020) stressed the need for more empirical research on the management of cybersecurity risks in SMEs. They explained that since SMEs have been advised to take advantage of new technology including technology like cloud computing in order to advance and grow their businesses, there is a widespread misunderstanding of their security threats among management. Small businesses' underestimation of cybersecurity issues increases their vulnerabilities and subsequently risks, which, unfortunately, might turn into real issues for them and other linked parties.

One unique research on cybersecurity risks was conducted in the area of Augmented Reality (AR) by (Dissanayake, 2020). The author talks mainly about AR threats that have not yet emerged but will do so in the future. This study explains that the data collected by AR devices from its users must be guarded. Like any other Internet of Things device, AR devices are vulnerable to risks because all IoT devices interact with the internet and the data they collect from users is stored and used by third-party organisations, even though these devices are transparent about how the collected data is stored. So, the need to protect these data from cyber risks is extremely important. In an augmented reality world, this review indicates that effective cyber security risk mitigation strategies are required.

In the area of robotics Priyadarshini (2018) conducted research on how cybersecurity risks have been on the rise in this domain. The author in this study highlighted the importance of cyber security in robotics, robotics and its current state of security, and some current scenarios showing the cybersecurity risks faced in robotics. The research went on to discuss mitigation strategies that can be employed to secure the robotics domain after identifying numerous vulnerabilities that lead to risks in robotics.

Cyber Security Issues: Attacks and Crimes of the Covid-19 Pandemic

Cybercrime is defined by the World Economic Forum [WEF] (2020) as all malicious computer-mediated activities to a company's or an individual's information. Cybercriminals acquire unauthorized access to information systems in order to steal, misuse, and jeopardize the integrity of data for personal benefit.

One of the things organisations had to do during the pandemic was to make room for employees to work from home. Groenendaal and Helsloot (2021) argued that not only did Covid-19 force many people to work from home, using their personal computers, with their own routers, virus protection, and so on but the lack of cyber security safeguards that individuals can have against hacker attacks, particularly for highly sensitive data, can be limited. Wang and Alexander (2021) further argued that the number of cyber-attacks has increased dramatically since the start of the Covid-19 pandemic.

Patterson, (2021) has stated that businesses were obliged to move to cloud services because of the rise in remote work during the pandemic and cybercriminals quickly followed suit. Threat actors modified their tactics to target employees using Covid-themed phishing and social engineering activities during the period of transition and disruption, capitalizing on the stress and fear of the pandemic crisis. He further stated that financial services, health care, government, and retail employees have been shown to be the most targeted by fraudsters.

Because there are no security protocols for offsite connections, according to researchers, cybercriminals are breaking into systems or internet-enabled gadgets for persons working from faraway locations. Internet espionage, phishing campaigns, distributed denial of service (DDoS) attacks, and fake news portals and applications are all being used to acquire highly sensitive information from unwary individuals, government officials, and organisations.

Dolezal in 2021 states that during Covid-19, 81 percent of global organisations encountered elevated cyber threats, and 79 percent of organisations experienced lost time because of cybersecurity risk all through peak season. A BCI's Supply Chain Resilience Report 2021, 27.8 percent of organisations had more than 20 supply chain interruptions in 2020, up from only 4.8 percent in 2019. The loss of production and logistics capacity, as well as labour-power, has provided the ideal attack path for cybercriminals: a potentially vulnerable and at-risk infrastructure to breach.

Global internet expenditure is anticipated to climb by 11% to $910 billion in 2021, according to Adobe's 2021 Digital Economy Index. This industry is facing more threats than ever before, thanks to store closures and a surge in internet buying, as well as limited product availability and shipping difficulties. The global retail business accounts for 5.2 percent of all detected cyber threats, according to the McAfee Enterprise Covid-19 dashboard. Compromised payment identifications and cloud storing, as well as other types of retail scams and theft, are examples of such concerns.

Airports, airlines, travel websites, and ride-sharing applications have all been targets of cyber-attacks in the past. This year, though, it stands out since the business has been in limbo due to pandemic-related health concerns and travel limitations Dolezal, (2021). Coronavirus-related losses are estimated to surpass $137.7 billion in 2020, according to the International Air Transport Association (IATA), with total industry losses expected to reach $201 billion in 2020-2022. Cybercriminals are keeping a close eye on the industry as it grapples with new challenges such as workforce shortages, supply chain issues, travel bans, and required vaccinations – and benefitting as much as they can from these vulnerabilities.

In the area of finance cyberattacks and threats against financial institutions soared by more than 238 percent globally between February and April 2020, at a time when the global economy was working feverishly to combat Covid-19 outbreaks. The Covid-19 issue provided the ideal environment for cybercriminals. During that time, ransomware attacks increased nine-fold, with phishing emails serving as the primary source (PwC 2020). Because hackers have a greater understanding of Financial Institutions' rules and procedures, they can readily find the financial institution's blind spots and continue to launch cyberattacks and threats.

One sector that saw a massive increase in cyber-attacks and crimes during the pandemic was the health care sector (Chigada & Madzinga, 2020c). The majority of healthcare organisations rely on ICT applications to provide e-healthcare services to patients and healthcare workers. The Covid-19 pandemic has brought these e-healthcare services to light, heightening the fight that healthcare institutions are now fighting, resulting in overstretched resources and employees reacting to the novel coronavirus

(Khan et al. 2020). DDoS attacks on the CDC and other healthcare facilities in the United States have resulted in millions of connection requests. Malicious assaults were also launched against the WHO at a crucial period for global reaction and a fundamental component of collective resilience. The attack on the WHO damaged key services, as fraudsters imitated the WHO and CDC in spear-phishing attempts, leveraging the epidemic to disseminate malware and ransomware, as well as build bogus websites to prey on people (Balsom & Dixon 2020).

The hospital in the Czech Republic that conducts the majority of the country's Covid-19 testing was held hostage and forced to shut down its IT network. A DDoS attack was launched against the US Department of Health and Human Services (HHS) (WHO 2020a). Cybercriminals \shave been targeting healthcare firms that are at the forefront of tackling the Covid-19 pandemic, including hospitals, research organisations, laboratories, and pharmaceutical corporations. Healthcare records are attractive for criminals intending to perpetrate fraud, identity theft, or credit card scams (Chigada 2020b) (Chigada 2020b). Covid-19 misinformation has been spreading across several channels, causing panic and anxiety.

Hackers who gained access to the WHO server exposed more than 450 email addresses and passwords, according to the WHO (2020a). Fake news and the propagation of disinformation are key factors to the threat, particularly in Asia.

According to Interpol (2020), cybercriminals are concentrating their efforts on government organisations and large corporations in order to create irreversible harm to information systems infrastructure. Because of the exponential growth of cyber threats and attacks, focusing on the pandemic and shifting cyber threat landscape places an additional load on law enforcement authorities around the world. Cyberattacks and threats are strengthened by capitalizing on the anxiety and uncertainty generated by the Covid-19 pandemic's fragile social and economic environment (Interpol 2020). Furthermore, fraudsters are aware of the security weaknesses in teleconferencing tools and platforms because they are used in virtual office spaces.

It can be concluded from the above that most research focus on identifying cybersecurity risks, mitigating these risks from an external and technical perspective. This research is devoid of the internal (human factors) that are part of the daily business processes of these organisations. It can be concluded that one of the reasons cybercrimes surged during the pandemic was because cyber criminals leveraged on these gaps between the awareness of cybersecurity risks and actual processes of managing these risks.

Common Types of Cyber-attacks During the Covid-19 Pandemic

This section will explain the most prevalent cyber-attacks during the Covid-19 pandemic.

1. **Malicious Sites:** Cybercriminals have created bogus domains on the internet and continue to do so in order to deceive their victims. According to Khan, Brohi, and Zaman (2020), a multitude of duplicating domains confuses internet users, resulting in attacks. More than 4000 domains associated with coronavirus were up and running by the end of January 2020. According to Checkpoint Risk Intelligence (2020), 3% of these domains are malicious, while the remaining 5% are suspicious. These rogue domains are used by hackers to con people and obtain personal information for evil purposes (Chigada 2020a).
2. **Denial of Service:** During the Covid-19 pandemic, the WHO (2020a) reported an increase in cyberattacks against government and healthcare organisations. Hackers disrupt government and healthcare communication channels by flooding the networks with millions of users at the same

time. The United States Department of Health and Human Services has lately been targeted. Cybercriminals have targeted Life Healthcare in South Africa, affecting all 66 of its hospitals. Admissions, corporate systems, and email servers were all harmed as a result of the attacks (White 2020).

3. **Unauthorised Websites:** Hackers and con artists establish unauthorized websites that people visit, despite the fact that they are illegal. More than 86 000 rogue domains containing Covid-19-related material have been developed to entice unsuspecting computer users to disclose sensitive data. When you visit a secure website, your browser looks at the certificate to see if it's genuine. Threat actors, on the other hand, can properly obtain a certificate with a particular character in the domain name that will deceive all major browsers into thinking the attacker is authentic (PwC 2020; WEF 2020).
4. **Spam Emails:** Several spam emails containing Covid-19-related phony messages for malicious attacks have been sent out. Hackers utilize spoofing to dupe their victims into donating bitcoins under the false pretence that the emails are coming from the WHO. The World Health Organisation (2020a) warned users that their official website ends in ".int" rather than ".org," and that they should be wary of emails from bogus websites.
5. **Ransomware:** Ransomware has infected hospitals, schools, and other public organisations. Hackers can afford to lock people out of their systems as a result of work from home or remote location access to business networks, and cybercriminals are hopeful that these institutions would pay a ransom (Khan et al. 2020). Infecting an information system is most commonly done by email attachments, links, and compromised credentials. Coronavirus is a new ransomware that was created and disseminated through system optimization software websites, persuading victims to download a bogus setup file. The ransomware Coronavirus takes passwords, encrypting data that cannot be decrypted later (Cook 2020).
6. **Fake social media:** In the sharing of information, video, and expertise, social networking sites play a significant role. Hackers, on the other hand, are obtaining access to Facebook, WhatsApp, and other social media sites for malicious purposes. Numerous examples of impersonation and phony Facebook profiles have resulted in the spread of false information. In addition, hackers entice their victims into signing up for free Netflix premium accounts. When the victim clicks the link, they are taken to a social media phishing website, where their login credentials are stolen (Cook 2020). Currently, social networking platforms are being used as a delivery mechanism, and advanced attacks are reportedly leveraging users' contacts, location, and commercial activity.
7. **Applications:** Smartphones allow users to quickly surf the net or access the internet from anywhere and at any time. Cybercriminals, on the other hand, have created a phony surfing program that claims to spread Covid-19 information and claims to come from WHO. Users are enticed to download and install the application through malicious links embedded in D-Link or Linksys routers, which automatically open browsers, out of fear and eagerness to get first-hand knowledge (The Australian Criminology Institute 2020). The user is offered to download a Covid-19 Info app, through which their credentials are stolen without their knowledge.
8. **Compromise of Business Emails:** Intruders are taking advantage of the Covid-19 pandemic, according to Dixon and Balson (2020), by employing coronavirus as a technique to persuade targets to execute transactions with an intruder posing as a legitimate employee in the same organisation. Business email compromise and hacking have recently targeted First National Bank, Standard Bank, and Nedbank. In February 2020, more than 1.7 million user accounts of Nedbank were

stolen. However, due to the sensitivity of cybersecurity, there was little information disclosed in the Nedbank cyberattack to indicate the scope of the harm (Isa 2020).

Cybersecurity Risk Assessment

The process of identifying, analyzing, and evaluating cybersecurity risks is known as risk assessment (ISO/IEC, 2018; NIST, 2011). Following a risk assessment, a list of prioritized cybersecurity threats that may affect an organisation or its environment is compiled (NIST, 2011). Risks are identified, recognized, and documented during risk identification, which includes the identification and description of risk events, their sources, and causes, as well as their repercussions (ISO/IEC, 2011). The goal of risk analysis is to have a better knowledge of the risks and to determine the risk level. The results of risk analysis are compared to risk criteria during risk appraisal to determine which risks are acceptable or bearable (ISO/IEC, 2011).

Risk assessment is an important aspect of risk management, which is a multi-step process that includes, among other things, risk treatment. (National Institute of Standards and Technology, 2011). The goal of a cybersecurity assessment is to figure out how secure an examined entity (an assessment object) is (Dalalana Bertoglio & Zorzo, 2017; Qassim et al., 2019). It provides an answer to the question of how well the entity achieves particular security goals. It is a cyclical process in which assets are confronted with their cybersecurity requirements, taking into account potential risks, threat repercussions, and associated costs (IEC, 2007). While it is not their primary focus, cybersecurity assessments can aid in the detection of cybersecurity threats (Dalalana, Bertoglio, & Zorzo, 2017). Simultaneously, the risks identified and analysed throughout the risk assessment process are frequently used to organize security assessment operations (Felderer et al., 2016).

In general, testing, examination, or interviews are used to assess cybersecurity (Chapple, Stewart & Gibson 2018). Testing entails putting an evaluated system or component through its paces in a controlled setting. It could be either passive or active. Active cybersecurity testing allows interactions to trigger and evaluate system reactions, whereas passive cybersecurity testing does not. Checklist-based evaluations, compliance checks, identifying vulnerabilities and analysis, penetration testing, simulation or emulation-based testing, formal analysis, and reviews are the most prevalent types of cybersecurity assessments (Leszczyna, 2021). These methods are explained below:

1. Evaluation using a checklist: The assessment process is organized around a list of activities, functions, or properties. The elements are then selected from the list, and the evaluated system's security status is tested against them (You & Lee 2016). Checklist-based evaluation can be seen as a special form of compliance checking. It assesses whether the assessment objects are consistent with the cybersecurity objectives, requirements, or assumptions (Leszczyna, 2021).
2. Compliance testing is typically carried out in accordance with specifications defined in standards or regulations (Chapple et al.; ISO/IEC, 2013).
3. Vulnerability identification seeks to spot weaknesses in the target entity that could lead to a cyberattack. Vulnerability analysis is the manual or automated examination of identified vulnerabilities in order to confirm their presence and to comment on the repercussions of their exploitation.
4. Simulated or emulation-based testing makes use of simulation and emulation techniques to aid the testing process. The strategies are typically employed to simulate or recreate the assessment

object's context or environment. They can, however, be used to mimic the assessment object itself, for example, when operating conditions impede on-site testing (Gupta & Akhtar, 2017).

5. Model-based testing is focused on simulating the examined system or component, as well as its surrounding context (Felderer et al., 2016). In addition, formal analysis limits this approach to models that are strictly mathematical or stated formally to allow manual or automatic examinations that approximate the proof of mathematical theorems and provide equivalent strength of argument.
6. Penetration testing uses techniques and approaches similar to those used by hostile attackers, however, it is done with the permission of the organisation being tested (Oriyano, 2017).
7. Passive, generally manual, evaluations of documentation pertaining to the assessed object are included in reviews. Technical specifications, logs, rules, and configuration files are some of the documents routinely inspected during security assessments (ISO/IEC, 2013).

Cybersecurity Risk Management Frameworks

Numerous authors and researchers have come to the consensus that risks-including cybersecurity risk-management framework falls into two categories; quantitative and qualitative (Algarni, Thayananthan, & Malaiya, 2021; Lee, 2020; Rios Insua et al., 2021). The first part of this section will list and explain qualitative risk management frameworks.

The International Organisation for Standardization (ISO) and the International Electro technical Commission (IEC) developed ISO/IEC 27005 as a set of standards (IEC). It gives managers tools and instructions for implementing and controlling information security threats. While ISO/IEC 27005 offers an organised structure of activities, it does not openly use any explicit risk management method, and organisations are normally to outline their own risk management method based on the nature of information security management system they have, risk management state, and the security issues specific to their industry.

The National Institute of Standards and Technology (NIST) Cybersecurity Framework. is a high-level, easy-to-understand guide designed for organisations to personalize. The framework core, implementation layers, and framework profile make up the framework. The cybersecurity program's main functions are described in the framework core. The implementation tiers explain how well an organisation's cybersecurity management practices demonstrate the tiers' specific cybersecurity capabilities. By comparing a "Present" Profile to an "Intended" Profile, a business can utilize the framework profile to find chances for improving its cybersecurity status. Risk management issues are only given minimal considerations with the NIST Cybersecurity Framework although it ascertains that activities involved with managing cybersecurity risk are specific to the organisation.

The Cyber Maturity Platform of the CMMI Institute uses the same risk management technique as existing cybersecurity risk frameworks. A risk-based guide, which is a customized rundown of action items ordered centred on the risks most significant to the organisation, is a unique component of the Cyber Maturity Platform. The Cyber Maturity Platform does a security gap analysis to compare existing maturity to the desired maturity and prioritizes security projects based on the organisation's cybersecurity risk profiles to create the risk-based roadmap.

The Cyber Kill Chain Methodology (CKC) is a seven-stage risk management framework established by Lockheed Martin. The model examines cybersecurity risk from the point of view of a cyber-attacker and what they would do to achieve their goals and suggests means of countering the attack by the defender both early on and later on to break the chain. The framework focuses primarily on the technical aspects of cybersecurity, such as attackers and defenders, but one of its drawbacks is that it does not address the human and organisational aspects of cyber risk, such as errors by humans and threats internal to the organisation. Additionally, it offers no explicit guidance for making cybersecurity investment decisions (Martin 2009).

The CERT(R) Coordination Centre in the USA established the Operationally Critical Threat, Asset, and Vulnerability Evaluation (OCTAVE) security evaluation framework OCTAVE assists an organisation in identifying and ranking essential IT assets, weighing risks to those assets, analysing vulnerabilities and impacts, and developing security priorities to decrease risk to IT assets. The concept of self-direction, in which a small, interdisciplinary team formed from an organisation's own departments conducts the review process, lies at the heart of this framework. To make the framework easier to implement in an organisation, the original version was modified to "OCTAVE Allegro". Without requiring considerable risk assessment knowledge, OCTAVE Allegro enables an all-encompassing assessment of an organisation's working risk environs in a workshop-style collaborative context (Alberts and Dorofee, 2002; Caralli, Stevens, Young, & Wilson, 2007).

Consensus Audit Guidelines (CAG) are published by the Centre for Internet Security (CIS) and consist of 20 key activities, known as critical security controls (CSC), that businesses should take to avoid or mitigate cyberattacks. The CAG's objectives include leveraging cyber offense to inform cyber defence, focusing on high-payoff areas, ensuring that security investments are targeted at the most serious threats, making the most of the use of computerisation to implement security controls, and using an agreement procedure to gather the best ideas. CAG comprises Implementation Groups (IGs), that are related to the NIST Cybersecurity Framework's implementation tiers. In terms of resources and cybersecurity knowledge, IG 1 is the least advanced, while IG 3 is the most advanced. The IGs are intended to assist businesses in determining their cybersecurity maturity level, prioritizing control implementation, and developing a successful cybersecurity program.

The remaining part of this section will explain some of the available quantitative cybersecurity risk frameworks. Since the most common know frameworks are qualitative this section will draw from literature studies that have come up with a novel quantitative method or a combination method with a qualitative framework. Quantitative methods have a tendency to limit the scope of studies to cyber risk assessment (Lee, 2020).

Aksu et al. 2017 created a quantitative CVSS-based cyber security risk assessment approach for IT systems. Because of the ever-increasing cyber risks within our ever-growing IT systems, the study focuses on risk assessment on IT systems. They came up with a new risk assessment approach for IT systems. The model is quantitative, focuses on assets and vulnerabilities, and identifies low and high-risk levels. The authors provide a full explanation of each category's formulations and have made this framework freely available for organisations interested in implementing the recommended methodology in their IT systems.

Added a Bayesian decision network (BDN) to a network security risk management framework. This framework consisted of things that should be done efficiently to better the security level of a network. Processes in this framework include; risk assessment, mitigation, and validation. During the risk mitigation process, customized Bayesian inference techniques are used to do a cost-benefit analysis of the risk mitigation. Because of the precise risk assessment and suitable risk reduction, their trials show that their approach considerably improves network security (Khosravi-Farmad & Ghaemi-Bafghi, 2020).

Algarni et al. (2021) developed a quantitative assessment of cybersecurity risks for preventing data breaches in commercial networks. The authors state that no significant research examining, comparing, and evaluating the methodologies employed by risk calculators to investigate data breaches have been done. Since these systems are linked to cybersecurity risks because of the large amount of business and industry data they hold. They suggested a mathematical cybersecurity risk model to prevent data breaches posed by cybersecurity threats such as cyber-attacks on database storage, processing, and management. They came to the conclusion that the models' outcomes dynamically reduce data breaches in potential and future business systems.

A cost-benefit analysis was incorporated into the NIST Cybersecurity Framework after it was realized that the framework lacked a financial basis for justifying cybersecurity projects. The research shows how cost-benefit analysis may aid firms in selecting the most appropriate NIST Implementation Tier level, as well as the relationship between NIST Implementation Tier levels and a firm's suitable level of cybersecurity spending. This study, though, does not offer operational specifics for spending decisions or describe how financial resources might be distributed across numerous cybersecurity projects (Gordon, Loeb, & Zhou 2020).

The AVARCIBER risk assessment framework expands on the specific characteristics of ISO 27005. Begin the risk assessment, identify assets and assess assets, identify threats to cybersecurity, assess the level of damage to the vulnerable asset, quantify the risk, and perform mitigations are all steps in the framework's execution. In comparison to ISO 27005, the entire process is not unique. More thorough activities and practical guidelines, on the other hand, are supplied. The framework's implementation was validated using a case study (Rea-Guaman, Mejía, San Feliu, & Calvo-Manzano 2020).

SOLUTIONS AND RECOMMENDATIONS

Traditionally, the IT department has been in charge of cybersecurity. IT professionals, on the other hand, have long argued that maintaining a company's network security is truly everyone's responsibility. In securing an organisations asset from attacks and damage organisations should follow these steps:

1. The first step organisations should take in managing/mitigating cyber risks is to figure out precisely where the risks are. The information to be guarded and what should be done when sensitive data is breached. Organisations should examine external dangers posed by other companies and vendors they collaborate with. Despite the fact that industry-specific research suggests that a significant portion of security breaches begin with a trusted insider within the organisation, organisations have a tendency to worry about their vulnerabilities to outsider threats when compared to their weaknesses to insider threats (Gundu, 2019).
2. Following this, organisations should come to a consensus based on their cybersecurity state after equipping themselves with industrial practices and standard and their vulnerabilities. The next phase is for the organisation to determine its objectives and define a strategic layout on how to collaborate with every department to figure out when these objectives can be fulfilled.
3. The next step the organisation needs to take is to categorize risk levels as low, medium, or high. If a high-level risk exists in one of the organisations locations, they will need to put a momentary stop-gap in place until they can more completely address the matter. Jeong, Mihelcic, Oliver, and Rudolph (2019) suggest taking into consideration human factors since they are the hardest to classify when categorizing risks.

4. The recommended industrial practise advices organisations to manage the risk that they can, take note of the cyber-attacks they cannot prevent, be quick to respond to any attacks, and try to gauge where the next attack may emerge from in order to prevent it.
5. When it comes to training and compliance, businesses must understand what the industry requirements are for cybersecurity in their area. They must ensure that they are in accordance with these requirements once they have completed their research. Organisations must keep their training and compliance up to speed with the current developments in their industry.
6. organisations should undertake cybersecurity response-readiness drills in the same way that they conduct fire or emergency drills in their buildings. If there are any flaws during these drills in the security network, they fix them for future use and retest and repeat as needed. Agreeing with this, Hasan et al. (2021) conducted research to find out factors that affect the cybersecurity readiness of organisations and how organisations performances are affected by these factors. They came up with a model for how businesses might better prepare themselves to prevent and mitigate cyber-attacks.
7. Businesses must also invest in human resources, such as security personnel and leadership, in addition to technology. This includes putting money into ongoing training for the people in these roles. Examining the organisation's budget to see if there are any areas where money can be saved to help reinvest in security issues would be a step in the right direction for organisations.
8. All levels of management, from the CEO to the board of directors, must follow sound cybersecurity practices. This will serve as a model for the rest of the workforce. Talking about the role of the board of directors on the management of risks, Lipton et al. (2020) agree that corporate risk management is more than just a business and operative duty for a company's management team; it's also a governance issue that falls under the board's control.

FUTURE RESEARCH DIRECTIONS

The Covid-19 pandemic saw an increase in the number of cyber-attacks and crimes. While all these attacks are not new to the cyber world, businesses must prepare themselves to handle any disruption of business processes, information security, and cyber-related risk of great magnitude. While most researchers agree that the pandemic has led to a greater susceptibility to cyber-threats Groenendaal and Helsloot (2021) conducting a case study on a financial institution found that by employing Hollnagel's four abilities for resilient performance the institution was able to manage cyber risks even though the threats it faced were not of high impact and the four potentials of the theory were developed before the Covid-19 pandemic. Of which, organisations cannot tell when an attack-cyber or not-will occur, the best practice is to already have implemented security managing strategies in place. Business leaders need to re-evaluate their plans, tactics, and strategies to better manage cybersecurity risk during and after the pandemic. Since organisations cannot tell when there will be another pandemic or give a precise report about how long the impact of any unforeseeable disaster will affect their business operations. They need to create mock drills to know how to respond in case any such situation arises. Many organisations have incorporated remote work into their regular business procedures one cyber-attack they have to tackle post the pandemic is social engineering. On a distracted and susceptible workforce, social engineering approaches are even more effective. Leaders need to create more awareness programs for employees as suggested by (Aldawood & Skinner, 2019a). When it comes to cybersecurity awareness extra care should be taken to make sure that the objective of the awareness is met and the target audience adheres to its teachings this is because a study conducted in 2014 by Bada et al. pointed to the fact that most cybersecurity awareness campaign fails to have the desired impact is because people need to be motivated and have a thorough understanding about why they should have a behavioural change. In this era of rapid technology innovation, governments and the commercial sector should collaborate to create uniform cybersecurity awareness campaigns. Everyone should be informed and aware of cyber threats at all times: an increase in employee awareness at all levels regardless of industry will help to curb issues related to cyber risk. One sector that was severely affected during the pandemic was the health sector a literature review by Nifakos et al. (2021) outlined "cyber hygiene habits" healthcare professionals can adopt when using social media platforms, as well as management techniques used by some healthcare organisations to combat the impact of social engineering attacks. Government and corporate leaders should consider the reversal of Covid-19's drive for individuals and businesses to look to digital substitutes for physical meetings. Organisations must have disaster recovery and continuity strategies in place to ensure they can continue to operate in the case of a sudden loss of digital tools and systems. The importance of worldwide, investor collaboration was highlighted at the Covid-19 pandemic. Collaboration between public and private sector leaders is also crucial, especially in terms of mitigation. Cybersecurity necessitates international cooperation, and there is a need to build confidence between governments and industry, as well as between industries and workers, at all levels. In the future, there may be a new deadly virus or common adversary in cyberspace; thus, collaboration at the policy, technical, and law implementation levels will be critical to safeguard everyone engaged and allow for a synergy that aids in the development of management and mitigation strategies. Future research should employ a socio-technical perspective in tackling cybersecurity risks because based on the conclusions drawn from this chapter research tends to focus on the technical aspects of cybersecurity risks and gloss over the human aspects or classify cyber risks as an IT department problem or management problem.

CONCLUSION

This chapter presents cybersecurity risks, cases of cyber-attacks in different sector, and assessment and mitigation strategies to tackle cybersecurity risk. This chapter stresses the fact that cybersecurity should not be addressed only from the technical aspect. The literature shows that cyber criminals target humans and organisations where humans are more vulnerable and likely to commits mistakes (hospitals, schools etc.). Cybersecurity assessment and management strategies are only effective if those involved know what to do. Due to a lack of in-depth study in this field including human factors or interdisciplinary perspective many organisations still continue to suffer from cyber-attacks and threats. This can be overcome with awareness programs, and involving everyone in the organisation in the risk (cyber risk) management process.

REFERENCES

Aksu, M. U., Dilek, M. H., Tatli, E. I., Bicakci, K., Dirik, H. I., Demirezen, M. U., & Aykir, T. (2017). A quantitative CVSS-based cyber security risk assessment methodology for IT systems. In *Proceedings - International Carnahan Conference on Security Technology* (pp. 1–8). 10.1109/CCST.2017.8167819

Alahmari, A., & Duncan, B. (2020). Cybersecurity Risk Management in Small and Medium-Sized Enterprises: A Systematic Review of Recent Evidence. *2020 International Conference on Cyber Situational Awareness, Data Analytics and Assessment.* 10.1109/CyberSA49311.2020.9139638

Alberts, C., & Dorofee, A. (2002). Introducing OCTAVE Allegro: Improving the Information Security Risk Assessment Process. In *Managing Information Security Risks: The OCTAVESM Approach*. Addison Wesley. http://citeseerx.ist.psu.edu/viewdoc/download?doi=10.1.1.461.7807&rep=rep1&type=pdf

Aldawood, H., & Skinner, G. (2019a). Educating and Raising Awareness on Cyber Security Social Engineering: A Literature Review. In *Proceedings of 2018 IEEE International Conference on Teaching, Assessment, and Learning for Engineering, TALE 2018* (pp. 62–68). IEEE. 10.1109/TALE.2018.8615162

Aldawood, H., & Skinner, G. (2019b). Reviewing cyber security social engineering training and awareness programs-pitfalls and ongoing issues. *Future Internet*, *11*(3), 73. Advance online publication. doi:10.3390/fi11030073

Algarni, A. M., Thayananthan, V., & Malaiya, Y. K. (2021). Quantitative assessment of cybersecurity risks for mitigating data breaches in business systems. *Applied Sciences (Switzerland)*, *11*(8), 3678. Advance online publication. doi:10.3390/app11083678

Allodi, L., & Massacci, F. (2017). Security Events and Vulnerability Data for Cybersecurity Risk Estimation. *Risk Analysis*, *37*(8), 1606–1627. doi:10.1111/risa.12864 PMID:28800378

Bada, M., Sasse, A. M., & Nurse, J. R. (2014). Cyber Security Awareness Campaigns: Why They Fail to Change Behavior. *International Conference on Cyber Security for Sustainable Society*, 38. Retrieved from http://www.cs.ox.ac.uk/publications/publication9343-abstract.html%0Ahttp://discovery.ucl.ac.uk/1468954/1/Awareness CampaignsDraftWorkingPaper.pdf

Chigada, J., & Madzinga, R. (2020). Cyberattacks and threats during COVID-19 : A systematic literature review Coronavirus Disease-2019. *South African Journal of Information Management*, *23*(1), 1–11.

Dissanayake, V. (2020). *A review of Cyber security risks in an Augmented reality world.* Retrieved from https://www.researchgate.net/publication/339941469_A_review_of_Cyber_security_risks_in_an_Augmented_reality_world

Fedele, A., & Roner, C. (2022). Dangerous games: A literature review on cybersecurity investments. *Journal of Economic Surveys*, *36*(1), 157–187. doi:10.1111/joes.12456

Groenendaal, J., & Helsloot, I. (2021). Cyber resilience during the COVID-19 pandemic crisis: A case study. *Journal of Contingencies and Crisis Management*, *29*(4), 439–444. doi:10.1111/1468-5973.12360

Gundu, T. (2019). Acknowledging and reducing the knowing and doing gap in employee cybersecurity compliance. *14th International Conference on Cyber Warfare and Security, ICCWS 2019*, 94–102.

Hasan, S., Ali, M., Kurnia, S., & Thurasamy, R. (2021). Evaluating the cyber security readiness of organizations and its influence on performance. *Journal of Information Security and Applications*, *58*, 102726. doi:10.1016/j.jisa.2020.102726

Humayun, M., Niazi, M., Jhanjhi, N., Alshayeb, M., & Mahmood, S. (2020). Cyber Security Threats and Vulnerabilities: A Systematic Mapping Study. *Arabian Journal for Science and Engineering*, *45*(4), 3171–3189. doi:10.100713369-019-04319-2

Jeong, J., Mihelcic, J., Oliver, G., & Rudolph, C. (2019). Towards an improved understanding of human factors in cybersecurity. In *Proceedings - 2019 IEEE 5th International Conference on Collaboration and Internet Computing, CIC 2019* (pp. 338–345). 10.1109/CIC48465.2019.00047

Kure, H. I., Islam, S., & Razzaque, M. A. (2018). An integrated cyber security risk management approach for a cyber-physical system. *Applied Sciences (Switzerland)*, *8*(6), 898. Advance online publication. doi:10.3390/app8060898

Lee, I. (2020). Internet of Things (IoT) cybersecurity: Literature review and iot cyber risk management. *Future Internet*, *12*(9), 157. Advance online publication. doi:10.3390/fi12090157

Lee, I. (2021). Cybersecurity: Risk management framework and investment cost analysis. *Business Horizons*, *64*(5), 659–671. doi:10.1016/j.bushor.2021.02.022

Leszczyna, R. (2021). Review of cybersecurity assessment methods: Applicability perspective. *Computers & Security*, *108*, 102376. Advance online publication. doi:10.1016/j.cose.2021.102376

Lipton, M., Neff, D. A., Brownstein, A. R., Rosenblum, S. A., Savarese, J. F., Emmerich, A. O., … Lu, C. X. W. (2020). *Risk Management and the Board of Directors* (Vol. 47). Academic Press.

Nifakos, S., Chandramouli, K., Nikolaou, C. K., Papachristou, P., Koch, S., Panaousis, E., & Bonacina, S. (2021). Influence of human factors on cyber security within healthcare organisations: A systematic review. *Sensors (Basel)*, *21*(15), 1–25. doi:10.339021155119 PMID:34372354

Pandey, S., Singh, R. K., Gunasekaran, A., & Kaushik, A. (2020). Cyber security risks in globalized supply chains: Conceptual framework. *Journal of Global Operations and Strategic Sourcing*, *13*(1), 103–128. doi:10.1108/JGOSS-05-2019-0042

Park, C., Shi, W., Zhang, W., Kontovas, C., & Chang, C. H. (2019). Cybersecurity in the maritime industry: A literature review. In *20th Commemorative Annual General Assembly, AGA 2019 - Proceedings of the International Association of Maritime Universities Conference, IAMUC 2019* (pp. 79–86). Academic Press.

Pranggono, B., & Arabo, A. (2021). COVID -19 pandemic cybersecurity issues. *Internet Technology Letters*, *4*(2), 4–9. doi:10.1002/itl2.247

Priyadarshini, I. (2018). Cyber security risks in robotics. In *Cyber Security and Threats* (pp. 1235–1250). Concepts, Methodologies, Tools, and Applications. doi:10.4018/978-1-5225-5634-3.ch061

Rea-Guaman, A. M., San Feliu, T., Calvo-Manzano, J. A., & Sanchez-Garcia, I. D. (2018). Systematic review: Cybersecurity risk taxonomy. *Advances in Intelligent Systems and Computing*, *688*, 137–146. doi:10.1007/978-3-319-69341-5_13

Rios Insua, D., Couce-Vieira, A., Rubio, J. A., Pieters, W., Labunets, K., & Rasines, G., D. (. (2021). An Adversarial Risk Analysis Framework for Cybersecurity. *Risk Analysis*, *41*(1), 16–36. doi:10.1111/risa.13331 PMID:31183890

Sadok, M., Alter, S., & Bednar, P. (2020). It is not my job: Exploring the disconnect between corporate security policies and actual security practices in SMEs. *Information and Computer Security*, *28*(3), 467–483. doi:10.1108/ICS-01-2019-0010

Sardi, A., Rizzi, A., Sorano, E., & Guerrieri, A. (2020). Cyber Risk in Health Facilities: A Systematic Literature Review. *Sustainability*, *12*(17), 1–16. doi:10.3390u12177002

Ulven, J. B., & Wangen, G. (2021). A systematic review of cybersecurity risks in higher education. *Future Internet*, *13*(2), 1–40. doi:10.3390/fi13020039

Wang, L., & Alexander, C. A. (2021). Cyber security during the COVID-19 pandemic. *AIMS Electronics and Electrical Engineering*, *5*(2), 146–157. doi:10.3934/electreng.2021008

ADDITIONAL READING

Aksu, M. U., Dilek, M. H., Tatli, E. I., Bicakci, K., Dirik, H. I., Demirezen, M. U., & Aykir, T. (2017). A quantitative CVSS-based cyber security risk assessment methodology for IT systems. In *Proceedings - International Carnahan Conference on Security Technology* (pp. 1–8). 10.1109/CCST.2017.8167819

Alahmari, A., & Duncan, B. (2020). Cybersecurity Risk Management in Small and Medium-Sized Enterprises: A Systematic Review of Recent Evidence. In *2020 International Conference on Cyber Situational Awareness, Data Analytics and Assessment*. 10.1109/CyberSA49311.2020.9139638

Aldawood, H., & Skinner, G. (2019a). Educating and Raising Awareness on Cyber Security Social Engineering: A Literature Review. In *Proceedings of 2018 IEEE International Conference on Teaching, Assessment, and Learning for Engineering, TALE 2018* (pp. 62–68). IEEE. 10.1109/TALE.2018.8615162

Aldawood, H., & Skinner, G. (2019b). Reviewing cyber security social engineering training and awareness programs-pitfalls and ongoing issues. *Future Internet*, *11*(3), 73. Advance online publication. doi:10.3390/fi11030073

Algarni, A. M., Thayananthan, V., & Malaiya, Y. K. (2021). Quantitative assessment of cybersecurity risks for mitigating data breaches in business systems. *Applied Sciences (Switzerland)*, *11*(8), 3678. Advance online publication. doi:10.3390/app11083678

Allodi, L., & Massacci, F. (2017). Security Events and Vulnerability Data for Cybersecurity Risk Estimation. *Risk Analysis*, *37*(8), 1606–1627. doi:10.1111/risa.12864 PMID:28800378

Bada, M., Sasse, A. M., & Nurse, J. R. (2014). Cyber Security Awareness Campaigns: Why They Fail to Change Behavior. *International Conference on Cyber Security for Sustainable Society*, 38. Retrieved from http://www.cs.ox.ac.uk/publications/publication9343-abstract.html%0Ahttp://discovery.ucl.ac.uk/1468954/1/Awareness CampaignsDraftWorkingPaper.pdf

Chigada, J., & Madzinga, R. (2020). Cyberattacks and threats during COVID-19 : A systematic literature review Coronavirus Disease-2019. *South African Journal of Information Management*, *23*(1), 1–11.

Dissanayake, V. (2020). *A review of Cyber security risks in an Augmented reality world.* Retrieved from https://www.researchgate.net/publication/339941469_A_review_of_Cyber_security_risks_in_an_Augmented_reality_world

Fedele, A., & Roner, C. (2022). Dangerous games: A literature review on cybersecurity investments. *Journal of Economic Surveys*, *36*(1), 157–187. doi:10.1111/joes.12456

Groenendaal, J., & Helsloot, I. (2021). Cyber resilience during the COVID-19 pandemic crisis: A case study. *Journal of Contingencies and Crisis Management*, *29*(4), 439–444. doi:10.1111/1468-5973.12360

Gundu, T. (2019). Acknowledging and reducing the knowing and doing gap in employee cybersecurity compliance. *14th International Conference on Cyber Warfare and Security, ICCWS 2019*, 94–102.

Hasan, S., Ali, M., Kurnia, S., & Thurasamy, R. (2021). Evaluating the cyber security readiness of organizations and its influence on performance. *Journal of Information Security and Applications*, *58*, 102726. doi:10.1016/j.jisa.2020.102726

Humayun, M., Niazi, M., Jhanjhi, N., Alshayeb, M., & Mahmood, S. (2020). Cyber Security Threats and Vulnerabilities: A Systematic Mapping Study. *Arabian Journal for Science and Engineering*, *45*(4), 3171–3189. doi:10.100713369-019-04319-2

Jeong, J., Mihelcic, J., Oliver, G., & Rudolph, C. (2019). Towards an improved understanding of human factors in cybersecurity. In *Proceedings - 2019 IEEE 5th International Conference on Collaboration and Internet Computing, CIC 2019* (pp. 338–345). 10.1109/CIC48465.2019.00047

Kure, H. I., Islam, S., & Razzaque, M. A. (2018). An integrated cyber security risk management approach for a cyber-physical system. *Applied Sciences (Switzerland)*, *8*(6), 898. Advance online publication. doi:10.3390/app8060898

Lee, I. (2020). Internet of Things (IoT) cybersecurity: Literature review and iot cyber risk management. *Future Internet*, *12*(9), 157. Advance online publication. doi:10.3390/fi12090157

Lee, I. (2021). Cybersecurity: Risk management framework and investment cost analysis. *Business Horizons*, *64*(5), 659–671. doi:10.1016/j.bushor.2021.02.022

Leszczyna, R. (2021). Review of cybersecurity assessment methods: Applicability perspective. *Computers & Security*, *108*, 102376. Advance online publication. doi:10.1016/j.cose.2021.102376

Lipton, M., Neff, D. A., Brownstein, A. R., Rosenblum, S. A., Savarese, J. F., Emmerich, A. O., … Lu, C. X. W. (2020). *Risk Management and the Board of Directors* (Vol. 47).

Nifakos, S., Chandramouli, K., Nikolaou, C. K., Papachristou, P., Koch, S., Panaousis, E., & Bonacina, S. (2021). Influence of human factors on cyber security within healthcare organisations: A systematic review. *Sensors (Basel)*, *21*(15), 1–25. doi:10.339021155119 PMID:34372354

Pandey, S., Singh, R. K., Gunasekaran, A., & Kaushik, A. (2020). Cyber security risks in globalized supply chains: Conceptual framework. *Journal of Global Operations and Strategic Sourcing*, *13*(1), 103–128. doi:10.1108/JGOSS-05-2019-0042

Park, C., Shi, W., Zhang, W., Kontovas, C., & Chang, C. H. (2019). Cybersecurity in the maritime industry: A literature review. In *20th Commemorative Annual General Assembly, AGA 2019 - Proceedings of the International Association of Maritime Universities Conference, IAMUC 2019* (pp. 79–86). Academic Press.

Pranggono, B., & Arabo, A. (2021). COVID -19 pandemic cybersecurity issues. *Internet Technology Letters*, *4*(2), 4–9. doi:10.1002/itl2.247

Priyadarshini, I. (2018). Cyber security risks in robotics. In *Cyber Security and Threats* (pp. 1235–1250). Concepts, Methodologies, Tools, and Applications. doi:10.4018/978-1-5225-5634-3.ch061

Rea-Guaman, A. M., San Feliu, T., Calvo-Manzano, J. A., & Sanchez-Garcia, I. D. (2018). Systematic review: Cybersecurity risk taxonomy. *Advances in Intelligent Systems and Computing*, *688*, 137–146. doi:10.1007/978-3-319-69341-5_13

Rios Insua, D., Couce-Vieira, A., Rubio, J. A., Pieters, W., Labunets, K., & Rasines, G., D. (. (2021). An Adversarial Risk Analysis Framework for Cybersecurity. *Risk Analysis*, *41*(1), 16–36. doi:10.1111/risa.13331 PMID:31183890

Sadok, M., Alter, S., & Bednar, P. (2020). It is not my job: Exploring the disconnect between corporate security policies and actual security practices in SMEs. *Information and Computer Security*, *28*(3), 467–483. doi:10.1108/ICS-01-2019-0010

Sardi, A., Rizzi, A., Sorano, E., & Guerrieri, A. (2020). Cyber Risk in Health Facilities: A Systematic Literature Review. *Sustainability*, *12*(17), 1–16. doi:10.3390u12177002

Ulven, J. B., & Wangen, G. (2021). A systematic review of cybersecurity risks in higher education. *Future Internet*, *13*(2), 1–40. doi:10.3390/fi13020039

Wang, L., & Alexander, C. A. (2021). Cyber security during the COVID-19 pandemic. *AIMS Electronics and Electrical Engineering*, *5*(2), 146–157. doi:10.3934/electreng.2021008

KEY TERMS AND DEFINITION

Cyber Attack: A cyber-attack is a cybercriminal attack that uses one or more computers to target a single or numerous computers or networks. A cyber-attack can be used to intentionally disable machines, steal data, or launch additional attacks from a compromised computer.

Cyber Threats: A cyber threat or cybersecurity threat is a harmful act aimed at causing data damage, data theft, or disruption to digital life in general. Computer viruses, data breaches, DoS assaults, and other attack vectors are all examples of cyber dangers.

Cybersecurity: The practice of securing systems, networks, and programs from digital threats and attacks is known as cybersecurity. These cyberattacks are typically aimed at gaining access to, altering, or destroying sensitive data, extorting money from users, or disrupting normal corporate activities.

Cybersecurity Risk: Cybersecurity risk refers to the possibility of being exposed, losing vital assets and sensitive information, or suffering reputational damage as a result of a cyberattack or breach within an organisation's network.

Risk: The likelihood of anything unpleasant occurring. Uncertainty regarding the effects/consequences of an activity on something that humans value, with a concentration on negative, unwanted outcomes, is referred to as risk.

Risk Assessment: Risk assessment is the process of determining what dangers are present in the workplace or may develop in the future. A risk assessment identifies which dangers in the workplace are most likely to harm employees and visitors.

Risk Management: It entails assessing risks and vulnerabilities, as well as taking administrative and thorough measures to ensure that a business is effectively secured. Traditional risk management principles are applied to digital systems and infrastructure in cybersecurity risk management.

Risk Management Framework: Organisations utilize the Risk Management Framework as a blueprint and guideline for identifying, eliminating, and minimizing risks. It establishes a road map of activities and objectives relevant to risk (cybersecurity risk) management's primary duties.

Chapter 10
Healthcare Informatics During the COVID-19 Pandemic

Philip Eappen
https://orcid.org/0000-0002-8120-8449
University of Toronto, Canada

ABSTRACT

This chapter explores how healthcare organizations utilized innovative healthcare informatics during the pandemic and how technology helped reduce healthcare delivery challenges. The unprecedented healthcare challenges created by the pandemic certainly warrant new and innovative tools to deal with healthcare requirements. Healthcare informatics undoubtedly played a significant role in smoothening healthcare operations during the pandemic, and it is expected to play a critical role in future healthcare operations. Health informatics tools such as telemedicine helped healthcare professionals to avoid unnecessary exposure to COVID patients, thus preventing many infections in healthcare organizations. This chapter presents healthcare informatics applications developed and used globally, including telemedicine, drug delivery portals, drones, robots, big data, AI, and many other sophisticated applications for remote healthcare access to patients.

INTRODUCTION

Developing and developed countries faced a severe threat in healthcare delivery during the past two years of the pandemic due to limited healthcare resources such as professionals, in-patient bed space, and personal protective devices (Rao et al., 2020). The Pandemic affected many lives, and the number of death due to the pandemic was massive in many parts of the world during the initial days and during multiple peak levels of the pandemic. A novel technology to manage healthcare requirements was inevitable when more and more Coronavirus disease cases were reported across the globe, and fewer staff members were available to provide healthcare. Despite all preventive and mitigative initiatives taken initially during the pandemic, healthcare providers faced severe staff shortages due to increased ICU admissions, crowded emergency rooms, and sick frontline healthcare workers (Abate et al., 2020). Each challenging experience during the pandemic made clinicians, policymakers, and patients think differently.

DOI: 10.4018/978-1-6684-5279-0.ch010

The crisis motivated them to use existing technologies and invest more in refining and revamping innovative health informatics techniques such as telemedicine and virtual care for patients (Obeid et al., 2020).

While the long-term solution to the pandemic is still non-existing, social distancing, face masks usage, vaccination, and new treatment modalities helped reduce the burden on healthcare institutions; however, emerging variants create long-term uncertainty as well as increased morbidity and mortality (Abate et al., 2020). The emergence of new variants promotes and warrants innovative health informatics technology and encourages clinicians to use it widely for future healthcare delivery. Telehealth and virtual care are the most rapidly growing areas in healthcare; thus, it is inevitable to expect more innovative health informatics technologies and applications than currently existing mere audiovisual technologies such as video conferencing using smartphones and tablets (Rao et al., 2020).

The main objective of this study is to promote healthcare informatics and provide easy, contact-free high-quality access between patients and healthcare providers. This chapter also looks at challenges faced during care provision and discusses recommendations and solutions for future health informatics and virtual care delivery during the pandemic, endemic, and beyond. Innovative ideas and techniques using healthcare informatics are vital because many people prefer using technologies to avoid hospital and pharmacy visits, especially during the pandemic. In addition, the CDC recommends avoiding or minimizing hospital visits and encourages patients to use telemedicine and remote technologies as much as possible to prevent crowded healthcare units (Leite et al., 2020). Although some medical examinations require face-to-face contact, it is wise and ideal to avoid face-to-face contact with clinicians and patients as much as possible to manage and reduce the pandemic burden (Hakim et al., 2020). Thus, promoting more innovative health informatics technologies for better healthcare provision is inevitable, and it creates a better path to manage cost-effective future healthcare operations during the pandemic and beyond using limited recourses.

BACKGROUND

The Coronavirus disease crisis compelled healthcare organizations and governments to accept and create rapid transformations to provide virtual patient care. To mitigate the effects of an unprecedented pandemic, the Centre for Disease Control, United States, created a "Framework for Healthcare Systems Providing Non-COVID19 Clinical Care" to assist healthcare providers in determining when in-person acute care is appropriate. Similarly, Canada, the United Kingdom (UK), and Australian healthcare accrediting bodies created guidelines to provide virtual care during pandemics (Anthony Jnr, 2020). Many countries such as India, China, and Arab countries also promoted virtual care with existing and new technologies; moreover, they invested heavily to transform healthcare service delivery. It is convincing that providers will continue to use advanced technologies and virtual care after the pandemic due to the merits of technology and innovations that happened during the pandemic. In addition, patient feedback after consulting online is better than expected in many parts of the globe to a large extent, as per various studies. Telehealth certainly can advance healthcare delivery in the future; however, it is essential to lift low-income countries to use innovative technologies by providing newer and affordable technologies and to get an advantage for patients across the globe.

Considering the increased pressure and cost of healthcare provision due to the pandemic, virtual and digital innovations could be a tool to reduce the cost and stress of healthcare professionals and organizations across the world. Remotely available virtual care programs help better manage the pandemic situation and allow patients to access care from their comfort zone; moreover, virtual care provision avoids unnecessary travels that may inadvertently expose them to the pandemic and infections (Leite et al., 2020). Hospitals across the developing countries, primarily, the United States, Canada, Australia, Denmark, and the United Kingdom, are investing heavily in innovative health informatic technologies to reduce Coronavirus disease spread in emergency rooms, intensive care units, surgical units, pediatric units, and other departments (Leite et al., 2020). In addition, hospitals also implement wearable technologies to remotely monitor patients' blood pressure, temperature, blood glucose, and heart rate rather than inviting them physically to a hospital setting (Torous et al., 2020). Monitoring vital signs such as blood pressure, temperature, and blood glucose is critical for patients with chronic diseases such as cardiac, hepatic, renal, and many other conditions. Digital health and wearable devices can keep healthcare practitioners informed and empower patients with real-time clinical alerts, and quick and live decision support (Yahia Zaki & Daniel John, 2020).

MAIN FOCUS OF THE CHAPTER

The emergence of new interoperable electronic health records (EHR) is beneficial during and after the pandemic. Patients can access medical records, treatment, and medical advice from anywhere, and it avoids boundaries and borders during travel restrictions across the globe (Reeves et al., 2021). Patients can collect drugs from pharmacies after a virtual consult, thus avoiding crowded hospitals, physicians' offices, pharmacies, and ERs. EHRs can significantly reduce the time for care provision, streamline operations, and decrease discharge time (Reeves et al., 2021). EHR also reduces medical errors by providing easy access to medical documentation for clinicians from many locations, including hospitals, physician offices, ERs, and their homes if required. EHR saves space for storing physical files, avoids difficulty in finding and documenting physical files, and avoids repeated as well as missing documentation. It is evident that EHR reduced considerable time used in documentation by care providers, and it is much easier to retrieve patients' documents from multiple healthcare locations than from a single site (Peek et al., 2020).

High-speed internet connectivity is inevitable for high-quality healthcare informatics programs and devices. 5th generation wireless communication (5G) facilities can certainly make health informatics easier and faster to use. It can provide a more reliable network, improve communication infrastructure, and stable as well as dependable connections to manage massive files. 5G can also help monitor virus spread, offer better communication systems, digital technology for managing Coronavirus disease, provision of e-learning during the pandemic, and digital technology-driven pandemic control (Hossain & Muhammad, 2018). For instance, 5 G can provide better connectivity and accuracy during a robotic surgery due to its high-quality streaming and uninterrupted services. 5G can also offer high-quality streaming for video calls between patients and providers without any lag; thus, more efficient and improved video calling, low latency, and interruptions. It is evident that more and more patients and clinicians will use virtual care when 5G is available due to its extraordinary speed and quality of video streaming without interruptions.

The coronavirus disease pandemic has pushed the healthcare sector to use innovations and technology to curtail and flatten the infection curve. Various governments temporarily waved numerous data protection rules and regulations related to telehealth to make it easily accessible for patients due to its usefulness (Torous et al., 2020). Existing laws and regulations related to privacy acted as a major barrier to the deep penetration of virtual healthcare services to communities in many developed countries. Professionals from the US, Canada, UK, and Australia use telehealth to prescreen patients before giving them an in-person appointment at the hospital (Leite et al., 2020). Pre-screening prevents symptomatic patients from visiting hospitals, thus safeguarding admitted patients, visitors, and professionals from getting infected to a certain extent. Hospitals also use sensors and GPS devices to locate patients and people exposed to viruses (Torous et al., 2020). Virtual care asynchronous units use information pages consisting of virtual information, such as the Johns Hopkins Coronavirus disease website. Johns Hopkins Coronavirus disease tracker has been beneficial in providing reliable details of Coronavirus disease case data across the globe.

It is critical to note that many countries such as Australia and Canada started using telemedicine and virtual health for providing primary healthcare after using it during the initial days of the pandemic. The coronavirus disease pandemic has given a chance to test virtual care for such countries and strengthened the position of the virtual care systems, and facilitated the development of virtual models in primary care for the future. The use of virtual care has increased more than 38 times during the pandemic considering pre-pandemic numbers. The second, third, and other waves only helped to reinforce the use of virtual care, especially in countries with high case numbers. Similarly, attitude towards telehealth has changed during the pandemic, and more and more patients are convinced to use virtual care as an alternative to hospital visits. Also, investments in virtual care provision and telehealth skyrocketed during the pandemic, and in addition, telehealth took over a significant percentage of outpatient visits across the world.

Virtual care, along with EHR, provides better efficiency for health care organizations and the health maintenance of patients. Public health initiatives are also taking the virtual care model after seeing the success of virtual care in primary care; it is anticipated to witness virtual care and increased use of innovations across the healthcare sector during and beyond the pandemic.

Although EHRs are made available in different parts of the globe, data privacy and data protection regulations made them inaccessible for most research members. On the other hand, pandemics encouraged many researchers to use informatics systems to upload research and data through collaborative efforts and made it broadly available on websites (Dagliati et al., 2021). Knowledge of health and healthcare has been improved, instead made available through various works of literature. A copious amount of clinical and epidemiological research data collected from EHRs is made available in standardized formats through open portals. Research and work related to the pandemic and other science filed have increased drastically due to available resources on the websites during the pandemic. Innovative technologies such as EHR played a critical role during this pandemic and made research data accessible to many researchers and students without meeting people face to face during the pandemic. EHR has helped create massive research across the globe by providing accessible data without human contact.

TECHNOLOGIES USED DURING THE PANDEMIC

Health informatics and EHRs greatly supported clinical research during the pandemic. Collecting and using data considering lockdowns and social distancing norms made research and data collection challenging; however, EHR and other informatics systems made it easier to manage data remotely without much face-to-face contact (Dagliati et al., 2021). EHR data-supported research maintained drug stocks and held logistic needs during challenging times. Data interoperability shared procedures to access data, and data privacy regulations are the most critical aspects governments and healthcare agencies dealt with during the pandemic (Dagliati et al., 2021).

In addition, blockchain can create predictive systems, predict infection rates, manage preventive activities, and reduce clinical risk (Fusco et al., 2020). Blockchain has improved the rapid collection and sharing of health data from interoperable systems during the pandemic without violating privacy and security. Blockchains provide decentralized data management technology; thus, data transactions happen in a decentralized manner. Blockchain has helped in various ways during the pandemic, such as contact tracing, supply chain, online education, and patient information sharing (Kalla et al., 2020). Blockchains also record patient symptoms, vital signs, vaccination status, face mask fit, and so on during the pandemic. Blockchains are a possible solution for preserving security, privacy, and sharing clinical information with trusted agents quickly and efficiently, as blockchains helped prevent and mitigate many challenges during the pandemic. Blockchains are used in many countries to tackle Coronavirus disease and manage healthcare operations during the pandemic, and it may continue to help manage operations in the future.

Contact Tracing and Screening

Effective contact tracing is critical in Coronavirus disease pandemic control. Various countries developed many applications to conduct contact tracing. Healthcare informatics applications can monitor, capture and record Coronavirus disease patients' movements and track their primary and secondary contacts, thus preventing the widespread of the deadly virus (Thomas et al., 2021). Australia, India, Canada, and Spain used GPS or Bluetooth-enabled technologies such as AROGYASETU, NOVID 20, OPEN CORONAVIRUS, and so on to track and monitor primary and secondary contacts of Coronavirus disease patients (Dar et al., 2020). These applications reduce human work requirements and errors to a significant extent and make it easy to conduct proper contact tracing with much more efficiency than earlier. These decentralized applications provide security, privacy, effective tracing, and help in disease control and prevention. Such applications are increasingly established in different parts of the world, including developing countries. Such applications are widely used to reduce human contact and carry contact tracing during the pandemic and beyond.

Many countries created applications with the help of innovative technologies to monitor and implement strict quarantine enforcement. Network mapping facilities through smartphones were used to track people who are doing quarantine, and it helped prevent violations to a certain extent (Thomas et al., 2021). Arab countries and a few Asian countries have used this technique to manage quarantine effectively. Colour-coded mobile applications helped recognize individuals at high risk or who are contagious with a red screen. In contrast, people with a green screen are considered less risky or less infectious (Whitelaw et al., 2020). Organizations also used colour-coded applications to assess Coronavirus disease risk by asking employees to check every day. Universities implemented colour-coded applications to prevent and stop symptomatic and unvaccinated students from entering campus, thus mitigating infections on campus. These applications helped individuals monitor their symptoms and health; they also notified the control room if they left the quarantine or geolocation without approval. Applications to watch people in quarantine helped healthcare workers avoid human contact and reduce exposures by effectively ensuring people follow quarantine requirements.

Many companies developed health informatics applications to do employee self-screening before they start working in offices, and it helped to prevent office infections to a large extent. "Team Sense" in Canada and "Prework Screen" in the United States are examples of two successful applications used during the pandemic for self-screening employees before their shift (Thomas et al., 2021). "Check Your Mask" is another application developed to check consistent mask-wearing of employees and customers by assessing a selfie video or picture of the client. Thermal scanning and face recognition at the airport and hospitals were seen from the beginning of the pandemic; It helped control it and collect data with fewer human contacts (Thomas et al., 2021). QR-coded vaccine verification equipment at the entrance of buildings and organizations is trendy after vaccine mandates become in force in multiple countries. Applications were also designed to allow safe state and international border crossing during the lockdown and throughout the pandemic. These applications are used in hospitals, airports, shopping complexes, and many other settings to consistently screen and detect patients with temperature, assess masks, and prevent pandemic restriction violations in different locations.

Mental Health Services

Mental health during the pandemic was another severe challenge faced by healthcare providers as well as people who stayed at home due to various reasons such as lockdowns, working from home, and so on. Many applications and services were invented and rolled out during the pandemic, and those services were very helpful in alleviating people's mental health challenges to a certain extent (Thomas et al., 2021). Mental health applications are one way of providing mental health and counselling services without meeting them face to face. It also prevents crowded hospitals by avoiding in-person visits for most mental health appointments. The development of applications helped clinicians manage less severe mental issues through virtual consultation and invite those who require in-person consultations to hospitals (Marshall et al., 2020). Mental health care providing applications also helped patients access their providers from their comfort zone and helped to avoid unwanted contacts during the pandemic. It is easy to access and use compared to hospital visits, and more and more patients are opting for mental health applications rather than hospital visits.

Healthcare workers were subjected to massive amounts of mental stress and emotional hardship due to increased hospitalizations and deaths due to the pandemic. Clinicians' mental health was primarily affected due to daily ICU deaths, lack of bed space for critical patients and resources were required to provide mental health support systems during the crisis (Chen et al., 2020). Various platforms and websites were created to internally support nurses and other healthcare professionals in need. Android and IOS applications were also developed to provide easy smartphone access to employees of healthcare organizations (Chen et al., 2020). "Be + Against COVID" was a digital platform made in China for healthcare workers, and it successfully met the mental health demands of the healthcare workers during the pandemic (Mira et al., 2020). Social media and newsletters were also used to further disseminate information on the applications and encourage the use of mental health resources during the crisis (Chen et al., 2020). Many other healthcare organizations used applications to provide mental health through various applications and websites throughout the pandemic, and a significant percentage of healthcare employees well accepted it. Two years after the beginning of the pandemic showed mental health deterioration in healthcare staff members, and it warrants more and more technologies to provide mental healthcare for healthcare employees. It is evident that more and more mental health support programs must be provided considering emerging new Coronavirus disease variants and to manage the pandemic burden on healthcare staff members and hospitals.

Innovations in Educational Sector

Nurses play a vital role in Covid pandemic mitigation and management; however, nursing schools and education for nursing students were affected mainly by the pandemic. Nursing schools worldwide, especially in the US and Canada, ramp up digital education for nursing students to provide high-quality training during the pandemic. Remote clinical experience was provided in many hospitals for nursing students with the help of pre-recorded and virtual meetings (Manakatt et al., 2021). Digital technologies were utilized to offer digital curricular resources for nursing students across the country during the past two years (Manakatt et al., 2021). Medical colleges also used the same technologies to keep their student engagement to a certain extent. Multiple webinars and virtual meetings were arranged to continue high-quality medical and nursing education throughout the pandemic.

Online learning becomes part of everyone during the pandemic. Many healthcare conferences and research seminars were arranged virtually using the internet and other digital technologies, and participants across the world met and discussed various pandemic scenarios. Organizations such as CDC and WHO consistently provided virtual meetings to enlighten communities regarding the pandemic, and those meetings certainly provided much knowledge to people across the globe. Healthcare leaders also used the virtual medium to meet with healthcare staff members multiple times every day and week. Such meetings helped convey messages from the management to professionals and helped keep seamless operation. Online learning is still common in many parts of the world, and it is undoubtedly helping to reduce the Coronavirus disease spread in classrooms without adequate ventilation and students without proper masking. Considering new variants and a massive number of cases in different parts of the world, more and more institutions are heavily investing in online teaching.

Genetic Counselling

Genetic counsellors in different parts of the world, specifically from the United States and Canada, struggled to care for their patients during the pandemic. Genetic counselling requires a lot of resources, and rapport between the counsellor and patient is an extremely important factor in determining the success of the therapy. Telehealth services were used in the US and Canada, and the number of patients patronizing services has rapidly increased due to high-quality telehealth services (Ma et al., 2021). A rapid shift to virtual care with an increased number of counsellors using telehealth to provide services changed the dynamics of service delivery. Many other countries are following the success path of the United States and Canada and implementing teleservices for genetic counselling. Moreover, positive feedback after using teleservices from counsellors and patients made it evident that telehealth is a feasible way of service provision for the future (Ma et al., 2021).

Drone and Robotic Technologies

Many developed countries such as the United States, Japan, and Canada implemented drones and robots in hospitals and airports to manage the pandemic. Similarly, drones avoided crowds, monitored travel areas, and disinfected crowded regions and logistic operations. Robots and drones were employed worldwide to control and manage the pandemic with the help of innovative healthcare informatics technologies (Thomas et al., 2021). During the pandemic, drones and robots delivered food, drugs, vaccines to patients, and many other medical supplies to various locations in different hospital settings. More and more healthcare institutions are heavily investing in robots and drones to equip their facility with the latest technology and make it more efficient with less human contact. Drones and robots help reduce healthcare providers' workload and can be used in highly infectious areas where human beings are not safe to work. Drones and robots have drastically reduced the workloads of healthcare staff members in many healthcare operations during the pandemic, and they will remain highly contributing to future healthcare service delivery.

Due to increased case numbers and decreased staffing during the initial days of the pandemic, field hospitals were built, and robots were used to manage staffing shortages. The use of medical robots and technologies may not replace doctors and nurses; however, they can drastically reduce the workload of clinicians and prevent unwanted exposure from infected patients (Lanza et al., 2020). Robots can check vital signs, provide pills, and supply food on time, with less human interaction, thus managing short-staffed healthcare operations efficiently and effectively. Robotic surgeries are more common due to their innovative skills and accuracy; many surgeons use robotic technologies to avoid close contact with patients during the pandemic. Robotic surgeries have been in place much before the pandemic; however, more and more hospitals and surgeons are turning towards using innovative robotic technologies to conduct part of the surgery or complete surgery. Robotic surgeries can be performed from a distance, and it is highly effective for trained surgeons and has better results for patients. Robotic surgeries require less human interaction and work; thus, they can manage short-staffed operation theatres and hospitals more effectively and efficiently.

Drones and robots were used in the medical sector much before the pandemic, but the pandemic reinforced the use of drones for medicine delivery and healthcare logistic requirements. The "Ava" robot has been used in hospitals for high-quality video interfaces and telemedicine (Saffari et al., 2015). It has sensors, and high-quality cameras to avoid obstacles in its path; thus, it acts as a perfect solution for healthcare requirements (Saffari et al., 2015). It has a simple design; therefore, it is easy to clean and manage in hospital settings. Ava can move from bed to bed and from patient to patient and provide individualized care with the help of clinicians. Ava can also do a video call between patients and clinicians using its high-quality video system, thus avoiding contact between patients and healthcare professionals. Robots were used in Kerala, India, to deliver food to patients in individual rooms during the pandemic. It is evident that drones and robots helped manage short-staffed healthcare operations during this pandemic, and indeed, those will play a significant role in future healthcare delivery.

China has developed a drone to handle and transport highly infected oropharyngeal and nasopharyngeal swabs of Covid patients. This technology helps avoid human contact during sample transportation and drastically reduces the cost of logistics (Angurala et al., 2020). Hospitals can use drones to transport highly infectious and dangerous samples from one location to another using drones and robots, thus reducing the risk for healthcare workers and transportation teams. Similarly, few countries have developed drones utilizing the Internet of Things (IoT) to collect and deliver blood, stool, and other samples from labs and hospitals to processing stations, thus avoiding human contact and reducing hospital-induced cross infections (Angurala et al., 2020). Robotic-assisted surgeries are also widely used with the help of IoT during the pandemic to prevent cross infections in healthcare organizations.

Sterilization and Sanitization

Frequent high-quality sanitization of common areas to reduce the risk of contracting viruses, bacteria, and other pathogens is prioritized during the pandemic. Disinfecting robots using health informatic technology have disinfected many hospitals and crowded areas by spraying disinfectants and ultraviolet rays during this pandemic. Such robots were also used to sterilize masks and personal protective devices during the pandemic's initial days, limiting personal protective supplies (Kim, 2020). Disinfecting robots can also sterilize operation theatres after each surgery and manage many sterile settings without healthcare staff members' intervention. Disinfecting robots have been sterilizing operation theatre equipment before and after robotic surgeries and reducing workloads for overburdened healthcare staff members. Many companies developed disinfecting robots using UV radiation and hydrogen peroxide to sterilize highly infected areas of hospitals during the pandemic, and those will be widely used during and after the pandemic. Those robots will help sterilize areas with no human contact, and these robots will do cleaning and sterilizations across hospitals at a lesser cost compared to having employees do the sterilization and cleaning job. The initial cost of owning these robots might be high; however, long-term benefits outweigh the initial cost.

Innovations in Radiology Field

Health informatics systems also helped radiologists to work from home during the pandemic. PACS (picture archiving and communication system) was used primarily in healthcare organizations during the pandemic to store securely and digitally transmit electronic images and clinically relevant reports (Towbin et al., 2021). The radiology informatics team set up PACS in homes for radiologists to work from home, thus avoiding contact with clinical spaces and crowded radiology departments. Informatic teams were also able to set up the required hardware and servers to manage the pandemic and massive demand from work-from-home settings (Towbin et al., 2021). Using PACS remotely was a revolutionary idea, and it proved that radiologists could also work from home and away from patients as they report from films and slides; this can not only decongest hospital offices but also help in cost saving. Due to the scarcity of radiologists across the globe, many radiology departments are short-staffed; this invention can help hospitals send documents through PACS to an available radiologist in another location and document assessments in the future. Remotely operating PACS would encourage more and more radiologists and hospitals to use remote services to reduce the cost of operation and manage short-staffed departments with increased efficiency.

Mobile Devices

Healthcare workers use mobile devices across Africa, and applications were installed for surveillance and reporting purposes during the pandemic (Owoyemi et al., 2021). A user administrated triage tool was developed and provided to the community in Nigeria to report symptoms, assess risk, and make informed decisions for patients (Owoyemi et al., 2021). These applications collect geo locations, collect anonymous data, present it to data processing centers, thus helping in data analytics and decision making. Some applications in Africa also came in multiple languages, and it helped to penetrate local communities due to its accessibility and user-friendliness (Owoyemi et al., 2021). Many applications were not effective in Africa due to poor networks and lack of broadband services in rural areas; however, more populations are using applications after the arrival of 4 G networks and broadband connections. More and more affordable applications must be developed after understanding the requirements of the developing countries as well as better internet connectivity must be provided for future healthcare delivery. It is evident that such applications and better networks such as 5G can change healthcare provision in Africa during and beyond the pandemic.

Internet of Things (IoT)

IoT has been changing the lifestyle of people during the pandemic. More and more people are trying to be health-conscious during the pandemic by using IoT devices to do daily exercises, track steps, and calories consumption as well as usage. Wearable devices connected with IoT will influence lifestyle and health directly; moreover, they can provide valuable information about patients to clinicians without meeting patients physically. Multibillion smartphones are connected to the internet, and it is viable to get the Covid data from smartphones more accessible these days (Jahmunah et al., 2021). Smart devices linked to IoT can provide many valuable pieces of information during this pandemic, and healthcare has been using it to manage patients' health from a distance and manage short-staffed departments and organizations by avoiding inpatient visits to hospitals. More and more people are buying intelligent wearable devices during the pandemic, and they are trying to achieve more physical activity than ever before. More exercises will help the population stay healthy and prevent lifestyle diseases to a certain extent during the pandemic. It is undoubtful that wearable devices would penetrate more people when it is more affordable and readily available.

Artificial Intelligence (AI)

AI has been another game-changer in the healthcare field during the pandemic. Several websites are available to see data sets and predictions related to Coronavirus disease, and AI plays a significant role in creating those useful websites. Also, images of CT scans and MRIs of Covid patients are available as resources for medical professionals due to AI inference activity. AI-based technologies are also used to classify Covid patients according to their case intensity to help care providers (Malik et al., 2020). Algorithms used by AI can check the intensity and number of cases by checking various data sets and by checking similar pneumonia symptoms (Malik et al., 2020). AI has been widely used to do Coronavirus disease case number predictions of specific months and seasons in various countries. AI can also look at some areas of the map and predict outbreaks after analyzing present scenarios of exposure and the number of current cases. AI also helps in vaccine manufacturing, drug production, disease diagnosis, and prediction of the Coronavirus disease pandemic.

Artificial intelligence helped analyze and predict the pandemic waves and found an unusual cluster of pneumonia cases in Wuhan, China, later diagnosed as the Coronavirus disease outbreak (Li et al., 2020). AI is used in many countries to find clusters of diseases as well as to analyze and predict future outbreaks of Coronavirus disease. AI has been widely used to create drugs, vaccines, and other symptomatic and experimental drugs to control and manage the Coronavirus pandemic (Li et al., 2020). AI applications also helped manage the pandemic by creating symptom checking devices, vaccine passport software, and Covid negative certificate checkers.AI helps in monitoring for new variants by highlighting new symptoms, new clusters, and an increased number of cases from one area or region. In addition, AI helped in data sharing, studying virus mutations, clinical outcomes of the drugs, research, and vaccine trials (Peek et al., 2020).

ISSUES, CONTROVERSIES, AND PROBLEMS

There are several policy issues, controversies, and problems with healthcare informatics and its implementation during the pandemic. Clinicians were not convinced about using the SNOMED list in many EHR systems; the unreliable list of medical issues made consultation rather tricky and challenging. Another challenge was the absence of guidelines for reviewing a problem list and removing a problem from EHR. Discussion on keeping privacy during the digital era has been a hot topic, and clinicians are worried about keeping HIPAA requirements and privacy policies with some EHR systems. It is critical to address the concerns of clinicians regarding the security and privacy of patient medical records to foster confidence in clinicians and patients in virtual care delivery.

Clinicians view AI and big data not as bias-free nor value-neutral innovations. Physicians and epidemiologists suggest that big data and AI cannot explore their own cognitive and epistemic limits, and critical thinking cannot be replaced by AI because it is a human thought property. Clinicians also argue that AI and big data are great tools; however, they cannot be used in healthcare areas without clinicians; thus, clinicians are not replaceable. Moreover, many clinicians express a lack of confidence in using AI and big data due to confidentiality issues.

Barriers

Even though there are many benefits, there are many barriers to practising healthcare informatics and virtual care during this pandemic. Many patients cannot access telehealth and virtual care due to a lack of consistent and reliable networks. Limited electronics skills, low income, low health literacy, and disability to use services are some other barriers to accessing virtual care (Hilbert, 2011). Many patients do not have access to smart devices to connect with telehealth agents and clinicians. There is a massive disparity between people with internet connectivity in rural and urban areas; thus, people in rural areas do not always have good internet connectivity to access telehealth. Many patients are not confident enough to try virtual care due to a lack of experience in using smart devices and a lack of knowledge in using innovative gadgets.

More Issues, Controversies, Problems

Patient dissatisfaction and lack of motivation in using telehealth is another issue, and many patients are not satisfied because of a lack of ideas on how to use resources. The lack of digital security and privacy of confidential data is a significant concern for many patients (Hilbert, 2011). Patients worry about reimbursement and coverage from insurance companies; thus, many avoid using telehealth channels (Chowdhury et al., 2020). Social media helped sensitize people throughout the pandemic; however, much fake news and misinformation were spread through social media during the pandemic, which rather demotivated many patients in using technological advancements (Chowdhury et al., 2020).

SOLUTIONS AND RECOMMENDATIONS

Recommendations

Expansion of ICT access, development of infrastructure to provide services, provision of care in local languages, providing training, and increasing awareness for patients are very critical areas to consider for encouraging more patient participation during this pandemic and in the future. Increasing patient satisfaction by providing high-quality virtual care is, in fact, critical and helpful in promoting telehealth and boosting confidence in patients as well as providers. Insurance companies' reimbursement policies for telehealth should be regularised to encourage more patient participation (Chowdhury et al., 2020).

Even though telehealth can provide customized and personalized healthcare, new technologies change the relationships between clinicians and patients due to a lack of face-to-face contact. Healthy relationship building between the patient and provider is not occurring through virtual healthcare platforms, unlike face-to-face meetings before the pandemic. Human touch and other forms of nonverbal communication fostered empathy and emotional connection between patients and providers; those are certainly lacking during teleconsultation (Kaplan & Litewka, 2008). More tech-savvy clinicians may become more accessible to patients, but clinicians with significantly higher experience may not be tech-savvy; thus, they cannot provide telehealth consultations.

Technology management and the confidentiality of patient records are significant concerns of patients and clinicians; thus, it is critical to provide services on secure platforms to protect patient privacy and confidentiality. More investment should be made to secure and protect systems from invaders and from security risks. Providers should also find concrete steps to provide a higher bandwidth internet connection to provide high-quality video streaming and a better experience for patients and clinicians. The arrival of 5G could significantly improve patient and clinicians' experience by giving high-quality video streaming without service interruptions.

Increased public awareness regarding telemedicine and other virtual care platforms is inevitable to attract more patients to virtual care and health informatics platforms. Disseminating positive experiences from patients to other patients would encourage others to try and use virtual care. Learning from others and getting educated can change the attitude towards telemedicine and health informatics programs. Also, training should be provided to providers that would encourage clinicians to explain the new technology to prospective patients and encourage them to try and continue using virtual care.

IT infrastructure and simple-to-use end-user applications are vital in providing virtual healthcare. Access to stable broadband internet connectivity is another requirement for a seamless virtual care experience. Patient records' privacy and data protection must be taken seriously to earn patients' trust in virtual healthcare programs and other healthcare informatics services. Providing 24/7 technical support to patients and clinicians is another aspect to consider while planning healthcare informatics services. IT support staff must always be available, and a clinician who can handle virtual platforms and other informatics applications should always be available. Training must be provided to all clinicians to operate various applications, and support systems to provide the required assistance to patients must always be available.

Healthcare transformation through informatics requires money, and it is crucial to have funds for a smooth transition and process. Privileges to prescribe and license to practice online are essential aspects of healthcare applications and organizations; more and more countries should create laws and policies to support healthcare informatics and telehealth, which will boost virtual care. Compliance requirements should be followed while providing virtual care to avoid complications and legal proceedings in the future. Credentialing and licensing of applications are also critical to getting refunds from insurance companies while encouraging and providing care for all. Insurance companies should be open in accepting virtual care to ease healthcare provision, and they should create policies to provide seamless virtual care within policies and legal boundaries. Elder and some other tech-savvy patients may be apprehensive about using technology, and it is essential to get permission and consent from them before providing virtual care. Insurance companies should recognize virtual care provision and adjust compensations and reimbursement packages accessible and easy to operate to patients and virtual care providers.

It is critical to assess patients and care providers' user readiness and willingness to use virtual care and health informatics solutions. Active participation of patients is inevitable for high-quality and satisfactory consultation. The patient's consent should be obtained before care provision, and the risk and benefits of receiving medical care should be explained before the consultation. Health informatics and virtual care certainly help provide and manage medical care provision, but it is imperative to consider multiple determinants that affect its adoption. Finally, massive coordination is required to provide high-quality healthcare through healthcare informatics systems. It is inevitable to have all required team members provide seamless service to patients, and seamless service can certainly encourage more participation and provide high-quality care and create highly satisfied patients.

CONCLUSION

Health informatics played a critical role in managing healthcare operations during the pandemic. EHR helped store and manage patient data securely throughout the pandemic and provided easy access to patient records for clinicians from different healthcare organisations and locations. Interoperable systems made it easy to access healthcare anywhere rather than visiting their primary centre during the pandemic. Bigdata helped manage vast and hard-to-manage volumes of data and easy to analyse resources for future healthcare predictions. AI managed operations during the pandemic and made it possible for machines to act like intelligent mechanisms and perform human-like tasks. Drones helped deliver samples, drugs, and other healthcare supplies to patients and organisations with less human contact. Robots managed many jobs, such as providing drugs, food, and supplies to patients without human interactions. Many other healthcare informatics devices made healthcare operations during crises easy and possible. Healthcare informatics will lead future healthcare delivery and make healthcare delivery accessible for prospective patients during future pandemics.

The benefits of using health informatics are countless; however, drawbacks such as confidentiality, lack of high-speed internet, and lack of patient confidence in using services are significant challenges. Most of the benefits, such as contact-free services delivery, cost-effectiveness, availability of service from any location, and affordability, outweigh the challenges faced during virtual healthcare. Acceptance of innovations and healthcare technologies based on AI, IoT, and big data can influence healthcare delivery during the pandemic and beyond. Wearable devices will undoubtedly change the way people use them to advance their health and health maintenance, especially by doing more physical exercises. Robots and drones certainly changed healthcare delivery dynamics to a large extent and changed the face of healthcare delivery. All advancements made before and during the pandemic using healthcare informatics and virtual care provision will provide smooth access for patients to healthcare systems remotely and ensure a seamless operation with limited staff members and resources. It is evident that more and more health informatics inventions, technologies, and innovations will change the face of healthcare delivery during and after the Coronavirus disease pandemic. Even though there are few demerits to using virtual care and health informatics during the pandemic, the benefits outweigh the risks; thus, we can see drastic growth and innovations in healthcare provision during the pandemic and beyond.

REFERENCES

Abate, S. M., Ahmed Ali, S., Mantfardo, B., & Basu, B. (2020). Rate of intensive care unit admission and outcomes among patients with coronavirus: A systematic review and meta-analysis. *PLoS One*, *15*(7), e0235653. Advance online publication. doi:10.1371/journal.pone.0235653 PMID:32649661

Angurala, M., Bala, M., Bamber, S. S., Kaur, R., & Singh, P. (2020). An internet of things assisted drone-based approach to reduce the rapid spread of COVID-19. *Journal of Safety Science and Resilience*, *1*(1), 31–35. doi:10.1016/j.jnlssr.2020.06.011

Anthony, B. Jnr. (2020). Implications of telehealth and digital care solutions during COVID-19 pandemic: A qualitative literature review. *Informatics for Health & Social Care*, *46*(1), 68–83. doi:10.1080/17538157.2020.1839467 PMID:33251894

Chen, Q., Liang, M., Li, Y., Guo, J., Fei, D., Wang, L., He, L., Sheng, C., Cai, Y., Li, X., Wang, J., & Zhang, Z. (2020). Mental health care for medical staff in China during the COVID-19 Outbreak. *The Lancet. Psychiatry*, *7*(4), e15–e16. Advance online publication. doi:10.1016/S2215-0366(20)30078-X PMID:32085839

Chowdhury, S. R., Sunna, T. C., & Ahmed, S. (2020). Telemedicine is an important aspect of healthcare services amid the Covid-19 outbreak: Its barriers in Bangladesh and strategies to overcome. *The International Journal of Health Planning and Management*, *36*(1), 4–12. doi:10.1002/hpm.3064 PMID:32857887

Dagliati, A., Malovini, A., Tibollo, V., & Bellazzi, R. (2021). Health Informatics and EHR to support clinical research in the COVID-19 pandemic: An overview. *Briefings in Bioinformatics*, *22*(2), 812–822. doi:10.1093/bib/bbaa418 PMID:33454728

Dar, A. B., Lone, A. H., Zahoor, S., Khan, A. A., & Naaz, R. (2020). Applicability of mobile contact tracing in fighting pandemic (COVID-19): Issues, challenges, and solutions. *Computer Science Review*, *38*, 100307. doi:10.1016/j.cosrev.2020.100307 PMID:32989380

Fusco, A., Dicuonzo, G., Dell'Atti, V., & Tatullo, M. (2020). Blockchain in Healthcare: Insights on COVID-19. *International Journal of Environmental Research and Public Health*, *17*(19), 7167. doi:10.3390/ijerph17197167 PMID:33007951

Hakim, A. A., Kellish, A. S., Atabek, U., Spitz, F. R., & Hong, Y. K. (2020). Implications for the use of telehealth in surgical patients during the COVID-19 pandemic. *American Journal of Surgery*, *220*(1), 48–49. doi:10.1016/j.amjsurg.2020.04.026 PMID:32336519

Hilbert, M. (2011). The end justifies the definition: The manifold outlooks on the digital divide and their practical usefulness for policymaking. *Telecommunications Policy*, *35*(8), 715–736. doi:10.1016/j.telpol.2011.06.012

Hossain, M. S., & Muhammad, G. (2018). Emotion-aware connected healthcare big data towards 5G. *IEEE Internet of Things Journal*, *5*(4), 2399–2406. doi:10.1109/JIOT.2017.2772959

Jahmunah, V., Sudarshan, V. K., Oh, S. L., Gururajan, R., Gururajan, R., Zhou, X., Tao, X., Faust, O., Ciaccio, E. J., Ng, K. H., & Acharya, U. R. (2021). Future IoT tools for COVID -19 Contact Tracing and prediction: A review of the state-of-the-science. *International Journal of Imaging Systems and Technology*, *31*(2), 455–471. doi:10.1002/ima.22552 PMID:33821093

Kalla, A., Hewa, T., Mishra, R. A., Ylianttila, M., & Liyanage, M. (2020). The role of blockchain in to fight against COVID-19. *IEEE Engineering Management Review*, *48*(3), 85–96. doi:10.1109/EMR.2020.3014052

Kaplan, B., & Litewka, S. (2008). Ethical challenges of telemedicine and Telehealth. *Cambridge Quarterly of Healthcare Ethics*, *17*(4), 401–416. doi:10.1017/S0963180108080535 PMID:18724880

Kim, A. (2020, October 2). *The Atlanta Falcons will use 'disinfecting drones' to sanitize the team's stadium when it welcomes back fans this month*. CNN. Retrieved December 30, 2021, from https://edition.cnn.com/2020/10/01/tech/drone-stadium-sanitize-spt-trnd/index.html

Lanza, F., Seidita, V., & Chella, A. (2020). Agents and robots for collaborating and supporting physicians in healthcare scenarios. *Journal of Biomedical Informatics*, *108*, 103483. doi:10.1016/j.jbi.2020.103483 PMID:32603793

Leite, H., Gruber, T., & Hodgkinson, I. R. (2020). Flattening the infection curve – understanding the role of telehealth in managing covid-19. *Leadership in Health Services*, *33*(2), 221–226. doi:10.1108/LHS-05-2020-084

Leite, H., Hodgkinson, I. R., & Gruber, T. (2020). New development: 'healing at a distance'—telemedicine and COVID-19. *Public Money & Management*, *40*(6), 483–485. doi:10.1080/09540962.2020.1748855

Li, L., Qin, L., Xu, Z., Yin, Y., Wang, X., Kong, B., Bai, J., Lu, Y., Fang, Z., Song, Q., Cao, K., Liu, D., Wang, G., Xu, Q., Fang, X., Zhang, S., Xia, J., & Xia, J. (2020). Using artificial intelligence to detect COVID-19 and community-acquired pneumonia based on pulmonary CT: Evaluation of the diagnostic accuracy. *Radiology*, *296*(2), E65–E71. Advance online publication. doi:10.1148/radiol.2020200905 PMID:32191588

Ma, D., Ahimaz, P. R., Mirocha, J. M., Cook, L., Giordano, J. L., Mohan, P., & Cohen, S. A. (2021). Clinical genetic counsellor experience in the adoption of telehealth in the United States and Canada during the Covid-19 pandemic. *Journal of Genetic Counseling*, *30*(5), 1214–1223. doi:10.1002/jgc4.1516 PMID:34757671

Malik, Y. S., Sircar, S., Bhat, S., Ansari, M. I., Pande, T., Kumar, P., Mathapati, B., Balasubramanian, G., Kaushik, R., Natesan, S., Ezzikouri, S., Zowalaty, M. E., & Dhama, K. (2020). How artificial intelligence may help the Covid-19 pandemic: Pitfalls and lessons for the future. *Reviews in Medical Virology*, *31*(5), 1–11. doi:10.1002/rmv.2205 PMID:33476063

Manakatt, B. M., Carson, Z. W., Penton, R. L., & Demello, A. S. (2021). Virtual learning experiences in population health nursing course during the COVID-19 pandemic. *International Nursing Review*, *68*(4), 557–562. doi:10.1111/inr.12725 PMID:34697806

Marshall, J. M., Dunstan, D. A., & Bartik, W. (2020). The role of digital mental health resources to treat trauma symptoms in Australia during COVID-19. *Psychological Trauma: Theory, Research, Practice, and Policy*, *12*(S1), S269–S271. Advance online publication. doi:10.1037/tra0000627 PMID:32496103

Mira, J. J., Vicente, M. A., Lopez-Pineda, A., Carrillo, I., Guilabert, M., Fernández, C., Pérez-Jover, V., Martin Delgado, J., Pérez-Pérez, P., Cobos Vargas, A., Astier-Peña, M. P., Martínez-García, O. B., Marco-Gómez, B., & Abad Bouzán, C. (2020). Preventing and addressing the stress reactions of health care workers caring for patients with covid-19: Development of a digital platform (BE + against COVID). *JMIR mHealth and uHealth*, *8*(10), e21692. Advance online publication. doi:10.2196/21692 PMID:32936769

Obeid, J. S., Davis, M., Turner, M., Meystre, S. M., Heider, P. M., O'Bryan, E. C., & Lenert, L. A. (2020). An artificial intelligence approach to COVID-19 infection risk assessment in virtual visits: A case report. *Journal of the American Medical Informatics Association: JAMIA*, *27*(8), 1321–1325. doi:10.1093/jamia/ocaa105 PMID:32449766

Owoyemi, A., Ikpe, R., Toye, M., Rewane, A., Abdullateef, M., Obaseki, E., Mustafa, S., & Adeosun, W. (2021). Mobile Health Approaches to disease surveillance in Africa; Wellvis Covid Triage Tool. *Digital Health*, *7*, 205520762199687. doi:10.1177/2055207621996876 PMID:33680485

Peek, N., Sujan, M., & Scott, P. (2020). Digital Health and care in pandemic times: Impact of covid-19. *BMJ Health & Care Informatics*, *27*(1), e100166. Advance online publication. doi:10.1136/bmjhci-2020-100166 PMID:32565418

Rao, S. S., Loeb, A. E., Amin, R. M., Golladay, G. J., Levin, A. S., & Thakkar, S. C. (2020). Establishing telemedicine in an academic total joint arthroplasty practice: Needs and opportunities highlighted by the COVID-19 pandemic. *Arthroplasty Today*, *6*(3), 617–622. doi:10.1016/j.artd.2020.04.014 PMID:32328510

Reeves, J. J., Pageler, N. M., Wick, E. C., Melton, G. B., Tan, Y.-H. G., Clay, B. J., & Longhurst, C. A. (2021, August). The clinical information systems response to the COVID-19 pandemic. *Yearbook of medical informatics*. Retrieved December 29, 2021, from https://www.ncbi.nlm.nih.gov/pmc/articles/PMC8416224/

Saffari, E., Meghdari, A., Vazirnezhad, B., & Alemi, M. (2015). Ava (a social robot): Design and performance of a robotic hearing apparatus. *Social Robotics*, 440–450. doi:10.1007/978-3-319-25554-5_44

Thomas, M. J., Lal, V., Baby, A. K., Rabeeh, V. P. M., James, A., & Raj, A. K. (2021). Can technological advancements help to alleviate the COVID-19 pandemic? A Review. *Journal of Biomedical Informatics*, *117*, 103787. doi:10.1016/j.jbi.2021.103787 PMID:33862231

Torous, J., Jän Myrick, K., Rauseo-Ricupero, N., & Firth, J. (2020). Digital Mental Health and COVID-19: Using technology today to accelerate the curve on access and quality Tomorrow. *JMIR Mental Health*, *7*(3), e18848. Advance online publication. doi:10.2196/18848 PMID:32213476

Towbin, A. J., Regan, J., Hulefeld, D., Schwieterman, E., Perry, L. A., O'Brien, S., Dhamija, A., OConnor, T., & Moskovitz, J. A. (2021). Disaster planning during SARS-COV-2/COVID: One radiology informatics team's story. *Journal of Digital Imaging*, *34*(2), 290–296. doi:10.100710278-021-00420-x PMID:33604808

Whitelaw, S., Mamas, M. A., Topol, E., & Van Spall, H. G. (2020). Applications of digital technology in COVID-19 pandemic planning and response. *The Lancet. Digital Health*, *2*(8), e435–e440. Advance online publication. doi:10.1016/S2589-7500(20)30142-4 PMID:32835201

Yahia Zaki, A., & Daniel John, D. (2020). Telehealth in the time of Corona: 'doctor in the House.' *Internal Medicine Journal*. Retrieved December 29, 2021, from https://pubmed.ncbi.nlm.nih.gov/33354885/

ADDITIONAL READING

Alassaf, B., Bah, S., Almulhim, F., AlDossary, N., & Alqahtani, M. (2021). Evaluation of official healthcare informatics applications in Saudi Arabia and their role in addressing covid-19 pandemic. *Healthcare Informatics Research*, *27*(3), 255–263. doi:10.4258/hir.2021.27.3.255 PMID:34384208

KEY TERMS AND DEFINITIONS

5G: 5th generation wireless communication with higher speed, lower latency than previously available networks.

AI: Artificial intelligence is a simulation of human intelligence in machines, and they are programmed to think and act like humans.

EHR: Electronic health records are digital versions of patient records in a hospital or healthcare organisation.

HIPAA: Health Insurance Portability and Accountability Act of 1996 protects sensitive patient health information and prevent disclosing health information without the patient's consent.

ICU: Intensive care unit treats critically ill patients with high medical and machine support if necessary.

IoT: The Internet of things are physical objects with sensors that collect process and exchange data.

SNOMED: Stands for Systemized Nomenclature of Medicine and it has systematically organised terms and codes used in medical care.

Chapter 11
Consequences in Acceptance and Application of Big Data Analytics in Micro, Small, and Medium Enterprises (MSMEs) in India

Rajasekhara Mouly Potluri
https://orcid.org/0000-0002-6935-1373
College of Business, Al Ghurair University, Dubai, UAE

ABSTRACT

This chapter elucidates the consequences of accepting and applying big data analytics in the micro, small and medium enterprises (MSMEs) in India. The author delineated research by administering multiple ways to garner the reactions from middle and top-level managers working in 50 organizations from five diverse vital commercial sectors. The application of big data analytics put forward numerous substantial problems for small companies as an investment in hardware and software resources are significant. The author presented the findings based on the experimental evidence on five critical challenges faced by the Indian MSMEs in accepting and instigating big data analytics: lack of human resources, data privacy and security, shortage of technological resources, deficiency of awareness, and financial implications. This research study highlights Indian MSMEs' diverse consequences while supporting big data analytics gains. The findings will help MSME organizational leadership plan and evolve short-term and long-term information systems approach.

INTRODUCTION

Data is a very privileged resource in the highly competitive business world, which is essentially required to resolve the number of challenges everyday businesses face. Based on the current imperative situation of the vast data related to finance, marketing, operations, and human resources associated with specific

DOI: 10.4018/978-1-6684-5279-0.ch011

target markets, particularly in the developing world, businesspeople are eying big data and its analytics these days. Irrespective of the magnitude, sector, and range, multinationals to MSMEs investigate avenues to burden and exploit the data. The application of big data analytics and its technologies is adjusting how businesses crosswise over enterprises work. Therefore, there is a desperate requirement for MSMEs to genuinely consider significant data adoption to address their voluminous data challenges. Big data includes several data types, including traditional enterprise data, machine-generated data, and social data (Opresnik & Taisch, 2015). Machine-generated data could consist of several formats, including weblogs, smart meters, and data originating from multiple sources. Big data contains data in both structured and unstructured data having five dimensions: namely volume, variety, velocity, integrity, and value. Capacity refers to the terabytes and Exabytes of data generated every day, while speed refers to creating big data quickly in real-time (Coleman et al., 2016). Variety refers to the numerous data sources, including textual data, image data, and much more. In contrast, veracity refers to detecting and correcting noisy and unreliable information (Coleman et al., 2016; Zheng et al., 2013).

Big data analytics analyzes big data to uncover hidden patterns, unknown correlations, and other information using sophisticated algorithms (Zheng et al., 2013). SMEs can benefit substantially from big data analytics, but the challenges associated with significant investment in technology and the workforce hinder these firms from benefiting from big data analytics (Zulkernine, Bauer & Aboulnaga, 2013). Agreeing to (Assuncao et al., 2015), more than 70% of large enterprises and 56% of SMEs in advanced countries have either already deployed or are intending to implement big data projects. According to Dobre and Xhafa (2014), 2.5 exabytes of data are produced every day, with more than 90% of the data generated in the last few years. However, Coleman et al. (2016) indicated that SMEs in developing and emerging economies are slow in embracing big data analytics because of several challenges. Unless these challenges are addressed, there is a risk that MSMEs will be left behind in benefitting from this new technology. Since MSMEs are the backbone of developing countries' economies, such a lapse can prove detrimental to developing countries' growth.

According to Zheng et al. (2013), data volume doubles every two years, and with several setups forming the core of SMEs in the last two years, more than 90% of their data was generated in the previous two years. Big data analytics involve considerable investment in hardware and software resources. A potential explanation for these challenges is in the form of cloud computing technology, which enables omnipresent and accessible provisioning of computing resources (Zulkernine et al., 2013). Cloud computing could offer these challenges through computing resources' pervasive and scalable provisioning (Zulkernine et al., 2013). The researchers have initiated this book chapter to know the Indian Micro, Small, and Medium Enterprises (MSMEs) challenges based on the Big-Data's significance. A similar kind of study was also conducted in Iran, and the results offer evidence of a big data analytics mediation effect in the relationship between technological, organizational, and environmental contexts and SMEs performance (Maroufkhani et al., 2020).

BACKGROUND

Literature Review

Micro, Small, and Medium Enterprises (MSMEs) in India

India is projected to appear as one of the world's major economies over the following decade or two, considering a constructive political, trade, and industry situation. The Micro, Small & Medium Enterprises (MSME) sector is anticipated to play a substantial role in developing the Indian economy. This sector's progress is enormously vital to meet the national priorities of financial presence and create many employment levels across urban, peri-urban, and rural areas across the nation. Furthermore, the sector's progress can encourage and back new generation entrepreneurs who can build internationally viable businesses from India. The Indian MSMEs can be the mainstay for the prevailing and potential lofty growth businesses with national and foreign companies participating in the 'Make in India' program and creating meaningful indigenization influence. The 'Make in India with zero defect and effect' is a substantial prospect. The new wave of MSMEs should empower the expansion of a business ecosystem that facilitates and persistently backs a business pitching to introduce the right product, the right quality, the right solution, and the exemplary service at an affordable and competitive price in local and global markets. The 'Digital India' transformation also provides a massive opportunity to encourage MSMEs' involvement in the Information, Communication, and Telecommunication (ICT) sector, in line with the government's vision. It is equally vital that the MSMEs expand in both manufacturing and services. The MSME segment will act as a catalyst for this socio-economic transformation (KPMG, 2015). In the Indian economy, the primary workforce is contributed from rural areas where most of the population is involved in tiny businesses and contributes a significant share to our society. Over time, these small businesses have become the driving force for overall industrial development. The Micro, Small, and Medium Scale Enterprises have contributed to improving India's gross domestic product (GDP) and lifted people from below the poverty line. Of late big data has become a revolution; it has completely changed the way of decision making and implementing policies at both micro and macro levels of the Indian economy (Dixit et al., 2021).

India has nearly 60.3 million MSMEs. As per data from the MSME Ministry, as of November 26, 2021, the Udyam Registration portal registered 5,767,734 MSMEs, replacing the former filing process for a Udyog Aadhaar Memorandum (UAM). Registered micro-enterprises stood at 5,441,220 (94.34%), followed by small enterprises at 293,555 (5.09%) and midsized enterprises at 32,959 (0.57%). As of November 26, 2021, under the top five state-wise Udyam registrations, Maharashtra recorded a maximum number of registrations with 12.18 lakh units, followed by Tamil Nadu (6.23), Gujarat (4.86), Rajasthan (4.68), and Uttar Pradesh (4.45). New online system of MSME/Udyam Registration launched by the Union MSME Ministry, w.e.f. July 01, 2020, successfully registered >5.7 million MSMEs until November 2021. The Indian MSMEs sector contributes about 29% of the GDP through national and international trade (IBEF, 2021).

There are approximately 63.39 million Micro, Small, and Medium Enterprises across the manufacturing, trading, and service sectors, employing 112 million people. The principal obligation of the marketing and advancement of MSMEs is the state authorities. Still, the Government of India supplements the efforts of the State Governments through various initiatives. The Ministry of MSME and its organizations' role is to help the states in their attempts to promote entrepreneurship, employment, and livelihood opportunities and enhance the competitiveness of MSMEs in the changed economic scenario (Government of India-MSME Annual Report, 2019-20). Corresponding to the World Bank, Micro, Small, and Medium Enterprises (MSMEs) are defined as micro-enterprises: 1–9 employees; small: 10–49 employees; and medium: 50–249 employees. However, the local definition of MSMEs varies from country to country. It is based on the number of employees and other variables such as turnaround and assets. MSMEs play an essential role in the broader ecosystem of firms. In many countries, start-ups and young firms, generally small or micro, are the principal source of net job innovation and are the guiding force of invention and sustainability in the private sector. There are about 365-445 million MSMEs in emerging markets: 25-30 million are formal SMEs, 55-70 million are standard micro, and 285-345 million are unofficial enterprises (World Bank, 2021). According to Dalberg (2011), MSMEs account for over 95% of firms, 60–70% of total employment, and 55% of GDP in the Organization for Economic Cooperation and Development (OECD) economies. Savrul et al. (2014) analyzed that the MSMEs' size has put them in a disadvantageous position. The author defined the micro-enterprises with an annual turnover of around 50 million Indian rupees, 50 to 750 million as small enterprises, and 750 to 2500 million Indian rupees turnover as medium-sized enterprises. The author also defined these based on the investment, especially for the service sector. The micro-enterprises shall not exceed one million Indian rupees, from one million to 20 million investment as small enterprises. From 20 million to 50 million investment service companies are considered medium enterprises.

The Ministry of MSMEs, a division of India's Government, is the executive body for articulating rules, regulations, and laws relating to India's micro, small and medium enterprises. The definition of MSMEs in India is standardized by the Micro, Small & Medium Enterprises Development (MSMED) Act of 2006 (EISBC, 2017). According to this Act, SMEs are categorized into two enterprises, namely, manufacturing enterprises and service enterprises. For manufacturing enterprises, if a firm invests up to 25 lakh INR (equivalent to around $62,500) in plant and machinery, then the firm is categorized as a micro-enterprise. At the same time, the firm is classified as a small enterprise for investments above 25 lakh INR and up to 5 crore INR (equivalent to $1.25 million) (DCMSME, 2017). A firm is categorized as a medium-sized enterprise if the investment in plant and machinery is above five crore INR but less than ten crore INR (equivalent to $2.5 million) (DCMSME, 2017). For service enterprises, if a firm invests up to 10 lakh INR (equivalent to around $25,000) in plant and machinery, then the firm is classified as a micro-enterprise. At the same time, the firm is classified as a small enterprise for investments above 10 lakh INR and up to 2 crore INR (equivalent to $0.5 million). A firm is ranked as a medium-sized enterprise if the investment in plant and machinery is above two crore INR but less than five crore INR (equivalent to $1.5 million) (EISBC, 2017).

Risks Facing by the MSMEs in India

With globalization's inception in the last two to three decades, the Indian Micro, Small, and Medium Enterprises (MSMEs) are trailing behind their competitors. The main reason for this is the lack of modernized technology and other remarkable reasons. Henceforth, this is the time to identify various risks facing and take urgent action to take corrective action to nullify the effect of those identified risks. It is an open fact that the absence of sophisticated and appropriate technology will diminish the competing abilities of MSMEs, decrease the demand for the product, switch to superior quality, and lower profit margin. Therefore, there should be a robust emphasis on executing the latest age technology through better awareness, adopting best practices, developing indigenous technology, and technological cooperation with universal partners. The Government of India has been introducing numerous MSME schemes related to technology from time to time. Still, further needs to be done, mainly implementing big data analytics. From both central and different state governments, the MSME sector is expecting more committed efforts in the form of higher investment in progressive technology and research and development, sophisticated usage of digital and technology-enabled platforms, transfer of technology, more investment in human resources, improved access to finance, reduced infrastructural gaps, lesser stringent business regulations that can help in improving the competitiveness of the MSMEs (Mukherjee, 2018). Even though the Indian MSMEs are operating in the high growth rate markets with alluring potential, they are still subjected to many constraints or risks like lack of timely credit support, procurement of raw materials at a competitive cost, inadequate infrastructure facilities, including power, water, transportation, and scarcity of skilled workforce. Compared to all these, technological backwardness in this new millennium is considered the most significant risk identified by the MSME sector.

The Indian MSMEs lack up-to-date information and are frequently oblivious about the latest technologies in the international market. These firms often lack managerial skills, entrepreneurial knowledge, and technology-intensive education to run competently with proper planning, directions, and control. The lacking organizational skills primarily exist in the rural-based firms in this sector. It is said that Information and Communication Technology (ICT) can play a more prominent role for MSMEs as they face tougher competition from their rival neighboring countries (China, Indonesia, Philippines, and Thailand). Thus, the need of the hour is the up-gradation of technology. For Indian MSMEs to become competitive, they must adopt the best international practices and continually upgrade their technology. The main challenge for many Small and Medium Enterprises (SMEs) is to cultivate the right skills and management practices for launching and incorporating expertise produced by outside partners with in-house procedures and innovation processes (OECD 2013).

Despite the tremendous corrective actions and support measures introduced by the Government of India and different state governments, the Indian MSMEs face numerous risks even after raising a novel economic policies like liberalization, privatization, and globalization. The following notable risks are discussed below: a) High cost of credit: The MSMEs in India are not adequately accessing adequate and timely credit at a reasonable cost, which is considered a vital and most crucial risk identified by the sector. The researchers (Levy 1993, Basu 2004, Seshasayee 2006, Das 2008, and Nagpal et al. 2009) with their studies proved the same. The principal rationale for this has been the banks' high-risk perception of this sector and the high transaction costs for loan appraisal. Moreover, the sector firms are also not apposition to provide collateral to loans from banks and are denied access to credit. b) Purchasing of raw materials at a reasonable cost: The required capability and raw materials to put entrepreneurial ideas into practice, to be economical, endure during adverse circumstances, and grow. This is a mounting challenge this sector faces as procurement for raw materials is brought out within local regions due to their monetary limitations, and procurements are many minor quantities in scale compared to large-scale industry. c) Insufficient infrastructure facilities, including power, water, and roads. Lack of power/electricity infrastructures adversely impacts manufacturing MSMEs' productivity and profitability (Adelekan 2005; Akinwale 2010; Doe and Asamoah 2014). To ensure the competitiveness of the MSMEs, the availability of infrastructure, technology, and skilled workforce must be fine-tuned with the worldwide trends. MSMEs are either stationed in industrial estates set up many years ago or are operating within city areas, or have come up in a disorganized approach in countryside areas. The infrastructure, including power, water, and roads, is flawed and unreliable. d) Lack of competent workforce for manufacturing, services, marketing: Shortcomings in the domestic market situation are the leading reason for MSMEs' malfunctions and rotate in organizational skills, understanding of finance, and nominal proficiency in the promotion and human resources (Ligthelm and Cant 2002). Even though India has the advantage of a massive human resources pool, the industry continually faces scarcity in the skilled workforce required for manufacturing, marketing, servicing, and other business functions. The eruption of COVID-19 has afflicted the world's economic and social activities. There is no exemption even for the Indian economy. Out of different economic activities, micro, small and medium enterprises (MSMEs) are affected in India. This article attempts to measure the contribution of MSMEs to the Indian economy and find out the challenges and problems in pre-and during the COVID period. The researchers used different descriptive statistics to measure MSMEs' impacts and used correlation and co-integration to measure the relationship among the variables such as the number of MSMEs, investment amount, employment, and output. This pandemic is an exceptional shock for MSMEs (Behera et al., 2020). Another group of researchers also highlighted those consequences are wide and open, like loss of jobs, reduction in revenue generation, declined sales, and a cut back in the income of the working class (Hariharan et al., 2021). The COVID-19 pandemic has impacted all the economic sectors, especially the MSME sector. The epidemic has created many challenges and severely impacted MSMEs' production, supply chain, liquidity, demand, workers, etc. So, the primary purpose of the research is to understand the impact of COVID-19 on the MSME sector in India. The lockdown has led to various issues like financial crunch, low production, lack of workforce, lack of supply, etc. (Banu & Suresh, 2020)

Big Data Analytics for MSMEs

Big data is not just for only large corporates with massive budgets. In this new millennium, even MSMEs can reap the advantages of the enormous quantities of online and offline information to make wise, data-driven choices to expand their businesses. The data accessibility and improved analytics revolution ignite prospects for new firms and existing MSMEs to discover the latest methods to harness the power of the growing aggregation of digital data. These immense opportunities generated by capturing and analyzing data create new companies every day. The power of data is not limited to start-ups but also applies to existing business models across industries. The application of digital data and analytical tools enables SMEs to extend their products and services and create new ones (Ogbuokiri 2015). Researchers like Ogbuokiri and others (2015) comprehensively expounded the big-data solution features in the MSMEs like flexibility and choice, simplicity, and cost.

Big data analytics can present sizable advantages to Indian MSMEs with an escalating change in the international business milieu from an "industry economy" to a "service economy" (Zheng, Ahu, & Lyu, 2013). According to Zheng et al. (2013), this swing is more substantial in developing countries, exceeding 70% of the business productivity. However, examining big data is a question for many applications because of the complexity and scalability of underlying algorithms supporting such procedures (Siddiqa et al., 2016). Big data comprises numerous kinds of service-generated data, containing trace logs and Quality of Service (QoS) data, extending a wealth of information for SMEs (Zheng et al., 2013). MSMEs' organizational leadership can make well-informed decisions by mining big data from data generated within the firm and confidentially obtained and openly accessible big data. However, building separate systems for analyzing big data is not feasible in the time and cost involved in such an effort. MSMEs can use big data analytics to offer either ultimate or exploratory outcomes, allowing them to make conscious judgments. Sizable firms mainly use grid technology for distributed mapping while analyzing large data sets. MSMEs cannot utilize network processing as this know-how is not accessible and is also pretty pricey. The research conducted by academicians Seseni and Mbohwa (2021) in South Africa found that big data SMEs are more profitable, productive, and innovative. However, SMEs find it difficult to use big data tools and technologies. This study recommends that institutions of higher learning should introduce short learning programs or continuing education programs to train SMEs on how to use big data tools and technologies. The government should provide financial and non-financial support to SMEs to use advanced technologies and compete with big corporations.

Big Data Analytics Service

Big data analytics entails in-depth analyses of data generated over petabyte levels from long-term accretion (Chen et al., 2016). A crucial concern with big data analytics is using the applicable paradigm for large-magnitude data analysis. Consequently, acquiring handy information from big data requires scalable analytics algorithm techniques. In this case, massive cloud infrastructure and applications are necessary to handle data parallelism (Siddiqa et al., 2016). The purpose of data parallelism is quite involved in the case of big data and does not inherently require quicker administering of data. Contemplating that data comes from different sources and speeds (5 'V's of big data), compound data analytics facilities should be improved to cope with big data. Therefore, cloud computing could be an ideal solution for managing this complexity. Cloud computing's system structure involves the main characteristics of cloud computing services, the deployment models, and the service models. The main aspects of cloud computing services include on-request self-service, extensive network access, resource pooling, rapid elasticity, and measured service (Chen et al., 2016). The four utilization models of cloud computing services include public clouds, private clouds, community clouds, and hybrid clouds (Chen et al., 2016). The three service models in cloud computing include the utilization of software as a service (SaaS), platform as a service (PaaS), and infrastructure as a service (IaaS) (Chen et al., 2016). In addition, Chen et al. (2016) recommended a cloud-based system outline built on Bigtable and MapReduce as the data storage and processing concepts. This web-based service permitted viewing, storing, and analyzing significant information models, including big data.

Based on the above discussion, the researchers have chosen the following list of hypotheses:

1. Financial implications are the core challenge in administering the big data for most MSMEs in India.
2. Lack of awareness of big data is the least crucial challenge to Indian MSMEs next to the other reasons.
3. Indian MSMEs have the most difficulty in getting quality technological resources.

MAIN FOCUS OF THE CHAPTER

Issues, Controversies, Problems

The questionnaire was designed, and pilot tested, and it was successfully retested with 50 MSME proprietors and executives working in MSMEs in India. The division of these firms throughout the key sectors is listed in Table 1. The study was restricted to south India's Andhra Pradesh and Telangana states. The researchers used a convenience random sampling technique to gather the required information based on the rationale that these two Indian states led in invention and development among all the other Indian states. We intended to generalize our findings to MSMEs in India and to be able to conclude these outcomes in other Indian states with similar political and economic conditions. Therefore, these two states were selected for the study as they were among the top-five territories in the Gross State Domestic Product (GSDP). The selected two south Indian states, Andhra Pradesh and Telangana, were one single state before the bifurcation in 2014. Andhra Pradesh state in India stood seventh regarding geographic area and 10th regarding population among the 29 Indian states. Data were collected from 50 MSME participants using an online survey instrument. The survey questions captured demographic characteristics. The survey recorded most of the answers as a dichotomous two-scale simple data type (yes or no)—the confidence level set at 95%. Minitab version 18 was employed for the tests and to organize the findings.

Table 1. Participating sector-wise MSMEs

Sector of MSMEs	Participating Companies (%)
Construction	30
Tourism	20
Information and Communication Technology (ICT)	15
Food Processing	20
Others	15

The research questions guiding the research to prepare the book chapter are the following:

1. How can Indian MSMEs leverage big data analytics to enhance productivity and performance?
2. What are the challenges that MSMEs face while implementing big data analytics?

SOLUTIONS AND RECOMMENDATIONS

Low data quality is one of the critical challenges SMEs faces while using big data. Data security is another crucial challenge in cloud computing, and the usefulness of cloud computing facilities for big data analytics would boost similar protection worries (Zulkernine et al., 2013). Corresponding to Garg et al. (2016), big data encompasses a massive amount of information, some of which might include personally identifiable information (PII). The PII might consist of account particulars, plastic money, and confidential data. Therefore, ample security must be in place to avoid this enormous data volume loss or theft. Zulqernine (2013) and his counterparts recommended a Cloud-based Analytics-as-a-Service (CLAaaS), which will provide on-demand data storage and analytics services via personalized user interfaces and apply Service Level Agreements (SLAs) to provide controlled access to domain-specific software and data resources. Hiring significant data practitioners and training the existing users on big data is another overhead for most SMEs (Zheng et al., 2016). Handling big data-related services requires expertise in big data analytics and subject matter professionals in the specialized field (Zhou et al., 2016); hence, hiring and training such experts might be challenging, especially for MSMEs. The demographic statistics of the respondents are listed in the following Table 2.

Table 2. Demographic statistics

Category	Criteria	Representation of Respondents (%)
Gender	Male	67%
	Female	33%
Age	20-30 years	38%
	30-40 years	22%
	40-50 years	26%
	>50 years	14%

The respondents identified five critical challenges: the scarcity of workforce, data privacy and security, lack of technological resources, lack of awareness, and financial implications. The subjects were provided with all the options and were allowed to select one or more challenges they felt were crucial while executing big data analytics. The application of cloud computing services and infrastructure could address these critical challenges. MSMEs do not have to worry about the maintenance and the financial implications of managing significant technological support. MSMEs can benefit from using big data services and cloud computing infrastructure. They do not have to invest significantly in traditional grid computing solutions but instead use the existing facilities and cloud infrastructure. The usage of cloud computing infrastructure and services will also help SMEs handle the costs of maintaining support and hiring and training the qualified workforce.

The research was limited to the MSMEs from five key Andhra Pradesh and Telangana. India is a vast country, so this study's findings on MSMEs' challenges and limitations may vary. As only 50 micro, small and medium-sized enterprises are included in this study, this study's results may be biased toward significant companies and some distant and specific sector MSMEs. Furthermore, the participants' responses limit the research during interviews and the time available to conduct the investigation. Therefore, the study's validity is limited to the instruments' reliability. Also, as the MSMEs represent India's five major economic sectors, some findings may not apply to other industrial areas. Astonishingly, 84.91 percent of respondents emphatically said that lack of technical resources is the core challenge identified by the SMEs in India, against just 15.09 percent who were not sure about the problems related to administering big data. Simultaneously, around 66 percent of SMEs have identified a lack of quality human resources against 54.72 percent with financial implications. Only 35.85 percent of MSMEs in India also identified data privacy and security even a considerable challenge, along with another 18.87 percent who noticed a lack of awareness about big data.

The following Table 3 illustrates the implementation of the proportionality hypothesis testing on the above-observed percentile values. The P-Value from this statistical test result will approve or disprove the stated three hypotheses.

Table 3.

Hypothesis S. No.	Null and Alternative Hypothesis (H0 & H1)	Hypotheses Test Result	Interpretation
1.	**H0**: Financial implications are not the core challenge in administering the big data for most MSMEs in India. **H1**: Financial implications are the core challenge in administering the big data for most MSMEs in India.	S = 54.72, N = 100 P-Value:0.39 X–Squared value: 0.72 95% Confidence Interval: [0.44 – 0.64]	Since the P-value is statistically significant (>0.5), the null hypothesis (H0) fails to reject. Thus, the financial implications are not the core challenge.
2.	**H0**: Lack of awareness of Big Data is not the least crucial challenge to Indian MSMEs, next to the other reasons. **H1**: Lack of awareness of Big Data is the least crucial challenge to Indian MSMEs, next to the other reasons.	S = 18.87, N = 100 P-Value: 9.012 x e^{-10} X–Squared value: 37.528 95% Confidence Interval: [0.12 – 0.28]	Since the P-value is not statistically significant (<0.5), the null hypothesis (H0) is rejected. Thus, the lack of awareness of Big Data is challenging.
3.	**H0**: Indian MSMEs do not have the most difficulty getting quality technological resources. **H1**: Indian MSMEs have the most difficulty in getting quality technological resources.	S = 84.91, N = 100 P-Value: 5.902 x e^{-12} X–Squared value: 47.362 95% Confidence Interval: [0.76 – 0.91]	Since the P-value is not statistically significant (<0.5), the null hypothesis (H0) is rejected. Thus, the MSMEs in India have identified an enormous difficulty in getting quality technological resources.

The statistical analysis results prove that the observed percentile values are accurate upon testing the three hypotheses. Based on the above hypotheses testing results, financial implications in implementing big-data analytics in the Indian MSMEs are not the core challenge. Except for very few MSMEs in the country, most firms have considerable information about big data analytics and its advantages. However, most businesses in this segment have identified that lack of awareness is not the core challenge. Only Indian MSMEs have identified a massive difficulty in getting sufficient and economical technological resources related to big-data analytics to suit their business requirement.

CONCLUSION AND FUTURE RESEARCH DIRECTIONS

Relatively new to the MSMEs, big data has been recognized as one of the present-day and potential research frontiers and has also been listed among Gartner's top ten strategic technology trends. This study's findings will help the managerial leadership in MSMEs devise strategies to leverage big data analytics benefits using cloud computing services. The research implications will benefit the organizational leadership of MSMEs in organizing and developing their short-term and long-term information systems strategies. Future research should focus on examining each of these identified challenges and solutions in the context of Indian SMEs. This study was just limited only to two south-east Indian territories; thus, upcoming exploration could be expanded to a more significant sample that would include all the Indian states so that the findings of this study can be generalized. The application of big data has slowly gained momentum among the Indian MSMEs based on multiple purposes with structured and unstructured data. Including the corporate sector, MSMEs also evidently recognized the importance of big data with accurate analysis to make timely decisions. Better, confident decisions with great pace can mean greater operational efficiencies, cost reduction, and reduced MSMEs risks. Therefore, the paper thoroughly discussed how MSMEs could benefit from applying big data and implementing the same with analytical practice. The book chapter also emphasized the significance of big data to the selected sector, a backbone of the world's economy, and examined big data analytics that can enhance MSMEs' performance. In India, the MSME sector should look at big data's structural potential for improved decision-making and policy formation in markets and business models and begin to explore the opportunities. The immense data analytics value signifies an exceptionally strategic and lucrative prospect for MSMEs. To be successful in the highly competitive business world where its regions are motivated by innovation and attractiveness, it is necessary to foster the development and wide-scale adoption of Big Data Value technologies, successful use cases, and data-driven business models.

REFERENCES

Adelekan, I. O. (2005). Gender, economic policy, and domestic energy use in Nigeria. *Ibaden Journal of the Social Sciences*, *3*(1), 1–16.

Akinwale, A. A. (2010). The menace of inadequate infrastructure in Nigeria. *African Journal of Science, Technology, Innovation and Development*, *2*(3), 207–228.

Assunção, M. D., Calheiros, R. N., Bianchi, S., Netto, M. A. S., & Buyya, R. (2014). Big data computing and clouds: Trends and future directions. *Journal of Parallel and Distributed Computing*, *79-80*(01), 3–15.

Banu, S., & Suresh, B. (2020). COVID-19 and its impact on micro, small and medium enterprises in India. *Mukt Shabd Journal*, *9*(X), 606–617.

Basu P (2004). Providing better access to finance for SMEs in India. *Access Finance, 2.*

Behera, M., Mishra, S., Mohapatra, N., & Behera, A. R. (2020). COVID-19 Pandemic and Micro, Small and Medium Enterprises (MSMEs): Policy Response for Revival. *SEDME (Small Enterprises Development, Management & Extension Journal), 47*(3), 213-228.

Chen, H.-M., Chang, K.-C., & Lin, T.-H. (2016). A cloud-based system framework for performing online viewing, storage, and analysis on big data of massive BIMs. *Automation in Construction*, *25*(1), 1–15. doi:10.1016/S0926-5805(99)00010-2

Dalberg, H. (2011). *Report on support to SMEs in Developing Countries Through Financial Intermediaries*. https://www.eib.org/attachments/dalberg_sme-briefing-paper.pdf

Das, K. (2008). SMEs in India: Issues and Possibilities in Times of Globalisation. In H. Lim (Ed.), *SME in Asia and Globalization, ERIA Research Project Report 2007-5* (pp. 69–97). Available at https://www.eria.org/SMEs%20in%20India_Issues%20and%20Possibilities%20in%20Times%20of%20Globalisation.pdf

DCMSME. (2017). *What are Micro, Small & Medium Enterprises?* http://www.dcmsme.gov.in/ssiindia/defination_msme.htm

Dixit, A., Sharma, S. K., & Sharma, D. P. (2021). Impetus on Big Data to Boost Indian MSME Sector and Economy using Cloud Storage. *International Journal of Computer Applications, 174*(21).

Dobre, C., & Xhafa, F. (2014). Intelligent services for big data science. *Future Generation Computer Systems*, *37*(1), 267–281. doi:10.1016/j.future.2013.07.014

Doe, F., & Asamoah, E. S. (2014). The effect of electric power fluctuations on the profitability and competitiveness of SMEs: A study of SMEs within the Acera Business District of Ghana. *Journal of Competitiveness*, *6*(3), 32–48. doi:10.7441/joc.2014.03.03

EISBC. (2017). *Definition of Indian SMEs*. http://www.eisbc.org/definition_of_indian_smes.aspx

Garg, N., Singla, S., & Jangra, S. (2016). Challenges and techniques for testing big data. *Procedia Computer Science*, *85*(1), 940–948. doi:10.1016/j.procs.2016.05.285

Government of India. (2020). *Annual Report-2019-20, Ministry of Micro, Small and Medium Enterprises*. https://msme.gov.in/sites/default/files/FINAL_MSME_ENGLISH_AR_2019-20.pdf

Hariharan, A., Thomas, S., & Viswanathan, P. K. (2021). Impact of COVID-19 on the Performance of Micro, Small and Medium Enterprises (MSMEs) In India–A Case Study in Kerala. *Annals of the Romanian Society for Cell Biology*, 14797–14816.

IBEF. (2021). *MSME Industry in India*. https://www.ibef.org/industry/msme.aspx#login-box

KPMG. (2015). *The new Indian MSME: An action agenda for growth*. https://assets.kpmg/content/dam/kpmg/pdf/2016/03/The-new-wave-Indian-MSME.pdf

Levy, B. (1993). Obstacles to Developing Indigenous Small and Medium Enterprises: An Empirical Assessment. *The World Bank Economic Review*, *7*(1), 65–83. doi:10.1093/wber/7.1.65

Ligthelm, A. A., & Cant, M. C. (2002). *Business success factors of SMEs in Gauteng: A proactive entrepreneurial approach*. Bureau of Market Research, University of South Africa.

Maroufkhani, P., Ismail, W. K. W., & Ghobakhloo, M. (2020). Big data analytics adoption model for small and medium enterprises. *Journal of Science and Technology Policy Management.*, *11*(4), 483–513. doi:10.1108/JSTPM-02-2020-0018

Mukherjee, S. (2018). Challenges to Indian micro, small scale and medium enterprises in the era of globalization. *Journal of Global Entrepreneurship Research*, *8*(28), 28. Advance online publication. doi:10.118640497-018-0115-5

Nagpal, Saini, & Gupta. (2009). *Problems faced by Small and Medium enterprises: SME in transitional economics-challenges and opportunities*. Deep and Deep Publications.

OECD. (2013). *Skills development and training in SMEs, OECD Skill Studies*. OECD Publishing. doi:10.1787/9789264169425-

Ogbuokiri, B. O., Udanor, C. N., & Agu, M. N. (2015). Implementing big data analytics for small and medium enterprise (SME) regional growth. *IOSR Journal of Computer Engineering*, *17*(6), 35–43.

Opresnik, D., & Taisch, M. (2015). The value of big data in servitization. *International Journal of Production Economics*, *165*(1), 174–184. doi:10.1016/j.ijpe.2014.12.036

Savrul, M., Incekara, A., & Sener, S. (2014). The potential of e-commerce for SMEs in a globalizing business environment. *Procedia: Social and Behavioral Sciences*, *150*, 35–45. doi:10.1016/j.sbspro.2014.09.005

Seseni, L., & Mbohwa, C. (2021). The Significance of Big Data in the Success of SMEs in Emerging Markets: A Case of South Africa. *Proceedings of the 11th Annual International Conference on Industrial Engineering and Operations Management.*

Seshasayee, R. (2012, Mar. 9). Financing SMEs: An industry perspective. *Business World.*

Siddiqa, A., Hashem, I. A. T., Yaqoob, I., Marjani, M., Shamshirband, S., Gani, A., & Nasaruddin, F. (2016). A survey of big data management: Taxonomy and state-of-the-art. *Journal of Network and Computer Applications*, *71*(1), 151–166. doi:10.1016/j.jnca.2016.04.008

World Bank. (2021). *Micro, small, and medium-sized enterprises (MSMEs) and their role in achieving the sustainable development goals.* Department of Economic and Social Affairs (DESA). https://sustainabledevelopment.un.org/content/documents/25851MSMEs_and_SDGs_Final3120.pdf

Zheng, Z., Ahu, J., & Lyu, M. R. (2013). Service-generated big data and big data-as-a-service: an overview. *IEEE International Congress on Big Data*. 402-410. 10.1109/BigData.Congress.2013.60

Zhou, K., Fu, C., & Yang, S. (2016). Big data-driven smart energy management: From big data to big insights. *Renewable & Sustainable Energy Reviews*, *56*(1), 215–225. doi:10.1016/j.rser.2015.11.050

Zulkernine, F., Bauer, M., & Aboulnaga, A. (2013). Towards Cloud-based analytics-as-a-service (CLAaaS) for big data analytics in the cloud. *Proceedings of the IEEE Congress on Big Data*. 62-69. 10.1109/BigData.Congress.2013.18

ADDITIONAL READING

Jha, R. S., & Sahoo, P. R. (2021). Influence of big data capabilities in knowledge management—MSMEs. In *ICT Systems and Sustainability* (pp. 513–524). Springer. doi:10.1007/978-981-15-8289-9_50

Potluri, R. M., & Potluri, L. S. (2016). A structural compendium on perceptual displays of rural India towards the role and impact of ICT. *Journal of Asian Finance, Economics, and Business*, *3*(4), 81–90. doi:10.13106/jafeb.2016.vol3.no4.81

Potluri, R. M., & Vajjahala, N. R. (2018). A study on application of web 3.0 technologies in Indian small & medium enterprises (SMEs). *Journal of Asian Finance. Economics and Business*, *5*(2), 73–79.

Potluri, R. M., & Vajjhala, N. R. (2021). Risks in Adoption and Implementation of Big Data Analytics: A Case of Indian Micro, Small, and Medium Enterprises (MSMEs). *International Journal of Risk and Contingency Management*, *10*(3), 1–11. doi:10.4018/IJRCM.2021070101

KEY TERMS AND DEFINITIONS

Big Data Analytics: Big data analytics is a practice applied to obtain significant understandings, such as concealed patterns, unidentified correlations, market movements, and customer inclinations.

Medium Enterprises: Medium-enterprises have 750 to 2500 million Indian rupees annually.

Micro Enterprises: Micro-enterprises with around 50 million Indian rupees in the manufacturing segment.

Service Sector Medium Enterprises: Medium-service sector enterprises' investment ranges from 20 million to 50 million Indian rupees.

Service Sector Micro Enterprises: Micro-service sector enterprises are firms that do not exceed one million Indian rupees investment.

Service Sector Small Enterprises: Small scale service sector enterprises are firms with an investment range from one million to 20 million.

Small Enterprises: Small enterprises in manufacturing have an annual turnover of around 50 to 750 million.

Chapter 12
The Influence of Risks Associated With Organizational Factors on Women's Professional Growth During COVID-19 in the UAE

Rajasekhara Mouly Potluri
https://orcid.org/0000-0002-6935-1373
College of Business and Communication, Al Ghurair University, Dubai, UAE

Sophia Johnson
Al Ghurair University, Dubai, UAE

ABSTRACT

The core objective of this chapter is to explore the risks associated with organizational factors influencing the professional growth of women in the United Arab Emirates (UAE) during the pandemic. The collected data were summarized and coded using software R Studio, and the variables were encoded and reduced using the one-hot encoding method and principal component analysis (PCA). The researchers identified that organizational and situational factors have a high degree of impact on women's professional development, which creates a significant effect of discontent over the mindset of women employees even in uncertain conditions. The study covers women employees working only in two emirates, Dubai and Sharjah. It includes telecom, banking, education, and other governmental and non-governmental organizations. This chapter is valuable to all the policymakers of the entire corporate sector and government authorities to set the right things by observing diverse organizational factors that influence women employees.

DOI: 10.4018/978-1-6684-5279-0.ch012

INTRODUCTION

The woman – the most incredible creation of Mother Nature and most inspiring community on the globe inevitably deserves the enthusiastic approach from all corners of the society for her committed, dedicated, and steadfast approach towards the surroundings of her existence. The women never hesitate to dedicate themselves to taking care of their loved family members, along with intense zeal and zest, to extend their support to their professional responsibilities. In providing more big money to their families, most women work these days, particularly in the last two to three decades. The trend of women employment throughout the globe has received phenomenon growth, including the traditional Islamic world also. Whatever may be the reason, and wherever women are working, they have been showing their mark in their professional career with their untiring commitment by perfectly balancing personal, social, and professional responsibilities. Women receive equal employment opportunities from private and public sector organizations with emotional intelligence, patience, compassion, intuition, adaptability, and networking skills. Modern-day professionally managed organizations identified women's strengths and capacities, treated them as bigwigs, and successfully offered a slot in their think-tanks. However, the pace is very minimal, and an insufficient number of women-only has received the kind of opportunities to get significant spaces in companies' organizational structures. The corporate world should develop uniform policies, plans, programs, and strategies with high confidence to throw away gender discrimination by proffering equal employment opportunities based on the skill and ken-level of the employees. Many career studies have primarily focused on either the western or Asian context. Gender discrimination has long been an extensively debatable issue (Arrow 1971; Lazear and Rosen, 1990; Bernard and Laband, 1995). Though globalization and equal employment opportunity regimes have opened several paths of company positions, so far, females are still less represented when it comes to climbing the corporate ladder (Grout et al. 2009), International Labor Organization (ILO), (2010a, 2010b). The world observed the signs of active participation of women leaders at all levels of decision-making in political, economic, and public life with equal opportunity (Osborn et al., 2015). Even with increasing participation in education and the labor force (United Nations (U.N.), 2015), women are stuck to higher posts in their careers. This trend presented a "glass ceiling" metaphor to the corporate world. The crucial research question to be answered in this paper is: What are the various organizational/situational factors that influence the UAE women's professional success? To address the critical research question, the researchers identified diverse organizational factors affecting professional growth in different parts of the globe with an extensive germane literature survey. The novel coronavirus (COVID-19) pandemic has brought about extraordinary challenges in diverse aspects of life. The current pandemic has presented immense challenges; other factors also shape the business landscape across the supply chain. The existing epidemic may be described as a global stress event that tests organizations' financial, operational and commercial resilience. They linked those factors with the UAE by collecting the opinions of five hundred women working in different public and private sector organizations only from Dubai and Sharjah emirates.

BACKGROUND

Several descriptions have been invented to illuminate impediments to women's career advancement, comprising the glass ceiling, glass cliff, maternal wall, glass escalator, and the sticky floor (Smith et al., 2012). Many metaphors relate to perspectives; for example, the maternal wall (Crosby et al., 2004;

Williams, 2005) and the motherhood penalty (Budig and Hodges, 2010; Correll et al., 2007) refer to the unique workplace challenges experienced by mothers. The glass escalator refers to advancement advantages of men over women in female-dominated occupations (Maume, 1999; Williams, 1992), and the glass cliff refers to the appointment of women to leadership positions when organizational conditions are risky or precarious (Haslam and Ryan, 2008; Ryan et al., 2011). Also, the career ladder refers to a single pathway to high positions, and the jungle gym conveys the possibility of lateral and upward movement (Sandberg, 2013). The glass ceiling is the most extended allegory in the intellectual domain compared to the remaining parables for women's barriers to professional advancement. Marilyn Loden coined the term glass ceiling in 1978 (Business Publishing, 2013; Pelican Bay Post, 2011). According to the Wall Street Journal, Marianne Schriber and Katherine Lawrence spelled the glass ceiling at Hewlett-Packard. However, the metaphor glass ceiling entered the corporate world by Carol Hymowitz and Timothy Schechellhardt in the Wall Street Journal's 24 March edition in 1986 (Jain and Mukherji, 2010). The glass ceiling is an invisible barrier (Dimovski et al., 2010a, b) which impedes a woman on advancement to a senior management position (Bolat et al., 2011) or on seeking employment to some organizations (Kolade and Kehinde, 2013) and a device for capturing and explaining the symbolic dimensions of discrimination against women (Bendl and Schmidt, 2010). The widespread acceptance of the term is evident from the establishment in 1991 of the bipartisan Glass Ceiling Commission, which was mandated to investigate biases against women and minorities that blocked their advancement to corporate management and to make recommendations on methods of eliminating the glass ceiling (Federal Glass Ceiling Commission, 1995a). The Federal Glass Ceiling Commission (1995b) established in the United States comprehensively defined the term as the unseen yet unbreachable barrier that keeps minorities and women from rising to the upper rungs of the corporate ladder, regardless of their qualifications or achievements. Researchers like Albrecht, Björklund, and Vroman (2003), Arulampalam, Booth, and Bryan (2004), and Pendakur and Pendakur (2005) also defined broadly the concept of the glass ceiling as an intangible barrier that determines the altitude to which women or a marginalized/under-represented demographic minority can come up in an organization.

Most of the career studies mainly focused on the western part of the world, particularly those interested in women's career success and, at the same time, very minimum number studies in non-western settings such as Asia (Xian and Woodhams, 2008; Granrose, 2007) or the Arab Middle East (AME) (Al-Marzouqi and Foster, 2011; Itani et al., 2011; Omair, 2010; Syed et al., 2010; Tlaiss and Kauser, 2010). Mainly, after considering professions of women and members of other minority groups, there have been numerous appeals to implementing a multi-level relational approach that incorporates the macro-national, organizational, and micro-individual levels of analysis and moves away from single-level explanations (Syed and Ozbilgin, 2009; Nishii and Ozbilgin, 2007). Despite these studies, few research studies contextualize the professional practices of women in the Arab Middle East (AME) region using a relational approach. In reply to these research studies, this study draws on empirical data from women employees from different public and private sectors in the unique meso-organizational contexts of the United Arab Emirates (UAE). The researchers explore the diverse organizational factors that impact the careers of Emirati women in this specific research framework. At the corporate level, various factors significantly impact the professional growth of all employees in general, including women and other minority sections of the organization. Just like weaker sections in the organization, women are also subject to discrimination in macro-contextual settings (Leinonen, 2012; Syed and Ozbilgin, 2009). Konrad (2003) contends that as organizations are dependent on environmental influences, they often imitate the conventional social discriminations in the allocations of the organizational result. Many researchers presumed that perceptions in societies and organizations are interrelated (Berry and Bell, 2012; Metcalfe and Rees, 2010). It does not come as disbelief that the more significant inequalities and discrimination encountered in the Arab societies (Tlaiss and Kauser, 2011; Omair, 2008) entrenched in the cultures and structures of organizations in the UAE as structural and attitudinal barriers (Al-Marzouqi and Foster, 2011; Randeree and Gaad, 2008; Rhode and Kellerman, 2007). Rhode and Kellerman (2007) noticed that women face more restraints than their male associates in the workplace because of gender categories. The McKinsey and Co. research shows that women have a worse experience than men, especially in the COVID pandemic. They are 1.5 times more likely than fathers to spend an additional three or more hours per day on housework and childcare. One in three mothers has considered leaving the workforce because of COVID-19 (Paulice, 2021). Work from home and work stress are associated with depressive symptoms among women having children between the ages of six and twenty-four months (Subha, 2021).

At the same time, Al-Marzouqi and Foster (2011) also noticed that women in the UAE IT sector recognize gender discrimination as a structural and attitudinal barrier obstructing their career progression. Prasada et al. (2020) focused on women working remotely in the I.T. sector and proved that occupational stress affected women's psychological well-being in the I.T. industries. Diverse studies on women's attitudes in the organizations report that the "think male-think manager" stereotype continues to be widespread within Arab countries (Tlaiss and Kauser, 2010; Omair, 2010; Al-Lamki, 1999). The discernment is also exceedingly noticeable in the salaries and wage gap. The Arab Human Development Office prepared an Arab Human Development Report (AHDR, 2006). It revealed that if women get employed, they earn less than their male counterparts because men are socially expected to be financially responsible for their families and should be paid more. The ratio of female to male earned income in the UAE is 0.24 (UNDP, 2006). Therefore, some of the recent studies which looked at Arab women's satisfaction with their salary and benefits in the services (Tlaiss and Mendelson, 2013) and the banking sector (Tlaiss, 2013) noticed that women in these sectors are dissatisfied with the monetary aspects of their career. These variations are prominent at the organizational level. At the same time, Randeree and Gaad (2008) discussed that for the economy of the UAE to achieve its potential and grow, the participation of women in the labor force and management should substantially increase in intensity. Even though the gender inequality index rank of the UAE is 26th in the world with a value of 0.113 as per the Human Development Report (UNDP, 2019), still female and male income differences are not competent with the developed world.

MAIN FOCUS OF THE CHAPTER

Professional growth or career success has received considerable attention from researchers in different parts of the world. Everyone in the corporate sector, along with the government, must know that a substantial number of reasons have influenced the professional growth of women and other minority sections in public and private sector organizations. The same has been proved in several types of research completed, even in the UAE and the Arab Middle East (AME). Though career success is a recognizable concept (Ballout, 2008), perceive it as a most difficult term to conceptualize, define, or operationalize, which has been proved by researchers (O'Neil et al., 2008; Ballout, 2007, 2008, 2009; MacDonald et al., 2005; Mainiero and Sullivan, 2005; Kim, 2004; Simpson et al., 2004; Judge et al., 1995; White, 1995; Powell & Mainiero, 1992; Gattiker & Larwood, 1988, 1989). The literature on career orientation highlights two types of success: objective and subjective (Nabi, 2003, 2001). Contrarily, real career success is characterized by vertical progression through climbing the corporate pyramid (Hall, 1996). The kind of professional accomplishment concentrates on organizational achievements, the scientific aspects of success (Powell & Mainiero, 1992), and society's monetary view of success and achievement (Nabi, 2001). It is believed that career success is independently established, applying "observable exoteric metrics such as salary and number of promotions" (Judge et al., 1995). It is hence assessed and specified through extrinsic or objective factors such as title or job status (Kim, 2004; Simpson et al., 2004; Gattiker & Larwood, 1988, 1999), promotions (Hall, 1996; Rosenbaum, 1979; Wilensky, 1964), the number of developments and upward career mobility (Baruch, 2006; Nabi, 2001), and monetary rewards such salary or income growth (Hall, 1996; Judge & Bretz, 1994; Rosenbaum, 1979; Wilensky, 1964). O'Neil et al. (2008) claimed that "male-defined" structures of success perpetuate a male-defined perspective on work and careers, over-rely on objective measures such as income, and fail to capture women's perceptions and actions of career success.

The glass ceiling affects employee commitment (Dost et al., 2012), and glass ceiling factors influence women's career development (Bombuwela & Alwis, 2013). Several researchers contributed extensively in identifying various glass ceiling factors like personal factors (Lerner et al., 1997; Jain & Mukherji, 2010; Pillai et al., 2011; Goveas & Aslam, 2011; Bombuwela & Alwis, 2013; Napasri & Yukongdi, 2015; Permanasri, 2013), social-role factors (Jamali et al. 2005; Gorbani & Tung, 2007; Jain & Mukherji, 2010; Pillai et al., 2011; Goveas & Aslam, 2011; Yang, 2011; Bombuwela & Alwis, 2013; Napasri & Yukongdi, 2015; Al-Manasra, 2013), interaction-centered factors (Lerner et al. 1997; Appelbaum, 2011b; Pillai et al., 2011; Goveas & Aslam, 2011), human capital factors (Lerner et al. 1997; Pillai et al., 2011), preference factors (Afza & Newaz, 2008; Jain & Mukherji, 2010; Pillai et al., 2011; Goveas & Aslam, 2011; Bombuwela & Alwis, 2013; Napasri & Yukongdi, 2015; Yang, 2011; Sumarto & Permanasri, 2013; Al-Manasra, 2013). Despite the UAE society's attributes, specifically tribal affiliations and patriarchy, the government implemented numerous radical policies to encourage women to participate more in the workforce and women's domination in higher education (Alibeli, 2015). Omair (2010) clearly explained in his study the four different types of career development for women in the UAE. These are progressive, moderate, idealistic, and facilitated careers. The first two categories are mostly related to middle-class women, and the last two, viz., ideological and facilitated jobs opted mainly by the upper-class women in the UAE. Social connections or "wasta" plays a pivotal role in women's careers in the UAE. The same study also revealed family relationships act as a significant boost for some women's jobs. Still, lack of contacts hinders their professional development, and the study finally supported that women face gender-based hurdles in their career progression (Omair, 2010). At the same time, the researchers identified the following list of organizational factors highly influenced by the literature review, as mentioned below, and considered those for the study.

Table 1. Organizational factors influence the career growth of women

Organizational Factors	Source
Organizational factors	Miles (2002)
Lack of security and stability	Looney (2005)
Lack of work opportunity	Looney (2005)
Corporate culture favoring men, Exclusion from networks	Jamali et al. (2005)
Lack of corporate support mechanism,	Jamali et al. (2005)
Perceived lack of commitment	Jamali et al. (2005)
Management perception, Organizational policy	Afza and Newaz (2008)
Sexual harassment at work, work environment	Afza and Newaz (2008)
Corporate culture, climate, and corporate practice	Dimovski and Man (2010)
Non-supportive corporate culture	Jain and Mukherji (2010)
Impact of work environment	Appelbaum et al. (2011a)
Seniority within the company	Appelbaum et al. (2011b)
Timely evaluation and promotion	Appelbaum et al. (2011b)
Human resource policies and strategies	Goveas and Aslam (2011)
Absence of peer colleague support and	Pillai et al. (2011)
Unfavorable company policies	Pillai et al. (2011)
Career self-efficacy and Work-related masculinity values	Bolat et al. (2011)
Old boy networks	Ghorbani and Tung (2007);
Old boy networks	Napasri and Yukongdi (2015)
Organizational practices	Al-Manasra (2013)
Management style and corporate policy	Bombuwela and Alwis (2013)
Difficult working relationship and	Napasri and Yukongdi (2015)
Human resource policies and practices	Napasri and Yukongdi (2015)

Alternatively, personal career success stresses the emotional aspects of success that are individually perceived and not confined to the organizational perspective. Different from the objective career success, the subjective view believes the assessment of professional growth from outside the corporate settings, converging on the contexts of career success idiosyncratic to an individual in terms of personal preferences and accommodation of work and family issues (Chudzikowski, 2012; Vincent-Hoper et al., 2012; Arthur et al., 2005; Clark, 2000). Distinct from real professional growth, personal professional development is internally oriented and defines success in terms of essential rewards. Primarily, organizations that have plans to avail the services of most committed women should develop flexible schedules, which helps them achieve productive contributions and work as part of a team to accomplish the anticipated outcomes (Jain & Mukherji, 2010). Cooper Jackson (2001) disclosed that corporate culture impedes women's professional development, and in most masculine-led companies, purposeful old boy groups exist, which eliminate females. Inadequacies incorporate practices like networking, mentoring, flexible working hours, and family-friendly initiatives to strengthen the existence of a glass ceiling in the organizations in Singapore (Dimovski et al., 2010a). High career self-efficacy provides women a way to reach their career aspirations, and low career self-efficacy blocks women. In a masculine culture, the gender gap is more substantial, and little equal opportunity (Bolat et al., 2011). Many women are uninterested in developing their self-efficacy because of the impact of the work environment (Appelbaum et al., 2011a). The higher the women climb the organization's ladder, the higher the chances of seeing more hurdles (Simpson & Altman, 2000). Looney (2005) said that lack of security, stability and work opportunity are the major hurdles for Iraqi women's career progression.

In contrast, working with superiors, colleagues, subordinates, and old-boy networks are the main barriers women employees face in Thailand and organizational policies (Napasri & Yukongdi, 2015). Moreover, different management styles and discriminatory promotion policies serve as crucial regulatory hurdles for women's career progression (Bombuwela & Alwis, 2013). At the same, in the case of Bangladesh, sexual harassment at the workplace, namely, oral, gesture, or unwanted emails, also work as factors along with management perceptions like male domination in higher positions and not to assign challenging projects to women hinder women's career progress (Afza & Newaz. 2008).

Issues, Controversies, Problems

1. Organizational policies and practices have a considerable effect on the career development of women in the UAE.
2. Working relations, peer support, and sexual harassment substantially impact UAE women's professional development.
3. Organizational factors significantly influence the UAE women's professional growth.

The researchers started this research to identify the various organizational or situational factors that influence the professional development of women in the UAE. The researchers thought that empirical study is essential to examine the problem statement with more clarity comprehensively and intended to determine significance for the development of the women's career progression in the UAE. The researchers collected more than forty research and review papers based on which extensive literature review and theoretical framework were completed to identify the diverse glass ceiling factors that influenced the career progression of women and minorities. Following a detailed, pertinent literature review and conceptual framework, the researchers selected three hypotheses and prepared a two-part questionnaire. The first part of the study highlights information about the demographic profile of respondents, whereas the second provides information about the various organizational factors. The researchers managed a stratified random sampling method to gather the opinion of five hundred women employees working in education, banking, telecom, and non-governmental organizations. Ultimately, the researchers received only 490 questionnaires with proper responses to all the columns. The gathered data was meticulously condensed, coded, and controlled using Software R Studio and Microsoft Excel. The variables obtained were encoded and lessened by applying the One-Hot Encoding Method and Principal Component Analysis (PCA). The selected three hypotheses were examined by employing the Kruskal-Wallis (K-W) Hypotheses technique.

Along with the above, the researchers also conducted brief personal interviews with the accepted 112 women employees for their time intending to know more about other organizational factors influence and their degree of impact. They analyzed the collected opinion by using a simple percentile. Internal consistency reliability, also called homogeneity, measures how well a test directs various constructs and provides reliable scores. For instance, in a series of questions that ask the subjects to rate their response between one and seven, Cronbach's alpha gives a score between zero and one, with 0.7 and above being reliable. Cronbach alpha (a) is the most used measure of internal consistency reliability (Litwin, 1995) and note that the reliability coefficient (alpha) can range from 0 to 1, with 0 representing a questionnaire that is not reliable and 1 representing a reliable questionnaire. A reliability coefficient (alpha) of 0.70 or higher is considered acceptable reliability.

This section of the article presents the analytical results of primary data in three categories. Under category one, the researchers offered the information about the demographical profile of the total respondents; category two highlights information about the respondents' response on organizational factors influencing the UAE women's career progression; in the final, presented the three hypotheses testing results.

Table 2. Demographic profile of the respondents percentage (N=490)

Demographic Variable	Classification	N=490	Percentage
1. Age (in years)	Less than 33	120	24.49
	Higher than or Equal to 33 and Less than 42	190	38.78
	Higher than or Equal to 42	180	36.73
	Total	**490**	**100.00**
2. Marital Status	Married	440	89.80
	Unmarried	50	10.20
	Total	**490**	**100.00**
3. Emirate at Work	Dubai	340	69.39
	Sharjah	150	30.61
	Total	**490**	**100.00**
4. Total Experience (in years)	Less Experienced (<10)	130	26.53
	Moderately Experienced (>=10 & <15)	160	32.65
	Highly Experienced (>=15)	200	40.82
	Total	**490**	**100.00**
5. Experience with Current Employer (in years)	Less Experienced (<8)	230	46.94
	Moderately Experienced (>=8 & <10)	40	08.16
	Highly Experienced (>=10)	220	44.90
	Total	**490**	**100.00**

Source: Survey results

The collected raw data from 490 respondents with the support of a two-part questionnaire was cleaned and analyzed statistically using the R language in R Studio. Data cleaning is implemented in Microsoft Excel before importing it into R Studio's statistical computing tool. The dependent variable in the data, the organizational factors that influence decisions towards their professional growth, illustrates the analysis path in this research. This dependent variable in the data determines the ultimate professional growth influence as per the opinion of the 490 UAE women respondents who participated in this research. The organizational factors influencing the decision variable demonstrate the respective career growth of each UAE woman who participated in this analysis. Three hundred and ten (310) UAE women responded that there is an impact of different organizational factors on their professional career growth in their organizations as against the remaining 180 UAE women opted that there is not that much influence of the organizational elements. The researchers first introduced a two-part survey for a pilot study with a sample of just 25 to check the internal consistency reliability. The researchers applied Cronbach's alpha test for nine constructs based on the collected data. The internal consistency reliability coefficient (alpha) measures these nine organizational factors that influence professional growth reported between 0.776

and 0.889. Organizational factors like sexual harassment and abusive language, company policies and practices, corporate culture, and climate have received Cronbach's alpha value of 0.776.

In contrast, lack of security, stability, work opportunity, work culture favoring men, and the impact of the work environment, management styles, and perceptions have a value of 0.882. And finally, factors like lack of corporate support mechanism, complicated working relationships, absence of peer support, and timely evaluation and promotions have a reliability coefficient value of 0.889. With several options, the respondents answered nine questions under different organizational/situational factors. The answers were selected using the 'select one or more options' format. The categorical data within each question was transformed using the One-Hot Encoding method for statistical analysis. This research uses the One-Hot encoding method to convert non-numeric categories into numbers. This method uses a group of bits to represent a possible category. If the variable cannot belong to multiple categories at once, only one bit in the group can be "on." Each of the bits is a feature.

For instance, a categorical variable questioning the responders' person-centered factors with nine possible categories is encoded as a feature vector of length nine (Zheng & Casari, 2018). The vital part of the dataset, the answers to all the six questions, were in the form of numerical data. Analyzing the data with several individual vectors for six questions was challenging to interpret due to the many dimensions statically. Subsequently, the dimensionality reduction technique, Principal Component Analysis (PCA), was implemented on the data to avoid this type of scenario. PCA focuses on the notion of linear dependence. Linearly dependent features are a waste of space and computation power because the information could have been encoded in much fewer features. To avoid this situation in this research, PCA tries to reduce such "fluff" by squashing the data into a much lower dimensional linear subspace. PCA computes a new set of variables known as principal components and expresses the data and its variance in these new variables.

The first principal component (PC1) explains the most variance spread in the data. Accordingly, the respective first principal component, PC1, for each of the six questions in this research describes the highest possible variation created by the multiple categorical options chosen by the responders. Thus, each selected PC1 for each of the six questions was further analyzed to prove or disprove the created hypothesis in this research (Zheng & Casari, 2018). Eventually, after collecting the data, which is ready to test and determine the driven assumptions, Kruskal-Wallis (K-W) Hypothesis testing is used in this research. The K-W test also called a one-way Analysis of Variance (ANOVA), tests whether samples originate from the same distribution in the data (Kruskal & Wallis, 1952). This technique compares two or more independent models of equal or example sizes. The researchers employed the K-W test to examine the chosen hypotheses, which illustrates the relation between a dependent variable, the final decision of women employees, and the remaining independent variables stated in the premises. The researchers were also involved in unstructured personal interviews with women who were willing to offer their time along with the questionnaires. Based on those interactions, researchers identified, along with the discussed glass ceiling factors, 94 percent of respondents whispered that religious, cultural, racial, national, and geographic factors also severely affected the career progression, which leads to serious discontentment. At the same time, 68 percent of subjects also reiterated that discrimination in the workplace severely affected their mental and physical health with substantial stress and deterrent factors like job satisfaction, social reputation, economic benefits, and self-esteem. Simultaneously, 75 percent of female employees expressed dissatisfaction with the corporate world's patriarchal social structures and male-dominant cultures. People who are in influential positions consciously create impediments to their career advancement. In these situations, women are often prevented from reaching the apex positions by revealing irrelevant causes or cock and bull stories about company situations even though highly qualified and efficient knowledge sources are available in the country. Finally, 90 percent of women respondents felt that their professional capabilities and commitments towards their careers are ignored and highly discounted, resulting in injustice and total hindrance in getting into higher echelons of managerial positions.

The following Table 3 illustrates the implementation of the Kruskal-Wallis hypothesis testing, which strengthens the data collected statistically and meaningfully. The P-Value from the result of this statistical test will decide to either approve or disprove the stated hypotheses.

Table 3. Testing of hypotheses

Hypothesis S. No.	Null and Alternative Hypothesis (H0 & H1)	Proportionality Test Result	Interpretation
1	**H0**: Organizational policies and practices **do not** have a considerable effect on the career development of women in the UAE. H1: Organizational policies and practices have a considerable effect on the career development of women in the UAE.	K–W Chi-Squared value: 3.07 P-Value: 0.084	Since the P-value is statistically significant (>0.05), the null hypothesis (H0) is failed to get rejected. Thus, organizational policies and practices do not have a significant impact on the career development of women in the UAE
2	**H0**: Working relations, peer support, and sexual harassment **do not** substantially impact the UAE women's professional development. H1: Working relations, peer support, and sexual harassment substantially impact UAE women's professional development.	K–W Chi-Squared value: 0.05 P-Value: 0.82	Since the P-value is statistically significant (>0.05), the null hypothesis (H0) is failed to get rejected. Thus, Person-Centered factors do not influence the career progression of UAE women.
3	**H0**: The UAE women's professional growth **does not** significantly influence the organizational factors. H1: Organizational factors significantly influence the UAE women's professional growth.	K–W Chi-Squared value: 6.25 P-Value: 0.01	Since the P-value is not statistically significant (<0.5), the null hypothesis (H0) is rejected. Thus, these factors significantly influence UAE women employees' career growth.

The researchers implemented the K-W hypothesis testing technique to ascertain whether the chosen factors affected the career growth of UAE women. If this P-value, resultant from the K-W hypotheses testing, has a value of greater than 0.05, the null-hypotheses (H0) is approved. In the other case, if P-value is less than or equal to 0.05, the alternative hypotheses (H1) are accepted. In explaining the overall results in this research, Organizational factors (P-value 0.01) significantly impact the UAE women's career growth. On the other hand, the remaining elements, such as working relations, peer-support, and sexual harassment (P-value 0.82), and the organizational policies and practices (P-value 0.084) do not significantly impact the UAE women's professional career growth or on seeking employment in an organization.

SOLUTIONS AND RECOMMENDATIONS

The UAE is prominent for fairness in access and privileges for men and women regarding jobs and wages (UAE Labor Law, 2007). However, the study conclusions disclose that organizational factors significantly affected women's career progress in this part of the globe. Based on the research outcome, the policymakers can review the existing administrative and situational factors to proffer meaningful opportunities to the women community. Women require government support to include women in leadership and supply chain in private and public sectors, constitutional rights, effective judicial laws, and policies to promote gender equality. The corporate sector in the UAE reviews its existing H.R. policies, plans, procedures, strategies, and budgets to proffer equal employment opportunities and redesign its system to avail the services of a highly committed women community. The research findings provide valuable insights regarding how women perceive the glass ceiling factors that influence their career progression for human resource departments of educational institutions, telecom companies, and banking companies.

Furthermore, every company's HR departments need to step up to redefine recruitment, selection, and promotional policies for women employees based on their qualifications, skills, and experiences. An encouraging redefinition of the company's plans in getting the most active women community to generate its productivity in many ways is always beneficial to any organization. Along with the above, companies also repeatedly initiate training and development prospects to build a multi-skill approach among women, improving self-confidence. Most women these days engage in multi-tasking and play numerous roles in upholding their families with the support of their professions by strengthening their financial capability. The study's findings also help governmental agencies and policymakers review their current gender discrimination policies at a broader level. This research also supports all public sector organizations introducing a more rigorous counteractive mechanism to eliminate gender discrimination and grant women a fair representation in their professional growth. The study observed that almost all organizational factors discussed in the chapter severely hamper the professional development of the UAE women in normal conditions and with an extra degree of impact affected during the pandemic. So many organizations have indefinitely stopped the promotions by introducing policy modifications and pink slip circulations.

FUTURE RESEARCH DIRECTIONS

The researchers should concentrate on legislation and government approaches towards the career development of women, lack of satisfaction with their salaries, promotion, and development programs. A similar kind of qualitative and comparative research in other Gulf Cooperation Council (GCC) countries like Bahrain, Kuwait, Saudi Arabia, Oman, and Qatar in the Middle East with a broader scope in the future may be taken up. Further extensive pragmatic studies with more samples on other factors like person-centered, social-role, interaction-centered, human capital, and preference factors may offer a vivid insight into women's leadership and its barriers, influencing women's career growth.

CONCLUSION

The research identified numerous organizational factors that significantly influenced the professional growth of the UAE women, primarily working in the country's public and private sectors, particularly in banking, telecom, education, governmental organizations, and some non-governmental organizations. Compared to the remaining parts of the world, UAE women have prominently enjoyed career progression due to governmental policies. Legal support and some social and cultural concerns also helped here. The study investigated the opinions of women employees from different public and private sectors, primarily located in the Dubai and Sharjah emirates of the UAE. The study highlighted two critical issues organizational factors that significantly influence the career progression of UAE women. Still, working relations, peer support, and sexual harassment have little influence. The research identified that 82 percent of women employees who responded to the survey said organizational factors severely influenced their professional growth. There is enormous scope for expanding this kind of research in other emirates to get a more general opinion of the entire working women in the country.

REFERENCES

Afza, S. R., & Newaz, M. K. (2008). Factors determining the presence of glass ceiling and influencing women career advancement in Bangladesh. *BRAC University Journal*, *5*(1), 85–92.

Al-Lamki, S. (1999). *Paradigm shift: A perspective on Mani women in management in the Sultanate of Oman, advancing women in leadership*. Available at www.advancingwomen .com/awl/spring99/Al-Lamki/allamk.html

Al-Manasra, E. A. (2013). What are the 'glass ceiling' barriers effects on women's career progress in Jordan? *International Journal of Business and Management*, *8*(6), 40–46. doi:10.5539/ijbm.v8n6p40

Al-Marzouqi, A. H., & Foster, N. (2011). An exploratory study of the under-representation of Emirate women in the United Arab Emirates information technology sector. *Equality, Diversity and Inclusion*, *30*(7), 544–562. doi:10.1108/02610151111167016

Albrecht, J., Björklund, A., & Vroman, S. (2003). Is there a glass ceiling in Sweden? *Journal of Labor Economics*, *21*(1), 145–177. doi:10.1086/344126

Alibeli, M. A. (2015). Gender and attitudes toward women in the United Arab Emirates. *Perspectives on Global Development and Technology*, *14*(1-2), 109–125. doi:10.1163/15691497-12341335

Appelbaum, S. H., Asham, N., & Argheyd, K. (2011a). Is the glass ceiling cracked in information technology? A qualitative analysis: Part 1. *Industrial and Commercial Training*, *43*(6), 354–361. doi:10.1108/00197851111160487

Appelbaum, S. H., Asham, N., & Argheyd, K. (2011b). Is the glass ceiling cracked in information technology? A qualitative analysis: Part 2. *Industrial and Commercial Training*, *43*(7), 451–459. doi:10.1108/00197851111171881

Arab Human Development Report (AHDR). (2006). *Towards the Rise of Women in the Arab World*. United National Development Program, Regional Bureau for the Arab States, National Press.

Arrow, K. J. (1971). *The Theory of Discrimination in labor markets.* Available at http://econ2.econ.iastate.edu/classes/econ321/rosburg/Arrow-TheTheoryofDistrimination.pdf

Arthur, M. B., Khapova, N., & Wilderom, C. P. M. (2005). Career success in a boundaryless career world. *Journal of Organizational Behavior, 26*(2), 177–202. doi:10.1002/job.290

Arulampalam, W., Booth, A. L., & Bryan, M. L. (2007). Is there a glass ceiling over Europe? Exploring the gender pay gap across the wage distribution. *Industrial & Labor Relations Review, 60*(2), 163–186. doi:10.1177/001979390706000201

Ballout, H. (2007). Career success: The effects of human capital, person-environment fit and organizational support. *Journal of Managerial Psychology, 22*(8), 741–765. doi:10.1108/02683940710837705

Ballout, H. (2008). Work-family conflict and career success: The effects of domain-specific determinants. *Journal of Management Development, 27*(5), 437–466. doi:10.1108/02621710810871781

Ballout, H. (2009). Career commitment and career success: Moderating role of self-efficacy. *Career Development International, 14*(7), 655–670. doi:10.1108/13620430911005708

Baruch, Y. (2006). Career development in organizations and beyond: Balancing traditional and contemporary viewpoints. *Human Resource Management Review, 16*(2), 125–138. doi:10.1016/j.hrmr.2006.03.002

Bendl, R., & Schmidt, A. (2010). From glass ceiling to firewalls – different metaphors for describing discrimination. *Gender, Work and Organization, 17*(5), 612–634. doi:10.1111/j.1468-0432.2010.00520.x

Bernard, F. L., & Laband, D. N. (1995). *Sex discrimination in the legal profession.* Quorum Books.

Berry, D., & Bell, M. P. (2012). Inequality in organizations: Stereotyping, discrimination, and labor law exclusions. *Equality, Diversity and Inclusion, 31*(3), 236–248. doi:10.1108/02610151211209090

Bolat, T., Bolat, O. I., & Kilic, T. (2011). Career self-efficacy and the glass ceiling: Moderating effect of work-related masculinity values. *Interdisciplinary Journal of Contemporary Research in Business, 2*(10), 57–68.

Bombuwela, P., & Alwis, A. A. (2013). Effects of glass ceiling on women career development in private sector organizations – case of Sri Lanka. *Journal of Competitiveness, 5*(2), 3–19. doi:10.7441/joc.2013.02.01

Budig, M. J., & Hodges, M. J. (2010). Differences in disadvantage: Variation in the motherhood penalty across white women's earnings distribution. *American Sociological Review, 75*(5), 705–728. doi:10.1177/0003122410381593

Business News Publishing. (2013). Summary: Full Frontal PR: Review and Analysis of Laermer and Prichinello's Book. Pimento.

Chudzikowski, K. (2012). Career transitions and career success in the 'new' career era. *Journal of Vocational Behavior, 81*(2), 298–306. doi:10.1016/j.jvb.2011.10.005

Clark, S. (2000). Work-family border theory: A new theory of work/family balance. *Human Relations, 56*(6), 747–761. doi:10.1177/0018726700536001

Cooper Jackson, J. (2001). Women middle managers' perception of the glass ceiling. *Women in Management Review*, *16*(1), 30–41. doi:10.1108/09649420110380265

Correll, S. J., Benard, S., & Paik, I. (2007). Getting a job: Is there a motherhood penalty? *American Journal of Sociology*, *112*(5), 1297–1338. doi:10.1086/511799

Crosby, F. J., Williams, J. C., & Biernat, M. (2004). The maternal wall. *The Journal of Social Issues*, *60*(4), 675–682. doi:10.1111/j.0022-4537.2004.00379.x

Dimovski, V., Skerlavaj, M., & Man, M. M. K. (2010a). Comparative analysis of mid-level women managers perception of the existence of glass ceiling in Singaporean and Malaysian organizations. *International Business & Economics Research Journal*, *9*(8), 61–77. doi:10.19030/iber.v9i8.613

Dimovski, V., Skerlavaj, M., & Man, M. M. K. (2010b). Is there a 'glass ceiling' for female managers in Singapore organizations? *Management*, *5*(4), 307–329.

Dost, M. K., Ur-Rehman, Z., & Tariq, S. (2012). The organizations having high level of glass ceiling has lower productivity due to lack of employee commitment. *Kuwait Chapter of Arabian Journal of Business and Management Review*, *33*(843), 1–11.

Federal Glass Ceiling Commission. (1995a). *A Solid Investment: Making Full Use of the Nation's Human Capital: Recommendations of the Federal Glass Ceiling Commission*. U.S. Glass Ceiling Commission.

Federal Glass Ceiling Commission. (1995b). *Solid Investments: Making Full Use of the Nation's Human Capital*. U.S. Department of Labor, November.

Gattiker, U. E., & Larwood, L. (1988). Predictors for managers' career mobility, success, and satisfaction. *Human Relations*, *41*(8), 569–591. doi:10.1177/001872678804100801

Gattiker, U. E., & Larwood, L. (1989). Career success, mobility and extrinsic satisfaction of corporate managers. *The Social Science Journal*, *26*(1), 75–92. doi:10.1016/0362-3319(89)90039-6

Ghorbani, M., & Tung, R. L. (2007). Behind the veil: An exploratory study of the myths and realities of women in the Iranian workforce. *Human Resource Management Journal*, *17*(4), 376–392. doi:10.1111/j.1748-8583.2007.00051.x

Goveas, S., & Aslam, N. (2011). A role and contributions of women in the Sultanate of Oman. *International Journal of Business and Management*, *6*(3), 232–239. doi:10.5539/ijbm.v6n3p232

Granrose, C. S. (2007). Gender differences in career perceptions in the People's Republic of China. *Career Development International*, *12*(1), 9–27. doi:10.1108/13620430710724802

GroutP. A.ParkI. U.SondereggerS. (2009). An economic theory of glass ceiling. http://www.bris.ac.uk/Dept/CMPO/workingpapers/wp183.pdf

Hall, D. T. (1996). Protean careers of the 21st century. *The Academy of Management Executive*, *10*(4), 8–16. doi:10.5465/ame.1996.3145315

Haslam, S. A., & Ryan, M. K. (2008). The road to the glass cliff: Differences in the perceived suitability of men and women for leadership positions in succeeding and failing organizations. *The Leadership Quarterly*, *19*(5), 530–546. doi:10.1016/j.leaqua.2008.07.011

International Labor Organization (ILO). (2010a). Global employment trends. Geneva: International Labor Office.

International Labor Organization (ILO). (2010b). *Women in labor markets: measuring progress and identifying challenges*. International Labor Office.

Itani, H., Sidani, Y., & Baalbaki, I. (2011). United Arab Emirates female entrepreneurs: Motivations and frustrations. *Equality, Diversity and Inclusion*, *30*(5), 409–424. doi:10.1108/02610151111150654

Jain, N., & Mukherji, S. (2010). The perception of the glass ceiling in Indian organizations: An exploratory study. *South Asian Journal of Management*, *17*(1), 23–42.

Jamali, D., Sidani, Y., & Safieddine, A. (2005). Constraints facing working women in Lebanon: An insider view. *Women in Management Review*, *20*(8), 581–594. doi:10.1108/09649420510635213

Judge, T. A., & Bretz, R. D. Jr. (1994). Political influence behavior and political success. *Journal of Management*, *20*(1), 43–65. doi:10.1177/014920639402000103

Judge, T. A., Cable, D. M., Boudreau, J. W., & Bretz, R. D. (1995). An empirical investigation of the predictors of executive career success. *Personnel Psychology*, *48*(3), 485–519. doi:10.1111/j.1744-6570.1995.tb01767.x

Kim, N. (2004). Career success orientation of Korean women bank employees. [Research Note]. *Career Development International*, *9*(6), 595–608. doi:10.1108/13620430410559179

Kolade, O. J., & Kehinde, O. (2010). Glass ceiling and women career advancement: Evidence from the Nigerian construction industry. *Iranian Journal of Management Studies*, *6*(1), 71–99.

Kruskal, W. H., & Wallis, W. A. (1952). Use of ranks in one-criterion variance analysis. *Journal of the American Statistical Association*, *47*(260), 583–621. doi:10.1080/01621459.1952.10483441

Labor Law U. A. E. Article 32. (2007). Available at https://www.moid.gov.ae/Laws/UAE_Labour_Law.pdf

Lazear, E. P., & Rosen, S. (1990). Male-female wage differentials in job ladders. *Journal of Labor Economics*, *8*(1).

Leinonen, M. (2012). Challenging and reinforcing gender boundaries at work. *Equality, Diversity and Inclusion*, *31*(7), 633–645. doi:10.1108/02610151211263469

Lerner, M., Brush, C., & Hisrich, R. (1997). Israeli women entrepreneurs: An examination of factors affecting performance. *Journal of Business Venturing*, *12*(4), 315–339. doi:10.1016/S0883-9026(96)00061-4

Litwin, M. (1995). *How to Measure Survey Reliability and Validity*. Sage Publications. doi:10.4135/9781483348957

Looney, R. (2005). The economics of coping: The plight of women in Iraq's informal economy. *The Journal of Social, Political, and Economic Studies*, *30*(3), 285–304.

MacDonald, P., Brown, K., & Bradley, L. (2005). Have traditional career paths given way to protean ones? Evidence from senior managers in the Australian public sector. *Career Development International*, *10*(2), 109–129. doi:10.1108/13620430510588310

Mainiero, L. A., & Sullivan, S. E. (2005). Kaleidoscope careers: An alternate explanation for the 'opt-out' revolution. *The Academy of Management Executive*, *19*(1), 106–123. doi:10.5465/ame.2005.15841962

Maume, D. J. Jr. (1999). Glass ceilings and glass escalators: Occupational segregation and race and sex differences in managerial promotions. *Work and Occupations*, *26*(4), 483–509. doi:10.1177/0730888499026004005

Metcalfe, B. D., & Rees, C. J. (2010). Gender, globalization and organization: Exploring power, relations, and intersections. *Equality, Diversity and Inclusion*, *29*(1), 5–22. doi:10.1108/02610151011019183

Miles, R. (2002). Employment and unemployment in Jordan: The importance of the gender system. *World Development*, *30*(3), 413–427. doi:10.1016/S0305-750X(01)00123-1

Nabi, G. (2001). The relationship between HRM, social support and subjective career success among men and women. *International Journal of Manpower*, *22*(5), 457–474. doi:10.1108/EUM0000000005850

Nabi, G. (2003). Situational characteristics and subjective career success: The mediating role of career-enhancing strategies. *International Journal of Manpower*, *24*(6), 653–671. doi:10.1108/01437720310496148

Napasri, T., & Yukongdi, V. (2015). A study of Thai female executives: Perceived barriers to career advancement. *Review of Integrative Business and Economics Research*, *4*(3), 108.

Nishii, L. H., & Ozbilgin, M. F. (2007). Global diversity management: Towards a conceptual framework. *International Journal of Human Resource Management*, *18*(11), 1883–1894. doi:10.1080/09585190701638077

O'Neil, D., Hopkins, M., & Bilimoria, D. (2008). Women careers at the start of the 21st century: Patterns and paradoxes. *Journal of Business Ethics*, *80*(4), 727–743. doi:10.100710551-007-9465-6

Omair, K. (2008). Women in management in the Arab context. *Education, Business and Society*, *1*(2), 107–123. doi:10.1108/17537980810890293

Omair, K. (2010). Typology of career development for Arab women managers in the United Arab Emirates. *Career Development International*, *15*(2), 121–143. doi:10.1108/13620431011040932

Osborn, D., Cutter, A., & Ullah, F. (2015). *Universal sustainable development goals: understanding the transformational challenge for developed countries*. Report of a Study by Stakeholder Forum.

Pelican Bay Post. (2011). *Marilyn Loden on feminine leadership*. Available at http://www.ecatalognow.com/article/Marilyn+Loden+On+Feminine+Leadership/766271/73810/article.html

Pendakur, K., & Pendakur, R. (2005). *Glass ceilings for ethnic minorities*. Vancouver Centre of Excellence. https://pdfs.semanticscholar.org/c144/0b7801d0928de18568f5462a26cbef15687f.pdf

Permanasari, R. (2013). Understanding of Women in Indonesia: Motivation to lead, work-family conflict, and ambition. *International Journal of Human Resource Studies*, *3*(3), 24–38. doi:10.5296/ijhrs.v3i3.4220

Pillai, K. R., Prasad, S., & Thomas, J. (2011). Why do women still experience downward gravitation in the corporate ladder? A close look at the glass ceiling in Bahrain. *Research and Practice in Human Resource Management*, *19*(1), 1–10.

Powell, G. N., & Mainiero, L. M. (1992). Cross-currents in the river of time: Conceptualizing the complexities of women's careers. *Journal of Management*, *18*(2), 215–237. doi:10.1177/014920639201800202

Prasada, K. D. V., Vaidyab, R. W., & Mangipudi, M. R. (2020). Effect of occupational stress and remote working on the psychological well-being of employees: An empirical analysis during Covid-19 pandemic concerning information technology industry in Hyderabad. *Indian Journal of Commerce & Management Studies.*, *11*(2), 1–13. doi:10.18843/ijcms/v11i2/01

Randeree, K., & Gaad, E. (2008). Views on the 'knowledge economy project' of the Arabian Gulf: A gender perspective from the UAE in education and management. *The International Journal of Diversity in Organisations, Communities and Nations*, *8*(2), 69–77. doi:10.18848/1447-9532/CGP/v08i02/39546

Rhode, D. L., & Kellerman, B. (2007). Women and leadership: the state of play. In B. Kellerman & D. L. Rhode (Eds.), *Women and Leadership: The State of Play and Strategies for Change* (pp. 1–62). John Wiley & Sons.

Rosenbaum, J. L. (1979). Tournament mobility: Career patterns in a corporation. *Administrative Science Quarterly*, *24*(2), 221–241. doi:10.2307/2392495

Ryan, M. K., Haslam, S. A., Hersby, M. D., & Bongiorno, R. (2011). Think crisis–think female: The glass cliff and contextual variation in the think manager–think male stereotype. *The Journal of Applied Psychology*, *96*(3), 470–484. doi:10.1037/a0022133 PMID:21171729

Sandberg, S. (2013). Lean. In *Women, Work and the Will to Lead*. WH Allen.

Simpson, R., & Altman, Y. (2000). The time-bounded glass ceiling and young women managers: Career progress and career success–evidence from the U.K. *Journal of European Industrial Training*, *24*(2/3/4), 190-198.

Simpson, R., Sturges, J., Woods, A., & Altman, Y. (2004). Career progress and career barriers: Women MBA graduates in Canada and the U.K. *Career Development International*, *9*(4/5), 459–477. doi:10.1108/13620430410550736

Smith, P., Caputi, P., & Crittenden, N. (2012). A maze of metaphors around glass ceilings. *Gender in Management*, *27*(7), 436–448. doi:10.1108/17542411211273432

Subha, B., Madhusudhanan, R., & Thomas, A. A. (2021). An investigation of the impact of occupational stress on mental health of remote working women I.T. professionals in urban Bangalore, India. *Journal of International Women's Studies*, *22*(6), 139–149.

Syed, J., Burke, R. J., & Acar, P. (2010). Re-thinking 'tanawwo' (diversity) and 'musawat' (equality) in the Middle East. *Equality, Diversity and Inclusion*, *29*(2), 144–149. doi:10.1108/02610151011024466

Syed, J., & Ozbilgin, M. (2009). A relational framework for international transfer of diversity management practices. *International Journal of Human Resource Management*, *20*(12), 2435–2453. doi:10.1080/09585190903363755

Tlaiss, H. (2013). Determinants of job satisfaction in the banking sector: The case of Lebanese managers. *Employee Relations*, *35*(4), 377–395. doi:10.1108/ER-10-2011-0064

Tlaiss, H., & Kauser, S. (2010). Perceived organizational barriers to women's career advancement in Lebanon. *Gender in Management*, *25*(6), 462–496. doi:10.1108/17542411011069882

Tlaiss, H., & Kauser, S. (2011). The impact of gender and family on career advancement: Evidence from Lebanese women. *Gender in Management*, *26*(1), 8–36. doi:10.1108/17542411111109291

Tlaiss, H. A., & Mendelson, M. B. (2013). Predicting women's job satisfaction with personal demographics: Evidence from a Middle Eastern country. *International Journal of Human Resource Management*, *25*(3), 434–458. doi:10.1080/09585192.2013.792859

UNDP. (2006). *Human Development Report 2006: Beyond Scarcity: Power, Poverty, and the Global Water Crisis*. UNDP.

UNDP. (2019). *Human Development Report 2019: Beyond Income, Beyond Averages, Beyond Today: Inequalities in Human Development in the 21st Century*. UNDP.

United Nations. (2015). *The millennium development goals report 2015*. United Nations. https://www.undp.org/content/dam/undp/library/MDG/english/UNDP_MDG_Report_2015.pdf

Vincent-Hoper, S., Muser, C., & Janneck, M. (2012). Transformational leadership, work engagement, and occupational success. *Career Development International*, *17*(7), 663–682. doi:10.1108/13620431211283805

White, B. (1995). The career development of successful women. *Women in Management Review*, *10*(3), 4–15. doi:10.1108/09649429510085053

Wilensky, H. L. (1964). The professionalization of everyone. *American Journal of Sociology*, *70*(2), 137–158. doi:10.1086/223790

Williams, C. L. (1992). The glass escalator: Hidden advantages for men in the "female" professions. *Social Problems*, *39*(3), 253–267. doi:10.2307/3096961

Williams, J. C. (2005). The glass ceiling and the maternal wall in academia. *New Directions for Higher Education*, *130*(130), 91–105. doi:10.1002/he.181

Xian, H., & Woodhams, C. (2008). Managing careers: Experiences of successful women in the Chinese I.T. industry. *Gender in Management*, *23*(6), 409–425. doi:10.1108/17542410810897535

Yang, Y. (2011). Gender and engineering career development of hotel employees in China. *Systems Engineering Procedia*, *1*, 365–371. doi:10.1016/j.sepro.2011.08.055

Zheng, A., & Casari, A. (2018). *Feature engineering for machine learning: principles and techniques for data scientists*. O'Reilly Media, Inc.

ADDITIONAL READING

Alketbi, A. H. S. B., Jimber del Rio, J. A., & Ibáñez Fernández, A. (2022). Exploring the role of human resource development functions on crisis management: The case of Dubai-UAE during Covid-19 crisis. *PLoS One*, *17*(3), e0263034. doi:10.1371/journal.pone.0263034 PMID:35259185

Dessler, G. (2020). *Human resource management.* Pearson Education.

Dodo, F., Potluri, R. M., & Gazara, S. (2017). Sustainable entrepreneurship among rural women in Nigeria: An assessment of benefits. *The Journal of Industrial Distribution & Business*, *8*(3), 5–9. doi:10.13106/ijidb.2017.vol8.no3.5.

Duran, S., Celik, I., Ertugrul, B., Ok, S., & Albayrak, S. (2021). Factors affecting nurses' professional commitment during the COVID-19 pandemic: A cross-sectional study. *Journal of Nursing Management*, *29*(7), 1906–1915. doi:10.1111/jonm.13327 PMID:33794061

Francis, V. (2017). What influences professional women's career advancement in construction? *Construction Management and Economics*, *35*(5), 254–275. doi:10.1080/01446193.2016.1277026

Guan, Y., Deng, H., & Zhou, X. (2020). Understanding the impact of the COVID-19 pandemic on career development: Insights from cultural psychology. *Journal of Vocational Behavior*, *119*, 103438. doi:10.1016/j.jvb.2020.103438 PMID:32382162

Olga, Y., Potluri, R. M., Gulfiya, N., & Aizhan, S. (2020). Women's unpaid work as a factor of gender inequality: A case of Kazakhstan. *Asian Journal of Business Environment*, *10*(2), 17–21. doi:10.13106/jbees.2020.vol10.no2.17

Potluri, R. M., Abikayeva, M. D., Yanovskaya, O. G., & Potluri, L. S. (2016). Kazakhstan's Gender Policy: Problems and Prospects. *The Journal of Industrial Distribution & Business*, *7*(2), 21–24. doi:10.13106/ijidb.2016.vol7.no2.21.

Potluri, R. M., Sophia, J., & Ullah, R. (2020). An investigative treatise on the success story of women entrepreneurs in tribal areas of India. *The Journal of Industrial Distribution & Business*, *11*(9), 17–24.

Ulrich, D., Becker, B. E., & Huselid, M. A. (2001). *The H.R. scorecard: Linking people, strategy, and performance.* Harvard Business School Press.

Ulrich, D., Younger, J., Brockbank, W., & Ulrich, M. (2012). *H.R. from the outside in: Six competencies for the future of human resources.* McGraw Hill Professional.

KEY TERMS AND DEFINITIONS

Kruskal-Wallis Hypothesis Technique: Kruskal-Wallis test, offered by Kruskal and Wallis in 1952, is a nonparametric testing method whether samples are initiated from the identical distribution. The null hypothesis of the Kruskal-Wallis test is that the mean ranks of the groups are the same.

Organizational Factors: Organizational factors contribute to the success of the information system according to the users. Mainly these factors are structure and philosophy, team resources and administrative support, and communication and coordination mechanisms.

Principal Component Analysis: Principal component analysis, or PCA, is a statistical procedure that allows you to summarize the information in large data tables employing a smaller set of "summary indices" that can be more easily visualized and analyzed. In addition, it is a statistical process that transforms the observations of correlated features into a set of linearly uncorrelated components with the help of orthogonal transformation.

Professional Growth: Professional growth implies gaining new skills and work experience to help you reach a goal in your career and practicing units to achieve a career goal or carrying out course work, workshops, or seminars to improve job skills or advance.

Chapter 13
COVID-19 Pandemic, Distance Learning, and Educational Inequality in Rural Ethiopia

Degwale Gebeyehu Belay
Bahir Dar University, Ethiopia

ABSTRACT

Due to the COVID-19 outbreak, schools are closed in many countries worldwide. China is the first to develop a distance learning program of 'Schools Out, But Classes On' not to disrupt learning. Ethiopia closed schools on 16 March 2020 after it confirmed the first coronavirus on 13 March 2020. To avoid learning disruption, the Ethiopian Ministry of Education has tried to develop strategies to resume classes at home. Accordingly, radio and TV education programs are designed for primary education, secondary education programs, and online teaching for higher education. This chapter aimed to explore the educational inequality of rural students of Ethiopia using situational analysis. The findings unveil the multiple inequalities of rural students that make them disadvantaged compared to urban students. The available distance learning programs homogenize students, which can create educational inequality.

INTRODUCTION

In late December 2019, a new virus emerged in China in the province of Wuhan (He et al., 2020; Wise et al., 2020). The World Health Organization (WHO) used the term 2019 novel coronavirus to refer to a coronavirus that affected the lower respiratory tract of patients with pneumonia in Wuhan, China, on 29 December 2019 (Adhikari et al., 2020). The first case of COVID-19 in Ethiopia was confirmed on 13 March 2020. On 16 March 2020, the Ethiopian Prime Minister's office announced that schools, sporting events, and public gatherings shall be suspended for 15 days until further notification. However, due to the increased outbreak of the virus, Ethiopia declared a state emergency on 10 April 2020 for the next five months. This intensified the closure of schools nationwide. As of 03 June 2020 (4:00 PM GMT), worldwide, 6,482,695 confirmed cases, 383,072 deaths and 3,089,101 recoveries were reported1. From

DOI: 10.4018/978-1-6684-5279-0.ch013

the same report, it is possible to understand that 1486 cases were confirmed in Ethiopia, 17 deaths and 246 recoveries.

As a result of COVID-19, schools were closed, which resulted in educational disruption. Despite this, it is difficult to know the exact number of students who disrupted education due to COVID-19; over one billion students are affected. This decision to temporarily close schools was prompted by the principle that large gatherings of persons constitute a serious risk to safeguarding public health during a pandemic (IESALC, 2020). As of 25 March 2020, 150 countries reported the closure of schools. In secondary schools, longer school closures could increase dropout risk for youth, particularly from lower-income groups (World Bank, 2020a). World Bank (2020b) stated the disruption of education as 'learning poverty'. The report of the World Bank further indicated that with the spread of COVID-19, among many disruptions to normal life, more than 160 countries have mandated temporary school closures, leaving 1.6 billion children and youth out of school. This article aims not to analyze the socioeconomic consequences of educational disruption due to COVID-19 but to analyze how distance learning interventions are exclusive and expose many students to educational inequality. The interventions taken homogenize students while the reality on the ground is different. The article also glimpses how the world is unfair in the distribution of resources, making the declaration of 'education for all' pseudo and futile.

The length of closure of schools and higher education institutions depends on the ability of the country to control the pandemic. No one knows for sure how long these closures are likely to last. Initial measures taken by many governments have ranged from 15 to 30 days, but one can easily anticipate that they will be extended until the pandemic subsides (IESALC, 2020). Although the pandemic poses a global challenge, it adds further complexity to countries with poor growth, inequality, and public financing (IESALC, 2020). The problem of COVID-19 on education is not proportionally fallen on poor and rich countries. Even in emerging countries, the problem is not the same in urban and rural areas. Being a citizen of an emerging country, living in a rural area, having a low-income family, being a girl, and having a certain disability have different levels of inequality in socioeconomic aspects. Hence, devising distance learning mechanisms, which are new models of education after the pandemic, which consider such differences of students is vital.

Infrastructure and familiarity with the tools drive successes (and challenges) in delivering learning. While schools are closed, many countries have turned to distance learning to mitigate lost time in continuing education services. Some countries are simply putting resources on their website and making available more products, but not necessarily online classes. While countries with robust connectivity deliver distance classes effectively, others who lack them find it difficult to reach all students equally (World Bank, 2020a). According to the report of the World Bank (2020b), while some African countries (Kenya, Rwanda, South Africa, Senegal, Botswana, and Gambia) have reasonable connectivity, and there are devices like tablets, most African countries' access to mobile devices is optimized.

Using smartphones requires partnership with private providers to allow zero charges for content downloaded from the Ministry of Education (or any agency that hosts learning resources platforms). In addition to infrastructure and connectivity, teachers' and administrators' familiarity with the tools and processes are also key factors in providing distance learning. International organizations have paid particular attention to the issue of "Education Response in Crises and Emergencies" (Huang et al., 2020). The Chines government was the first to make a deal with disrupted education since the pandemic was first found in China. The Chinese Ministry of Education has launched an initiative entitled "Disrupted Classes, Undisrupted Learning" to provide flexible online learning to hundreds of millions of students from their homes (Cheng, 2020; Huang et al., 2020). This strategy was "School's Out, But Class's On" (Cheng, 2020). This is the pioneering work of online education in China and worldwide (Zhou et al., 2020).

Cheng (2020) stated that although "School's Out, But Class's On" was a measure for home study during the pandemic, its essence was still a continuation of school education. Schools are the leading implementers of "School's Out, But Class's On". This aimed at "suspending classes without stopping teaching and learning" (pp.502). Schools and departments should be organized to ensure that teachers undertake online teaching, tutoring, and homework corrections. Therefore, it is of great significance to use information technology to promote education and teaching reform, "School's Out, But Class's On" is a kind of broad-based learning. Online teaching is only one format, and it cannot wholly replace classroom teaching (Ministry of Education of the People's Republic of China, 2020).

Different countries worldwide have introduced various solutions to continue the education process during the pandemic. Online libraries, TV broadcasts, guidelines, resources, video lectures, and online channels were introduced (Basilaia & Kvavadze, 2020). From their study in Georgia, Basilaia and Kvavadze (2020) stated that based on the first-week online teaching process at one of the private schools, the transition from the traditional to the online education systems at the school was successful. However, in the case of the USA, Dorn et al. (2020) stated that despite teachers, administrators, and parents have worked hard to keep learning alive, these efforts are not likely to provide the quality of education that's delivered in the classroom.

With the help of UNICEF, the Ethiopian government developed a coasted distance learning plan, with a focus on radio learning, particularly in primary education (UNICEF, 2020a). The Ethiopian Ministry of Education has introduced radio and TV programs to primary education, TV program to secondary and online teaching to higher education (see Table 1). Although some initiatives are taken worldwide, the problem of distance education is different between and among students in developed and developing countries. From their study in the USA, Dorn et al. (2020) found out that school shutdowns disproportionately affect black and Hispanic students compared to whites. These scholars further stated that there is more dropout among these disadvantaged students. This article focuses on rural students who suffer from multiple inequalities that lead to educational disadvantages compared to urban students.

Being a rural student, having a poor family, being a girl and other social dimensions intersect each other and affect students disproportionately. Therefore, the aim of this article is to unveil intersectional problems and educational inequality among urban and rural students in Ethiopia. This article focused on rural-urban divisions because the interventions of distance learning program during the pandemic, needs contextualization to be effective; unless it can create educational inequality between urban and rural students. This does not mean that there are no differences among rural and urban students themselves. The findings of this study can help governments and other national and international organizations to consider different dimensions to make distance learning effective in time of emergency like COVID-19.

Table 1. Remote learning means during COVID-19

Levels of Education	Means of Distance Learning
Early childhood	TV and Radio
Primary	TV, radio, and online videos Teachers can communicate their students via SMS and social media
Secondary	Predominantly online but can be supplemented sometimes with radio and TV
Higher education	Entirely online

Source: World Bank (2020b, p. 3)

METHODOLOGY

This chapter adopted a qualitative research methodology of situational analysis. Situational analysis (Clarke, 2005) is a research methodology that uses the situation broadly conceived as the unit of analysis. Clarke (2005) further stated that situational analysis can be used to produce a thick analysis of discourses, texts, "symbolisms of the nonhuman". As a research method, situational analysis is designed to (a) illustrate the complexities found within and surrounding social situations as they change, become stable, and create patterns and positions, (b) reveal subjugated knowledge' and marginalized perspectives, and (c) empirically decenter "the knowing subject" (Clarke, 2005). Situational analysis extends and goes beyond grounded theory (Clarke et al., 2015). Unlike g rounded theory which focuses on action, situational analysis focuses on the situation of inquiry broadly conceived; the ultimate unit of analysis, and understanding its elements and their relations (Whisker, 2018). Situational analysis constructs "the situation" empirically by making three unique ecological-relational maps: situational maps, social worlds/ arenas maps, and positional maps (Clark, 2005).

This methodology helps me to integrate my personal and professional experiences related to the issue as an integral component of critical research design and continued analysis. In the situational mapping, the author considers human and nonhuman elements that shape effectiveness of distance learning during the pandemic. For example, availability internet connectivity, TV, and Radio, mobile phone and other digital devises are important nonhuman elements. While availability educated parents and other family members and teachers are important human elements of the situational map. The social world map helps to interpret the relation between students, parents, and teachers that helps effective continual of the disrupted school. The positional map helps to explain how different positions affect distance learning. Social stratification i.e., sex, child labour demands by parents, socioeconomic status (occupation, income, and educational attainment) are important elements in the positional map.

This chapter is based on a hypothesis: 'All students are equally benefited from distance l earning during COVID-19'. In order to prove this hypothesis, the author had research questions of: do all students have equal access to internet, TV, and Radio? How the socioeconomic statuses of parents affect distance learning? What is the role of student-parent- teachers' relation in the effectiveness of distance learning during the pandemic? In order to answer these questions, the author has considered different reports and literatures to contextualize and analyse the data. Besides, the author has gathered data using informal discussions, email, and phone call that helps me in making the situation analysis. Due to the state of emergency of COVID-19, the author did not make a rigorous research method. Both quantitative and qualitative aspects were not addressed well. How students and their parents feel about children education is not well considered from parents as well as students perspective. Lack of theoretical and empirical literatures on educational situation during COVID19 in Ethiopia limits this article.

Focusing on rural-urban divide does not mean that all urban students are better-off than rural students in a complete manner. So, this article is limited in showing such complexes found between urban-rural settings, and among rural as well as urban settings themselves. However, through its relational understanding, the article can serve as a nice glimpse how socioeconomic difference create educational disadvantage between students during the periods of pandemic. It also depicts how rural students are in a more disadvantage position due to multiple inequalities compared to urban students in a relative speaking. Therefore, the author recommends a further comprehensive study in Ethiopia how distance learning modalities were practiced in urban and rural areas by incorporating the view of schools, students, and parents using a rigorous research method.

THEORETICAL FRAMEWORK

COVID-19 and Distance Learning

Different countries use different terms like 'flexible learning', 'open learning', and 'remote learning', and 'distance learning' which are alternative means to usual ways of teaching-learning process. For the matter of uniformity, this article uses 'distance learning' afterwards. Just like COVID-19 is first found in China, the strategy of 'School's out. But Class's ON' was started in China and later spread to the world to practice undisrupted learning (Zhou et al., 2020). Countries like Singapore have made early preparation of training teachers with expectation of closure of schools. Some countries like Lebanon have opted to send kids home with lessons as homework, promoting independent distance learning with the help of parents and peers (World Bank, 2020a).

As COVID-19 continues spreading in many countries of world, how to keep learning in disruption has become a major challenge to the global education community (Huang, et al., 2020). Using the China's strategy of 'School's Out, But Class On', UNESCO has designed a 'handbook on facilitating flexible learning'. UNESCO has designed a flexible learning approach which can offer choices in the educational environment, as well as customizing a given course to meet the needs of individual learners (Huang et al, 2020). The handbook has provided a comprehensive guide on how to use online teaching in a flexible manner. Though the handbook noted the limitations of Chinese experience of not addressing distance learning in areas with no internet connectivity TV cables, it did not address how the disrupted class can proceed in such disadvantaged situations. Distance learning aims to make learners more self-determined and independent, while teachers became more as learning facilitators (Wiki, 2019). Learners can be offered choices based on their needs (e.g., study during evenings or weekends) (Huang et al., 2020). The location of learners to carry out learning activities and access learning materials can also be flexible anywhere at any time via mobile devices, such as at campus, home, public transport, airport or even on a plane (Collis et al., 1997; Gordon, 2014; McMeekin, 1998).

Different technologies like email and social networks can be used to conduct flexible learning. Online education as a subset of distance learning (which also includes TV, radio, and other means which do not require internet) has always been concerned with providing access to education experience that are at least more flexible in time and in space than campus-based education (Huang et al., 2020). Online learning is defined as learning experiences in synchronous or asynchronous environments using different devices (e.g., mobile phones, laptops, etc.) with internet access. In these environments, students can be anywhere (independent) to learn and interact with instructors and other students (Singh & Thurman, 2019). In online learning, learners can interact directly with the learning content that they find in multiple formats (e.g., video, audio, document, etc.). Additionally, they can also choose to have their own learning sequenced, directed, and evaluated with the assistance of a teacher (Huang et al., 2020). Google meet and zoom are important online means of teaching (Basilaia & Kvavadze, 2020). The countries that are having the limited technologies have problems in schools are not ready for the complete implementation of the countrywide online education (Basilaia & Kvavadze, 2020; Sintema, 2020).

On April 2020, World Bank has provided guidance on distance learning; which is better inclusive compared to UNESCO handbook. The bank has provided different strategies of distance learning for different levels of education. Distance learning approach of World Bank has the 'aim to ensure all children and youth have access to a quality education' (World Bank, 2020b:1). Distance learning can ensure that students continue learning through a variety of avenues. From Table 1, it is possible to understand that the bank has considered different means of learning depending on the levels of education. In other words, the appropriate means of learning at each level of education has been suggested by the bank. Hence, how to conduct learning at different levels in countries with poor internet connectivity and digital infrastructures like Ethiopia was not given high consideration. Moreover, the bank did not consider the infrastructural facilities to students at all levels are almost similar except graduate students who are mostly self-dependent and might have access to internet and capacity to buy laptops, desktops, and smart phones. However, in developing countries like Ethiopia, there are higher education students of first degree from rural areas where there is no internet access and even electricity. Notwithstanding that UNESCO and World Bank has provided guidelines to proceed the disrupted class, there is uncertainty about when face-to-face classes, exams, assessment procedures and, of course, enrolments that are part of the cycle of any academic year can be resumed. At the moment, it is impossible to make predictions. However, as indicated in the study of IESALC (2020), most Spanish and Italian Universities are expected to open their doors in September 2020/21 academic calendar.

Distance Learning and Rural-urban Divide

In developing countries, education inequality is still widely observed between rural and urban areas. Income disparity, various institutional barriers, and different parenting styles, among others, are regarded as potential causes of education inequality (Zhang et al., 2015). Most parents in the rural areas do not take much interest in their children's schoolwork (Litheko, 2012). There is 'digital divide' between rural and urban students to access to technology and opportunities to learn ICT skills. There is no hardware, software, the Internet and technology support within public schools. There is also difference on how frequently students and teachers use technology within the classroom (Wang, 2013). The rural-urban infrastructure disparities indicate that urban areas can boast electricity and telecommunications capabilities, but rural areas remain unconnected and hence disadvantaged (Gulati, 2008). The lack of ready access to technology is a key barrier to technology integration for developing areas (Wang, 2013).

Both teachers and students in rural are disadvantageous in technological facilities, with regard to teachers, the study of Clark (2000) shows that urban teachers in the U.S. have positive reactions towards technology integration. The findings include three points: 1) urban teachers feel confident about their ability to use technology; 2) urban teachers believe that technology is an integral part of their classroom; and 3) urban teachers want more software and equipment in their classrooms. However, research indicates that rural schools do not have teachers with the same qualifications and confidence levels in technology integration as urban schools do. Lacking experienced and skilled teachers and technical training have been an on-going problem for rural schools (Herselman, 2003). With regard to students, as indicated in Wang (2013), students from rural schools score lower on all the Internet inequality indicators (digital access, autonomy of use, social support, Internet use and self-efficacy) and are therefore more disadvantaged in Internet usage status than their urban peers. Researchers have also argued that students in low-income areas often use computers for repetitive activities, whereas students in high-income areas often use technology for higher-order thinking, problem solving, and other intellectually challenging activities (Songer, Lee, & Kam, 2002 in Wang, 2013).

The Challenges of Online Learning

In the handbook of UNESCO (2020) and World Bank (2000b) guideline, online teaching has given great focus particularly to secondary and higher education. Higher education institutions have chosen to continue offering regular courses using virtual platforms and always with the guarantee of credit transfer. Here, however, there is a huge difference between those HEIs that have their own capacities both technological and in teaching resources and, above all, experienced teachers and those that do not (IESALC, 2020, p. 33). In comparison, online teaching cannot achieve the face-to-face emotional communication between teachers and students, and lacks real-time feedback of information and classroom constraints (Cheng, 2020). Moreover, if the closure long lasts, achieving the objectives of course will be very difficult (IESALC, 2020).

As stated in World Bank (2020b), while digital technologies can offer a wide set of capabilities for distance learning, most education systems in low- and middle-income countries, including schools, children and/or teachers, lack access to high-speed broadband or digital devices needed to fully deploy online learning options. As such, education systems need to consider alternative ways for students to continue learning when they are not in school, like in the current COVID-19 crisis. Online libraries, TV broadcasts, guidelines, resources, video lectures, online channel are important alternatives of face-to-face learning (Basilaia & Kvavadze, 2020; World Bank, 2020b). As stated in Huang et al. (2020), several challenges were reported during the application of online learning in the global wide according to the literature and international experts. For example, (a) Internet connection can be unreliable if there are thousands of learners learning simultaneously; (b) Some instructors can find it difficult to find online resources that are the most suitable in their teaching contexts because thousands of resources are published online; (c) Several instructors and learners do not have the appropriate digital skills to teach and learn online. This can make the online teaching/learning experience inconvenient for them; (d) Several learners lack crucial learning competencies, such as adaptation, independent study, and self-regulation, which are key factors for successful online learning; and, (e) Several instructors simply use direct instructions without considering important features of online learning, such as interactivity, social presence, and cognitive presence, resulting in unmotivating learning experiences.

Radio education and Television education are important broadcast distance learning models (World Bank, 2020b). However; as analysed in the coming section, in countries like Ethiopia where the large number of people in live rural areas with no electricity, TV and radio programs might not be applicable.

MAIN FOCUS OF THE CHAPTER

Intersectionality and Educational Disadvantage of Rural Students

Intersectionality considers different intersecting inequalities. Intersectionality posits that social divisions interrelate in terms of the production of social relations and in terms of people's lives. This term is used for the first time by Kimberley Crenshaw to mean overlapping categories of discrimination (Crenshaw, 1994). There are different specific criteria for social categorization i.e., sex difference, sexuality, ethnicity, race, age, height, educational achievements, appearance, and colour of eyes (Anthias, 2012). Social inequality, power, and politics have been primary concerns of intersectionality since its inception (Collins, 2012).

Anthias (2012) further states that such differences are not fixed elements of social landscape. This requires social policies that can consider multiple inequalities. Collins (2012, p. 446) comprehensively stated that 'social structures such as neighbourhoods, schools, jobs, religious institutions, recreational facilities, and physical and cyberspace marketplaces are the institutional expressions of social inequalities of race, class, gender, age, ethnicity, religion, sexuality, and ability'. Collins (2012) further stated that these different structures offer different opportunities and rewards. These different characteristics of people create different conditions of life. Using the term of Lohmann and Ferger (2014), with regard to education, the rural students suffer from absence of equality of conditions leads to 'educational poverty', and 'educational inequality' due to absence of equal opportunities.

Individuals from low-income families tend to invest less in education than those from high-income families (Botezat, 2016). From human development perspective, education is more than an instrument of development; it is a development by itself (Tilak, 2001). Rural areas are not just suffered from income poverty. What is revealing in rural Ethiopia is human poverty; people are denied of choices and opportunities for living a tolerable life (See: UNDP, 1992, p. 2). In this regard, World Bank (1994, p.2) also indicated that 'poverty is not only a problem of low incomes; rather it is a multi-dimensional problem that includes low access to opportunities for developing human capital and to education'. Using the notion of Amartya Sen, students in the rural areas lack capabilities; freedom that a person has in terms of choices and opportunities 'to lead lives they have reason to value' (Sen, 1999). The school situation before the closure of schools due to COVID-19 is not the concern of this article though it might have an influence on the effectiveness of distance learning after the closure. Educational inequality for rural students is discussed on how different modes of distance learning i.e., online, TV, and Radio are applicable compared to urban students. The socioeconomic background of students and student-parent-school relations are also important conditions that create educational inequality particularly to rural students.

Paradoxes of Distance Learning in Ethiopia

While internet use is widespread in everyday life and work for many in high income countries, this is not the case in most low- and middle-income countries (UNICEF, 2020b). As stated in IESALC (2020), from the seven continents, Africa is by far low in connectivity (17%) followed by Latin America (47%). Similarly, Internet World Stats (2020a) indicated that Africa has the least internet coverage; only 39.3% by far followed by Asia (53.6%). This makes African students not to have access to connectivity when they return home. In Africa in general and Ethiopia in particular there are more mobile lines than connected homes.

Ethiopia is formally connected to the Internet in January 1997, with the ISP being the then Ethiopian Telecommunication Corporation, now ethio-telecom (Atnafu, 2014). Compared to the rate of developments for Internet access in the rest of the world, it is difficult to say that access to Internet and the Internet penetration in Ethiopia has developed well. As indicated in Internet World Stats (2013), despite Ethiopia constitutes 9% of the Africa's population, it accounts only to less than 1% of African Internet access. Internet World Stats (2020a) also indicated that it is only 17.8% of the Ethiopia's population who have access to internet service. As indicated in World Bank, (2019), while the coverage of grid electricity in urban areas of Ethiopia is 97%, it is only 12% in rural areas. In the report of OECED (2020), despite students are supposed to have smartphones than laptops, the case is worst in rural Ethiopia; where students lack smartphones too. The haves are curious about how to get fast internet connections where most students are connected. However, in poor countries like Ethiopia, students lack internet connections at all particularly in rural areas. In Ethiopia rural area refers to locality having less than 2000 inhabitants (CSA, 2007). Moreover, in this study rural area is characterized by occupation, where agriculture is a dominant sector; lack of electricity and internet connectivity.

By 2014 the internet penetration rate in Ethiopia was less than 2% the social networking statistics shows that Facebook penetration in Ethiopia is comparable to the country's Internet penetration rate despite it is low compared to Facebook penetration in some African countries, which is 34.63% in Tunisia and 17.16% in Egypt (Atinafu, 2014). Internet Society (2019) also reported that many people in developing countries still do not use a mobile phone. And when the unconnected do gain access, such access may not be of adequate quality or low enough cost to be meaningful to them.

Online teaching is performed at higher education institutions. For graduate students, reading materials, assignments, and home take exams are sent via emails. In some universities, defences of Thesis and dissertation are made face-to-face with respect to the rules of the national state emergency due to COVID-19. In some other universities, defences are made using Zoom, and Google Meet. However, there are electric power and internet interruptions that affect effectiveness of this practice. In case of undergraduate students, despite the Ethiopian Ministry of Science and Higher Education (MOSHE) has planned to precede distance learning online, none of the universities are effective due to lack of internet access to the majority of students. Moreover, most undergraduate students do have email address to communicate.

As stated somewhere in the next sections, primary and secondary school students of private schools have better access to internet connectivity and ability to afford for digital devices. This is because, students of private schools have better socioeconomic background and these schools are located dominantly in major cities. Unlike public schools, private schools better distributed reading materials on applications of Telegram and WhatsApp. Private schools also conducted home-take final exams which are distributed in hard copies and returned back a week after. Moreover, the Ethiopian Ministry of Education designed online teaching to higher education which is not functioning effectively. Also, National Model Exams of Grade 8 and grade 12 model exams of 2020 academic year are reported to be conducted on Telegram. It is said that the question will stay online for few days to make it accessible to students with different accessibility challenges including power interruption. However, alternative mechanisms are not presented for rural areas that don't have access to internet as well as smart phone at all. This can create educational inequality and discrimination against the rural students.

In addition to the large inequities in access to the internet, TV and radio access varies considerably both across and within countries. In the context of Sub-Saharan Africa, TV and radio ownership rates among urban households were more than double that of rural households with the largest disparities appearing in sub-Saharan Africa (UNICEF, 2020b). UNICEF (2020b) further stated that Ethiopia is the lowest in Sub-Saharan Africa in which only 28% of the population have radio ownership. With this condition, it is obvious that rural students cannot be benefited from TV and radio programs as well. On 09 June 2020 UNICEF has made a report on how education is keep going during COVID-19 using TV and Radio platforms in Ethiopia. From the report some students who do have access to TV and educated parents have better advantage of perusing their study at home (Sewnet, 2020). However, the report does not clearly mention how students in rural areas spent their time during the pandemic.

Family Background and Children's Education

Family background has a great impact on the performance of children's schooling. Among this difference, being the resident of rural area is the glimpse of other socioeconomic differences with the urban people. Beyond, being children of rural family, poor family background of children creates multidimensional challenges to effectively perform education. Particularly during the time of COVID-19 where students are advised to stay and learn at home, students can't have access to reading materials such as text books, and other relevant infrastructures. As stated in Ayoroa et al. (2010), the poor don't send their children to school because they cannot scarify the financial support that these children provide through home labour. In Ethiopia, the study of ILO (2018) indicated that school attendance of children aged 7-14 is 82.4% in urban areas while 56.7% in rural areas. Therefore, it cannot be difficult to imagine that children of the rural poor who stayed at home due to COVID19 will be highly requested the labour. School closure disproportionately affect female students since they engaged in common household chores include babysitting, cleaning, cooking, shopping and caring for sick household members (ILO, 2018).

The poorer regions of the world, namely Sub-Saharan Africa, and South and West Asia experienced the lowest literacy rates (UNESCO, 2011). Financial security within the family plays a key role in how parents and their children make decisions about educational choices and provision which is related to the socioeconomic status of the family, which in turn is greatly influenced by the education level of parents (Drajea & O'Sullivan, 2014, p. 149). Similarly, Nelson (2009) stated that parents who have not attended college, on the other hand, tend to have less direct knowledge of the economic and social benefits of a post-secondary education. Thus, some of these parents may prefer that their children to work rather than to attend college. Christine Eden comprehensively stated that poverty, in terms of low family income affects children in several ways: the absence of learning habits and experiences at home; a lack of access to computers; lack of a sense of self-esteem through appropriate interactions with parents; poor housing; an unhealthy diet; possible mental health issues within the family; domestic violence; and the stress associated with low pay or unemployment (Eden, 2013, p. 35 cited in Drajea and O'Sullivan, 2014).

Student-parent-school Relation and Distance Education

During the time of COVID-19 strong school administration, parents, and teachers' support is important. However, in the context of Ethiopia, school administration and teachers' supervision to students is different between public and private schools. Private schools are concentrated in urban areas. Urban schools have qualified teachers and attractive salaries compared to their counter parts of government schools in both rural and urban areas. Curriculum difference is found between private and urban schools rather than in specialty. Rural schools have poor facilities as well as poor school-parent relation. McCracken and Barcinas (1991) stated that urban schools were larger; had more teachers, administrators, and support staff; and offered more courses and extra-curricular activities. This is a great implication that there is weak support to rural students compared to students in urban areas. From their study in China, Ayoroa and his colleagues stated that rural/urban education disparity is thus perpetuated as areas with lower quality education are provided with less-qualified teachers' (Ayoroa, et al., 2010). This is partly due to low salaries and few teaching and learning supplies for rural schools.

COVID-19, Learning at Home and Parents' Help to Children

Families background i.e., occupation, level of education, and family size have significant impact on students' educational attainment. This creates difference urban and rural areas. Most of the rural people in Ethiopia are agrarians who seek the labour of their children. Therefore, when schools are closed due to COVID-19, this is a good opportunity for rural parents to use the labour of students. Besides, unlike the urban parents, who mostly have behaviour of guiding their children to study, rural parents don't have such experience. Particularly female students will be engaged in household chores and will not be given time to study compared to their counterparts. Due to weak guidance culture of parents, the rural students to spend their time in plying than studying even in their free times.

It is not surprizing that children of educated family have an opportunity to get different support from their parents. Such parents can demonstrate positive attitude about education, monitor their children's videos, games, and internet use, encourage their children to read, help them in doing assignments and correcting them, and guide their children to be effective in their education career. The influence of family background on children's educational experiences has a curious place within the field of sociology of education (Lareau, 1987). The higher the social class, the higher the income, education, material possessions, and status (Evans & Herr, 1978, p. 119-120).

Kotrlik and Harrison (1989) concluded that students perceive that their parents influence their career choice more than any other person, and the mother is more influential than the father. That is why urban students have better educational and occupational aspiration compared to rural students (McCracken & Barcinas, 1991). Lareau (1987, p. 76) also stated that 'Many factors-e.g., parents' educational attainment, the amount of non-work time parents can invest in their children's schooling-affect the kind and degree of parental involvement'. Lareau further stated that parents' involvement in the education of their children is vital for their academic achievements. Education capability of parents and information about schooling are determinant factors that shape parents' participation in their children's schooling (Gooding, 2001; Lareau, 1987). Moreover, parents of rural students were less likely to expect their children to advance their education (McCracken & Barcinas, 1991).

Education capability of parents determines their involvement and assistance to children's education. The less educational capability of the parent, the more the parents turn the responsibility for education to teachers. In the middle-class community, parents had extensive information about classroom and school life (McCracken & Barcinas, 1991). Similarly, Parental education is consisting on different activities like the supervision of their children's social settings, activities and friends (Rizwan et al., 2014). It should also be noted that distance education requires more discipline and commitment on the part of the student, which perhaps explains why it is more successful among older people, that is, postgraduates, compared to undergraduates (IESALC, 2020). Students of rural areas who do have parents engaged in agricultural activities and peaty trading require labour of the students than helping them to study their subjects.

The face-to-face experience is particularly important for vulnerable students who have often had fewer opportunities for interaction in areas such as that offered by a university campus that allows them to strengthen their social skills, so that, if the closure is prolonged, they will be more disadvantaged than other students (IESALC, 2020, p. 16).

COVID-19 and the Situation of Distance Learning in Ethiopia

Following the school closures and the response plan set by the Ministry of Education, the respective regional education bureaus have initiated the continuity of education using various media, including using educational radio programmes and television learning programmes provided by the Ministry of Education. In addition, some private schools, mostly in urban areas, have been focusing on engaging parents and their students in learning through a Telegram mobile application, which is more widely used in Ethiopia (Hailu, 2020; Tiruneh, 2020).

However, the Ethiopian Ministry of Education has taken strategies that homogenises students. The Ministry suggested Radio and TV programs for primary education, TV education program to secondary education, and online teaching to higher education. These strategies would benefit only the advantaged students from urban areas and do have educated family background. Others who are the majority live in rural areas and cannot be benefited from all suggested strategies. Even, these distance learning strategies are not provided effectively.

As stated in Tiruneh (2020), radio and television lessons may work for some children in urban areas. However, the Ministry as well as regional education bureaus do not have clear evidence on how many parents in rural areas have access to radios and satellite television. Given that more than 80% of the Ethiopian population lives in the rural areas with limited or no access to electricity, it is least likely that radio and television lessons would reach all primary and secondary school children in the rural areas. Even when radio and television lessons reach some of the rural children, it is unlikely that those children get sufficient support from their parents at home because their parents have never been to school. This makes the existing strategies very limited that do not consider the existing situation of the majority students who are exposed to multiple inequalities. For sure, this can perpetuate educational inequality between the urban advantaged and the rural disadvantaged students.

As a default, the Ethiopian Ministry of Education has been encouraging schools and parents to help all children continue to learn from home through remote learning. However, there are limited mechanisms in place to ensure that ALL children can continue to learn at home. As indicated in Cordry and Wilson (2005), educational researchers argue that parental involvement in the education of their children at home is equally important. Despite it is impossible to say that the unschooled rural parents do not help their children at all (Ejaz, 2009), the nature of family's work, and the norm of coaching their schooling is different between schooled and unschooled parents (Lareau, 1987). Trineh (2020) also stated that homeschooling is particularly challenging in low-income countries like Ethiopia because many parents have not themselves been to school and there is a lack of the necessary infrastructure to support remote learning.

In most private schools of Ethiopia which are concentrated to the cities of capital of the country and regional states i.e., Addis Ababa, Bahir Dar, Hawassa, Adama, and Mekele, students have better advantage of learning at home via Telegram. The schools provide different worksheets to students and perform better compared to students of public schools. Some private schools also provide home take exams. Here, it is good to mention that students of private schools have better family background at least in terms of income, and education. As stated by Tiruneh (2020), there are no efforts by the public schools in urban and rural areas to keep their students learning from home. It is understandable that most of the public-school teachers and parents have limited or no access to Internet connectivity, but most importantly the teachers lack the preparedness to work in such unprecedented circumstances. Therefore, though the focus of this article is on rural students who are the majority, the urban poor students also in a disadvantaged position. However, the rural students are the most disadvantaged whom multiple inequalities intersect.

The problem of distance learning is not limited to primary and secondary education. Higher education programs for undergraduate, graduate, and post graduate students are not also clearly functioning. Masters and PhD students who are doing their thesis and dissertations are communicating with advisors on emails. The ministry of education also directed that graduation will be made to these students. However, there is no clear direction and also functioning to other students. From my data gathered some universities share materials to students (particularly to Masters) via email. Despite this, there is no clear direction how students will be assessed and how long such uneven practices will stay.

SOLUTIONS AND RECOMMENDATIONS

At the time of COVID-19, students were encouraged to stay at home and read there. This was great challenge to students of the rural society. Because; for rural children, school is everything; it is a place to learn, to study, and to have fun. Once they return home, there is no a comfortable environment to study. As indicated in Nelson (2014), children of parents who did not pursue higher education are less likely to have frequent observational learning opportunities to develop dedicated study habits. Hence, rural students have not a model to look around or they don't have someone to coach them to study. Therefore, government organizations, non-governmental organizations, and other concerned bodies should consider the existing realities of students and devising mechanisms to reach them. Particularly, the rural parents have to be oriented to encourage their children to study at home. A temporary arrangement should be made for students in rural areas to receive reading materials and read it to reduce risks of school closure.

As indicated in World Bank (2020b), there is digital technology access difference among students. Hence, policymakers have to consider equity concerns; as the most vulnerable students are most probably affected disproportionately hard and most likely lack the ability to access digital resources. Beyond developing new content, it would be better to focus on curating existing (especially free, 'open') content and aligning it to the curriculum. In addition, government guidelines should clearly state how students can be evaluated. As noted above, despite intermittently given, there are some practices of teaching on TV, radio, and online. But it is not clear direction how to evaluate them properly. Therefore, how and when students should be tested or alternate assessment requirements should be set properly. This will give students a better focus on their learning.

FUTURE RESERCH DIRECTIONS

Future research should focus on unfailing the socioeconomic differences between and among different section of the society. This is because, during the time of crisis, risks are unevenly distributed among different groups. That means the interventions should different in accordance with the severity of risks. Accordingly, citizens can be treated equally. So, future researches should have different lenses i.e., gender, economic class, level of education of parents, rural and urban nature of school while studying the risks associated with education disruption during crisis.

CONCLUSION

Due to COVID-19, face-to-face learning has been disrupted. It is also impossible to predict when the normal face-face-learning will be resumed (IESALC, 2020). This makes the China's model of 'School is Out, But Class's On' to be conducted effectively. However, the Ethiopian government failed to make interventions to support the marginalized rural students of any level of education. Particularly the rural students who do have family background of little or no schooling are at great disadvantaged position. Hence, considering different dimension and devising means to make student active learners is vital.

In rural areas where there is no internet and electricity, the existing government intervention is not functioning to the majority rural students. Despite distribution is the challenge, printed materials to students to study at home are important (World Bank, 2020b). However, in case of Ethiopia, since there was no any preparation before the closure of schools, institutions were not ready to provide reading materials to their students before they go home. There is also no monitoring from schools and local governments in Ethiopia that, how distance learning is functioning by addressing the diverse needs of children with multiple inequality. Beyond, rural character of students, there are many primary and secondary school children in Ethiopia with special educational needs, who may not benefit equally from the radio and television lessons.

The cultural experiences in the home facilitate children's adjustment to school and academic achievement, thereby transforming cultural resources into what he calls cultural capital (Bourdieu 1977a, 1977b cited in Lareau, 1987). Students in rural areas are more or less homogeneous which limits their opportunity to share experience unlike urban students (McCracken & Barcinas, 1991). This makes information gap between the access haves and the have-nots regarding different government decisions. Hence, as indicated in World Bank (2020b) and IESALC (2020), long-time closure of schools might lead to drop out of students which worst rural students' educational inequality.

REFERENCES

Anthias, F. (2012). Intersectional what? Social divisions, intersectionality and levels of analysis. *Ethnicities*, *13*(1), 3–19. doi:10.1177/1468796812463547

Atnafu, S. (2014). *Local Internet Content: The Case of Ethiopia*. In *12th Globelics International Conference*, Addis Ababa, Ethiopia.

Ayoroa, P., Bailey, B., Crossen, A., & Geo-JaJa, M. A. (2010). Education in China: The urban/rural disparity explained. In J. Zajda (Ed.), *Globalisation, ideology and education policy reforms* (pp. 89–113). Springer. doi:10.1007/978-90-481-3524-0_7

Basilaia, G., & Kvavadze, D. (2020). Transition to online education in schools during a SARS-CoV-2 coronavirus (COVID-19) pandemic in Georgia. *Pedagogical Research*, *5*(4), 1–9. doi:10.29333/pr/7937

Botezat, A. (2016). *Educational poverty*. The Gh. Zane Institute for Economic and Social Research of the Romanian Academy, Iasi Branch.

Cheng, X. (2020). Challenges of "School's Out, But Class's On" to School Education: Practical Exploration of Chinese Schools during the COVID-19 Pandemic. *Sci Insigt Edu Front*, *5*(2), 501–516. doi:10.15354ief.20.ar043

Clark, K. D. (2000). Urban middle school teachers' use of instructional technology. *Journal of Research on Computing in Education*, *33*(2), 178–193. doi:10.1080/08886504.2000.10782308

Clarke, A. E. (2005). *Situational analysis: Grounded theory after the postmodern turn*. SAGE., doi:10.4135/9781412985833

Clarke, A. E., Friese, C., & Washburn, R. (Eds.). (2015). *Situational analysis in practice: Mapping research with grounded theory* (Vol. 1). Left Coast Press. doi:10.4324/9781315420134

Collins, P. H. (2012). Social inequality, power, and politics: Intersectionality and American pragmatism in dialogue. *The Journal of Speculative Philosophy*, *26*(2), 442–457. doi:10.5325/jspecphil.26.2.0442

Collis, B., Moonen, J., & Vingerhoets, J. (1997). Flexibility as a key construct in European training: Experiences from the TeleScopia project. *British Journal of Educational Technology*, *28*(3), 199–217. doi:10.1111/1467-8535.00026

Cordry, S., & Wilson, J. D. (2004). Parents as first teacher. *Education*, *125*(1), 56–62.

Crenshaw, K. (1994). Mapping the margins: intersectionality, identity politics and violence against women of color. In M. A. Fineman & R. Mykitiuk (Eds.), *The Public Nature of Private Violence* (pp. 93–118). Routledge.

CSA. (2007). *Population and Housing Census of Ethiopia*. Administrative Report.

Dorn, E., Hancock, B., Sarakatsannis, J., & Viruleg, E. (2020). *COVID-19 and student learning in the United States: The hurt could last a lifetime*. McKinsey & Company.

Drajea, A. J., & O'Sullivan, C. (2014). Influence of parental education and family income on children's education in rural Uganda. *Global Education Review*, *1*(3), 149–166.

Ejaz, M. (2009). Contribution of unschooled parents in the education of their children: An analysis. *Pakistan Journal of Social Sciences*, *29*(2).

Fu, T. M. (2005). Unequal primary education opportunities in rural and urban China. *China Perspectives*, *2005*(60). doi:10.4000/chinaperspectives.500

Gooding, Y. (2001). *The relationship between parental educational level and academic success of college freshmen* [Dissertation]. Iowa State University.

Gordon, N. A. (2014). *Flexible Pedagogies: Technology-enhanced learning*. In The Higher Education Academy. doi:10.13140/2.1.2052.5760

Gulati, S. (2008). Technology-enhanced learning in developing nations: A review. *International Review of Research in Open and Distance Learning*, *9*(1), 1–16. doi:10.19173/irrodl.v9i1.477

Hailu, B. H. (2020). *Education Response to COVID-19: How Can Basic Education Be Implemented in Ethiopia?* Retrieved from https://riseprogramme.org/blog/COVID-19-ETH-Basic-Education

He, F., Deng, Y., & Weina, L. (2020). Coronavirus disease 2019: What we know? *Journal of Medical Virology*, *2020*(7), 1–7. doi:10.1002/jmv.25766 PMID:32170865

Herselman, M. E. (2003). ICT in Rural Areas in South Africa: Various Case Studies. *Proceedings of Informing Science*, 945-955. doi:10.28945/2680

Huang, R. H., Liu, D. J., Tlili, A., Yang, J. F., & Wang, H. H. (2020). *Handbook on Facilitating Flexible Learning During Educational Disruption: The Chinese Experience in Maintaining Undisrupted Learning in COVID-19 Outbreak*. Smart Learning Institute of Beijing Normal University.

IESALC. (2020). *COVID-19 and higher education: Today and tomorrow. Impact analysis, policy responses and recommendation*. Author.

ILO. (2018). Ethiopia National Child Labour Survey. Ethiopia National Child Labour Survey 2015 / International Labour Office, Fundamental Principles and Rights at Work Branch (FUNDAMENTALS); Central Statistical Agency (CSA).

Internet Society (2019). *Internet Society Global Internet Report: Consolidation in the internet economy*. Author.

Internet World Statistics. (2013). *Usage and Population Statistics*. Retrieved from https://www.internetworldstats.com/stats1.htm

Internet World Statistics. (2020b). *Internet Usage Statistics. World Internet Users and 2020 Population Stats*. Retrieved from https://www.internetworldstats.com/stats.htm

InternetWorld Statistics. (2020a). *Usage and Population Statistics*. Retrieved from https://www.internetworldstats.com/stats1.htm

Lareau, A. (1987). Social class differences in family-school relationships: The importance of cultural capital. *Sociology of Education*, *60*(2), 73–85. doi:10.2307/2112583

Litheko, S. R. S. (2012). The difference in performance between schools situated in the urban areas and those in the rural areas of Lesotho. *Electronic Journal for Inclusive Education*, *2*(9), 2.

Lohmann, H., & Ferger, F. (2014). *Educational Poverty in a Comparative Perspective: Theoretical and Empirical Implications*. SFB882 Working Paper Series, No. 26.

McCracken, J. D., & Barcinas, J. D. T. (1991). Differences between rural and urban schools, student characteristics, and student aspirations in Ohio. *Journal of Research in Rural Education*, *7*(2), 29–40.

McMeekin, A. (1998). *Flexible Learning and Teaching and IT*. Keynote address to the 1998 Monash University Flexible Learning and Technology Conference.

Ministry of Education of the People's Republic of China. (2020). *Notice on Several Issues concerning Targeted Teacher Work during the Pandemic Prevention and Control*. Retrieved from http://www.moe.gov.cn

Nelson, J. K. (2009). *Impact of Parent Education on Student Success*. Online Submission.

Rizwan, M., Ur-Rehman, A., Shabbir, S. W., & Warriach, I. A. (2014). Explorative study of parents' education effect on the socialization of their children (A case of district Muzaffargarh*). Research on Humanities and Social Sciences*, *4*(26), 81–86.

Sandholtz, J. H., Ringstaff, C., & Dwyer, D. C. (1992). Teaching in high-tech environment: Classroom management revisited. *Journal of Educational Computing Research*, *8*(4), 479–505. doi:10.2190/Y5NE-V9RQ-FD63-WC2N

Sen, A. K. (1999). *Development as Freedom*. Oxford University Press.

Sewnet, Z. (2020). *Ethiopia: Keeping children learning during COVID-19*. UNICEF. Available at https://www.unicef.org/ethiopia/stories/ethiopia-keeping-children-learning-during-covid-19

Singh, V., & Thurman, A. (2019). How Many Ways Can We Define Online Learning? A Systematic Literature Review of Definitions of Online Learning (1988-2018). *American Journal of Distance Education*, *33*(4), 289306. doi:10.1080/08923647.2019.1663082

Sintema, E. J. (2020). Effect of COVID-19 on the Performance of Grade 12 Students: Implications for STEM Education. *Eurasia Journal of Mathematics, Science and Technology Education*, *16*(7), em1851. doi:10.29333/ejmste/7893

Tilak, J. B. G. (2001). Household Expenditure on Education in India: A Few Stylized Facts. In S. M. Dev, P. Antony, V. Gayathri, & R. P. Mamgain (Eds.), *Social and Economic Security in India* (pp. 191–218). Institute for Human Development.

Tiruneh, D. T. (2020). *COVID-19 School Closures May Further Widen the Inequality Gaps between the Advantaged and the Disadvantaged in Ethiopia*. Retrieved from https://www.riseprogramme.org/blog/COVID-19_ethiopia_school_closures

UNDP. (1997). *Human Development Report*. Oxford University Press.

UNI CEF. (2020a). *Ethiopia COVID-19*. Situational Report No. 5.

UNICEF. (2020b). *Promising practices for equitable remote learning Emerging lessons from COVID-19 education responses in 127 countries*. Innocent Research Brief.

Whisker, C. (2018). Review: Adele E. Clarke, Carrie Friese & Rachel S. Washburn (2018). Situational analysis: Grounded theory after the interpretive turn (2nd ed.). Forum Qualitative Sozialforschung / Forum: Qualitative Social Research, 19(3), Art. 35. doi:10.17169/fqs-19.3.3138

Wiki. (2019). *Open learning*. Retrieved from https://en.wikipedia.org/wiki/Open_learning

Wise, T., Zbozinek, T., Michelini, G., Hagan, C. C., & Mobbs, D. (2020). Changes in risk perception and protective behavior during the first week of the COVID-19 pandemic in the United States. doi:10.31234/osf.io/dz428osf.io/dz428

World Bank. (1994). Poverty Reduction in South Asia. Academic Press.

World Bank. (2019). *International Bank for Reconstruction and Development*. 2019-Tracking SDG7-The Energy Progress Report. Retrieved rom https://trackingsdg7.esmap.org/data/files/download-documents/2019-Tracking%20SDG7-Full%20Report.pdf

World Bank. (2020a). *Guidance Note on Education Systems' Response to COVID19*. Retrieved from http://pubdocs.worldbank.org/en/450881585235950757/COVID19-Education-Sector-Guidance-Note-March26.pdf

World Bank. (2020b). *The World Bank Education Global Practice Guidance Note: Remote Learning & COVID-19*. Author.

Zhang, D., Li, X., & Xue, J. (2015). Education inequality between rural and urban areas of the People's Republic of China, migrants' children education, and some implications. *Asian Development Review*, *32*(1), 196–224. doi:10.1162/ADEV_a_00042

Zhou, L., Li, F., Wu, S., & Zhou M. (2020). "School's Out, But Class's On", The largest online education in the world today: Taking China's practical exploration during the COVID-19 epidemic prevention and control as an example. *Best Evid Chin Edu, 4*(2), 501-519. doi:10.15354/bece.20.ar023

ADDITIONAL READING

Colvin, M. K., Reesman, J., & Glen, T. (2022). The impact of COVID-19 related educational disruption on children and adolescents: An interim data summary and commentary on ten considerations for neuropsychological practice. *The Clinical Neuropsychologist*, *36*(1), 45–71. doi:10.1080/13854046.2021.1970230 PMID:34495815

Dwivedi, Y. K., Hughes, D. L., Coombs, C., Constantiou, I., Duan, Y., Edwards, J. S., Gupta, B., Lal, B., Misra, S., Prashant, P., Raman, R., Rana, N. P., Sharma, S. K., & Upadhyay, N. (2020). Impact of COVID-19 pandemic on information management research and practice: Transforming education, work and life. *International Journal of Information Management*, *55*, 102211. doi:10.1016/j.ijinfomgt.2020.102211

Fry-Bowers, E. K. (2020). Children are at risk from COVID-19. *Journal of Pediatric Nursing*, *53*, A10–A12. doi:10.1016/j.pedn.2020.04.026 PMID:32386796

Gurdasani, D., Alwan, N. A., Greenhalgh, T., Hyde, Z., Johnson, L., McKee, M., Michie, S., Prather, K. A., Rasmussen, S. D., Reicher, S., Roderick, P., & Ziauddeen, H. (2021). School reopening without robust COVID-19 mitigation risks accelerating the pandemic. *Lancet*, *397*(10280), 1177–1178. doi:10.1016/S0140-6736(21)00622-X PMID:33713595

Liu, J., Chen, Q., & Dang, J. (2021). Examining risk factors related to digital learning and social isolation: Youth visual acuity in COVID-19 pandemic. *Journal of Global Health*, *11*, 11. doi:10.7189/jogh.11.05020 PMID:34484707

Lu, Q., Cai, Z., Chen, B., & Liu, T. (2020). Social policy responses to the Covid-19 crisis in China in 2020. *International Journal of Environmental Research and Public Health*, *17*(16), 5896. doi:10.3390/ijerph17165896 PMID:32823833

Rodrigues, M., Franco, M., & Silva, R. (2020). COVID-19 and disruption in management and education academics: Bibliometric mapping and analysis. *Sustainability*, *12*(18), 7362. doi:10.3390u12187362

KEY TERMS AND DEFINITIONS

COVID-19 Pandemic: An infectious disease caused by the SARS-CoV-2 virus which was founded in Wuhan China in 2019.

Distance Learning: Modality of leaning as an alternative to face-face-face learning.

Educational Inequality: Inequality between students in access to quality education due to disruption of schools caused by COVID-19 pandemic.

Multiple Inequalities: A state of inequality that someone faces due to his/her different socioeconomic status.

Online Learning: Mode of distance teaching-learning process using internet.

Rural Ethiopia: Countryside of Ethiopia that is located outside towns and cities and is characterized by poor or no access to electricity and internet.

Situational Analysis: It is a research method used to analyse internal and external factors of something; educational inequality in this chapter.

Chapter 14
Managing Risk in Wealth Building Through Residential Real Estate Business in Canada

Mahendra Singh Rawat
https://orcid.org/0000-0002-4247-8219
MSR Holdings International Inc., Canada

Mudit Singh Rawat
MSR Holdings International Inc., Canada

ABSTRACT

Many Canadians have built their wealth through the real estate business. There are two types of real estate: commercial real estate and residential real estate. In this chapter, risks relating to only residential real estate have been discussed due to two main reasons. Firstly, residential real estate occupies an important place in the income of the household sector. Secondly, in comparison to commercial real estate, it requires a smaller capital to do the business and build wealth. Residential real estate investors build wealth by investing in investment properties and generating current income through capital appreciation. However, there are multiple risks that an investor faces in managing investment properties. This chapter discusses how some risks can be averted before and after buying an investment property. The chapter points out that the essential part of the business is to buy the right property at the right place and at the right time.

INTRODUCTION

Gazing through the economic history of the developed world for the last three decades, it is observed that North American economies, like US and Canada, went through a severe financial crisis at least four times in the previous few decades. In 1990-91, a recession was rampant in these countries due to low demand and high unemployment rate – Canada reached a double-digit unemployment rate. Then in 2000, there was a burst of the Dot Com Bubble due to the failure of several start-up technology companies,

DOI: 10.4018/978-1-6684-5279-0.ch014

and the wealth of several investors were eroded (Phillips et al., 2021). In 2008 due to an overheated real estate market and large-scale loss of mortgages, the financial crisis disrupted many developed world economies. They continue to impact the developed and the developing world economies, restricting their growth and expansion. Lastly, the global pandemic of 2020 is keeping the world uncertain, and when it is finally over, it is still not known with certainty.

A scrutiny of the above-mentioned economic crisis reveals two trends. Firstly, a financial crisis occurs at an approximate interval of one decade. While they may trigger in one country, they soon spread to other countries because today, all economies are closely integrated with other economies due to globalization. Secondly, markets get adversely affected due to these crises, and asset valuations come down sharply. Falling valuations create a panic in the market, inducing the investors to sell their assets. This panic selling further erodes the valuations. As a result of these two trends, the low valuations of assets provide an opportunity to buy them and build wealth for the future.

BACKGROUND

Commonly, there are five broad classes of assets (Phillips et al., 2021) in which rich people invest to build their wealth. These are Equities (Stocks), Fixed Income (Bonds or Debt Instruments), Cash and cash equivalent liquid assets, Commodities and currencies, and Real Estate. A new sixth asset class has emerged in recent times, mainly being explored by the younger generation. This asset is called 'Digital Asset" often represented by digital products like crypto currency.

Although cash is generally considered as an asset or a liquid asset, but wealthy investors believe it to be an asset only after it is invested into an income earning asset (Kiyosaki, 1997). It remains a liability as cash kept in the vault does not bring any income, on the other hand it has a carrying cost. Each of the class, mentioned above, has its own merits and demerits (Akhilesh, 2022), and their popularity differs at different times. For example, during the COVID-19 global the stock market flooded with many investors, making the equity class the most sought-after asset class. However, wealth is not built-in a few days or few months. It is said "Money making is short term, creating wealth is long term" (Dilmaghani, 2019). It is always a long-term investor who builds the wealth. Therefore, it is time that will tell who made their wealth from these investments in the long run. Canadians also invest in all these assets for building their wealth like any other people in the world.

For centuries, the rich have been investing in real estate which is considered a tradable asset class. It can be bought and sold in the market like any other types of financial assets (Harvey, 1982). Real estate usually constitutes a household's largest financial asset, and investing in an owner- occupied home, is often how the middle class accumulates wealth (Khan et al., 2021). There are three main reasons (Haila, 1991) for investors to invest in real estate. Firstly, it is considered to be a good hedge against inflation, Secondly, it provides a good diversification to an asset portfolio along with stocks and bonds, Thirdly, investment in real assets provides better tax benefits than in other assets (Dilmaghani, 2019; Hebb, Hamilton & Hachigian, 2010).

Further, it is not only the most visible tangible asset among different asset classes, but it is also an asset that creates the status of an individual in the society. An article published on 1st October 2019 in www.cnbc.com quoted Mr. Andrew Carnegie, the owner of the Carnegie Steel Corporation, one of the biggest steel plants in America and one of the world's wealthiest persons in the early 20th century, as having said that 90% of millionaires have built their wealth by investing in real estate. So that is the power of real estate, which Canadians also use. To understand the importance of real estate as an asset class in Canada, it is good to look at the different types of assets in which Canadians invest to build their wealth.

REVIEW OF LITERATURE

Different Asset Classes That Build Wealth in Canada

Government of Canada, Statistic Department gives importance to the following classes of assets in the Household sector. It categorizes four broad asset classes of wealth:

1. Financial Assets like Life Insurance Plans, Pension Plans, including employers, Pension plans, etc.
2. Other Financial Assets like Investments in Equities, Bonds and Debentures, Currencies and Deposits, Foreign Investments, etc.
3. Non-Financial Asset - Real Estate
4. Other Non-Financial Assets like Intellectual Property, Machinery, Equipment, Consumer Durables, etc.

The following pie chart shown in Figure 1 shows how wealth is distributed in the Canadian household sector, as per asset class categories mentioned above. It's clear from the pie chart that Real Estate enjoys the maximum share in the total household sector.

Figure 1. Net worth indicators

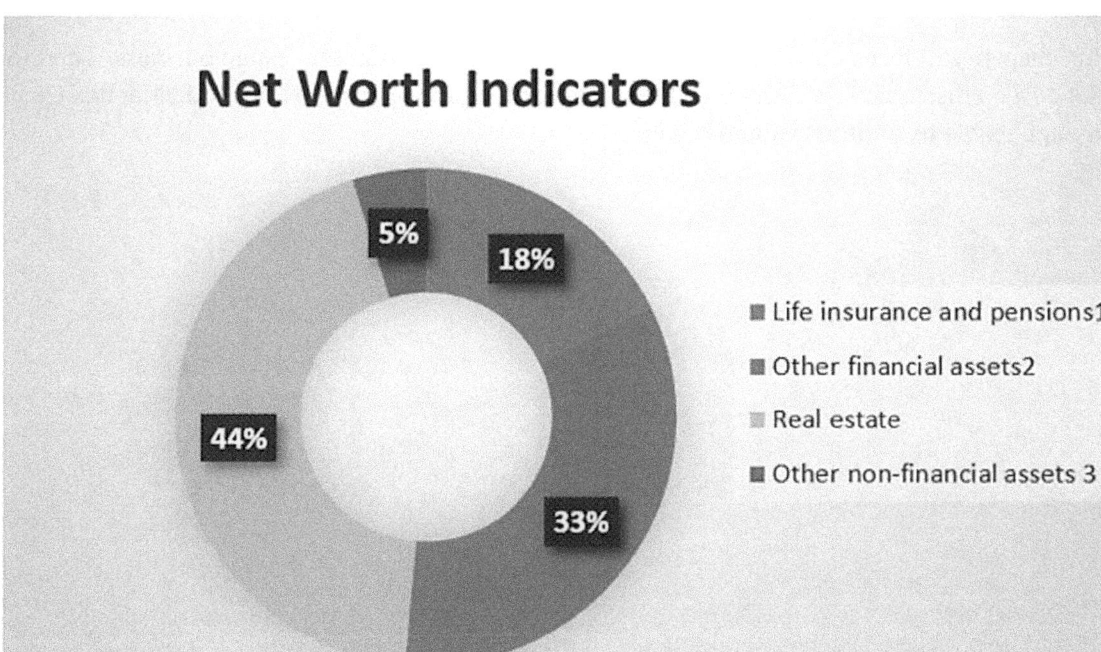

1. Life insurance and pensions include the value of all life insurance and employer pension plans termination basis. This excludes public plans administered or sponsored by governments: Old Age Security (OAS), including the Guaranteed Income Supplement (GIS) and the Spouse's Allowance (SPA), as well as Canada and Quebec Pension Plans (CPP/QPP).
2. Other financial assets include total currency and deposits, Canadian short-term paper, Canadian bonds and debentures, foreign investments in paper and bonds, mortgages, equity and investment funds, and other receivables.
3. Other non-financial assets include consumer durables, machinery and equipment, and intellectual property products. This excludes the accumulation of value of collectibles, including coins, stamps, and artwork.

Figure 2 shows how the real estate share in wealth building has gone up during the last five years, from 40.5% in 2019 to 43.8% (nearly 44%) in 2021.

Types of Real Estate Business in Canada

In Canada as well as elsewhere, the real estate sector is segmented into commercial and residential subsectors and into distinctive property types such as office, industrial and retail (Hebb, Hamilton & Hachigian, 2010).

1. Commercial Real Estate consists of commercial complexes – offices, shopping centres, factory buildings, fulfillment centers, multi-story apartments and mix buildings etc.
2. Residential Real Estate consists of residential units like Detached or Semi-Detached Houses, Town Houses, Condos, multiplexes (up to 4 story building) or single-family units.

This chapter will focus on wealth building through the residential real estate business. Therefore, it will not cover a discussion on commercial real estate, though many aspects of residential real estate are equally applicable to commercial real estate.

Figure 2. Net worth indicators as % of household economic accounts & wealth indicators, Canada (2010 - 2021)

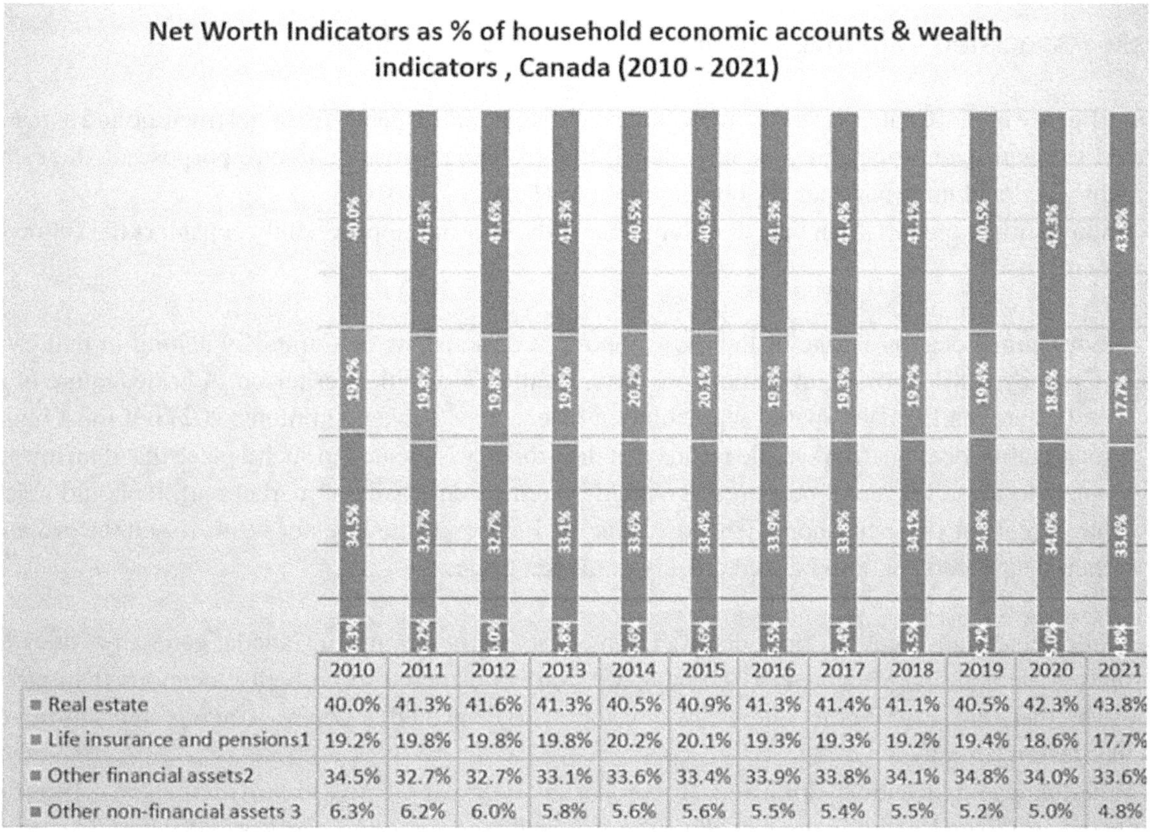

	2010	2011	2012	2013	2014	2015	2016	2017	2018	2019	2020	2021
Real estate	40.0%	41.3%	41.6%	41.3%	40.5%	40.9%	41.3%	41.4%	41.1%	40.5%	42.3%	43.8%
Life insurance and pensions1	19.2%	19.8%	19.8%	19.8%	20.2%	20.1%	19.3%	19.3%	19.2%	19.4%	18.6%	17.7%
Other financial assets2	34.5%	32.7%	32.7%	33.1%	33.6%	33.4%	33.9%	33.8%	34.1%	34.8%	34.0%	33.6%
Other non-financial assets 3	6.3%	6.2%	6.0%	5.8%	5.6%	5.6%	5.5%	5.4%	5.5%	5.2%	5.0%	4.8%

Risks in Residential Real Estate Business in Canada

While real estate in Canada has been a popular way to build wealth, there is no doubt that it is also fraught with multiple risks. Some risks, arising out of tradability, divisibility and portability features of real estate, (Charney, 2001), are quite common and can be controlled, but some risks, like high level of Radon gas emission (Khan et. al 2021) from buildings, particularly constructed between 2010-2020, are quite complicated, and they also require government intervention. Therefore, it is imperative to create a mechanism for removing or reducing all such risks. However, before actually diving into the various risks involved in this business, one has to differentiate between a Primary Home property and an investment property.

A Primary home property is primarily used for own living (self-occupied) and not for earning income on capital employed. Thus, a primary home is generally kept out of the real estate business (Charney, 2001). However, it gradually helps in building equity through repayment of the monthly mortgage and this equity, when invested in an investment property, helps in building wealth. An investment property is one in which capital is invested with the sole purpose of earning income through recurring cash flows as well as through capital appreciation. All the properties mentioned above in residential real estate have their specific challenges. However, some of the risks discussed below are common to all types of investment properties in real estate.

Risks Associated With Investment Property at Buying Stage

Due diligence of real estate, covers all micro and macroeconomic aspects, financial (income and expenses related to owning and managing estates), legal, tax, technical, organizational, purpose of the estate, psychological and informational (Hebb, Hamilton & Hachigian, 2010).

An investment property can be a wealth builder if the investor appropriately considers the following aspects.

1. **Location**: Location is one of the most important dimensions of Capital switching in real estate (Charney, 2001). For an investment property, location is a critical criterion. A basic feature of the real estate market is its spatial segmentation (Mensah & Tucker-Simmons, 2021). It must be in a marketable location. Marketable means that the property is located in such a place that if an investor wants to use it for rental purposes, it should be rented out easily at market rent. It should neither have frequent vacancies nor extended vacancies. Further, if the investor wants to sell the property, then the property should be sold quickly at market price.

While selecting a location, first identification of city is important. In Canada, generally Cities like Toronto, Montreal and Vancouver (Charney, 2001) are considered to be better locations than others. However, there are several other cities now developing in Canada like Ottawa, Calgary and sub-urb cities in Greater Toronto.

When choosing a location within a city, for properties, with an objective to earn reasonable market rent, it is necessary to be located in populated areas and where amenities like markets, educational institutes, hospitals, recreational centers, etc., are available at nearby places. Suppose an investor is investing in real estate with an objective of getting a return through capital appreciation. In that case, location should be identified with future projections, considering how long one intends to hold the property. In places like Toronto and Vancouver cities in Canada, property prices rise at an average compound rate of over 15% per annum (CREA, 2021). Thus, in such a market, one can have an objective of doubling the capital in 6 to 7 years. If that is the goal, then an appropriate exit strategy can be adopted.

2. **Identification of suitable property**: After identifying a good location, identifying the property in such a location is the next important step. Investment properties are determined primarily by going through listings on various real estate websites, called market deals. Sometimes properties are also found by directly approaching potential sellers, called off-market deals.

The objective of investing in an investment property is to generate a positive cash flow (Irvin, 2018). Positive cash flow is generated when the net of all expenses relating to property (e.g., taxes, insurance, utility bills, maintenance and repairs, monthly mortgage payments, etc.) from the income (generated from the rent) is more than zero. Such investment properties are most profitable to possess (Mensah & Tucker-Simmons, 2021). However, sometimes a property may not generate a positive cash flow immediately, in the short term. Still, investment in such properties can be considered, if it can generate positive cash flow after a reasonable period of 6 to 12 months. Some properties have the characteristic of faster capital appreciation due to some new developments in the area; then, such properties may be considered after evaluating an individual's capacity to hold it for an extended period.

Some of the aspects that are worth considering, while identifying the property with objective of mitigating risks as well as with objective of generating more income are as follows:

a. Importance of Multiplex. A multiplex residential house, with multi-independent units, will give more rental income than a single-family home, though it may be marginally more expensive, yet more rewarding. Therefore, for earning more rental income, a multiplex residential house is more desirable than a family home, as an investment property.
b. Lot Size: The size of the lot on which the property is built is another essential property feature. The bigger the lot size, the chances of the property having higher future capital appreciation increases. It also provides scope for creating further expansion of the property. However, if the property is purchased to extend the existing dwelling or add a new dwelling, the investor must ensure that it meets the zoning requirements and the investor can obtain permits to expand the property. The investor must take expert opinion from an architect before buying the property.
c. Price of Property: In buying any asset, the asset price is one of the main factors. Since, in real estate, significant investment is required, price becomes the most critical deciding factor once location and property features are acceptable. An investor will generally negotiate to get the lowest price in the deal. However, there may be limitations to negotiating power of the investor due to the prevalence of certain market conditions. In recent years the Canadian real estate market has been more often in the mode of a seller's market than in a buyer's market. Due to it, the prices have been rising at double-digit figures in the sought-after popular cities, leaving almost no scope for the investor to negotiate.

Usually, it is believed that the real estate market is a seller's market if the inventory of residential units, aftermarket listing, gets sold within three months. The market is considered neutral or balanced if the inventory of residential units remains in the market between 3 to 6 months. The market is viewed as a buyer's market if the inventory of residential units in the market remains for more than six months. In recent years in Canada, the inventory has been sold within three months in most major cities, making Canada a seller's market.

The following factors are the main reason for such a price sensitivity situation in the market:

i. According to Canada government's Immigration Levels Plan 2022-24, in 2022 alone, 432,000 immigrants are likely to land with Permanent Resident Status in Canada, as against 405.000 landings in 2021. (CIC News 10 Feb, 2022) Thus Canada Government is targeting more than 400,000 immigrants every year. These immigrants mostly try to settle in cities like Toronto, Vancouver, Montreal, etc. due to the availability of more job opportunities in these cities. Hence, immigrants are creating demand for residential units in these cities. Initially, the demand is for rental units, and after a few years, they demand residential units for their permanent living once they are settled in this country (Dilmaghani, 2017).
ii. Generally, the supply of residential units is less than the demand in the market. In cities like Toronto, after its listing in the market, a residential unit remains listed only for 10 to 15 days (Mensah & Tucker-Simmons, 2021), after which it is sold. In other nearby cities, residential units sell in one to two months of being listed.

iii. The Bank of Canada lowered its interest rates due to the pandemic in the last two years. This decrease in rates led the banks' lending mortgage loans at rates as low as 1% per annum and encouraged many home buyers and investors to buy residential units. This increased demand encouraged homeowners to sell their homes at inflated prices. In March 2022, the Bank of Canada announced raising of interest rate gradually during the year. Though this has slightly corrected the market but still the demand for housing will continue to remain in the market,

Although the description mentioned above shows limitations to the buyer's negotiation power, a prudent investor can still take pricing decision from other factual information available in the market. Many websites, like Zocasa.ca, housesigma.com, zolo.ca etc also give actual prices of similar properties sold in the past, in nearby locations, or they mention the average market prices of all similar properties. A prudent buyer would always try to find a property priced below the average cost to lower his risk against any downslides in real estate prices. Another aspect that the investors in this business believe is that as long as the property after purchase provides a positive cash flow from rental income, the fall in prices will not hurt very much because sooner or later, the prices in real estate tend to rise (Liu, Rosenthal & Strange, 2018).

1. **Age of property**: A property constructed a few years ago and built many years ago will have different maintenance requirements (Liu, Rosenthal & Strange, 2018). An old property will require higher maintenance than a recently made property. Therefore, while identifying a property, one must consider the property's age. Another essential aspect when buying a condo or an apartment is the maintenance cost charged by the property management company keeps increasing year after year. This increase occurs even if no repairs are needed in the apartment because the maintenance cost is determined based on the cost of maintaining the entire building and not on the maintenance cost of the specific apartment one owns. This increased cost is not present in independent houses where one must incur expenditure on maintenance when repairs are required.
2. **Property Taxes**: Taxes on properties vary from city to city; some have only federal taxes, and some have federal and provincial taxes. Besides property taxes, there are also sewage taxes. Therefore, in le calculating the cash flow, one in investment properties must consider the burden of payment of total taxes.
3. **Financial Ratios**: In the real estate business, like in any other business, specific financial ratios help understand the company's profitability. They also allow investors to make comparisons of returns with similar properties and make an investment decision. The most common ratio is the cap rate or capitalization rate. The net operating income divided by the full value of the asset or the total cost at which it has been purchased, multiplied by 100, gives us the cap rate. When we detect all the operating expenses from the total rental income received during the year, we get the t net active income (NOI). From the discussion in the paragraph mentioned above, it is clear that the property's rental income directly influences the cap rate. The higher the rental income, the higher will be cap rate. As rental income from multistoried homes is more than from single-family homes, the cap rate for multistoried homes will always be higher. Thus, an investor will prefer to buy a multistoried home over a single-family home. The Cap rate will differ from city to city. Within Greater Toronto Area (GTA), in cities like Toronto, Mississauga, Brampton, etc., the cap rate for multiplexes is around 4% to 5%. For other cities in GTA, the cap rate for multistoried homes is 6% to 7%. However, capital appreciation of properties in such cities is lesser than the capital apprecia-

tion of properties in cities like Toronto, Mississauga, and Brampton. Many investors prefer to use positive cash flow to determine their net cash profit. A positive cash flow is determined by deducting operating expenses and payment of monthly mortgages from the total rental income received. Some investors further divide this surplus cash obtained annually by their down payment to get the mortgage and call it their annual return on capital. Whatever surplus is left is called positive cash. While the financial ratios mentioned above are not complete in themselves for making an investment decision, but they throw some light on the return that an investor is likely to get from his investment. Therefore, these ratios are used only as an indicator and not as a significant factor in making the investment decision.

4. **Miscellaneous**: Some of the items to be investigated are the number of covered or uncovered car parking spots. Further, does the dwelling has a basement. If the basement exists, is it a legal basement or an illegal basement? If it is a legal basement, then whether it is a finished basement or an unfinished basement. These aspects create value in the investment property and should be examined more carefully.

Risks Associated With Investment Property at Holding Stage

Once the property is purchased and ownership transferred to the investor, all the risks associated with the withholding of the property are also transferred. Good management of these risks will enable the investor to earn income and build wealth. Inadequate management of these risks will affect the property's income generation and reduce the opportunity for wealth building. These risks are broadly categorized into three categories, viz, Income risk, operating risks, and marketing risk.

1. **Income risk:** Income risk is also called a cash flow risk. The main objective of investment property is to get positive cash flow. This positive cash flow is derived from rental income received from tenants who pay rent for the use of the property. Therefore, identifying tenants who can pay the rent regularly is critical. A thorough identification of prospective tenant's is absolutely necessary. Prospective tenant's Credit check, their source of income, and, if possible, their history as a tenant should be verified by the owner. One must determine if the rent control act is applicable where the investment property is located (Gillies, 1952). In Canada, the rent control act is applicable in most provinces; therefore, the investor must have a complete understanding of the provisions of this act, as such acts are more favorable to tenants than to landlords.
    a. After taking all measures and precautions, the investor may still land into a troublesome tenant If such tenants are not paying the rent regularly, it may not be desirable to keep them in the building. They may also behave indecently like disturbing other tenants living in the same building. The investor would like the tenant to leave the building in such circumstances. There could be another situation where an investor may have lower income issues. Sometimes, an investor may buy a suitable property where tenants live for an extended period and pay lower than market rent. In both the cases mentioned above, the investor would want the tenants to leave the building and replace them with well-paying good tenants. However, replacing tenants in the building is never straightforward, especially when the Rent Control Act favors the tenant. To mitigate their future income risk by getting rid of such tenants, some intelligent investors use a method known as the "Cash to Key" method. In this method, the investor offers a certain amount in cash to the tenant to vacate the occupied premises and give back the key

to the investor. Since the investor pays cash to get around the key and possession of beliefs, it is called the cash required method.

2. **Operational Risk:** There are various challenges in managing an investment property. Robert Kiyosaki, the famous author of Rich Dad and Poor Dad, says it is easy to buy a property, but it is challenging to manage it. If the property is managed poorly, then not only will the cash flow get affected, but the value of the property will also deteriorate, and future appreciation will slow down. Usually, Properties do have multiple issues arising from time to time. It is common to get problems relating to plumbing repairs, rectifying electrical faults, leakages, dampness on walls, defects on heating systems, leakages in roofs, etc. A landlord must understand that these issues are common, and therefore the landlord must have a regular arrangement for managing these issues on the property. If the owner has multiple investment properties, it is advisable to engage a proper professional Management Services Company to look after such matters. Alternatively, if the owner has one property or a few properties, the owner must promptly engage someone to manage these issues. In the short run, it may be a cost to the owners, but in the long run, it will reward the owners with a good capital appreciation for the property. Further, the tenants appreciate such professional arrangements and are willing to pay market or above-market rent for such properties.
3. **Market risk:** There is no doubt that the real estate business is an excellent source for wealth-building in the long term. However, like any other business, the real estate business also faces Market risk. We mentioned at the beginning of this chapter that the 2008 Global financial crisis was caused by the failure of the real estate market. Therefore, a real estate investor must understand that real estate market prices increase and decrease according to market demand and supply trends. However, there may be occasions when there may be a crash in the market. Some shrewd investors wait for such events and enter the market to buy low-priced properties. Hence, it is crucial to recognize that the real estate business game is a long-term game, not a short-term one. The valuations of the properties in the long-term always increase, and in the short-term, there may be occasions when the prices may fall. Therefore, an investor must look for a long-term business horizon in the real estate business.
   a. One of the ways by which the Market risk in prices can be avoided Is by way of refinancing the property from a bank. Regarding refinancing, we will be discussing in detail when we discuss the different strategies to be adopted in the real estate business. Another Market risk that a real estate investor, who rents out property, may face is when the property remains vacant due to the non-availability of tenants. Usually, the property will become vacant when the present tenant is leaving. Usually, a minimum of one month's notice is required to vacate the property by a tenant. This one month should be extensively used to find the new tenant either by advertisement or any other means of publicity. Alternatively, when the property is vacant, it can be used for repairs and renovation. These repairs and renovations would improve the quality of the property and command a higher rent making up for the loss of vacant period.
   b. Market risk also arises in exceptional circumstances, such as the global pandemic of 2020 - 21. During the pandemic, the real estate business also suffered like many other businesses. One of the unique features that evolved during the pandemic was that people started working from their own homes. Many left the cities or residential places near their offices to work from their homes. This created a situation where many tenants left their rental residences, which became vacant for a long time, depriving the landlords of their regular rental income. Even those landlords who were using their apartments or condos for Airbnb purposes also

suffered as travel mobility reduced drastically. While the global pandemic provided exceptional circumstances when rents came down, it also offered a unique opportunity for some investors to buy properties whose prices had come down. However, except few places, property prices did not remain low for a long time. They recovered soon and reached newer heights by the end of 2021 in all big cities. Market risk can also arise due to changing valuations of the investment property. There is no doubt that the property's price is the most critical factor influencing the buying or selling decision. An investment property buyer would not only be considering the current price of the property but would also be concerned about the future potential of the property. Therefore, a property investor must understand the valuations of the property. Although the valuation of properties is a complete chapter, we will briefly discuss the various methods used for valuing a property.

As per the Municipal Property Assessment Corporation (MPAC) that administers property assessment and appeals in the province of Ontario, there are three methods to evaluate properties:

1. The first method is the cost approach, under which properties are being constructed or have just been completed and are evaluated. In this method, the cost of land per square foot plus the cost of building the total area per square foot, plus 10% to 12% for locational advantages and approximately 20% for the builder's profit, are added together to determine the market value of the property.
2. The second method is called the direct comparison approach. In this method, comparable prices of similar properties sold in the recent past are considered, and then the cost of close property in the market is estimated. If no matching property is found to be sold in the recent past, then prices of similar properties sold in the last year are traced. The average Sale price of such properties becomes the base price. Then, some amount for the inflation for the period passed is added to the base price at the total price is taken to be the property's fair market value.
3. The third method is the Income or rental yield method. This method is the most common method used among investors who invest in properties to get continuous rental income. They hold the property for a long time. This way, they earn an excellent current income and take benefit of capital appreciation after a considerable long time. They determine the rental yield by dividing the gross rent received during a year by the total investment made on the property and multiplying it by 100 to get the percentage yield. This rental yield May differ from place to place. Still, it is generally accepted that rental yield in high-density cities like Toronto would be around 4% to 5%, and in other cities with lesser densities, it would vary from 6% to 8%. These rental yields will cover all property expenses and leave some cash surplus. Thus, an investor has a tool of rental yield that helps the investor value the property. For example, let's presume that the rental yield in a place is 5%. An investor finds a property in that place and knows that the annual rent available on that property is $50,000. Then at a 5% rental yield, this property valuation would be $ 1,000,000. So, the investor should buy this property at an approximate price of $ 1 million, the correct valuation for this property as per the rental yield method.

Mitigating Risks Through Various Business Strategies in Residential Real Estate Market

Investors use several strategies in the residential real estate market to mitigate the risks and build their wealth. Some of them are discussed below:

- Buy and Hold Strategy (B & H Strategy): Under this strategy, an investor buys the property and holds it for an extended period. How long should the holding period be? Some believe that it should be five years, but others believe that it should not be less than ten years. While there is no rule for determining the reasonable holding period, general practice is to sell the property when its appreciation reaches the targeted level of profit for the investor.
- BRRRR Strategy: BRRRR acronym stands for Buy, Renovate (or Rehabilitate), Rent, Refinance and Repeat. In this strategy, an investor buys an old uninhabitable property or a depleted property at a low price that requires complete rehabilitation or restructuring. Then the property is fully renovated and rented out, enhancing the valuation of the property at a significantly higher level than its original level. Once the renovated property comes up in its new structure with a higher valuation, the investor gets it refinanced at a lower interest rate from a commercial bank. Investors will use personal funds or takes high-cost private funding to reach this level. Further, the investor can get back the entire funds invested initially due to a higher valuation. Let us understand the importance of this strategy with the help of an example. Suppose that an investor buys a depleted property for $200,000 by putting their funds. After that, the investor obtains $400,000 from a private funding source and renovates the entire property. Thus, investor spends a total amount of $600,000. After the property is fully renovated and a new structure comes up, the property's value gets enhanced to $750,000. A commercial bank will quickly provide a mortgage loan of $600,000 (80% of the property value). Thus, the investor will get back the entire amount spent on renovating the property. If the property is rented out and rent received can meet all monthly expenses, including the monthly mortgage, the property gives income at zero investment. The beauty of this strategy is that with zero investment, an investor can earn recurring revenue and create equity in the property due to a monthly mortgage payment through rental income.
- Fix and Flip Strategy: An investor buys a property below the market rate under the fix and flip strategy. Then the investor makes some Improvements to the property either by renovating it or creating an additional facility in the property. For example, an investor can create another residential unit by remodeling the basement or creating additional covered car parking, repainting the entire property, and doing facelifting work. This enhances the value of the property. After improving the property's value, the investor sells the property at a higher price. In summary, an investor buys property under market price and enhances its value by fixing some property's shortcomings or creating additional facilities, increasing its market value. Then the property is sold at a higher market price, thereby giving a substantial profit to the investor.
    - Another form of this strategy is the flip strategy, which is mainly used in condos preconstruction. Here the investor books a condo at its preconstruction stage. Condos take 3 to 4 years to complete construction, and during the construction period, the investor has to pay only 20% of the total cost in different phases. So, by the time condos are ready for delivery after 3-4 years, the prices of condos appreciate by 25% to 30%. At that time, the investor flips it by selling it to another buyer. The significant advantage of this strategy is that while the investor

invests only 20% of the price in the phase, he benefits from a higher sale value on 100% of the property. There is significant Leverage in this strategy.

- House hacking strategy: This strategy is suitable for beginners in the real estate business. In this strategy, a property consisting of different units is purchased. The investor or the property owner lives in one of the units, and in other units, the investor keeps tenants. The investor lives in the same property, which the investor is also using partially for the rental income. This helps the investor in repaying the mortgage partially from rents received. At the same time, when the investor is living in the same property, the investor also understands the issues relating to the management of the property. For a beginner in the real estate business, this could be a great learning experience for running the business successfully.
- Wholesale selling strategy: This strategy is suitable for people who are either beginners or do not have enough capital to start a real estate business. This strategy is generally conducted as off Market deal. This means that the property is not advertised or listed in the market by the seller. The person intending to do a whole selling business in real estate will approach the seller directly and negotiate a sale price for the property (Downs, 1996). Then after paying a small deposit by the entire seller to the property seller, a contract will be signed between them in which it would be agreed that the whole seller can sell the property to anyone before the closing date. Thus, there would be a free assignment clause in the contract in favor of the wholesaler. The whole seller will then search for a suitable buyer who can buy the property above the contracted price with the seller before the closing date. The difference between the contracted price with the seller and the price paid by the ultimate buyer will be the profit of the whole seller. Thus, the wholesaler does not have to invest significant money in this strategy. However, one must have the capability to arrange a final buyer before the closing date. Otherwise, one will run into the risk of a big financial problem.
- REITs strategy: REITs stands for Real Estate Investment Trusts. Specifically, REIT is a trust fund collected from many investors by issuing shares or certificates of income, real estate investment management by specialized investment institutions, and distributing income as regulated to investors The REIT system is designed like a mutual fund, to provide opportunities for small and medium investors to invest in real estate. This strategy is suitable for those who do not want to own and manage properties, and it is also ideal for those who do not have significant funds to invest in real estate but want to take advantage of the growth in the real estate business. Big companies that own substantial real estate businesses issue REIT units for the real estate value they hold. Investors apply for the unit as per the funds they want to invest, thereby getting the fractional ownership in that real estate business. Such units owned by the investors can be traded in the market like stocks of companies are sold in the stock market. Thus, REITs offer opportunities even to a small investor to invest in the real estate business and enjoy its growth benefits. REITs also allow security investors to invest in one more tradable security to diversify their portfolios.

SOLUTIONS AND RECOMMENDATIONS

Financing of Residential Real Estate Business in Canada

Since real estate business requires a significant investment, financing plays a crucial role in developing real estate business. Multiple financial institutions have supported the real estate business in Canada by providing liberal mortgage loans at a meager interest rate. The Canadian residential mortgage market is dominated by the big six banks (RBC, CIBC, Scotiabank, Bank of Montreal, TD and National Bank of Can ada), which together hold approximately 75 per cent of the value of outstanding mortgages .These large banks have diversified their lending across all the major regions of Canada. Commercial Banks provide up to 95% of the total value of the property as a mortgage loan if the property is being purchased as a primarily residential home. If the property is being purchased as a residential investment property, then Banks provide finance up to 80% of the total value of the property. The most common mortgage in Canada has a fixed interest rate for a 5-year term, although there is a range of alternative mortgage products. Over 95 per cent of mortgages have a term of between six months and five years, and approximately one-third of outstanding mort- gages have a variable interest rate.

The federal regulatory and supervisory framework has a strong impact on the underwriting standards of lenders and the types of mortgage products available in Canada. About 80 per cent of mortgages are originated by lenders that are federally regulated by the Office of the Superintendent of Financial Institutions (OSFI). These lenders follow two major components of the federal policy guideline:

1. The primary basis for a loan decision should be the borrower's demonstrated willingness and capacity to make debt payments on a timely basis.
2. The lender has to purchase insurance for mortgages that exceed 80 per cent of the value of the residential property (i.e., with a down payment that is less than 20 per cent of the purchase price). The cost of the insurance is passed on to the borrowers

Further, banks carry out an independent appraisal of the property to satisfy themselves that the property's value has been determined as a fair market value and the value sufficiently covers the entire outstanding amount of the mortgage loan. Commercial banks are the "A" grade financial institutions that provide mortgage loans for residential real estate. However, they adhere to their bank's guidelines under which they provide loans only to customers who meet the criteria of creditworthiness, loan to value, and other eligibility criteria. So many people cannot get mortgage loans from banks due to either having bad credit or not having enough funds to meet the down payment criteria. The government allows withdrawal from the RRSP (Registered Retirement Savings Plan) account up to the limit of $ 25,000 for paying as a down payment for first-time homebuyers.

In addition to schedule "A" lenders, many schedule "B" and "C" grade financial institutions, commonly known as mortgage lenders, provide mortgage loans to customers who are not eligible for bank finance. These include Mortgage Finance companies (MFC), Mortgage Investment Corporations (MIC), and private investors. MFCs are non-depository financial institutions that underwrite and administer mortgages sourced through brokers. Their lending is funded mainly through MCAP Financial Corporation, First National Income Trust, Paradigm Quest Inc., and Merix Financials are some of the leading MFCs present in the Canadian market.

MICs and other private investors typically provide uninsured and highly customized mortgage products that are not available through traditional banks. These products include non-prime loans, second mortgages and very short-term mortgages. MICs typically do not require high credit scores but need a First Mortgage, preferably a second mortgage, to protect their credit risk and a creditable repayment plan. As the investors in the MICs take on greater risk, they charge quite a high-interest rate, from 10% to 15%, depending upon whether it is a first mortgage charge or a second mortgage charge. Some MICs even provide 100% financing provided one is prepared to pay a high-interest rate and offer a first mortgage along with additional security.

Besides "A" grade commercial Banks, "B" and "C" great financial institutions, there are some other sources of finance that are available for the real estate business in Canada. These sources are collectively known as OPM - Other People Money. The first such source is Owners financing, also called VTB or Vendor Take Back financing. In this financing method, the seller finances the buyer a certain percentage of the property price (say 20%) at a specific interest rate to secure the sale of the property. The remaining amount is sponsored by some financial institution or a private lender. The buyer then uses some small amount of personal funds to facelift the property by repainting the property or fixing and repairing some basic amenities. Then puts some tenants on the property. After that, the buyer takes refinancing from a bank or financial Institution and repays the owner and other lenders. Thus, this financing method allows the buyer to own a property by investing only a small amount.

The second method of OPM is by entering into joint venture partners who have some funds and want to participate in the real estate business but do not have enough time to look after the real estate business due to their preoccupation elsewhere. So, they participate in trade with experienced people and preferably work full time in the real estate business by lending their funds to them and sharing the proportionate income or profit from the company. Such joint venture partners are also called Money Partners, and the other partner is called Working partners.

Like Joint venture partners, private lenders are ready to lend their funds for the short term at high-interest rates but do not join the business as partners, and their interest is limited to earning interest. Usually, such loans are high-risk loans, as they are not secured against any mortgage and are given against Promissory Notes, and hence it carries a higher interest rate for taking higher risks.

Lastly, one of the less known sources of financing under OPM is a loan against RRSPs. The mortgage can be a first mortgage or second mortgage, or a pari-passu mortgage charge, where all lenders share risk proportional to their finance. There is a provision for taking a loan from another person's RRSPs, provided the loan is secured against the mortgage.

Risk Management Through Creation of a Reliable Network of Professionals

There is no doubt that the real estate business is lucrative in the long run. However, an investor is dependent on several functionaries in the real estate business, and therefore, an investor must create a reliable network of experts in various business operations. Firstly, an investor must have an excellent real estate agent who can support the investor in identifying good investment properties, preferably below the market price for the investor to invest. This will mitigate the risk of values going down below a certain level in a depressed market, although upside valuation possibilities will always exist in the long run. Since real estate agents are continuously in need, an expert and reliable agent will always help an investor identify the right property at the right location at the right price.

For any Investor in the real estate business, having expert Solicitors or Lawyers in their network always helps mitigate any legal risk due to their expertise in conducting due diligence on the property.

They also efficiently organize the sale transaction by coordinating with the land and registration office, seller's real estate agent, seller's solicitors, mortgage bankers, and investors. It is understood that the real estate business requires large-scale funds, which are arranged through OPM or lending institutions. However, an essential link between the lending institutions and the investors is a person known as Mortgage Broker. There are two types of mortgage brokers. First, those who are employees of a financial institution, and these brokers work for their Institutions and help the investor get mortgage loans from their Institutions. The second type of mortgage broker is those who work as independent brokers and have an agency relationship with multiple lending institutions. In the investor's interests, these brokers shop around different institutions and get the mortgage loan at very suitable terms to the investor. The second type of mortgage broker is beneficial for the investors, who either have a low credit rating or adopt the BRRRR strategy in their real estate business model.

As mortgage brokers are virtual channels for the availability of funds to real estate investors, they must maintain a relationship with multiple mortgage brokers and keep them an essential part of the network. Such a relationship helps the investor minimize his risk of shortage of adequate funds for expanding his business. After a property is purchased, an investor will either renovate the entire property or carry out some fixes and repairs to make it look like an excellent habitable property. For such activities, a real estate investor keeps a relationship with good property inspectors, architects, and contractors in his network. Using such experts enables the investor to mitigate two risks.

Firstly, these experts will identify and fix any significant shortcomings in the property right at the beginning, avoiding any inconvenience or dissatisfaction to tenants at a later stage and giving mental peace to the investor. Secondly, a suitable property will always invite stable, well-paying tenants, reducing the risk of nonpayment of rent or long property vacancy. Good quality tenants are the essence of the regular flow of income in the real estate business. Good quality tenants will always be attracted to that property known for providing good maintenance facilities. In rental properties, it is common to have frequent issues relating to plumbing faults, electrical faults, water leakages, etc. A timely rectification of these faults keeps tenants happy, and they are less prone to vacating the property. Therefore, to stay good long-term tenants and keep the property well maintained, the investor must possess a good team of plumbers, electricians, and other maintenance experts or contract with a maintenance company to provide timely maintenance services. This will lower the risk of tenant vacancy, thereby ensuring the regular inflow of income and reducing the risk of damage to the property due to persisting faults.

Like any other business, the real estate business also requires an accountant. An expert accountant's professional knowledge can help manage income and expenses so that the risk of paying high-income tax and paying high capital gains tax at the time of selling the property can easily be reduced. Finally, the investor's network needs to have suitable insurance advisors. There is a risk of fire, floods, earthquakes, and damage from any other calamity to buildings. A valid comprehensive insurance policy covering all possible risks should be taken with the guidance of an expert insurance advisor.

FUTURE RESEARCH DIRECTIONS

It is essential to understand the taxation aspect of the real estate business. There are two types of income in the real estate business, i.e., current income and income from capital appreciation. There are two types of taxes applicable to this business—tax on current income and tax on capital appreciation. Taxes also depend upon the type of real estate one has. There will be no income from primary home properties because an owner must live in the primary home. Hence no income tax liability will arise. However, Primary Home has the most significant tax advantage because there is no tax on the income from capital appreciation, irrespective of the capital appreciation amount. Due to this advantage, interest paid on a mortgage is not considered a tax-deductible expense.

Respect for investment properties is different. All expenses, including interest paid on mortgages, are considered tax-deductible expenses. All rental income after deducting tax-deductible expenses is taxable, and it is regarded as current income and is taxable as per the investor's tax slab. The income derived from Capital appreciation is also taxable. In this case, 50% of the capital appreciation is allowed to be tax-free, and the remaining 50% is taxed as per the investor's tax slab. To avoid the risk of high taxation, many investors do not sell their properties. They keep on taking refinancing in 3–4-year intervals from the banks as the market price of their properties keeps on increasing. In this way, they can withdraw cash profit from the property and still do not have to pay tax on the capital appreciation. Meanwhile, they keep on getting the current income from their property. This is considered a good strategy for mitigating the risk of high taxation.

CONCLUSION

Canadian real estate business is booming because real estate business is a profitable business in the long run. Many affluent Canadians have created vast wealth by seriously engaging themselves in real estate. However, multiple risks and challenges must be overcome to succeed in the business. The essential part of the business is to buy the right property at the right place and at the right time. Several risks are involved in the business, like credit, operational, and Market risk. An investor must make use of several strategies to overcome these risks. This business requires a significant investment of funds, and therefore this business is carried out using high Leverage on borrowed funds. The investor must rely upon multiple lending institutions to get funds and utilize them in the business. A meaningful way to mitigate risk in this business is to keep a strong network of expert people in different business functions. The more robust the network of experts, the more vital the chances of the business to be successful in creating long-term wealth.

REFERENCES

Charney, I. (2001). Three dimensions of capital switching within the real estate sector: A Canadian case study. *International Journal of Urban and Regional Research*, *25*(4), 740–758. doi:10.1111/1468-2427.00342

Dilmaghani, M. (2019). Religious identity and real estate wealth accumulation: Evidence from Canada. *Housing Studies*, *34*(10), 1690–1720. doi:10.1080/02673037.2017.1364714

Downs, A. (1996). Why invest in commercial real estate. *Urban Land September, 30*(3), 62-67.

Gillies, J. (1952). Residential Real Estate in Canada O. J. *Firestone. In*, *42*, 211–212.

Haila, A. (1991). Four types of investment in land and property. *International Journal of Urban and Regional Research, 15*(1), 343–365. doi:10.1111/j.1468-2427.1991.tb00643.x

Harvey, D. (1978). The urban process under capitalism: A framework for analysis. *International Journal of Urban and Regional Research, 2*(1), 101–131. doi:10.1111/j.1468-2427.1978.tb00738.x

Hebb, T., Hamilton, A., & Hachigian, H. (2010). Responsible property investing in Canada: Factoring both environmental and social impacts in the Canadian real estate market. *Journal of Business Ethics, 92*(2), 99–115. doi:10.100710551-010-0636-5

Khan, S. M., Pearson, D. D., Rönnqvist, T., Nielsen, M. E., Taron, J. M., & Goodarzi, A. A. (2021). Rising Canadian and falling Swedish radon gas exposure as a consequence of 20th to 21st century residential build practices. *Scientific Reports, 11*(1), 1–15. doi:10.103841598-021-96928-x PMID:34475435

Liu, C. H., Rosenthal, S. S., & Strange, W. C. (2018). The vertical city: Rent gradients, spatial structure, and agglomeration economies. *Journal of Urban Economics, 106*(2), 101–122. doi:10.1016/j.jue.2018.04.001

Mensah, J., & Tucker-Simmons, D. (2021). Social (in)justice and rental housing discrimination in urban Canada: The case of ethno-racial minorities in the Herongate community in Ottawa. *Studies in Social Justice, 15*(1), 81–101. doi:10.26522sj.v15i1.2239

Phillips, S., Dalziel, K., & Sjogren, K. (2021). Donor advised funds in Canada, Australia and the US: Differing regulatory regimes, differing streams of policy drift. *Nonprofit Policy Forum, 12*(3), 409-441. 10.1515/npf-2020-0061

ADDITIONAL READING

Benson, E., Hansen, J., Schwartz, A., & Smersh, G. (1997). The Influence of Canadian Investment on U.S. Residential Property Values. *Journal of Real Estate Research, 13*(3), 231–249. doi:10.1080/10835547.1997.12090880

Le Moigne, C., & Viveiros, É. (2008). The Inflation-Hedging Ability of Canadian Direct Real Estate Return and its Components, Income, and Appreciation. *Journal of Real Estate Portfolio Management, 14*(2), 141–154. doi:10.1080/10835547.2008.12089802

Lin, P., & Fuerst, F. (2014). Volatility Clustering, Risk-Return Relationship, and Asymmetric Adjustment in the Canadian Housing Market. *Journal of Real Estate Portfolio Management, 20*(1), 37–46. doi:10.1080/10835547.2014.12089961

Rherrad, I., Bago, J.-L., & Mokengoy, M. (2021). Real estate bubbles and contagion: New empirical evidence from Canada. *New Zealand Economic Papers, 55*(1), 38–51. doi:10.1080/00779954.2020.1791940

Schneider, S. (2004). Organized crime, money laundering, and the real estate market in Canada. *Journal of Property Research, 21*(2), 99–118. doi:10.1080/0959991042000328801

Chapter 15
From the Risk Society to COVID-19:
Analysis of Beck's Risk Society – Towards a New Modernity

Maximiliano Emanuel Korstanje
https://orcid.org/0000-0002-5149-1669
University of Palermo, Argentina

ABSTRACT

Ulrich Beck, a German sociologist who does not need prior presentation, cast his diagnosis of risk society as a new emerging ethos where social class and hierarchies blurred before the figure of risk. Although he shed light on the post-industrial society of the 1990s, today, the society he studied seems pretty different. Hence, a new fresh insight should be placed. This chapter introduces readers to the conceptual foundations of Thana Capitalism, as it was critically debated in the author's book The Rise of Thana Capitalism and Tourism. The risk society sets the pace for a new facet of capitalism where the other´s pain remains the main commodity to exchange. Far from being a more egalitarian society, as Beck said, in the days of Thana capitalism, a ruling elite governs the destiny of a precaritized workforce. The novel The Hunger Games represents perfectly how this society works. Additionally, the author brings some reflection on the connection of Thana capitalism and the spectacle beyond the recent COVID-19 pandemic.

INTRODUCTION

Doubtless, social scientists in general and sociology, in particular, should pay homage to Ulrich Beck not only in view of his main innovative contributions to the fields of modern sociology but also because his ideas shed light on the postmodern sociology. Beck has introduced innovative argumentations that invariably has shaken the sociology from the slumber it was. These new ideas and concepts discussed by Beck in the fields of sociology were of paramount importance to imagine a society marked by higher levels of uncertainness and fear. His conception of risk and contingency has relevance for sociology even

DOI: 10.4018/978-1-6684-5279-0.ch015

today. Let´s remind readers that Beck publishes the first edition of Risk Society: towards new modernity in 1992. In this book he unfolds elegantly all his genius to expand the current understanding of global modernity. For some reasons, which are very hard to precise here, Beck dates back the origin of risk society to Chernobyl´s accident. As he notes, Chernobyl should be understood as a founding event which laid the foundations of a new stage of capitalism. As a disrupting event, Chernobyl shows two important aspects of modern society. Technology which occupies a central position in human security paved the ways for the rise of the apocalypses unless dully regulated. Secondly, the risk society moves in a climate of uncertainty and complexity as never before. To wit, risk plays a leading role drawing the social institutions of a new society. Having said this, society has made from the notion of risk its centrepiece. As an accident of global impacts, Chernobyl created a paradoxical situation where the same technology disposed to make of human life safer led gradually toward an apocalyptic disaster. This paradox seems to be no other thing than the essence of technology in a risk society, as Beck adheres.

Starting from the premise that risk became in the epicentre of the world, Beck holds the thesis that the organization of society resulted in an egalitarian line of authority, which defied the already-existent hierarchies, paving the ways for the rise of a collective culture, where risks mediated between citizens and social institutions. Although Risk Society inaugurated a set of different studies revolving around risk perception, no less true is that the already existent sharp contrast between probabilists and culturalists has been enlarged. Today`s sociologists do not agree with a unified conception about risk. Whilst probabilists understand the risk as an objective condition that places the system or the self in jeopardy (Bernstein, 1996; Sunstein, 2005)-no matter than it is perceived or ignored- culturalists dangles the cultural nature of risks, which not only are linguistically conditioned but resonates differently depending of culture and context (Douglas & Wildavsky 1983; Slovic 1993; Boholm, 2003; Korstanje 2015). Equally important are the assumptions formulated by German sociologist Niklas Luhmann in cataloguing risks as inherently-enrooted into the principle of contingency. That way, Luhmann presents the distinction between risk and threats as his tug-of-war in the discussion ignited with other sociologists. Risk, paragraphing Luhmann, should be defined as something else than a simple calculation -as probabilists do- or a cultural construal. Since ancient civilization fleshed out different techniques and protocols to mitigate the negative effects of quakes, floods and so forth, they were unable to produce risks. It is important not to lose the sight for Luhmann, the risk is created by a previous decision-making process which is open to the contingency -this means that it can be avoided. Instead, threats are often externally imposed on the self or community without any possibilities for victims to elude them. Such a provoking-thought argument envisages that whilst the privileged ruling elite creates the risks, the rank-and-file workers face the aftermaths (Luhmann 1993). Hence, though Luhmann blames Beck to be alarmist in the diagnosis, he recognizes that only modern cultures produce risks. Produced-Knowledge is the key factor that explains risks. Whether ancient cultures devoted their loyalties to the cult of Gods, modern society appealed to reason to understand its environs. At some extent, risk assessment adjoins to a much deeper process of secularization initiated during the Industrial Revolution (Korstanje 2015). This moot point was widely criticised by another Senior sociologist, Sir Anthony Giddens, who not only opposed to Luhmann`s thesis but also interrogated on the nature of risk as ever-present in society, no matter the responsibilities of decision-maker. As Giddens (1991) eloquently observes, in a society where information and knowledge are systematically produced, packaged and disseminated to all classes, there is no place to surmise-as Luhmann precludes- that risk is strictly subject to individual or collective decision-making processes. Who would escape to the hegemony of risk? Giddens adds. Through the hyper-connected society, in the digital days, we are deciding even when we stop to do it. In consonance with Beck, our British sociologist acknowledges that “we are living our days” in runaway capitalism, where complexity and reasoning opened the doors to a process of reflexibility, unless duly-regulated by the risk-prevention programs and risk-management, may very well usher mankind in an imminent tragedy (Giddens 1999; 2011).

As the previous backdrop, some intriguing points of convergence in Giddens and Luhmann still remain open, which suggest that risks seem to be a modern-sounding theme, unknown by our ancient ancestors. The turn of the century witnessed the rise of different risks and threats, which range from terrorism towards lethal virus outbreaks (like COVID-19) without mentioning devastating quakes and tsunamis, which over recent years placed the public opinion in the alert (Skoll & Korstanje 2012). The present book chapter is structured according to three clear-cut themes. Preliminary we discuss in depth the nature and the evolution of risk as a sociological (probabilist) conceptualization. We place some authorative voices coming from different fields of social science. The notion of risk has been approached by different disciplines, each one kept its own definition and notion of what a risk means. Secondly, we introduce readers in the epistemological tenets of what we dubbed as “thana-capitalism”. The term was coined to give a fresh understanding of the rise of a new type of capitalism that replaces the risk society originally imagined by Bech. In this new morbid stage, the “Other´s suffering” is packaged and commoditised in form of dark spectacle. Lastly, we describe the spectacle beyond the recent COVID-19 pandemic which not only whipped the Western and Eastern economies but also ground the global trade into an unparalleled halt.

THE QUESTION OF RISK: BACKGROUND

Specialists and pundits’ debate to what extent risk is a new modern phenomenon or has been culturally enrooted in our civilization from its outset. In the discussion it is vital to distinguish between fear, risk or angst as well as the different definitions used in the threshold of time. Without any doubt, Aristotle, who was a pioneering voice, focused on the emotional nature of fear and its impacts on society. To a closer look, he holds the thesis that human behaviour is previously determined by imposed habits -which given some conditions- might be corrupted by human passions. Although Aristotle never cited the term risk in his texts, he signalled to fear as an emotional excess of bravery. Of course, men are often subject to a precautionary nature which protect them from external dangers, but when this nature becomes in excess, the hero passes to be a coward. Our tendency to pleasure-maximization –as a fundamental passion- paves the ways for the rise of fear (Hoffe 2010).

As this backdrop, Aristotle´s legacy was continued and redefined by another philosopher, who laid the theoretical foundations of modernity: Thomas Hobbes. The concept of Leviathan appears to be inspired by the needs of maximizing pleasure whilst minimizing pain. The subject is torn between contrasting trends. On one hand, it looks to dispossess others from their properties at the time, it avoids to be exploited by others. The urgency of avoiding a violent death as opposed to the needs of accumulating and dispossessing others from their properties. Given the problem in these terms, The figure of Leviathan speaks to us of the monopolization and the use of force as well as the application of the law that ultimately impedes the “War of All Against All”. Per Hobbes, the structure of nation-state is based on a long-dormant fear, which far from disappearing, mutates towards subtle political forms. The fear, echoing Hobbes, is the touchstone of modern society (Hobbes 2006). Over recent years, psychology has widely shown that the sentiment of fear should be understood as a basic emotion historically adapted to grant the subject´s survival. However, one the fear is domesticated through the articulation of repetitive habits, it can be manipulated to determine the autonomy of the subject. Fear triggers an inner drive which disposes the agent to paralysis, the attack or the flight before an external danger (Levenson, Ekman & Friesen, 1990; Strongman 1996). Undoubtedly, the psychological fear and the biological evolution of the agent are inextricably intertwined. Despite the agreement of psychology to reach a shared definition on risk, not all disciplines are in agreement of what risk means. Whilst modern philosophy turned the attention to the figure of angst which situated as the tug of war of existentialism, anthropology and sociology focused on risk as a cultural construal which is culturally cemented. Some ethnographies reveal how some aborigines are reluctant to the introduction of technology to measure the volcano activity because it triggers the rage of Gods which is the real reason behind the natural disasters. Rather, for western science, technology is often used to save lives. Two cosmologies, two different ways of interpreting the origin of disasters. The quake which whipped Lisbon in the eighteen century was seen for the Catholic Church as the sign of the moral fall, no less true is that for others it represented the start of modern seismography.

In this vein, the figure of angst seems to be associated with the rise and expansion of modernity as a cultural project. As Martin Heidegger puts it, whilst the notion of fear is enrooted in the presence of a visual (palpable) threat, angst –instead- operates in the constellations of diffuse horizons once the self meets with the nothingness. The dasein (being-there) moves according to a climate where its decisions open the doors to the idea of contingency. The figure of angst derives from the freedom given to the dasein which engages with the desire of living. (Heidegger, 1996). Anthony Giddens (1991) hotly debates to what extent the reclusion of religion to the advance of modernity left a gap which was finally filled by the risk. Today, we have no certainties, no firm horizons nor all-encompassing epistemologies which guide our destinies. Modernity can be compared to a "runaway train" which not only has not a fixed direction but also goes out of control (Giddens 2011). The paradox of technology is a clear example of this. Whereas western technology is unfolded to find and mitigate external risks which may place the society in jeopardy, no less true is that new emerging unseen risks are engendered (Beck 1992). In his seminal book, The Society under Siege, Zygmunt Bauman (2013) bemoans that the risk was a cultural construct, which introduced by modernity, allowed to capital owners to control (or at least imagine) the not-so-distant future. In the medieval times, the idea of happiness was strictly reserved to a ruling elite, who experienced by a long period of material deprivation. Happiness cannot be understood without the pain. Medieval philosophers toyed with the belief that nobody felt happiness if before they experienced the dark side of sadness. What is equally important, modernity as political project upended this logic maximizing happiness no matter the costs. To put the same in other words, modernity changed the interplay of happiness-sadness forever. The revolution in America and its subsequent independence from Great Britain not only deals with a traumatic experience with Britons, but it pivots the ways happiness is valorised. The founding parents of the United States declared unilaterally that all men have the same right to feel happiness (contrasting to the aristocrat conception forged in Europe), whilst the nation-state should devote its resources to achieve a climate of collective happiness. The old medieval doctrine of asceticism which postulates that nobody may reach happiness if the pain is undermined sets the pace to a new (modern) ideology. The invention of the nation-state, as well as the conception of nationhood, were two key factors towards a new understanding of happiness. The nation should be the watchdog that ensures collective freedom which is the precondition to happiness. To wit, the state should devote affordable resources in order for their citizens to meet the individual goals. In so doing, a just distribution of goods should be organised for all those abide the law. Likewise, as Bauman brilliantly observes, modern philosophers envisaged a new cosmology where pleasure should be repressed in order for an atmosphere of happiness can be sustained in a long-lasting term. Paradoxically, the quest of happiness created an uncanny obsession for the future, whereas the development of technology paved the ways for the needs of domesticating the uncertainness. This means that the quest of happiness might be an ideal to follow in so far as it reproduces a climate of mistrust and discomfort dotted with higher levels of anxiety. Having said this, it is important not to lose the sight of the fact that the dilemma left by Hobbes and Beck remains open to date. Robert Castel, the French philosopher, adventured to resolve this issue in different texts. It is unfortunate that Castel was never translated to English and what can be read is in Spanish or French. Our efforts to pass Castel to English are not an easy task but it deserves our time. Castel argues convincingly that risk should be studied according to the cultural background of postmodernity. The notion of risk not only comes from the modern form of production but also from the modern form of labour organizations. To put this in bluntly, the triumph of risk as a dominant discourse of the privileged class coincides with the precaritization of working unions and the labour relations worldwide. Whilst the social ties were undermined through the stimulation of labour competence, the ontological security of the citizens withered away. In the medieval days, the peasant was surely subject to countless deprivations, to real dangers and early death. However, even in these grim days, religion worked as a protective cocoon which offered a better life in heaven. The introduction of modernity not only offered an expansion of life expectancy but the decline of religion. As a result of this, numerous risks loomed human existence as never before. The paradox of risk relates to the following axiom: despite the material benefits-oriented to make of this modern life a safer place, further insecurities certainly surfaced (Castel 1997; 2006; 2010). As Korstanje (2014; 2015) puts it, English speaking countries seem to be more sensitive to risk perception than Spanish speaking cultures. This happens simply because the Protestant faith has developed a strange urgency to domesticate future, as preconditioned by the divinity. The predestination played a crucial role in the configuration of the capitalist ethos, which derives from the Protestantism –as Weber brilliantly asserted. The Church-centered faith which characterised the political stability of medieval times gradually passed to a tailored theology, designed to be adjusted to the individual whim. The idea of predestination, which is enrooted in the Protestantism, proffered a closed view of the future. In this respect, Anglo-Saxons were aimed at controlling the future supported by the technological breakthrough which led invariably to the industrial revolution.

In parallel, recent studies discuss the role of communication in the formation and perception of risks (Fischoff, 1995; Morgan 2002). The professionalization of culture was widely explored by B. Bledstein who acknowledges that the culture of individualism, as it was cultivated in the United States during eighteen century, is the platform for thousands of young students in quest of social upward. The process of educating the lay-citizen assured the necessary cultural background for the reproduction of a new burgeoning class redesigning new professions to locate and solve problems that affect daily life. The society of risk cannot be dissociated to the modern science (Bledstein 1978; Gustafsod, 1998; Johnson & Powell, 1994; Flynn, Slovic & Mertz, 1994; Mitchells, 1998; Fothergill, Maestas, & Darlington, 1999; Kahan et al. 2007). Nonetheless, some points here suggest that lay-person perceive different risk than experts. The question of whether experts are educated and trained to make a clear diagnosis of the risk, one might speculate that they fail to communicate efficiently their knowledge to the rest of the community. As Sjoberg (1999) highlighted, the impact of risk on the lay-persons not only depend on their previous experience but also by their biographical background. The specialists develop a rational understanding of the situation, which is based on objective proofs and observable evidence, whilst persons often fall prey of emotional distortions. The net of experts plays two different roles at the time of communicating risks: protectors and promoters. Whilst the former signals to those agents trained to conduct a formal debate revolving around the causes and effects of different problems, the latter are moved by the needs of communicating what are the potential risks that threaten the society all. Sjoberg goes on to write,

The conflict between Protectors and Promoters is often a theme in fiction or movies. Take the movie Jaws as an example. Here the Protector is a police officer who is concerned about the safety of the population in a beach resort town. Finding traces of a Big White on the shore he blows the whistle. The mayor of the town, however, is a Promoter of the tourist trade. To him, the alarm is very misplaced because it threatens that trade. Hence he does not believe in the warnings, ridicules or even fires the police officer, etc, etc. Many other examples could be given. The story is nearly always the same. The whistleblower, or Protector, is ignored or harassed by Promoters who have large vested interests in some kind of business. A final disaster is then avoided or mitigated by the heroic deeds of the Protector who is finally recognised by everyone as having been right all the time (Sjoberg, 1999: 4).

In terms of Cass Sunstein (2005), the inflation of risk explains by the emphasis put by the precautionary doctrine in events of high-impact which are improbable. In his book Laws of Fear: beyond the precautionary principle, he says overtly that the borders between security and insecurity are culturally drawn by the political system. Democracies, per his outcomes, or better said, deliberative democracies are characterised by the pluralism of voices, whereas in dictatorships or demagogic populism decisions are made by top officials. Though experts play a leading role in the discussion of those matters that can place the society in jeopardy, no less true is that the state of disaster can be avoided if decisions are collectively discussed. This belief would explain the reasons as to why democratic societies have more instruments to face disasters than totalitarian or authoritarian ones. Whereas the latter does not provide their citizens with the necessary steps to evaluate the pre-existing risks, the former invests a considerable amount of capital in the process of mitigation and preparedness for natural catastrophes. It is important not to lose the sight of people seems to be prone to face serious risks in matters they feel safer, whereas, in other conditions, which have further negative consequences, risks are glossed over. In this token, the precautionary principle, which is based on the European model, obscures more than it clarifies. In fact, the precautionary principle sometimes gives the necessary conditions for risks to be multiplied. The bombing of risk-containing news, far from enabling commitment in population, creates paralysis. Underpinned in the ethical quandary, which superposes knowledge-production to risk-assessment –as the critical literature argued-, Sunstein clarifies the worst happens when even experts follow their surmises and diagnoses irrationally. He coins the neologism, risk-neglect to theorise on the effects of irrational decisions, which are conditioned by populist demands or incorrect diagnosis. The current inflation of risks derives from two psychological mechanisms, the neglect of probability and the heuristic of risk. Given by emotional dispositions, people are trapped into some preconceived beliefs that from keep away from rational evaluations. With the benefits of hindsight, Sunstein contends that the probability neglect shows how some persons fall in the worst feasible situation without evaluating properly the probabilities the disaster happens whilst in others conditions the real reasons for disasters are ignored. The heuristic of risks exhibits a tendency to misjudge risks by the potential effects instead of probabilities. This means that some serious risks are trivialised whereas others are over-valorised (Sunstein 2002; 2003).

One of the contributions of Sunstein on the studied theme consists of reminding the importance of risk as something else than a cultural construal alone. Although communication is of paramount importance to give risks specific meanings and interpretations, further investigation is needed in a combined model that alternates quality-conducted ethnography that helps to grasp the biography of subjects with probability-based models to expand the current understanding of risk (Goodwin & Strang 2012; Strang 2015).

FUTURE CHALLENGES IN THE DARK SOCIETY

In our days, the society of risks examined by Giddens and Beck has gone forever, or at least it has mutated into a new form, Thana-Capitalism. Risk-Capitalism essentially was associated with biopolitics and the needs of life, Thana Capitalism centres on the opposite, death. In sharp contrast to Medieval Age, in Thana-Capitalism people have a high expectancy of life, but live frightened by the possibility of death. Consumers are fascinated to witness spectacles where others are affected, killed or tortured. Death has become the main cultural value in this new society, where 24 hours per day, TV and Journalism only transmit news linked to death. News that oscillates between disasters, terrorist attacks or local crimes daily captivates an audience more interested to feel more special than consternated for a run-a-way World. In many newscasts, it appears a message that says "images may hurt your sensibility", or Warning, videos and images not for children". At a closer look, even if the audience in the developed societies are bombarded to catastrophic news with the end of keeping the society in an on-going state of emergency, no less true is that death has become in a form of entertainment (Korstanje 2016). The manifest impossibility of the precautionary principle to prevent the risk before it takes place leads gradually to a new society where the disaster is visually packaged, disseminated and commoditised as a form of consumption. This new climate opens the doors to new a fictionality, narratives and discourses oriented to domesticate the global audience. To some extent, the disaster has become a spectacle. From terrorism to climate change, the media produces new narratives tilted at presenting the Other´s pain as a source of pleasure for the anaesthetised self. Of course, Beck never imagined a (dark) society where the Other´s death situates as the main commodity to exchange. The Thana-capitalism started with a founding event the 9/11 which marked the American society. Altheide reminds brilliantly how the US is not a dictatorial power in itself but the obsession for security is leading towards more despotic and radicalised discourses which may jeopardize democracy in a short-run. This is the case of some extremists like Donald Trump that reached the presidency thanks to the climate of terror and mistrust Americans day-to-day experience after 9/11. D. Altheide argues convincingly that from its inception, America debated between the fear of strangers and the needs of alternating check and balance institutions with egalitarianism. During the Cold War, the red-scare reanimated this old fear to the non-western "Other" to the extent the political resources were mobilised to protect the nation. Once the Soviet Union collapsed, this place was occupied by international terrorism and the figure of rogue states. Basically, the popular culture was historically oriented to demonize the alterity to provide Americans with a form of entertainment. Today, democracy is in danger because the respect for institutions and the division of powers is ceding to the populist demands for more security, Altheide concludes (Altheide 2017).

Another good example is the theatralization around the problem of climate change as the main risk for society. In the turn of the century, countless global risks and dangers loom the tourist and hospitality industries. These threats oscillate from radicalised terrorist cells to natural disasters prompted by climate change. Precisely this latter captivated the attention of scholars over the recent years. At a closer look, big problems –like Climate change- required from a big solution. Here two assumptions should be done. On one hand, theorists speculated on the urgency to create a cosmopolitan spirit to coordinate efforts towards a more sustainable and global society. After two major wars, the ideals of the Kantian peace seemed to within reach. Of course, since the Kyoto protocol and the agreements of Copenhagen and Paris, developing nations adopted an eco-friendly attitude whilst developed ones shudder to think in the possibilities to reduce their greenhouse gases to the atmosphere. The material asymmetries between developed and underdeveloped economies which characterize the history of capitalism was certainly crystalised in the successive failures to reach an international consensus. Finally, the Paris Agreement included a major consensus with the exemption of the US (just after D. Trump would be elected president).

On another, some scholars agree that there was a dissociation between what people concern and the practical steps to revert their individual behaviour. Whilst a majority of interviewed tourists express a manifest concern for climate change, no less true they were uncertain about what to do in reverting the contamination or the necessary steps towards a more sustainable economy (Gossling et al 2012; Korstanje & George 2012).

This begs a more than the puzzling question: is climate change a major threat for humankind existence or simply a new artefact of popular entertainment?

Though an answer seems not to be easy, one might speculate that a clear hint can be precisely found in the logic of popular entertainment. During decades, ethnographers and anthropologists of all stripes agree that the turn of the century brings often millennial fears and anxieties which relate to the end of the world (at least as we know it). Just after the beginning of the twentieth-one century, countless global threats woke up Occident from the slumber it was. In this context, the climate change situates as a global hazard which not only jeopardizes the capitalist system but the earth as mankind´s home. The industry of entertainment –materialised in movies, novels, videogames and other popular industries- is culturally formatted to give hypothetical answers to those mysteries that concern humanity. To set an example, one of the goals of horror and disaster-movies orient to provide concrete lessons to be followed in post-disaster contexts. Not surprisingly the lack of firm answers and shared coordination by the side of governments engaged to reduce the greenhouse gases opened the doors in order for the climate change to be commoditised and sold as a cultural product. In so doing, the audiences experience a combination of fear and fascination for the possibilities of witnessing the end of the world. The act of gazing implies a certain privilege that reinforces their own status. When we watch a horror or a disaster movie, we feel pleasure simply because the real danger has been certainly exorcised if not encapsulated. Enmeshed in a climate of controlled risk, horror movies paralyze whilst entertaining the global audiences worldwide. It is unfortunate that the same applies to climate change. Needless to say, the entertainment industries have a double function. On one side, they immobilize the critical thinking of the spectatorship enhancing its resilience spirit. On another, it dissociates what people feel from what they finally can do. What is the nature of a spectacle?

The idea of the spectacle comes from an unresolved mystery, a thorny-question, which though causes higher levels of anxieties, has not been resolved and opposes to our sense of existence. Ethically speaking, the spectacle (i.e a play-work) leaves an open question which is interpreted and negotiated by the spectatorship according to its discretion. At the bottom, the goals of the spectacle are aimed at conditioning the audience to embrace their social institutions. Here two additional problems arise. Firstly, the cultural entertainment industry and the obsession for climate change recreate fictional stories, explanations and expectancies that are aimed at replicating the logic of the system that produces it. Whilst paradoxically we feel worried about the potential effects of natural disasters, at the bottom we do not believe we are the next victims. Secondly and most important, since the causes of the problem are never tackled (which is the precondition for the spectacle transcends in the threshold of time), the possibilities new disasters repeat with more intensity seems to be higher. Doubtless, climate change is a big problem for the planet, but no less true is that we are far from reaching an all-pervading solution to the problem. In this respect, climate change interrogates us and our capacities to change or to succumb to the society of spectacle which hides the material asymmetries generated by global capitalism.

THE SPECTACLE OF COVID-19

The first cases of COVID-19 (SARSCOv-2) were originally reported in Wuhan, China in 2019. Although originally the governments disposed of restrictive measures to contain the infection, it rapidly disseminated worldwide (Fotiadis, Polyzos & Huan, 2021; Butcher 2021). These measures included the border and airspaces closure, as well as the imposition of lockdown and social distancing without mentioning the closure of hotels, theatres and public offices. Beyond the real economic impacts of the pandemic, which led global capitalism to the brink of collapse, there was a type of macabre spectacle mounted to entertain the audiences. In this respect, the media, journalists and TV programs transmitted COVID-19 related news 24/7. Whilst one must confess the world finally stopped, lay-people who were forced to stay at home consumed the morbid spectacle of COVID-19 all the time. Each day, news anchor said the number of infected, hospitalised patients and the fatal victims. What is more important, the COVID-19, far from being a foundational event, reaffirmed a tendency originally forged just after 9/11 where the "Other" becomes in an undesired guest. The attacks to WTC in 2001 not only inaugurated a new society (as clearly explained in the former sections) but also undermined the Western civilization from within, affecting one of its cultural values: the sacred law of hospitality. In the days after 9/11, anyone can be a potential terrorist, a friend, a colleague or a neighbour. "The Other" becomes in a potential invisible enemy who plans in secrecy the next attack. Western societies which are mainly marked by higher levels of mobility closed their borders whilst imposing serious restrictions to migrants and different travel bans. At the same time, echoing Altheide, terrorism was commoditised as a great mega spectacle which combines fear and pleasure. The same applies for the COVID-19 pandemic. Nowadays, all we are potential (terrorists) carriers of a lethal virus. Without any doubt, we witness not only the decline of hospitality where the "Other" is not welcomed, but also a process of feudalization characterised by geopolitical tensions, racist or separatist discourse, and the tourist-phobia, which means a much deeper sentiment of hate directed against foreign tourists (Korstanje & George, 2021; 2022).

CONCLUSION

Ulrich Beck, German sociologist who does not need previous presentation, casted his diagnosis about risk society as a new emerging ethos where social class and hierarchies blurred before to the figure of risk. Although he shed light on the post-industrial society of the 90s decade, today the society he studied seems to be pretty different. Hence, a new fresh insight should be placed. This paper introduces readers on the conceptual foundations of Thana Capitalism, as it was critically debated in our book *The Rise of Thana Capitalism and Tourism.* Per our conception, the risk society sets the pace to a new facet of capitalism where the Other´s pain remains as the main commodity to exchange. Far from being a more egalitarian society, as Beck said, in the days of Thana-capitalism a ruling elite governs the destiny of a precaritised work-force. The novel *The Hunger Games* represents perfectly how this society works.

Additionally we bring some reflection on the connection of Thana-capitalism and the Spectacle beyond the recent COVID-19 pandemic.

REFERENCES

Altheide, D. (2017). *Terrorism and the Politics of Fear*. Rowman & Littlefield.

Bauman, Z. (2013). *Society under siege*. John Wiley & Sons.

Beck, U. (1992). *Risk society: Towards a new modernity* (Vol. 17). Sage.

Bernstein, P. L. (1996). *Against the gods: The remarkable story of risk*. Wiley & Sons.

Bledstein, B. (1978). The Culture of Professionalism. In The middle class and the higher education in America. Norton.

Boholm, Å. (2003). The cultural nature of risk: Can there be an anthropology of uncertainty? *Ethnos, 68*(2), 159–178. doi:10.1080/0014184032000097722

Butcher, J. (2021). Covid-19, tourism and the advocacy of degrowth. *Tourism Recreation Research*, 1–10. doi:10.1080/02508281.2021.1953306

Castel, R. (1997). *The Metamorphosis of the Social Question. A Chronicle of the Salariado* [La Metamorfosis de la Cuestión social. Una Crónica del salariado]. Paidos.

Douglas, M., & Wildavsky, A. (1983). *Risk and culture: An essay on the selection of technological and environmental dangers*. University of California Press. doi:10.1525/9780520907393

Fischhoff, B. (1995). Risk perception and communication unplugged: Twenty years of process. *Risk Analysis, 15*(2), 137–145. doi:10.1111/j.1539-6924.1995.tb00308.x PMID:7597253

Flynn, J., Slovic, P., & Mertz, C. K. (1994). Gender, race, and perception of environmental health risks. *Risk Analysis, 14*(6), 1101–1108. doi:10.1111/j.1539-6924.1994.tb00082.x PMID:7846319

Fothergill, A., Maestas, E. G., & Darlington, J. D. (1999). Race, ethnicity and disasters in the United States: A review of the literature. *Disasters, 23*(2), 156–173. doi:10.1111/1467-7717.00111 PMID:10379098

Fotiadis, A., Polyzos, S., & Huan, T. C. T. (2021). The good, the bad and the ugly on COVID-19 tourism recovery. *Annals of Tourism Research, 87*, 103117. doi:10.1016/j.annals.2020.103117 PMID:33518847

Giddens, A. (1991). *Modernity and self-identity: Self and society in the late modern age*. Stanford University Press.

Giddens, A. (1999). Risk and responsibility. *The Modern Law Review, 62*(1), 1–10. doi:10.1111/1468-2230.00188

Giddens, A. (2011). *Runaway world*. Profile Books.

Goodwin, Y., & Strang, K. D. (2012). Socio-cultural and multi-disciplinary perceptions of risk. *International Journal of Risk and Contingency Management, 1*(1), 1–11. doi:10.4018/ijrcm.2012010101

Gössling, S., Scott, D., Hall, C. M., Ceron, J. P., & Dubois, G. (2012). Consumer behaviour and demand response of tourists to climate change. *Annals of Tourism Research*, *39*(1), 36–58. doi:10.1016/j.annals.2011.11.002

Gustafsod, P. E. (1998). Gender Differences in risk perception: Theoretical and methodological erspectives. *Risk Analysis*, *18*(6), 805–811. doi:10.1111/j.1539-6924.1998.tb01123.x PMID:9972583

Heidegger, M. (1996). *Being and time: A translation of Sein und Zeit*. SUNY Press.

Hobbes, T. (2006). *Leviathan*. A&C Black.

Höffe, O. (Ed.). (2010). *Aristotle's "Nicomachean Ethics"*. Brill. doi:10.1163/ej.9789004177628.i-259

Johnson, J. E., & Powell, P. L. (1994). Decision making, risk and gender: Are managers different? *British Journal of Management*, *5*(2), 123–138. doi:10.1111/j.1467-8551.1994.tb00073.x

Kahan, D. M., Braman, D., Gastil, J., Slovic, P., & Mertz, C. K. (2007). Culture and identity-protective cognition: Explaining the white-male effect in risk perception. *Journal of Empirical Legal Studies*, *4*(3), 465–505. doi:10.1111/j.1740-1461.2007.00097.x

Korstanje, M., & George, B. (2021). *Mobility and Globalization in the Aftermath of COVID19: Emerging New Geographies in a Locked World*. Palgrave Macmillan. doi:10.1007/978-3-030-78845-2

Korstanje, M. E. (2014). Why risk-research is more prominent in English speaking countries in the digital society. *International Journal of Cyber Warfare & Terrorism*, *4*(1), 8–18. doi:10.4018/ijcwt.2014010102

Korstanje M E (2015) *A Difficult World: Examining the roots of capitalism*. Nova Science.

Korstanje, M. E. (2016). *The Rise of Thana Capitalism and Tourism*. Routledge. doi:10.4324/9781315457482

Korstanje, M. E., & George, B. (2012). Global warming and tourism: Chronicles of apocalypse? *Worldwide Hospitality and Tourism Themes*, *4*(4), 332–355. doi:10.1108/17554211211255684

Korstanje, M. E., & George, B. (2021). The Nature and Future of tourism: In a post COVID-19 context. Apple Academic Press.

Levenson, R. W., Ekman, P., & Friesen, W. W. (1990). Voluntary facial expression generates emotions-specific nervous system activity. *Psychophysiology*, *27*, 363–384. doi:10.1111/j.1469-8986.1990.tb02330.x PMID:2236440

Luhmann, N. (1993). *Communication and social order: risk: a sociological theory*. Transaction Publishers.

Mitchell, V. W. (1998). Buy-phase and buy-class effects on organisational risk perception and reduction in purchasing professional services. *Journal of Business and Industrial Marketing*, *13*(6), 461–478. doi:10.1108/08858629810246779

Morgan, M. G. (2002). *Risk communication: A mental models approach*. Cambridge University Press.

Sjoberg, L. (1999). Risk Perception by The Public and By Experts: A dilemma in risk management. *Human Ecology Review*, *6*(2), 1–9.

Skoll, G. R., & Korstanje, M. E. (2012). Risks, totems, and fetishes in Marx and Freud. *Sincronía*, *2*, 11–27.

Slovic, P. (1993). Perceived risk, trust, and democracy. *Risk Analysis*, *13*(6), 675–682. doi:10.1111/j.1539-6924.1993.tb01329.x

Strang, K. D. (2015). Developing a goal-driven research strategy. In *The Palgrave Handbook of Research Design in Business and Management* (pp. 31–45). Palgrave Macmillan US. doi:10.1057/9781137484956_3

Strongman, K. T. (1996). *The Phsychology of Emotions: theories of emotions in perspective*. Willey and Sons.

Sunstein, C. R. (2002). Probability neglect: Emotions, worst cases, and law. *The Yale Law Journal*, *112*(1), 61–107. doi:10.2307/1562234

Sunstein, C. R. (2003). Terrorism and probability neglect. *Journal of Risk and Uncertainty*, *26*(2-3), 121–136. doi:10.1023/A:1024111006336

Sunstein, C. R. (2005). *Laws of fear: Beyond the precautionary principle* (Vol. 6). Cambridge University Press. doi:10.1017/CBO9780511790850

ADDITIONAL READING

Arendt, H. (1963). *Eichmann in Jerusalem*. Penguin.

Ariès, P. (1975). *Western attitudes toward death: from the Middle Ages to the present* (Vol. 3). JHU Press.

Barro, R. J., & Ursua, J. F. (2008). Consumption disasters in the twentieth century. *The American Economic Review*, *98*(2), 58–63. doi:10.1257/aer.98.2.58

Baudrillard, J. (1995). *The Gulf War did not take place*. Indiana University Press.

Bauman, Z. (1988). Sociology after the Holocaust. *The British Journal of Sociology*, *39*(4), 469–497. doi:10.2307/590497

Bauman, Z. (1989). *Modernity and the Holocaust*. Cornell University Press.

Bernstein, R. J. (2002). *Radical Evil: A Philosophical Interrogation*. Blackwell publishers.

Bloxham, D. (2001). *Genocide on trial: war crimes trials and the formation of Holocaust history and memory*. Oxford University Press. doi:10.1093/acprof:oso/9780198208723.001.0001

Chan, E. (2003). War and Images: 9/11/01, Susan Sontag, Jean Baudrillard, and Paul Virilio. *Film International*, *5*, 128–147.

Derrida, J. (2000). Of Hospitality: Anne Dufourmantelle Invites Jacques Derrida to Respond, trans. Rachel Bowlby. Stanford Univ. Press.

Feierstein, D. (2014). *Genocide as Social Practice: reorganizing society under Nazis and Argentina's Military Juntas*. Rutgers University Press. doi:10.26530/OAPEN_625248

Friedrichs, D. O. (2000). The crime of the century? The case for the Holocaust. *Crime, Law, and Social Change*, *34*(1), 21–41. doi:10.1023/A:1008322402290

Giddens, A. (1999). Risk and responsibility. *The Modern Law Review*, *62*(1), 1–10. doi:10.1111/1468-2230.00188

Hofstadter, R. (1944). *Social Darwinism in American thought.* Beacon Press.

Ignatieff, M. (2003). *Human rights as politics and idolatry*. Princeton University Press.

Klein, N. (2007). *The shock doctrine: The rise of disaster capitalism*. Macmillan.

Korstanje, M. (2014). Chile helps Chile: Exploring the effects of earthquake Chile 2010. *International Journal of Disaster Resilience in the Built Environment*, *5*(4), 380–390. doi:10.1108/IJDRBE-01-2012-0002

Korstanje, M. E. (2016). *The Rise of Thana Capitalism and Tourism*. Routledge. doi:10.4324/9781315457482

Korstanje, M. E. (2017). The Allegory of Holocaust: The Rise of Thana Capitalism. In *Ideological Messaging and the Role of Political Literature* (pp. 177–199). IGI Global. doi:10.4018/978-1-5225-2391-8.ch010

Korstanje, M. E. (2018). A Paradoxical World and the Role of Technology in Thana-Capitalism. In *Encyclopedia of Information Science and Technology* (4th ed., pp. 4761–4773). IGI Global.

Korstanje, M. E., & George, B. (2017). *Virtual Traumascapes and Exploring the roots of Dark Tourism*. IGI global.

Lang, B. (1999). *The future of the Holocaust: between history and memory*. Cornell University Press. doi:10.7591/9781501727559

Lara, M. P. (2007). *Narrating evil: A postmetaphysical theory of reflective judgment*. Columbia University Press. doi:10.7312/lara14030

Levi, P. (2017). *The drowned and the saved*. Simon and Schuster.

Levinas, E. (1988). *Useless suffering. In The provocation of Levinas: Rethinking the other*. Routledge.

Lipstadt, D. (1993). *Denying the Holocaust, the growing assault of truth and memory*. Free Press.

Luhmann, N. (2017). *Trust and power*. John Wiley & Sons.

Malamud Goti, J. (1996). *A Game without end*. Oklahoma University Press.

Mayer, M. (2013). *They thought they were free: The Germans, 1933-45*. University of Chicago Press.

Nussbaum, M. C. (2001). *The fragility of goodness: Luck and ethics in Greek tragedy and philosophy*. Cambridge University Press. doi:10.1017/CBO9780511817915

KEY TERMS AND DEFINITIONS

Dark Consumption: It is type of consumption where the "Other´s death" is commoditised and exchanged in society.

Risk Society: It is a term coined by Sociologist Ulrich Beck to denote the change to a new stage of capitalism mainly marked by the proliferation of risks.

Thana Capitalism: It is a term developed by Maximiliano Korstanje to explain the next stage of global capitalism which passed from risk society to Thana-capitalism.

Ulrich Beck: Was a German sociologist dedicated to the study of modern capitalism and society.

Chapter 16
Terrorism, Automated Hosts, and COVID-19:
Critical Film Review of the HBO Saga *Westworld*

Maximiliano Emanuel Korstanje
https://orcid.org/0000-0002-5149-1669
University of Palermo, Argentina

ABSTRACT

The reign of terror ignited by 9/11 and the resulting War on Terror has accelerated the effects on social imaginary. Beyond the economic aftermaths, 9/11 recreated the conditions towards a monopoly of radicalized discourse, which was mainly oriented toward demonizing the "Non-Western Other." Terrorism allowed the introduction of a conspiracy plot that marked some minority ethnicities as an enemy living within. At the bottom, these narratives punctuated that Muslim communities hate the society they inhabit. Such discourse changed forever the ways the "Other" is imagined. The chapter deals with HBO Saga Westworld, a futurist and dystopian world where robots (hosts) are subjected to torture, violence, and even sadist practices at the hands of wealthy tourists (guests). The formula in "Robots We Must Trust" is placed under the critical lens of scrutiny.

INTRODUCTION

Over recent years, some voices have enthusiastically applauded the idea of introducing robots and artificial intelligence to improve the guest-host relations (Ivanov, Webster & Berezina, 2017; Ivanov & Webster 2019). To some extent, the recruitment of robots –as a potential hotel or housekeeping staff- to meet tourists´ demands not only escapes to the ethical debates which denote the subordination of hosts to guests´ desires but also situate as a promising opportunity to enhance the destination performance in the next decades (Yeoman & Mars, 2012). Starting from the premise that robots do not feel, nor have deeply-enrooted emotions such as rage, fear, or love, these studies hold thesis that technology offers a

DOI: 10.4018/978-1-6684-5279-0.ch016

fertile ground towards a new revolution if it is oriented to service industries (Murphy, Hofacker & Gretzel, 2017; Buckley et al, 2015). At a closer look, one might speculate that robots are machines that do not need to sleep or rest, which supposes that the process of systematization of tourist services will create smarter and more robust destinations tailored mainly to what tourists often demand (Tung & Law, 2017; Murphy, Gretzel & Hofacker, 2015; Yeoman 2012). What is more promising, robots and technology can be used to develop more sustainable destinations worldwide (Ivanov & Webster 2019; de Kervenoael et al, 2019; Dalgic & Bidir, 2020). As Sangwon Park puts it, tourism research should particularly focus on the significant role of robots in enhancing tourist´s satisfaction, as well as a direct contribution to local economies. The increasing fascination for robots allows multiplication of segments and multifaceted performances while reinforcing the institution-based trust (Park 2020). Before the so-called scourge of terrorism, robots and technology offer the opportunities to have safer destinations. The recently originated COVID-19 virus outbreak not only placed the tourism industry between the wall and the much blue sea but paved the ways for the rise of acclaimed authors to venerate robots as potential hotel staff immune to the pandemics (Jiang & Wen 2020; Sigala 2020). Some voices have argued that COVID-19 is the continuation of terrorism as well as the corollary of 9/11. Basically, terrorism not only opened the doors to a new stage where the fear played a leading role in the construction of a new stage of capitalism but also marked the end of hospitality (Korstanje 2017). As a major risk which interrogates society terrorism appeals to a much deeper closure with the "Other" (Korstanje 2019a; 2019b). The decline of hospitality is characterized by the adoption of Artificial intelligence disposed to deal with guests (Korstanje 2019b). Of course, the success of artificial intelligence to be applied in tourism services depends on two main factors. On one hand, the systematization of robots resulted from the recent technological breakthrough which was accelerated by the digital world. On another, the increasing volume of tourists without mentioning mass tourism saturated the international destinations creating anti-tourist discourses, or phobias against foreigner tourists (Korstanje & George, 2020; Mantecon & Velazco, 2020). Tourist-phobia seems to be a term probably associated with problems of mass tourism. Doubtless, the adoption of robots saturated destinations may very well placate the discontent of hosts paving the pathways for the rise of smarter destinations (Karyotakis et al 2018). Nevertheless, some detractors have alerted on the ethical problems to adopt robots in the service and hospitality industries (Korstanje & Seraphin 2018). Tourist practices should not be divorced from ethics, no matter the consequences over the hosts. Proponents and exegetes of robot tourism argue erroneously that there are no moral quandaries in exploiting robots simply because they do not feel, they are no humans. This standpoint, which comes from philosophical pragmatism, overlooks the fact that moral issues are not judged by the real effects on the victim, but by the intentions. To set an example, well-illustrated by Harry Frankfurt, I can drive my car while stopping to drink some whiskies. I have no clear intention to crash or to harm a passerby. I get drank after drinking two-litre of finest whisky. By keeping on my trip I finally had a tragic accident where other driver lost his life. As Frankfurt observes, for pragmatism I had no guilty because I had not the intention to kill but as he notes, I am guilty because I imagined the consequences when opted to drink. The opposite is equally true I plan an assassination which is finally thwarted by the police. I failed to kill a person, though I am guilty to try to kill a person. Frankfurt starts from the premise that one of the philosophical limitations of pragmatism consists in believing ethics should be formed by the direct effects over the victim, or the type of victim (if the crime involves a person or an animal), instead of the intentions behind (Frankfurt 1982; 2002).

The present book paper is aimed at unpacking the ethical limitations revolving around the employment of robots in the tourism and hospitality industries, as well as presenting a critical film review of the HBO Saga, Westworld. In this dystopian world, humanoids are deposed to fill our guests´ -even the most sadist- desires. The first section of this film review brings reflection on the problems of the West to imagine and accept the "Non-Western Other". Robots tourism evinces a clear sign or tendency initiated after the attacks to WTC in 2001, which indicates the decline of Western hospitality. In a second section, we examine in-depth the plot of HBO Saga, Westworld. The chapter holds the thesis that terrorism inaugurated a new epochal period where the fear for the stranger occupied a primordial position. This tendency stimulated a culture of fear which was closed by the recent virus outbreaks known as Covid19. Both terrorism and viruses are invisible enemies to struggle, potential dangers, which living within, lurk the society. The war against Terror has set the pace to the war against a virus. This position evinces the end of hospitality which nourishes the urgency of adopting technology to create safer worlds. However, technology does not warrant an ethical solution to the problem of "alterity". What Westworld amply evinces, a much deeper process of depersonalization which invariably affected the hospitableness has been started after 9/11 and the resulted securitization process. The vaunted Wall in the US, Brexit or Windrush scandal, Bolsonaro or Trump´s discourses, Islamophobia, White supremacist riots, Touristphobia are clear signs of the end of hospitality.

THEORETICAL DEBATE: THE CULTURE OF FEAR AND TECHNOLOGY

One of the pioneering voices interested by the consequences of technology in society was Jacques Ellul. He centered on a Weberian model, which punctuated that technology, far from emancipating the lay citizen, oppresses the daily human life, commoditizing it in standardized processes. One of the success strategies of capitalism, as a global project, consisted of disorganizing the social ties while re-channeling the manpower to a depersonalized and individual atmosphere of extreme competition (Ellul 1964). For some reason, which is very hard to precise here, Ellul has never bided well in the American sociology, but no less true is that his legacy stood the test of time, even to date (McLuhan & Zingrone 1997; Mitchan & Mackey, 1971). Ellul´s works not only have shed light on the problem of modern technology and capitalism but has ignited interesting discussions in the fields of social sciences. In McLuhan´s legacy, technology is defined as an instrument geared to potentiate the five senses of the man (i.e. smell, vision, hearing, touch and taste). Technology not only makes things for human easier but accelerated a radical transformation in the economic cycles of production (McLuhan 1997). To some extent, as Baudrillard inferred, the current world, at the best as we know it, is far from being stable and fixed. It mutates constantly towards what he dubbed as "simulacra". The present acts are regulated from an emptied future which operates energetically through the precautionary logic. Technology plays a leading role in fictionalizing the real world, creating *pseudo-events* which mean to events that never take place in reality. Domination plays a leading role in Baudrillard (1994) studies. The old cause-consequence causality sets the pace to the hegemony of flat-screen where facts are fabricated, packaged and surely disseminated to be consumed by global spectatorship. The spectacle of terror marks the beginning of a new form of cultural entertainment intended to commoditize disasters, at the same time, a politics of risk-inflation that paralyzes and subverts human interactions (which doubtless means the real polity). What is the connection between the virtual world and terror?

Slavoj Zizek (2007) argues convincingly that technology irreparably ushers culture into a virtualized world where the pain is reduced. In this world, where humans are comfortably dumb, only the risk (of dying) wakes them from the slumber they are. One of the philosophical dilemmas of 9/11 and terrorism does not associate the instilled panic, but the sense of reality this event imposes. The US and West were certainly interrogated by terrorism to the extent the critical thinking proper of political sciences seems to be sedated. The so-called War on Terror became in buzzword and a panacea within the constellations of political studies. Complementarily, as Zygmunt Bauman eloquently observes, technology lays the foundations towards a much deeper process of *diaforization,* which means to the ethical dissociation between the goals and the collateral damages of the proper actions. The soldier from his desk controls a drone that kills hundreds of innocent victims after an attack is not legally responsible for his actions. Even he is an error and this tragic event is reported as *collateral damage.* As Bauman puts it, this is the best example to understand how diaforization works. The obsession for amassing profits at no cost, an ideal finely-inscribed in the capitalist culture, paves the ways for the rise of a manifest impossibility to understand the "Other" and his being in this world (Bauman 2011). In a nutshell, the agency only evolves when it is cannibalized by the capitalist system. The position of alterity is reduced, and limited through the articulation of surveillance technology.

In his recently-published book, Korstanje holds the thesis that technology -for good or bad- has placed mankind over the rest of the animal kingdom while empowered him to administrate rationally the world. The Western rationality, which characterizes modern capitalism, centers on the belief that the natural world can be intervened according to the laws of progress and economic prosperity. The liberal doctrine punctuates that the man not only administers this world but he can improve it through his labor. Progress, democracy and economic prosperity seem to be inextricably interlinked in the liberal discourse. When some event threatens mankind, the rational discipline easily locates and removes the risk. But this viewpoint, which is supported by technology, wakes up some fears and anxieties which are originated in the culprit sentiment. The fear of terrorism, the fear of strangers, or the fear of an invisible enemy like a virus means the same thing: the end of hospitality leading occident to an inevitable lockdown. West has closed itself because of the fear instilled by terrorism and in so doing, the *Non-Western Other,* who in other epochs was a subject of curiosity, sets the pace to new radicalized cosmology where its presence is neglected. The "Other" has been re-codified in an *undesired-guest* (Korstanje 2019a; 2019b). This point begs a more than an interesting question: how can terrorism change the cultural entertainment industry?

The answer was formulated by Korstanje & Olsen (2011), and Korstanje & Tarlow (2012), who have carefully scrutinized more than a dozen horror movies plots. These researchers come to conclude that the concept of evilness derives from the perverse core of those who give hospitality to cannibalize the guest. As they remark, hospitality can be offered or neglected, but there is a third liminal alternative when the villain –for example Dracula- hosts a guest to consume its vital energy. Narratives of horror movies are indeed inserted in a tradition where rogues torture, cannibalize and kill innocent tourists. A banquet, a good shelter, pretty women or simply a drink are signs of this perverse hospitality.

Over recent years, some critical scholars as George Ritzer (2019) and Tom Selwyn (2019) acknowledge that hospitality is in a complete decline. While the world has been flattened leading the national borders to be blurred in a global ethos an emerging sentiment of hostility against the foreigner surfaces. This very well applies to white supremacist discourses, to Brexit, Windrush scandal and the anti-migration policies adopted by main important economies. In this new epoch, the alterity is seen as an object of suspicion simply because the world should be ordered and organized according to the matrix of Western (capitalist) rationality. Given the problem in other terms, capitalism moved to a new stage where efficiency and the standardization make from humans real machines. Above all, capital owners applaud not only the introduction of robots in the productive sector while sending workers to home with a check. The relegation and exploitation of the workforce seem to be nothing news in the capitalist system, but what remains important is the obsession of prediction to avoid economic losses. This logic of rationality and prediction, as these authors agree, is unconditionally contrary to the essence of hospitality. While hospitality was finely-encrypted as a foundational value for West, nowadays the *Non-Western Other* was decoded as an *undesired-guest.* This point coincides with my concerns remarked in *Terrorism, Tourism and the end of hospitality in the West.* As a foundational event, 9/11 not only shocked the world setting a new neoliberal agenda in the fields of economics but ignited a new culture of fear where the enemy does not loom from the outside, now he lives with us, looks like us and probably waiting for the moment to attack. This discourse, which culturally aligned with a theory of living with the enemy within, ushers society in a sentiment of mistrust respecting the alterity. To some extent, terrorism erodes one of the mainstream cultural values of Western civilization: *the sacred laws of hospitality* (Korstanje 2017).

Technology and the Otherness

As the previous backdrop described in the introductory section, it is important to mention that some studies have emphasized the urgency to place the idea of robots tourism under the critical lens of scrutiny. In fact, the use of digital technology, which includes artificial intelligence and robots, leads invariably to unethical practices because the local "Other" is negated. As Derrida eloquently observes, hospitality starts with two radical questions where the "Other" is interrogated: who are you and what do you want? (Derrida, 2000). Hospitality fulfils a double function. Originally it is designed to mitigate the fear of hosts and guests because the intentions of the "Other" remain covert, but secondly, it places both in egalitarian conditions –starting a much deeper process of gift-exchange (O´ Gorman, 2007; Ritzer, 2019; Selwyn, 2019. In a seminal book entitled, Lord of All The World, Anthony Pagden reminds the dark side of hospitality, or the risks not to accept the universal rights of hominem viatores, at least as it was forged in the European ethnocentrism. As Pagden explains, far from being a universal phenomenon, hospitality was not recognized nor practices by some aborigines tribes in the Americas. The legitimacy of Spanish King was under suspicion and review by some French and British philosophical circles. These philosophers questioned to what extent the Pope who issued the bulls (known as Alexander´s bull) in favor of the King, had real authority over people who have not shared the Catholic faith. Even within the Spanish circles, some discrepancies revolving around the authority of the King in the Americas were common-placed. Finally, the dispute was solved when some rumors came from the new World. These stories told that some aboriginal cultures did not recognize the right of free transit and the right of hospitality. Spanish travelers (hominem viatores) who needed to trespass a territory to reach other destination were attacked or locked down by some tribes. This news not only shocked Spanish philosophers but gave the excuse to legitimate the authority of the King and the subsequent dispossession of their lands. The Salamanca School enthusiastically claimed that Indians were sub-humans because they ignored the *sacred law of hospitality* (Pagden 1995). What Pagden suggests is that the ideals of western hospitality legitimated the conquest of the Americas.

In the recent decades, to be more exact after 9/11 and the so-called "War On Terror", West seems to close its borders to the "Non-Western Other" creating a crisis which erodes the system from within (Korstanje 2018). No matter than its nature, the host is radically commoditized, exploited and cannibalized so the guest to expand its ego.

The problem of sustainability is proportional direct to de-growth tourism (Canavan 2014). This means that the obsession for achieving standardized destinations, accompanied by the ends of creating more sustainable destinations without losing profits, led scholars to propose robot tourism as a valid and fresh alternative. However, far from developing more sustainable destinations, this position negates the position of the "Other" affecting seriously the host guests exchanges. What is more important, robot tourism undermines the essence of hospitality as the genuine human encounter subject to "the contingency" (Derrida, 2000; Korstanje 2019; Korstanje & Seraphin, 2018). This controversy, far from being resolved, aligns with the main goal of the present film review, which centers on Westworld, the recent HBO Saga. From the outset, tourism and technology were inextricably intertwined. Technically, the industry was successfully expanded through the articulation of novel technological inventions which revolutionized classical transport means (Likorish & Jenkins, 2007). These radical changes –technology buttressed efficiently - accelerated some legal reforms oriented to obtain further free time, and better wages without mentioning the right to strike and paid-holidays. Today, digital technology and artificial intelligence open the doors to a new 4.0 society where cultures, customs, and people are commoditized to be gazed by international tourism (Lash & Urry 1994). Mass-production, which characterized the industrial world, sets the pace to new decentralized means of production associated with an economy of signs (Lash & Urry, 1994). The arrival of robots to the industry revolves around a long-dormant discussion where locals, more of them geographically located in underdeveloped nations, are subordinated to the pleasure of travelers who come from developed ones. The old colonial center-periphery dependency is now re-affirmed through the material asymmetries generated by global capital and technology.

METHODOLOGICAL DISCUSSION

The present film review continues the ethical dilemma about the use of robots at luxury complexes and hotels. As a relational process that places host and guest in equal conditions, hospitality accepts the presence of the "alterity" even he interrogates furtherly on the own cultural values. The introduction of robots not only affects the egalitarian essence of hospitality but endorses guests with the capacity to violate the law to maximize their pleasure. In Westworld, there is no ethical border to transgress, because hosts lack fundamental rights. They are often subject to sadist experiences commanded by the rich guests. Hosts not only are androids –designed by a commercial corporation- to meet guests´ desires but though they feel, they are considered "sub-humans", machines dispossessed from the sense of freedom. We use visual (cinema) ethnography as a valid method which helps to provoke a critical engagement in the quest for meaning and further understanding of complex matters originally enrooted in the profundity of the cultural ethos. To put things simply, visual ethnography –as a qualitative instrument- facilitates the articulation of ideals types to infer hypotheses that can be validated empirically in a later stage. Visual or Cinema ethnography places practices and theory at the same level. Cinema-ethnography can be considered a sub-discipline of ethnography, mainly originated to understand cosmologies or sophisticated arguments that are repressed in the culture (Oksiloff, 2016). As Rodanthi Tzanelli put it, the fabricated cinematic representations are often externally drawn and imposed or negotiated internally by actors. The access to these narratives should be successfully achieved thanks to cinematic ethnography (Tzanelli, 2007; 2013; 2016). This reminds that ethnography should be understood as a qualitative methodological alternative that transcends what tourists overtly say. Needless to say, the established quantitative methods, which are enthralled in the fields of tourism, often have some evident limitations to grasp complex social topics. Sometimes interviewed tourists are unfamiliar with the inner-world or what is worse, they lie to protect their interests. In sharp contrast to interviewees or close-ended questionnaires that focused on what tourists feel, (cinema) ethnography is based on hearing, watching and writing.

The analysis centers on two important questions: is the adoption of robots in tourism a clear sign that marks the end of hospitality?, is hospitality possible with a *non-human "Other",* and to what extent, the exploitation of Non-human hosts escape to the ethical mandate?

The present film review intends to decipher the main ideal types encrypted in the argument and plot of HBO Saga, Westworld, a TV series created by Jonathan Nolan & Lisa Joy. The Saga can be very well divided into three seasons: *The Maze (2016), The Door (2018), The New World (2020).* The Maze focuses primarily on the nature of enslavement and its direct effects on the ethics of tourism consumption, in a world where tourists and vagabonds –citing Bauman (2017)- offer two contrasting cultural landscapes. Rich tourists, who are legally encouraged to cross the national borders, travel worldwide enjoying the multicultural products everywhere while lodging inexpensive hotels. Rather, migrants are forced to remain immobile probably living with nothing. Not only nation-state deploys surveillance technology to locate and deport migrants, but the rights of hospitality are negated for them (Bauman, 2017). The enslavement of hosts, returning to Westworld, effaces the principle of hospitality because the "Other" is limited to satisfy all the guest´s desires. Contrariwise, the second season, the Door shows the urgency to be "free" questioning essentially the nature of mankind. Artificial intelligence alludes to the intersection between freedom and consciousness. The world that humans created is finally and inevitably inherited by the enslaved androids. This moot point is treated in the third episode, the New World, where hosts not only struggle for their freedom but shakes the dogmatism of Westworld prompting a terminal crisis.

Last but not least, Westworld exhibits a futurist scenario amounted to fictionalize the daily life in the far West. Humanoids are disposed to serve all guests´ needs, even the most sadist ones. This highly-demanded tourist place receives rich tourists who not only are in quest of unique but extreme experiences. Some of them satisfy their darkest drives killing, torturing or even rapping humanoids. Artificially created to fulfil all the tourists (guests) need, these humanoids are named as hosts. Naturally programmed not to attack tourists, hosts are often subjected to sadist practices or harmed once and once again only for entertainment purposes. The entertainment parks invite rich guests who probably are motivated by different reasons but all they look to have a unique and outstanding experience.

Westworld, which locates in the 2058 B.C, is controlled by a private corporation Delos Inc. Four themed-parks are orchestrated to emulate life in the Far-West. Almost impossible from being distinguished from humans hosts are unable to hurt their clients. What is more important, all host-guest interactions are subject to a matrix which repeats cyclical forms of relationships in the day. Some operators occupy the stage in an operational hub known as Central Mesa.

Westworld

Westworld is an HBO saga, recently starred and directed by Michael Chrichton. The plot eloquently describes in a dystopian world which is technologically built to emulate the daily life in the Far West. For the social imaginary, a stereotype fed back by historical novels, the far-west is seen as a dangerous place where violence and murdering daily coexist. In consonance with this archetype, Westworld is a recreational park that often receives thousands of tourists (known as a guest) who are high purchasing power. These high-paying guests not only move freely within the park but also can kill, torture and kidnap –among other crimes- hosts who are humanoids systematically fabricated to meet all guest´s desires, including the darkest ones. In Westworld, anything goes while hosts are programmed not to retaliate or attack tourists. The saga has a great cast of the caliber of Anthony Hopkins, Ed Harris, James Marsden, and Ben Barnes only to name a few. As a recreational park which is part of a system –formed by other five parks- Westworld is carefully designed to protect the integral security of guests. Regardless of what they do, guests cannot be judged nor killed by hosts. When something goes wrong, which means the host puts a guest in a dangerous situation, the host is reprogrammed and his memory erased. This creates a primordial rule that reminds guests are legally legitimated to dispose of, consume and even kill hosts, but hosts cannot attack their visitors. Although some are cruel and ruthless, other guests are altruistic, sympathetic and open to hosts. Each one, in this futurist world, is what he or she wants to be. Though there are women, males are predominantly the segment of guests, this dangerous place targets. The sense masculinity, which centralizes the capacity to kill others, predominates in Westland as a dominant discourse. In this dystopian futurist park, any type of ethical rule can be suspended, breached or negotiated according to the logic of the guest (the master). Needless to say, hosts (who are androids) look like humans, but they are not legally considered humans. For this reason, the crimes against them are never punishable. Once assassinated, their memories are wiped and recycled, but in some point, a particular glitch led Dolores to rememorize part of the traumatic experiences she lived. Past traumatic events are somehow replicated even in fragments which are recurrent in the Saga. The host-guest dependency speaks to us of the asymmetries in the current tourism industry, as well as the risks of adopting robots as slaves of humans. Many Science fiction plots such as Battlestar Galactica, Matrix or Terminator warn on the problems of dealing with Artificial intelligence, in fact, sooner or later, robots struggle for their autonomy throwing down humans, but in Westland, the figure of what we dubbed as neglected hospitality plays a crucial role. The "Other" not only is subordinated but disposed of any right. What is more important, when *masters* cannot be regulated nor controlled, sadism is the only rule. This does not impede that Williams, for example, falls in love of Dolores but these relations center on a subordinated position which can be unilaterally cancelled at the discretion of the guest.

Furthermore, Westworld reminds not only the risk of exploitation –fomented by technology- but the end of hospitality as an ethical law without mentioning the emergence of a new sadist sentiment of pleasure when the "Other" suffers. In earlier approaches, we used the term *Thana-capitalism* to frame a new stage of capitalism where the Other´s pain is the main commodity to exchange. The morbid spectacle of death is not present only in dark tourism but in many other cultural entertainment industries as literature, movies and even video-games. The modern citizen sees the world in a Darwinist narrative where only the strongest man survives. The winner wins and takes all! By consuming the Other´s death gives pleasure and uniqueness because after all, the gazer is still live in the trace. This cosmology, which was imposed after 9/11 and the so-called culture of fear, not only replaced the risk society imagined by classic sociologists but is possible because of the resistance of modern man to die. The survivor feels special when he or she escapes from death her or his fate confers a mission in this world. The survivor is saved by destiny because of a so-called superiority, less regulated may ushers society to ethnocentrism. The best ways of feeling as a super-man coincide with the urgency of gazing Other´s death or torturing hosts (Westworld or Hostel are a clear example of the trend); in such a cosmology the hospitality dies. In these landscapes, killing "Other" is the best ways to avoid being killed (Korstanje 2016). Is Westworld replicating the cultural background of Thana-Capitalism?

Having said this, hosts are desired only to be consumed and exploited as wasting pieces of a more global machine. Sooner these androids show certain sign of consciousness mainly associated with their free choice but also to their memories. This particularly concerns Dr Ford who is the director of the recreational site. Repression and sadism as values fitted against altruism occupy a central position in this plot has been repeated in a second episode when two friends appear in scene Logan, a sadist killer who spend their time drinking and killing people and William, a young altruist visitor. William sooner disobeys Logan´s orders while develops an empathy for Dolores. Here the idea of consciousness seems vital to understand part of the Saga. In the first episode (The Original, season 1), the Marshall experiences some technical problems and suddenly it is reviewed by the staff. He is fallen apart from Westland to revise the origin of the glitch. Specialists discover interesting outcome androids are dreaming of creating an incipient anomaly in their programming. These dreams, in some way experts cannot precise, conserves a partial memory of past traumas. Dolores´ father, at the next day, gathers a picture a traveler involuntarily drops. At the time he watches the picture, some repressed feelings perturb him. A similar event repeats in the second episode (Chestnut, season 1) when Maeve, one of the prostitutes of the tavern, talks with Dolores. In this conversation, Dolores says Maeve she has premonitory visions. Automatically once it is heart, Maeve experiences through a situation similar to the Marshall. As the protocols mark, Maeve is retired from the circulation of Westworld to determine the reasons behind her malfunctioning. Dr Stone acknowledges that androids are experiencing a type of rememorations which allow accessing to their past. At the time she is being revised, Maeve wakes up and tries to escape from the complex. She is horrified to witness how doctors experiment with some of her partners. She realizes how the deceased hosts are repaired, tested and returned to Westland. This is the foundational event that led Maeve to see how she is a prisoner of her consciousness. She feels the needs to escape from the park where she is a slave. In this respect, Maeve told Felix and Sylvester about an occult algorithmic program inside each host which can be activated. Meanwhile, William takes Dolores to escape from the park. Chestnut evinces the conflict between hosts (androids), who gradually acquire a consciousness waking them from slumber and guests (humans narcoticized by their sadism).

The successive chapters in the first season show the interests of hosts to take control of Delos and humans who monopolizes the surveillance technology. The first season, *the Maze,* is characterized by a much deeper tension between subordination and pleasure-maximization, a philosophical debate inserted in the Western rationality. Rather, the second season (The Door) explores Dolores´ motivations to recruit other hosts to confront directly Dr Ford and Delos. She suspects that beyond the borders of the park there is a phantom nation which is the key to reach the outside world. This goal will be successfully met by Dolores and her partners. The question of whether the Maze reflects the old philosophical dilemma of the existence where the self-here is juxtaposed to "the Other-there, no less true is that in the Door hosts take a proactive position. To put the same in bluntly, the slave has been liberated putting all the system in risk. The Maze is performed in a Hobbesian ethos where the human orders dispose of humanoids to fill all human desires regardless of their ethical connotations. But once Dolores empowers herself, she heads a revolution in quest of a new place to dwell. She moves through the desert to locate the phantom nation where she hopes to be well-received. This imagined hospitality, at least in Dolores´ mind, equates to the archetype of lost-Eden. Westworld proffers a more than interesting dialogue with the limitations and controversies the adoption of robots in tourism industry pose.

CONCLUSION

Terrorism has, doubtless, generated direct and indirect consequences on the social imaginary of western societies. To the economic shutdown, just after 2001, other durable effects associated to paranoia, the culture of fear and the hostility for the "Non-Western Other" are only examples of what accompanied the daily life in Occident. Terrorism not only eroded the right of hospitality from within but the trust in the neighbor. The present chapter deals with the dilemma of introducing robots in the industry of tourism and service sectors.

It is important to mention that digital technologies are changing the means of production as well as the nature of tourism, at the best as we know it (Gale 2009). Doubtless, the economy, as well as tourism, seems to be changing given the introduction of new technologies. In an early publication, Korstanje & Seraphin (2018) exerted a radical criticism to the fields of robots tourism because of two main reasons. On one hand, robots are exploited, submitted and subjugated to satisfy their masters. In Hegelian terms, there is a slave-master dependency which is almost impossible to break. This position, which is far from ethics, emulates the old relations between white masters and aborigines which were proper of colonialism. On another, robots unequivocally exhibit the tendency initiated after 9/11 we have examined in previous works: *the end of hospitality*. In a culture of fear, 9/11 instilled an unspeakable panic which gradually closed the Western civilization to the uncertainness, to the *Non-Western Other.* As a result of this, terrorism started a tendency to mine one of the symbolic touchstones of West: hospitality.

It is important not to lose the sight of the fact, not only the tourism industry but society faced major threats after the turn of the century, risks which oscillate from terrorism to climate change, obviously without mentioning the recent virus outbreak COVID-19, that recently shocked the world. All these events re-founded internally the social ties of Western citizens closing themselves to the *non-Western Otherness.* In this respect, the turn of the century witnessed the rise of a radicalized discourse orchestrated to hate the foreigner. Islamophobia, tourist-phobia and the anti-migration-led discourses were only part of the tendency. Those political speeches oriented to demonize migrants, including the accessibility of Donald Trump to the US presidency firmly associate to an emerging sentiment of fear to strangers which closed the borders. The digital technology disposed to surveillance this type of *undesired guest* erodes gradually and from inside the *sacred laws of hospitality.* Digital surveillance, adjoined to robots and drones serve the government to control strangers who are seen as potential enemies living within.

REFERENCES

Baudrillard, J. (1994). *Simulacra and simulation*. University of Michigan Press.

Bauman, Z. (2011). *Collateral damage: Social inequalities in a global age*. Polity Press.

Bauman, Z. (2017). Tourists and vagabonds: Or, living in postmodern times. In *Identity and social change* (pp. 19–32). Routledge. doi:10.4324/9780203789339-3

Buckley, R., Gretzel, U., Scott, D., Weaver, D., & Becken, S. (2015). Tourism megatrends. *Tourism Recreation Research, 40*(1), 59–70. doi:10.1080/02508281.2015.1005942

Canavan, B. (2014). Sustainable tourism: Development, decline and de-growth. Management issues from the Isle of Man. *Journal of Sustainable Tourism, 22*(1), 127–147. doi:10.1080/09669582.2013.819876

Dalgic, A., & Birdir, K. (2020). Smart Hotels and Technological Applications. In *Handbook of Research on Smart Technology Applications in the Tourism Industry* (pp. 323–343). IGI Global. doi:10.4018/978-1-7998-1989-9.ch015 de Kervenoael, R., Hasan, R., Schwob, A., & Goh, E. (2020). Leveraging human-robot interaction in hospitality services: Incorporating the role of perceived value, empathy, and information sharing into visitors' intentions to use social robots. *Tourism Management*, *78*, 104042. doi:10.1016/j.tourman.2019.104042

Derrida, J., & Dufourmantelle, A. (2000). *Of hospitality*. Stanford University Press.

Ellul, J. (1964). *The technological society* (Vol. 303). Vintage Books.

Frankfurt, H. (1982). The importance of what we care about. *Synthese*, *53*(2), 257–272. doi:10.1007/BF00484902

Frankfurt, H. G. (2002). *Contours of agency: Essays on themes from Harry Frankfurt*. MIT Press.

Gale, T. (2009). Urban beaches, virtual worlds and 'the end of tourism'. *Mobilities*, *4*(1), 119–138. doi:10.1080/17450100802657996

Ivanov, S., & Webster, C. (2019). Perceived appropriateness and intention to use service robots in tourism. In *Information and communication technologies in tourism 2019* (pp. 237–248). Springer. doi:10.1007/978-3-030-05940-8_19

Ivanov, S., & Webster, C. (2019). Economic Fundamentals of the Use of robots, artificial intelligence, and service Automation in travel, tourism, and hospitality. In *Robots, artificial intelligence, and service Automation in travel, tourism and hospitality*. Emerald Publishing Limited.

Ivanov, S. H., Webster, C., & Berezina, K. (2017). Adoption of robots and service automation by tourism and hospitality companies. *Revista Turismo & Desenvolvimento*, *27*(28), 1501–1517.

Jiang, Y., & Wen, J. (2020). Effects of COVID-19 on hotel marketing and management: A perspective article. *International Journal of Contemporary Hospitality Management*, *32*(8), 2563–2573. doi:10.1108/IJCHM-03-2020-0237

Karyotakis, M. A., Antonopoulos, N., Veglis, A., & Kiourexidou, M. (2018). Tourist go home: Communication and Propaganda on YouTube. *Journal of Media Critiques*, *4*(14), 323–337.

Korstanje, M. E. (2016). *The Rise of Thana Capitalism and Tourism*. Routledge. doi:10.4324/9781315457482

Korstanje, M. E. (2017). *Terrrorism, Tourism and the end of hospitality in the West*. Palgrave-Macmillan.

Korstanje, M. E. (2019a). *Terrorism, Technology and Apocalyptic Futures*. Springer. doi:10.1007/978-3-030-13385-6

Korstanje, M. E. (2019b). The Society 4.0, Internet, Tourism and the War on Terror. In Digital Labour, Society and the Politics of Sensibilities. Palgrave Macmillan.

Korstanje, M. E., & George, B. P. (2020). Education as a Strategy to Tackle Over Tourism for Overtourism and Inclusive Sustainability in the Twenty-First Century. In *Overtourism* (pp. 341–359). Palgrave Macmillan. doi:10.1007/978-3-030-42458-9_18

Korstanje, M. E., & Olsen, D. H. (2011). The discourse of risk in horror movies post 9/11: Hospitality and hostility in perspective. *International Journal of Tourism Anthropology*, *1*(3), 304–317. doi:10.1504/IJTA.2011.043712

Korstanje, M. E., & Seraphin, H. (2018). Awakening: A critical discussion of the role of robots in the rite of hospitality. In M. Korstanje (Ed.), *Tourism and Hospitality: Perspectives, Opportunities and Challenges* (pp. 59–77). Nova Science Publishers.

Korstanje, M. E., & Tarlow, P. (2012). Being lost: Tourism, risk and vulnerability in the post-'9/11'entertainment industry. *Journal of Tourism and Cultural Change*, *10*(1), 22–33. doi:10.1080/14766825.2011.639455

Lash, S., & Urry, J. (1994). *Economies of signs and space*. SAGE.

Lickorish, L. J., & Jenkins, C. L. (2007). *Introduction to tourism*. Routledge.

Mantecón, A., & Velasco, M. (2020). Beyond Tourismphobia: Conceptualizing a New Framework to Analyze Attitudes Towards Tourism. In *Handbook of Research on the Impacts, Challenges, and Policy Responses to Overtourism* (pp. 60–74). IGI Global. doi:10.4018/978-1-7998-2224-0.ch004

McLuhan, E., & Zingrone, F. (1997). *Essential McLuhan*. Routledge. doi:10.4324/9780203992968

Mitcham, C., & Mackey, R. (1971). Jacques Ellul and the technological society. *Philosophy Today*, *15*(2), 102–121. doi:10.5840/philtoday197115218

Murphy, J., Gretzel, U., & Hofacker, C. (2017, May). Service robots in hospitality and tourism: investigating anthropomorphism. In *15th APacCHRIE conference* (Vol. 31). Academic Press.

Murphy, J., Hofacker, C., & Gretzel, U. (2017). Dawning of the age of robots in hospitality and tourism: Challenges for teaching and research. *European Journal of Tourism Research*, *15*, 104–111. doi:10.54055/ejtr.v15i.265

O'Gorman, K. D. (2007). The hospitality phenomenon: Philosophical enlightenment? *International Journal of Culture, Tourism and Hospitality Research*, *1*(3), 189–202.

Oksiloff, A. (2016). *Picturing the primitive: Visual culture, ethnography, and early German cinema*. Springer.

Pagden, A. (1995). *Lords of all the World: Ideologies of Empire in Spain, Britain and France c. 1500-c. 1800*. Yale University Press.

Park, S. (2020). Multifaceted trust in tourism service robots. *Annals of Tourism Research*, *81*, 102888.

Ritzer, G. (2019). Inhospitable hospitality. In Experiencing hospitality. Nova Science.

Selwyn, T. (2019). Hostility and Hospitality: connecting Brexit, Grenfell and Windrush. In Experiencing hospitality. Nova Science.

Sigala, M. (2020). Tourism and COVID-19: impacts and implications for advancing and resetting industry and research. *Journal of Business Research*.

Tung, V. W. S., & Law, R. (2017). The potential for tourism and hospitality experience research in human-robot interactions. *International Journal of Contemporary Hospitality Management*.

Tzanelli, R. (2007). *The cinematic tourist: Explorations in globalization, culture and resistance*. Routledge.

Tzanelli, R. (2013). *Heritage in the digital era: Cinematic tourism and the activist cause*. Routledge.

Tzanelli, R. (2016). *Thanatourism and Cinematic Representations of Risk: Screening the End of Tourism*. Routledge.

Yeoman, I. (2012). *2050-tomorrow's tourism* (Vol. 55). Channel View Publications.

Yeoman, I., & Mars, M. (2012). Robots, men and sex tourism. *Futures*, *44*(4), 365–371.

Zizek, S. (2007). *The universal exception* (Vol. 2). A&C Black.

ADDITIONAL READING

Atkins, B., Chew, J. K., Gschwlnd, D., & Parker, A. (2003). The impact of terrorism on tourism and hospitality business: An online debate by experts in the field. *Tourism and Hospitality Research*, *4*(3), 262–267. doi:10.1177/146735840300400306

Garg, A., Block, C., Jalan, P. J. S., & Jaya, P. (2009). Crisis in Hospitality and Tourism: A study on the impacts of terrorism on Indian Hospitality and Tourism Industry. *MM University Journal of Management Practices, 3*(1).

Harb, A. (2016). Impact of War And Terrorism on Tourism and Hospitality Sector in Lebanon. *Annual of Sofia University St. Kliment Ohridski, 109*(2).

Korstanje, M. E. (2011). The fear of traveling: A new perspective for tourism and hospitality. *Anatolia*, *22*(2), 222–233. doi:10.1080/13032917.2011.597935

Korstanje, M. E. (2016). The spirit of terrorism: Tourism, unionization and terrorism. *Pasos Revista de Turismo y Patrimonio Cultural*, *14*(3), 239–250.

Korstanje, M. E. (2020). Passage from the tourist gaze to the wicked gaze: a case study on Covid-19 with special reference to Argentina. In *International case studies in the management of disasters*. Emerald Publishing Limited. doi:10.1108/978-1-83982-186-820201012

Korstanje, M. E., Raj, R., & Griffin, K. (Eds.). (2018). *Risk and safety challenges for religious tourism and events*. CABI. doi:10.1079/9781786392282.0000

Peter, C., Poulston, J., & Losekoot, E. (2014). Terrorism, rugby, and hospitality: She′ ll be right. *Journal of Destination Marketing & Management*, *3*(4), 253–261. doi:10.1016/j.jdmm.2014.03.001

Skoll, G. R., & Korstanje, M. E. (2014). Terrorism, homeland safety and event management. *International Journal of Hospitality and Event Management*, *1*(1), 95–110. doi:10.1504/IJHEM.2014.062869

KEY TERMS AND DEFINITIONS

Artificial Intelligence: The term signals to the signs of intelligence showed by robots and machines.
Hospitality: It is defined as the relation between hosts and guests.

Robots: It is a machine capable of achieving complex designed tasks.

Terrorism: It is a type of political (illegal) violence against innocent targets to extortionate governments.

Tourism: It is a service industry that often stimulates the pleasure for traveling.

Compilation of References

Abate, S. M., Ahmed Ali, S., Mantfardo, B., & Basu, B. (2020). Rate of intensive care unit admission and outcomes among patients with coronavirus: A systematic review and meta-analysis. *PLoS One*, *15*(7), e0235653. Advance online publication. doi:10.1371/journal.pone.0235653 PMID:32649661

Adams, L. M., & Berry, D. (2012). Who Will Show Up? Estimating Ability and Willingness of Essential Hospital Personnel to Report to Work in Response to a Disaster. *Online Journal of Issues in Nursing*, *17*(2), J1. doi:10.3912/OJIN.Vol17No02PPT02 PMID:22686116

Adelekan, I. O. (2005). Gender, economic policy, and domestic energy use in Nigeria. *Ibaden Journal of the Social Sciences*, *3*(1), 1–16.

Adirondack. (2016). *Discover the Adirondack Park*. Adirondack Council. Retrieved December 30, 2016, from the World Wide Web: https://www.adirondackcouncil.org/

Afum, E., Agyabeng-Mensah, Y., Acquah, I. S. K., Baah, C., Dacosta, E., Owusu, C. S., & Amponsah Owusu, J. (2021). Examining the links between logistics outsourcing, company competitiveness and selected performances: The evidence from an emerging country. *International Journal of Logistics Management*, *32*(3), 1068–1090. doi:10.1108/IJLM-05-2020-0205

Afza, S. R., & Newaz, M. K. (2008). Factors determining the presence of glass ceiling and influencing women career advancement in Bangladesh. *BRAC University Journal*, *5*(1), 85–92.

Ahmadian, R., & Falconer, R. A. (2012). Assessment of array shape of tidal stream turbines on hydro-environmental impacts and power output. *Renewable Energy*, *44*(1), 318–327. doi:10.1016/j.renene.2012.01.106

Ahmadian, R., Falconer, R. A., & Bockelmann-Evans, B. (2014). Comparison of hydro-environmental impacts for ebb-only and two-way generation for a Severn Barrage. *Computers & Geosciences*, *71*(C), 11–19. doi:10.1016/j.cageo.2014.05.006

Ahmadian, R., Falconer, R., & Bockelmann-Evans, B. (2012). Far-field modelling of the hydro-environmental impact of tidal stream turbines. *Renewable Energy*, *38*(1), 107–116. doi:10.1016/j.renene.2011.07.005

Akinwale, A. A. (2010). The menace of inadequate infrastructure in Nigeria. *African Journal of Science, Technology, Innovation and Development*, *2*(3), 207–228.

Aksu, M. U., Dilek, M. H., Tatli, E. I., Bicakci, K., Dirik, H. I., Demirezen, M. U., & Aykir, T. (2017). A quantitative CVSS-based cyber security risk assessment methodology for IT systems. In *Proceedings - International Carnahan Conference on Security Technology* (pp. 1–8). 10.1109/CCST.2017.8167819

Alahmari, A., & Duncan, B. (2020). Cybersecurity Risk Management in Small and Medium-Sized Enterprises: A Systematic Review of Recent Evidence. *2020 International Conference on Cyber Situational Awareness, Data Analytics and Assessment*. 10.1109/CyberSA49311.2020.9139638

Alberts, C., & Dorofee, A. (2002). Introducing OCTAVE Allegro: Improving the Information Security Risk Assessment Process. In *Managing Information Security Risks: The OCTAVESM Approach*. Addison Wesley. http://citeseerx.ist.psu.edu/viewdoc/download?doi=10.1.1.461.7807&rep=rep1&type=pdf

Albrecht, J., Björklund, A., & Vroman, S. (2003). Is there a glass ceiling in Sweden? *Journal of Labor Economics*, *21*(1), 145–177. doi:10.1086/344126

Aldawood, H., & Skinner, G. (2019a). Educating and Raising Awareness on Cyber Security Social Engineering: A Literature Review. In *Proceedings of 2018 IEEE International Conference on Teaching, Assessment, and Learning for Engineering, TALE 2018* (pp. 62–68). IEEE. 10.1109/TALE.2018.8615162

Aldawood, H., & Skinner, G. (2019b). Reviewing cyber security social engineering training and awareness programs-pitfalls and ongoing issues. *Future Internet*, *11*(3), 73. Advance online publication. doi:10.3390/fi11030073

Algarni, A. M., Thayananthan, V., & Malaiya, Y. K. (2021). Quantitative assessment of cybersecurity risks for mitigating data breaches in business systems. *Applied Sciences (Switzerland)*, *11*(8), 3678. Advance online publication. doi:10.3390/app11083678

Alhakami, A. S., & Slovic, P. (1994). A psychological study of the inverse relationship between perceived risk and perceived benefit. *Risk Analysis*, *14*(6), 1085–1096. doi:10.1111/j.1539-6924.1994.tb00080.x PMID:7846317

Alibeli, M. A. (2015). Gender and attitudes toward women in the United Arab Emirates. *Perspectives on Global Development and Technology*, *14*(1-2), 109–125. doi:10.1163/15691497-12341335

Al-Lamki, S. (1999). *Paradigm shift: A perspective on Mani women in management in the Sultanate of Oman, advancing women in leadership*. Available at www.advancingwomen .com/awl/spring99/Al-Lamki/allamk.html

Allodi, L., & Massacci, F. (2017). Security Events and Vulnerability Data for Cybersecurity Risk Estimation. *Risk Analysis*, *37*(8), 1606–1627. doi:10.1111/risa.12864 PMID:28800378

Al-Manasra, E. A. (2013). What are the 'glass ceiling' barriers effects on women's career progress in Jordan? *International Journal of Business and Management*, *8*(6), 40–46. doi:10.5539/ijbm.v8n6p40

Al-Marzouqi, A. H., & Foster, N. (2011). An exploratory study of the under-representation of Emirate women in the United Arab Emirates information technology sector. *Equality, Diversity and Inclusion*, *30*(7), 544–562. doi:10.1108/02610151111167016

Aloini, D., Dulmin, R., & Mininno, V. (2012). Risk assessment in ERP projects. *Information Systems*, *37*(3), 183–199. doi:10.1016/j.is.2011.10.001

Alora, A., & Barua, M. K. (2021). The effect of supply chain disruptions on shareholder wealth in small and mid-cap companies. *Supply Chain Management*, *26*(2), 212–223. doi:10.1108/SCM-05-2020-0200

Alsaqqa, S., & Almajali, S. (2020). Blockchain Technology Consensus Algorithms and Applications: A Survey. *International Journal of Interactive Mobile Technologies*, *14*(15), 142. Advance online publication. doi:10.3991/ijim.v14i15.15893

Altheide, D. (2017). *Terrorism and the Politics of Fear*. Rowman & Littlefield.

Altheide, D. L. (2020). Pandemic in the time of Trump: Digital Media Logic and Deadly Politics. *Symbolic Interaction*, *43*(3), 514–540. doi:10.1002ymb.501

Andrews, D. W. K. (1993). Tests for parameter instability and structural change with unknown change point. *Econometrica*, *61*(4), 821–856. doi:10.2307/2951764

Angurala, M., Bala, M., Bamber, S. S., Kaur, R., & Singh, P. (2020). An internet of things assisted drone-based approach to reduce the rapid spread of COVID-19. *Journal of Safety Science and Resilience*, *1*(1), 31–35. doi:10.1016/j.jnlssr.2020.06.011

Anthias, F. (2012). Intersectional what? Social divisions, intersectionality and levels of analysis. *Ethnicities*, *13*(1), 3–19. doi:10.1177/1468796812463547

Anthony, B. Jnr. (2020). Implications of telehealth and digital care solutions during COVID-19 pandemic: A qualitative literature review. *Informatics for Health & Social Care*, *46*(1), 68–83. doi:10.1080/17538157.2020.1839467 PMID:33251894

Antonioni, G., Spadoni, G., & Cozzani, V. (2009). Application of domino effect quantitative risk assessment to an extended industrial area. *Journal of Loss Prevention in the Process Industries*, *22*(5), 614–624. doi:10.1016/j.jlp.2009.02.012

Appelbaum, S. H., Asham, N., & Argheyd, K. (2011a). Is the glass ceiling cracked in information technology? A qualitative analysis: Part 1. *Industrial and Commercial Training*, *43*(6), 354–361. doi:10.1108/00197851111160487

Appelbaum, S. H., Asham, N., & Argheyd, K. (2011b). Is the glass ceiling cracked in information technology? A qualitative analysis: Part 2. *Industrial and Commercial Training*, *43*(7), 451–459. doi:10.1108/00197851111171881

Arab Human Development Report (AHDR). (2006). *Towards the Rise of Women in the Arab World.* United National Development Program, Regional Bureau for the Arab States, National Press.

Arias, J. C., & Stern, R. (2011). Review of risk management methods. *Business Intelligence Journal*, *4*(1), 51–78.

Armstrong, A., & Bulkeley, H. (2014). Micro-hydro politics: Producing and contesting community energy in the North of England. *Geoforum*, *56*(1), 66–76. doi:10.1016/j.geoforum.2014.06.015

Arrow, K. J. (1971). *The Theory of Discrimination in labor markets*. Available at http://econ2.econ.iastate.edu/classes/econ321/rosburg/Arrow-TheTheoryofDistrimination.pdf

Arthur, M. B., Khapova, N., & Wilderom, C. P. M. (2005). Career success in a boundaryless career world. *Journal of Organizational Behavior*, *26*(2), 177–202. doi:10.1002/job.290

Arulampalam, W., Booth, A. L., & Bryan, M. L. (2007). Is there a glass ceiling over Europe? Exploring the gender pay gap across the wage distribution. *Industrial & Labor Relations Review*, *60*(2), 163–186. doi:10.1177/001979390706000201

Ashok, S. (2007). Optimised model for community-based hybrid energy system. *Renewable Energy*, *32*(7), 1155–1164. doi:10.1016/j.renene.2006.04.008

Assunção, M. D., Calheiros, R. N., Bianchi, S., Netto, M. A. S., & Buyya, R. (2014). Big data computing and clouds: Trends and future directions. *Journal of Parallel and Distributed Computing*, *79-80*(01), 3–15.

Asterisk. (2020). https://www.asterisk.org/

Atlason, R., & Unnthorsson, R. (2014). Ideal EROI (energy return on investment) deepens the understanding of energy systems. *Energy*, *67*(1), 241–245. doi:10.1016/j.energy.2014.01.096

Atnafu, S. (2014). *Local Internet Content: The Case of Ethiopia*. In *12th Globelics International Conference*, Addis Ababa, Ethiopia.

Aven, T. (2010). On how to define, understand and describe risk. *Reliability Engineering & System Safety*, *95*(6), 623–631. doi:10.1016/j.ress.2010.01.011

Awan, S., Ahmed, S., Nawaz, A., Maghdid, S., Zaman, K., Ali, M. Y., Khan, Z., & Saeed, S. (2020). BlockChain with IoT, an Emergent Routing Scheme for Smart Agriculture. *International Journal of Advanced Computer Science and Applications, 11*(4). Advance online publication. doi:10.14569/IJACSA.2020.0110457

Ayoroa, P., Bailey, B., Crossen, A., & Geo-JaJa, M. A. (2010). Education in China: The urban/rural disparity explained. In J. Zajda (Ed.), *Globalisation, ideology and education policy reforms* (pp. 89–113). Springer. doi:10.1007/978-90-481-3524-0_7

Bada, M., Sasse, A. M., & Nurse, J. R. (2014). Cyber Security Awareness Campaigns: Why They Fail to Change Behavior. *International Conference on Cyber Security for Sustainable Society*, 38. Retrieved from http://www.cs.ox.ac.uk/publications/publication9343-abstract.html%0Ahttp://discovery.ucl.ac.uk/1468954/1/Awareness CampaignsDraftWorkingPaper.pdf

Bai, J., & Perron, P. (2003). Computation and analysis of multiple structural change models. *Journal of Applied Econometrics, 18*(1), 1–22. doi:10.1002/jae.659

Baker, S., Ponniah, D., & Smith, S. (1999). Risk response techniques employed currently for major projects. *Construction Management and Economics, 17*(2), 205–213. doi:10.1080/014461999371709

Balcilar, M., Ozdemir, Z. A., & Shahbaz, M. (2018). On the time-varying links between oil and gold: New insights from the rolling and recursive rolling approaches. *International Journal of Finance & Economics, 24*(3), 1047–1065. doi:10.1002/ijfe.1704

Ballout, H. (2007). Career success: The effects of human capital, person-environment fit and organizational support. *Journal of Managerial Psychology, 22*(8), 741–765. doi:10.1108/02683940710837705

Ballout, H. (2008). Work-family conflict and career success: The effects of domain-specific determinants. *Journal of Management Development, 27*(5), 437–466. doi:10.1108/02621710810871781

Ballout, H. (2009). Career commitment and career success: Moderating role of self-efficacy. *Career Development International, 14*(7), 655–670. doi:10.1108/13620430911005708

Bannerman, P. L. (2008). Risk and Risk management in software projects: A reassessment. *Journal of Systems and Software, 81*(12), 2118–2133. doi:10.1016/j.jss.2008.03.059

Bansal, A. K., Kumar, R., & Gupta, R. A. (2013). Economic analysis and power management of a Small Autonomous Hybrid Power System (SAHPS) using Biogeography Based Optimization (BBO) algorithm. *IEEE Transactions on Smart Grid, 4*(1), 638–648. doi:10.1109/TSG.2012.2236112

Banu, S., & Suresh, B. (2020). COVID-19 and its impact on micro, small and medium enterprises in India. *Mukt Shabd Journal, 9*(X), 606–617.

Banyahmad, H. (2011). *Key challenges of information technology project risk management*. Academic Press.

Barbour, E., Radcliffe, J., Ding, Y., Li, Y., & Wilson, I. A. G. (2016). A review of pumped hydro energy storage development in significant international electricity markets. *Renewable & Sustainable Energy Reviews, 61*(1), 421–432. doi:10.1016/j.rser.2016.04.019

Baruch, Y. (2006). Career development in organizations and beyond: Balancing traditional and contemporary viewpoints. *Human Resource Management Review, 16*(2), 125–138. doi:10.1016/j.hrmr.2006.03.002

Basilaia, G., & Kvavadze, D. (2020). Transition to online education in schools during a SARS-CoV-2 coronavirus (COVID-19) pandemic in Georgia. *Pedagogical Research, 5*(4), 1–9. doi:10.29333/pr/7937

Basnyat, M. B. (2004). Rural electrification through renewable energy in Nepal. *World Review of Science, Technology and Sustainable Development*, *1*(1), 74–80. doi:10.1504/WRSTSD.2004.004857

Basu P (2004). Providing better access to finance for SMEs in India. *Access Finance, 2.*

Baudrillard, J. (1994). *Simulacra and simulation*. University of Michigan Press.

Bauman, Z. (2011). *Collateral damage: Social inequalities in a global age*. Polity Press.

Bauman, Z. (2013). *Society under siege*. John Wiley & Sons.

Bauman, Z. (2017). Tourists and vagabonds: Or, living in postmodern times. In *Identity and social change* (pp. 19–32). Routledge. doi:10.4324/9780203789339-3

Baumeister, C., & Kilian, L. (2016). Forty years of oil price fluctuations: Why the price of oil may still surprise us. *The Journal of Economic Perspectives*, *30*(1), 139–160. doi:10.1257/jep.30.1.139

Baur, D. G., & Glover, K. (2012). A gold bubble? SSRN *Electronic Journal.* Retrieved from https://papers.ssrn.com/sol3/papers.cfm?abstract_id=2166636 doi:10.2139/ssrn.2166636

Baur, D. G., Dimpfl, T., & Kuck, K. (2018). Bitcoin, gold and the US dollar–A replication and extension. *Finance Research Letters*, *25*, 103–110. doi:10.1016/j.frl.2017.10.012

Bazaeea, G., Hassanib, M., & Shahmansouri, A. (2020, September). Identifying Blockchain Technology Maturity's Levels in the Oil and Gas Industry. *Petroleum Business Review*, *4*(3), 43–61.

Beck, U. (1992). *Risk society: Towards a new modernity* (Vol. 17). Sage.

Behera, M., Mishra, S., Mohapatra, N., & Behera, A. R. (2020). COVID-19 Pandemic and Micro, Small and Medium Enterprises (MSMEs): Policy Response for Revival. *SEDME (Small Enterprises Development, Management & Extension Journal), 47*(3), 213-228.

Bendl, R., & Schmidt, A. (2010). From glass ceiling to firewalls – different metaphors for describing discrimination. *Gender, Work and Organization*, *17*(5), 612–634. doi:10.1111/j.1468-0432.2010.00520.x

Bernard, F. L., & Laband, D. N. (1995). *Sex discrimination in the legal profession*. Quorum Books.

Bernstein, P. L. (1996). *Against the gods: The remarkable story of risk*. Wiley & Sons.

Berntzen, L. (2013). Citizen-centric eGovernment Services. In *CENTRIC 2013, The Sixth International Conference on Advances in Human oriented and Personalized Mechanisms, Technologies, and Services.* ThinkMind.

Berry, D., & Bell, M. P. (2012). Inequality in organizations: Stereotyping, discrimination, and labor law exclusions. *Equality, Diversity and Inclusion*, *31*(3), 236–248. doi:10.1108/02610151211209090

Bettendorf, T., & Chen, W. (2013). Are there bubbles in the Sterling-Dollar exchange rate? New evidence from sequential ADF tests. *Economics Letters*, *120*(2), 350–353. doi:10.1016/j.econlet.2013.04.039

Bialkowski, J., Bohl, M. T., Stephan, P. M., & Wisniewski, T. P. (2015). The gold price in times of crisis. *International Review of Financial Analysis*, *41*, 329–339. doi:10.1016/j.irfa.2014.07.001

Biedenbach, T., & Müller, R. (2011). Paradigms in project management research: Examples from 15 years of IRNOP conferences. *International Journal of Managing Projects in Business*, *4*(1), 82–104. doi:10.1108/17538371111096908

Bier, T., Lange, A., & Glock, C. H. (2020). Methods for Mitigating Disruptions in Complex Supply Chain Structures: A Systematic Literature Review. *International Journal of Production Research*, *58*(6), 1835–1856. doi:10.1080/00207543.2019.1687954

Blakemore, M. (2006). *Think Paper 2: Customer-centric, citizen centric. Should Government learn directly from business?* Working paper, prepared for the e-Government unit, DG Information Society and Media, European Commision. Available at http://europa.eu.int/e-Government_research

Blakers, A. (2015). Sustainable Energy Options. *Asian Perspective*, *39*(4), 559–590. doi:10.1353/apr.2015.0025

Bledstein, B. (1978). The Culture of Professionalism. In The middle class and the higher education in America. Norton.

Bobinaite, V., & Juozapaviaiene, A. (2011). Assessment of performance efficiency of enterprises producing electricity in hydro and wind power plants. *Business: Theory and Practice*, *12*(2), 193–202.

Boholm, Å. (2003). The cultural nature of risk: Can there be an anthropology of uncertainty? *Ethnos*, *68*(2), 159–178. doi:10.1080/0014184032000097722

Boicea, V. A. (2014). Energy storage technologies: The past and the present. *Proceedings of the IEEE*, *102*(11), 1777–1794. doi:10.1109/JPROC.2014.2359545

Boin, A., Hart, P., Stern, E., & Sundelius, B. (2006). *The Politics of Crisis Management: Public Leadership Under Pressure*. Cambridge University Press.

Bolat, T., Bolat, O. I., & Kilic, T. (2011). Career self-efficacy and the glass ceiling: Moderating effect of work-related masculinity values. *Interdisciplinary Journal of Contemporary Research in Business*, *2*(10), 57–68.

Bollinger, R. (2010). *Lean Risk Management*. Project Management Institute.

Bombuwela, P., & Alwis, A. A. (2013). Effects of glass ceiling on women career development in private sector organizations – case of Sri Lanka. *Journal of Competitiveness*, *5*(2), 3–19. doi:10.7441/joc.2013.02.01

Botezat, A. (2016). *Educational poverty*. The Gh. Zane Institute for Economic and Social Research of the Romanian Academy, Iasi Branch.

Bouri, E., Shahzad, S. J. H., & Roubaud, D. (2019). Co-explosivity in the cryptocurrency market. *Finance Research Letters*, *29*, 178–183. doi:10.1016/j.frl.2018.07.005

Brändström, A., & Kuipers, S. (2014). *From 'Normal Incidents' to Political Crises: Understanding the Selective Politicization of Policy Failure*. Cambridge University Press. doi:10.1111/1477-7053.t01-1-00016

Breckenridge, J. N., Zimbardo, P. G., & Sweeton, J. L. (2010). After years of media coverage, can one more video report trigger heuristic judgments? A national study of American terrorism risk perceptions. *Behavioral Sciences Of Terrorism & Political Aggression*, *2*(3), 163–178. doi:10.1080/19434471003768826

Broock, W. A., Scheinkman, J. A., Dechert, W. D., & LeBaron, B. (1996). A test for independence based on the correlation dimension. *Econometric Reviews*, *15*(3), 197–235. doi:10.1080/07474939608800353

Brooks, C., Prokopczuk, M., & Wu, Y. (2015). Booms and busts in commodity markets: Bubbles or fundamentals? *Journal of Futures Markets*, *35*(10), 916–938. doi:10.1002/fut.21721

Browne, M. W., & Cudeck, R. (1993). Alternative ways of assessing model fit. In J. S. Long (Ed.), *Testing Structural Equation Models*. Sage.

Bruninx, K., Delarue, E., Dhaeseleer, W., Dvorkin, Y., Kirschen, D. S., & Pandzic, H. (2016). Coupling Pumped Hydro Energy Storage with Unit Commitment. *IEEE Transactions on Sustainable Energy*, *7*(2), 786–796. doi:10.1109/TSTE.2015.2498555

Bryman, A., & Bell, E. (2011). *Business research methods*. Oxford University Press.

Buckley, R., Gretzel, U., Scott, D., Weaver, D., & Becken, S. (2015). Tourism megatrends. *Tourism Recreation Research*, *40*(1), 59–70. doi:10.1080/02508281.2015.1005942

Budig, M. J., & Hodges, M. J. (2010). Differences in disadvantage: Variation in the motherhood penalty across white women's earnings distribution. *American Sociological Review*, *75*(5), 705–728. doi:10.1177/0003122410381593

Business News Publishing. (2013). Summary: Full Frontal PR: Review and Analysis of Laermer and Prichinello's Book. Pimento.

Butcher, J. (2021). Covid-19, tourism and the advocacy of degrowth. *Tourism Recreation Research*, 1–10. doi:10.1080/02508281.2021.1953306

Butt, A.S. (2021). Strategies to mitigate the impact of COVID-19 on supply chain disruptions: a multiple case analysis of buyers and distributors. *The International Journal of Logistics Management*. . doi:10.1108/IJLM-11-2020-0455

Cairney, P. (2020). *Understanding Public Policy: Theories and Issues*. MacMillan International/Red Globe Press.

Callahan, C., & Soileau, J. (2017). Does Enterprise risk management enhance operating performance? *Advances in Accounting*, *37*(1), 122–139. doi:10.1016/j.adiac.2017.01.001

Canavan, B. (2014). Sustainable tourism: Development, decline and de-growth. Management issues from the Isle of Man. *Journal of Sustainable Tourism*, *22*(1), 127–147. doi:10.1080/09669582.2013.819876

Caspi, I., Phillips, P. C. B., & Shi, S. (2018). *Real time monitoring of asset markets with psymonitor*. R package version 0.0.1. https://itamarcaspi.github.io/psymonitor

Castel, R. (1997). *The Metamorphosis of the Social Question. A Chronicle of the Salariado* [La Metamorfosis de la Cuestión social. Una Crónica del salariado]. Paidos.

Chakraborty, T., Misra, I. S., & Prasad, R. (2019). Overview of VoIP Technology. In *VoIP Technology: Applications and Challenges. Springer Series in Wireless Technology*. Springer. doi:10.1007/978-3-319-95594-0_1

Chapman, C., & Ward, S. (2007). *Project risk management: processes, techniques and insights*. John Wiley & Sons.

Chapman, R. J. (2001). The controlling influences on effective risk identification and assessment for construction design management. *International Journal of Project Management*, *19*(3), 147–160. doi:10.1016/S0263-7863(99)00070-8

Charney, I. (2001). Three dimensions of capital switching within the real estate sector: A Canadian case study. *International Journal of Urban and Regional Research*, *25*(4), 740–758. doi:10.1111/1468-2427.00342

Chaudhry, A. M., Raza, R., & Hayat, S. A. (2009). Renewable energy technologies in Pakistan: Prospects and challenges. *Renewable & Sustainable Energy Reviews*, *13*(6-7), 1657–1662. doi:10.1016/j.rser.2008.09.025

Cheah, E. T., & Fry, J. (2015). Speculative bubbles in Bitcoin markets? An empirical investigation into the fundamental value of Bitcoin. *Economics Letters*, *130*, 32–36. doi:10.1016/j.econlet.2015.02.029

Cheng, X. (2020). Challenges of "School's Out, But Class's On" to School Education: Practical Exploration of Chinese Schools during the COVID-19 Pandemic. *Sci Insigt Edu Front*, *5*(2), 501–516. doi:10.15354ief.20.ar043

Chen, H.-M., Chang, K.-C., & Lin, T.-H. (2016). A cloud-based system framework for performing online viewing, storage, and analysis on big data of massive BIMs. *Automation in Construction*, *25*(1), 1–15. doi:10.1016/S0926-5805(99)00010-2

Chen, Q., Liang, M., Li, Y., Guo, J., Fei, D., Wang, L., He, L., Sheng, C., Cai, Y., Li, X., Wang, J., & Zhang, Z. (2020). Mental health care for medical staff in China during the COVID-19 Outbreak. *The Lancet. Psychiatry*, *7*(4), e15–e16. Advance online publication. doi:10.1016/S2215-0366(20)30078-X PMID:32085839

Chhetri, A. B., Islam, M. R., & Pokharel, G. R. (2009). Sustainability of micro-hydrosystems - A case study. *Energy & Environment*, *20*(4), 567–585. doi:10.1260/095830509788707356

Chigada, J., & Madzinga, R. (2020). Cyberattacks and threats during COVID-19 : A systematic literature review Coronavirus Disease-2019. *South African Journal of Information Management*, *23*(1), 1–11.

Chionis, D., Karanikas, N., Iordan, A. R., & Svensson-Dianellou, A. (2022). Risk perception and communication factors in aviation: Insights from safety investigators. *Journal of Risk Research*, 1–16. doi:10.1080/13669877.2022.2038246

Chiu, C. L., & Yeh, C. C. (2019). Whether the multiple bubbles exist in the bond markets of developed countries? *International Journal of Information and Management Sciences*, *30*, 271–282.

Chobanova, E. (2014). *Why You Should Share Your Risk With Business Partners*. Available at: http://www.executiveboard.com/it-blog/why-you-should-share-your-risk-with-business-partners/?utm_source=Tech&utm_medium=CIO-Banner&v2=banner

Choi, T.-M. (2020). Innovative 'Bring-Service-Near-Your- Home' Operations under Corona-Virus (COVID-19/SARSCoV-2) Outbreak: Can Logistics become the Messiah? *Transportation Research Part E: Logistics and Transportation*, *140*, 101961. doi:10.1016/j.tre.2020.101961 PMID:32346356

Chowdhury, S. R., Sunna, T. C., & Ahmed, S. (2020). Telemedicine is an important aspect of healthcare services amid the Covid-19 outbreak: Its barriers in Bangladesh and strategies to overcome. *The International Journal of Health Planning and Management*, *36*(1), 4–12. doi:10.1002/hpm.3064 PMID:32857887

Chudzikowski, K. (2012). Career transitions and career success in the 'new' career era. *Journal of Vocational Behavior*, *81*(2), 298–306. doi:10.1016/j.jvb.2011.10.005

Ciorciari, M., & Blattner, P. (2008). *Enterprise risk management maturity-level assessment tool*. Paper presented at the 2008 Enterprise risk management symposium, Chicago, IL.

Clark, W., & Harley, A. (2020). *How COVID-19 has changed public policy*. Harvard Kennedy School. https://www.hks.harvard.edu/faculty-research/policy-topics/public-leadership-management/how-covid-19-has-changed-public-policy

Clarke, A. E. (2005). *Situational analysis: Grounded theory after the postmodern turn*. SAGE., doi:10.4135/9781412985833

Clarke, A. E., Friese, C., & Washburn, R. (Eds.). (2015). *Situational analysis in practice: Mapping research with grounded theory* (Vol. 1). Left Coast Press. doi:10.4324/9781315420134

Clark, K. D. (2000). Urban middle school teachers' use of instructional technology. *Journal of Research on Computing in Education*, *33*(2), 178–193. doi:10.1080/08886504.2000.10782308

Clark, S. (2000). Work-family border theory: A new theory of work/family balance. *Human Relations*, *56*(6), 747–761. doi:10.1177/0018726700536001

Collins, P. H. (2012). Social inequality, power, and politics: Intersectionality and American pragmatism in dialogue. *The Journal of Speculative Philosophy*, *26*(2), 442–457. doi:10.5325/jspecphil.26.2.0442

Collis, B., Moonen, J., & Vingerhoets, J. (1997). Flexibility as a key construct in European training: Experiences from the TeleScopia project. *British Journal of Educational Technology*, *28*(3), 199–217. doi:10.1111/1467-8535.00026

Connolly, D., Leahy, M., & MacLaughlin, S. (2010). Development of a computer program to locate potential sites for pumped hydroelectric energy storage. *Energy*, *35*(1), 375–381. doi:10.1016/j.energy.2009.10.004

Cooper Jackson, J. (2001). Women middle managers' perception of the glass ceiling. *Women in Management Review*, *16*(1), 30–41. doi:10.1108/09649420110380265

Corbet, S., Lucey, B., & Yarovaya, L. (2018). Datestamping the Bitcoin and Ethereum bubbles. *Finance Research Letters*, *26*, 81–88. doi:10.1016/j.frl.2017.12.006

Cordry, S., & Wilson, J. D. (2004). Parents as first teacher. *Education*, *125*(1), 56–62.

Correll, S. J., Benard, S., & Paik, I. (2007). Getting a job: Is there a motherhood penalty? *American Journal of Sociology*, *112*(5), 1297–1338. doi:10.1086/511799

CouchDB as the State Database. (2020). *CouchDB as the State Database — Hyperledger - Fabricdocs Master Documentation*. https://hyperledger-fabric.readthedocs.io/en/release-1.4/couchdb_as_state_database.html

Crawford, D. (2003). *The Invisible Enemy: A Natural History of Viruses*. Oxford University Press.

Crawford, J. K. (2006). The Project Management Maturity Model. *Information Systems Management*, *23*(2), 50–58. doi:10.1201/1078.10580530/46352.23.4.20060901/95113.7

Crenshaw, K. (1994). Mapping the margins: intersectionality, identity politics and violence against women of color. In M. A. Fineman & R. Mykitiuk (Eds.), *The Public Nature of Private Violence* (pp. 93–118). Routledge.

Creswell, J. W. (2007). *Qualitative enquiry and research design: Choosing among five approaches*. Sage publications Ltd.

Crosby, F. J., Williams, J. C., & Biernat, M. (2004). The maternal wall. *The Journal of Social Issues*, *60*(4), 675–682. doi:10.1111/j.0022-4537.2004.00379.x

CSA. (2007). *Population and Housing Census of Ethiopia*. Administrative Report.

Dagliati, A., Malovini, A., Tibollo, V., & Bellazzi, R. (2021). Health Informatics and EHR to support clinical research in the COVID-19 pandemic: An overview. *Briefings in Bioinformatics*, *22*(2), 812–822. doi:10.1093/bib/bbaa418 PMID:33454728

Dalberg, H. (2011). *Report on support to SMEs in Developing Countries Through Financial Intermediaries*. https://www.eib.org/attachments/dalberg_sme-briefing-paper.pdf

Dale, R. S., Johnson, J. E., & Tang, L. (2005). Financial markets can go mad: Evidence of irrational behaviour during the South Sea Bubble. *The Economic History Review*, *58*(2), 233–271. doi:10.1111/j.1468-0289.2005.00304.x

Dalgic, A., & Birdir, K. (2020). Smart Hotels and Technological Applications. In *Handbook of Research on Smart Technology Applications in the Tourism Industry* (pp. 323–343). IGI Global. doi:10.4018/978-1-7998-1989-9.ch015

Dallat, C., Salmon, P. M., & Goode, N. (2017). Risky systems versus risky people: To what extent do risk assessment methods consider the systems approach to accident causation? A review of the literature. *Safety Science*.

Daniel, W. W. (1990). Applied Nonparametric Statistics (2nd ed.). PWS Kent.

Dar, A. B., Lone, A. H., Zahoor, S., Khan, A. A., & Naaz, R. (2020). Applicability of mobile contact tracing in fighting pandemic (COVID-19): Issues, challenges, and solutions. *Computer Science Review*, *38*, 100307. doi:10.1016/j.cosrev.2020.100307 PMID:32989380

Das, K. (2008). SMEs in India: Issues and Possibilities in Times of Globalisation. In H. Lim (Ed.), *SME in Asia and Globalization, ERIA Research Project Report 2007-5* (pp. 69–97). Available at https://www.eria.org/SMEs%20in%20India_Issues%20and%20Possibilities%20in%20Times%20of%20Globalisation.pdf

Davis, B. R., & Mentzer, J. T. (2006). Logistics service driven loyalty: An exploratory study. *Journal of Business Logistics, 27*(2), 53–73. doi:10.1002/j.2158-1592.2006.tb00217.x

Dawotola, A. W., Gelder, P. H., & Vrijling, J. K. (2012). Design for acceptable risk in transportation pipelines. *International Journal of Risk Assessment and Management, 16*(1-3), 112–127. doi:10.1504/IJRAM.2012.047570

DCMSME. (2017). *What are Micro, Small & Medium Enterprises?* http://www.dcmsme.gov.in/ssiindia/defination_msme.htm

de Bakker, K., Boonstra, A., & Wortmann, H. (2011). Risk management affecting IS/IT project success through communicative action. *Project Management Journal, 42*(3), 75–90. doi:10.1002/pmj.20242

de Bakker, K., Boonstra, A., & Wortmann, H. (2012). Risk managements' communicative effects influencing IT project success. *International Journal of Project Management, 30*(4), 444–457. doi:10.1016/j.ijproman.2011.09.003

de Bakker, K., Boonstra, A., & Wortmann, H. (2014). The communicative effect of risk identification on project success. *International Journal of Project Organisation and Management, 6*(1-2), 138–156. doi:10.1504/IJPOM.2014.059749

de Boer, H. S., Moll, H., Benders, R., & Grond, L. (2014). The application of power-to-gas, pumped hydro storage and compressed air energy storage in an electricity system at different wind power penetration levels. *Energy, 72*(1), 360–370. doi:10.1016/j.energy.2014.05.047

De Groot, K., & Thurik, R. (2018). Disentangling risk and uncertainty: When risk-taking measures are not about risk. *Frontiers in Psychology, 9*, 2194. doi:10.3389/fpsyg.2018.02194 PMID:30498464

de Kervenoael, R., Hasan, R., Schwob, A., & Goh, E. (2020). Leveraging human-robot interaction in hospitality services: Incorporating the role of perceived value, empathy, and information sharing into visitors' intentions to use social robots. *Tourism Management, 78*, 104042. doi:10.1016/j.tourman.2019.104042

Dell, G., Egger, C., & Grabl, A. (1996). Renewable energy in Austria. *Renewable Energy, 9*(1-4), 1116-1119.

Derks, K., de Swart, J., van Batenburg, P., Wagenmakers, E.-J., & Wetzels, R. (2021). Priors in a Bayesian audit: How integration of existing information into the prior distribution can improve audit transparency and efficiency. *International Journal of Auditing, 25*(3), 621–636. doi:10.1111/ijau.12240

Derrida, J., & Dufourmantelle, A. (2000). *Of hospitality*. Stanford University Press.

Diba, B. T., & Grossman, H. I. (1988). Explosive rational bubbles in stock prices? *The American Economic Review, 78*(3), 520–530.

Dickey, D. A., & Fuller, W. A. (1979). Distribution of the estimators for autoregressive time series with a unit root. *Journal of the American Statistical Association, 74*(366a), 427–431.

Dilmaghani, M. (2019). Religious identity and real estate wealth accumulation: Evidence from Canada. *Housing Studies, 34*(10), 1690–1720. doi:10.1080/02673037.2017.1364714

Dimovski, V., Skerlavaj, M., & Man, M. M. K. (2010a). Comparative analysis of mid-level women managers perception of the existence of glass ceiling in Singaporean and Malaysian organizations. *International Business & Economics Research Journal, 9*(8), 61–77. doi:10.19030/iber.v9i8.613

Dimovski, V., Skerlavaj, M., & Man, M. M. K. (2010b). Is there a 'glass ceiling' for female managers in Singapore organizations? *Management*, *5*(4), 307–329.

Dissanayake, V. (2020). *A review of Cyber security risks in an Augmented reality world*. Retrieved from https://www.researchgate.net/publication/339941469_A_review_of_Cyber_security_risks_in_an_Augmented_reality_world

Dixit, A., Sharma, S. K., & Sharma, D. P. (2021). Impetus on Big Data to Boost Indian MSME Sector and Economy using Cloud Storage. *International Journal of Computer Applications, 174*(21).

Dobre, C., & Xhafa, F. (2014). Intelligent services for big data science. *Future Generation Computer Systems*, *37*(1), 267–281. doi:10.1016/j.future.2013.07.014

Doe, F., & Asamoah, E. S. (2014). The effect of electric power fluctuations on the profitability and competitiveness of SMEs: A study of SMEs within the Acera Business District of Ghana. *Journal of Competitiveness*, *6*(3), 32–48. doi:10.7441/joc.2014.03.03

Dohale, V., Ambilkar, P., Gunasekaran, A., & Verma, P. (2021). Supply Chain Risk Mitigation Strategies during COVID- 19: Exploratory Cases of 'Make-to-Order' Handloom Saree Apparel Industries. *International Journal of Physical Distribution & Logistics Management*. Advance online publication. doi:10.1108/IJPDLM-12-2020-0450

Do, Q. N., Mishra, N., Wulandhari, N. B. I., Ramudhin, A., Sivarajah, U., & Milligan, G. (2021). Supply chain agility responding to unprecedented changes: Empirical evidence from the UK food supply chain during COVID-19 crisis. *Supply Chain Management*, *26*(6), 737–752. doi:10.1108/SCM-09-2020-0470

Dorn, E., Hancock, B., Sarakatsannis, J., & Viruleg, E. (2020). *COVID-19 and student learning in the United States: The hurt could last a lifetime*. McKinsey & Company.

Dost, M. K., Ur-Rehman, Z., & Tariq, S. (2012). The organizations having high level of glass ceiling has lower productivity due to lack of employee commitment. *Kuwait Chapter of Arabian Journal of Business and Management Review*, *33*(843), 1–11.

Douglas, M., & Wildavsky, A. (1983). *Risk and culture: An essay on the selection of technological and environmental dangers*. University of California Press. doi:10.1525/9780520907393

Downs, A. (1996). Why invest in commercial real estate. *Urban Land September, 30*(3), 62-67.

Drajea, A. J., & O'Sullivan, C. (2014). Influence of parental education and family income on children's education in rural Uganda. *Global Education Review*, *1*(3), 149–166.

Ehnberg, S. G. J., & Bollen, M. H. J. (2005). Reliability of a small power system using solar power and hydro. *Electric Power Systems Research*, *74*(1), 119–127. doi:10.1016/j.epsr.2004.09.009

EISBC. (2017). *Definition of Indian SMEs*. http://www.eisbc.org/definition_of_indian_smes.aspx

Ejaz, M. (2009). Contribution of unschooled parents in the education of their children: An analysis. *Pakistan Journal of Social Sciences*, *29*(2).

Elahee, M. K. (2013). Potential of hydropower in mauritius: Myth or reality? *Energy Sources. Part A, Recovery, Utilization, and Environmental Effects*, *35*(10), 921–925. doi:10.1080/15567036.2010.514592

Ellegaard, C. (2008). Supply risk management in a small company perspective. *Supply Chain Management*, *13*(6), 425–434. doi:10.1108/13598540810905688

Elli, A., Barger, A., Bortnikov, V., Cachin, C., Christidis, K., De Caro, A., & Enyeart. (2018). Hyperledger Fabric: A Distributed Operating System for Permissioned Blockchains. *Proceedings of the Thirteenth EuroSys Conference on - EuroSys '18*, 1–15. 10.1145/3190508.3190538

Ellul, J. (1964). *The technological society* (Vol. 303). Vintage Books.

Emblemsvåg, J., & Kjølstad, L. E. (2006). Qualitative risk analysis: Some problems and remedies. *Management Decision, 44*(3), 395–408. doi:10.1108/00251740610656278

Emekter, R., Jirasakuldech, B., & Went, P. (2012). Rational speculative bubbles and commodities markets: Application of duration dependence test. *Applied Financial Economics, 22*(7), 581–596. doi:10.1080/09603107.2011.619496

Enoksen, F. A., Landsnes, C. J., Lučivjanská, K., & Molnár, P. (2020). Understanding risk of bubbles in cryptocurrencies. *Journal of Economic Behavior & Organization, 176*, 129–144. doi:10.1016/j.jebo.2020.05.005

Erdogdu, E. (2011). An analysis of Turkish hydropower policy. *Renewable & Sustainable Energy Reviews, 15*(1), 689–696. doi:10.1016/j.rser.2010.09.019

Fantazzini, D. (2016). The oil price crash in 2014/15: Was there a (negative) financial bubble? *Energy Policy, 96*, 383–396. doi:10.1016/j.enpol.2016.06.020

Fedele, A., & Roner, C. (2022). Dangerous games: A literature review on cybersecurity investments. *Journal of Economic Surveys, 36*(1), 157–187. doi:10.1111/joes.12456

Federal Glass Ceiling Commission. (1995a). *A Solid Investment: Making Full Use of the Nation's Human Capital: Recommendations of the Federal Glass Ceiling Commission.* U.S. Glass Ceiling Commission.

Federal Glass Ceiling Commission. (1995b). *Solid Investments: Making Full Use of the Nation's Human Capital.* U.S. Department of Labor, November.

Figuerola-Ferretti, I., McCrorie, J. R., & Paraskevopoulos, I. (2020). Mild explosivity in recent crude oil prices. *Energy Economics, 87*, 104387. doi:10.1016/j.eneco.2019.05.002

Fischhoff, B. (1995). Risk perception and communication unplugged: Twenty years of process. *Risk Analysis, 15*(2), 137–145. doi:10.1111/j.1539-6924.1995.tb00308.x PMID:7597253

Flynn, J., Slovic, P., & Mertz, C. K. (1994). Gender, race, and perception of environmental health risks. *Risk Analysis, 14*(6), 1101–1108. doi:10.1111/j.1539-6924.1994.tb00082.x PMID:7846319

Foley, A. M., Leahy, P. G., McKeogh, E. J., Li, K., & Morrison, A. P. (2015). A long-term analysis of pumped hydro storage to firm wind power. *Applied Energy, 137*(1), 638–648. doi:10.1016/j.apenergy.2014.07.020

Fonseca, J. A., & Schlueter, A. (2013). Novel approach for decentralized energy supply and energy storage of tall buildings in Latin America based on renewable energy sources: Case study of informal vertical community Torre David, Caracas - Venezuela. *Energy, 45*(2), 131–143. doi:10.1016/j.energy.2013.02.019

Fothergill, A., Maestas, E. G., & Darlington, J. D. (1999). Race, ethnicity and disasters in the United States: A review of the literature. *Disasters, 23*(2), 156–173. doi:10.1111/1467-7717.00111 PMID:10379098

Fotiadis, A., Polyzos, S., & Huan, T. C. T. (2021). The good, the bad and the ugly on COVID-19 tourism recovery. *Annals of Tourism Research, 87*, 103117. doi:10.1016/j.annals.2020.103117 PMID:33518847

Frankfurt, H. (1982). The importance of what we care about. *Synthese, 53*(2), 257–272. doi:10.1007/BF00484902

Frankfurt, H. G. (2002). *Contours of agency: Essays on themes from Harry Frankfurt.* MIT Press.

Fu, T. M. (2005). Unequal primary education opportunities in rural and urban China. *China Perspectives*, *2005*(60). doi:10.4000/chinaperspectives.500

Fung, A. (2020). *How COVID-19 Has Changed Public Policy*. Harvard Kennedy School. https://www.hks.harvard.edu/faculty-research/policy-topics/public-leadership-management/how-covid-19-has-changed-public-policy

Fusco, A., Dicuonzo, G., Dell'Atti, V., & Tatullo, M. (2020). Blockchain in Healthcare: Insights on COVID-19. *International Journal of Environmental Research and Public Health*, *17*(19), 7167. doi:10.3390/ijerph17197167 PMID:33007951

Gale, T. (2009). Urban beaches, virtual worlds and 'the end of tourism'. *Mobilities*, *4*(1), 119–138. doi:10.1080/17450100802657996

Garg, N., Singla, S., & Jangra, S. (2016). Challenges and techniques for testing big data. *Procedia Computer Science*, *85*(1), 940–948. doi:10.1016/j.procs.2016.05.285

Gattiker, U. E., & Larwood, L. (1988). Predictors for managers' career mobility, success, and satisfaction. *Human Relations*, *41*(8), 569–591. doi:10.1177/001872678804100801

Gattiker, U. E., & Larwood, L. (1989). Career success, mobility and extrinsic satisfaction of corporate managers. *The Social Science Journal*, *26*(1), 75–92. doi:10.1016/0362-3319(89)90039-6

Gaudenzi, B., & Borghesi, A. (2006). Managing risks in the supply chain using the AHP method. *International Journal of Logistics Management*, *17*(1), 114–136. doi:10.1108/09574090610663464

Gauthier, J.-B., & Ika, L. A. (2012). Foundations of Project Management Research: An Explicit and Six-Facet Ontological Framework. *Project Management Journal*, *43*(5), 5–23. doi:10.1002/pmj.21288

Gemici, E. (2020). Testing for multiple bubbles in cryptocurrency market. In A. Akinci (Ed.), *Interdisciplinary Public Finance, Business and Economics Studies* (Vol. 3, pp. 107–118). Peter Lang Publishing.

Geth, F., Brijs, T., Driesen, J., Belmans, R., & Kathan, J. (2015). An overview of large-scale stationary electricity storage plants in Europe: Current status and new developments. *Renewable & Sustainable Energy Reviews*, *52*(1), 1212–1227. doi:10.1016/j.rser.2015.07.145

Geuder, J., Kinateder, H., & Wagner, N. F. (2019). Cryptocurrencies as financial bubbles: The case of Bitcoin. *Finance Research Letters*, *31*, 179–184. doi:10.1016/j.frl.2018.11.011

Ghadikolaei, H. M., Ahmadi, A., Aghaei, J., & Najafi, M. (2012). Risk constrained self-scheduling of hydro/wind units for short term electricity markets considering intermittency and uncertainty. *Renewable & Sustainable Energy Reviews*, *16*(7), 4734–4743. doi:10.1016/j.rser.2012.04.019

Gharib, C., Mefteh-Wali, S., & Jabeur, S. B. (2021). The bubble contagion effect of COVID-19 outbreak: Evidence from crude oil and gold markets. *Finance Research Letters*, *38*, 101703. doi:10.1016/j.frl.2020.101703 PMID:32837382

Gholami, S. (2012). Critical risk factors in outsourced support projects of IT. *Journal of Management Research*, *4*(1), 1.

Ghorbani, M., & Tung, R. L. (2007). Behind the veil: An exploratory study of the myths and realities of women in the Iranian workforce. *Human Resource Management Journal*, *17*(4), 376–392. doi:10.1111/j.1748-8583.2007.00051.x

Giddens, A. (1991). *Modernity and self-identity: Self and society in the late modern age*. Stanford University Press.

Giddens, A. (1999). Risk and responsibility. *The Modern Law Review*, *62*(1), 1–10. doi:10.1111/1468-2230.00188

Giddens, A. (2011). *Runaway world*. Profile Books.

Gillies, J. (1952). Residential Real Estate in Canada O. J. *Firestone. In*, *42*, 211–212.

Ginn, R. D. (1989). *Continuity Planning: Preventing, Surviving and Recovering from Disaster*. Elsevier Science Publishers Ltd.

Gkillas, K., Bouri, E., Gupta, R., & Roubaud, D. (2020). Spillovers in higher-order moments of crude oil, gold, and Bitcoin. *The Quarterly Review of Economics and Finance*, *x*, xxx–xxx. doi:10.1016/j.qref.2020.08.004

Goel, P. K., Singh, B., Murthy, S. S., & Kishore, N. (2011). Isolated wind-hydro hybrid system using cage generators and battery storage. *IEEE Transactions on Industrial Electronics*, *58*(4), 1141–1153. doi:10.1109/TIE.2009.2037646

Gök, R. (2021). Identification of Multiple Bubbles in Turkish Financial Markets: Evidence From GSADF Approach. *Marmara Üniversitesi İktisadi ve İdari Bilimler Dergisi*, *43*(2), 231–252.

Goldfinch, S., Gauld, R., & Taplin, R. (2021). Trust in Government Soars in Australia and New Zealand During Pandemic. *The Conversation*. https://theconversation.com/trust-in-government-soars-in-australia-and-new-zealand-during-pandemic-154948

Gooding, Y. (2001). *The relationship between parental educational level and academic success of college freshmen* [Dissertation]. Iowa State University.

Goodwin, Y., & Strang, K. D. (2012). Socio-cultural and multi-disciplinary perceptions of risk. *International Journal of Risk and Contingency Management*, *1*(1), 1–11. doi:10.4018/ijrcm.2012010101

Gordon, N. A. (2014). *Flexible Pedagogies: Technology-enhanced learning*. In The Higher Education Academy. doi:10.13140/2.1.2052.5760

Gössling, S., Scott, D., Hall, C. M., Ceron, J. P., & Dubois, G. (2012). Consumer behaviour and demand response of tourists to climate change. *Annals of Tourism Research*, *39*(1), 36–58. doi:10.1016/j.annals.2011.11.002

Goveas, S., & Aslam, N. (2011). A role and contributions of women in the Sultanate of Oman. *International Journal of Business and Management*, *6*(3), 232–239. doi:10.5539/ijbm.v6n3p232

Government of India. (2020). *Annual Report-2019-20, Ministry of Micro, Small and Medium Enterprises*. https://msme.gov.in/sites/default/files/FINAL_MSME_ENGLISH_AR_2019-20.pdf

Granrose, C. S. (2007). Gender differences in career perceptions in the People's Republic of China. *Career Development International*, *12*(1), 9–27. doi:10.1108/13620430710724802

Groenendaal, J., & Helsloot, I. (2021). Cyber resilience during the COVID-19 pandemic crisis: A case study. *Journal of Contingencies and Crisis Management*, *29*(4), 439–444. doi:10.1111/1468-5973.12360

GroutP. A.ParkI. U.SondereggerS. (2009). An economic theory of glass ceiling. http://www.bris.ac.uk/Dept/CMPO/workingpapers/wp183.pdf

Gulati, S. (2008). Technology-enhanced learning in developing nations: A review. *International Review of Research in Open and Distance Learning*, *9*(1), 1–16. doi:10.19173/irrodl.v9i1.477

Gundu, T. (2019). Acknowledging and reducing the knowing and doing gap in employee cybersecurity compliance. *14th International Conference on Cyber Warfare and Security, ICCWS 2019*, 94–102.

Guo, X., Lu, F., & Wei, Y. (2021). Capture the contagion network of Bitcoin–Evidence from pre and mid COVID-19. *Research in International Business and Finance*, *58*, 101484. doi:10.1016/j.ribaf.2021.101484 PMID:34518717

Gupta, A., Saini, R. P., & Sharma, M. P. (2010). Steady-state modelling of hybrid energy system for off grid electrification of cluster of villages. *Renewable Energy*, *35*(2), 520–535. doi:10.1016/j.renene.2009.06.014

Gupta, A., Saini, R. P., & Sharma, M. P. (2011). Modelling of hybrid energy system-Part I: Problem formulation and model development. *Renewable Energy*, *36*(2), 459–465. doi:10.1016/j.renene.2010.06.035

Gürkaynak, R. S. (2008). Econometric tests of asset price bubbles: Taking stock. *Journal of Economic Surveys*, *22*(1), 166–186. doi:10.1111/j.1467-6419.2007.00530.x

Gustafsod, P. E. (1998). Gender Differences in risk perception: Theoretical and methodological erspectives. *Risk Analysis*, *18*(6), 805–811. doi:10.1111/j.1539-6924.1998.tb01123.x PMID:9972583

Gu, Y., Bakke, J., Zhou, Z., Osborn, D., Bo, R., & Guo, T. (2014). A novel market simulation methodology on hydro storage. *IEEE Transactions on Smart Grid*, *5*(2), 1119–1128. doi:10.1109/TSG.2013.2289915

Hacker, S., & Hatemi-J, A. (2012). A bootstrap test for causality with endogenous lag length choice: Theory and application in finance. *Journal of Economic Studies (Glasgow, Scotland)*, *39*(2), 144–160. doi:10.1108/01443581211222635

Haila, A. (1991). Four types of investment in land and property. *International Journal of Urban and Regional Research*, *15*(1), 343–365. doi:10.1111/j.1468-2427.1991.tb00643.x

Hailu, B. H. (2020). *Education Response to COVID-19: How Can Basic Education Be Implemented in Ethiopia?* Retrieved from https://riseprogramme.org/blog/COVID-19-ETH-Basic-Education

Hakim, A. A., Kellish, A. S., Atabek, U., Spitz, F. R., & Hong, Y. K. (2020). Implications for the use of telehealth in surgical patients during the COVID-19 pandemic. *American Journal of Surgery*, *220*(1), 48–49. doi:10.1016/j.amjsurg.2020.04.026 PMID:32336519

Hall, D. T. (1996). Protean careers of the 21st century. *The Academy of Management Executive*, *10*(4), 8–16. doi:10.5465/ame.1996.3145315

Hariharan, A., Thomas, S., & Viswanathan, P. K. (2021). Impact of COVID-19 on the Performance of Micro, Small and Medium Enterprises (MSMEs) In India–A Case Study in Kerala. *Annals of the Romanian Society for Cell Biology*, 14797–14816.

Hartley, J. (2004). *Case study research*. SAGE Publications.

Harvett, C. M. (2013). *A Study of Uncertainty and Risk Management Practice Related to Perceived Project Complexity* [PhD thesis]. Bond University.

Harvey, D. (1978). The urban process under capitalism: A framework for analysis. *International Journal of Urban and Regional Research*, *2*(1), 101–131. doi:10.1111/j.1468-2427.1978.tb00738.x

Harvey, D. I., Leybourne, S. J., Sollis, R., & Taylor, A. R. (2016). Tests for explosive financial bubbles in the presence of non-stationary volatility. *Journal of Empirical Finance*, *38*, 548–574. doi:10.1016/j.jempfin.2015.09.002

Harwood, I. A., Ward, S. C., & Chapman, C. B. (2009). A grounded exploration of organisational risk propensity. *Journal of Risk Research*, *12*(5), 563–579. doi:10.1080/13669870802497751

Hasan, S., Ali, M., Kurnia, S., & Thurasamy, R. (2021). Evaluating the cyber security readiness of organizations and its influence on performance. *Journal of Information Security and Applications*, *58*, 102726. doi:10.1016/j.jisa.2020.102726

Haslam, S. A., & Ryan, M. K. (2008). The road to the glass cliff: Differences in the perceived suitability of men and women for leadership positions in succeeding and failing organizations. *The Leadership Quarterly*, *19*(5), 530–546. doi:10.1016/j.leaqua.2008.07.011

Hazen, B. T., Russo, I., Confente, I., & Pellathy, D. (2021). Supply chain management for circular economy: Conceptual framework and research agenda. *International Journal of Logistics Management*, *32*(2), 510–537. doi:10.1108/IJLM-12-2019-0332

Hebb, T., Hamilton, A., & Hachigian, H. (2010). Responsible property investing in Canada: Factoring both environmental and social impacts in the Canadian real estate market. *Journal of Business Ethics*, *92*(2), 99–115. doi:10.100710551-010-0636-5

He, F., Deng, Y., & Weina, L. (2020). Coronavirus disease 2019: What we know? *Journal of Medical Virology*, *2020*(7), 1–7. doi:10.1002/jmv.25766 PMID:32170865

Heidegger, M. (1996). *Being and time: A translation of Sein und Zeit*. SUNY Press.

Herselman, M. E. (2003). ICT in Rural Areas in South Africa: Various Case Studies. *Proceedings of Informing Science*, 945-955. doi:10.28945/2680

Heyerdahl, A. (2022). Risk assessment without the risk? A controversy about security and risk in Norway. *Journal of Risk Research*, *25*(2), 252–267. doi:10.1080/13669877.2021.1936610

Hilbert, M. (2011). The end justifies the definition: The manifold outlooks on the digital divide and their practical usefulness for policymaking. *Telecommunications Policy*, *35*(8), 715–736. doi:10.1016/j.telpol.2011.06.012

Hillson, D. A. (1997). Towards a risk maturity model. *The International Journal of Project and Business Risk Management*, *1*(1), 35–45.

Hobbes, T. (2006). *Leviathan*. A&C Black.

Höffe, O. (Ed.). (2010). *Aristotle's "Nicomachean Ethics"*. Brill. doi:10.1163/ej.9789004177628.i-259

Holzmann, V. (2012). *Analyzing Lessons Learned to Identify Potential Risks in new Product Development Projects*. Paper presented at the 6th European Conference on Information Management and Evaluation, Cork, Ireland.

Homm, U., & Breitung, J. (2012). Testing for speculative bubbles in stock markets: A comparison of alternative methods. *Journal of Financial Econometrics*, *10*(1), 198–231. doi:10.1093/jjfinec/nbr009

Hopkinson, M. (2012). *The project risk maturity model: measuring and improving risk management capability*. Gower Publishing, Ltd.

Hossain, M. S., & Muhammad, G. (2018). Emotion-aware connected healthcare big data towards 5G. *IEEE Internet of Things Journal*, *5*(4), 2399–2406. doi:10.1109/JIOT.2017.2772959

Hosseini, S., Ivanov, D., & Dolgui, A. (2019). ReviewofQuantitativeMethods for Supply Chain ResilienceAnalysis. *Transportation Research Part E, Logistics and Transportation Review*, *125*, 285–307. doi:10.1016/j.tre.2019.03.001

Huang, R. H., Liu, D. J., Tlili, A., Yang, J. F., & Wang, H. H. (2020). *Handbook on Facilitating Flexible Learning During Educational Disruption: The Chinese Experience in Maintaining Undisrupted Learning in COVID-19 Outbreak*. Smart Learning Institute of Beijing Normal University.

Huang, Y.-C., Yang, M.-L., & Wong, Y.-J. (2016). Institutional pressures, resources commitment, and returns management. *Supply Chain Management*, *21*(3), 398–416. doi:10.1108/SCM-04-2015-0144

Hull, T. (2010, April). A deterministic scenario approach to risk management. In *2010 Enterprise Risk Management Symposium* (pp. 1-7). Academic Press.

Humayun, M., Niazi, M., Jhanjhi, N., Alshayeb, M., & Mahmood, S. (2020). Cyber Security Threats and Vulnerabilities: A Systematic Mapping Study. *Arabian Journal for Science and Engineering*, *45*(4), 3171–3189. doi:10.100713369-019-04319-2

Huynh, T. L. D., Ahmed, R., Nasir, M. A., Shahbaz, M., & Huynh, N. Q. A. (2021). The nexus between black and digital gold: Evidence from US markets. *Annals of Operations Research*, 1–26. doi:10.100710479-021-04192-z PMID:34316086

Hyperledger - Fabricdocs Master Documentation. (2020). *Introduction — Hyperledger-Fabricdocs Master Documentation.* https://hyperledger-fabric.readthedocs.io/en/release-1.4/blockchain.html

Hyperledger. (2020). *Hyperledger – Open Source Blockchain Technologies.* https://www.hyperledger.org/

IBEF. (2021). *MSME Industry in India.* https://www.ibef.org/industry/msme.aspx#login-box

IEA. (2015). Key world energy statistics. International Energy Association (IEA).

IESALC. (2020). *COVID-19 and higher education: Today and tomorrow. Impact analysis, policy responses and recommendation.* Author.

ILO. (2018). Ethiopia National Child Labour Survey. Ethiopia National Child Labour Survey 2015 / International Labour Office, Fundamental Principles and Rights at Work Branch (FUNDAMENTALS); Central Statistical Agency (CSA).

International Labor Organization (ILO). (2010a). Global employment trends. Geneva: International Labor Office.

International Labor Organization (ILO). (2010b). *Women in labor markets: measuring progress and identifying challenges*. International Labor Office.

Internet Society (2019). *Internet Society Global Internet Report: Consolidation in the internet economy*. Author.

Internet World Statistics. (2013). *Usage and Population Statistics*. Retrieved from https://www.internetworldstats.com/stats1.htm

Internet World Statistics. (2020b). *Internet Usage Statistics. World Internet Users and 2020 Population Stats*. Retrieved from https://www.internetworldstats.com/stats.htm

InternetWorld Statistics. (2020a). *Usage and Population Statistics*. Retrieved from https://www.internetworldstats.com/stats1.htm

Islam, M. S., Karim, S. A., Rahman, M. G., Gupta, S. D., & Masum, M. S. (2013). A case study of the notion and model of micro hydro power plant using the kinetic energy of flowing water of Burinadi and Meghna Rivers of Bangladesh. *Engineering Journal (New York)*, *17*(4), 47–60.

Issaoui, Y., Khiat, A., Bahnasse, A., & Ouajji, H. (2020). Smart Logistics: Blockchain trends and applications. *Journal of Ubiquitous Systems and Pervasive Networks.*, *12*(2), 9–15. doi:10.5383/JUSPN.12.02.002

Itani, H., Sidani, Y., & Baalbaki, I. (2011). United Arab Emirates female entrepreneurs: Motivations and frustrations. *Equality, Diversity and Inclusion*, *30*(5), 409–424. doi:10.1108/02610151111150654

Ivanov, S., & Webster, C. (2019). Economic Fundamentals of the Use of robots, artificial intelligence, and service Automation in travel, tourism, and hospitality. In *Robots, artificial intelligence, and service Automation in travel, tourism and hospitality.* Emerald Publishing Limited.

Ivanov, D. (2020a). Predicting the Impacts of Epidemic Outbreaks on Global Supply Chains: A Simulation-Based Analysis on theCoronavirusOutbreak (COVID-19/SARS-CoV-2) Case. *Transportation Research Part E, Logistics and Transportation Review*, *136*, 101922. doi:10.1016/j.tre.2020.101922 PMID:32288597

Ivanov, D. (2020b). Viable Supply Chain Model: Integrating Agility, Resilience and Sustainability Perspectives – Lessons from and Thinking Beyond the COVID-19 Pandemic. *Annals of Operations Research*. Advance online publication. doi:10.100710479-020-03640-6 PMID:32836614

Ivanov, D. (2021a). Supply Chain Viability and the COVID- 19 Pandemic: A Conceptual and Formal Generalisation of Four Major Adaptation Strategies. *International Journal of Production Research*, *59*(12), 3535–3552. doi:10.1080/00207543.2021.1890852

Ivanov, S. H., Webster, C., & Berezina, K. (2017). Adoption of robots and service automation by tourism and hospitality companies. *Revista Turismo & Desenvolvimento*, *27*(28), 1501–1517.

Ivanov, S., & Webster, C. (2019). Perceived appropriateness and intention to use service robots in tourism. In *Information and communication technologies in tourism 2019* (pp. 237–248). Springer. doi:10.1007/978-3-030-05940-8_19

Jafar, M. (2000). Renewable energy in the South Pacific - Options and constraints. *Renewable Energy*, *19*(1-2), 305–309. doi:10.1016/S0960-1481(99)00045-2

Jahmunah, V., Sudarshan, V. K., Oh, S. L., Gururajan, R., Gururajan, R., Zhou, X., Tao, X., Faust, O., Ciaccio, E. J., Ng, K. H., & Acharya, U. R. (2021). Future IoT tools for COVID -19 Contact Tracing and prediction: A review of the state-of-the-science. *International Journal of Imaging Systems and Technology*, *31*(2), 455–471. doi:10.1002/ima.22552 PMID:33821093

Jain, N., & Mukherji, S. (2010). The perception of the glass ceiling in Indian organizations: An exploratory study. *South Asian Journal of Management*, *17*(1), 23–42.

Jamali, D., Sidani, Y., & Safieddine, A. (2005). Constraints facing working women in Lebanon: An insider view. *Women in Management Review*, *20*(8), 581–594. doi:10.1108/09649420510635213

Jamil, M., Ahmad, F., & Jeon, Y. J. (2016). Renewable energy technologies adopted by the UAE: Prospects and challenges - A comprehensive overview. *Renewable & Sustainable Energy Reviews*, *55*, 1181–1194. doi:10.1016/j.rser.2015.05.087

Jen, R. (2009). *Visual Ishikawa Risk Techique (VIRT) - An Approach to Risk Management*. PMI Virtual Library.

Jeong, J., Mihelcic, J., Oliver, G., & Rudolph, C. (2019). Towards an improved understanding of human factors in cybersecurity. In *Proceedings - 2019 IEEE 5th International Conference on Collaboration and Internet Computing, CIC 2019* (pp. 338–345). 10.1109/CIC48465.2019.00047

Jha, A., Sharma, R. R. K., Kumar, V., & Verma, P. (2021). Designing supply chain performance system: a strategic study on Indian manufacturing sector. *Supply Chain Management: An International Journal*. . doi:10.1108/SCM-05-2020-0198

Jiang, Y., & Wen, J. (2020). Effects of COVID-19 on hotel marketing and management: A perspective article. *International Journal of Contemporary Hospitality Management*, *32*(8), 2563–2573. doi:10.1108/IJCHM-03-2020-0237

Jimanez, A., Capilla, J. A., Carrian, J. A., & Alameda-Hernandez, E. (2016). Optimal site selection for upper reservoirs in pump-back systems, using geographical information systems and multicriteria analysis. *Renewable Energy*, *86*(1), 429–440. doi:10.1016/j.renene.2015.08.035

Johnson, J. E., & Powell, P. L. (1994). Decision making, risk and gender: Are managers different? *British Journal of Management*, *5*(2), 123–138. doi:10.1111/j.1467-8551.1994.tb00073.x

Johnstone, D. (2018). Accounting Theory as a Bayesian Discipline. *Foundations and Trends in Accounting*, *13*(1-2), 1–266. doi:10.1561/1400000056

Joustra, S. B. (2010). *Towards the effective management of project risk in complex projects: A case study review*. Retrieved from www.sk.tbm.tudelft.nl

Judge, T. A., & Bretz, R. D. Jr. (1994). Political influence behavior and political success. *Journal of Management*, *20*(1), 43–65. doi:10.1177/014920639402000103

Judge, T. A., Cable, D. M., Boudreau, J. W., & Bretz, R. D. (1995). An empirical investigation of the predictors of executive career success. *Personnel Psychology*, *48*(3), 485–519. doi:10.1111/j.1744-6570.1995.tb01767.x

Kadiyala, A., Kommalapati, R., & Huque, Z. (2016). Evaluation of the life cycle greenhouse gas emissions from hydroelectricity generation systems. *Sustainability (Switzerland)*, *8*(6), 12–25. doi:10.3390u8060539

Kahan, D. M., Braman, D., Gastil, J., Slovic, P., & Mertz, C. K. (2007). Culture and identity-protective cognition: Explaining the white-male effect in risk perception. *Journal of Empirical Legal Studies*, *4*(3), 465–505. doi:10.1111/j.1740-1461.2007.00097.x

Kalla, A., Hewa, T., Mishra, R. A., Ylianttila, M., & Liyanage, M. (2020). The role of blockchain in to fight against COVID-19. *IEEE Engineering Management Review*, *48*(3), 85–96. doi:10.1109/EMR.2020.3014052

Kallakuri, C., Vaidyanathan, S., Kelly, M., & Cluett, R. (2016). *The 2016 International Energy Efficiency Scorecard* (E1602). Washington, DC: American Council for an Energy-Efficient Economy (ACEEE).

Kang, S. H., McIver, R. P., & Hernandez, J. A. (2019). Co-movements between Bitcoin and Gold: A wavelet coherence analysis. *Physica A*, *536*, 120888. doi:10.1016/j.physa.2019.04.124

Kaplan, B., & Litewka, S. (2008). Ethical challenges of telemedicine and Telehealth. *Cambridge Quarterly of Healthcare Ethics*, *17*(4), 401–416. doi:10.1017/S0963180108080535 PMID:18724880

Karyotakis, M. A., Antonopoulos, N., Veglis, A., & Kiourexidou, M. (2018). Tourist go home: Communication and Propaganda on YouTube. *Journal of Media Critiques*, *4*(14), 323–337.

Kawa, A., & Światowiec-Szczpańska, J. (2021). Logistics as a value in e-commerce and its influence on satisfaction in industries: a multilevel analysis. *Journal of Business & Industrial Marketing*. . doi:10.1108/JBIM-09-2020-0429

Kazem, H. A. (2011). Renewable energy in Oman: Status and future prospects. *Renewable & Sustainable Energy Reviews*, *15*(8), 3465–3469. doi:10.1016/j.rser.2011.05.015

Keppel, G., & Wickens, T. D. (2004). *Design and Analysis: A Researcher's Handbook* (4th ed.). Pearson Prentice-Hall.

Khan, O., & Burnes, B. (2007). Risk and supply chain management: Creating a research agenda. *International Journal of Logistics Management*, *18*(2), 197–216.

Khan, S. M., Pearson, D. D., Rönnqvist, T., Nielsen, M. E., Taron, J. M., & Goodarzi, A. A. (2021). Rising Canadian and falling Swedish radon gas exposure as a consequence of 20th to 21st century residential build practices. *Scientific Reports*, *11*(1), 1–15. doi:10.103841598-021-96928-x PMID:34475435

Kim, A. (2020, October 2). *The Atlanta Falcons will use 'disinfecting drones' to sanitize the team's stadium when it welcomes back fans this month*. CNN. Retrieved December 30, 2021, from https://edition.cnn.com/2020/10/01/tech/drone-stadium-sanitize-spt-trnd/index.html

Kim, N. (2004). Career success orientation of Korean women bank employees. [Research Note]. *Career Development International*, *9*(6), 595–608. doi:10.1108/13620430410559179

Kleinfeld, R. (2020). *Do Authoritarian or Democratic Countries Handle Pandemics Better?* Carnegie Endowment for International Peace. https://carnegieendowment.org/2020/03/31/do-authoritarian-or-democratic-countries-handle-pandemics-better-pub-81404

Kolade, O. J., & Kehinde, O. (2010). Glass ceiling and women career advancement: Evidence from the Nigerian construction industry. *Iranian Journal of Management Studies*, *6*(1), 71–99.

Koleva, E. G., & Mladenov, G. M. (2014). Renewable energy and energy efficiency in Bulgaria. *Progress in Industrial Ecology*, *8*(4), 257–278. doi:10.1504/PIE.2014.066798

Koohi-Kamali, S., Rahim, N. A., Mokhlis, H., Tyagi, V. V., & Panwar, N. L. (2013). Emergence of energy storage technologies as the solution for reliable operation of smart power systems: A review. *Renewable & Sustainable Energy Reviews*, *25*(1), 135–165. doi:10.1016/j.rser.2013.03.056

Korstanje M E (2015) *A Difficult World: Examining the roots of capitalism.* Nova Science.

Korstanje, M. E. (2019b). The Society 4.0, Internet, Tourism and the War on Terror. In Digital Labour, Society and the Politics of Sensibilities. Palgrave Macmillan.

Korstanje, M. E., & George, B. (2021). The Nature and Future of tourism: In a post COVID-19 context. Apple Academic Press.

Korstanje, M. E., Strang, K. D., & Tzanelli, R. (2019). Tourism security after climate change. In M. E. Korstanje (Ed.), *The Anthropology of Tourism Security*. https://eprints.whiterose.ac.uk/147935/

Korstanje, M. E. (2014). Why risk-research is more prominent in English speaking countries in the digital society. *International Journal of Cyber Warfare & Terrorism*, *4*(1), 8–18. doi:10.4018/ijcwt.2014010102

Korstanje, M. E. (2016). *The Rise of Thana Capitalism and Tourism*. Routledge. doi:10.4324/9781315457482

Korstanje, M. E. (2017). *Terrrorism, Tourism and the end of hospitality in the West*. Palgrave-Macmillan.

Korstanje, M. E. (2019a). *Terrorism, Technology and Apocalyptic Futures*. Springer. doi:10.1007/978-3-030-13385-6

Korstanje, M. E., & George, B. (2012). Global warming and tourism: Chronicles of apocalypse? *Worldwide Hospitality and Tourism Themes*, *4*(4), 332–355. doi:10.1108/17554211211255684

Korstanje, M. E., & George, B. (2021). *Mobility and Globalization in the Aftermath of COVID-19: Emerging New Geographies in a Locked World*. Palgrave MacMillan. doi:10.1007/978-3-030-78845-2

Korstanje, M. E., & George, B. P. (2020). Education as a Strategy to Tackle Over Tourism for Overtourism and Inclusive Sustainability in the Twenty-First Century. In *Overtourism* (pp. 341–359). Palgrave Macmillan. doi:10.1007/978-3-030-42458-9_18

Korstanje, M. E., & Olsen, D. H. (2011). The discourse of risk in horror movies post 9/11: Hospitality and hostility in perspective. *International Journal of Tourism Anthropology*, *1*(3), 304–317. doi:10.1504/IJTA.2011.043712

Korstanje, M. E., & Seraphin, H. (2018). Awakening: A critical discussion of the role of robots in the rite of hospitality. In M. Korstanje (Ed.), *Tourism and Hospitality: Perspectives, Opportunities and Challenges* (pp. 59–77). Nova Science Publishers.

Korstanje, M. E., & Tarlow, P. (2012). Being lost: Tourism, risk and vulnerability in the post-‘9/11’ entertainment industry. *Journal of Tourism and Cultural Change*, *10*(1), 22–33. doi:10.1080/14766825.2011.639455

KPMG. (2015). *The new Indian MSME: An action agenda for growth.* https://assets.kpmg/content/dam/kpmg/pdf/2016/03/The-new-wave-Indian-MSME.pdf

Krane, H. P., Olsson, N. O. E., & Rolstadås, A. (2012). How Project Manager-Project Owner Interaction Can Work Within and Influence Project Risk Management. *Project Management Journal*, *43*(2), 54–67. doi:10.1002/pmj.20284

Kruskal, W. H., & Wallis, W. A. (1952). Use of ranks in one-criterion variance analysis. *Journal of the American Statistical Association*, *47*(260), 583–621. doi:10.1080/01621459.1952.10483441

Kure, H. I., Islam, S., & Razzaque, M. A. (2018). An integrated cyber security risk management approach for a cyber-physical system. *Applied Sciences (Switzerland)*, *8*(6), 898. Advance online publication. doi:10.3390/app8060898

Kusakana, K. (2016). Optimal scheduling for distributed hybrid system with pumped hydro storage. *Energy Conversion and Management*, *111*(1), 253–260.

Labor Law U. A. E. Article 32. (2007). Available at https://www.moid.gov.ae/Laws/UAE_Labour_Law.pdf

Lambert, D. M., & Schwieterman, M. A. (2012). Supplier relationship management as a macro business process. *Supply Chain Management*, *17*(3), 337–352. doi:10.1108/13598541211227153

Lamberti, L. (2013). Customer centricity: The construct and the operational antecedents. *Journal of Strategic Marketing*, *21*(7), 588–612.

Lancet (2022). *Estimating excess mortality due to the COVID-19 pandemic: A systematic analysis of COVID-19-related mortality, 2020–21*. doi:10.1016/S0140-6736(21)02796-3

Lanza, F., Seidita, V., & Chella, A. (2020). Agents and robots for collaborating and supporting physicians in healthcare scenarios. *Journal of Biomedical Informatics*, *108*, 103483. doi:10.1016/j.jbi.2020.103483 PMID:32603793

Lareau, A. (1987). Social class differences in family-school relationships: The importance of cultural capital. *Sociology of Education*, *60*(2), 73–85. doi:10.2307/2112583

Lash, S., & Urry, J. (1994). *Economies of signs and space*. SAGE.

Lazear, E. P., & Rosen, S. (1990). Male-female wage differentials in job ladders. *Journal of Labor Economics*, *8*(1).

Lee, I. (2020). Internet of Things (IoT) cybersecurity: Literature review and iot cyber risk management. *Future Internet*, *12*(9), 157. Advance online publication. doi:10.3390/fi12090157

Lee, I. (2021). Cybersecurity: Risk management framework and investment cost analysis. *Business Horizons*, *64*(5), 659–671. doi:10.1016/j.bushor.2021.02.022

Leinonen, M. (2012). Challenging and reinforcing gender boundaries at work. *Equality, Diversity and Inclusion*, *31*(7), 633–645. doi:10.1108/02610151211263469

Leite, H., Gruber, T., & Hodgkinson, I. R. (2020). Flattening the infection curve – understanding the role of telehealth in managing covid-19. *Leadership in Health Services*, *33*(2), 221–226. doi:10.1108/LHS-05-2020-084

Leite, H., Hodgkinson, I. R., & Gruber, T. (2020). New development: 'healing at a distance'—telemedicine and COVID-19. *Public Money & Management*, *40*(6), 483–485. doi:10.1080/09540962.2020.1748855

Lerner, M., Brush, C., & Hisrich, R. (1997). Israeli women entrepreneurs: An examination of factors affecting performance. *Journal of Business Venturing*, *12*(4), 315–339. doi:10.1016/S0883-9026(96)00061-4

Leszczyna, R. (2021). Review of cybersecurity assessment methods: Applicability perspective. *Computers & Security*, *108*, 102376. Advance online publication. doi:10.1016/j.cose.2021.102376

Levenson, R. W., Ekman, P., & Friesen, W. W. (1990). Voluntary facial expression generates emotions-specific nervous system activity. *Psychophysiology*, *27*, 363–384. doi:10.1111/j.1469-8986.1990.tb02330.x PMID:2236440

Leveson, N. (2004). A new accident model for engineering safer systems. *Safety Science*, *42*(4), 237–270. doi:10.1016/S0925-7535(03)00047-X

Levine, D. M., Stephan, D., Krehbiel, T. C., & Berenson, M. L. (2005). *Statistics for Managers using Microsoft Excel* (4th ed.). Pearson Prentice-Hall.

Levy, B. (1993). Obstacles to Developing Indigenous Small and Medium Enterprises: An Empirical Assessment. *The World Bank Economic Review*, *7*(1), 65–83. doi:10.1093/wber/7.1.65

Li, Q., Yan, R., Zhang, L., & Yan, B. (2021). Empirical study on improving international dry port competitiveness based on logistics supply chain integration: evidence from China. *The International Journal of Logistics Management*.

Liang, F.-Y., Ryvak, M., Sayeed, S., & Zhao, N. (2012). The role of natural gas as a primary fuel in the near future, including comparisons of acquisition, transmission and waste handling costs of as with competitive alternatives. *Chemistry Central Journal*, *6*(1), 1–24. doi:10.1186/1752-153X-6-S1-S4 PMID:22540989

Lickorish, L. J., & Jenkins, C. L. (2007). *Introduction to tourism*. Routledge.

Ligthelm, A. A., & Cant, M. C. (2002). *Business success factors of SMEs in Gauteng: A proactive entrepreneurial approach*. Bureau of Market Research, University of South Africa.

Li, L., Qin, L., Xu, Z., Yin, Y., Wang, X., Kong, B., Bai, J., Lu, Y., Fang, Z., Song, Q., Cao, K., Liu, D., Wang, G., Xu, Q., Fang, X., Zhang, S., Xia, J., & Xia, J. (2020). Using artificial intelligence to detect COVID-19 and community-acquired pneumonia based on pulmonary CT: Evaluation of the diagnostic accuracy. *Radiology*, *296*(2), E65–E71. Advance online publication. doi:10.1148/radiol.2020200905 PMID:32191588

Lipton, M., Neff, D. A., Brownstein, A. R., Rosenblum, S. A., Savarese, J. F., Emmerich, A. O., … Lu, C. X. W. (2020). *Risk Management and the Board of Directors* (Vol. 47). Academic Press.

Litheko, S. R. S. (2012). The difference in performance between schools situated in the urban areas and those in the rural areas of Lesotho. *Electronic Journal for Inclusive Education*, *2*(9), 2.

Litwin, M. (1995). *How to Measure Survey Reliability and Validity*. Sage Publications. doi:10.4135/9781483348957

Liu, C. H., Rosenthal, S. S., & Strange, W. C. (2018). The vertical city: Rent gradients, spatial structure, and agglomeration economies. *Journal of Urban Economics*, *106*(2), 101–122. doi:10.1016/j.jue.2018.04.001

lo Storto, C., & Capano, B. (2014). Productivity changes of the renewable energy installed capacity: An empirical study relating to 31 European countries between 2002 and 2011. *Energy Education Science and Technology, Part A. Energy Science and Research*, *32*(5), 3061–3072.

Lohmann, H., & Ferger, F. (2014). *Educational Poverty in a Comparative Perspective: Theoretical and Empirical Implications*. SFB882 Working Paper Series, No. 26.

Looney, R. (2005). The economics of coping: The plight of women in Iraq's informal economy. *The Journal of Social, Political, and Economic Studies*, *30*(3), 285–304.

Lucey, B. M., & O'Connor, F. A. (2013). Do bubbles occur in the gold price? An investigation of gold lease rates and Markov Switching models. *Borsa Istanbul Review*, *13*(3), 53–63. doi:10.1016/j.bir.2013.10.008

Luhmann, N. (1993). *Communication and social order: risk: a sociological theory*. Transaction Publishers.

MacDonald, P., Brown, K., & Bradley, L. (2005). Have traditional career paths given way to protean ones? Evidence from senior managers in the Australian public sector. *Career Development International*, *10*(2), 109–129. doi:10.1108/13620430510588310

Ma, D., Ahimaz, P. R., Mirocha, J. M., Cook, L., Giordano, J. L., Mohan, P., & Cohen, S. A. (2021). Clinical genetic counsellor experience in the adoption of telehealth in the United States and Canada during the Covid-19 pandemic. *Journal of Genetic Counseling*, *30*(5), 1214–1223. doi:10.1002/jgc4.1516 PMID:34757671

Maier, A. M., Moultrie, J., & Clarkson, P. J. (2012). Assessing organizational capabilities: Reviewing and guiding the development of maturity grids. *Engineering Management. IEEE Transactions on*, *59*(1), 138–159.

Mainiero, L. A., & Sullivan, S. E. (2005). Kaleidoscope careers: An alternate explanation for the 'opt-out' revolution. *The Academy of Management Executive*, *19*(1), 106–123. doi:10.5465/ame.2005.15841962

Majdara, A., & Nematollahi, M. R. (2008). Development and application of a Risk Assessment Tool. *Reliability Engineering & System Safety*, *93*(8), 1130–1137. doi:10.1016/j.ress.2007.09.007

Malik, Y. S., Sircar, S., Bhat, S., Ansari, M. I., Pande, T., Kumar, P., Mathapati, B., Balasubramanian, G., Kaushik, R., Natesan, S., Ezzikouri, S., Zowalaty, M. E., & Dhama, K. (2020). How artificial intelligence may help the Covid-19 pandemic: Pitfalls and lessons for the future. *Reviews in Medical Virology*, *31*(5), 1–11. doi:10.1002/rmv.2205 PMID:33476063

Mallapaty, S. (2021). Laos Bats Host Closest Known Relatives of Virus Behind Covid. *Nature*, *24*(September). https://www.nature.com/articles/d41586-021-02596-2

Man, T.-J. (2007). *A framework for the comparison of Maturity Models for Project-based Management* [Unpublished MBA thesis]. Utrecht University.

Manakatt, B. M., Carson, Z. W., Penton, R. L., & Demello, A. S. (2021). Virtual learning experiences in population health nursing course during the COVID-19 pandemic. *International Nursing Review*, *68*(4), 557–562. doi:10.1111/inr.12725 PMID:34697806

Mantecón, A., & Velasco, M. (2020). Beyond Tourismphobia: Conceptualizing a New Framework to Analyze Attitudes Towards Tourism. In *Handbook of Research on the Impacts, Challenges, and Policy Responses to Overtourism* (pp. 60–74). IGI Global. doi:10.4018/978-1-7998-2224-0.ch004

Margeta, J., & Glasnovic, Z. (2010). Feasibility of the green energy production by hybrid solar + hydro power system in Europe and similar climate areas. *Renewable & Sustainable Energy Reviews*, *14*(6), 1580–1590. doi:10.1016/j.rser.2010.01.019

Margeta, J., & Glasnovic, Z. (2011). Exploitation of temporary water flow by hybrid PV-hydroelectric plant. *Renewable Energy*, *36*(8), 2268–2277. doi:10.1016/j.renene.2011.01.001

Marhavilas, P. K., Koulouriotis, D., & Gemeni, V. (2011). Risk analysis and assessment methodologies in the work sites: On a review, classification and comparative study of the scientific literature of the period 2000–2009. *Journal of Loss Prevention in the Process Industries*, *24*(5), 477–523. doi:10.1016/j.jlp.2011.03.004

Maria, D. B. (2020). *Maria DB 2020*. https://mariadb.org/documentation/

Maroufkhani, P., Ismail, W. K. W., & Ghobakhloo, M. (2020). Big data analytics adoption model for small and medium enterprises. *Journal of Science and Technology Policy Management.*, *11*(4), 483–513. doi:10.1108/JSTPM-02-2020-0018

Marshall, C., & Rossman, G. B. (2014). *Designing qualitative research*. Sage publications.

Marshall, J. M., Dunstan, D. A., & Bartik, W. (2020). The role of digital mental health resources to treat trauma symptoms in Australia during COVID-19. *Psychological Trauma: Theory, Research, Practice, and Policy*, *12*(S1), S269–S271. Advance online publication. doi:10.1037/tra0000627 PMID:32496103

Martínez Lamas, M., Quintas Ferrín, A., & Pardo Froján, J. (2012). *Project Risk Management in Automotive Industry. A Case Study.* Paper presented at the 6th International Conference on Industrial Engineering and Industrial Management.

Ma, T., Yang, H., & Lu, L. (2014). Feasibility study and economic analysis of pumped hydro storage and battery storage for a renewable energy powered island. *Energy Conversion and Management*, *79*(1), 387–397. doi:10.1016/j.enconman.2013.12.047

Maume, D. J. Jr. (1999). Glass ceilings and glass escalators: Occupational segregation and race and sex differences in managerial promotions. *Work and Occupations*, *26*(4), 483–509. doi:10.1177/0730888499026004005

Mazey, S., & Richardson, J. (2020). Lesson-Drawing from New Zealand and Covid-19: The Need for Anticipatory Policy Making. *The Political Quarterly*, *91*(3), 561–570. doi:10.1111/1467-923X.12893 PMID:32836413

McClure, D. (2007). *From the CIO trenches: Why some projects fail and others succeed.* Gartner Industry Research.

McConnell, A., & Stark, A. (2021). Understanding Policy Responses to COVID-19: The Stars Haven't Fallen from the Sky for Scholars of Public Policy. *Journal of European Public Policy*, *28*(8), 1115–1130. Advance online publication. doi:10.1080/13501763.2021.1942518

McConnell, D., Forcey, T., & Sandiford, M. (2015). Estimating the value of electricity storage in an energy-only wholesale market. *Applied Energy*, *159*(1), 422–432. doi:10.1016/j.apenergy.2015.09.006

McCracken, J. D., & Barcinas, J. D. T. (1991). Differences between rural and urban schools, student characteristics, and student aspirations in Ohio. *Journal of Research in Rural Education*, *7*(2), 29–40.

McDonald, N. (2006). *Think Paper 5: Is Citizen-centric the same as Customer-centric.* Ccegov Project. http://www. ccegov. eu/thinkpapers. asp

McLuhan, E., & Zingrone, F. (1997). *Essential McLuhan.* Routledge. doi:10.4324/9780203992968

McMeekin, A. (1998). *Flexible Learning and Teaching and IT.* Keynote address to the 1998 Monash University Flexible Learning and Technology Conference.

McNabola, A., Coughlan, P., & Williams, A. P. (2014). Energy recovery in the water industry: An assessment of the potential of micro-hydropower. *Water and Environment Journal: the Journal / the Chartered Institution of Water and Environmental Management*, *28*(2), 294–304. doi:10.1111/wej.12046

Mendelssohn, I. A., Andersen, A. L., Baltz, D. M., Caffey, R. H., Carman, K. R., Fleeger, J. W., Joye, S. B., Lin, Q., Maltby, E., Overton, E. B., & Rozas, L. R. (2010). Oil impacts on coastal wetlands: Implications for the Mississippi River Delta Ecosystem after the Deepwater HorizonOil Spill. *Bioscience*, *62*(6), 562–574. doi:10.1525/bio.2012.62.6.7

Mensah, J., & Tucker-Simmons, D. (2021). Social (in)justice and rental housing discrimination in urban Canada: The case of ethno-racial minorities in the Herongate community in Ottawa. *Studies in Social Justice*, *15*(1), 81–101. doi:10.26522sj.v15i1.2239

Messina, D., Barros, A. C., Soares, A. L., & Matopoulos, A. (2020). An information management approach for supply chain disruption recovery. *International Journal of Logistics Management*, *31*(3), 489–519. doi:10.1108/IJLM-11-2018-0294

Metcalfe, B. D., & Rees, C. J. (2010). Gender, globalization and organization: Exploring power, relations, and intersections. *Equality, Diversity and Inclusion*, *29*(1), 5–22. doi:10.1108/02610151011019183

Miles, R. (2002). Employment and unemployment in Jordan: The importance of the gender system. *World Development*, *30*(3), 413–427. doi:10.1016/S0305-750X(01)00123-1

Ministry of Education of the People's Republic of China. (2020). *Notice on Several Issues concerning Targeted Teacher Work during the Pandemic Prevention and Control*. Retrieved from http://www.moe.gov.cn

Mira, J. J., Vicente, M. A., Lopez-Pineda, A., Carrillo, I., Guilabert, M., Fernández, C., Pérez-Jover, V., Martin Delgado, J., Pérez-Pérez, P., Cobos Vargas, A., Astier-Peña, M. P., Martínez-García, O. B., Marco-Gómez, B., & Abad Bouzán, C. (2020). Preventing and addressing the stress reactions of health care workers caring for patients with covid-19: Development of a digital platform (BE + against COVID). *JMIR mHealth and uHealth*, *8*(10), e21692. Advance online publication. doi:10.2196/21692 PMID:32936769

Mishra, A. K. (2010). Alternate Sources of Energy Gadgets for the Sikkim State of NE Region. *Agricultural Engineering Today VO*, *34*(4), 29.

Mitcham, C., & Mackey, R. (1971). Jacques Ellul and the technological society. *Philosophy Today*, *15*(2), 102–121. doi:10.5840/philtoday197115218

Mitchell, V. W. (1998). Buy-phase and buy-class effects on organisational risk perception and reduction in purchasing professional services. *Journal of Business and Industrial Marketing*, *13*(6), 461–478. doi:10.1108/08858629810246779

Moncef, B., & Monnet Dupuy, M. (2021). Last-mile logistics in the sharing economy: Sustainability paradoxes. *International Journal of Physical Distribution & Logistics Management*, *51*(5), 508–527. doi:10.1108/IJPDLM-10-2019-0328

Morgan, M. G. (2002). *Risk communication: A mental models approach*. Cambridge University Press.

Mukherjee, S. (2018). Challenges to Indian micro, small scale and medium enterprises in the era of globalization. *Journal of Global Entrepreneurship Research*, *8*(28), 28. Advance online publication. doi:10.118640497-018-0115-5

Murphy, J., Gretzel, U., & Hofacker, C. (2017, May). Service robots in hospitality and tourism: investigating anthropomorphism. In *15th APacCHRIE conference* (Vol. 31). Academic Press.

Murphy, J., Hofacker, C., & Gretzel, U. (2017). Dawning of the age of robots in hospitality and tourism: Challenges for teaching and research. *European Journal of Tourism Research*, *15*, 104–111. doi:10.54055/ejtr.v15i.265

Nabi, G. (2001). The relationship between HRM, social support and subjective career success among men and women. *International Journal of Manpower*, *22*(5), 457–474. doi:10.1108/EUM0000000005850

Nabi, G. (2003). Situational characteristics and subjective career success: The mediating role of career-enhancing strategies. *International Journal of Manpower*, *24*(6), 653–671. doi:10.1108/01437720310496148

Nag, B., Han, C., & Yao, D. (2014). Mapping supply chain strategy: An industry analysis. *Journal of Manufacturing Technology Management*, *25*(3), 351–370. doi:10.1108/JMTM-06-2012-0062

Nagpal, Saini, & Gupta. (2009). *Problems faced by Small and Medium enterprises: SME in transitional economics-challenges and opportunities*. Deep and Deep Publications.

Namey, E., Guest, G., Thairu, L., & Johnson, L. (2008). Data reduction techniques for large qualitative data sets. *Handbook for Team-Based Qualitative Research, 2*, 137-161.

Napasri, T., & Yukongdi, V. (2015). A study of Thai female executives: Perceived barriers to career advancement. *Review of Integrative Business and Economics Research*, *4*(3), 108.

Narayanan, A., Bonneau, J., Felten, E., Miller, A., & Goldfeder, S. (2016). *Bitcoin and cryptocurrency technologies: a comprehensive introduction*. Princeton University Press.

Nelson, J. K. (2009). *Impact of Parent Education on Student Success*. Online Submission.

Nersesian, R., & Strang, K. D. (2013). Risk planning with discrete distribution analysis applied to petroleum spills. *International Journal of Risk and Contingency Management*, *2*(4), 61–78. doi:10.4018/ijrcm.2013100105

Nersesian, R., & Strang, K. D. (2017). Feasibility approaches to reduce the unreliability of gas, nuclear, coal, solar and wind electricity production. *International Journal of Risk and Contingency Management*, *6*(1), 54–69. doi:10.4018/IJRCM.2017010104

Niebecker, K. (2009). *Collaborative and cross-company project management within the automotive industry using the Balanced Scorecard* [PhD thesis]. University of Technology, Sydney.

Nifakos, S., Chandramouli, K., Nikolaou, C. K., Papachristou, P., Koch, S., Panaousis, E., & Bonacina, S. (2021). Influence of human factors on cyber security within healthcare organisations: A systematic review. *Sensors (Basel)*, *21*(15), 1–25. doi:10.339021155119 PMID:34372354

Nikolić, B., & Ružić-Dimitrijević, L. (2009). Risk Assessment of Information Technology Systems. *Issues in Informing Science & Information Technology, 6.*

Nishii, L. H., & Ozbilgin, M. F. (2007). Global diversity management: Towards a conceptual framework. *International Journal of Human Resource Management*, *18*(11), 1883–1894. doi:10.1080/09585190701638077

Nizamuddin, N., & Abugabah, A. (2021). Blockchain for automotive: An insight towards the IPFS blockchain-based auto insurance sector. *Iranian Journal of Electrical and Computer Engineering*, *11*(3), 2443–2456. doi:10.11591/ijece.v11i3.pp2443-2456

O'Gorman, K. D. (2007). The hospitality phenomenon: Philosophical enlightenment? *International Journal of Culture, Tourism and Hospitality Research*, *1*(3), 189–202.

O'Neil, D., Hopkins, M., & Bilimoria, D. (2008). Women careers at the start of the 21st century: Patterns and paradoxes. *Journal of Business Ethics*, *80*(4), 727–743. doi:10.100710551-007-9465-6

Obeid, J. S., Davis, M., Turner, M., Meystre, S. M., Heider, P. M., O'Bryan, E. C., & Lenert, L. A. (2020). An artificial intelligence approach to COVID-19 infection risk assessment in virtual visits: A case report. *Journal of the American Medical Informatics Association: JAMIA*, *27*(8), 1321–1325. doi:10.1093/jamia/ocaa105 PMID:32449766

OECD. (2013). *Skills development and training in SMEs, OECD Skill Studies*. OECD Publishing. doi:10.1787/9789264169425-

OECD. (2021). *Enterprise Risk Management Maturity Model Maturity Model.* OECD Tax Administration Maturity Model Series, OECD. Retrieved March 6, 2022, from www.oecd.org/tax/forum-on-tax-administration/publications-and-products/enterprise-risk-managementmaturity-model.htm

Ogbuokiri, B. O., Udanor, C. N., & Agu, M. N. (2015). Implementing big data analytics for small and medium enterprise (SME) regional growth. *IOSR Journal of Computer Engineering*, *17*(6), 35–43.

Oke, A., & Gopalakrishnan, M. (2009). Managing disruptions in supply chains: A case study of a retail supply chain. *International Journal of Production Economics*, *118*(1), 168–174. doi:10.1016/j.ijpe.2008.08.045

Okorie, D. I., & Lin, B. (2020). Crude oil price and cryptocurrencies: Evidence of volatility connectedness and hedging strategy. *Energy Economics*, *87*, 104703. doi:10.1016/j.eneco.2020.104703

Oksiloff, A. (2016). *Picturing the primitive: Visual culture, ethnography, and early German cinema*. Springer.

Olakunle, O., & Win, T. (2022). Cybersecurity and Data Privacy in the Digital Age: Two Case Studies. In M. Wynn (Ed.), Handbook of Research on Digital Transformation, Industry Use Cases, and the Impact of Disruptive Technologies (pp. 117-131). IGI-Global.

Olsen, J., Paasch, K., Lassen, B., & Veje, C. T. (2015). A new principle for underground pumped hydroelectric storage. *Journal of Energy Storage*, *2*(1), 54–63. doi:10.1016/j.est.2015.06.003

Olsen, M. D., & Roper, A. (1998). Research in strategic management in the hospitality industry. *International Journal of Hospitality Management*, *17*(2), 111–124.

Olsson, R. (2006). *Managing project uncertainty by using an enhanced risk management process* [Unpublished PhD thesis]. University of Västerås, Mälardalen.

Omair, K. (2008). Women in management in the Arab context. *Education, Business and Society*, *1*(2), 107–123. doi:10.1108/17537980810890293

Omair, K. (2010). Typology of career development for Arab women managers in the United Arab Emirates. *Career Development International*, *15*(2), 121–143. doi:10.1108/13620431011040932

Opresnik, D., & Taisch, M. (2015). The value of big data in servitization. *International Journal of Production Economics*, *165*(1), 174–184. doi:10.1016/j.ijpe.2014.12.036

Orr, S., & Jadhav, A. (2018). Creating a sustainable supply chain: The strategic foundation. *The Journal of Business Strategy*, *39*(6), 29–35. doi:10.1108/JBS-11-2017-0157

Osborn, D., Cutter, A., & Ullah, F. (2015). *Universal sustainable development goals: understanding the transformational challenge for developed countries*. Report of a Study by Stakeholder Forum.

Oseni, M. O. (2012). Improving households' access to electricity and energy consumption pattern in Nigeria: Renewable energy alternative. *Renewable & Sustainable Energy Reviews*, *16*(6), 3967–3974. doi:10.1016/j.rser.2012.03.010

Owoyemi, A., Ikpe, R., Toye, M., Rewane, A., Abdullateef, M., Obaseki, E., Mustafa, S., & Adeosun, W. (2021). Mobile Health Approaches to disease surveillance in Africa; Wellvis Covid Triage Tool. *Digital Health*, *7*, 205520762199687. doi:10.1177/2055207621996876 PMID:33680485

Ozgur, C., & Strasser, S. E. (2004). A Study of the Statistical Inference Criteria: Can We Agree on When to use Z Versus t? *Decision Sciences Journal of Innovative Education*, *2*(2), 177–192. doi:10.1111/j.1540-4609.2004.00043.x

Ozgur, O., Yilanci, V., & Ozbugday, F. C. (2021). Detecting speculative bubbles in metal prices: Evidence from GSADF test and machine learning approaches. *Resources Policy*, *74*, 102306. doi:10.1016/j.resourpol.2021.102306

Paciarotti, C., Piotrowicz, W. D., & Fenton, G. (2021). Humanitarian logistics and supply chain standards. Literature review and view from practice. *Journal of Humanitarian Logistics and Supply Chain Management*, *11*(3), 550–573. doi:10.1108/JHLSCM-11-2020-0101

Pagden, A. (1995). *Lords of all the World: Ideologies of Empire in Spain, Britain and France c. 1500-c. 1800*. Yale University Press.

Palang, D., & Tippayawong, K. Y. (2019). Performance evaluation of tourism supply chain management: The case of Thailand. *Business Process Management Journal*, *25*(6), 1193–1207. doi:10.1108/BPMJ-05-2017-0124

Pandey, S., Singh, R. K., Gunasekaran, A., & Kaushik, A. (2020). Cyber security risks in globalized supply chains: Conceptual framework. *Journal of Global Operations and Strategic Sourcing*, *13*(1), 103–128. doi:10.1108/JGOSS-05-2019-0042

Park, C., Shi, W., Zhang, W., Kontovas, C., & Chang, C. H. (2019). Cybersecurity in the maritime industry: A literature review. In *20th Commemorative Annual General Assembly, AGA 2019 - Proceedings of the International Association of Maritime Universities Conference, IAMUC 2019* (pp. 79–86). Academic Press.

Park, J.-H., Kim, C.-G., & Lee, Y.-H. (2016). Efficient energy storage method by multistage pump of the energy storage system using CFD. *International Journal of Energy Research*, *40*(5), 685–691. doi:10.1002/er.3432

Park, S. (2020). Multifaceted trust in tourism service robots. *Annals of Tourism Research*, *81*, 102888.

Patro, C. S., & Raghunath, K. M. K. (2015). Impetus to supply chain decisions with IT tools: An empirical study. *International Journal of Enterprise Information Systems*, *11*(3), 52–67. doi:10.4018/IJEIS.2015070104

Patterson, F. D. (2002). *Project risk management and its application into the automotive manufacturing industry* [PhD Thesis]. University of Warwick. Retrieved from http://search.ebscohost.com/login.aspx?direct=true&AuthType=ip,shib&db=edsble&AN=ethos.007151837&site=eds-live&scope=site&custid=s1123095

Patterson, F. D., & Neailey, K. (2002). A Risk Register Database System to aid the management of project risk. *International Journal of Project Management*, *20*(5), 365.

Paula, I. C., Campos, E. A. R., Pagani, R. N., Guarnieri, P., & Kaviani, M. A. (2020). Are collaboration and trust sources for innovation in the reverse logistics? Insights from a systematic literature review. *Supply Chain Management*, *25*(2), 176–222. doi:10.1108/SCM-03-2018-0129

Pedraza, J. M. (2012). The Current and Future Role of Renewable Energy Sources for the Production of Electricity in Latin America and the Caribbean. *International Journal of Energy and Environmental Engineering*, *20*(5), 415–477.

Peek, N., Sujan, M., & Scott, P. (2020). Digital Health and care in pandemic times: Impact of covid-19. *BMJ Health & Care Informatics*, *27*(1), e100166. Advance online publication. doi:10.1136/bmjhci-2020-100166 PMID:32565418

Peinado, J., Graeml, A. R., & Vianna, F. (2018). Operations management body of knowledge and its relevance to manufacturing and service organizations. *Revista de Gestão*, *25*(4), 373–389. doi:10.1108/REGE-03-2018-0049

Pelican Bay Post. (2011). *Marilyn Loden on feminine leadership.* Available at http://www.ecatalognow.com/article/Marilyn+Loden+On+Feminine+Leadership/766271/73810/article.html

Pendakur, K., & Pendakur, R. (2005). *Glass ceilings for ethnic minorities*. Vancouver Centre of Excellence. https://pdfs.semanticscholar.org/c144/0b7801d0928de18568f5462a26cbef15687f.pdf

Perifanis, T. (2019). Detecting west Texas intermediate (WTI) prices' bubble periods. *Energies*, *12*(14), 2649. doi:10.3390/en12142649

Permanasari, R. (2013). Understanding of Women in Indonesia: Motivation to lead, work-family conflict, and ambition. *International Journal of Human Resource Studies*, *3*(3), 24–38. doi:10.5296/ijhrs.v3i3.4220

Phillips, P. C., & Shi, S. (2020). Real time monitoring of asset markets: Bubbles and crises. In Handbook of Statistics 42 (pp. 61–80). Elsevier Science.

Phillips, S., Dalziel, K., & Sjogren, K. (2021). Donor advised funds in Canada, Australia and the US: Differing regulatory regimes, differing streams of policy drift. *Nonprofit Policy Forum, 12*(3), 409-441. 10.1515/npf-2020-0061

Phillips, P. C., & Perron, P. (1988). Testing for a unit root in time series regression. *Biometrika*, *75*(2), 335–346. doi:10.1093/biomet/75.2.335

Phillips, P. C., Shi, S., & Yu, J. (2015). Testing for multiple bubbles: Historical episodes of exuberance and collapse in the SP500. *International Economic Review*, *56*(4), 1043–1078. doi:10.1111/iere.12132

Phillips, P. C., Wu, Y., & Yu, J. (2011). Explosive behavior in the 1990s NASDAQ: When did exuberance escalate asset values? *International Economic Review*, *52*(1), 201–226. doi:10.1111/j.1468-2354.2010.00625.x

Phoenix, C., Osborne, N. J., Redshaw, C., Moran, R., Stahl-timmins, W., Depledge, M. H., . . . Wheeler, B. W. (2013). *Paradigmatic approaches to studying environment and human health: (Forgotten) implications for interdisciplinary research*. Retrieved from OAIster database.

Pillai, K. R., Prasad, S., & Thomas, J. (2011). Why do women still experience downward gravitation in the corporate ladder? A close look at the glass ceiling in Bahrain. *Research and Practice in Human Resource Management*, *19*(1), 1–10.

Pimenta, F. M., & Assireu, A. T. (2015). Simulating reservoir storage for a wind-hydro hydrid system. *Renewable Energy*, *76*(1), 757–767. doi:10.1016/j.renene.2014.11.047

Platteau, J. P., & Verardi, V. (2020). How to Exit COVID-19 Lockdowns: Culture Matters. CEPR.

Powell, G. N., & Mainiero, L. M. (1992). Cross-currents in the river of time: Conceptualizing the complexities of women's careers. *Journal of Management*, *18*(2), 215–237. doi:10.1177/014920639201800202

Pranggono, B., & Arabo, A. (2021). COVID -19 pandemic cybersecurity issues. *Internet Technology Letters*, *4*(2), 4–9. doi:10.1002/itl2.247

Prasada, K. D. V., Vaidyab, R. W., & Mangipudi, M. R. (2020). Effect of occupational stress and remote working on the psychological well-being of employees: An empirical analysis during Covid-19 pandemic concerning information technology industry in Hyderabad. *Indian Journal of Commerce & Management Studies.*, *11*(2), 1–13. doi:10.18843/ijcms/v11i2/01

Priyadarshini, I. (2018). Cyber security risks in robotics. In *Cyber Security and Threats* (pp. 1235–1250). Concepts, Methodologies, Tools, and Applications. doi:10.4018/978-1-5225-5634-3.ch061

Project Management.com. (2019). *Ineffective Risk Management – That's Risky!* White paper. PMI/Deltek. Retrieved January 19, 2022, from https://img.en25.com/Web/DeltekInc/%7Bb6abeb66-b499-4ee4-ae8d-022336a3b88e%7D_Ineffective_Risk_Management_%E2%80%93_That's_Risky_.pdf?elqTrackId=91ad96e2cb854183987f4c254d285ab0&elqaid=11820&elqat=2

Purvins, A., Papaioannou, I. T., Tzimas, E., & Oleinikova, I. (2012). Effects of variable renewable power on a country-scale electricity system: High penetration of hydro power plants and wind farms in electricity generation. *Energy*, *43*(1), 225–236. doi:10.1016/j.energy.2012.04.038

PwC. (2021). *Enterprise Risk Management*. Pricewaterhouse Coopers LLP. Retrieved March 6, 2022, from https://www.pwc.co.uk/audit-assurance/assets/pdf/enterprise-risk-management.pdf

Queralta, J. P., & Westerlund, T. (2019). *Blockchain-Powered Collaboration in Heterogeneous Swarms of Robots*. Cryptography and Security.

Rafele, C. (2004). Logistic service measurement: A reference framework. *Journal of Manufacturing Technology Management*, *15*(3), 280–290. doi:10.1108/17410380410523506

Raghunath, K. M. K., & Devi, S. L. T. (2018). Supply Chain Risk Management: An Invigorating Outlook. *International Journal of Information Systems and Supply Chain Management*, *11*(3), 87–104. doi:10.4018/IJISSCM.2018070105

Raghunath, K. M. K., Devi, S. L. T., & Patro, C. S. (2017). An Empirical Take on Qualitative and Quantitative Risk Factors. *International Journal of Risk and Contingency Management*, *6*(4), 1–15. doi:10.4018/IJRCM.2017100101

Raghunath, K. M. K., & Devi, S. T. (2018). Effectiveness of Risk Assessment Models in Business Decisions: Reinforcing Knowledge. *International Journal of Sociotechnology and Knowledge Development*, *10*(2), 35–53. doi:10.4018/IJSKD.2018040103

Raluy, R. G., Serra, L., & Uche, J. (2005). Life cycle assessment of desalination technologies integrated with renewable energies. *Desalination*, *183*(1-3), 81–93. doi:10.1016/j.desal.2005.04.023

Randeree, K., & Gaad, E. (2008). Views on the 'knowledge economy project' of the Arabian Gulf: A gender perspective from the UAE in education and management. *The International Journal of Diversity in Organisations, Communities and Nations*, *8*(2), 69–77. doi:10.18848/1447-9532/CGP/v08i02/39546

Rao, S. S., Loeb, A. E., Amin, R. M., Golladay, G. J., Levin, A. S., & Thakkar, S. C. (2020). Establishing telemedicine in an academic total joint arthroplasty practice: Needs and opportunities highlighted by the COVID-19 pandemic. *Arthroplasty Today*, *6*(3), 617–622. doi:10.1016/j.artd.2020.04.014 PMID:32328510

Raz, T., & Michael, E. (2001). Use and benefits of tools for project risk management. *International Journal of Project Management*, *19*(1), 9–17. doi:10.1016/S0263-7863(99)00036-8

Read, C. (2013). Key risk and uncertainty theories impacting contemporary financial economics. *International Journal of Risk and Contingency Management*, *1*(4), 22–41.

Rea-Guaman, A. M., San Feliu, T., Calvo-Manzano, J. A., & Sanchez-Garcia, I. D. (2018). Systematic review: Cybersecurity risk taxonomy. *Advances in Intelligent Systems and Computing*, *688*, 137–146. doi:10.1007/978-3-319-69341-5_13

Reeves, J. J., Pageler, N. M., Wick, E. C., Melton, G. B., Tan, Y.-H. G., Clay, B. J., & Longhurst, C. A. (2021, August). The clinical information systems response to the COVID-19 pandemic. *Yearbook of medical informatics*. Retrieved December 29, 2021, from https://www.ncbi.nlm.nih.gov/pmc/articles/PMC8416224/

Renn, O. (2017). *Risk governance: coping with uncertainty in a complex world.* Routledge. doi:10.4324/9781849772440

Rhode, D. L., & Kellerman, B. (2007). Women and leadership: the state of play. In B. Kellerman & D. L. Rhode (Eds.), *Women and Leadership: The State of Play and Strategies for Change* (pp. 1–62). John Wiley & Sons.

Ries, T. (Ed.). (2020). *2020 Edelman Trust Barometer Global Report.* https://www.edelman.com/trust/2020-trust-barometer

Ries, T. (Ed.). (2022). *2022 Edelman Trust Barometer Global Report.* https://www.edelman.com/trust/2020-trust-barometer

Rios Insua, D., Couce-Vieira, A., Rubio, J. A., Pieters, W., Labunets, K., & Rasines, G., D. (. (2021). An Adversarial Risk Analysis Framework for Cybersecurity. *Risk Analysis*, *41*(1), 16–36. doi:10.1111/risa.13331 PMID:31183890

Ritzer, G. (2019). Inhospitable hospitality. In Experiencing hospitality. Nova Science.

Rizwan, M., Ur-Rehman, A., Shabbir, S. W., & Warriach, I. A. (2014). Explorative study of parents' education effect on the socialization of their children (A case of district Muzaffargarh*). Research on Humanities and Social Sciences*, *4*(26), 81–86.

Rosenbaum, J. L. (1979). Tournament mobility: Career patterns in a corporation. *Administrative Science Quarterly*, *24*(2), 221–241. doi:10.2307/2392495

Rübesam, T. (2015). *Drug funding decision-making in hospital formulary committees in Germany* [Unpublished DBA thesis]. University of Gloucestershire.

Rubin, H. J., & Rubin, I. S. (2011). Qualitative interviewing: The art of hearing data. *Sage (Atlanta, Ga.).*

Ryan, M. K., Haslam, S. A., Hersby, M. D., & Bongiorno, R. (2011). Think crisis–think female: The glass cliff and contextual variation in the think manager–think male stereotype. *The Journal of Applied Psychology*, *96*(3), 470–484. doi:10.1037/a0022133 PMID:21171729

Sadok, M., Alter, S., & Bednar, P. (2020). It is not my job: Exploring the disconnect between corporate security policies and actual security practices in SMEs. *Information and Computer Security*, *28*(3), 467–483. doi:10.1108/ICS-01-2019-0010

Saffari, E., Meghdari, A., Vazirnezhad, B., & Alemi, M. (2015). Ava (a social robot): Design and performance of a robotic hearing apparatus. *Social Robotics*, 440–450. doi:10.1007/978-3-319-25554-5_44

Salam, M. A., & Khan, S. A. (2020). Lessons from the humanitarian disaster logistics management. *Benchmarking*, *27*(4), 1455–1473. doi:10.1108/BIJ-04-2019-0165

Salmon, P. M., Walker, G. H. M., Read, G. J., Goode, N., & Stanton, N. A. (2017). Fitting methods to paradigms: Are ergonomics methods fit for systems thinking? *Ergonomics*, *60*(2), 194–205. doi:10.1080/00140139.2015.1103385 PMID:26799501

Sandberg, S. (2013). Lean. In *Women, Work and the Will to Lead*. WH Allen.

Sandholtz, J. H., Ringstaff, C., & Dwyer, D. C. (1992). Teaching in high-tech environment: Classroom management revisited. *Journal of Educational Computing Research*, *8*(4), 479–505. doi:10.2190/Y5NE-V9RQ-FD63-WC2N

Sardi, A., Rizzi, A., Sorano, E., & Guerrieri, A. (2020). Cyber Risk in Health Facilities: A Systematic Literature Review. *Sustainability*, *12*(17), 1–16. doi:10.3390u12177002

Saunders, M., Lewis, P., & Thornhill, A. (2009). *Research methods for business students*. FT/Prentice Hall.

Savrul, M., Incekara, A., & Sener, S. (2014). The potential of e-commerce for SMEs in a globalizing business environment. *Procedia: Social and Behavioral Sciences*, *150*, 35–45. doi:10.1016/j.sbspro.2014.09.005

Segurado, R., Costa, M., Carvalho, M. G., & Duia, N. (2014). Integrated analysis of energy and water supply in islands. Case study of S. Vicente, Cape Verde. *Energy*, *92*(Part 3), 639–648.

Segurado, R., Madeira, J. F. A., Costa, M., Carvalho, M. G., & Duia, N. (2016). Optimization of a wind powered desalination and pumped hydro storage system. *Applied Energy*, *177*, 487–499. doi:10.1016/j.apenergy.2016.05.125

Selwyn, T. (2019). Hostility and Hospitality: connecting Brexit, Grenfell and Windrush. In Experiencing hospitality. Nova Science.

Sen, A. K. (1999). *Development as Freedom*. Oxford University Press.

Seseni, L., & Mbohwa, C. (2021). The Significance of Big Data in the Success of SMEs in Emerging Markets: A Case of South Africa. *Proceedings of the 11th Annual International Conference on Industrial Engineering and Operations Management*.

Seshasayee, R. (2012, Mar. 9). Financing SMEs: An industry perspective. *Business World*.

Seuring, S., & Müller, M. (2008). From a literature review to a conceptual framework for sustainable supply chain management. *Journal of Cleaner Production*, *16*(15), 1699–1710. doi:10.1016/j.jclepro.2008.04.020

Sewnet, Z. (2020). *Ethiopia: Keeping children learning during COVID-19*. UNICEF. Available at https://www.unicef.org/ethiopia/stories/ethiopia-keeping-children-learning-during-covid-19

Sharma, V., Raut, R. D., Govindarajan, U. H., & Narkhede, B. E. (2021). Advancements in urban logistics toward smart, sustainable reforms in developing enabling technologies and markets. *Kybernetes*. doi:10.1108/K-01-2021-0026

Sharma, S., & Escobari, D. (2018). Identifying price bubble periods in the energy sector. *Energy Economics*, *69*, 418–429. doi:10.1016/j.eneco.2017.12.007

Shin, Y., & Schmidt, P. (1992). The KPSS stationarity test as a unit root test. *Economics Letters*, *38*(4), 387–392. doi:10.1016/0165-1765(92)90023-R

Shi, S., Phillips, P. C., & Hurn, S. (2018). Change detection and the causal impact of the yield curve. *Journal of Time Series Analysis*, *39*(6), 966–987. doi:10.1111/jtsa.12427

Shokouhyar, S., Pahlevani, N., & Mir Mohammad Sadeghi, F. (2019). Scenario analysis of smart, sustainable supply chain on the basis of a fuzzy cognitive map. *Management Research Review*, *43*(4), 463–496. doi:10.1108/MRR-01-2019-0002

Siddiqa, A., Hashem, I. A. T., Yaqoob, I., Marjani, M., Shamshirband, S., Gani, A., & Nasaruddin, F. (2016). A survey of big data management: Taxonomy and state-of-the-art. *Journal of Network and Computer Applications*, *71*(1), 151–166. doi:10.1016/j.jnca.2016.04.008

Sigala, M. (2020). Tourism and COVID-19: impacts and implications for advancing and resetting industry and research. *Journal of Business Research.*

Silva, M. E., Alves, A. P. F., Dias, P., & Nascimento, L. F. M. (2019). The role of orientation towards sustainability in supply chains. *Benchmarking: An International Journal.* doi:10.1108/BIJ-07-2017-0184

Simonovi, S. P. (2010). *Systems approach to management of disasters: Methods and applications.* Wiley. doi:10.1002/9780470890363

Simpson, R., & Altman, Y. (2000). The time-bounded glass ceiling and young women managers: Career progress and career success–evidence from the U.K. *Journal of European Industrial Training*, *24*(2/3/4), 190-198.

Simpson, R., Sturges, J., Woods, A., & Altman, Y. (2004). Career progress and career barriers: Women MBA graduates in Canada and the U.K. *Career Development International*, *9*(4/5), 459–477. doi:10.1108/13620430410550736

Singh, V., & Thurman, A. (2019). How Many Ways Can We Define Online Learning? A Systematic Literature Review of Definitions of Online Learning (1988-2018). *American Journal of Distance Education*, *33*(4), 289306. doi:10.1080/08923647.2019.1663082

Sintema, E. J. (2020). Effect of COVID-19 on the Performance of Grade 12 Students: Implications for STEM Education. *Eurasia Journal of Mathematics, Science and Technology Education*, *16*(7), em1851. doi:10.29333/ejmste/7893

SIP. (2019). *RFC 3261 - SIP: Session Initiation Protocol.* https://tools.ietf.org/html/rfc3261#page-8

Sjoberg, L. (1999). Risk Perception by The Public and By Experts: A dilemma in risk management. *Human Ecology Review*, *6*(2), 1–9.

Skinner, D., Tagg, C., & Holloway, J. (2000). Managers and Research: The Pros and Cons of Qualitative Approaches. *Management Learning*, *31*(2), 163–179.

Skoll, G. R., & Korstanje, M. E. (2012). Risks, totems, and fetishes in Marx and Freud. *Sincronía*, *2*, 11–27.

Slovic, P. (1993). Perceived risk, trust, and democracy. *Risk Analysis*, *13*(6), 675–682. doi:10.1111/j.1539-6924.1993.tb01329.x

Slovic, P. (2016). *The perception of risk.* Routledge. doi:10.4324/9781315661773

Smith, P., Caputi, P., & Crittenden, N. (2012). A maze of metaphors around glass ceilings. *Gender in Management*, *27*(7), 436–448. doi:10.1108/17542411211273432

Stock, J. R., & Lambert, D. M. (1992). Becoming a "World Class" Company With Logistics Service Quality. *International Journal of Logistics Management*, *3*(1), 73–81. doi:10.1108/09574099210804822

Strang, K. D. (2015). Risk Management Research. In Research Methods: Concepts, Methodologies, Tools, and Applications (pp. 362-389). Information Resource Management Association (IRMA). doi:10.4018/978-1-4666-7456-1.ch017

Strang, K. D. (2015a). Exploring the relationship between global terrorist ideology and attack methodology. *Risk Management Journal, 17*(2), 65-90. https://link.springer.com/article/1010.1057/rm.2015.1058

Strang, K. D. (2015b). *Handbook of Research Design in Business and Management*. New York: Palgrave Macmillan. Retrieved from http://kennethstrang.com/ABIS/ResearchDesignHandbook[ISBN9781137484956]-Strang@Palgrave(2015).pdf doi:10.1057/9781137484956

Strang, K. D. (2009). Using recursive regression to explore nonlinear relationships and interactions: A tutorial applied to a multicultural education study. *Practical Assessment, Research & Evaluation*, *14*(3), 1–13.

Strang, K. D. (2015). Developing a goal-driven research strategy. In *The Palgrave Handbook of Research Design in Business and Management* (pp. 31–45). Palgrave Macmillan US. doi:10.1057/9781137484956_3

Strang, K. D. (2015). Developing prescriptive environmental protection models from descriptive human accident behavior. *International Journal of Disaster Resilience in the Built Environment*, *6*(4), 81–96. doi:10.1108/IJDRBE-08-2013-0029

Strang, K. D. (2017). Feasibility of a hidden renewable energy hydro power storage battery. *Journal of Energy Storage*, *13*(3), 164–175. doi:10.1016/j.est.2017.07.001

Strang, K. D., & Chan, C. E. L. (2010). Simulating e-business innovation process improvement with virtual teams across Europe and Asia. *International Journal of E-Entrepreneurship and Innovation*, *1*(1), 22–41. doi:10.4018/jeei.2010010102

Strang, K. D., & Nersesian, R. (2014). Nonparametric estimation of petroleum accident risk to improve environmental protection. *Journal of Environment. Systems and Decisions*, *34*(1), 150–159. doi:10.100710669-013-9476-z

Strang, K. D., Vajjhala, N. R., & Korstanje, M. E. (2018). Global risk and contingency management overview. In K. D. Strang, M. E. Korstanje, & N. R. Vajjhala (Eds.), *Research, Practices, and Innovations in Global Risk and Contingency Management* (pp. xxii–xxix). IGI-Global. doi:10.4018/978-1-5225-4754-9

Strongman, K. T. (1996). *The Phsychology of Emotions: theories of emotions in perspective*. Willey and Sons.

Subha, B., Madhusudhanan, R., & Thomas, A. A. (2021). An investigation of the impact of occupational stress on mental health of remote working women I.T. professionals in urban Bangalore, India. *Journal of International Women's Studies*, *22*(6), 139–149.

Subiyanto, E. (2021). Investigating the logistics costs model: Recent update in Indonesia. *Journal of Science and Technology Policy Management*, *12*(2), 331–350. doi:10.1108/JSTPM-03-2020-0034

Su, C. W., Li, Z. Z., Chang, H. L., & Lobonţ, O. R. (2017). When will occur the crude oil bubbles? *Energy Policy*, *102*, 1–6. doi:10.1016/j.enpol.2016.12.006

Sunstein, C. R. (2002). Probability neglect: Emotions, worst cases, and law. *The Yale Law Journal*, *112*(1), 61–107. doi:10.2307/1562234

Sunstein, C. R. (2003). Terrorism and probability neglect. *Journal of Risk and Uncertainty*, *26*(2-3), 121–136. doi:10.1023/A:1024111006336

Sunstein, C. R. (2005). *Laws of fear: Beyond the precautionary principle* (Vol. 6). Cambridge University Press. doi:10.1017/CBO9780511790850

Swale, R., & Collins, D. (2013). Carrier Grade Voice Over IP (3rd ed.). McGraw-Hill.

Sweeney, E., Grant, D. B., & Mangan, D. J. (2018). Strategic adoption of logistics and supply chain management. *International Journal of Operations & Production Management*, *38*(3), 852–873. doi:10.1108/IJOPM-05-2016-0258

Syed, J., Burke, R. J., & Acar, P. (2010). Re-thinking 'tanawwo' (diversity) and 'musawat' (equality) in the Middle East. *Equality, Diversity and Inclusion*, *29*(2), 144–149. doi:10.1108/02610151011024466

Syed, J., & Ozbilgin, M. (2009). A relational framework for international transfer of diversity management practices. *International Journal of Human Resource Management*, *20*(12), 2435–2453. doi:10.1080/09585190903363755

Taleb, N. N. (2007). *The black swan. The impact of the highly improbable*. Penguin.

Talet, A. N., Mat-Zin, R., & Houari, M. (2014). Risk management and information technology projects. *International Journal of Digital Information and Wireless Communications*, *4*(1), 1–10.

Tam, S. W., Blomquist, C. A., & Kartsounes, G. T. (2007). Underground pumped hydro storage—An overview. *Energy Sources*, *4*(4), 329–351. doi:10.1080/00908317908908068

Tang, C. S. (2006). Perspectives in supply chain risk management. *International Journal of Production Economics*, *103*(2), 451–488. doi:10.1016/j.ijpe.2005.12.006

Taylor, F. W. (1911). *The Principles of Scientific Management*. Harper and Brothers.

Thakkar, P., Nathan, S., & Viswanathan, B. (2018). Performance Benchmarking and Optimizing Hyperledger Fabric Blockchain Platform. In *2018 IEEE 26th International Symposium on Modeling, Analysis, and Simulation of Computer and Telecommunication Systems (MASCOTS)*. 10.1109/MASCOTS.2018.00034

Thomas, P. (2013). *The Risk of Using Risk Matrices* (Masters Master's thesis). University of Stavanger. Retrieved from https://brage.bibsys.no/uis/bitstream/URN:NBN:no-bibsys_brage_45899/1/Thomas_Philip.pdf

Thomas, M. J., Lal, V., Baby, A. K., Rabeeh, V. P. M., James, A., & Raj, A. K. (2021). Can technological advancements help to alleviate the COVID-19 pandemic? A Review. *Journal of Biomedical Informatics*, *117*, 103787. doi:10.1016/j.jbi.2021.103787 PMID:33862231

Thompson, H. (2012). Fracking boom spurs environmental audit: As hydraulic fracturing unlocks new gas reserves, researchers struggle to understand its health implications. *Nature*, *485*(5), 557–560.

Tilak, J. B. G. (2001). Household Expenditure on Education in India: A Few Stylized Facts. In S. M. Dev, P. Antony, V. Gayathri, & R. P. Mamgain (Eds.), *Social and Economic Security in India* (pp. 191–218). Institute for Human Development.

Tiruneh, D. T. (2020). *COVID-19 School Closures May Further Widen the Inequality Gaps between the Advantaged and the Disadvantaged in Ethiopia*. Retrieved from https://www.riseprogramme.org/blog/COVID-19_ethiopia_school_closures

Tlaiss, H. (2013). Determinants of job satisfaction in the banking sector: The case of Lebanese managers. *Employee Relations*, *35*(4), 377–395. doi:10.1108/ER-10-2011-0064

Tlaiss, H. A., & Mendelson, M. B. (2013). Predicting women's job satisfaction with personal demographics: Evidence from a Middle Eastern country. *International Journal of Human Resource Management*, *25*(3), 434–458. doi:10.1080/09585192.2013.792859

Tlaiss, H., & Kauser, S. (2010). Perceived organizational barriers to women's career advancement in Lebanon. *Gender in Management*, *25*(6), 462–496. doi:10.1108/17542411011069882

Tlaiss, H., & Kauser, S. (2011). The impact of gender and family on career advancement: Evidence from Lebanese women. *Gender in Management*, *26*(1), 8–36. doi:10.1108/17542411111109291

Torous, J., Jän Myrick, K., Rauseo-Ricupero, N., & Firth, J. (2020). Digital Mental Health and COVID-19: Using technology today to accelerate the curve on access and quality Tomorrow. *JMIR Mental Health*, *7*(3), e18848. Advance online publication. doi:10.2196/18848 PMID:32213476

Tortajada, C. (2015). Dams: An essential component of development. *Journal of Hydrologic Engineering*, *20*(1), 1–10. doi:10.1061/(ASCE)HE.1943-5584.0000919

Towbin, A. J., Regan, J., Hulefeld, D., Schwieterman, E., Perry, L. A., O'Brien, S., Dhamija, A., OConnor, T., & Moskovitz, J. A. (2021). Disaster planning during SARS-COV-2/COVID: One radiology informatics team's story. *Journal of Digital Imaging*, *34*(2), 290–296. doi:10.100710278-021-00420-x PMID:33604808

TowerGroup. (2014). Reducing Risk Management's Organizational Drag. Executive Guidance. CIO Executive Board.

Tran, T. B. N. (2017). Speculative bubbles in emerging stock markets and macroeconomic factors: A new empirical evidence for Asia and Latin America. *Research in International Business and Finance*, *42*, 454–467. doi:10.1016/j.ribaf.2016.02.004

Tsay, A. A., Gray, J. V., Noh, I. J., & Mahoney, J. T. (2018). A Review of Production and Operations Management Research on Outsourcing in Supply Chains: Implications for the Theory of the Firm. *Production and Operations Management*, *27*(7), 1177–1220. doi:10.1111/poms.12855

Tung, V. W. S., & Law, R. (2017). The potential for tourism and hospitality experience research in human-robot interactions. *International Journal of Contemporary Hospitality Management*.

Turnbull, J. (2014). *The Docker Book*. Lulu.com.

Tzanelli, R. (2007). *The cinematic tourist: Explorations in globalization, culture and resistance*. Routledge.

Tzanelli, R. (2013). *Heritage in the digital era: Cinematic tourism and the activist cause*. Routledge.

Tzanelli, R. (2016). *Thanatourism and Cinematic Representations of Risk: Screening the End of Tourism*. Routledge.

Uddin, N. (2012). *Geotechnical issues in the creation of underground reservoirs for massive energy storage*. Paper presented at the IEEE Geothermal Innovations, Birmingham, AL. 10.1109/JPROC.2011.2161969

Ulven, J. B., & Wangen, G. (2021). A systematic review of cybersecurity risks in higher education. *Future Internet*, *13*(2), 1–40. doi:10.3390/fi13020039

UNDP. (1997). *Human Development Report*. Oxford University Press.

UNDP. (2006). *Human Development Report 2006: Beyond Scarcity: Power, Poverty, and the Global Water Crisis*. UNDP.

UNDP. (2019). *Human Development Report 2019: Beyond Income, Beyond Averages, Beyond Today: Inequalities in Human Development in the 21st Century*. UNDP.

UNI CEF. (2020a). *Ethiopia COVID-19*. Situational Report No. 5.

UNICEF. (2020b). *Promising practices for equitable remote learning Emerging lessons from COVID-19 education responses in 127 countries*. Innocent Research Brief.

United Nations. (2015). *The millennium development goals report 2015*. United Nations. https://www.undp.org/content/dam/undp/library/MDG/english/UNDP_MDG_Report_2015.pdf

USBTS. (2022). *Oil Spills In and Around U.S. Waterways*. Bureau of Transportation Statistics, U.S. Department of Transportation.

Vaish, R., Agrawal, A., & Kapoor, S. (2021). *AI maturity framework for enterprise applications*. IBM Corporation.

Vasel-Be-Hagh, A., Carriveau, R., & Ting, D. S.-K. (2013). Energy storage using weights hydraulically lifted above ground. *The International Journal of Environmental Studies*, *70*(5), 792–799. doi:10.1080/00207233.2013.810043

Vasilopoulos, K., Pavlidis, E., & Spavound, S. (2018). *Econometric analysis of explosive time series*. R foundation for statistical computing. https://github.com/kvasilopoulos/exuber

Verma, N., Sharma, V., & Badar, M. A. (2021). Entropy-Based Lean, Energy and Six Sigma Approach to Achieve Sustainability in Manufacturing System. *Arabian Journal for Science and Engineering*, *46*(8), 8105–8117. doi:10.100713369-021-05826-x PMID:34189013

Vincent-Hoper, S., Muser, C., & Janneck, M. (2012). Transformational leadership, work engagement, and occupational success. *Career Development International*, *17*(7), 663–682. doi:10.1108/13620431211283805

Wagner, K. D., Brief, D. J., Vielhauer, M. J., Sussman, S., Keane, T. M., & Malow, R. (2009). The Potential for Ptsd, Substance Use, and HIV Risk Behavior Among Adolescents Exposed to Hurricane Katrina. *Journal of Substance Use & Misuse*, *44*(1), 1749–1767. doi:10.3109/10826080902963472 PMID:19895305

Wall, K. D. (2011). *The Trouble With Risk Matrices*. DRMI Working Papers Ongoing Research.

Wang, H., Chen, K., & Xu, D. (2016). *A maturity model for blockchain adoption. Financial Innovation, 2(12)*. doi:10.118640854-016-0031-z

Wang, H., Wang, L., Wang, X., & Yao, E. (2013). A novel pumped hydro combined with compressed air energy storage system. *Energies*, *6*(3), 1554–1567. doi:10.3390/en6031554

Wang, L., & Alexander, C. A. (2021). Cyber security during the COVID-19 pandemic. *AIMS Electronics and Electrical Engineering*, *5*(2), 146–157. doi:10.3934/electreng.2021008

Wang, M., Wang, B., & Chan, R. (2021). Reverse logistics uncertainty in a courier industry: A triadic model. *Modern Supply Chain Research and Applications*, *3*(1), 56–73. doi:10.1108/MSCRA-10-2020-0026

Whisker, C. (2018). Review: Adele E. Clarke, Carrie Friese & Rachel S. Washburn (2018). Situational analysis: Grounded theory after the interpretive turn (2nd ed.). Forum Qualitative Sozialforschung / Forum: Qualitative Social Research, 19(3), Art. 35. doi:10.17169/fqs-19.3.3138

White, B. (1995). The career development of successful women. *Women in Management Review*, *10*(3), 4–15. doi:10.1108/09649429510085053

Whitelaw, S., Mamas, M. A., Topol, E., & Van Spall, H. G. (2020). Applications of digital technology in COVID-19 pandemic planning and response. *The Lancet. Digital Health*, *2*(8), e435–e440. Advance online publication. doi:10.1016/S2589-7500(20)30142-4 PMID:32835201

White, R., Marinakis, Y., Islam, N., & Walsh, S. (2020). Is Bitcoin a currency, a technology-based product, or something else? *Technological Forecasting and Social Change*, *151*, 119877. doi:10.1016/j.techfore.2019.119877

Whittingham, M. S. (2012). History, evolution, and future status of energy storage. *Proceedings of the IEEE*, *100*, 1518-1534. 10.1109/JPROC.2012.2190170

Wiki. (2019). *Open learning*. Retrieved from https://en.wikipedia.org/wiki/Open_learning

Wilensky, H. L. (1964). The professionalization of everyone. *American Journal of Sociology*, *70*(2), 137–158. doi:10.1086/223790

Williams, C. L. (1992). The glass escalator: Hidden advantages for men in the "female" professions. *Social Problems*, *39*(3), 253–267. doi:10.2307/3096961

Williams, J. C. (2005). The glass ceiling and the maternal wall in academia. *New Directions for Higher Education*, *130*(130), 91–105. doi:10.1002/he.181

Wise, T., Zbozinek, T., Michelini, G., Hagan, C. C., & Mobbs, D. (2020). Changes in risk perception and protective behavior during the first week of the COVID-19 pandemic in the United States. doi:10.31234/osf.io/dz428osf.io/dz428

World Bank. (1994). Poverty Reduction in South Asia. Academic Press.

World Bank. (2019). *International Bank for Reconstruction and Development*. 2019-Tracking SDG7-The Energy Progress Report. Retrieved rom https://trackingsdg7.esmap.org/data/files/download-documents/2019-Tracking%20SDG7-Full%20 Report.pdf

World Bank. (2020a). *Guidance Note on Education Systems' Response to COVID19*. Retrieved from http://pubdocs.worldbank.org/en/450881585235950757/COVID19-Education-Sector-Guidance-Note-March26.pdf

World Bank. (2020b). *The World Bank Education Global Practice Guidance Note: Remote Learning & COVID-19*. Author.

World Bank. (2021). *Micro, small, and medium-sized enterprises (MSMEs) and their role in achieving the sustainable development goals*. Department of Economic and Social Affairs (DESA). https://sustainabledevelopment.un.org/content/documents/25851MSMEs_and_SDGs_Final3120.pdf

Wu, C. (2021). Social Capital and COVID-19: A Multidimensional and Multilevel Approach. *Chinese Sociological Review*, *53*(1), 27–54. doi:10.1080/21620555.2020.1814139

Wynn, M., Bakeer, A., & Forti, Y. (2021). E-government and digital transformation in Libyan local authorities. *International Journal of Teaching and Case Studies*, *12*(2), 119–139. doi:10.1504/IJTCS.2021.116139

Wynn, M., Turner, P., & Lau, E. (2013). E-business and process change: Two case studies (towards an assessment framework). *Journal of Small Business and Enterprise Development*, *20*(4), 913–933. doi:10.1108/JSBED-03-2012-0044

Xian, H., & Woodhams, C. (2008). Managing careers: Experiences of successful women in the Chinese I.T. industry. *Gender in Management*, *23*(6), 409–425. doi:10.1108/17542410810897535

Xu, J., Tian, Y., Ma, T., & Al-Nabhan, N. (2020). Najla Al-Nabhan. Intelligent manufacturing security model based on improved blockchain. *Mathematical Biosciences and Engineering*, *17*(5), 5633–5650. doi:10.3934/mbe.2020303 PMID:33120570

Yadav, V., Gahlot, P., Kaswan, M. S., Rathi, R., & Singh, M. (2022). Sustainable Green Lean Six Sigma Methodology and Application Status: A Perspective Review. In A. K. Dubey, A. Sachdeva, & M. Mehta (Eds.), *Recent Trends in Industrial and Production Engineering* (pp. 251–266). Springer Singapore. doi:10.1007/978-981-16-3135-1_26

Yahia Zaki, A., & Daniel John, D. (2020). Telehealth in the time of Corona: 'doctor in the House.' *Internal Medicine Journal*. Retrieved December 29, 2021, from https://pubmed.ncbi.nlm.nih.gov/33354885/

Yang, Y. (2011). Gender and engineering career development of hotel employees in China. *Systems Engineering Procedia*, *1*, 365–371. doi:10.1016/j.sepro.2011.08.055

Yeo, K., & Ren, Y. (2009). Risk management capability maturity model for complex product systems (CoPS) projects. *Systems Engineering*, *12*(4), 275–294.

Yeoman, I. (2012). *2050-tomorrow's tourism* (Vol. 55). Channel View Publications.

Yeoman, I., & Mars, M. (2012). Robots, men and sex tourism. *Futures*, *44*(4), 365–371.

Yıldırım, D. Ç., Cevik, E. I., & Esen, Ö. (2020). Time-varying volatility spillovers between oil prices and precious metal prices. *Resources Policy*, *68*, 101783. doi:10.1016/j.resourpol.2020.101783

Yin, R. K. (2012). *Applications of case study research*. SAGE Publications Ltd.

Yue, R. P. H., Lau, B. H., Chan, C. L., & Ng, S. M. (2021). Risk perception as a double-edged sword in policy compliance in COVID-19 pandemic? A two-phase evaluation from Hong Kong. *Journal of Risk Research*, 1–15. doi:10.1080/13669877.2021.1936612

Zafirakis, D., Chalvatzis, K. J., Baiocchi, G., & Daskalakis, G. (2013). Modeling of financial incentives for investments in energy storage systems that promote the large-scale integration of wind energy. *Applied Energy*, *105*(1), 138–154. doi:10.1016/j.apenergy.2012.11.073

Zafirakis, D., Chalvatzis, K. J., Daskalakis, G., & Baiocchi, G. (2016). The value of arbitrage for energy storage: Evidence from European electricity markets. *Applied Energy*, *149*(1), 150–161. doi:10.1016/j.apenergy.2016.05.047

Zavolokina, L., Ziolkowski, R., Bauer, I., & Schwabe, G. (2020). Management, Governance and Value Creation in a Blockchain Consortium. *MIS Quarterly Executive*, *19*(1), 1–17. Advance online publication. doi:10.17705/2msqe.00022

Zayed, T., Amer, M., & Pan, J. (2008). Assessing risk and uncertainty inherent in Chinese highway projects using AHP. *International Journal of Project Management*, *26*(4), 408–419. doi:10.1016/j.ijproman.2007.05.012

Zhang, D., Li, X., & Xue, J. (2015). Education inequality between rural and urban areas of the People's Republic of China, migrants' children education, and some implications. *Asian Development Review*, *32*(1), 196–224. doi:10.1162/ADEV_a_00042

Zhang, Y. J., & Yao, T. (2016). Interpreting the movement of oil prices: Driven by fundamentals or bubbles? *Economic Modelling*, *55*, 226–240. doi:10.1016/j.econmod.2016.02.016

Zhao, Y., Chang, H. L., Su, C. W., & Nian, R. (2015). Gold bubbles: When are they most likely to occur? *Japan and the World Economy*, *34*, 17–23. doi:10.1016/j.japwor.2015.03.001

Zheng, A., & Casari, A. (2018). *Feature engineering for machine learning: principles and techniques for data scientists*. O'Reilly Media, Inc.

Zheng, Z., Ahu, J., & Lyu, M. R. (2013). Service-generated big data and big data-as-a-service: an overview. *IEEE International Congress on Big Data*. 402-410. 10.1109/BigData.Congress.2013.60

Zhou, L., Li, F., Wu, S., & Zhou M. (2020). "School's Out, But Class's On", The largest online education in the world today: Taking China's practical exploration during the COVID-19 epidemic prevention and control as an example. *Best Evid Chin Edu, 4*(2), 501-519. doi:10.15354/bece.20.ar023

Zhou, K., Fu, C., & Yang, S. (2016). Big data-driven smart energy management: From big data to big insights. *Renewable & Sustainable Energy Reviews*, *56*(1), 215–225. doi:10.1016/j.rser.2015.11.050

Zimon, D., Madzik, P., & Sroufe, R. (2020). Management systems and improving supply chain processes. *International Journal of Retail & Distribution Management*, *48*(9), 939–961. doi:10.1108/IJRDM-04-2019-0107

Zizek, S. (2007). *The universal exception* (Vol. 2). A&C Black.

Zou, P. X., Chen, Y., & Chan, T.-Y. (2010). Understanding and improving your risk management capability: Assessment model for construction organizations. *Journal of Construction Engineering and Management*, *136*(8). Retrieved March 6, 2022, from https://ascelibrary.org/doi/abs/10.1061/%28ASCE%29CO.1943-7862.0000175

Zsidisin, G. A., Bresler, A., Hazen, B., Snider, K. F., & Wilkerson, T. H. (2020). Research in defense logistics: Where are we and where are we going? *Journal of Defense Analytics and Logistics*, *4*(1), 3–17. doi:10.1108/JDAL-07-2019-0012

Zubairu, N., Dinwoodie, J., Govindan, K., Hunter, L., & Roh, S. (2021). Supply chain strategies as drivers of financial performance in liquefied natural gas networks. *Supply Chain Management*, *26*(5), 579–591. doi:10.1108/SCM-08-2020-0389

Zulkernine, F., Bauer, M., & Aboulnaga, A. (2013). Towards Cloud-based analytics-as-a-service (CLAaaS) for big data analytics in the cloud. *Proceedings of the IEEE Congress on Big Data*. 62-69. 10.1109/BigData.Congress.2013.18

Zwikael, O., & Ahn, M. (2011). The effectiveness of risk management: An analysis of project risk planning across industries and countries. *Risk Analysis*, *31*(1), 25–37.

About the Contributors

Narasimha Rao Vajjhala is working at the Faculty of Engineering and Architecture at the University of New York Tirana, Albania. He is a senior member of ACM and IEEE. He is the Editor-in-Chief for the International Journal of Risk and Contingency Management (IJRCM). He is also a member of the Risk Management Society (RIMS), and the Project Management Institute (PMI). He has over 20 years of experience in teaching mainly programming and database-related courses at both graduate and undergraduate levels in Europe and Africa. He has also worked as a consultant in technology firms in Europe and has experience participating in EU-funded projects. He has supervised several undergraduate senior design projects and graduate theses. He has completed a Doctorate in Information Systems and Technology (United States); holds a Master of Science in Computer Science and Applications (India), and a Master of Business Administration with a specialization in Information Systems (Switzerland), and an undergraduate degree in Computer Science (India).

Kenneth David Strang has more than 290 mostly-sole-authored scholarly publications. He is a professor who teaches and supervises undergraduate, graduate and doctoral students across five disciplines: business administration, management information systems, marketing/consumer behavior, supply chain management and economics/statistics. Ken has a doctorate in project management (operations research), an MBA (strategic management), a BSBA (marketing), an AAS (IT) all with summa cum laude/honors plus he is an internationally licensed Project Management Professional (PMI, USA), a Certified Research Professional (IIPMR, USA), a Certified Network Administrator (Novell, USA), a Certified Supply Chain Specialist/Procurement Professional (IIPMR, USA) and a Fellow Life Management Institute with distinction (LOMA, USA). Dr. Strang has lifetime grant projects valued over $7 million+, and he has won several honors including a Behavior Energy Climate Change Fellowship from the American Council for an Energy-Efficient Economy, the Emerald Literati award and Duke of Edinborough community service medal, along with several presidential citations.

* * *

Degwale Gebeyehu Belay is an assistant professor at the Department of Governance and Development Studies, Bahir Dar University, Ethiopia. He holds a BA degree in Public Administration and Development Management from Addis Ababa University. He has a MA degree in 'Regional and Local Development Studies' from Addis Ababa University, Ethiopia. He also has an MA degree in Development Studies (Major in 'Social Policy for Development', specialization in 'Children and Youth Studies') from the International Institute of Social Studies of Erasmus University Rotterdam, the Netherlands.

Degwale's research interest lies in issues of children and young people's work, employment, migration, governance and democracy, and public policy.

Marenglen Biba is a full professor at the Department of Computer Science, Faculty of Engineering and Architecture, University of New York in Tirana (UNYT). Prof. Dr. Biba received a Ph.D. in Computer Science from University of Bari, Italy, and is currently the Dean of Faculty at UNYT where he joined in 2009 as Assistant Professor and later as Associate Professor from 2013 to 2022. From 2022 he is a full professor of Computer Science at UNYT. His main research area is Artificial Intelligence in general and Machine Learning in particular. He has published more than 70 papers in international journals and conferences and has participated in several national and international projects.

Enes Cela recently graduated from the University of New York Tirana with an M.Sc. in Computer Science as the topper of the class. Enes has more than three years of work experience in VoIP and open source technologies such as Asterisk, providing support and solutions. He is interested in Blockchain solutions to business problems, specifically in Hyperledger frameworks. Enes has experience in Fabric and is eager to explore other frameworks such as Sawtooth.

Edna Mngusughun Denga, is a graduate student at the School of Business and Entrepreneurship, American University of Nigeria, Yola. In 2014, she finished her MBA in Business Management specializing in Marketing. Her primary research interests are in digital marketing, brand tribalism, relationship marketing, and other related topics.

Philip Eappen is an experienced healthcare administrator and an adjunct faculty with a clear vision, plans, and strategies to manage healthcare operations. As a healthcare administrator, Dr. Eappen is always determined to achieve the requirement of healthcare organizations by giving the best and getting the best from employees. Dr. Eappen can create and manage a sustainable and profit-making operation with available resources. Dr. Eappen has a decade of experience in hospital and healthcare management. Currently, he is working as the Coordinator of Science Communication Skills at Cape Breton University. Dr. Eappen has completed a Doctorate in Healthcare Administration from Central Michigan University, the United States, and a Master of Business Administration in Health Care Management and Bachelor of Nursing from very reputed universities. He also has a post-graduate certificate in International Health from Central Michigan University and many other certifications from most reputed universities around the globe.

Natasha Cecilia Edeh works for EZ Career Consultant Pvt Ltd as an education consultant. Edeh's research focuses on human-centered topics such as open innovation, cybersecurity, and human-robot collaboration. She is now working on a chapter for the book Cybersecurity for Decision Makers on the topic "Cybersecurity frameworks and assessment models". Edeh graduated from the American University of Nigeria with a master's degree in Information Systems in 2018.

Remzi Gök has a PhD degree in Banking and Finance from Ankara Yıldırım Beyazıt University in Turkey (2018). He currently works at the Department of Business Administration, Dicle University. He does research in risk and financial management, mostly, through wavelet analysis technique.

Ibiene Idu is a certified Project Management Professional. She currently works as a Project Manager focused on Service delivery at Behaviorprise Consulting Inc.; An organization specialized in providing quality and individualized services to children and adults living with a diagnosis of Autism Spectrum Disorder (ASD) and other forms of developmental disabilities on the principle of applied behavior analysis (ABA). Ibiene's research focuses on human centered research that includes: Cybersecurity, Crisis intervention and management practices, Individual program adjustment (IPA), and Community Integration. Ibiene received her masters degree from the American University of Nigeria in 2018 and moved to Canada in 2019.

Jose Irizar completed his PhD in Business and Enterprise Management at the School of Business and Technology of the University of Gloucestershire, UK, and he also has a masters degree in Business Administration from the University of West Florida. Currently he is senior manager with ZF Friedrichshafen AG with over 20 years' experience in project management, and is also a lecturer in Business Information Systems at the SRH University, Heidelberg and project supervisor at the University of Gloucestershire. He has undertaken research in the fields of program and project risk management, and his current research activities include work on artificial intelligence, advanced analytics, and machine learning in different industrial sectors.

Maximiliano E. Korstanje is editor in chief of International Journal of Safety and Security in Tourism (UP Argentina) and Editor in Chief Emeritus of International Journal of Cyber Warfare and Terrorism (IGI-Global US). Korstanje is Senior Researchers in the Department of Economics at University of Palermo, Argentina. In 2015 he was awarded as Visiting Research Fellow at School of Sociology and Social Policy, University of Leeds, UK and the University of La Habana Cuba. In 2017 is elected as Foreign Faculty Member of AMIT, Mexican Academy in the study of Tourism, which is the most prominent institutions dedicated to tourism research in Mexico. He had a vast experience in editorial projects working as advisory member of Elsevier, Routledge, Springer, IGI global and Cambridge Scholar publishing. Korstanje had visited and given seminars in many important universities worldwide. He has also recently been selected to take part of the 2018 Albert Nelson Marquis Lifetime Achievement Award. a great distinction given by Marquis Who´s Who in the world.

Rajasekhara Mouly Potluri is a Professor of Management/Marketing with thirty years of industry/teaching experience in various universities on many continents. He has taught both marketing and management courses on BBA, MBA, EMBA, MS (Management), and Ph.D. programs. Dr. Potluri earned his Ph.D. in Marketing from Shivaji University in India and held four Master's degrees in Business Administration (Marketing), Commerce (Banking), Philosophy (Human Resources), as well as an MBA in Islamic Marketing from the International Islamic Marketing Association in the U.K. He has published more than eighty research articles, book chapters, and case studies in internationally ranked peer-reviewed journals indexed in Scopus, ABDC, SSCI, and KCI. Dr. Potluri has won eleven Best Research Paper Awards and ten Academic Service Excellence Awards in different International Conference presentations in Egypt, South Korea, Malaysia, USA, and UAE. He has extensive teaching and research experience in multi-cultural and multi-ethnic environments in India, Ethiopia, Kazakhstan, South Korea, Nigeria, and the United Arab Emirates. His research interests are Marketing, Islamic Marketing, CSR, HRM & OB, and Entrepreneurship.

K. Madhu Kishore Raghunath has obtained his Ph.D. in Management from the National Institute of Technology-Warangal and he is currently working as an Assistant Professor in the Department of Finance, GITAM institute of management, in GITAM (Deemed to be University) Visakhapatnam Campus. He has a Post-graduate degree in Management with Finance and Marketing specializations from Jawaharlal Nehru Technological University and has over 5 years of teaching experience in higher education along with CBSE-NET & AP & TS- SLET qualification. His research interests include subjects like Finance, Marketing, Risk Management, and Supply Chain Management.

Sandip Rakshit is an academician of versatile talents, involved in the education field with a teaching, consulting and research experience of more than 20 years. Prof. Rakshit has delivered more than 50 keynote addresses, invited seminars, and media briefings in IEEE, ACM, AIS, ISACA, Springer, Elsevier, Emerald conferences and has been actively involved in organizing more than 50 national and international conferences in various capacities. He has also conducted more than 50 MDP for Top Corporates and Army Officers in India and other countries. Dr. Rakshit also served as IEEE GOLD (Kolkata Section) Chairman for 2012 & 2013 two consecutive years and current Vice-chair ACM Yola Professional Chapter.

Mahendra Singh Rawat has completed his Masters in Economics from Garhwal University in India along with a Masters in Management Studies from Benaras Hindu University in India. He had worked as a Lecturer of Economics in Meerut University in India apart from a senior Management Position in State Bank of India for over 15 years. He had also worked as the Chief Executive Officer (CEO) of International Commercial Bank in Albania as well as an Adjunct Faculty at the University of New York in Tirana, Albania. He is currently an active Shareholder of MSR Holdings International Inc Canada (A Real Estate Company).

Mudit Singh Rawat is an Engineering Graduate from Birla Institute of Technology in India and an MBA from Schulich Business School, York University in Toronto. Mudit is a seasoned professional with over twelve years of experience working in the technology and retail sector, both as an entrepreneur and a corporate executive. Mudit is known in the Canadian tech industry as the founder of Urbery, Canada's first on-demand grocery and alcohol delivery platform. His second startup, Nexus Commerce, focused on enabling D2C eCommerce channels for large CPG brands like Nestlé and Unilever, was acquired in 2019 by a US-based supply-chain consulting firm (Tompkins International). At Planet Corp, he leads the M&A practice and also works closely on helping the acquired companies' leadership teams hit their corporate objectives. He is also one of the promoters of MSR Holdings Inc, a real estate company in Canada. Before becoming a full-time entrepreneur, he has worked in various strategy and business development roles in multi-national corporations like Oracle, CGI, and Sobeys. His rich mix of corporate and entrepreneurial experience gives him a unique perspective on ventures across different stages, and he is an active angel investor in early-stage tech startups like Swyft, Ukko, Scener and Kabo.

Colin Read is a Professor of Economics and Finance at the State University of New York College at Plattsburgh in Plattsburgh, New York, U.S.A. His Ph.D. was in urban economics and real estate finance at Queen's University in Kingston, Ontario. He also earned a J.D. in law from the University of Connecticut, a Master's of Accountancy at the University of Tulsa, and an M.B.A. from the University of Alaska Fairbanks. His undergraduate degree was in Physics from Simon Fraser University in Burnaby,

British Columbia. He served as Mayor of the City of Plattsburgh, New York, from 2017 to 2020. He conducts research in Money and Banking, environmental economics, and cryptocurrency.

Evis Trandafili, PhD, is a full-time lecturer at the Computer Engineering Department, Faculty of Information Technology, Polytechnic University of Tirana since 2009. She finished her PhD in 2014 in the field of Natural Language Processing in Albanian language. Furthermore, her research interests focus mainly on Artificial Intelligence, Machine Learning, Natural Language Processing, and other similar fields. Her works are published in different national and international conferences and journals. She has participated in several national and international projects. Currently, she holds the position of Vice Dean for Research in the Faculty of Information Technology, Polytechnic University of Tirana.

S. L. Tulasi Devi is an Assistant Professor in the School of Management at the National Institute of Technology- Warangal. She has over 29 years of experience in academic teaching in finance. Her areas of research interest are financial management, corporate finance, and financial econometrics.

Martin Wynn is Associate Professor in the School of Computing and Engineering, University of Gloucestershire, UK. He gained his BA and MA degrees at Durham University and his PhD at Nottingham Trent University. He then joined Glaxo Pharmaceuticals, where he led the end-user computing department. He moved to drinks company HP Bulmer, now part of the Heineken group, where he was Head of IT for 10 years. On his return to academia at the University of Gloucestershire, he first focussed on developing knowledge transfer activities for the University and played a major role in the leadership and management of this third-stream activity. He edited a recent book - "Digital Transformation, Industry Use Cases, and the Impact of Disruptive Technologies", published by IGI-Global in 2022.

Index

E

F

G

H

I

K

L

M

N

O

P

R

S

T

U

V

W

www.ingramcontent.com/pod-product-compliance
Lightning Source LLC
LaVergne TN
LVHW080633011026
849160LV00014B/1203